Afterimages

ARLENE CROCE

Afterimages

ADAM AND CHARLES BLACK
LONDON

First published in this edition in 1978 by
A & C Black Ltd
35 Bedford Row, London WC1R 4JH

ISBN 0 7136 1875 2

Most of these reviews originally appeared in The New Yorker. "Balanchine's Girls: The Making of a Style" was first published in Harper's Magazine; "The Pleasure of Their Company" first appeared in Playbill; and all of the selections in Part Two were originally published in The Dancing Times.

Grateful acknowledgment is made to the following for permission to reprint previously published selections by Arlene Croce:

Marcel Dekker, Inc.: For the following reviews, which were first published in Ballet Review: "The Other Royal Ballet (Moon Reindeer)," Spring 1966, Vol. 1, No. 3; "Ballets Without Choreography," Summer 1967, Vol. 2, No. 1; "Dancers and Dance Critics," Fall 1968, Vol. 2, No. 3; "The Avant-Garde on Broadway," Spring 1969, Vol. 2, No. 5; "Stuttgart's Ballet. New York's Myth," Fall 1969, Vol. 3, No. 1; "Eliot Feld and Company," Winter 1969, Vol. 3, No. 2; "The Royal Ballet in New York," Summer 1970, Vol. 3, No. 4; "Folies Béjart," Spring 1971, Vol. 3, No. 5; "Twyla Tharp's Red Hot Peppers," Winter 1971, Vol. 4, No. 1; and "The Relevance of Robbins," as "Waterloo," Spring 1972, Vol. 4, No. 2.

Harcourt Brace Jovanovich, Inc., and Faber & Faber Ltd.: For the brief excerpt from East Coker, from Four Quartets by T. S. Eliot.

Martin Secker & Warburg Ltd: For "Dance in Film," which will be appearing in A Critical Dictionary of the Cinema, to be published by Martin Secker & Warburg Ltd, London, and The Viking Press, Inc., New York, 1978

Printed in Great Britain by
Redwood Burn Ltd, Trowbridge and Esher

Contents

Preface ix

PART FOUR

On Occasion

Preface

Afterimage is defined as "the impression retained by the retina of the eye, or by any other organ of sense, of a vivid sensation, after the external cause has been removed." An afterimage is what we are left with when the performance is over. Dancing leaves nothing else behind—no record, no text—and so the afterimage becomes the subject of dance criticism. A dance critic tries to train the memory as well as the organs of sense; he tries to make the afterimage that appears in his writing match the performance. But often it doesn't match literally because the senses are assimilating impressions and not recording facts. When the critic revisits the theatre, he knows that things will probably seem different, in shape and in sequence, from the way they seemed before. It happens again and again. The dance critic resigns himself to doing a fool's job as best he can.

I have made no attempt to correct errors of this sort that crop up in the pages that follow. I have, however, cut or rewritten passages in the earlier material when a topic had lost its relevance or when the meanings were unclear. Here and there, again in the earlier material, I have restored data to a piece to bring it closer to what I hoped to have printed at the time.

This book covers a little over ten years. It is not intended to be the history of a decade but only a survey of my views as I was able to express them, more or less sporadically, writing for different publications and different deadlines. For a dance critic it is best to write as soon after the event as possible. Until *The New Yorker* gave me that opportunity in 1973, I often felt that I could not keep up with what was going on. Not only that; I felt it increasingly difficult to get into the real substance of what went on—namely, performing by dancers. I am grateful to William Shawn for opening his pages to me, and to my editors at *The New Yorker*, Rogers Whitaker and Susan Moritz, for helping me find the best way of saying what I wanted to say. To Mary Clarke, editor of *The Dancing Times* of London, my thanks for offering me a monthly beat at a time when it was impossible to publish on a regular basis in this country.

PART ONE

By the Week

1973-1977

Prizewinners

The Bolshoi Ballet's newest star, Nadezhda Pavlova, doesn't resemble her namesake, and she doesn't resemble any other dancer I've ever seen. At seventeen, she is an authentic original; she shows you the full grandeur of the style of classical dancing she has been trained in and, at the same time, the fullness of her own contribution to it. Other great dancers—for example, her fine partner Vyacheslav Gordeyev—announce themselves within a created style. They celebrate it, so to speak. Nadezhda Pavlova dominates and extends it. At least, that's what her impact on me at this minute suggests. Prodigies can burn out, or their talent can be wasted by choreographers, or they can be stifled by a repertory that has established its own set of models for change and growth. I wouldn't want to see Pavlova turned into another Lepeshinskaya, the great soubrette of the thirties and forties, and although she has a personality and technique that head her in that direction, she has a new vitality that heads her away from it. I hope to see her become the precedent for something as yet unformed and uncategorizable—what we might at some lucky future time be able to speak of as representing Bolshoi-ballerina style in the seventies.

In the meantime, I'd like to see Pavlova dance a whole ballet. The season the Bolshoi is presenting at the Metropolitan may not give us much more than a glimpse of her. Like the "Stars of the Bolshoi Ballet" season of 1968, it's a truck-and-bus sort of affair, with a reduced company, no full-evening ballets, and no major new productions. Besides all that, it seems to have been thrown together at the last minute. Programs and casts tend to remain uncertain right up to curtain time. Pavlova, who may or may not appear during the final weeks of the season, has been seen in two different pas de deux, neither of which was announced in advance. She has led the so-called Highlights section of the programs, but she hasn't danced every night, and people who have wanted to see her (or any of the other unfamiliar young stars who have been publicized as the engagement's main attraction) haven't known when to come. Those who have come on the right night have seen the most promising young Soviet ballerina to make a Western début since Alla Sizova in 1961.

Physically, Pavlova is a well-shaped, small girl with abnormal leg extensions and feet. Maybe it's the abnormality that gives her stage personality its "dark" intonation; even when the steps are light and zestful, she almost terrifies you. Like many phenomenal dancers when they first appear, she exaggerates elements of the classical style, so that they appear to carry new meanings, but nothing in the exaggeration violates the implicit sense of the style. Her leg in full extension is precisely that series of subtle S curves which is drawn in dotted lines in the dancing manuals. Although the leg is held perfectly straight, the eye can follow one large S (from the front of the thigh to the calf) laid upon another in reverse (from the back of the knee along the high arch of the foot to its point). This is how all ballet legs look in theory, but it is strange to see the principle enunciated so fully on the stage, and it is doubly strange to see these paradigmatic legs sweeping the air in their high-voltage arcs. The energy of the gesture seems to pulsate from hip to point as steadily as a beam from a lighthouse. The hip joint operates so freely that in the leg's release no part of the force that belongs to the leg is kept back. In the *Nutcracker* pas de deux, she completes each of a series of supported pirouettes by opening smoothly to the highest of high développés—a hundred and eighty degrees—and without tipping from the vertical axis to do it. That leg just seems to go home by itself. And when it comes to those Bolshoi split jetés, she doesn't kick the back of her head, à la Plisetskaya; she keeps her cat-stretch in the air with legs leveled straight across (the flying-carpet look), and then does it twice more without warning. It's jump, jump, and jump again. In arabesque penchée, there she is again—wide open in a plunge—and she may be supported or she may not.

It might be expected that so young a performer would be encompassed by her effects—that they'd look like "mere" effects, with nothing more in the picture for us to see. But Pavlova is the mistress of what she does, and she touched me in innumerable ways—most of all in the sweet unconcern with which she did the undoable, as if it meant nothing unusual to her. Nothing *more* unusual, that is, than what already exists in traditional technique to delight her imagination. A simple run on point seems to enchant her. She may be a bit flowery and, with her theatrical black eyebrows, even a bit of an old-fashioned coquette, but something outré has to have lingered from the generation of Russian dancers that taught her—a generation for whom développés past the ear were unwise, if not unknown. I

suspect that her precocity is the sort that will in time shed its premature sophistication, and that, like Gelsey Kirkland, she'll grow
younger as she grows older. Although there are a few things I would
take away from the picture she creates, there is nothing I would add
—especially after her ravishing performance with Gordeyev in the
pas de deux from *La Fille Mal Gardée* at the first Saturday matinée.
The big original effects she achieves were combined with what one
might call standard bravura, except that there was nothing standard
about the quality of execution; and the smoothness of the combination, once the shock of it has passed, is what makes her an intelligible
—an eloquent—new figure on the stage. I am dazzled, but I am
not confused.

A few weeks ago, Nadezhda Pavlova won the grand prize at the
International Ballet Competition that is held every four years in
Moscow. Vyacheslav Gordeyev and Alexander Godunov were given
gold medals—the next-highest award. While that decision justly
reflects Gordeyev's abilities in relation to Pavlova's, it is a far from
accurate indication of Godunov's in relation to Gordeyev's. Gordeyev
is the best male classical dancer to appear during the Bolshoi season,
and he must be one of the best male classical dancers in the world.
I don't presume to understand how ballet competitions are judged
("ballet" and "competition" are to me incompatible notions), but
when I see Gordeyev performing posés en relevé while sustaining
his ballerina in a shoulder lift; when I see him, in a solo such as
the one he does in the *Fille* excerpt, adding luster to a circuit of
already perfect jetés en tournant by changing the position of his
arms—then I know I'm seeing gold-medalmanship if ever it deserved
to exist. Gordeyev's dancing, both when he is a partner and when
he is a soloist, is full of those grace notes that weaker technicians
leave out, but in watching him I find myself wondering how much
pure technique, in the crass sense, actually has to do with it. Those
little extras of his seem to come from inside, as tokens of an ardent
sincerity toward his ballerina, his public, and the art of dancing.
He's not one of the thunderers of ballet—in looks and temperament
he's a lot like the Joffrey Ballet's Burton Taylor—and although he
is certainly strong, he doesn't tear your head off. Rather, he's a
stylist who projects strength of mind—the kind of dancer I'd like
to read a book about. As for Godunov, I have watched him for two
weeks, in things like the *Black Swan* and *Don Quixote* pas de deux

and *The Ocean and the Pearls*, without finding out why he dances. A lanky blond giant who sends the audience into frenzies with his high jumps and multiple turns, Godunov seems to dance not for the love of it but for the *fight* of it. With a poor line, turned-in thighs, and floppy feet, he has a conscripted—even an imprisoned— look, and his struggle against the odds is not without a gloomy majesty. The Moscow judges must have thought him as good in his own way as Gordeyev—he is a hammer, and Gordeyev is a dart— but I believe that his true gift is for dramatic roles.

Young Ludmila Semenyaka, a Kirov graduate, a bronze medalist in 1969, and Godunov's ballerina in *Black Swan*, is the same kind of dancer as Natalia Makarova, and therefore I expected to like her more than I do. Maybe when Semenyaka learns projection I will. It's easy to say that she has been cursed with a flawless body, and she does look complacent, but her problem, I think, is the opposite —overconscientiousness. Too rigid a concentration on details may be keeping her from making the rhythmic continuity of a role clear to an audience. Only when the details are clear in respect to an overall rhythm does the dancer herself start to come alive and look interesting. Semenyaka seems to work at her dancing bit by bit and then match the bits. And they are lovely. She even "dramatizes," but that close-range way of doing things deprives her of animation. In the Bolshoi's Act II of *Giselle*, she was carried (literally, too, of course) by that most gentle and loving of Albrechts, Nicolai Fadeyechev. Fadeyechev, as those of us know who have admired him for years, is a very instructive dancer to admire. He has never seemed to me a great artist, but he is a true artist in some things— not least in his partnering. And he is a true artist, too, in the way he presents himself. His chief virtue consists in doing nothing to disturb the impression we get of him as soon as he appears. He never makes an abrupt or angular gesture. He never forces an effect. Everything about him—his roundness of contour in face and body, his softness of bearing, his easy rhythm in dancing, and his elastic returns to the floor from a jump, the upper leg springing higher as he lands in arabesque—all these things form a consistent picture, so he persuades us of his reality as an imaginary character in a ballet. It's as if he could see himself from the last rows in the topmost balcony. Semenyaka, when she stepped out of the wings, seemed about to project a sharp rhythm, an almost neurotic tension, but then she didn't do it. Fadeyechev alone told a credible story of the grave and the lilies and the dead girl and her ghost.

Fadeyechev, at forty, is looking thick in the middle and rather blue in the jowls, but it was good to see him again, and odd to think how remote even an unemphatic storytelling style like his may be from the new generation of Bolshoi dancers. Those chiffon miniatures on the "Highlights" programs simply can't be performed as pure dance metaphors, though that is how several of the younger girls tried to perform them. Of course, we can't really know very much about the direction the company is moving in until we see it in full ballets, and the current repertory at the Met is offering only second acts and excerpts and divertissements, plus *Chopiniana*, *Walpurgis Night*, and a new version of *Ballet School*. *Chopiniana* doesn't work with either the old or the new dancers. The musical rhythms are pulled out of shape and the dancing is flat. *Walpurgis Night*, the nymphs-and-satyrs number, will probably never work again. The generation of ballerinas that made a ballet like that a piece of glorious trash is now past its prime. Raissa Struchkova, the season's prima ballerina, tried to give it her old high, loud laughter, but all we got was an echo. The main interest of the season isn't centered on that sort of thing or on her but on the young dancers—the prizewinners and a few rising soloists, and the Bolshoi Dance Academy, which is appearing alongside members of the regular company. In *Ballet School*, several of the girl students show legs almost as remarkable as Nadezhda Pavlova's—long and straight legs that swing with a solid force and are never crooked up in arabesque. Like the crooked-leg arabesque of former days, the new high, high développé seems to be an official insigne of style.

However, I didn't notice anyone else's knees lifting so vividly in a run as Struchkova's do. At one end of the scale is the young Pavlova, whom no one resembles yet; at the other is Struchkova, whom no one resembles anymore. On the opening night, after the prodigy had created a sensation, Struchkova came on and, by entirely different means, created another one. She did one of her lavender numbers—an *Étude*—entering in a lift two stories high. On the floor, she knelt in ecstatic tendu poses or was dipped deeply backward in her partner's arms. Then, of course, she ran toward him, but not like a bowling ball at a tenpin, as she does in *Moszkowski Waltz*. For each run, there was a new motive; the dramatic picture kept changing, and the force of each change struck you with an unearthly clarity. It was old-time acrobatic adagio transformed into a story about a woman's uncontrollable passion for (one could not help thinking) a younger man. And it was, on Struchkova's part, a magnificent illusion. We imagined we saw unedited personal emotion, as blamelessly vulgar as in real life. But one doesn't applaud an artist like Struchkova for the size of her feelings. She doesn't captivate by "letting herself go"; far from it. The completeness of her artistic control became unmistakable at the end, when the surge died as suddenly as it had come. On top of her partner's chest in a no-hands lift (but that was unimportant), she drew the whole house to her in a spellbound quiet, and there was nothing left but her face. —*July 16, 1973*

Swans

Some companies, mostly Russian, dance *Swan Lake* as if it were an abstract tone poem. Others, such as the American Ballet Theatre, would like to keep it a lyric tragedy, if they only knew how. When the Russian star Natalia Makarova dances Odette-Odile with Ballet Theatre, as she did in her single appearance this past season, she performs in her own style, and with such thrilling conviction that you wish the company's native ballerinas would follow suit. But when you see how far Cynthia Gregory has already gone in quite a different direction, you want to cheer her on. The performance I saw Gregory give this season was the second of two; after two weeks of cancellations owing to a knee injury, she was not at her best. I did see her at her best in the *La Sylphide* that followed a few days later, and just as I began to think the same thing about it as about her normally very fine *Swan Lake*—that she has everything but style—suddenly, in the second act, she did have it.

Gregory casts a wavering spell in the big classical roles. (In roles created by Antony Tudor or Eliot Feld, or even Alvin Ailey, she has no trouble.) Sometimes her attention seems to be split between the role and the audience; more often it's as if she didn't quite believe in the character (of Odette or the Sylphide), or else didn't believe in herself as that character. Style consists in maintaining a convincing reality all through a piece. It's like wearing a garment that looks as if it might have been made for you even if it wasn't. Martine van Hamel, who made a very successful début in *Swan Lake* this season, is in that respect farther along than Gregory, though she hasn't Gregory's impact and isn't as brilliant a dancer. Gregory—tall, elegant, and with the wittiest nose in ballet since Tanaquil LeClercq's —is better as Odile than as Odette, while for Van Hamel's regal fourth positions and fine shoulders Odette is a natural. One would like to see Gregory build the grand-scale tragic drama that is meant to begin in the second act. For example, in the famous diagonal variation Odette jumps—sissonne forward—once, twice, and, after a low bend in fourth, finishes with a développé passé to the back. The sissonnes have a peculiar poignancy about them, a kind of folly. The feet that spring apart and together and apart seem to tear themselves from the earth. The jump gathers no momentum; it halts dead each time. Odette looks as if she were trying to jump out of her skin. She tries again, and this time her effort is supreme. Crossing her wrists low to the ground, she rises and arches hugely into the passé back, balancing for a second with swept-back wings. The whole phrase, from the jump through to the passé that ends in arabesque, parallels one phrase of the music, but it is a complete thought and a completely clear image of freedom not won but desperately sought. Odette's plight is before you—her captivity, her straining for release from the swan form to which she has been condemned. We get a sense of yearning, perhaps of resignation. We get a picture. It happens to be a picture that none of Ballet Theatre's Odettes gave me, but it is one of the possibilities of style that they might develop.

Although sissonnes en avant and "winged" arabesques occur in hundreds of ballets, the images of struggle in bondage belong to *Swan Lake* alone. They are emotionally expressive in a way that relates uniquely to the large emotion of the story. But the images may not be so concrete in every style of performance—they may not even be apparent. The variety of nuance in classical dancing is such that meanings change even when steps do not. There is a train of imagery basic to *Swan Lake* that is distinctly different from the imagery that is transmuted in performance. In his book *Russian Ballets*, the late Adrian Stokes is fascinated by the swan nature of Odette, and describes the sissonnes thus: "Each time she jumps softly it is as if she drew the stage up with her, as if her feet were

prehensile." The description is absolutely true to what I can only
call the static symbolism of the role. But *Swan Lake* is not a drama
about birds—it's a drama about freedom. The kind of imagery that
makes Odette live as a character appears only as a result of a
dancer's rhythm in the part. The Western ballerinas from whom
I've formed my impression of Odette's step sequence have a strict
sense of rhythm and a sharp attack: they emphasize the clearly
different shapes that the phrase takes as it progresses to the music;
they stress the sudden scissorlike parting of the thighs in the jump.
I've no idea whether they put the same emotional construction on
the movements that I do, but those who really bend forward from
the waist before lifting the leg back through développé passé make
me see an image unfolding from bud to blossom. Sometimes, when
the balance goes all the way to a swept-wing arabesque, it's also
possible to see the duplicit images of the swan in flight and the arc
of the hunter's bow fitted with its arrow.

But an Odette may give us none of this and still be real. Makarova
has a legato rhythm by nature, and, like most Russian ballerinas,
she loves languishing tempos. She doesn't bite into a phrase—she
eases through it. She doesn't give us a sharply active beat—she
gives us a mild pressure and a variable flow. Against our Western
tradition of performance, Makarova's Odette stood forth in grand
relief. I had not seen her perform the role in two years; the change
was remarkable. She seemed more than ever to be a great dancer
and to have discovered that special repose of great dancers in which
dancing is not an act but a state of being. She presented a drama
about freedom in which there was almost no dramatic interest.
Odette appeared isolated, inviolable, already free in her totally
passive acceptance of her fate. It was the fate of a slave. Until the
last act she did not protest. As Odette, Makarova does not let you
feel the force of her personality; she seems personally uninvolved.
And the lightness of her attack has increased; it is now almost
impalpable. You feel, rather than see, the movement calmly radiating
from a still center. Mysteriously, it keeps radiating. The muscular
energy does not bind or retract. People in the audience remarked
that you could not see the beginning or the end of a step—that it
seemed to grow from nowhere and vanish. That sounds like a fancy
cliché, but there is always in Makarova's dancing that mysterious
extra stretch from the center—always that central support for the
force of a gesture—which remains invisible. Leg extensions at hip
height caused not the slightest disturbance in the torso or anyplace

else. So she appeared as if controlled by some exterior force—the sorcerer, perhaps.

If Odette is Makarova passive, Odile is Makarova active, but the two roles don't divide her capacities equally. As a dancer, she is more closely attuned to Odette. As an actress, she thrives in the third act —she is a whole new creature. And it's in the role of Odile that we feel the fullness of her presence for the first time. The contrasts in her personality are all on view, summed up, held in balance. She's all there. Makarova has a slyness that makes her a charming comedienne, and she's a devastating Odile. At one point, she rushed down to the front of the stage, held a soussus pose at full tension, and beamed her appealing rat-faced, toothy grin straight onto the audience. And there's that one magnificently horrid moment when, as Odile, she impersonates Odette in order to fool the hero. Makarova doesn't slip from one character into another—she slips from character into noncharacter. You see in a flash what the dual role means to her—how in one act she extends her natural genius as a dancer to create a semblance of a dramatic statement, and how in the next she really lives as an integrated theatrical personality. Since her escape from Russia, Makarova has triumphed mainly in the nineteenth-century ballets that she used to do there, and she has had great success, too, in Ballet Theatre's Tudor repertory. (She is the only dancer who has ever made me see the point of *Dark Elegies*.) But no choreographer, East or West, has created an important role for her. No one has helped to *explain* her as a personality. As Odile, she showed us that she can do just about anything; even the pirouettes, her only serious technical weakness, are getting better. Her dancing was as mysteriously controlled, as light and blandishing, as in the second act, but crisper in attack—oh, yes, she knows how to do it. And, but for that one moment at the footlights, everything was played to her partner, the extremely pleasant Ivan Nagy (who facially resembles her). The whole dirty trick was on him, for him, not for the audience. As one whose heart automatically sinks at the downbeat of the Black Swan pas de deux (especially in this production, where its placing causes a wrenching key change), I testify to the radiance of the dance on this occasion. Before it was over, the audience was on its feet.

The American Ballet Theatre is not, on the whole, the place to look for classical dancing, but it possesses a few impressive young dancers who peep out from their places in the corps or shine in soloist roles. Kim Highton seems to me the best of the girls, and Fernando Bujones is the outstanding male talent of the new generation in American ballet. Bujones is one of those rare straight-from-the-crib classical dancers, having fully turned-out hips, stretched and turned-over legs, and long, flexible feet that are amazing in their strength and delicacy. Flat on the floor, they seem to grip like talons (*there* are prehensile feet for you), and his three-quarter rise on toe is as narrowly based and as diamond-hard as any girl's point. His arms seem to start from his lower back and branch, forklike, from his spine. Bujones is built slightly but ideally; small but with a gift for expanding himself physically in space, he already has a very grand style. A lordly elf. One sees him jump to fierce heights, land, and rebound with no sign of shock or break in the continuity of his line. His zest saves his perfection from monotony, his grit saves it from prissiness.

The company has put Bujones into soloist roles: various pas de deux and de trois; Dennis Nahat's empty *Mendelssohn Symphony* (the "Italian"), in which he performs a long series of classroom exercises; Harald Lander's *Etudes*, in which he does the same; and a few character parts, like the Third Sailor in *Fancy Free*. He has looked smashing in everything, but isolated. There is a sense in which male classical dancers of talent are more isolated by their gifts than female dancers are. A girl can expand against the corps, or lean on a boy for support, but boys always protrude from their context. Male technique defines the figure as essentially a lonely one, sets it apart from everything and everyone else. The lone male figure in a stageful of women gains drama in isolation; it gains nothing from a stageful of men. And the practical consequence of this is that male stars are hard to cast. After the inevitable James in *La Sylphide* and Poet in *Les Sylphides* and Frantz in *Coppélia*, Bujones may go on to Siegfried and Albrecht, but those parts, considered the summit of male stardom, are primarily partnering roles. No amount of revision can disguise the fact that they were not meant to occupy a position equal to the woman's roles. Bujones at present outdances everybody else on the stage, and lovers of classical dancing will rush to see him in anything. And they will all clamor to see him in a new, custom-made *dancing* role. But if no one creates for Makarova, who will create for Bujones?   —*August 27, 1973*

Joffrey Jazz

As its name indicates, *Deuce Coupe* is a vehicle for two companies, and as a joint presentation of Twyla Tharp's company and the City Center Joffrey Ballet it was the hit of the entire spring season. Now it's back, in repertory, with much the same cast as before (a very smiley Nancy Ichino has gone in for Starr Danias, and there are one or two other minor replacements) and in even better performance condition. The audience loves it; I love it. But *Deuce Coupe* is more than a big hit, more than the best thing the Joffrey Ballet has ever done—it's the outstanding accomplishment to date of the ballet year.

For excitement and originality, none of the new works by major choreographers compares with it—not even Merce Cunningham's *Changing Steps*, which was included in a series of Events given last March at the Brooklyn Academy. I say "not even Cunningham" because there may well be a genealogical link between him and Twyla Tharp. I won't attempt to trace Twyla Tharp's line of descent —she seems to have absorbed something from nearly everybody who moves well—but, like Cunningham, she is routinely classified as an "avant-garde" choreographer, and only a few years ago she was one of those choreographers who were working without music and in nontheatrical and open spaces—either out-of-doors or in museums and gyms. The only element that she did not eliminate was dancing itself, and in this she was unique—defying the exponents of nondance and antidance. The way she danced was unique, too. The open-space movement in choreography goes on, and Twyla Tharp now has her imitators, but at that time nothing like her had ever been seen before. The finest of the post-Cunningham generation of choreographers, up until *Deuce Coupe*, she was thought to be also the most forbiddingly idiosyncratic. Even when, with her own small company, she started choreographing in more conventional surroundings to eighteenth-century music and to jazz, the burn of her intensely personal style didn't wear off, and her dancers seemed to be moved by a form of private communication which made them unlike any other dancers that one could see. I believe that the dances she has done for them—especially the great jazz ballets *Eight Jelly Rolls* and *The Bix Pieces* and *The Raggedy Dances*—are her best work. But *Deuce Coupe* is a good work, too. It isn't a great ballet, but it fills to abundance every need it was meant to fill, and, as far as ballet audiences are concerned, nothing like *it* has ever been seen before, either.

Deuce Coupe is a pop ballet and a great gift to the Joffrey company. Since 1968, when Robert Joffrey put his company on the cover of *Time* with a mixed-media/rock ballet called *Astarte*, it has been polishing its reputation as America's great swinging company. This is one half of the Joffrey company's Janus profile; the other is the image of custodian of modern-day classics from the international repertory. But the Joffrey's dual policy stretched the capacities of its dancers too far and broke them. Dancers live and progress on roles that are created for them. All those slick, empty, and violent ballets by Gerald Arpino that slammed the audience with the Dionysian ecstasy of dance or appealed to the audience's political convictions and hunger for "relevance" certainly did contribute to the shaping of a style, but it was a style that rendered Joffrey dancers unfit for anything better. As classical dancers, the Joffreys have no touch; they look squat, badly placed, hectic, and unmusical. When Joffrey, who has excellent taste in non-Joffrey ballets, imports a classic Danish ballet like *Konservatoriet*, his dancers can hardly get through it. At the moment, they are having serious problems with a production of Frederick Ashton's *The Dream*. (What dream is this? Their tendency to broaden and coarsen is like a bad dream of American ballet.) After seven years in residence at the City Center, the company had grown so unattractive that serious dance lovers stopped attending everything but the classic revivals—the choices were always interesting, even if the actual performances were not. What this withdrawal of attention meant was that the structure by which the company made its dancers grow was dead. Generally speaking, you can't feed dancers on imports and revivals. Imports and revivals please audiences; they seldom help the dancer, who can't be at his best in somebody else's old part.

It would be too much to claim that *Deuce Coupe* has saved the Joffrey, but it does give the dancers something genuine to respond to—something that's exactly suited to their talents—and it tidies up the company's self-image. It's just as if Twyla Tharp had said, "So you want pop? I'll give you pop," but what she has given the

Joffrey is so close to the real thing that part of the audience—the part that has decided what contemporary, orgiastic, youth-spirited, with-it ballet looks like—is taken by surprise. *Deuce Coupe* astounds by the utter unfamiliarity of familiar things. Its music is a tape collage of fourteen Beach Boys hits, starting with "Little Deuce Coupe" and ending with "Cuddle Up"—probably the last jukebox pop that *was* pop, and not Pop Art. Its décor is spray-can graffiti applied to a rolling backcloth while the ballet is in progress. And its dancing—that which gives it life and joy—is a peculiar Tharpian combination of classical ballet and the juvenile social dancing of the past decade. The ballet steps are like a primitive's-eye view of classical style, fascinating in their plainness and angularity, and the social dances are rich with crazy, campily corny suggestion. Neither type of dancing is what it would be in the hands of any other choreographer, and yet neither is what it ordinarily appears to be in its raw state—in the classroom, or in school gyms, ballrooms, and discothèques. Whatever the Tharp eye sees, it changes. (Even the graffiti, with their characteristic stilted lines, curly serifs, and locked edges, look as if they were intended for *Deuce Coupe*. And, oh, New York! Isn't it nice to see the stuff in a place where it belongs?) As a result, the whole ballet has this low-contrast choreographic weave that knits its separate scenes together, but there's so much action going on, and the action is so complicated and delicately timed, that the effect is never one of monotony. (There is one moment when the ballet seems to slump. At the end of "Don't Go Near the Water," we get one more roiling group instead of something we haven't seen before.) This complexity and delicacy can be undervalued. Most of the time in *Deuce Coupe*, the dancers appear to be behaving with such realism that we could believe they were making it up as they went along. People who don't often go to the ballet might recognize the validity of these dances at once and wonder why such a fuss was being made over them. People who go more regularly fall into the trap of their expectations, and *Deuce Coupe* looks formless to them—just taken off the street and thrown onto the stage. Actually, no one has put contemporary American popular dancing of quite this intensity and freedom on the stage before, and I am sure no one but Twyla Tharp would have known how to make these dances legible in the theatre. A hundred kids going berserk at a school prom is a powerful but not necessarily a theatrical spectacle. To be realized on the stage, such potency has to be objectified; the material has to be changed and heightened. In the process, it becomes beautiful, but "beauty" isn't the choreographer's object—clarity is. And Twyla Tharp does something that people dancing for recreation don't do: she makes a theatrical translation of the music. In "How She Boogalooed It," she doesn't give us the Boogaloo—she gives us something that looks more like snake dancing at top speed. "Alley Oop," "Take a Load Off Your Feet," "Long Tall Texan," and "Catch a Wave" are based as much on the lyrics as on the music, and include several obvious, Broadway-style jokes. In "Papa Ooh Mau Mau," the dancers mime smoking pot and freaking out. When the music isn't interesting enough, it's speeded up or two tracks are run side by side. We do get a long way from the school prom. The spontaneity and naturalness of the dances are a marvelous illusion, a secret of professional style. Everyone has had the experience in the theatre of the happy occurrence—some fantastically accurate inflection or bit of punctuation, so like a moment in life we think it couldn't happen again. Twyla Tharp's choreography is full of such moments that do happen again. In *Deuce Coupe*, I think of Nina Wiener's freak-out or Glenn White landing in fifth position right on the *pow!* of the downbeat in "Wouldn't It Be Nice." (The surprise is partly that you hadn't seen him jump.)

Deuce Coupe makes rather a special point of ballet versus pop dancing. In this, it's an extension of *The Bix Pieces*, which was composed two years ago for the Tharp company's formal Paris début. (Its most recent performances took place this past summer at Jacob's Pillow and a few weeks ago on the CBS Sunday-morning program *Camera Three*.) *The Bix Pieces*, named for Bix Beiderbecke, is based on jazz-band dance music of the 1920's. The dancing is a moody synthesis of the tap-toe-baton-acrobatic routines that millions of American children have been heirs to, and in the course of the work a narrator informs us, "The fundamental concepts of dance are few, but the stylistic appraisal of these concepts can produce infinite combinations and appearances. For example, 'slap, ball, change' is 'chassé' in ballet, or 'slap' ('tendu'), 'ball' ('piqué'), 'change' ('plié')." This is demonstrated, and the narrator goes on to say, "So, you see, all things can be profoundly and invisibly related, exactly and not at all the same." *Deuce Coupe* deals in a similar technical paradox—sometimes at too great a length. For example, it has a ballerina (Erika Goodman) performing a classical solo virtually all through the piece. Sometimes she's alone onstage and sometimes she's the eye of the hurricane, but she never stops dancing, and since there are other ballet dancers on the stage, I have sometimes wondered why she's there. She is eternal, the others are temporal? But I have never wished Miss Goodman off the stage while watching her on it. I like what she does, and she's doing it this season with unusual beauty. Erika Goodman is chubby and neckless, with big legs that wave in disproportionately high extensions. With her large-scale gesture and demonstrative warmth, she's becoming a baby Struchkova. But, like most of the Joffrey girls, she lacks something as a classical stylist, and her role—a taxing one, which consists of the ballet vocabulary performed alphabetically—is so Tharpian in conception that it really doesn't resemble classical ballet enchaînements at all. What we see in her random provocative movements is a parallel to the dislocated, familiar-unfamiliar movements that dominate the main action of the ballet. The two dance forms —ballet and popular—remain technically distinguishable but become stylistically fused. It's a Tharpian fusion, and the didactic point of *The Bix Pieces* disappears. All things are no longer so invisibly related.

There's a sense in which *Deuce Coupe* would be better if the Joffrey members of the cast were better classical dancers. Twyla Tharp has asked a lyricism of them, and a precision of épaulement, that they can't consistently supply. Yet in "Wouldn't It Be Nice," the most exhilarating of the Beach Boys songs, the steps are entirely classical, and this is the number I love best. From the opening port de bras to the quietly held preparations in fifth—held so long that when the jetés into attitude-front start popping like molecules around the stage the pressure appears to blow them into the air—there is a tender mystery to the dancing which seems equal to the best of *The Bix Pieces* and to the best classical ballet I know. *Deuce Coupe* makes the Joffrey dancers look human (at the first performance I had trouble recognizing most of them); it rescues them from the curse of pseudo ballet and gives them back their natural grace of movement. They look very much as they might have looked as children—which is right for the preteen, presexual world that the ballet invokes—and they are magically divested of their customary hard-sell performing style. Besides Miss Goodman and Mr. White, the Joffrey dancers who shine most vividly in this new light are (in order of their appearance): Rebecca Wright, William Whitener, Beatriz Rodriguez, Larry Grenier, Gary Chryst, Donna Cowen, and Eileen Brady.

As for the Tharp dancers, they always do what comes naturally.

Their stage personalities are so alive that we can follow them from ballet to ballet like characters in the Sunday comics. Twyla Tharp herself, with her sorrowful-baleful semihallucinated stare, is the Krazy Kat of the bunch. Sara Rudner is the Mysterious Lady (her *Deuce Coupe* solo "Got to Know the Woman" is ironically seductive, like an adolescent's vision of sexuality), and Rose Marie Wright, the "Long Tall Texan," has an instantaneous impact on the audience —it applauds her on sight. Kenneth Rinker, the lone male, is a brotherly, somewhat taciturn corduroy-cap type, and the two other girls, Isabel Garcia-Lorca and Nina Wiener, have a fashion-model elegance. The group dancing of the Tharp company suggests a federation of individuals, and you can see the same kind of freedom in the group dancing of *Deuce Coupe*. But the restlessness and pain of American children are in it, too. The end of the ballet—the long, slow crescendo of tossing arms, lunges in plié, and backward bourrées on point, with here and there a fall to the floor—is half truth, half myth. It sums up a kind of schmaltzy romanticism that young people love to wrap themselves in, and it is absolutely true to our experience of their world. The crescendo is ingeniously stage-managed, gaining might not by mass but by intensity, like a hum that gets louder, and it ends in a masterstroke—a freeze-pose blackout into silhouette. The cliché is the only possible schmaltz-climax. Then, gradually, it loosens, Miss Goodman takes a few hops forward, and *Deuce Coupe* continues somewhere in space as the curtain falls.

Deuce Coupe is fresh and exciting because it is closer to its source in popular culture than most pop or "jazz" ballets ever care to be. The music is the kind of music for which a dance idiom already exists. The choreography is in part a parody of that idiom, but it is authentic. In two other ballets in the Joffrey repertory, Eliot Feld's *Jive* and Arpino's *Trinity*, the music is concert-hall jazz and evangelical rock, respectively: two forms for which the dancing has to be invented, and in both ballets the choreography is more synthetic than the music. *Jive* is set to Morton Gould's "Derivations for Clarinet and Jazz Band"—the same score that Balanchine used for a piece called *Clarinade*, which is remembered solely because it was the first ballet he created at Lincoln Center. The music doesn't work any better for Feld, who transforms it into a tight, cheerless, and ambivalent pastiche of the fifties, the period of Jerome Robbins wearing sneakers. It ends with the dancers lurching at the audience and crying "Jive!" *Jive* (a forties title) represents a good choreographer working below his form. *Trinity* represents a bad choreographer working at the very top of *his*. The work is all big jumps and running lifts, and it is consumed with the fake piety of the beads-and-amulets era. At the end, the dancers place peace candles all over the stage. In the context of these two ballets, and of the Joffrey repertory generally, *Deuce Coupe* is a masterpiece. Not only is it musically sound and poetically convincing—its emotions are the kind that make civilized contact in the theatre possible. It doesn't bludgeon us for a response; when it throws out a manipulative net, it does so with a grin. It doesn't pretend that we share the life it depicts, or make us feel that we should. It is completely objective, but, beyond that (*Jive* is objective, too, and dead), it respects its material. *Deuce Coupe* is an adult ballet about kids.   —*October 29, 1973*

Ballroom Britannia

Arthur Murray, Inc., says that "touch" dancing, or dancing with partners, is coming back. For some people, it has never been away, and among those people are fifty-one highly trained couples whom the Murray organization, as hosts and local sponsors, brought to the Felt Forum last weekend to compete in the 1973 World's Professional Ballroom Dancing Championships. The competitors, who represented twenty-seven countries, included some old-timers (a few smooth imperial rovers, one or two hotcha grandmothers in popcorn curls), but the clear majority of the dancers were in their late twenties to middle thirties—young enough to have started their careers just at the time when the wave of spastic go-go solo dancing was carrying off the youth of all nations. Oddly, the country that provided the international pop-rock phenomenon with its standard of chic—Great Britain—is also the stronghold of traditional ballroom dancing. First prize in the Modern competition on Sunday (Saturday had been devoted to Latin American dances) was taken by a British couple, Richard and Janet Gleave, who were just nineteen when they began dancing together, in 1963, the year of the Beatles.

Altogether, Britain dominated the weekend, also taking second prize in both Modern and Latin. Its closest competitors were Austria (first prize, Latin) and West Germany, with Japan coming up strong on the outside. An American team, Vernon Brock and Beverly

Donahue, of Cherry Hill, New Jersey, was third in Latin, and we also won the Consolation Cha-Cha, an event held for the couples who didn't make the semifinals. These were conspicuous victories, but in the wrong contest. The standards that have been set for exhibition Latin dancing don't seem nearly as elegant as those set for exhibition Modern; the whole Saturday competition lacked style, and, in the sense that a New York Latin might understand the word, it lacked class. Surely the two splendid New York Latin bands, Machito's and Tito Puente's, that were among those hired to play for the occasion can seldom have looked down upon a more *jíbaro*—nonhip—scene. That might account for an almost total absence of Latin and black contestants. With a whole evening devoted to Latin American numbers—the cha-cha, the samba, the rumba, and the paso doble—the competition drew not a single entry from South America. (There was one Mexican couple, who didn't make much of a showing.) A publicity fact sheet pointed out that South America has no organized dancing, and organization does seem to be the key to representation. The International Council of Ballroom Dancing, with headquarters in London, runs the World's Championships, on the model of an annual Olympics, and the member countries also hold periodic championship dance-offs, for which contestants may qualify by passing a series of graded examinations set up by another London body, the Imperial Society of Teachers of Dancing. The average contestant couple are certified professionals—usually dance instructors in their home countries—who have not only mastered the successive stages of the ISTD syllabus but also studied for some time in London. The pervasive English influence on Latin dancing isn't apparent to the spectator—the dancing doesn't look "Anglo" —but *some* pervasive influence certainly is apparent, and it seems to have resulted in a tasteless domestication of those sensual and volatile elements that make Latin dances appealing. Not that exhibition Latin looks easy to perform; it merely looks difficult in the wrong way —grimly "flamboyant." And it is full of bizarre practices: corny flamenco, nightclub-jazz choreography, bits of ballet adagio, and a great many figure-skating exercises. I knew that the judges used the Olympic "skating system" of marking, but I didn't expect to see so much ballroom skating. There were flying-camel lifts, sit spins, slow-circling arabesques penchées performed by men holding on to girls' waists, and stationary penchées performed by girls opposite men in low fondu. Somehow, it all looks better on skates—sexier, too.

More anomalies presented themselves in the arrangement of the programs. The tango, classified as a "modern" dance, appeared in the Modern competition, and something called Boston jive appeared in the Latin competition. "Boston jive" at least ran true to form—the form of exhibition Latin: unstylish show-biz eclecticism, square execution. (Jack Hansen's orchestra, playing in the strict tempo prescribed by the competition, didn't help.) The tango, though, was London tango and nothing else but. I certainly *had* been surprised to read in the program, "Surprisingly, the tango has its origins in country dance of seventeenth-century England." But, with the way things are run at international ballroom-dance meets, who could doubt that the tango had made its way home again? Of the three known varieties the program went on to name—the Argentine, the Continental, and the English—the English, or "International or Competition," tango was the one we got. As it turns out, the English tango is, in its own subdued way, ravishing. There are no slinky postures, no lunges to the knee, no skulls pressed together or swooning-away dips to the floor. The basic step is a foxtrot sink-glide with a slight hesitation as the heads snap-lash in opposite directions. It is hypnotic and only a little bit silly. And it provided the one touch of exoticism in the Modern competition, which otherwise consisted of the waltz (the English or Boston), the slow foxtrot, the fast foxtrot (or quickstep), and the Viennese waltz.

What a marvelous program this Modern competition was! After Saturday's Latin-*cum*-jazz indigestibles, Sunday was like getting to a first-class English restaurant. No more bad, obfuscatory foreign matter; no more ice-skating. On Saturday, it hadn't really been possible to concentrate on the dancers. My eye had been taken by the chaotic and unbecoming things they were doing, and the excellence of the first-prize winners—Hans Peter and Inge Fischer, of Austria —had escaped me. But on Sunday pure-English dancing mastery asserted itself everywhere—not only in the supremacy of individual English couples, like the Gleaves, but in the schooling of all the dancers. London in the 1970's is to ballroom dancing what St. Petersburg in the 1890's was to ballet—the last outpost, the largest remaining authoritative professional center. In contrast to Russia, however, whose balletomanes were large in force but small in number, England has a huge ballroom-dance public; the strength of the English professional schooling derives in great part from a national passion that never died, as it did in this country. No American couple has ever won a World's Championship, but this year, with the competition held for the first time in the United States, hopes were high for last year's third-place winners in Modern, the Joe Jenkinses, of Washington, D.C. Unfortunately, Mrs. Jenkins had become physically disabled, and they bowed out. To an inexpert American eye—my own —there were no great bets among the American couples that did dance. They lacked the elementary free-breathing togetherness of the British couples—that look of being pinned securely at the breastbone, with the woman's torso handsomely lifted and arched. The mingled élan and restraint of the style eluded them, too. (The Japanese were wonderful at it.) At an unfamiliar spectacle, one gains expertise by watching that part of it one thinks is the best. I watched with great pleasure a bubble-light team from Tokyo, Tetsuo Kezuka and Chieko Yamamoto, until it became evident, even to me, that Miss Yamamoto's footwork wasn't as precise and arrowy as Mrs. Gleave's. Once onto the Gleaves, I never came off. In the slow foxtrot and the waltzes, where the trick is not to stay on the beat but to hang off it as daringly as possible, the dancers all tried for rubato phrasing, but none so successfully as the Gleaves. None were able to achieve such variety in the phrase—such prolonged, world-enough-and-time retards, such imperceptible recoveries and smooth renewals of impetus. In the quickstep, the Gleaves hovered and flew; sometimes their flights ended in a skid down the floor—a full chord pressed to the ground, after innumerable glancing strokes at inch height. Their tango was an absolute diagram of that dance. And in all the dances no other couple on the floor had their divine slow takeoff. It became a thrill to watch for—an independent signature of their style. What the Gleaves alone had is what ballroom dancing is about, and although the judges' scores were not posted after the rounds, no one in the audience seemed surprised when it was announced at the end of the day that the Gleaves had indeed won every dance. A good deal of sentiment was evident, though, for Kezuka and Yamamoto, who really deserved better than fourth place.

There was one area of expertise that I wish I could have possessed beforehand. Until their efficiency in motion became clear to me (and even then it became only somewhat clear), I didn't like the women's stylized balldresses—the tight bodices and extremely wide bouffant skirts, which are like a heavy caricature of ballet tutus. The pointed toes and near-stiletto heels on the shoes have a function also—to lend clarity to the footwork—but, like the skirts, they are aesthetically unattractive. (For the Latin dances, women wear the same shoes and cancan skirts with flounces just above the knee.) The effect of the female silhouette is to freeze time in the year 1960, when the World's Championships began. To a European dance aficionado, it may be part of an understood and accepted tradition, but to an American it looks as if someone were trying to turn the clock back.   —*November 12, 1973*

A Moment in Time

Twyla Tharp is the Nijinska of our time. *Deuce Coupe*, an un-idealized portrait of American youth in the 1960's, is her *Les Biches*, and *As Time Goes By*, an abstract fantasy about individuals against the blank canvas of a tribal society, is her *Les Noces*. Of course I'm generalizing, but not, I hope, idly. *As Time Goes By*, created this season for the Joffrey Ballet and employing an all-Joffrey cast and Haydn music, is a study of classical dancing. Its "tribal" ethos is that of young, hard-working New York–American dancers, subspecies Joffrey, and its light-speckled fancies and serene inversions of classical principles are as far from the iron wit of *Les Noces* as the heterogeneous home-style social dances of *Deuce Coupe* are from the monolithic encounters of that Riviera salon in *Les Biches*. Nevertheless, the parallel persists between Twyla Tharp and ballet's greatest woman choreographer. I think that, like Nijinska's, Twyla Tharp's work exacts a primitive force of expression from its subject, which is classical ballet. It seems to seek out first principles and turn them over with curiosity, finding new excitement in what lies on the other side of orthodoxy. And it gains a secondary kind of raw power from what seem deliberate lapses from ballet decorum and refinement. Sometimes a classical step is resolved with a new twist; it forms itself and then re-forms itself backward. But sometimes the step itself isn't all there; it seems truncated or only half-quoted; the effect is of a surgical cut, a slash at the fat body of unusable style. The negations and distortions of Nijinska's choreography cut away rhetorical flab. The turned-in toes and obsessive stiff pointwork of *Les Noces* were a radical distortion, necessary if women's feet and not simply their points were to become significant once more on the stage. In much the same way, Twyla Tharp is moving toward a new quality of plain speech in classical choreography. At times, she seems to be on the verge of creating a new style, a new humanity, for classical-ballet dancers. If she doesn't go all the way to a full enunciation of that style, that is probably because the ballet is not long enough. Time, in this ballet, goes by much too fast.

As Time Goes By is in four sections, quasi-dramatic in their progression. Beginning with the Individual, it moves on to the Group, then to the Mass, and finally back to the Individual. (These designations are my own; I prefer them to the unevocative titles in the program.) The opening solo is danced by Beatriz Rodriguez in silence. It is a concise statement of the material that will be developed, a ball of string that will be unwound. We see semaphore arms, snake hips, pirouettes stopped in mid-whirl, a paroxysm of flexions in relevé. Rodriguez, who looked childlike in *Deuce Coupe*, is transformed again. She is monumental, like a Nijinska iron woman. Three boys and two girls join her (Adix Carman, Henry Berg, William Whitener, Eileen Brady, and Pamela Nearhoof), and the music begins—the Minuet and Trio of Haydn's "Farewell" Symphony. The dance that accompanies it is not one dance but six—one for each member of the sextet. All six dances go on at the same time, now linking up, now separating, and all the while moving from one tight cellular cluster to another. This sextet, which builds up the fascination and the deadpan humor of a clockwork toy, is a classical arrangement of the Tharpian group dance and typically democratic. The multifocal viewpoint makes a special event of the partnering (which keeps changing hands). It also eliminates the conventional hierarchy of the ballet ensemble. No one here is a ballerina; anyone may partner or be partnered. The sextet builds up pressure, too. The little hexagonal unit seems to become more and more confining, but the sweet musicianship of the choreography keeps the scene clear, its density unharrowing.

The music breaks off, and one of the girls does a little walkaround in silence as new dancers enter. The Presto movement of the symphony starts. Suddenly, the stage seems to expand to unbelievable size. Dancers pour on and spread out. The broadened pattern has released us, but the tempo has stepped up the pressure, and we redouble our concentration. Now, against a complex background of moving dancers, solo variations occur; one, for Nearhoof, is galvanically funny, though at this breathless speed the laughs can't keep up with the jokes. Nor can we keep up with the ballet. There is no time to ponder the new logic of the steps—new in the way they combine close musical fit with a "natural" loose look suited to each individual dancer; there's just time enough to enjoy it. One would like the key to that new logic; what makes it work at this tempo? Whatever it is, the result is a hyper-kinesthesia that takes hold of the audience and doesn't let up until, once more, Haydn waves his wand and the dancers stroll nonchalantly away.

The end of the piece is as Haydn would have wished it. To the Adagio finale of the "Farewell"—so called because the instrumentation thins out until only two violins are left—a dancer (Larry Grenier, whose attenuated lyrical style is itself a statement of slackening force) moves alone while others set about disappearing in a fashion that is unpredictable and sometimes chancy. A girl leaves, only to return a moment later. A boy lifts a girl off, turning her twice in the air, so another girl has to duck three times to avoid being hit. Ultimately, Grenier is *all* alone, having spun out the last thin skein of movement.

As Time Goes By is not a pretentious enough ballet to make people feel that they have witnessed a heroic new undertaking in choreography. Its fifteen minutes are loaded with interest, but, like all of Twyla Tharp's work, the piece is peculiarly horizonless. Although each work she has made is self-contained and perfectly lucid in its own terms, each seems almost accidentally bound by the rise and fall of a curtain and to be part of a larger continuity that exists out of time—out of the time, that is, of this ballet we have just seen. Somewhere, perhaps, there are unseen dancers unrolling the patterns and following up every implication, but we in the audience are spared their tortuous zeal. Twyla Tharp makes us feel that a ballet is nothing more than divisions of a choreographer's time. Although she understands cheap sensation and uses it well, there is no gloss, no appeal for attention, no careerism, in her work. It's amusing to think of what a promoter like Diaghilev would have done with her. First, I think, he would retitle the sections of this ballet "Ariadne," "Athens," "The Labyrinth," and "Theseus." Cocteau would write the program notes and design the costumes. (The ones we have, by the Seventh Avenue designer Chester Weinberg, are examples of modest chic in shades of taupe.) Diaghilev would call the whole piece *The Minotaur*, because there's no Minotaur in it, and he would proclaim "La Tharp" the herald of a new age. Which she is. —*November 19, 1973*

Standing Still

When a choreographer can't follow up on a great success, it may be because he is not sure what success is made of. The Alvin Ailey City Center Dance Theatre has its one big hit in *Revelations*. It is always taking on new works and revivals, yet, year in and year out, nothing tops *Revelations*. Nothing that seems to have been intended to top it even gets halfway. And as *Revelations* looms in its increasingly solitary splendor, it becomes something that its admirers want to stay away from—a superhit that will win ovations and encores even when, as in this past season at the City Center, it isn't very well danced. At one time, *Revelations* was plausibly the signature work of the Ailey company, standing for what Ailey and his dancers could do best. Now it might almost be taken for a fluke. All the attempts to repeat its success have loaded the repertory with failures based on similar material. But the special power of *Revelations* doesn't come from its material, strong as that is; it comes from the structural tension and driving rhythm that Ailey built into the piece in the years when he was still working on the things that craftsmen care about. Ailey either doesn't realize or doesn't care anymore what makes *Revelations* so popular, and the work he now does is marked by an incredible inconsistency and slackness of design. However, Ailey is remarkably consistent in trying to capitalize on *Revelations* as if it were a *formula* success.

Among his failures one would have to list this season's two new productions—José Limón's *Missa Brevis* and John Butler's *Carmina Burana*. Ailey has apparently decided that the audience wants more ballets on religious or folk themes, with singing as well as dancing, and for the past few years he has been filling the orchestra pit with choristers and dressing his dancers in surplices and cowls. Not long ago he did a chaotic Roman Catholic version of *Revelations* with the jazz composer Mary Lou Williams. *Mary Lou's Mass* was not performed this season; its place was presumably taken by *Missa Brevis*. The music is the "Missa Brevis in Time of War" that Kodály wrote between 1942 and 1945; it isn't a requiem, but the mood of the choreography is one of heavy mourning dotted with passages of heavy "affirmation." When I first saw the work performed, in 1958, by Limón's company, with Limón himself as the Pastor, I thought that he had in mind a homage to the heroes of the Hungarian revolution in 1956. (There may actually have been a program note to that effect, or perhaps someone made the connection in a review.) I don't know what occasion is served by Ailey's revival of this bereaved flock worshiping in its bombed-out church. *Missa Brevis* is the kind of work one demands an explanation for, because the choreography, besides being unremittingly grim, has little intrinsic interest. Limón, honest workman that he was, does not betray his theme by any variation in texture. Every move is programmatic; everything is made of lead—even the lifts, in which girls are stood upright in the air or slung like sacks between two men.

In 1958, I thought, too, that Limón was Mindszenty. Now I guess we're meant to think of John Parks as José Limón. Parks, long and thin, has a shaved, bony skull and a big wingspread. He was a praying mantis of a Pastor; usually he looks like a dancing lobster. For a man of his size, his impact is weak. His spine is rigid, so his torso has no expressive play, and when he moves he seems to get smaller. The audience enjoys Parks. His oddities, and Ailey's need for male dancers, make him a star, and he has a great many leading roles, including one in *Carmina Burana*. When I saw it, the other male lead was taken by Hector Mercado, and the two of them gave performances that couldn't be described in professional terms as dancing. Mercado, stocky and muscle-bound, typifies a number of recent additions to the Ailey male corps. These men have difficulty stretching their bodies into the three-dimensional plastic configurations that distinguish a dancer's space from an athlete's, and if they can manage to stretch into their space they can't fill it with energy. Most of these helpless young men were on the stage in *Carmina Burana*, partnering women who were not much better. (The two female leads, Mari Kajiwara and Tina Yuan, were pretty dears who didn't seem to know what they were doing.) The choreography, like the music, is undergraduate flimflam, and it needs to be pushed along by the performers; I remembered it as meretricious rather than feeble. Can this be the *Carmina Burana* I saw done by the New York City Opera in 1959, with Carmen de Lavallade, Mary Hinkson, Scott Douglas, and Glen Tetley doing their damnedest to look delectable and roguish?

The Ailey dancers were so listless throughout this season that it was painful to hear them eulogized by intermission speakers calling upon the audience for financial support. Possibly the listlessness was due to the strain of trying to get too many ballets into too few rehearsal hours—the Ailey repertory is nothing if not extensive—and more money would buy the company more time. But many of the speakers didn't sell the company on the basis of its artistry; they sold its multiracial character, its native populism, its ecumenical repertory. They sold it, in short, as a cause for good liberal Americans. The Ailey audience is all-loving and all-forgiving and almost all-white. When the curtain went up on *Carmina Burana* (a kind of *Revelations* for humanists, with monks prowling the stage to Orff's "profane cantatas") I think the onlookers were pleased, and although they had to start stifling their yawns long before the piece ended, they cheered and applauded for minutes when it finally did end.

Masekela Langage ends to the same kind of enthusiastic applause, right after one of the characters, who has been beaten up offstage, dies and the others move down to the footlights and eye the audience accusingly. This whammying of the customers was a gigantic cliché five years ago, when the piece was new, but Ailey has kept it in, along with the jarring operatic convention of having the victim, bloody and broken, pirouette himself to death while the rest of the cast quickly makes up a chorus. The convention might work if up to then the action of *Masekela Langage* were not so consciously naturalistic. The bric-a-brac tavern set is unusually detailed even for Ailey, who loves atmospheric props, and the dancers lounging around in it, snapping at each other and playing South African jazz by Hugh Masekela on the jukebox, look as if they had specific characters to project. There is Sara Yarborough as a short-tempered teen-ager, Judith Jamison as a faraway Tennessee Williams-type lady, and Kelvin Rotardier as a debonair bum-about-town. *Masekela* might have ranked with *Blues Suite* (which it resembles) as Ailey's best work next to *Revelations*, but stylistic crudity and lack of coordination destroy it. Its big failure is that the dance monologues go on too long without developing characterizations. Rotardier is a mime of great elegance, in a class with Francisco Moncion and Derek Rencher. Ailey has given him lots of yardage here but no ball, and Rotardier can't keep *Masekela* from collapsing in the middle of his solo. Nor can Jamison pick up the pieces. Because of some extra poundage gained since last spring, Jamison did not dance effectively this season.

There wasn't much for her to dance. Jamison has become a star because the audience thinks she should be one. None of the roles that have been fashioned for her really lets her deliver. In *Cry*, the nearest thing she has to a vehicle, Ailey doesn't use her rich humor or her exuberant shimmy style until the last moment, and until that moment she is forced to do an unconscionable amount of barge-toting and bale-lifting. (Some of the blackface stereotypes Ailey deals in would be jeered at if they came from a white choreographer.) The best dancing of the season was done by the talented Sara Yarborough, and *Rainbow 'Round My Shoulder* was worth seeing for her. This is another of the folk-song ballets, and one of the better ones, although it can't be sat through very easily. The work songs of the chain gang were choreographed by Donald McKayle, and if you find the idea of chain-gang choreography repulsive you'd better not go. The prisoners come sidestepping on like a line of chorus boys. Within this gauzy frame there are a few sober vignettes about convicts and their dream woman, and one or two unforced moments of sweetness and pain, mostly contributed by Miss Yarborough.

The McKayle piece dates from 1959 and looks much older, as do portions of *Revelations*, which was first presented in 1960. The idea of combining folk songs or Negro spirituals with American concert-dance choreography wasn't new; the combination had been used by generations of dance recitalists. If you've ever seen one of those "Songs of My People" recitals, with dancers doubling themselves up to "Go Down, Moses" or earnestly miming their way through "He's Got the Whole World in His Hands," you know what the perils of the genre are. Black choreographers still embraced the expressionistic style at a time when white choreographers were abandoning it. Merce Cunningham and his descendants felt no need of that style, just as novelists of the fifties and sixties felt no need to write like Hemingway or Steinbeck. But the black choreographers did have a need for a "strong" statement of a "strong" theme, and they held on to the dance technique of the 1930's for the same reason many white choreographers were relinquishing it—because it was respectable. The dancing in the opening scenes of *Revelations* is neither fine art nor vernacular art, it's "cultured" folk art; and although I respond to the almost symbiotic attachment between this kind of movement and this kind of music, I can't escape feeling that the music is being subtly undermined, if not exactly cheapened. When I see that familiar pyramidal cluster, with the women planted straddle position and the many hands clasping and splaying to Heaven while the choir sings "I Been 'Buked and I Been Scorned," I don't believe it. Images made of Dynel sackcloth don't fit the simple majesty of the song. The wide plié and the upward-straining gestures are, however, basic to a kind of tacky sincerity that is the only strength of cultured folk art. Genuine folk art shocks; cultured folk art appeals. There's a very appealing duet to "Fix Me, Jesus"—the best Ailey has ever made. The central image is of a woman braced and struggling to rise tall on a man's outspread thighs (plié stance plus yearning arabesque). In a good performance, it is clear that he is a preacher and she the soul he's trying to save, but *save* isn't the same as *fix*. Ailey has no imagery for such amazing diction; his technique has to say "save." In the performance I saw this season, Dana Sapiro's high ballet extensions conveyed Ailey's point forcefully and she deserved every bit of her applause, but I feel it is worth pointing out that a great song like "Fix Me, Jesus" suffers a loss of power in proportion to its success as a dance number; it loses the humility of its sentiment as well as the precision of its utterance.

"I Want to Be Ready" is Dudley Williams in a series of perfectly pitched and controlled body lifts from the floor. He draws himself up and sinks back, never coming fully erect, never finding rest, and he finishes in a blazing star-pointed pose on one knee. This is dance metaphor on the level of "Fix Me, Jesus," but this time I find nothing wrong in it. It tells the story the song tells, and adds to it, because Williams's technique transfigures him and becomes, seemingly, the result of the religious idealism of the song—he *is* ready. There is a patness in the number I don't care for, but I can't pick it apart. The only trouble with "I Want to Be Ready" is that by the time it comes on I have seen something better than what this studio-fashioned technique can produce, even at its best, and that's the dancing in the baptism sequence, "Wading in the Water." The staging is a little *faux-naïf*—blue and white veils stretched low across the floor and shaken, white streamers, white netting, white gowns, and one big umbrella draped in white—but it hardly matters when Jamison is stepping through those waves and undulating her torso, and Rotardier and Yarborough are doing their forward-and-backward slow pelvic walk (and their one lovely burst as the walk changes to a skip). There aren't many times when one sits before the Ailey dancers and wonders, How do they do it? This is one of those times. The movement looks inimitable and untaught, like the perky little strut downstage and up that is done in the last two numbers—"You May Run Home" and "Rocka My Soul in the Bosom of Abraham."

That casual, loose style hasn't been cultivated since the decline of tap-dancing, and I know of no black choreographer who is cultivating it now. Ailey hasn't in years choreographed a gesture that looks colloquial or hip. His pantomime, which once seemed a fascinating private language used by his dancers, has become decorative chatter, done for us, not for them. Compare the stylized fight scene in *Masekela Langage* with any of several rough incidents in *Blues Suite*. In the former, the dancers appear to be always looking over their shoulders, to see if we're watching them. In the latter, they don't give a damn. There seem to be fewer jokes, too, with less point to them. Nothing matches the moment in *Revelations* when Ailey reverses the effects of the polished, conscientiously strained, effortlessly effortful style of movement by having the women turn their backs to us, go into their straddle stance, and slowly, slowly, fanning themselves the while, sit down on stools. That slow, heavy squat is good and rude, but Ailey seems to have lost interest in how people really move. There is no black colloquial dance in the theatre today. Most black choreographers are content to work in the received idioms of thirties-style expressionistic concert dance. Their forerunners aren't Bill Robinson or Buddy Bradley or Josephine Baker, or even Katherine Dunham, but Martha Graham and Doris Humphrey and Charles Weidman and, in Alvin Ailey's case, Lester Horton. One large reason for Ailey's success is that he has known how to profit from the gradual absorption of this generation's methods by Broadway. He is much more credible as the descendant of those choreographers who took over Broadway musicals in the forties than he is as a promulgator of the Horton technique. Expressionistic concert dance became respectable in Broadway musicals, as respectable as ballet. When choreographers began directing shows, the dance technique and the musical became more or less fused, and Ailey found that he was able to make his thirties-style religious dance suite as entertaining as a musical comedy. I never saw the original *Revelations* of 1960, but the printed program for it suggests that, in content, it did not greatly differ from the version we know today, except for the final section, which then included "Precious Lord," "Waters of Babylon," and "Elijah Rock." By 1962, these had been discarded in favor of the present selections—"The Day Is Past and Gone" and "Rocka My Soul." "You May Run Home" was inserted later, but "Sinner Man," originally a solo, had become a trio by 1962. It's in these numbers, plus "Wading in the Water," that Ailey's choreography breaks out of the church-basement dance-recital mold and attains the precision and showmanship that make *Revelations* a hit. When, to "The Day Is Past and Gone," the girls start coming on with their stools and floppy hats and palm-leaf fans, each girl wearing a long yellow gown that suggests the street dresses of the thirties, the heavy tent skirts and technique-laden dance movement of the opening numbers seem far away.

But all the scene-setting and music shuffling wouldn't have meant much without the tight organization. The original *Revelations* was forty-five minutes long. Now there isn't a wasted moment in the entire piece. The outline it has is that of a beautiful onrolling wave, rising to little crests of excitement and breaking just in time, or unfurling long climaxes that smash with an accumulated intensity. The "Rocka My Soul" finale used to leave audiences dizzy with happiness; now it—and sometimes the whole ballet—makes them dizzy with anticipation. Ailey keeps adding dancers to his finale, and the piece has become too much like a Broadway show, with too many dancers onstage punching their spirits too high. I think the audience lavishes its emotion on *Revelations* because it hasn't got anyplace else to put it. Ailey is a pop choreographer who no longer seems to train himself to the efficiency standards of popular art. He has made a few other pieces that look like Broadway shows, but they don't have the controlled energy of good entertainment, and his nonpop pieces are hopeless—all those overlong, attenuated lyrical ballets that seem to be taking place underwater. The boringly even rhythm and lack of tension are weakening the dancers, and Ailey doesn't have many good dancers to begin with. (He doesn't have one male dancer who can turn well in "Sinner Man.") The Ailey company is pressing its luck. It's loading up on religious and secular song suites, feeding its audience with a particular kind of material when all that matters is how that material—or *any* material—is assembled. With musicals slipping badly in recent years, the Ailey has been drawing a lot of people who think of it as a higher substitute for Broadway. They find what they are looking for in only one piece. It doesn't take them long to discover that *Revelations* is the higher substitute for the Ailey. —*January 7, 1974*

Sweetmeats

Except for the extraordinarily pretty costumes worn by some of the party guests in Act I, nothing new was added to the New York City Ballet's production of *The Nutcracker* this season. There were no débuts in any of the major roles, and no curious events such as Balanchine likes to stage from time to time—his addition last year of white mice to the corps of gray ones in the battle with the toy soldiers, for example, or his rearrangement the year before last of the scene in which the court of the Sugar Plum Fairy masses onstage to greet the children sailing up in their boat. There weren't any white mice this year, but Rouben Ter-Arutunian's frontcloth shows an angel and a comet, and in the season of Kohoutek this perhaps struck some people as a new inspiration. The changes Balanchine keeps making are usually in scenes that need no improvement. He tends to work at imperfections in the production that are invisible to everyone but him, while ignoring imperfections that are visible to the audience. One of the latter imperfections—I hate to call them flaws, since *The Nutcracker*, both in conception and in execution, seems to me as nearly flawless a work as the company has ever staged—is apparently ineradicable because it's a kind of negative imprint of one of the imperfections that exist only in Balanchine's mind. This is the imbalance in the grand pas de deux of Sugar Plum and her Cavalier which is brought about by having her dance her famous variation in the aura of the mystical soft radiance that Tchaikovsky creates at the start of the second act, instead of having her do it at the end, where Tchaikovsky placed it. Balanchine's solution—to dispense with the Cavalier's variation when the time comes for him to dance it—not only is unfair to dancers of the stature of Edward Villella and Peter Martins and Helgi Tomasson but doesn't correct the imbalance. Another solution Balanchine once tried, that of dispensing with the Cavalier altogether and having the ballerina supported in her adagio by four men from the divertissement—Sugar Plum's courtiers—was far worse. The drama of the pas de deux is one of a love relationship, and in terms of the symbolism of the ballet the Cavalier corresponds to the little-boy hero just as Sugar Plum corresponds to the little girl.

Balanchine does not lightly violate a composer's structure; when sense surpasses structure he attends to sense. The music for Sugar Plum's variation characterizes her uniquely (Tchaikovsky imported a new instrument from Paris, the celesta, in order to create those mysterious sounds), whereas the music for the Cavalier's variation is a tarantella that characterizes no one in particular and might have been written "in Italian" simply to round out the suite of national dances in the second act (Spanish, Arabian, Chinese, Russian). There is nothing in his music to suggest why the Russians originally chose to name the Cavalier Prince Koklush—Prince Whooping Cough.* (What instrument would have had to be imported for *those* mysterious sounds?) It almost seems a logical development of the music that Sugar Plum and her Cavalier are lovers but not coequals. Balanchine's version of the ballet widens the gap between them. He takes advantage of a musical imbalance to justify a structural one, and I think he does justify it. Not only does he give us the Land of Sweets as Sugar Plum's kingdom but he shows her taking possession of it at the start of the second act. And several years ago he heightened her supremacy with one of those embellishments of his— an embellishment no one had foreseen the need of until it was provided. This was the moment in the adagio in which we see the ballerina, with the merest fingertip support from her partner, hold an arabesque as motionless as a statue and yet move across the stage. Balanchine contrived this by moving the floor under her point, and, unlike some of his other novelties, it became a permanent feature— one of a number of magical stage illusions in *The Nutcracker*. It may also have been his final solution to the Cavalier problem—a way of implying that if a problem exists it is surely not that the Cavalier's role is too small but that the ballerina's role is. One can almost hear him saying, "Who cares about the Cavalier, anyway? Just look at this great woman!" In his other full-evening ballets, A *Midsummer Night's Dream* and *Don Quixote*, he has created superb roles for Titania and Dulcinea and given each of them a characterless Cavalier who does nothing more than lend support in the adagio. (But in those instances Balanchine didn't cast a star male dancer—he cast

---

* *Postscript* 1977: Several readers wrote, identifying "Koklush" as a Russian gallicism derived from *coqueluche*, whooping cough, but suggesting that the *Nutcracker* Cavalier was named after *coqueluche*, originally "a hooded bonnet of the Middle Ages worn by men of fashion" and hence a term for favorite, fashion, or rage, as in *coqueluche de la ville* (town dandy) or *coqueluche des dames* (ladies' man). No one has explained why the same word means whooping cough.

Conrad Ludlow, a Cavalier par excellence.) The audience may wonder who that fellow is, but I think Balanchine means him to be "not there," like a Bunraku puppeteer. No choreographer creates greater roles for women, and it sometimes seems as if Balanchine's vision of perfection consisted of one woman dancing at a peak of classical style for hours, unaided.

This season, the company didn't recover from the effects of its month-long strike in time for its first performance; it didn't really recover until after Christmas. On opening night, there was a dreadful moment when it seemed that Balanchine had decided to drop the coda of the pas de deux, in which the Cavalier gets his only opportunity to dance. But it turned out to have been dropped because Jacques d'Amboise, who was partnering Patricia McBride, had hurt his knee. In this performance, the children were excellent, as they always are —so completely wrapped up in the different things Balanchine has given them to do that they catch the *spirit* of absorption and just live onstage. They have a wonderful bit of business that you can catch if you sit close: when they cup their mouths and call out to Drosselmeier the magician, they actually whisper "Magic! Magic!" With Shaun O'Brien as Drosselmeier, and with Gelsey Kirkland, who was Dewdrop in the Waltz of the Flowers, they gave the performance what glow it had. Kirkland is the most spritelike of Dewdrops, and her combination of clear-mindedness and abandon makes her one of the most exciting young dancers in the world. She isn't as musical as Marnee Morris is, but she doesn't have the mannerisms that spoil Morris. As Sugar Plum, she is not ideally cast (only Allegra Kent is that), but she pours the role full of new love and new learning; you can see how much it means to her just in the way she holds her wand. McBride, whom I saw again on another night, was better but not at her best, giving the kind of nervous, overstimulated, exaggerated performance she often gives when her partner is Jean-Pierre Bonnefous. As for Kent, no other dancer I've ever seen can be so waywardly off her form and still enchant. Her entrance, weaving her way downstage among the ten-year-olds, whom she seemed to gather in lovingly as she went, summed up her enchantment (and it had to, for she danced the rest of the performance in a murmur).

There were other good performances to be seen in the New York City's production this season—Victor Castelli's as Candy Cane, Jean-Pierre Frohlich's as the Soldier, Susan Pilarre's as the Marzipan Shepherdess, Christopher d'Amboise's as the Nutcracker—but for too much of the season too many members of the company danced *The Nutcracker* as if they had been sentenced to it, so I went to Philadelphia to see what the Pennsylvania Ballet's production was like. The strong and enthusiastic dancers of this company had impressed me during a four-day season in November at the Brooklyn Academy, where they did a *Raymonda Variations* that surpassed all but the best performances by Balanchine's own company. The Pennsylvania's *Nutcracker* has a second act based on Balanchine's production, and many of the dances are quoted directly, but the company would have done better to take his first act instead. The Pennsylvania's Act I was the work of Osvaldo Riofrancos, who is known as a director of plays and operas but not as a choreographer, and it was so creaky and incoherent, and so appalling in its grotesquerie (at one point several large white plastic rats crept about on a table in a blue light), that in New York it would have passed for avant-garde art. The Snowflake Waltz, which ends the act, and the cantilena passage that precedes the Waltz were choreographed by Robert Rodham for a Snow King and Queen and a large, carefully rehearsed corps de ballet. The dances were not the worst things that could have been presented to an imagination already captured by Balanchine's wandering bed and choreographed blizzard, and the Waltz was enhanced by the singing of the All-Philadelphia Boys Choir, live in red jackets.

It was a pleasure to see the second-act dances done as well as they were—especially by Marcia Darhower, a robust Verdy type with a high, long jump, who was the Shepherdess at the matinée and the Dewdrop in the evening. The grand pas de deux (with the two variations side by side) was given conscientious, well-sculptured performances by Alba Calzada with Keith Martin and Barbara Sandonato with Lawrence Rhodes. But the power I remembered in the Brooklyn *Raymonda Variations* did not rise very far. The great strength of Balanchine's *Nutcracker* is not in his second act, and I think that what Cyril Beaumont wrote about the first London production of Ivanov's choreography, in 1934, applies also to Balanchine's (though Beaumont's sense of outrage does not): "It passes the understanding that 'Coffee' should be conveyed by a Stomach Dance in the manner of a dancer of the Ouled-Naïl, and that 'Tea' should be suggested by a couple of ridiculous Chinese whose 'number' seems to have been borrowed from a pantomime version of Aladdin."

Balanchine's divertissement dances aren't vulgar, but they are full of stock devices. The Waltz of the Flowers is the great—the very great—exception, so dazzling in the sweep of its imagery and so concentrated in its means that one might analyze it for days without coming to the end of what Balanchine knows about choreography. And one might do the same with the first act, starting with the mystery of that story and then going on to consider the marvelous craft with which that story is told—the sure sense of pace and climax, the brilliant use of the many different kinds of effect that spectacular theatre is capable of, the seductive blend, so typically Balanchinean, of real fantasy and fantastic realism. For years Balanchine's Act I has been taken for granted because it's so simple and "has no dancing." It contains the heart of his genius. When something in it doesn't seem right or has to be faked—like the firing of the candy from the toy cannon that doesn't work, or like the many little-boys' roles that have to be taken by little girls—the discomfort I feel is a testament to how deeply I have fallen under the spell Balanchine casts. When the little white bed that carries the sleeping heroine into the snow forest is making its journey around the stage, I try not to see the forest drops as they are being lowered; the undisguised flux of scenery mars the beauty of the stage picture. And for years I've tried not to think about why Drosselmeier, hearing nine chimes from the orchestra, sets the grandfather's clock at ten to seven or twenty past eight, or why the clock is not reset at midnight during the stage blackout that precedes the dream. And when the curtain rises on Act II, on that mountain of sweetglut that is Ter-Arutunian's idea of the Land of Sweets, I shut my eyes. It is all minor discord in a major theatrical experience.   —*January 21, 1971*

Care and Feeding

The life of a repertory company lies in the talents of its performers, and the success of a repertory season is measured in revealed talent. Ballets do not have a life of their own; dancers keep them alive, and dancers themselves are alive only when their talents are being revealed and extended. Good choreographers know this, and they know how to get a dancer's natural gift to work for them. Bad choreographers are unwilling to compromise the grandeur of their conception with the limitations of the performers who are available to them; they expose the limitations and shorten the performers' careers. About the most one can say for *Variations pour une Porte et un Soupir*—because this new piece of Balanchine's is one of the *least* ballets (and perhaps also one of the worst) he has done—is that it finds a good use for the talents of Karin von Arøldingen and John Clifford, two of the most awkwardly limited dancers in the New York City Ballet, and it exercises a modest sort of fascination on that account. I can't think of anything good to say about Jerome Robbins's latest piece for the company—the perplexing *Four Bagatelles*. Even though it is unmusical and inconsiderate of the dancers, it's not because Robbins is a bad choreographer who can't cope with dancers' limitations. He's a great choreographer who often behaves as if he were too great to be any good. It's his own limitations he can't cope with, or, let us say, since Robbins these days appears to be thinking in terms of Impossible Dream ballets, that it's the limitations of The Dance.

Four Bagatelles seems to be choreographed for two dancers who don't exist, to music that doesn't exist, either. It's all theory and no action. There's an excess of grandeur in the music Robbins has chosen—four of Beethoven's bagatelles for piano—and although I'm sure he knows this is "dance" music that wasn't meant to be danced to, he's gone ahead and set it as a standard pas de deux—adagio, two variations, coda—with "folk" touches such as might have been seen in the demi-caractère theatrical dancing of Beethoven's own time. Maybe he hoped to surprise Beethoven across the centuries, but the impression the piece leaves is of Beethoven and Robbins glumly outstaring one another across an abyss. Although the standard format seems plain enough, the driving idea behind the choreography seems to be that it's unperformable, and that its beauties are really ineffable. Some of these beauties consist of devices adapted from Balanchine (adapted, however, with only the faintest plausible connection to this music)—a complex dance figure occurring a moment ahead of or behind a complex figure in the music, so as to convey the effect of anticipation or echo; a long, *long* supported promenade for the ballerina in which she keeps altering pose. There are also those effects that interest Robbins in the workshop of his mind—deliberate effects of strained logic, antirhythm, noncausality. One could catalogue all the devices and write a term paper on choreography, but does one want to see a term-paper ballet? And who could dance it? Violette Verdy and Jean-Pierre Bonnefous, who gave *Four Bagatelles* in one preview performance here last spring, have certain eccentricities as dancers which helped cover up, or at least suggested a parallel to, the eccentricities of the choreography. They didn't, though, cover up the fact that the piece is pointlessly taxing to dance, and the cast I saw this season didn't either. Gelsey Kirkland and Helgi Tomasson are two dancers whose classically limpid style magnified every gnarl and gap and twist. They concealed nothing in Robbins's ballet and, with the sweetest of intentions, were merciless to it.

Kirkland's style, with its exceptional clarity and vitality, has its own element of concealment in the force of her impetus. She can fade gently into her own momentum, into a kind of steady-as-you-go, and as you watch her getting paler and milkier and more and more uninsistent, suddenly without a break in continuity she's on top of you in a huge, bounding jump. The scale changes with no apparent change in attack; the evenness of the reverie continues. Dancing like this is mesmerizing, but you wouldn't think so calm and clean and mild a style would be so popular. Kirkland isn't a colorful dancer and her feats are accomplished without a trace of personality projection, yet of all the New York City's girls who have been granted principal-dancer status in the last few years she's the only solid audience favorite and the only genuine ballerina, too. Karin von Aroldingen and Kay Mazzo and Sara Leland have been pushed up to their fullest capacities and beyond, but I can't accept any of them as ballerinas, and when the company has been hit as hard as it has been this season, by injuries to Verdy and Patricia McBride, and with less rehearsal time to make up for their absence than there would have been if there hadn't been a strike, it's little Miss Kirkland, taking on role after role, who's been the fountain of strength.

But the crisis has only proved what has been evident for some time—that the company hasn't enough ballerinas—and Balanchine without ballerinas is like Ziegfeld without stairs. Under normal circumstances, this is the season we would have been looking for the dancers who are Kirkland's juniors (in rank if not in years) to make their mark in significant parts—dancers like Colleen Neary and Christine Redpath, among others. But for a number of careers the season has been one big holding operation. Neary did get *Firebird*, but this is a role in which the main concern of the ballerina is not tripping over her train, and so far there have been no débuts that could be described as auspicious. Except for Gelsey Kirkland's. The Verdy role in the charming Delibes divertissement that Balanchine calls *La Source* was taken by both Kirkland (with Tomasson) and Mazzo (with Peter Martins), and because I'd always felt that the role is quintessential Verdy, full of firmly profiled arabesques and high relevés-passés that flattered Verdy's pulled-up thighs and sensitive feet, I didn't think either of the newcomers would have much success in it. And, in relation to Verdy, Mazzo's sketchy, fretful outline and infirm legs and feet weren't very interesting. Mazzo is easy to like, and some portion of the audience always responds romantically to her, but she's really good to look at only from the waist up. All her energy seems to go into securing that Victorian "princess" cameo framed by elegant arms. But with Kirkland the whole role was revitalized, and I forgot what it had been like as a Verdy vehicle. And with Tomasson assisting Kirkland in the beautiful lifts and performing the two male solos with the delicacy and style that no one has ever been able to give them before, I forgot that I'd been tempted to dismiss *La Source*, after the Mazzo-Martins performance, as just another pink ballet. Martins seemed cast solely to support Mazzo, and he danced the solos perfunctorily, as if he knew it. Casting Martins opposite Mazzo fulfills and extends Mazzo, but casting Martins, the tallest man in the company, opposite the tiny Kirkland (as in the *Tchaikovsky Suite No. 3*) isn't a good idea. Tomasson is more than a partner for Kirkland, but he doesn't give her anything she doesn't have. He doubles her strength, like a twin. Their *Tchaikovsky Pas de Deux* was another revelation—ingenuous, lambent, fleet, a world away from the powerhouse exhibition number we usually see.

Another remarkable thing about Kirkland is that, unlike the rest of the New York City's ranking dancers, she hasn't depended on specially tailored roles to help her grow (and she hasn't had many); she seems able to grow by herself. Von Aroldingen and Mazzo are at their best in the roles Balanchine has made for them—ingeniously fashioned roles that capitalize on every good point and cover every deficiency. They are both in the *Stravinsky Violin Concerto,* and both are completely convincing. Von Aroldingen must be the least compelling dancer Balanchine has ever worked with. She's tall and blocklike, with big muscles, a long torso, and proportionately short legs. She has the face of a Nordic movie goddess (the outdoor type) and a manner both placid and intense. Her granitic glamour is one of the things Balanchine has used well in the past, and now, in *Variations pour une Porte et un Soupir*, he makes her lack of transparency seem positive. Planted in the center of the stage, she's the Door that John Clifford, as the Sigh, is trying to enter. Of course, the two dancers never become involved (one shudders to think of it: this tank of a woman rolling over this eel of a man); they confront each other matter-of-factly, and the first third of the piece, in which the two alternate in passages of acrobatic mime, is a dourly funny Balanchine puppetoon. Clifford's role, which consists of a great many agonized contortionist poses and hairspring leaps, resembles such earlier Balanchine conceptions as the Todd Bolender role in the "Unanswered Question" section of *Ivesiana* and the Paul Taylor solo in *Episodes*, and Von Aroldingen's movements are those familiar mock-elegant gestures Balanchine has created for many of his female characters, beginning with his Siren in *The Prodigal Son*. What makes the parody movements funny is that they're exactly synchronized to the sounds of Pierre Henry's musique-concrète score. With a deliberately gawky, note-for-note (so to speak) literalness Balanchine would never think of applying to orchestral music, Clifford writhes to respiratory noises, and Von Aroldingen, insouciantly angled at knee, elbow, and wrist, swivels to the accompaniment of wrenched hinges and creaking wood. But the interest this creates—which isn't exactly a *high* interest—dies when the scenic element takes over the ballet, and the absurd solemnity of what we are seeing and hearing slips away into straight solemnity.

Musique concrète, a Paris export, was a hot item in this country in the fifties. The purpose that American choreographers found for it then doesn't seem to have affected the French and other European choreographers who have continued to make liberal use of it (Henry composed his score in 1963, and Béjart choreographed it in 1965), and it doesn't seem to have affected Balanchine's use of it now. Another feature of *Variations* seems shipped from Paris, too—the enormous train of black silk that stretches from Von Aroldingen's waist to the sides and back of the stage and that, when lifted in peaks and made to sway and billow, becomes animated décor. One thinks again of the Siren, a role Von Aroldingen performs and in which she not only has a cape that becomes part of the décor but walks on her hands, as she does here (and in the *Violin Concerto*). But if *Varia-*

tions suggests a deranged parody of *The Prodigal Son*, it also suggests innumerable ballets from Paris with capes in them (Loie Fuller, whom Mallarmé and Rodin praised, probably started the whole business with her manipulations of light and silk at the Folies-Bergère), and Balanchine's method of "dramatizing" musique concrète is not much above the sort of thing a Béjart or a Roland Petit would offer us. A peculiar characteristic of Balanchine's use of faddish material is that he doesn't place himself above it, he places himself entirely at its service, and generally the experiment fails, not because the material is outside his range but because it's beneath his gifts. I'm afraid *Variations* must be added to the short list of his works which might be headed "Fads and Foibles"—a list that includes such dim experiments of the past as *Electronics* and *Modern Jazz: Variants* (the titles indicate the areas of experimentation) and the more recent *PAMTGG* and *Slaughter on Tenth Avenue*.

A new talent of Edward Villella's was revealed in the *Pulcinella* on which Balanchine and Robbins collaborated for the Stravinsky Festival. Since the role makes very slight use of Villella as a dancer and striking use of his abilities as a comic actor, I'd like to think he could go on doing it years after he gets tired of dancing, but the ballet isn't good enough to last that long. It's amazing that it's lasted this long, and although Balanchine has revised it widely and wisely, it will never be right. The big, busy Eugene Berman set full of rafters and laundry, the score with its musicianly jokes, and the episodic action make the piece hard to follow and almost impossible to enjoy if you *can* follow it. The broad humor of the pantomime doesn't seem to come from the same world as the icily mirthful music. Balanchine finds the levity in Stravinsky in such a piece as the *Violin Concerto* and uses it gratefully; in *Pulcinella* he has to play against it. The only solution I have been able to come up with is to watch Villella closely. He's the one nonabstruse and totally nonfatuous element in the piece, and he does nothing outside the lexicon, if one may call it that, of the burlesque comedian. Villella has never had a role like this before; his style in it and his makeup and costume disguise him past recognition and perhaps release him as well. He goes through the piece like a speeding crab, as loose as Groucho and as funny as Harpo in Harpo's special way of being funny, and with more encouragement and more "bits" I think he could be funnier still. It takes two or three viewings to get through all the production and on to Villella, and at every performance the majority of the audience isn't laughing, which has a blanketing effect on the minority, which is. But I found myself, last time around, giggling happily (though quietly) at most of what Villella did, especially at his conducting of the onstage orchestra with wiggles of his hips and other gestures of inspiration.

At Natalia Makarova's first performance of the season, everyone put on a great show—the star by dancing gloriously, the company by rising with her, the audience by its keen attention and prompt response. The event was American Ballet Theatre's *Coppélia*. It is a pleasant production—bland, good-natured, in no way distinguished, yet never disappointing—and if it evades all the grander and more perilous emotions in the music, it doesn't offer us cheap substitutes. It was based by Enrique Martinez on a version he learned in Cuba, where Leon Fokine had staged it for Alicia Alonso. I'm glad the priest's role in the third act is now being done by Kenneth Hughes, who doesn't play it as a drunk; that lampoon is more intelligible in a Catholic-Communist country than it is in our own.

The choreography is pretty minimal, but Makarova leaves you feeling that it is pure rather than thin. She finds a rhythm in the part, a thread of consistency, and draws your eye along it, phrase by unwinding phrase. The dance rhythm becomes the bond between her and the audience—a complicity upon which she then comments with all the resources of a superb actress. This instinct for rhythmic continuity is also Gelsey Kirkland's great gift—one that is still in a state of abstract development. In Makarova, it's a fully achieved art, a means by which she creates dramatic suspense and the right psychological scale for the intimacy that is necessary to high comedy. Her mime is wonderful "talking" mime, distinct in its emphases, confiding in its tone. She has an individual way of breaking up in the middle of a gesture which suggests combustible high spirits. But in all her wit as an actress one sees the same gift for plastic expression that is in her dancing, and she's the same person in all three acts. In the climactic dances of the third act, she doesn't leave the peasant girl behind and change into a grand ballerina; she remains completely a comedy character in the daringly protracted balances and stretched penchées. Under all the risks lies a ripple of amusement.

The new Ballet Theatre *Apollo*, revived without Balanchine's supervision, is also an attractive production, but I noticed a few errors that could easily be corrected. In the birth scene, when one of the handmaidens cradles the baby Apollo and rocks him, he should open his mouth as if in a bawl. He probably shouldn't enter on the "plunk" in the music that signals the end of Leto's labor. In the Apotheosis, the moving-bridge sequence, with Apollo and the three Muses passing beneath each other's linked arms, should consist of three complete evolutions, not two, and the peacock pose should be held longer. At the end of the ballet, Leto should return with her handmaidens. Akira Endo should conduct every performance.

As for the dance performances, there were things in them that have always puzzled me about *Apollo* and things that puzzled me for the first time. I have always wondered why, in the giant leaps of the coda, so many Apollos omit the one detail that seems to me to make the leaps unique—twisting the hips at the top of the leap, like a pole-vaulter clearing the bar. (The choreography of *Apollo* comes to us from the twenties, the golden age of sport.) In Terpsichore's wide lunges, when she turns slowly through the body, Cynthia Gregory was steadfast about turning her points and then her flexed feet into the ground, and Makarova was steadfast about *not* doing it. But both gave fine performances, and so did the other female soloists—Martine van Hamel and Deborah Dobson in the Gregory cast, and Kim Highton and Hilda Morales in the Makarova cast. Of the Apollos I saw, Michael Denard looked the best, with his craggy rhythm and handsome, wily face; and he had the firmest conception. Apart from a few rashly mistimed moves, his impulses were sound, as they usually are. But they tended to be an actor's rather than a dancer's impulses, and my main criticism of his performance is my criticism of the production as a whole—that it's insufficiently musical.

The Ballet Theatre dancers who came closest to mastering the Bournonville style for a new production called *Divertissements from "Napoli"* were Gregory, Marianna Tcherkassky, and Warren Conover, and Fernando Bujones, who *over*mastered it. Because there were almost as many changes of cast as there were performances, we never got all these dancers at one time, and so the piece, which has solos for nine principals (including two who perform the *Flower Festival* pas de deux, lifted from another Bournonville ballet), never accumulated the power to get it even partly off the ground. The third act of *Napoli* is the signature work of the Royal Danish Ballet and, performed by Danish virtuosos, is one of the most joyous dance spectacles in existence. With the interpolation of *Flower Festival*, it's also one of the longest, but Copenhagen audiences may well demand more from their brilliant stars—more dancing to feast away the endless winter nights. The tarantella that goes on and on and finally concludes the piece is in the nature of an encore, but the Ballet Theatre casting didn't set up a tumult in my heart, and by the time the dancers ran out with their tambourines I was ready for the sunrise and a large snort of akvavit.   —*February 11, 1974*

The Big Click

American Genesis, the full-evening Paul Taylor work that was given its New York première at the Brooklyn Academy of Music, is like a bicentennial pageant dreamed up by the cleverest kids in the ninth grade. It's too inventive and bouncy to be sophomoric, but its lack of stature is disappointing. Taylor has taken the fables of Genesis—the Creation, the Fall, and the Flood—and staged them in terms of American history and culture. Everything is big, bright, and simple, and the parallels are theatrically so irresistible that the audience can easily start having ideas of its own. The trouble with the piece is that Taylor hasn't anticipated the fecundity of what he has set in motion; he hasn't kept the action moving ahead of the audience. There are moments when it actually lags—when we think we're much farther along than we are. Part of the difficulty derives from Taylor's restraint and good taste; he never sermonizes, never forces us to see things his way. All the ideas in the piece are stated provisionally, but the absence of tendentiousness is also an absence of rigor. We lose the beat just when we need to be smashed to pieces by it.

But Taylor's main problem is technical, and he lets it absorb too much of his energy. He has not only set himself the task of braiding his twinned epics in a single strand of visual suggestion, he has also tried to make a big-scale, consistently buoyant dance show with roles for all ten members of his company. Another choreographer—Martha Graham, for example—would have stopped at this point and commissioned a score. But Taylor has set the whole thing to a tape consisting of excerpts from Bach and Haydn, selections by the folk guitarist John Fahey, a whole Martinů concerto, and miscellaneous Gottschalk. The music constitutes a third force that determines the way the action will go, and although the appositeness of the accompaniment engages us as much as it did Taylor, he really could have done without this extra set of demands. Taylor has yielded to too many temptations at once; he's looking for the big click. When he has the Puritans landing at Plymouth Rock in their black and gray choir robes to fanfares from Bach's "Easter Oratorio," or when he envisions Noah as a Mississippi riverboat captain in a setting by Gottschalk, it's impossible not to feel his happiness; the stage is filled with the brimming wealth of discovery and the atmosphere is tonic. The sons of Noah and their wives are rebellious layabouts looking for a good time. They become the animals who board the Ark, doing wild scratching and pecking vaudeville-type dances to "Lassus Trombone," the one non-Gottschalk selection. An admirer of *Cakewalk*, I resisted Taylor's inventions for the music he shares with that ballet, but succumbed at the second performance. I've never been able to resist Taylor's big, simple rhythm. (And now he's given me big, simple ideas to go with it.) But he has more fun than I have with his hillbilly Eden, where Adam and Eve and their serpent friend cavort to a bluegrass guitar. Taylor is never unintentionally vulgar; it's just that his dance style and dance manners here are things I don't care for. This trio for a girl and two boys is stronger in context than it was when Taylor presented it as an independent piece last year; as a perfectly equilateral triangle it has noncasuistic implications that are important to the story of *American Genesis*. But in the Haydn and Martinů sections one has to grope for the threads of the scenario. Specific symbols and patterns of association fade into arbitrary ones. The music is a trap for Taylor's ambitions, and he never pulls free of it.

American Genesis is not at all a hard piece to watch—it's very close to being family entertainment—and the second time I saw it, it was clear that its few ambiguities arose not from the complexity of Taylor's ideas but from the structure of their execution. Taylor doesn't really have anything very profound to say. He's fashioned a spectacle of coloring-book simplicity, all outlines and harmless exaggerations without depth, but such simplicity is difficult to arrive at cleanly. Confusions crop up at those points where two or more elements in Taylor's grand design collide instead of meshing. Sometimes the music dictates the choreography to such an extent that the story hangs while the dance pattern is filled out. Sometimes extraneous characters appear for no reason, one feels, except that certain dancers need roles. And sometimes the casting sets up problems of its own. Taylor apparently couldn't resist following the Plymouth Rock scene with a Colonial-era minuet to a Haydn quartet, in which Lilith is introduced to Adam. But we have no way of knowing (unless we've read the program) that Carolyn Adams is Lilith or Greg Reynolds Adam, and because they are both black dancers we may think at first that they're supposed to be slaves. When we consult the program to find out who the other two (white) dancers in the minuet are, we read "Other Adam and Lilith," which simply won't do. Taylor doesn't use his black dancers for their blackness, and he seems deliberately to have avoided turning the Cain-Abel story into the Civil War. Yet the logic of the scenario is such that we expect certain explicit encounters and events to occur; we're compelled to seek links in the action where Taylor provides none. The story of Lilith doesn't develop, and the Cain-Abel story, set to the Martinů concerto, is carried out on too cosmic a scale and in the "wrong" setting—a Western sin city, with dance-hall girls who call up nothing but old de Mille and Loring ballets. Cain murders and murders; Abel (Greg Reynolds again) is borne on repeatedly en cortège. By the time we begin to suspect that Reynolds *is* being used for his blackness, and that it may be the story of American racial warfare in whatever era, the curtain descends. Taylor's intentions are always simpler than you think. If he weren't trying to be so absolutely schematic, his intentions would be easier to follow. But success on his terms means that the piece has to be a tour de force from start to finish (like his *Orbs*, which made Beethoven quartets sound like Taylor music), and force is exactly what the piece doesn't have. Taylor seems to have wanted magic instead—the miracle of parts clicking naturally into a coherent whole.

Much of the time, though, the piece does succeed on Taylor's terms; it's a semimiracle. He keeps the dual conceits building through the piece. Ultimately—shakily—they do add up. The black costume Taylor wears as Lucifer is topped in the first scene by a high Puritan Father hat and a black opera cloak lined in crimson. Taylor's thesis—that Puritanism encompasses good and evil alike—is hardly original, but his costume, which plays with the resemblance between two kinds of high hat and, I think, *is* original, catches that meaning precisely. Opposite himself Taylor has cast tall, straight-backed

Bettie deJong as Michael, the defending angel—another stroke of symbolic counterpoint. I thought it just as appropriate that deJong scarcely changes her costume in successive eras while Taylor adopts lace ruffles or a satin vest. In the Flood scene, both appear, all shocked rectitude, as the Reverend and Mrs. Noah. For Lucifer and Michael and Gabriel (Eileen Cropley), who flutters through the piece, heralding, reconciling, consoling, there are three props—a pitchfork, a sword, and a clarion—wrapped in tinfoil. The meaning of a fourth prop, also foil-wrapped, isn't disclosed until the end of the Flood, when it turns out to be the olive branch. George Tacit, the designer of the costumes, also provided an all-purpose portable décor—a semicircular construction, painted on one side with a gray-and-silver rainbow à la Frank Stella. In the first scene, it's Plymouth Rock, and also, perhaps, the dawn of a new nation. With its back to the audience, and with Eve straddling its curve, it frames compartments in which Cain and Abel are born, each curled toward the other. Laid flat, the piece becomes a go-go platform for one of Lucifer's solos. And it reappears in a new guise as Noah's barnyard fence, his helm, and—upended—the wheel of his paddleboat. There hasn't been so much fun in the visual design of a dance work since Martha Graham abandoned her intricately functional forms and went decorative.

My chief complaint about the dancing is that there isn't enough of Carolyn Adams, the company's best dancer. Nicholas Gunn, as the Serpent, as Cain, and as a would-be song-and-dance man, has the biggest role, and attacks it hard, with thick-muscled pertinacity. I enjoyed him, but I think he might profitably seek out a few soft tones in his material. DeJong, Reynolds, Cropley, and the rest I liked as much as ever—Taylor, too, although he was so ill with the flu on the opening night that the performance had to be stopped. When I saw him again, he still hadn't recovered. His dancing has always interested me for the way his bulk dwindles as the force of a gesture travels through an arm or a leg, diminishing until the fly-away hand or foot looks as if it were attached to nothing at all. And he is marvelous actor. He's played the Devil before, but *American Genesis* is a better piece than *Agathe's Tale*. It should be seen, and seen twice.

It has been a fine if somewhat reclusive season for Merce Cunningham and his company, who are now in the midst of a series of performances in New York. The series, which began in February and will continue through late April, constitutes the longest sustained exposure to the work of this great dancer and choreographer that local followers have enjoyed for some time, but, except for a two-day engagement early in March at the Brooklyn Academy and a lecture-demonstration last week at Town Hall, all the performances have been held, on weekends, at the Cunningham studio in Westbeth, which has a seating capacity of about seventy. Reservations are absolutely necessary and early arrival is recommended. The performance generally does not run more than seventy-five minutes, and there are no intermissions. Various sound accompaniments are provided, but, as is the custom with this company, they bear no relation to the dancing. On a Sunday evening recently, John Cage read a deranged version of portions of Thoreau's *Journals*, in a voice that sounded like Vincent Price performing in Kabuki. The sound on other evenings has ranged from pleasant to tolerable, and its pitch seldom rises above a murmur. The only aural gaffe I've encountered occurred in the course of the Brooklyn Academy run when, during one of Cunningham's solos, as he strolled about shaking his wrists, a tape of a talk-show conversation about impeachment was played. It made Cunningham appear to be reacting to the remarks.

Cunningham's hands are like chords of music; full articulation flows straight to the electric extremities. He really does seem to have more in his little finger than most dancers have in their whole bodies. And the diversity and specificity of nuance of which his body is capable, after more than thirty-five years of professional dancing, are amazing. His performing this season has been limited mostly to quiet solos of great tension and delicacy, though I recall vividly one burst of allegro when he danced against the group in a different rhythm. The solo I mentioned is called *Loops*; another is just called *Solo* but is commonly referred to as "the animal solo" because of a passage in which Cunningham seems to turn by degrees into a furry beast. No obviously representational gestures are made. Cunningham seems to get *inside* the animal and reproduce its senses in different states of consciousness. Nor does he lose his humanity; he could be an old man or a dreaming baby.

Because Cunningham choreography dissolves conventional stage space, it is best seen not in theatres but in big, open rooms. I also prefer it at close range. The Lepercq Space at the Brooklyn Academy is a fine location for a Cunningham dance, but there the audience, seated on opposite sides of the dance floor, was often forced to look through one dance to see another. At the Westbeth studio, the audience occupies a narrow margin along one wall, and it's easier to hold on to simultaneous dances when they're spread out in front of you. Like the Styrofoam molds that cushion appliances in custom-built packing cases, this grand, spacious room, its floor an expanse of inviolate maple (visitors must remove shoes before entering), its high ceiling hung with stage lights, its row of windows giving onto a skyline view, seems to contain the dances in their pristine beauty. *TV Rerun* and *Landrover,* two of Cunningham's recent works, had largely escaped me when I first saw them performed onstage at the Academy. In the studio they were both ravishing.

So far, no new works are being presented this season. Instead, Cunningham puts together sections of some of his recent pieces, changing the order from week to week. The performances are billed as "Events" and given numbers. That Sunday was Event No. 95 (Event No. 1 took place in Vienna in 1964), and it consisted of parts of *Canfield, Changing Steps, Signals,* and *Solo.* I regret the absence of Robert Morris's lighting design for *Canfield* and Richard Nelson's for *Signals,* which were among the most beautiful and ingenious of late years, but even out of the theatre *Canfield* generates its peculiar nervous force. The force hasn't a chance to collect, as it does in the theatre; already we are into the various duets and small groups of *Changing Steps,* performed two or three at a time. The dances are full of odd happenings (and odd steps, a couple of which seem based on *Giselle*). Two girls face to face do a solemn wigwag with squared elbows. A girl sits on a boy's back and remains seated as he rolls over. Later, the same girl (Valda Setterfield, who looks like a Van Dongen lady) is hilarious trying to interrupt or join a couple in a maniacal stomping dance. There is a pause as Cunningham completes *Solo,* which he had begun during *Canfield.* The dance is made almost wholly of tiny, slightly twitchy movements and stillnesses too active to be poses. Lying on his side, he makes one or two pawlike passes around his head, then another. Suddenly alert, he stares for a long, suspended moment into the forest. The room is in complete silence. Beyond the windows, which rattle in the wind, a helicopter passes.

The mysterious drama of this dance is unique in the Cunningham repertory at the moment. There are often implied situations and relationships in the dances the company does, but none that have a dramatic impact. Incidents aren't stressed; the dancers don't use that kind of timing. One is entertained solely by the formal values of dancing—by what Cunningham in his Town Hall lecture described as "the passage of movement from moment to moment in a length of time." Those who aren't disposed toward this dry sort of interest probably shouldn't risk a night at Westbeth, but those who get pleasure from the sheer physical act of dancing and from its cultivation by experts will find their pleasure taking an endless variety of forms, and, several times in the course of an evening, they may even be moved to ecstasy.

Cunningham's choreography has no external subject, and as an object it removes itself irrevocably and more swiftly than dancing that is set to music—music is a powerful fixative and memory aid. Although its basic vocabulary comes from classical ballet and its style is more precise than that of most ballet choreography, the dancing is by classical standards nonsequential. It faces in all directions. It does not draw toward and away from climaxes. At first, it seems to have no markers that pass the eye smoothly along. But soon the sense of it as a series of growing actions becomes deeply absorbing. Individual dancers begin to fascinate and can be studied like progress charts. The present company includes many new or newish dancers, among them two excellent boys, Chris Komar and Robert Kovich, who are sharply complementary. None of the girls have yet arrived in a class with Susanna Hayman-Chaffey, a magnificent dancer, whose look of luscious contentment in impossible positions never fails to astonish me. It is she who consoles me for the loss of Sandra Neels and the irreplaceable Carolyn Brown.

Performers like this, and choreography that attempts to rid dancing of familiarity, dullness, and inertia, antagonize some people. At Town Hall, as we watched the company going through some new virtuosic combinations, an irritated voice called out, "We came here to see dancing. When are you gonna *dance?*" Cunningham has lost none of his power.   —*April 1, 1974*

The Blue Glass Goblet, and After

Martha Graham has a gift for utterance, and now that she no longer dances, audiences are responding with renewed excitement to her eloquence as a public speaker. Her appearance onstage to introduce her company on its opening night at the Mark Hellinger Theatre was the high point of the evening and the season's most glamorous occasion. Her delivery is casual but precise; she seems to speak thoughts that have just come into her mind, but many of them obviously have been formed from a lifetime's meditation and are almost as well known as the passages she loves to quote from T. S. Eliot or St. John Perse or the Church Fathers. "Theatre is a verb before it is a noun, an act before it is a place," she tells us, in her disconcertingly lazy, musical little voice, and although she also tells a lot of jokes (with enviable wit and timing), it is upon these philosophical heights that she places us for our view of her own work. Unfortunately, Graham's theatre these days is all too often a noun before it is a verb.

"Freedom to a dancer means only one thing—discipline," she also says, and one sometimes feels that she chose a dancer's life because of the severity of its discipline. It was the way of a Puritan, and, at Graham's moment in history, it was also the way of an artist. Dancing, the domain of the frivolous, had to be reshaped; the pull of gravity could not be denied; and discipline must be revealed to the audience as a sign of the dancer's new vitality and her new seriousness. Under Graham's command, dancers now did onstage what they customarily did only in the studio—struggled, wasted themselves, fell, and rose again. Effort was not concealed, it was dramatized, and although the sense of toil in dancing was not Graham's invention, the sense of its drama was. Self-discipline in the dancer is spiritual as well as physical; Graham, most powerfully among her contemporaries, was able to relate that fact to the expressionist movement then taking hold of the American stage. In Graham

Theatre, as purely and outstandingly American an artifact as Eugene
O'Neill Theatre or Robert Edmond Jones Theatre, the drama within
became a dance drama and the dancer became generically a tragic
heroine.

But the tragic heroine is also a triumphant heroine. Implicit in
the rigor of her self-discipline is the certainty of her reward—self-
discovery. No Graham heroine dies unillumined. The difference between her and the fated heroines of nineteenth-century ballet—a
Giselle or an Odette—is that the Graham heroine possesses, herself,
the key to her mystery. She does not entrust it to the hero; she herself must unlock the inner door. In a Graham ballet, this is precisely
what happens. The heroine, discovered at her life's supreme point of
crisis, summons her forces, resolves her dilemma, and moves into the
light. The arc of the narrative rises upward, sometimes looping backward to gather up evidence from the past before reaching its apex,
which is the moment of illumination. On this moment the curtain
falls. We always leave the heroine a step ahead of the point at which
we found her. Clytemnestra, at the start of the action, has already
died. In the Underworld, she meditates, relives her past, and pursues
its meaning to an ultimate acceptance of her position among the
dead. Like Jocasta (in *Night Journey*) and St. Joan (in *Seraphic
Dialogue*), she must understand why she is where she is. The outcome of the tragedy is upbeat, and although the illumination, in
the instance of Jocasta, is unbearable, it does constitute a victory. If
one were to adopt a maxim for Graham Theatre, it would be
"Know Thyself." Even Medea, the blackest of Graham's heroines,
by extinguishing her humanity discovers the essence of her being. In
Cave of the Heart, she becomes the evil she feeds upon, and in the
perfection of her translation (and its brilliant realization on the
stage) hers may be the biggest victory of them all.

The tragic-triumphant heroine is a relatively late development in
Graham's theatre, and I think it postdates the period of her greatest
work. In the repertory the company is now showing at the Hellinger,
that period is represented by *Letter to the World* (1940–41), *Deaths
and Entrances* (1943), and *Appalachian Spring* (1944). In all three
of these works, the dancing has that mysterious spiritual force that
appears to arise from the discipline of Graham technique, but the
heroine, who possesses more of it than anybody else, does not yet
know the meaning of her inner treasure, and we in turn are not sure
she will discover it before the curtain comes down. There is a loose-

ness, an uncalculated tension, an openness to life in these works that is lacking in the so-called Greek period that began in the late forties and, for many people, epitomizes the theatre of Martha Graham. Perhaps the "Greek" works are esteemed because of the grandeur of the Greek legends, but they're all a bit Hollywood, especially *Clytemnestra*, which is often spoken of as Graham's masterpiece. (It's merely her longest work, with a prologue and two acts—a Graham blockbuster.) Graham, who made the dancer's self-discipline part of the poetic language of the theatre—who put effort on the stage as a positive theatrical idea—seems to have felt the need to establish a dramatic corollary to her technique of movement, and those moments of illumination and critical "instants" of self-recognition began to proliferate until they became the stock framing device of Graham drama.

The affirmative endings of *Letter to the World* and *Deaths and Entrances* and *Appalachian Spring* are freely arrived at, but already, in *Deaths and Entrances*, one sees the beginning of the turn toward the symbolic and the second-rate that was completed in the fifties. At the end of this long, marvelously charged, complex work, the heroine all at once decides to move a prop, a blue glass goblet, which she has been toying with for the better part of an hour. The move is entirely consistent with the woman's frenzied, impulsive character as we have watched it develop through her dancing, but the telltale bit of symbolism gives the audience a chance to perceive what it might not have noticed already—"See! She has the courage to change!" And in her later pieces Graham increasingly "explained" her movement to the audience by further externalizing its implications, so that we could turn to one another and say, "See, it means *this*." In 1948, Stark Young could still write of Graham's choreography, "We have the sense that, no matter what has been left out, nothing has entered a composition that has not grown into it organically." But by the fifties what was growing organically into Graham's compositions was Noguchi's props, and, much as I admire Noguchi, particularly the Noguchi of Graham's theatre, I find all the symbol-making a little deadening to sit through season after season. The ballets are tight and dry—exquisitely shaped and adamantly sealed. It is difficult for us to evaluate them, even with new casts, because so little of the drama can be affected by the different emphases of this or that dancer. Since the work "means" only one thing (what it says in the program), since it has been molded toward a predetermined end, the audience responds not to its moment-by-moment power but to the smoothness of its trajectory, which we observe from a distance. We aren't drawn mentally into the action, as we are in Graham's best pieces. We stand at the corner and wait for it to catch up.

Of course, even second-rate Graham may be immensely enjoyable, and I include in this category three other pieces in the Hellinger repertory that I usually enjoy—*Errand into the Maze* (based on the myth of the Minotaur); *Seraphic Dialogue*, which, though not one of the "Greek" numbers, can be classified among the more mechanically contrived Graham works; and *Diversion of Angels*, which has no plot but does have a gooey layer of desperately acted-out and dearly cherished emotion poured over the dances by the company. (It's good choreography; why can't it just be danced instead of hugged to death?) One clue to the inferiority of these first two pieces is that the heroine's big moment is not really there for an audience to see. Although I sometimes imagine I have seen it in *Errand into the Maze*, all that happens onstage is that the heroine suddenly finds the strength to clobber her antagonist. Where this strength comes from is not explained. The transfiguration of Joan of Arc in *Seraphic Dialogue* is a plot event rather than a dance event, and so is the "rebirth" of Clytemnestra. The complicated dénouement of the *Oresteia* is too much to handle without words, and in Graham's version Apollo and Athena preside at a tribunal that decides nothing. When Clytemnestra seizes the black sceptres from Hades and dances out along the forecurtain, we're meant, I'm sure, to see that her spirit has attained peace at last, but Graham has no way of showing what she would like to show—that Clytemnestra's peace comes not from the vindication she sought but from a realization of her own guilt and complicity in the bloody system of retributive justice. In the latter-day Graham Theatre, it often seems that movement is trying, and failing, to take the place of words; in the epochal Graham Theatre of the forties, movement expressed what no words could.

The decline in the repertory is linked inescapably to Graham's own physical decline as a dancer. I don't think she began preferring props to dances, or grew rigid in her thinking, or became literary by choice; my point is that her physical technique, which once buoyed her through a series of theatrical adventures such as the world had never seen, was eroded with the years, and this erosion forced her to seek other means of expression and inevitably to invent on a lower level. This is not a tragedy; Graham's lower level would often be another choreographer's stratosphere, and one lesson the present repertory teaches us is that this most imitated of modern choreographers has seldom been imitated in the right things. Others have ripped off her style of gesture, her technical discoveries, her manner of presentation, her subjects, even her hairdos, but very few of her predators have learned to organize space and time as well as she has or trained themselves to build suspense abstractly, as she does in such a piece as *Deaths and Entrances*.

Possibly the most damaging aspect of the decline in her theatre has been the intrusion of all the clanging affirmations and moments of truth. Compare, for example, *El Penitente* (1940), a gentle, sunny "minor" classic, with the Silver and Bronze Age "masterpieces," and you'll see the difference between a secure work of art, asking nothing, insisting on nothing, and a series of post-Victorian exhortations designed for the moral enrichment of mankind. Perhaps the temptation to exhort was always present in Graham, and I've suggested that a kind of doctrinal heroism is a special attribute of her technique. I'd also suggest that their invigorating moral atmosphere is what makes a lot of the second-rate Graham works so appealing; more than one observer has felt himself rising on the yeastiness of their good intentions. It's almost like being in church. But this "exalting" aspect of Graham is one, I think, that we should avoid enjoying too heartily. It builds up our worship of a gone world and keeps us from seeing the things in her art that are really liberating and contemporary. At times, Graham presents herself not as the first of the moderns but as the last of the Victorians. *Letter to the World* and *Deaths and Entrances* and *Appalachian Spring* are all views of the nineteenth century, but they're distanced views; the ballets themselves are of their own time, and some of the things in them may strike us, even today, as avant-garde. Of course, they've all been stolen blind, but this hasn't made them stale. The really amazing thing about them is that their freshness of feeling, which seems to come from behind the dances like a light, is still there after thirty years.

The only answer I can give to those who ask how much these pieces lose by not having Graham in them is that *Appalachian Spring* loses least. *Letter* and *Deaths* are portraits of woman as artist; *Appalachian Spring* is a portrait of woman as wife. Long ago, when Graham was still dancing the part of the bride, I thought she had miscast herself, and when Ethel Winter and then Phyllis Gutelius took the role over, I felt sure of it. Gutelius does it now with William Carter as the husband, David Hatch Walker as the preacher, and Janet Eilber in the mysteriously effective role of the pioneer woman. All of them are excellent; it's the cast to see. Gutelius fills out her role with suggestions of things that are not explicit in the choreography. She's refined and vulnerable—a city-bred girl, one feels, who has had servants, and the mother-to-be of children who will surely die. Nothing in her past has prepared her for the frontier except the necessity of making so hard a choice and the courage to see it through. Gutelius also does the principal sister in *Deaths and Entrances*, with more range than depth. In those powerful plunges into madness, she doesn't go down very far. But then this was unquestionably Graham's greatest role, and one can still contemplate the sheer size of it with awe, even though, in its present version, it seems to have been deliberately shrunken in scale. The roles of the two other sisters, taken by Eilber and Diane Gray, seem to have been scaled down proportionately. They're now conventional villainesses, like Cinderella's stepsisters.

There are works of Graham I no longer care to see, because of the flattening out of certain details. Medea does not feed the red ribbon into her mouth, as Graham used to do, but folds it into her bodice, and the famous solo looks altered in other respects. This was another role in which Graham tore up the stage, and the one Graham performance of which I have the most vivid recollection. The dancers who now do the role aren't able to extract the right dance values from it, and so miss its spirit. However much they squeeze and contort themselves, they never seem really pulled together inside and can't work up much more than a vague, catlike spitting and clawing, whereas Graham aimed and struck like a cobra, all in one piece. Graham as Medea didn't spill over into melodrama, yet the younger dancers always do. Because they don't have this gift for wholeness of emphasis in movement, they can't hold on to the seriousness of Medea. What would be called integrity in an actress is in a dancer a secondary virtue. Many of the Graham dancers have it, but not all of them have it as dancers.

Although Graham's program notes are almost as famous as her dances, sometimes it's advisable not to read them. The program suggests that *Deaths and Entrances* is about the Brontës, but "Emily Brontë" is really a Grahamesque metaphor for the anarchic female spirit struggling in a prison of cultural stereotypes. The four characters of *Embattled Garden*, a straight-faced suburban sex comedy, are identified as Adam and Eve and Lilith and the Stranger (i.e., the Devil); this throws off the dancers as well as the audience. But I'm afraid there's no getting away from the program in *Chronique*. With its St. John Perse text read aloud from the orchestra pit, the piece is one long, bloviating program note. *Chronique*, a revision of last year's *Mendicants of Evening*, is one of two new works Graham is presenting this spring, and in it she seems to be giving us not so much a ballet as her ideas for one. It's like a living enactment of a page from *The Notebooks of Martha Graham*, the volume published by Harcourt last year, to the sorrow and confusion of many of her admirers. Graham's mind is infinitely more fascinating than this anthology of scholarly jottings suggests, and the publication, together with *Chronique*, unhappily reinforces the present-day image of Graham as that of a bookish lady who puts on dances. Visually, *Chronique* is a swirl of draperies and fragmentary choreographic studies. It's not bad to look at, but it never comes off the page.

Graham's mind has been revealed to us first through her great dances, then through the ingenious but ever more restrictive means she found when her body could no longer speak for her mind. The Graham company does not contain Martha Graham, but, like a giant picture puzzle, it does contain images of her, and one must seek them out. Trying to authenticate those images amid all the distortions of the revived works and the compromises of the later ones is a hazardous job, and Graham, who will be eighty next week, is still choreographing. But for the final, authentic image of Martha Graham it is we and not Graham who bear the responsibility.

—*April 22, 1974*

Forces of Harlem

The Dance Theatre of Harlem, an ensemble of twenty-seven black dancers trained in the academic classical style, has a point to make—that black Americans can dance ballet as well as white Americans. It makes this point within minutes and then rushes on to make a larger one—that classical style is basically noncompetitive, that it's its own reason for being. Throughout their two-week season at the ANTA Theatre—their first extended solo run in Manhattan—the dancers were so good, so happy and alive in the strength of their schooling, that one's social conscience was just tickled away. Four years ago, when the company was founded by Arthur Mitchell, the New York City Ballet's outstanding black soloist, it existed as a somewhat shakily experimental division of black dance. Today it is an expression of American ballet and potentially one of the richest.

The way these dancers take the stage lets you know they were born to it. Thanks to the season at the ANTA, we're now aware of a dozen or more new ballet personalities—of Laura Brown and Paul Russell, who danced the best American *Corsaire* pas de deux to date (I recommend it especially to anyone who saw the version given by the Harkness Ballet); of Lydia Abarca and Virginia Johnson, two elegant, long-lined beauties; of Susan Lovelle and Ronald Perry, whose miraculous bodies have joints seemingly lined with plush; of fiery William Scott and suave Homer Bryant and bold Gayle Mc-Kinney; of Derek Williams, a noble partner, and Roslyn Sampson, a charming soubrette with a fine jump. In none of the dancers does the classical technique look grafted on; it bubbles up luxuriantly from the inside. The women's placement, timing of accent, and general style derive from the New York City Ballet. The look is forward and up, with lovely upper-body carriage, soft arms, and open hips that let legs sweep easily into high arabesque. Arm and hand positions are stricter than in the New York City; details of footwork aren't yet as refined. The men have improved astonishingly since the company's earliest days. Though they're less accomplished than the women, it is they who give the ensemble its refreshing glow and solidity of impact. There is not one flighty or spindly boy among them, and one never has the impression that the ranks have been picked thin for soloists or partners. With Russell its star and Perry its most gifted comer, this is the most virile male corps in American ballet.

Unlike many star dancers who turn to choreography, Arthur Mitchell hasn't tried to make the dancers into replicas of himself. He's remarkably sensitive to individual talent and to his company's need for increased challenges and variety of expression. The works he has made—from *Rhythmetron* to *Tones* and *Biosfera*, from *Fête Noire* to *Holberg Suite*—display the young dancers in a pleasant array of formula ballets. The choreography is never less than serviceable, and some of it—*Holberg Suite*, the finale of *Fête Noire* (which has nothing *noire* about it except the color of the dancers' skins)—is distinguished. Mitchell, who hasn't set out to establish himself as a choreographer, is better at his craft than many more celebrated choreographers, and in the sub-Balanchine style at which he excels he shows an understanding, rare among young male choreographers, of how women use their points. His ballets are "teacherly" but not dull; they get the dancers working objectively and responsibly as theatre artists. However, the dancers have already outgrown most of Mitchell's challenges, and they're even beginning to look a little complacent in Balanchine's *Concerto Barocco*. *Wings*, a remodeled Louis Johnson piece, is a good company workout but not much of a ballet, and John Taras's *Design for Strings* (which used to be called *Designs with Strings*; the music is Tchaikovsky's Trio, Opus 50) is another sub-Balanchine exercise, more pretentious but less well focused than Mitchell's own work.

At the head of the classical section of the repertory stands *Agon* —world-conquering *Agon*. Not the highest but certainly not the least of its many glittering achievements was that it made Arthur Mitchell a star, and now, seventeen years after its première, Mitchell has a company that can return the compliment. *Agon* with these dancers has the ease and majesty it had in the first years of its performance by the New York City Ballet, when we became aware that in it Balanchine and Stravinsky had consolidated the modern American virtuoso style in ballet. In the New York City Ballet, *Agon* has shaken down into a routine repertory item, but the Harlem dancers' precision of attack restores the old balance between security and audacity. *Agon* contains an element of New York Afro-Latin rhythm to which the dancers respond excitingly, just as they respond to the syncopation and jazzlike counterpoint of *Concerto Barocco*. Both ballets were wise choices on Mitchell's part, but both were performed with areas of deadness. In the two great pas de deux, the dancers didn't sense an inner drama. If *Concerto Barocco* seems a little wintry for their temperament, *Agon* should have set off a spark or two, but it didn't. The company in its present stage hasn't joined its dance power to its dramatic instinct. It can give *Le Corsaire* plenty of both, but the hot style of the piece provokes that anyway.

During the ANTA season, *Le Corsaire* led the field in hot, or exotic, numbers. Half the trouble with the more outright "ethnic" ballets in the repertory is that although the pressure of the beat is often huge, they don't become very large to the eye. In Geoffrey Holder's *Dougla*, the drums pounded galvanically while the dancers waggled their heads, fingers, or hips. I didn't find the contradiction entertaining, but Holder is a great colorist, and his *scènes d'Afrique* gave the company its most handsome decorative piece. *Caravansarai*, by Talley Beatty, was full of diffuse, gnatlike activity—one of those pieces in which the dancers keep running across the stage and out before anything can happen. *Ancient Voices of Children*, set to George Crumb's popular score of that title, is the work of the Yugoslav choreographer Milko Sparemblek, and involves six bare-chested men and their idol-priestess in some amusing pretzel routines. The audience of children with whom I watched the piece wasn't misled by the fake ritualism.

The dancers' style is so unaffected that they can perform even works such as Beatty's and Sparemblek's with dignity. But one doesn't want to see them having to do it, or having to go on much longer with what seems to be their signature work, *Forces of Rhythm*. This casserole of a ballet, devised by Louis Johnson especially for the Dance Theatre of Harlem, is a great audience favorite—after *Le Corsaire* the greatest—and it's wild enough to grip at every performance. But the mental age of the piece is about ten, and there's a whiff of condescension in it. The form is like that of a lecture-demonstration showing you the relatedness of ballet, jazz, tribal dancing, French drugstores, and the Oklahoma Land Rush. Johnson has thrown everything into it and tied none of it together. Four girls from *Concerto Barocco* consort with the four men from *Agon* to snatches of Tchaikovsky's Fifth and Sixth, and they get all mixed up with four Africans in red loincloths. From somewhere—Katherine Dunhamland or Alvin Aileyland—come four ladies in turbans and long, ruffled skirts. The music, on tape, veers from pop to Tchaikovsky and back. There's a revivalist number, danced very differently by William Scott or Virginia Johnson, and Paul Russell has a solo vaguely combining all the leading motifs. To take the piece seriously is to expect more than it can deliver. Perhaps all forms of cultivated dancing *are* interrelated, but this is a point that can be demonstrated only at the highest level, and no single element in the piece is as good as the best of what it reminds you of. Like most ballets the company does, *Forces of Rhythm* is saved by the dancers, but saving it doesn't require enough of them. Even as an unserious chunk of entertainment, the ballet is too facile. Paul Russell's solo is, for me, the reason to see it. Russell is the greatest performer the company has. His body is handsome (the back especially so) and brilliantly controlled. He seems able to stop dead in the middle of a rush. He's radiant and funny, and what he makes of his bit in *Forces of Rhythm*—a comic star turn—does bring out something of what the piece is meant to be about. On the television show *Soul Train*, one can see every Saturday young amateur dancers for whom dancing isn't merely a recreation but an expression of a personal fantasy. Every now and then, one of the boys will hurl himself into a saut de basque—playing at ballet—and Russell's sense of fantasy is communicable in much the same way. He has the greatness and the naturalness to remind you of something in real life.   —*May 13, 1974*

ℛoyal Jitters

With the Western world passing through a crisis of leadership, it hardly seems worthwhile to exaggerate the perils of the Royal Ballet under the direction of Kenneth MacMillan. Three times in the last three years, London has been agitated by a MacMillan production on which, we were told, the fate of the company depended. The first of these, *Anastasia*, was liberally mocked, but I didn't find it nearly as awful as the word from London had led me to expect. The Mac-Millan version of *The Sleeping Beauty* was so despised that the company hasn't taken it on its current American tour. And now we have the controversial *Manon*, opening the Royal's season at the Met. It is neither as good nor as bad as advance reports had suggested, and its smooth mediocrity is alarming only because it seems to derive from a fear of offending public opinion. Once the company recovers from its attack of the frights, it should survive *Manon* very well.

At its worst, as in Act III, *Manon* is like a bad opera. The chorus jumps into its dance, the stars jump into their climactic point-of-death duet. Irrelevant characters, inexplicably lingering on from previous drafts of the libretto, get their big chance minutes before the curtain falls. At its best—a pas de trois in Act I, in which Manon is sold by her brother to Monsieur G. M.; the brothel scene in Act II, with its rich collection of variations and group dances—the ballet really does seem to be giving us, in dance terms, some of the mood and tension of Abbé Prévost's story about the luxury prostitute who loved a poor man. Of that love itself, and of its consequences for Des Grieux, the ballet has virtually nothing to say. The several pas de deux for the lovers are the big washouts of the piece—nonsensically pure in form, unvarying in expression. We see a girl; we see her meeting a boy. He dances for her in adagio tempo, then they dance together in the same tempo. A moment later, they do it again. They are separated and come back together. Again they do their dance. The story content in all this is so badly focused that it might as well not be there at all. For some in the audience, and possibly for Mac-Millan, too, the content of these dances is filled by the performers. On opening night, when Des Grieux introduced himself to Manon, he seemed to be saying, "Madame, I am Anthony Dowell. Notice my turns, my perfect développé into attitude front." And her answer was "If you're Anthony Dowell, I must be Antoinette Sibley. Let's have a Sibley-Dowell pas de deux." And they did.

MacMillan's direction appears to suffer from two kinds of pressure—the need to support a star system with star vehicles, and the need to maintain a progressive standard in choreography. Both kinds of pressure operate to destructive effect in *Manon*, because, in his anxiety to satisfy public taste, MacMillan has brought them into conflict with his principal obligation, which was to tell a great dramatic story. International trends in story ballets decree that dancing shall replace mime. But in the best examples we have of mimeless drama the dances fill the dramatic purpose of mime; they don't wash the drama away. The audience that long ago stopped looking for literal meaning in dance movement has now stopped looking for *any* meaning. No matter how mechanical and inexpressive the dancing may be, as long as dancing is happening, it's a ballet. If dancing is not happening, it's dumb show, a silent movie, a museum piece. *Manon*, like so many other modern story ballets, panders to this prejudice. Its stars are so busy dancing they haven't time to fill out their characterizations or advance the plot. There's an absurd moment in the third act when Manon is being led by the jailer to his private lair and Des Grieux follows abstractedly along doing slow pirouettes. At least, audiences can't say they haven't seen Dowell (or Wayne Eagling or Rudolf Nureyev) *dance*. Or Sibley dance with him. (Or Jennifer Penney dance with Eagling, or Merle Park with Nureyev.)

The big acrobatic pas de deux that brings the ballet to a close has so many running lifts and body flips and catches in the air that old-style, literal-minded audiences might well have supposed that Manon dies of overexertion. And they might have wondered why the only bit of sex that occurs in any of the pas de deux is the hint of fellatio with the jailer.

It's the old story: Poverty of Means goes to the ball dressed up as Purity of Expression. We're supposed to be too sophisticated to notice the masquerade or to want anything better even if we do notice it. The cover for this is the theory that everybody knows the story anyway—from Massenet's and Puccini's operas if not from Prévost's novel—and people have paid to see dancing. But I don't know any people who would pay to see meaningless dancing, even if they don't recognize it when they do see it. And if it's true that we all know the story, isn't it likely that we know it because it's a great eternal story that people have never tired of telling? Surely the pleasure the audience expects to get from a three-act ballet version lies in having *Manon Lescaut* told to it all over again in a new form. MacMillan leaves too much of the story out. He has discovered no means of conveying the sensuality and poverty that Prévost made seem mutually exclusive. Nicholas Georgiadis's basic setting for all three acts is a wall of rags, but this symbolic reminder of the poverty that terrifies Manon so is itself aesthetically appealing. The rags are beautiful, as stage rags always are. And MacMillan gives us nothing of the character of Des Grieux or of his corruption through his passion for Manon. He remains a sweet, innocent boy to the last. Without Des Grieux's fall, the story comes to little more than an account of foolish young people who wanted nice things.

The Royal fields its star teams with lavish ease. Of the two Manons I saw during the first week, Sibley was the more rapacious, Penney the more touchingly frail. Manon would have been a great role for Sibley if MacMillan hadn't been so timid about characterizing it in dance. Temperamentally, it suits her as well as anything she has done since Titania in *The Dream*, but MacMillan hasn't responded to her gifts as well as he responded to Lynn Seymour's in *Romeo and Juliet* and *Anastasia*. *The Dream* was the ballet in which Ashton launched Sibley's partnership with Dowell. MacMillan pays homage to that partnership in *Manon*; he hasn't analyzed or extended it, and Sibley seems a little imprisoned by her stardom. I can't help wondering what would have happened if the entire role had been choreographed on Penney. The most talented of the Royal's junior ballerinas, Penney is still in that overprolonged nascent stage of development peculiar to so many Royal Ballet dancers. It's time she had a big, custom-built role to make her a big star. Dowell, paraded about in his nothing of a part, looked handsome. Eagling, whose self-assertiveness shatters the Royal mold, did not look lost.

The ballet has been much abused for its music. My ear doesn't cringe unless it is attacked, and it approved the use of Massenet's "Elégie" as the lovers' theme song in three different orchestrations. The score, based on MacMillan's own scenario, is made up of miscellaneous Massenet pieces that include nothing from the opera *Manon*, and succeeds in sounding very much as if Massenet were working on commission for the choreographer—a feat for which MacMillan and his musical collaborators, Leighton Lucas and Hilda Gaunt, deserve congratulations. MacMillan's *Manon* is another in a series of attempts to extort from the nineteenth century the ballets it somehow failed to produce—a series that began with John Cranko's *Eugene Onegin*, set to music by Tchaikovsky which is not in the opera score—and each time I've seen one of these operatic ballets I've been impressed by their triviality in relation to the operas. Musically, the trick is turned, but dramatically there's no contest. Operas are able to encompass much more of the literary works on which they're based than ballets are, and usually, when a ballet succeeds in exploring literary material, rather than just defining it in dance form, it's because the choreographer has re-created the material. MacMillan's first-act trio is one example of this process, and the high point of the brothel scene, admirably set to the Nocturne from *La Navarraise*, is a dance for Manon and eight men—an emblem of her career as a courtesan which triumphantly compresses the repetitious incidents of the novel. MacMillan has also invented a mistress for Lescaut, Manon's brother, and given her two bitterly proud solos, in high contrast to Manon's fresh seductiveness. Many of MacMillan's surprises, though, are restatements of earlier works. *Romeo and Juliet* seems to have lent its marketplace to the opening scene of *Manon*, and Lescaut is very much a Mercutio figure. Act III, with its sad little deportees debarking at the Louisiana penal colony, and its "hallucinations" accompanying the final pas de deux, seems drawn from *Anastasia*.

Of the three full-evening ballets MacMillan has produced so far,

Anastasia seems to me the best, not so much because of what it achieves as because of what it attempts. In *Romeo*, MacMillan had before him both Leonid Lavrovsky's version for the Bolshoi and Cranko's for the Stuttgart; in *Manon* he is again working à la Cranko. But in *Anastasia* he produced a personal fantasy about a global cataclysm entirely from nothing. I don't think he was being pretentious, and the insults that were showered upon him for missing the mark themselves missed the mark. MacMillan's taste, musical instinct, and technical skill place him first among those British and European choreographers whose careers began in the fifties. *Manon* shows a loss of confidence. The steely bravura of *Anastasia* is missing. But, at forty-four, MacMillan is just entering his maturity, and I think we have a right to expect him to fulfill it.

The Royal's first week also unveiled a friendly *Swan Lake*, shorn of most of the neologisms that disfigured it in the past. Yet again there was a puzzling reticence, a strange modesty, that marred the performance. Merle Park, the first of the Swan Queens, was letter-perfect, musically sound, and gratifyingly unaffected in style. But she wasn't very exciting, and the second act went as if she were determined not to scale heights but to remain humbly in the foot-hills of the role. As Odile, she brought out her Joan Greenwood personality, but it didn't project. Park has an "unclassical" physique, and in the British view of things she is a soubrette and nothing but a soubrette. I don't agree with this; type-casting may be as much a matter of psychological as of physical conditioning. Jennifer Penney, on the other hand, is one of those ballerinas who has the role of Odette by inheritance. No one can ever have looked more beautiful in the part, more marvellously right in every move—or more fearful of imposing herself on the audience. In the black act, she seemed unsure of herself. I don't think she knows how good she is. She doesn't lack bite, but she does lack something in tenacity. With her "Russian" back and higher-than-high arabesques, she represents a break in the line of ballerina-models that stems from Fonteyn, and the company would do well to encourage her.

The two Siegfrieds I saw, Nureyev with Park and David Wall with Penney, were both extremely pleasing, Nureyev steadily loosen-ing and gearing up his style (and providing Park with deluxe sup-port), and Wall acting and dancing with consistent, full-bodied spon-taneity. Ashton's heavenly pas de quatre, which used to be given in

Act I, has been moved to Act III, where it naturally becomes the highlight before the big star turn. Two objections: The sets and costumes, by Leslie Hurry, look as if they'd been taken out of cold storage, and the choreography for Act IV, restored to its old patterns, continues to disturb me with its naturalistic details—the kissing that goes on between the two principals, Odette being tugged back from the suicide brink by Siegfried, or being pulled between Siegfried and Von Rothbart. Just as the Count di Luna should never sit down (said G. B. Shaw), Odette should never be caught standing any way except point tendu back.   —*May 27, 1974*

Glimpses of Genius

Mikhail Baryshnikov, the legendary young star of Leningrad's Kirov Ballet, is making his first appearances on this continent this summer, touring in Canada with a contingent of Bolshoi dancers. Baryshnikov became a legend even before he was admitted to the Kirov, in 1967; he was the pupil—the best, many said, and one of the last, as it turned out—of Alexander Pushkin, the great Leningrad teacher who had trained Yuri Soloviev and Rudolf Nureyev. In 1970, the year Pushkin died, Baryshnikov appeared in London, and from the way the London critics threw around the word "genius" I began to get an uncomfortable feeling about him: either he wouldn't live up to his notices or he would so fully justify them that he'd be, as a phenomenon, unrecognizable. True genius doesn't fulfill expectations, it shatters them, and the initial experience of it can be disturbing. Now that I've seen Baryshnikov perform in Montreal, I can't remember what I expected him to be like. Something on the order of Soloviev, I suppose, only smaller, higher, and faster. (That would have been genius enough.) Well, Baryshnikov is all three, but he's unlike anyone else, and he does things I've never seen any other dancer do. I was confounded, and the audiences at the Salle Wilfrid-Pelletier were, too. Although they gave him ovations, I think they really didn't get him. Probably they, like me, were bemused by the purity of Baryshnikov's style. He carries the impeccable to the point where it vanishes into the ineffable. One can't see where the dazzle comes from. When he walks out onto the stage, he doesn't radiate

—doesn't put the audience on notice that he's a star. His body, with its short, rounded muscles, isn't handsome; he's no Anthony Dowell. His head and hands are large, and his face—pale, with peaked features and distant eyes—is the face of Petrouchka. He attends carefully to his ballerina and appears utterly unprepossessing. When he dances, the illusion—its size and glow—comes so suddenly that it takes you by surprise. You think from the looks of him that he might be a maverick, which would make him easy to accept, but he doesn't dance like one. Any hope of idiosyncrasy or impertinence is dashed the instant he leaves the floor. And yet there's no mistaking his phenomenal gifts. It's obvious that Pushkin has turned out not the last of a line but a new and unique classical virtuoso.

Baryshnikov is able to perform unparalleled spectacular feats as an extension of classical rather than character or acrobatic dancing. Lovers of flashy entertainment, of sport, of raw prowess, may not take to him at once, but lovers of classical style will go mad. He gets into a step sequence more quickly, complicates it more variously, and prolongs it more extravagantly than any dancer I've ever seen. And he finishes when he wants to, not when he has to. Perhaps his greatest gift is his sense of fantasy in classical gesture. He pursues the extremes of its logic so that every step takes on an unforeseen dimension. His grande pirouette is a rhapsody of swelling volume and displaced weight. He does not turn; he is turned—spun around and around by the tip of his toe. Like the young prodigy Nadezhda Pavlova, whom the Bolshoi introduced to American audiences last year, Baryshnikov both summarizes and extends the resources of classical expression. The three performances I saw him give in Montreal were of standard pas de deux (two *Nutcrackers* and one *Don Quixote*), and while it would be absurd to judge his range on so short an acquaintance, one can certainly assume that he possesses many qualities he had no chance to display in Montreal. I can believe, for example, that he is the fine actor he's reputed to be, because of the way he altered his style to suit each of the pas de deux. In the *Nutcracker*, he was an image of elfin Mozartean grace; in the *Don Quixote*, he was diabolical, dancing with a livid force. And the dance pictures he produced in these different styles—particularly one of a high, slow jeté passé in which he arched his back at the peak of the jump—will linger long in memory.

His partner in the two *Nutcrackers* was none other than Irina Kolpakova, the Kirov's great prima ballerina, and she also appeared, unannounced and partnered by Nicolai Fadeyechev, in the Gluck *Melody*—one of those wafty adagios-with-a-veil that seem to mean so much (but what?) to the Russians. Kolpakova is the kind of star who does radiate, although when I last saw her, ten years ago, she had nothing like the rosy confidence and direct manner toward the audience that she has now. The lovely legs are as eloquent, the style as correct, the phrasing as musical as ever. Like Baryshnikov, and like her former colleague Natalia Makarova, she dances from a center of mysterious calm, and with an all but invisible attack. A knee injury prevented her from giving us her famous soaring jump in the *Nutcracker*, but she did breathtaking unsupported double pirouettes with arms en couronne.

A word about the company that Baryshnikov and Kolpakova are traveling with. Basically, it's a provincialized version of the one, led by Raissa Struchkova, that appeared in American cities last summer, when it was augmented by an array of new-generation talent. Except for Baryshnikov, who comes late to these shores, Canadian audiences aren't getting much in the way of new talent. Besides Struchkova, Fadeyechev, Yaroslav Sekh, and two or three not very well-prepared young soloists, the roster includes many of the same aging second- and third-raters seen here last year, and the company performs the same excerpts and divertissements from the Bolshoi repertory—but a less extensive and demanding selection than it showed here. In its *Walpurgis Night*, the four satyrs in fur breeches are oddly replaced by four bacchantes (who then have to chase the nymphs); its *Spring Waters* is far below standard; and it gives a duet called *Dolls* that was actually performed in New York by the children of the Bolshoi Dance Academy. (Another "highlight"—six girls linked together like the cygnets in *Swan Lake* and bouncing to the "pizzicato" variation from *Sylvia*—is worse than childish.) Fadeyechev, now grown enormously fat in the hips, partners the younger women in the second acts of *Swan Lake* (the hideous Gorsky version) and *Giselle* (the great Lavrovsky version), and the backcloths for the two ballets are flip versions of each other—dull-blue swamps obviously rendered by the same incompetent hand. Yet all the tackiness and substitutions don't kill the Bolshoi spirit or its talent. Struchkova is in roaring form (especially opposite Baryshnikov in *Don Quixote*), Fadeychev still has his spring (his big bottom seems filled with helium), and the corps in *Giselle* shows its magnificent schooling in every step. But it was Baryshnikov and Kolpakova I had come to see. In their Bolshoi setting, the two Kirov stars cast a distinctively different, tantalizing spell. What artists they are, and what a way to see them! If it weren't for the wretched Panov affair, which wasn't resolved until the eve of the Bolshoi engagements in Canada and London (where the main company is appearing), they would be dancing with their own company in New York right now. —*July 8, 1974*

Makarova's Miracle

A breathless week—in dance—for American-Soviet relations. Mikhail Baryshnikov, about whose appearances in Montreal I wrote two weeks ago, defects in Toronto—the greatest male dancer to have escaped Russia since Nijinsky got himself fired by the Imperial Ballet in 1911. Three days after Baryshnikov's break, Natalia Makarova's staging of *La Bayadère* is presented by American Ballet Theatre. It is an astounding success—more evidence that self-exiled Russian stars have as much to give as to gain in the West. *La Bayadère* (short for *La Bayadère*, Act IV: "The Kingdom of the Shades") is an old Petipa classic of which most Westerners were unaware until the Kirov Ballet toured it in 1961. When Rudolf Nureyev, who defected on the same tour, produced it two years later for the Royal Ballet, it seemed that a miracle of transposition had taken place. Makarova has wrought an even greater miracle. She's not only reproduced a masterpiece of choreography, she's taken Ballet Theatre's corps— hardly the most sensitive choreographic instrument in the world— and recharged it from top to bottom. In place of the lifeless gray ensemble that has skated through *Giselle* and *Swan Lake* all these many years, there is now in *La Bayadère* an alert, disciplined, and expressive corps de ballet, trembling with self-discovery.

The process of transformation is as yet incomplete, but never in my experience had the company danced a classical piece in so strict a style, on so broad a scale, and with such clarity of rhythm. Without these qualities, *La Bayadère* wouldn't be fun—it wouldn't even be *La Bayadère*—and what's *most* fun about this production is that every girl on the stage seems to be aware of the sensational progress she's making. When the famous single-file entrance down the ramp began, at the back of the State Theatre stage, I looked at those un-

conditioned thighs and jelly waists and thought, They'll never manage it—their backs won't hold, their legs won't keep lifting free.
But they did manage it, and not so much by force of will as by
force of energy correctly sensed. If the bodies looked underbred,
they didn't look strained, and the losses of control that appeared at
one or two points were minor. It isn't easy for these girls to take a
développé to the peak of a diagonal and hold it, unsupported, at full
turnout. One day it will be easier and the backs will be stronger and
more beautiful, too. What matters now is that the motor impulse is
there, solidly pumping energy into the right channels.

Makarova's direction has been faithful and revealing. That motor
impulse is basic to Petipa's exposition of movement flowing clean
from its source. It flows from the simple to the complex, but we are
always aware of its source, deep in the dancer's back, and of its vibration as it carries in widening arcs around the auditorium. This is
dancing to be felt as well as seen, and Petipa gives it a long time to
creep under our skins. Like a patient drillmaster, he opens the piece
with a single, two-phrase theme in adagio tempo (arabesque, cambré
port de bras), repeated over and over until all the dancers have filed
onto the stage. Then, at the same tempo, with the dancers facing us
in columns, he produces a set of mild variations, expanding the
profile of the opening image from two dimensions to three. Positions
are developed naturally through the body's leverage—weight, counter-
weight. Diagonals are firmly expressed. Returning to profile, the
columns divide and flutter one by one to the rear. The final pose is
of two long columns facing the wings with annunciatory arms. Now,
to a collection of beer-garden tunes (the composer is Ludwig Minkus), Petipa sets dances for five soloists—a ballerina, a danseur, and
three principal Shades—while behind them the vast, tireless corps
responds in echoes, diverges, vanishes, regathers into garlands, into
gateways, tosses, and freezes. The choreography is considered to be
the first expression of grand-scale symphonism in dance, predating
by seventeen years Ivanov's masterly designs for the definitive *Swan
Lake*. But our first reaction is not to how old it looks but to how
modern. Actually, the only word for this old-new choreography is
"immemorial." *La Bayadère* (1877) looks like the first ballet ever
made: like man's—or, rather, woman's—first imprint in space and
time.

The subject of "The Kingdom of the Shades" is not really death,
although everybody in it except the hero is dead. It's Elysian bliss,

and its setting is eternity. The long, slow repeated-arabesque sequence creates the impression of a grand crescendo that seems to annihilate all time. No reason it could not go on forever. And in the adagio drill that follows, the steps are so few and their content is so exposed that we think we'll remember them always—just like dancers, who *have* remembered them for a hundred years and for who knows how long before Petipa commemorated them in this ballet. Ballets, passed down the generations like legends, acquire a patina of ritualism, but *La Bayadère* is a true ritual, a poem about dancing and memory and time. Each dance seems to add something new to the previous one, like a language being learned. The ballet grows heavy with this knowledge, which at the beginning had been only a primordial utterance, and in the coda it fairly bursts with articulate splendor. My favorite moment comes in the final waltz, when the three principal Shades are doing relevé-passé, relevé-attitude cambré to a rocking rhythm, and the corps, seeing this, rush to join them in the repeat. They—the corps —remember those cambré positions from their big dance.

It's the corps' ballet—a fact the management should recognize by allowing a company call after, as well as before, the soloists have taken their bows. But the soloists in the performance I saw—Cynthia Gregory, Ivan Nagy, Karena Brock, Deborah Dobson, and Martine van Hamel—deserved their applause. Gregory was at her greatest. She took her grand port de bras the way it was meant to be taken— straight up out of the floor and through the body. Van Hamel, who may be the most talented of the company's younger ballerinas, did her variation the hard way by not coming off point until she was well up and into arabesque, and the excessively slow tempo made it even harder. Nagy has a way of filling a role superlatively without actually doing the steps. In his variation, he gathered himself powerfully and unfurled something that started like double assemblés and ended halfway to double sauts de basque. In the pas de deux with the veil, he didn't parallel the ballerina's steps and poses—but this is one of the differences between Makarova's staging and Nureyev's. Another difference is that she doesn't stroke the upbeat, or break the path of a gesture in order to "point" it. The way these two have staged the piece corresponds to their styles as performers—hers, musically more fluid; his, more emphatic. Also, her arabesques are not penchées, the solos are arranged in a different order, and she ends the ballet with the corps stretched along the floor in a semicircle rather than back-bent in a sunburst. I prefer the Royal Ballet's orchestration, with its drumrolls and its protracted climax that accompanies the sunburst, and I think I prefer the sunburst, but apart from those things there's little to choose between these productions. They're both marvelous. Marcos Paredes's costumes for Ballet Theatre are in the Victorian style traditional to this ballet, and I liked his headdresses for the women—beaded circlets à la Anna Pavlova.

La Bayadère is a ballet to grow on. Because there is no retreat from its severities—it must be performed with rigor and concentration or not at all—it is an excellent fortifier of technique. That's the way it has served the Royal Ballet for over a decade, and now, thanks to Makarova, Ballet Theatre has a base on which to rebuild its style in *Giselle, Swan Lake,* and the rest of the classical repertory. On the previous night, the company introduced another Petipa excerpt, staged by David Blair—Act III of *The Sleeping Beauty*—but what *it* was meant to serve I can't imagine. Blair's interpolations include two men's variations in the precious-gems-and-metals quartet that are grueling rather than rigorous. Aurora and the Prince are brought on early, in heavy costumes, to dance the Sarabande with their wedding guests and then leave during it, but the music that Tchaikovsky wrote for bringing them on isn't used. Nor are we given the lovely dance he wrote for Cinderella and Prince Charming, though these two are among the guests. Cuts of this sort are usually made in full-length productions of the ballet, but in an excerpt they are unaccountable. The Bluebird pas de deux was taken at half-tempo, which robbed it of all spontaneity, and it looked like a weak compromise between the Royal and Kirov versions. Makarova seemed to be dancing a version she'd learned as a little girl but had lost the point of, and Fernando Bujones's magnificence as the Bluebird had no impact at this speed. Gregory, as Aurora, had no trouble at all, but in her variation she cut her sissonnes at a groaning tempo, and the conductor followed her instead of leading. (This business of following tempi set by the dancers is one Kirov trait I'd rather not see imported.)

Although it's a brand-new production, with scenery by Oliver Smith and costumes by Miles White, this *Sleeping Beauty* seems straight from the warehouse (and someone should blow the dust from those orchestral parts in the Mazurka). Why not put on an authentic warehouse production instead? In the forties, the company used to do a *Princess Aurora* in which both costumes and scenery were executed "after original designs by Léon Bakst." A contemporary observer, Grace Robert, wrote of this production, which I never saw, that it was "the most beautifully mounted classic revival yet to be seen in New York. . . . It was evident that this was to be no semiresurrection in bargain-basement costumes, but a full-dress production worthy of the ballet's status in the history of the dance." Reverse that judgment and you get a picture of what Smith and White have done.

As for Baryshnikov, news of whom travels all too slowly, word comes as I write this that he will make his American début with Ballet Theatre on July 27, partnering Makarova in *Giselle*.

—July 22, 1974

Baryshnikov's Day

Because his performances are as exciting for what they portend as for what they contain, it's impossible to see all there is of Mikhail Baryshnikov at the moment and to see him complete. The feeling he leaves you with is one of intense pleasure mingled with the ache of frustration, and you can't capture him whole by seeing him again. To watch Baryshnikov dance for the first time is to see a door open on the future—on the possibilities, as yet untold, of male classical style in this century. The second time, and the third and the fourth, it's the same—that same dazzling vista, crowded with prophetic shapes and rhythms; we see it clearly in a flash, and then it's like trying to recall the content of a dream we only feel the emotion of: we get the same ache. Although Baryshnikov is in no sense an unfinished artist—at twenty-six he is in his prime—every performance confirms his potential, and part of the anguish we feel comes from the fear that his potential may be wasted. He harbors the future, but his roles keep him from exploring it. If ever a dancer needed new roles, it is he, and I don't mean roles from the modern Western repertory which would be new just to him; I mean his own new roles, with advanced choreography, that would be new to us as well. Baryshnikov begins where other dancers leave off, and to confine him to an existing repertory—no matter how amply he might ornament it—would be to suppress his essential genius.

Baryshnikov crams traditional roles with new vitality, and in them he seems literally to be flying out of the nineteenth into the twentieth century. In his début performances this season with the American Ballet Theatre, he danced "on top of" the solos in *Giselle* and *La Bayadère*, giving us two and three times as much to look at as anyone had ever given us in the same unit of musical time. High-concentrate dancing is what the most progressive twentieth-century choreography is all about, but the idea has never been expressed before by a performer on so high a level of virtuosity. For Baryshnikov, a double pirouette or air turn is a linking step, and preparations scarcely exist. In the *Bayadère* variation, he turned a grande pirouette in second, in passé, in attitude—nine or ten revolutions in all, and all from one preparation. In a traveling version of the same thing, he swept from low grand jeté into an air turn à la seconde and, on landing, continued to turn in a series of perfectly placed pirouettes en dedans. His finishes are achieved in a faultless diminuendo or a sudden clean stop. He gives a new urgency to commonplace allegro steps like brisés (in the two speeding diagonals of *Giselle*), and an ordinary jump appears in all its compound splendor as grand jeté dessus en tournant battu—redefined almost past recognition, and about a mile off the ground, too. Occasionally, because the traditional dance rhetoric comes so easily to him, the pressure gets a little thin. In the coda to *La Bayadère* and in his *Don Quixote* solo, he does a circuit of barrel turns (tour de reins) that must be unmatched for height, evenness, and cleanness of execution, but the ease of his style deprives the step of the raw impact it can have when it is done by lesser dancers. He also performs invented steps. One is a turning jeté in which, at the last second, he changes the foot he's going to land on and his legs flash past each other in the air. Or, on the way to one of his pinpoint landings in assemblé, he will suddenly flex his knees. It looks like provincial hot stuff. Baryshnikov's promise lies not in novel steps but in his power to push classical steps to a new extreme in logic, a new density of interest. He is a modern classical dancer. Unfortunately, at Ballet Theatre he plays to an audience that identifies classicism with the nineteenth century or with empty displays of technique. On the evening of his first *La Bayadère*, Baryshnikov was cheered, but Cynthia Gregory was cheered twice as loudly for perverting her own beautiful style in a simpering, stunt-filled exercise called *Grand Pas Classique*.

Baryshnikov's ballerina in all four of his performances was Natalia

Makarova—a partnership that is not heaven-sent. Makarova is hard to partner, especially in *La Bayadère*. She needs Ivan Nagy, who can commit himself to her completely. But in *Giselle* and in the *Don Quixote* pas de deux Makarova and Baryshnikov were wonderful to have together on the same stage. Stylistically, these two former stars of the Kirov Ballet are beautifully matched, and their Giselle and Albrecht were as psychically fused as Cathy and Heathcliff. (In the second *Bayadère*, this psychic fusion turned a bit anxious and a gray something descended which I can only describe as Kirov funk.) In the second act, Makarova's slightly rigid head positions and the line from the nape to the extended instep in fourth position had an entrancing pathos. It was her only *Giselle* of the season; she gave it up to Baryshnikov for his first appearance in America. He, in turn, played to her all evening with fervent devotion. At the end, he scattered lilies in a trail from the grave, then lay facing it as the curtain fell.   —*August 19, 1974*

The Two Trockaderos

The art of female impersonation, thousands of years old, enters a new dimension when the females impersonated are ballerinas. The basis of the parody is not gender alone but a stylization of gender, and the subject is—or properly should be—not Woman but Woman as Dancer. It was Mallarmé who said that a ballerina is not a woman dancing, because she isn't a woman and she doesn't dance. In this he was drawing a critical distinction between dancing and the ballet. The ballet, in Mallarmé's view, is dancing adapted to the theatre; it is "preeminently the theatrical form of poetry," and the ballerina is a metaphor, one who writes poems with her body, who appears before us as a vessel teeming with abstract preliterate suggestions—forever a symbol, never a person. For Mallarmé, whose ideal in dance was the purity of expression we have since come to recognize in great abstract choreography, the signature of the classical ballerina was her ability to summon up elemental visions—"a sword, cup, flower, etc." was the way he put it, and he didn't need to add that the ballet was not a mere business of noodling around on point. Drag ballet, or men on point and in tutus, has to be expressive in the same way as straight ballet is, or it loses the essence of its parody. There are two companies doing drag ballet in New York. I didn't go to either of them expecting to be reminded of Mallarméan first principles, but the difference between the companies is so basic that only Mallarmé's great paradox will do, like a gleaming cleaver, to separate them. In one company, the Trockadero Gloxinia Ballet, the subject is gender and nothing more; it's drag-queen display, dressing up, noodling around on point. In the other company, Les Ballets Trockadero de Monte Carlo, the subject is ballet. In the Gloxinia, the travesty is formless and unfunny. In the Monte Carlo, it is dead on target and hilarious.

It's axiomatic that in any parody the more serious you are the funnier you will be. The Gloxinia, the larger and sleeker of the two companies, is serious about all the inessential things—makeup and wigs and jewelry and costumes (which look expensive enough for the Harkness). It hands out a lovely little hand-bound printed program. A good portion of its corps de ballet—which includes one woman—gets up on point. But its choreography, which is unattributed, is neither imitation nor invention. It's weak improvisation, an amateur's blurred impression of things seen on the real ballet stage, and in the ballet-blanc numbers the purposefully dim lighting actually draws our attention to the repetitious vague steps instead of to the intended primary effect—the exquisite clouds of tulle. Unfortunately, there is no way to parody ballet without doing it—without, that is, a certain technique, however rudimentary it may be. Some may take the Gloxinia for a parody of decadent ballet, but in fact when ballet has been truly decadent it has elevated technique above everything else; it hasn't suppressed it. The Gloxinia puts all its effort into illusion, and the illusion covers all bases except home plate. Most of the routines, such as *Russian Snowflakes* and *Raymonda, Act III*, use costumes and music and lights to set up a definite look, or a hint of an idea, but then the thing starts to move and goes nowhere. Although the Gloxinia has been around for a few years and has acquired a reputation as a "fun" evening, I can't believe that a dance audience for it exists. On the night I saw it, a few weekends ago, at the La Mama, the audience seemed impressed, especially by the meticulous cosmetic preparations, but it also seemed ripe for the sort of thing the Gloxinia doesn't offer—accurate caricature of an art form. New York, "the dance capital of the world," has long needed a company of madmen to break us all up, and until I actually saw it I half believed the Gloxinia was it. But it's really just one more bad ballet company, and its appeal as a drag act depends less, I think, on one's taste for such things than on one's willingness to put up with its pretensions as a ballet. And with all the murky lighting. The Gloxinia's is the art that conceals. In one of its rare lights-up numbers, four soloists take turns doing a little something to the "Four Seasons" music of Prokofiev's *Cinderella*. Each wears a Botticellian tunic, boxily cut and thickly layered to disguise the wearer's physique. You could almost swear you were watching girls, but you'd never think you were watching dancers. The Gloxinia is so good at being girls that, for me, it's boring theatre. There's not much difference between the show it puts on and a show by inept women dancers, but its ineptness isn't a comic ineptness; it's merely evasive and unaware.

The parody company we've been needing may have just arrived, with the Trockadero de Monte Carlo. Its début season last month, in a loft owned by the West Side Discussion Group, a homophile society on Fourteenth Street, could not have been more of a success, and it took everyone by surprise, not least the Gloxinia, of which it is a rebellious outgrowth. One evening with the Monte Carlo (the name, of course, is in memory of the Colonel de Basil-René Blum rivalry of the thirties) and you see the reason for the rebellion. The Monte Carlo is the creation of ballet fanatics. They've seen the performances, memorized the steps, read the books (this shows in the program notes), listened to the music (this shows in the editing of the taped scores), and turned the whole scorching experience inside out. If it weren't for the long white gloves, a Trockadero trademark, there'd be nothing the two companies have in common.

Unlike the Gloxinia, which aims for a chilly beauty, the Monte Carlo seems to have an affection for broken-down, touring-trunk, desperate-last-stand ballet (its *Swan Lake, Act II* owes something to the production of Denham's Ballet Russe de Monte Carlo, the survivor of both De Basil and Blum), and it believes in war-horses —not only *Swan Lake* but *Don Quixote*, whose third act is arranged to look like the entire ballet. The big surprise is how much of this standard choreography the company is actually able to present— more than you'd believe possible, considering its numbers (corps de ballet of five), its handkerchief-size stage, and the fact that only the two leading artists can dance on point and that in the classics one appears as the other's cavalier. A female performer appears in this company, too, but—wisely, I think—only in mime roles. The rest of the company totter, gallop, or bourrée in a flatfooted scuffle through the scene, or else lumpily decorate it in poses; although they do what they do brutally, they never do it sloppily. The essence is preserved, because it has been observed. The Monte Carlo has a great ballerina in Tamara Karpova (Antony Bassae), but by and large it isn't technically more proficient than the Gloxinia; it's only more—much more—observant of and faithful to its models. The Monte Carlo's sharp-eyed artistic direction constitutes its main technical resource. It's so damned all-seeing that I don't think anything in ballet can be safe from it for long. Take, for example, the miraculously compact *Don Quixote*—the way it casually opens, with its peppery, sullen señoritas doing their lounging walks around the marketplace, tossing away bits of over-the-shoulder mime, then suddenly grabbing brooms and sweeping the upbeat like maniacs for the first *danse générale*. No two mime scenes are alike, and no two dances; the whole gamut of classical-folk clichés is there, whirling on the head of a pin.

There are also two good pieces of original satire. *The Queen's Revenge*, a baroque ritual about a gamboling quartet of lovers in which *The Moor's Pavane* is heavily implicated, has choreography and costumes by Bassae, music by Purcell, and a narrator hissing couplets from the side of the stage ("See how civil each one is— breeding always tells! / Yet underneath they're writhing in their own private hells"). On a lower level—its lunacies might have been planned for a deep-provincial dance-school recital in 1926—but just as pleasing is *Loïe Flutter*, the story of a giant blond peony that loses its petals. A "Danse Chinoise" from *The Nutcracker* is too brief to make an impact, and *Clair de Lune*, an exotic nude solo à la Josephine Bak*air*, is pure Continental Baths. The only uncharacteristic number in the show, it might well be dropped, or sent to the Gloxinia in exchange for the Isadora Duncan and Martha Graham takeoffs, which are the only uncharacteristic (and the best) numbers in *its* show. Both Duncan and Graham are the work of Olga Plushinskaya (Richard Goldberger). A thick-set and starkly made-up lady, she caught Graham's manner (c. 1965) but not her method of making a piece. As Isadora, however, she triumphed, feverishly sewing the last stars onto an American flag as the revolution approached in the form of the "1812 Overture"; then (ready at last) streaming into battle like the Winged Victory; *then*, draped in the flag and defying the cannonballs, being shot, being shot again, being dead, and finally being buried—under the flag.

Though apparently she is not, like Plushinskaya and the Monte Carlo's Tchikaboumskaya, a born comedienne, La Karpova, "the black rhinestone of Russian Ballet," is a mistress of style and the finest of the travesty performers. She's built like a pug version of Lou Costello, and on point looks a little like a bulldog standing on its hind legs, but she's musical and soft and rounded in the *Swan Lake*, smoothly vivacious in the *Don Quixote*. And in the notorious *Don Quixote* pas de deux—notorious because it is always being performed and almost always *barbarously* performed—Karpova, I believe, gave a better performance than the Bolshoi's Nina Sorokina, who was at the time dancing it at the Met. Though the two performances are not to be compared technically, there was more wit, more plasticity, more elegance, and even more femininity in Karpova's balances and kneeling backbends than in all of Sorokina's tricks, and the way Karpova used her snap-open fan put Sorokina to shame. Antony Bassae's mimicry of a ballerina is not a personal fantasy; it's an immaculately deadpan rendering of what a ballerina actually does, and at the same time a critical comment on what she should do. As a theatrical figure, Karpova has it all over the more fabled Ekathrina Sobechanskaya, prima of the Gloxinia (Larry Ree). Sobechanskaya styles herself after pictures of Anna Pavlova, but she does only the things she feels like doing, namely, walk a lot on point, take teetery little balances, and wave bye-bye to the audience. Ree's Sobechanskaya believes in herself; Bassae's Karpova believes in her role. The difference between them is the difference between the boudoir and the stage.

Watching ballet in drag can be instructive. If it really *is* ballet, it can have moments that are astonishingly close to the experience of straight ballet; the impersonality of it doesn't change, yet of course everything is wrong end to. Drag ballet provides one answer to the question of why men impersonating women are funny, while women impersonating men are not; it has to do with gravity. (A heavy thing trying to become light is automatically funnier than a light thing trying to become heavy.) And watching the two Trockaderos forced me to reponder certain aspects of sex in regard to ballet. It is partly because a ballerina isn't a woman but an abstraction of one that ballet attracts homosexuals in large numbers, but the

Gloxinia may be partial evidence that at least some homosexuals think the ballerina *is* the woman and not an abstraction at all. Naturally, if you believe the powerful, supremely theatricalized being on the stage is Woman, you'll never understand much about real women. And, like those feminists who feel that ballet traduces women, you'll never understand much about ballet, either. There are homosexual balletomanes who celebrate ballet for its distortions of women, while insulted feminists denounce it, but the two groups operate—from opposite ends—on the same scale of confusion. Both exaggerate the sexuality of ballet. Both are blind to ballet as a world of signs and designs. Because most of the great imagery in ballet has come to us through the courtesy of women's bodies, even people who aren't sexually prejudiced may grow confused and overconcerned with sex, but to impute sexist meanings to standard ballet usages (such as the supported adagio, which shows the woman as the man's puppet, Germaine Greer tells us, when, with equal prejudice and less paranoia, she might have seen the man as the woman's slave) is to indulge in fantasyland explorations at the Disneyland level. Ballet is fantasy, true, but even when it is erotic fantasy its transfigured realism reorders the sensations that flow from physical acts, and our perceptions change accordingly. The arabesque is real, the leg is not.

New York has never seen coarser and less attractive Soviet dancers, appearing in drearier programs, than the bunch that turned up here billed as "Stars of the Bolshoi Ballet," and I'm sorry to say that New York audiences behaved as if they did not know it. I exempt Maya Plisetskaya, the only genuine star of the engagement; though Plisetskaya's touch has never been especially delicate, and though the vehicles that have been fashioned for her by non-Soviet choreographers—*Carmen Suite*, by Alberto Alonso, and *La Rose Malade*, by Roland Petit—are hardly superior to the homemade junk she has appeared in for years, she was nevertheless the only performer who justified the audience's gaga reaction. Her glamour seems to have taken on a tinge of heaviness and sadness; this wasn't the old, fortifying Maya, but one had to admire her courage, returning to please the idiots by signing that long white autograph, *The Dying Swan*, over and over again.

—*October 14, 1974*

How to Be Very, Very Popular

When the Royal Ballet brought Frederick Ashton's *Monotones* to New York, in 1967, audiences slept through it and woke up to the rabid applause of a minority. The applause caught on, and the piece was given a grudging ovation. These things sometimes happen, and sometimes nothing helps. That was also the year the New York audience disgraced itself by its massive rejection of Nijinska's *Les Noces*, one of the most significant revivals of the decade. *Les Noces* never came back to New York, but *Monotones* got a second season. I remember the first trio (the piece is composed of two pas de trois, one set to the "Three Gnossiennes" and the other to the "Three Gymnopédies" of Satie), danced by Brian Shaw and Diana Vere and Georgina Parkinson in brick-red costumes. The second trio was even better. Anthony Dowell and Vyvyan Lorrayne and Robert Mead wore samite white; their dance was a fascinating cross-weave of static and dynamic patterns, all set to the same slow, tick-tock cadence. "Deadly dull," said a woman near me; I remember that, too, and also what a constancy of devotion to details of classical style the piece represented. Good old British Cecchetti technique—all chaste and flowing arabesques, limpid contrapposto harmonies, impervious balances, and (especially ravishing to the deprived American eye) strict épaulement. These company virtues had reached one of their periodic flowerings in the production of the "Shades" scene from *La Bayadère*, and Ashton not long after made the "Gymnopédies" in what must have been a moment of direct inspiration. The influence on *Monotones* of the corps's opening dance in *La Bayadère* is as marked as the echoes of *Symphonic Variations*, the ballet that established Ashton's postwar reputation. Although *Symphonic Variations* (1946) still has a place in the Royal's repertory, its chief importance is to its period. As a spiritual image of British postwar austerity, it undoubtedly hit home, but next to *Monotones* it is plaster-cast classicism. *Monotones* is Ashton's ultimate distillation of English classical style. It is also a luminous, peculiar, and disturbing ballet, and—for the average ballet audience —an uncompromising experiment in concentration. I've described something of its history because of what has now happened to it at the Joffrey Ballet.

The Joffrey production of *Monotones* was reconstructed for the fall season by Faith Worth, the Royal's notation expert. I arrived nervous. Would the package marked "Fragile" be full of broken glass, like last year's *The Dream?* Would the audience detest it? The "Gnossiennes" came on with Burton Taylor, Rebecca Wright, and Starr Danias, dressed in replicas of the original costumes (all-over tights) in their original color—pale green—with matching helmets. It was rough going. Splinters and chips appeared, all of them unavoidable. The dancers made a brave effort in an alien style. They did a lovely series of back-curving lunges into tight attitude, and other élancé passages came off well. Taylor's bearing was, as ·always, admirably correct, and he could clear his head and shoulders in oblique positions (croisé-effacé) with his arms above his head, which was something the girls couldn't do. None of them could maintain an unsupported balance. (In one passage they are required to hold an attitude-back balance, fold the leg through to attitude front, and hold *that*.) These were blood-sweat-and-tears "Gnossiennes." The "Gymnopédies" were something else. Sheathed in white unitards and wearing beanies that deliciously exposed the ears' (these "saltimbanque"-style costumes are of Ashton's own design), the dancers had the right look—long, lean, and flexible —and the right kind of unpresumptuous authority. With the marvelous young Pamela Nearhoof partnered by a highly promising newcomer, Kevin McKenzie, and by Robert Thomas, who seemed to be recovering some of the form he had when he joined the company, the dancing took on the calm transparency and sustained momentum Ashton meant it to have. This section contains his finest composing; the continuity of his line is like that of a master draftsman whose pen never leaves the paper. A line so steadily traced makes it difficult to speak of climaxes or even of "moments," but there are twists or whorls that do stand out, like the girl being promenaded at arm's length as she holds an arabesque while the second boy keeps backing under the bridge formed by the arms, backing and circling her as she turns. The promenade winds to a finish with all three dancers in tandem extending parallel développés to the back, completing the pose with a little "there-you-have-it" gesture of upturned palms. In contrast to this convolution is the simple changement from a left to a right diagonal, performed three abreast. It comes, hair-raisingly, on a key change in the second "Gymnopédie," and the powerful effect it has is out of all proportion to the humility of its means. It's like a shock to the senses.

Henri Sauguet said of the Satie music that it "seems to come from very far and from very high." The same might be said of the choreography. It is not the kind of piece out of which a choreographer hopes to get a hit, yet the Joffrey audience received it with rapture. Of course, half the cast is not quite up to the challenge, and American audiences are quick to sympathize with dancers in trouble, but I can't credit the Joffrey audience with that keen a perception of technical awkwardness. I wish I could. You practically have to fall down for most people to notice anything wrong. As for things like the absence of épaulement or the absence of security and stretch in the classical silhouette, the Joffrey repertory hasn't trained its audience to see stylistic faults any better than it has trained the majority of its dancers to correct them. No, the audience adored all of *Monotones,* and if it preferred the "Gymnopédies" (stepped-up applause, yells) it was probably because it is the better of two tightrope acts. The ballet, in the context of the Joffrey repertory, appears bracing in a way it isn't when you see it on a Royal program. The Joffrey audience might have caught that edge of an aesthetic difference, and it might have enjoyed having its faculties tested. (My own concentration breaks in the third "Gymnopédie.") The aristocratic reticence of the ballet, its inward-gazing manner and level, "deadly-dull" rhythm, didn't seem to bother anyone.

So an unlooked-for triumph took place, and for the first time I find myself complimenting the Joffrey on the production of a contemporary ballet not by Twyla Tharp. Still, what does this production of *Monotones* mean? When the ballet is danced by its Royal casts, you feel the whole strength of the company rising behind it. It comes out of a tradition they know intimately. When it is danced by the Joffrey, it's an isolated, precarious undertaking that depends for success on the singular abilities of a few dancers. The difference between the Royal's *Monotones* and the Joffrey's is that the Royal practices style and the Joffrey only professes it. What it practices is consumer relations in ballet. As the season went on, I noticed that the Joffrey audience tends to applaud everything just about equally, and I wondered what you have to do to fail here. The audience seems perfectly willing to let the management dictate its range of taste; it has confidence in the product, and there are levels of product for levels of taste. The Joffrey produces a shoddy line of goods on its own (see this year's, any year's, Gerald Arpino ballet) and buys better wares for those who are tired of shopping in the basement. The upstairs merchandise has big names attached to it. A Hurok audience may sneeze at an Ashton ballet that hasn't got Fonteyn or Nureyev in it, but Ashton at the Joffrey carries the cachet of the whole Royal Ballet—plus the Joffrey imprimatur. (At the Royal, *The Dream* succeeded as a Sibley-Dowell vehicle. In the Joffrey production, nothing works but the comedy relief, and the audience loves the ballet just the same.) There are the stillborn Massine revivals, the Diaghilev revivals, the bits of Bournonville, Jooss, and Limón, and the nostalgia revivals—Jerome Robbins in job lots. Although some of these pieces are well performed, most of them serve the audience better than they do the dancers. A season at the Joffrey is better than a browse through the dance-history books. Who wants to read about foreign ballets and dead ballets when you can see them?

The desire is perfectly understandable, and I not only respect it, I share it. If somebody announces *Parade* or *Le Beau Danube*, I will certainly go. Curiosity drags me. But chances are I won't go back. The dancing isn't always to blame. Ballets that belong to other times and other customs aren't negotiable, and dancers can't save them. Gary Chryst is very good as the Chinese Conjurer in *Parade* (and as Petrouchka); his makeup is fine and his mime is wonderfully specific. And Donna Cowen as the Little American Girl has clarified a lot of the details in her role which were obscure. But Satie's score remains for me the liveliest part of this wilted show. The Franco-Russian performing style so necessary to *Le Beau Danube* did not survive the Second World War. I hope never to see a worse version than the Joffrey's, or a better one than the performance that exists on a sixteen-mm. film made in the thirties—badly shot, without a sound track, but with an all-star cast: Massine, Danilova, Baronova, Riabouchinska, Lichine, all of them in their prime. Dramatically, the Joffrey *Petrouchka* is superior to American Ballet Theatre's, but not scenically. This season's Massine revival, *Pulcinella*, is a bummer. It's not that the ballet has ceased to be radioactive, like *Parade*; it's that one can't believe it ever was.

Pulcinella, created in 1920 and revived under the choreographer's supervision, is a very pretty spectacle, rather on the quaint side, and pervaded by the fruitless nervous energy that Massine's followers used to mistake for rhythm. As in the recent Balanchine-Robbins version, the music seems unsuited to a straightforward, unfiltered depiction of the traditional Neapolitan street theatre. Despite the authenticity of the Pergolesi fragments he orchestrated, Stravinsky's score has his own mandarin personality. The Picasso scenery is what might be called Cubist-Primitive—childlike in its qualities of freshness and simplicity but sophisticated in its treatment. To their visual and aural backgrounds the dances return no kind of comment. They're innocent of any point of view, innocent of style. Tediously they press a vague plot interest without developing any interest of their own. Picasso and Stravinsky seem to have been in on a joke that excluded Massine and Diaghilev. The joke didn't go far enough. Picasso's set, brilliant as it is, achieved nothing in radical theatre design that had not been achieved by *Le Tricorne* the year before. Perhaps Picasso should have insisted on keeping his original scheme, which called for a stage within a stage and for the classic pantomime characters to be impersonated by "real" nineteenth-century Neapolitans. Cocteau appears to have been the only member of Diaghilev's circle who felt that Picasso's first thoughts were his best. He suggests that Picasso's intention was to "rejuvenate" the old farces "as Stravinsky rejuvenated the music of Pergolesi," and he described the outcome ruefully: "After making a score of designs showing a theatre with its chandelier, its boxes and a stage set, Picasso's taste led him to suppress all that he had striven for and to fill the whole of the real stage with the décor which was previously on the tiny inner stage. Red plush was abandoned for the illusion of moonlight and a Neapolitan street."

As a museum exhibit, the production is worth seeing, along with *Parade*, the décor of which had been disfigured, until this season, by blundering execution. It has been repainted, and it looks approximately credible as the work of Picasso. The Neapolitan street of *Pulcinella*, leading to a bayside view of Vesuvius, is flanked by tall houses in Cubistic perspective; the colors are white, black, blue, and gray. There is a white floorcloth and a drop curtain, which was never used by Diaghilev. It shows a Pulcinella parting a juicy red theatre curtain. Rouben Ter-Arutunian's restorations are skillful. I wondered only about the platinum-blond Mae West wigs worn by the two seventeenth-century gallants. The costumes are more conventional in design and less organically related to the set than the costumes in *Parade* and *Le Tricorne*. (Strange that Stravinsky once called *Pulcinella* "a coherent and homogenous whole.") One recognizes them as Picassoesque because of their unerring sweet-sour color contrasts and their association with his paintings and drawings. The ballet was Picasso's favorite of those he designed; he had been portraying clowns, acrobats, and commedia-dell'arte characters since the earliest years of the century. But what these figures meant to him as symbols of men's souls didn't get into the ballet. At moments —the mock funeral, for example—Picasso's poetic fancy seems alive on the stage. The choreography can double the pictorial force of his images, but it can't give them theatrical depth. The ballet doesn't have Picasso's spirit. It takes his themes and turns them back into the raw material he drew on. There's more Picasso in *Monotones* than there is in *Pulcinella*.

There are signs that the management is getting a little impatient with the dreck ballets of its resident choreographer, Gerald Arpino, and is seeking a classier house line. Its two Twyla Tharp commissions, *Deuce Coupe* and *As Time Goes By*, gave the company custom-tailored choreography, a genuinely contemporary identity, and a chance to make history in its own right. But Robert Joffrey's heart seems to belong to the safe, the respectable, the genteel "art" ballet. Last year, he choreographed *Remembrances*, a maundering, dusky affair set to Wagnerian concert lieder, with endless visions of the young in one another's arms. This season he got Jonathan Watts, the director of the Joffrey junior company, to do it all again, to Schumann's "Davidsbündlertänze." And it is not as if we hadn't already seen countless examples of this frail, fragrant, piano-*cum*-partners type of thing done by every ballet company in the land. It has become a fixation as deeply rooted as *The Moor's Pavane*. Watts's ballet, called *Evening Dialogues*, is the genre seen from the peculiarly effaced viewpoint of the male partner: the women are caught, turned, held, lifted, but their images in space are never in any way incised by the presence of the men assisting them; they're just women dancing and being propped. Watts as a dancer was a fine partner (and still is; he appeared in the première performances of *Remembrances*). As a choreographer he hasn't much to say.

Arpino still has a lot to say; the man simply won't down. *The Relativity of Icarus*, his first ballet in almost two years, is in four parts: (1) a hard-driving solo for the Sun, danced by the company fireball, Ann Marie DeAngelo; (2) a very long and very slow gymnastic pas de deux for Icarus and Daedalus (Russell Sultzbach in the air, Ted Nelson on the ground); (3) reprise for DeAngelo; (4) finale, in which Icarus kills Daedalus and the Sun rules in triumph. The pas de deux is an endless vision of the young and gay in one another's crotches, and for the insanely credulous a verse meditation on the Greek myth is sung during the action. Arpino has gone pretty far this time, and probably will go farther still. The audience was thrilled. Arpino gave the company its first flash of nudity back in the sixties. He was into male love as long ago as *Olympics*, in 1966. He has done rock orgies and peace vigils, Doomsday Machine holocausts and Jesus-freak weddings—all of which remain in repertory to maintain the company's reputation as popular, accessible, and hip. He ought to do a full-evening opus called *Zeitgeist*. His last ballet before *The Relativity of Icarus* was *Jackpot*, a duet for Erika Goodman and Glenn White. The subject was orgasm and the décor was a box that lit up every time. The pro-Arpino critics were getting restless, and the ballet was dropped. But *Jackpot* was, I think, Arpino's best ballet—a straight dirty joke built around a few good inside jokes that the critics didn't want to laugh at. White's part, and the piece as a whole, were closely modeled on the work of Murray Louis, the Grand Street Marcel Marceau. Besides that, *Jackpot* was unabashed, unsolemnized porn. Arpino's work is howlingly vulgar, but *Jackpot* showed that it might be amusing if it didn't take itself so seriously so much of the time. Most of the fake significance in *Icarus* comes in at the ear, but it's still a pretty pompous as well as a pretty blatant piece of choreography. A popular theory of pornography holds that its appeal is enhanced by pretensions to art and culture. That may be the reason people are willing to pay $8.95 to see gay porn at the ballet when they can get it with wraps off at the movies right across the street.

Ann Marie DeAngelo's performance in this ballet couldn't really be called dancing, because Arpino's arrangement of her solos doesn't go beyond the barest presentation of her technique. She enters·in a high split-jump à la seconde and then proceeds to do all by herself and in about two minutes what another dancer would need a whole Black Swan pas de deux for. Her leg, wheeling high in rond de jambe from a steady-as-a-rock base, is like the swing of a cannon in its turret, and her specialty—throwing a leg up past her ear and promenading on point—is astounding. She's too touchingly young to look brutal, but that's how Arpino means her to look—not really for dramatic reasons but because brutality is his idea of powerful expression. Dancers in Arpino choreography customarily look hard as nails, driving themselves small distances on an absurdly big scale. Steps come in successive bursts, not in linked phrases. In adagio the body looks flung apart. In allegro it jabs in all directions. Arpino's "classical" ballets, such as *Viva Vivaldi!* and *Kettentanz*, are as abrasive as his sex extravaganzas and testaments of our time. They're indeed worse, because the music exposes his extraordinary tin ear. His choreography wrecks dancers; that's the worst single thing I can say about it. It makes them feel movement as a series of violent strategies rather than as an emanation from a calm center. I think it shortens their tendons. Their Bournonville is hopeless because they have no ballon.

The dancers have an easier time with *Moves* and *New York Export, Opus Jazz* than with *Interplay*, which is pop ballet with a classical base. The airiness had left Robbins in the fifties. He was adopting more and more of Anna Sokolow's ironclad gesture and combining it with his own nervous intensity. It's a lethal combination in the *Opus Jazz* piece; the Sokolowisms aren't nearly as well integrated in *Moves*, and I'd like to see the piece danced without all the histrionic touches and rude manners. In *Opus Jazz* the dancers are locked into their impersonations of those fictitious teenagers who on stage or screen are ever with us. They have two moods: sullen and larky. The ballet is as synthetic and sentimental as anything Robbins has made, and as entertaining. I watch it—the first three sections of it—with a light head and a guilty heart. It has Pamela Nearhoof as the girl who provokes five boys unspeakably and gets thrown off a tenement roof. With this and *Monotones* and *As Time Goes By*, in which she still does the part of the girl in white whose feet run away with her and who looks around to see if anyone has noticed, Nearhoof (a good name for a dancer) has become the princess of the company. The mantle seemed to drop across her handsome shoulders after her first minute or so in *Monotones* had passed. Nearhoof has something few young dancers have —relaxed power. She can wrap herself in a stage illusion and appear as if she were dancing for no one in the world but herself—and still sting you with her presence. She hasn't yet been overhauled by the Arpino repertory. Sexy-elegant, with an indispensable touch of brass, Nearhoof represents the Joffrey's image of itself in something like its ideal state.

The Joffrey has yet to put its various identities together in one crisp package like Pamela Nearhoof. That's why it is a third-rate company, but a successful third-rate company. When the New York City Ballet has failures, they are failures by its own standards. But because the Joffrey audience is stratified, different *audience* standards are at work and everything, or almost everything, is a hit. The audience may not be as stratified as I've made it sound, but there's no way I know of to check except by taking a poll. You can't judge by familiar and unfamiliar faces in the audience which people are going where, because the movement from one station to another is down as well as up. You can't tell by people's ages; there are masses of young people who may have become interested in the prestige attractions through their schoolwork and then found themselves in Arpino. And evidently there are always enough people in transit between levels to give the applause that baffling sound of unanimity. When I happen to enjoy what's on the stage, the Joffrey Ballet is a great place to be. The atmosphere around the company is a happy one, like a jammed party at which no one knows for sure, or cares, what's being celebrated. We have in this country three major ballet companies. The New York City Ballet, in its present period of slipped ideals, is a second-rate first-rate company. Ballet Theatre, our most conservative company, is just second-rate. But the Joffrey is first-rate at being third-rate. It's the only one that doesn't let down the side.

People in search of intelligent lyrical entertainment on Broadway could not have done better than to buy a ticket to the Paul Taylor company during its week at the Alvin. There were two programs— a mixed bill that included a new work called *Sports and Follies*, alternating with *American Genesis*, the evening-length ballet about our vicissitudes as a Puritan nation. There wasn't a dull moment in either show. *American Genesis* has some structural flaws and it lacks the seriousness one might expect of its theme, but it is a fine example of Taylor's capacity to set a stage abundantly flowing with ideas by means of a few props and gestures he seems to have pulled out of a hat. The piece is good to see again when you've digested the ideas, which are not difficult. Then its rhythmic continuity becomes even more powerful and sensuously exciting.

Sports and Follies, a suite for uncertain athletes set to a Satie miscellany, is expertly made and silly, the kind of Paul Taylor silly

I enjoy. Carolyn Adams has a jumping solo in which she never seems to touch down or take a breath. The high point of the week was a revival of *Churchyard*, a hypnotically morbid piece, as engulfing as a good horror movie. There were those long, rolling rhythms again, but here the ideas—if they are ideas—never come unstuck from the nightmare of what we're seeing: people piling onto and around each other in frenzies, their lower bodies covered with tumors. Taylor, who was abandoned years ago by the snobbishly avant-garde audience, has become the master of a kind of popular theatre without losing any of his integrity.

Yes, Rudolf Nureyev appeared with the Taylor company, and no, he is not a Paul Taylor dancer, but who ever said he was? Fifteen years ago, I would have given anything to see Taylor dance *Apollo*. He was not a classical dancer then, any more than he is now, and I don't think his presence in the ballet would have done it anything but good. Nureyev's presence in *Aureole* was a little like the Joffrey doing *Monotones*; he didn't get it all, but it was surprising how much of it he did get. And more impressive than his dancing was the way he put himself imaginatively at the service of the choreography and the company, even changing the way he takes his bows. Nureyev is the kind of dancer who causes categories to have a nervous breakdown. It's his personality rather than his technique that does it. He seems able to go anywhere and do anything, and even those who have never seen him on the stage have an impression of him as an extraordinary unconfined being. The impression stems, naturally, from his defection to the West, but he no longer seems especially Russian. He seems, instead, the man from nowhere, the man with an erased past and a completely restructured new life.

And when he arrived in the West, it was at a moment of upheaval in public morals and popular culture. Nureyev's behavior on- and offstage appeared related to a new trend, and he may even have instigated it, in part. It was amazing how many British rock stars suddenly turned up looking like him. He has never really belonged to the Royal Ballet; he has said that he is an interloper wherever he goes and that he will go anywhere if he is asked. I'm not even sure that he belongs to the dance profession, and it's always a bit of a surprise to see him turn up for his entrances on cue. A picture book devoted to his career would be dull if it were limited to pictures of Nureyev just dancing. When Nureyev comes out onto the stage, he brings this large, magical aura of freedom with him. It is greater than any gift he has as a dancer, and it is an aura very different from the one he projected when we first saw him, twelve years ago. Then it was his pride and idealism, which sometimes took the form of defensiveness, that were so moving. Nureyev has got the world to accept him exactly as he is, because that is how he accepts himself. There's plenty of showmanship in his makeup but not an ounce of self-deception. He has chosen to live as a gentleman of the West.

—*November 11, 1974*

Teddy and Topsy

The theme that runs through *Your Isadora*, Francis Steegmuller's edition of Isadora Duncan's correspondence with Gordon Craig, is that of two lovers who, to use Isadora's words in her autobiography, *My Life*, "were not two, but one, that one amazing being of whom Plato tells . . . two halves of the same soul." In *Your Isadora* (Random House and the New York Public Library), the theme is expressed in one of the first and most beautiful of Isadora's letters to Craig: "We were born in the same star and we came in its rays to earth, & for a little I was in your heart & then I wandered far away & now I am back. That is our History. No one could understand it—but us." This note, dashed off while she was packing for Russia, is typical of the lyrical Isadora, and she never stops singing to Craig, even when he has her strained to the breaking point. The same theme expressed in Craig's writings to and about Isadora appears to take on different aspects of his personality—aspects that tumble through the book and never quite cohere in a solid whole. There is Craig quicksilver ("She is just simple, lovely, & we seem to be just about *one*"), Craig leaden ("We were made for each other"), and Craig gaseous (a passage that begins "Suppose one had been in a world with 'ones other half—once—and that world so wonderfully perfect; and then . . ." and then goes on for many mazy lines of description of "one's" various states and conditions without the other, ending with "and here she is—and here am I. Is not that marvellous? It is quite 'impossible,' being so very marvellous—with what a cry we come together"). That Craig may be smuggling deep personal meanings through this fog is evident, though the message is not clear; he was a man the truth of whose feelings he often managed to conceal from himself, and Steegmuller, who does not conceal his own intermittent rage at Craig, speaks with some force of his "stunted feelings."

Steegmuller is often angered on Isadora's account, but he's angered, too, by Craig's own treatment of himself, as when Craig, the penniless theatrical designer of genius, niggles away yet another lucrative carte-blanche contract. George Bernard Shaw observed that "Gordon Craig has made himself the most famous producer in Europe by dint of never producing anything." This was all but literally true. In the entire sixty-two-year course of his career in Europe, he was responsible for fewer than half a dozen productions. The two of these on which his fame rests were the *Rosmersholm* with Duse, given one performance only, in Florence in 1906, and the 1912 *Hamlet* for the Moscow Art Theatre, which remained years in repertory. Both these commissions were obtained through Isadora Duncan, who knew both Duse and Stanislavski, but, as Shaw also remarked, Craig could have obtained them—or any other commissions he wanted—on his own: "If ever there was a spoilt child in artistic Europe, that child was Teddy Craig. The doors of the theatre were wider open to him than anyone else." Craig was the son of Ellen Terry and the godson of Henry Irving, the most powerful and beloved acting team in England. He was also a visionary, whose proposals for theatrical reform and whose early revolutionary productions of operas and plays brought him a local fame but no money. He was utterly passive about practical matters; Ellen Terry subsidized him, and later Isadora did, too. With his gift for converting his vices into virtues, Craig in later life said, "I had no self-ambition whatever—it is this lack of popular sin which has always buoyed me up." (It isn't hard to imagine where Shaw—or Steegmuller—would begin a catalogue of the popular sins that Craig *didn't* lack.) During his days with Isadora, he tried to absorb her "American *push*," and spoke often of his need for a good business manager. The Steegmuller volume is perhaps unfair to Craig, because it offers less material for his side of the affair. Against "every scrap—ribbon—ticket—letter & card" that Isadora ever gave him (save ten "too personal" letters, which he burned) there are only the few drafts of his letters to her that he also retained, together with the notes on her he kept adding to all his life. (Isadora's copies of the letters from Craig have apparently perished.) But the book is not a distorted picture of Craig. It is a picture of Craig with all his self-distortions, the worst among them being his positive appetite for failure, which, masked as idealism, he foisted time and again on the trustful, the loving, and the all too successful Isadora.

Edward Gordon Craig met Isadora Duncan in December of 1904, when she was twenty-six and he was thirty-two. They were in Berlin, which Isadora, whose name was already a byword throughout half of Europe, had made the magnetic center of her art. It was here that she had published her lecture *The Dance of the Future*, had founded a school, and had become the subject of a popular cult in which the whole German nation came to share. Craig was a newcomer to all this; in Weimar—but only in Weimar—where he had first been introduced to the artistic circles that clustered around his sponsor, Count Harry Kessler, it was the custom to speak disparagingly of Isadora. Wrote Craig, "I had heard that there was a sort of governess who had taken to dancing in an artistic manner," and his impression on meeting Isadora at the Duncans' salon in Berlin was of "a nice Greekish lady by art & a fine American girl by nature, and I am sure I shall be bored by her dancing." He went to see her perform and was overwhelmed. "I sat still and speechless," he wrote. In a few days, they celebrated their "marriage night" (his words) on the floor of his studio.

Count Kessler, the diplomat and amateur of the arts who had sought to bring Craig into contact with theatrical producers in Germany, wrote of Isadora in his memoirs, "I did not have a great opinion of her as a dancer in her early days; she was clumsy, amateurish, and uncultivated. She learned a lot from Gordon Craig." Whether this is true or not—Isadora herself was pleased to report to Craig the opinion of the German papers three years later that her dancing showed *"grosse Fortschritt"* ("great progress")—Craig never took any credit. Although in many ways Craig played an ignoble, even a destructive, role in Isadora's life, that was one crime against her he didn't commit. He never supposed that she was any less great than he. He never ceased to praise her as an artist, and he never violated her autonomy. (Nor would he permit her to violate his. He refused to collaborate with her and went into fits over her famous blue-curtain backdrops because, he said, she let people think he had designed them.) There were myriad offenses against both flesh and spirit which Isadora survived. He accepted her love and returned it; he also accepted her money, in return for which he acted, incompetently, as her manager, drawing up crackpot contracts and inhuman tour schedules. He became the father of her first child, but he neglected her so badly during her pregnancy that she tried to commit suicide. After the baby was born (harrowingly; readers of *My Life* will be prepared for this birth scene), and too soon for the good of her health, he forced her back on tour, and reproached her when a second tour, in the dead of summer, proved profitless. All this Isadora endured. She even, in time, rose above the knowledge that dawned, well into the affair, of Craig's having already fathered eight children by three other women, whom he had then deserted. The eighth of these children, Edward A. Craig (who in 1968 published a scathingly objective biography of his father), was born in London to Craig's faithful mistress, Elena Meo, during the initial stage of Craig's love idyll with Isadora in Berlin. But it was his insistence on seeing the love and the deep natural sympathy that existed between them as an understanding between equal stars whirling in their separate courses that broke her heart. By the autumn of 1907, Isadora no longer had a lover, or a father for her child. Craig had set himself up at last, in Florence, with a workshop and a printing press. When the child, Deirdre, died, in 1913, along with Isadora's second child (by Paris Singer), in the car that fell into the Seine, Craig was too busy to go to the funeral, and he received a wire from Elena and his mother reminding him to send condolences. He had done so, and later he wrote again, reviving the old theme: "For my heart and your heart are one heart and an utterly incomprehensible thing it is."

Steegmuller's connecting text offers a number of useful speculations on Craig's abrupt changes of attitude toward Isadora over the years. "Transference of guilt" is the only possible interpretation of Craig's savage assertion that the children's death was caused by Isadora's carelessness. Other speculations involve Craig's apparent need to perpetuate his illegitimacy (his father, the designer and architect Edward Godwin, neither married Ellen Terry nor supported his children by her, and Craig seems to have inherited his irresponsibility along with his talent), and the amazing similarities between Ellen Terry and Isadora Duncan—as Steegmuller lists them, "both beautiful, both famous, both enchanting privately and electrifying on the stage, both unashamedly bearing children outside marriage to the men they loved: a mother who had still been giving him an allowance of £500 a year when he was twenty-four...and who since then had been supporting two of his families; a mistress who danced herself half to death to support their child and further his work." And Steegmuller invites further speculation by suggesting that "the battering by Craig—by the tornado of egocentricity that was Edward Gordon Craig—had permanent effects on [Isadora's] personality and way of life." Perhaps nothing accounts for her terrible marriage to Sergei Esenin so well as grief for the wayward young "genius" husband she never had. Steegmuller's sensitive explorations of Craig-Duncan psychology are what make this book the superior example of theatre biography that it is, but he becomes so resentful of Craig toward the end that he fails to account sufficiently for what strikes me as a new note in the correspondence— Craig's pathos when, some months after the children's death, he writes two genuinely loving and extraordinarily humble letters to Isadora, in one of which he asks, "Can you forgive me for all the bad things? & can you forgive me for trying to live without you? You see I can't. So can you? It would open the sky for me." And there is his next-to-last letter, of 1917—his masterpiece—which begins by quoting her 1904 letter: "We were born in the same star. . . ."

Whether they were "one heart," as each of them always claimed, Craig and Isadora were in their artistic personalities virtually one and the same being. On paper, in formal print, both were rhapsodists, and they were not very helpful when it came to evoking each other's work. She wrote a ringing essay on his book *The Art of the Theatre* in which she keeps calling him Mr. Vesuvius Theatre Destroyer. Right after seeing her dance, he began a notebook about her which he called "Book Topsy." His recorded reactions to that first performance form part of the literature of intoxication that Isadora inspired wherever she went. Craig, unlike most observers, saw clearly enough what was happening, and he was even able to put some of it indelibly into words, but when he approaches the gut issue—how she actually moved—he fills in with such statements as "only just moving—not pirouetting or doing any of those things which we expect to see," and "she came to move as no one had ever seen anyone move before." These, for all their warmth and accuracy, are question-begging words. We are left to guess, by negative inference, at the things Isadora actually accomplished in movement. Craig didn't attempt further description; he seemed to feel that it was impossible. "She was speaking in her own language—do you understand? her own language: have you got it?—not echoing any ballet master. . . . And if she is speaking, what is it she is saying? No one would ever be able to report truly—or exactly—extraordinary, isn't it?—yet no one present had a moment's doubt." And no one ever did report Isadora exactly. Her reviewers a few weeks later in St. Petersburg, the citadel of classical ballet, were captivated, as Craig was, by her simple platform manner, her sense of the dramatic, her vividness as an actress. Poetry flowed from their pens when they wrote about Isadora's numbers, each of which had a dramatic program. She was a bird, an undine, a bacchante, a supplicant, a mourner. A dazzling spectrum of emotions passes before the eye together with a hint of surging thighs, a bit of veiling, and a flash of "thin, pale feet."

So it went throughout her career. People talked about the sensations she evoked; they didn't talk about the range, shape, duration, or attack of her movement, and Isadora, her whole substance reduced to the most enchanting gush, entered the dim galaxy of immortal dancing artists whose bodies are to subsequent generations a mere series of immaterial presences. Taglioni, Duncan, Pavlova—they might be perfumes, almost, each with her own tangy essence, each handily labeling the epoch in which she danced. When we read about these dancers today, it is the epoch that comes before us, not the woman—the epoch that unconsciously reflects itself in what it favors, and uses all the wrong words. In the case of Isadora Duncan, it speaks of Tanagra figurines or Attic vases when it might more comfortably have linked her with Art Nouveau and its own Rodin, who drew her; with Charles Darwin, whom she revered and whose *Expression of Emotions in Man and Animals* she undoubtedly knew; and with François Delsarte's *System of Expression*, a book she carried around like a bible. Yet Isadora's age did also recognize her as a contemporary, and the ecstatic, choked-up language it used about her was its tribute of recognition. No barrier of nationality kept this Californian from expressing meanings that, from Paris to Moscow, everyone seemed ready to accept. As William Bolitho wrote, in disapproval, "The feast of self-expression was in the oven; Isadora came in with the hors-d'oeuvres." But imagine the excitement of the starched and corseted audiences as they watched her racing around the stage in as near a natural state as decorum would permit—who can't imagine it?

To her own era Isadora came like the glad good friend who brings news of its inmost life. But in the immensity of her impact the individuality of her gesture is lost. What was original, what was borrowed, what was changed or deleted or heightened as she went through her period of *grosse Fortschritt* has never been documented. Even with Craig, who shared her mind as no other man in her life did, she seems never to have discussed her day-to-day work. In the more than two hundred letters that she wrote him, there is not a word about dancing. She speaks of composing new works, of rehearsing, of performing badly or well; she writes about the circumstances of her career, she complains about conditions on tour, she reports on audiences and receipts. But she never says what, exactly, she is up to during those rehearsal hours or what she had to do to progress, either as a dancer or as a choreographer. (The word was not then in use.) The only glimpse of choreographic effort in *Your Isadora* comes when Isadora requests, through Craig, some dance music from Martin Shaw, a conductor friend of his. "Can you write music on Greek rhythms," she asks, indicating the accents. "It must be a *Pastorale* with flutes and oboe. Something about Pan & satyrs. *Long* rhythms." And Craig chimes in, "Fine long rhythms & as noble as hell."

Because Isadora was almost entirely self-taught and had raised herself in her own style, Craig nicknamed her Topsy, and it has been suggested that her "choreography" consisted of improvising onstage. But this doesn't seem to have been the case at all. Annabelle Gamson's recent concert at the American Theatre Laboratory, which featured a suite of early, middle, and late Duncan solos, proved, first, that a body of teachable and hence nonimprovised Duncan material exists, and, second, that performed in the right style it might be as interesting today as any of the ballets have been which absorbed Duncan gesture—ballets ranging from *Les Sylphides* to *Walpurgis Night* and *Allegro Brillante*. Miss Gamson learned most of the choreography from Julia Levien, who had it from Anna and Irma Duncan, two of Isadora's pupils who took her name. Duncan dances were indeed made of steps, and steps full of the most surprising dynamic variety. The large bold ones that suddenly reversed their shape in the air are the ones I remember best. And there were lovely open gestures of the arms and hands that seemed to stress a tender kind of relationship between the dancer and the audience and all the space around her and us. Nothing about the movement looked fancy, but it did look tricky—hard to do well. Miss Gamson's staccato style made every image decisively clear whether it was based on a pantomime gesture or an abstract one, and there was enthusiastic applause for everything from the overflow audience. The Duncan suite was too short to do much more than announce its authenticity—and its authority. One would like a whole evening in which dances of this kind could build their own poignance and grandeur.   —*November 25, 1974*

Blind Fate

Balanchine's celebrated dictum "There are no mothers-in-law in ballet" may have stemmed from his experience producing Stravinsky's *Le Baiser de la Fée*. The hero of the ballet is a babe in arms in the Prologue. A fairy bewitches the baby with a kiss and after he is grown to manhood she returns disguised as a gypsy fortune-teller on the eve of his wedding. The young man awaits his bride; when she appears he lifts her veil and recognizes instead the fairy-gypsy, who has come to carry him away with her forever. How to show that the bridegroom is the child of the Prologue and the gypsy the fairy in disguise were problems that appeared to trouble Balanchine more than they did the audience. He has never believed in "mothers-in-law"—in transformations and relationships that aren't clear in visual terms. In *Tyl Ulenspiegel* he showed Tyl and his enemy, Philip II of Spain, growing to manhood by having the two crouch behind a table as children and stand up as adults. In *Baiser* he had to appeal, impurely, to the audience's intellect. But audiences have always known that the baby of the Prologue to *The Sleeping Beauty* is the sixteen-year-old Aurora of Act I and that Odile is not Odette in *Swan Lake*. The libretto of *Le Baiser de la Fée*, drawn from Hans Christian Andersen, was intended by Stravinsky to be an allegory about Tchaikovsky ("the Muse having similarly branded Tchaikovsky with her fatal kiss, and the magic imprint [having] made itself felt in all the musical creations of this great artist"), and the ballet used elements from the Tchaikovsky ballet classics, including a snow scene that recalled *The Nutcracker*, to create a theatrical fantasy as Tchaikovsky himself might have imagined it.

In this sense, there *are* mothers-in-law in ballet—precedents so well established in the mind of the audience that they become part of a choreographer's inheritance. I can understand Balanchine's having reservations about the libretto of *Baiser* in 1937, when he first choreographed the ballet and when American audiences weren't as familiar with the full-length Tchaikovsky classics as they are now, but I can't understand his continuing to have reservations about it or about the staging of the ballet's final scene, which presented genuine technical problems both in 1937 and in subsequent revivals. For this scene, in which the fairy draws the boy farther and farther into her kingdom, Stravinsky composed an extended, slow-moving melody that flows on and on in the manner of one of Tchaikovsky's panoramas, and Balanchine has described the accompanying stage effect that he tried to produce: "The fairy should appear to be suspended and the bridegroom, just below her, must seem to be swimming through space, as it were, to reach her." Balanchine's various attempts to achieve this illusion, including the one that most people remember—the hero slowly climbing a cargo net spread across a giant glacier—met with no success, because the action was invisible to the part of the audience sitting in the upper house, and after 1951 he gave up on the ballet. It seems a pity not to have one more attempt, at a time when Tristan and Isolde sail miles into the sky at the Met and John Neumeier (through American Ballet Theatre) gives us as the finale to his ridiculously encumbered and obtuse production of *Baiser* a tortuous zigzag around some traveling curtains strung on rods. Surely anything Balanchine might think up today would be better than that.

For his revival during the New York City Ballet's Stravinsky Festival in 1972, Balanchine used excerpts from the *Divertimento* —the concert suite Stravinsky made from his ballet score—and staged a suite of dances that had no reference to the libretto except for those who could find in the dances for Patricia McBride and a small female corps echoes of the ballet's bride and wedding attendants, and in Helgi Tomasson's moody solo an intimation of the hero's tragic destiny. The dances for the girls and the pas de deux are part of the wedding divertissement in the original ballet, and very likely they are what they would be in a full version of the ballet had Balanchine elected to stage it. But Tomasson's dance is something that probably couldn't occur in any other context—a statement that sums up, in non-narrative, emblematic form, the eerie mystery of the ballet as a whole. And the staging of the finale, which Balanchine has added to the *Divertimento* this season, is also something that couldn't occur in the full ballet. For this music, which begins with Stravinsky's lovely setting of "None But the Lonely Heart" and continues into his extended slow "panorama," Balanchine uses only the material of his *Divertimento* ballet—the corps of girls, in their now incongruous peasant dresses, acting as impersonal agents of fate to separate the two lovers, the lovers weaving their way toward each other through the corps's diagonal, passing each other blindly, and, still blinded, backing offstage in opposite directions as the curtain falls. Balanchine has managed this—the hundredth variation on his classic theme of blind fate—more handsomely than I can make it sound. The new scene matches Tomasson's solo in mood; the question is whether it's just a bit of tacked-on drama or an extension into new territory that resets the proportions of the *Divertimento* as we've known it up to now.

After one performance, I couldn't see that anything had really changed, and I couldn't take the expanded mystique of a story, which Balanchine has provided instead of the story itself, any more seriously than the three haunted-ballroom scenes with which he regales us while we're waiting for "Theme and Variations" in the *Tchaikovsky Suite No. 3*. When *Suite No. 3* was first done, a few years ago, all the barefoot dancing and long hair, together with the schematic lighting the piece then had, seemed to mean something in relation to "Theme"; what that was I no longer remember. The sober truth seems to be that Balanchine these days often sets pieces of music he happens to like without making ballets out of them. The *Divertimento from "Le Baiser de la Fée"* has always been something more than a divertissement and something less than a drama, but within its hybrid structure it had, and continues to have, a formal distinction in the relation of its parts that *Suite No. 3* lacks. There's a great difference between the blind-fate episode in the *Divertimento* and the one in the first movement of *Suite No. 3* (which, perhaps not coincidentally, also contains a variant of "None But the Lonely Heart"). In *Suite No. 3* it's a stock situation, weak in dance impetus and dangerously close to kitsch. In the *Divertimento* it is developed directly out of Tomasson's earlier pas de deux with McBride. Balanchine has taken McBride's signature attitudes and distorted them slightly to reveal their dark implications. In the earlier duet, she dipped and turned in different directions, pirouetting with a powerful swing of her leg to lock her partner behind her. Now, in the new scene, she freezes in low-slung arabesque and, as he turns her, gradually knots herself about him until the two are fused. The bride of the original tale becomes the fairy, and this, too, recalls a traditional Balanchine theme—the heroine whose aspect flickers between vampire and goddess. The sinister-sweet elements in McBride's nature are perfect for the role. But if the new developments seem to grow naturally out of what has gone before, I can't see that their refocusing of the piece in the general direction of conventional Balanchine dramatics is any great gift, especially to those of us who would have loved a revival of *Baiser* complete. The *Divertimento* is one of the most superbly crafted pieces that have come from Balanchine in recent years, and McBride, Tomasson, and the girls always perform it with exceptional polish, but it's basically footnote material, a collection of thoughts about a lost work of art.

McBride continues to perform, in "Theme and Variations," a role that doesn't suit her. It was created in 1947 for Alicia Alonso's fully turned-out legs and their bold precision in allegro. McBride, with her thin thighs and lesser turnout, can't be expressive in this demanding piece. The ballerina McBride most resembles (if film can be trusted) is Marie Jeanne. She's far happier meeting the terrors of *Tchaikovsky Concerto No. 2*—in a role originated by Marie Jeanne —but what terrors they are! No sooner has the ballerina entered than a pit yawns at her feet—the piano cadenza to which she must perform pirouettes of utmost difficulty, including several ground-skimming double pirouettes on quarter-point which, in their problems of traction, momentum, and braking, are practically unique in the ballerina repertory. Merrill Ashley, making her début in the role, swept through the cadenza with startling ease and, gaining confidence, went on to have a great success. Ashley is a tall dancer whose main strength is in her legs and in their frank power in big jumps. Because of a long, narrow torso and an oblong, somewhat sharp face, she can sometimes look tight and clawlike. Although her movement is large, it isn't full. Lack of amplitude is at the moment her only deficiency.

Of the other performances I have been able to see so far this season, the most impressive were by Colleen Neary in *Concerto No. 2* and *Serenade*, Victor Castelli and Tracy Bennett as Neary's matched pair of partners in *Concerto No. 2*, Edward Villella making a welcome return to the Stravinsky *Symphony in Three Movements,* and the new Danish dancer Peter Schaufuss, who gave, in *Scotch Symphony*, a very finished performance for a company début on short notice.

Tchaikovsky Concerto No. 2 and *Serenade* and *Scotch Symphony* are in good shape this season, with corps work that is unusually well rehearsed and keen-spirited. The ensemble will never be absolutely together, but now their stragglings are threaded through by something that looks like conscience. The mist of inaccuracy has lifted over parts of the *Symphony in Three Movements*, that 747 of ballets, and it isn't as irritatingly ticky as it has been, though it *is* as slick and glassy. An irritant that will never die, apparently, is the way the company looks in its putty T-shirts and lollipop leotards. Of all the ballets I saw during the first week, only *Scotch Symphony* and *Western Symphony* seemed adequately designed, dressed, and lit. The *Concerto No. 2*, as miraculous a ballet as it was when it was called *Ballet Imperial*, is decked out in acid combinations of turquoise and lemon yellow on an arctic stage, a vision that deadens the eye long before the piece is over. The color of *Serenade* is headache blue. Has there ever been a worse-dressed ballet company in the history of the world? Or a theatrical institution of renown that was more careless of the functions of costume and décor? Helgi Tomasson, in the *Divertimento*, dances his greatest role in the costume he wears in *Donizetti Variations*. There are those who say that the New York City Ballet dances all its ballets as if they were the same ballet— an assertion hard to counter except in individual cases (like Tomasson's). But it certainly can't help dancers to make distinctions in style when what they're given to wear is unstylish.

The excellent Pennsylvania Ballet brought its production of *Concerto Barocco*, starring Joanne Danto, back to the Brooklyn Academy for a brief season, along with a gutsy *Serenade* and three company premières. Hans van Manen's *Solo for Voice 1* was an attractive semi-Dada arrangement to a John Cage score, with a soprano (dressed like the incomparable Hildegarde) singing the title piece at two dancers in white (Michelle Lucci and Lawrence Rhodes), whose movements were skillfully timed reactions to the pitch and volume of her voice. *Zig Zag*, by Lar Lubovitch, used assorted dance shticks and mime shticks in one of those playtime ballets that one doesn't see anymore. Not a bad piece, but not interesting as dance. In *An American Rhapsody*, Robert Rodham set a large stage but never succeeded in filling it—the trap that usually awaits choreographers who try to stage the "Rhapsody in Blue." Gershwin's score is full of cues for movement and changes of scene, but it allows no time to build a climax. Rodham, who also appeared in the piece, as a spangled, tap-dancing Uncle Sam, came very close to it, though, and his greatest invention was an impeccably suave Veloz-and-Yolanda-like couple (Joanne Danto, Gregory Drotar) doing backbends to the slow theme while ice mist rolled around their feet. The Art Deco set and costumes, which were of the finest quality, were done by Robert Mitchell and Hal George.

Serenade, the Balanchine ballet that contains his best-known image of Fate propelling the Poet, was forty years old last June, and I'm glad I was able to see the Pennsylvania version before the anniversary year was out. It differs from the New York City Ballet version in several important and arguable respects—the tempi are slower, the movement is punchier, and it omits the extension of the *tema russo* that Balanchine supplied in 1964—but it is irresistibly well performed by a company that knows in every gesture how it wants this piece to look, and that is at least a workable definition of style. —*December 2, 1974*

Wrapped in an Enigma

On a desperate night in Stockholm, one can throw oneself into a canal or go to the Royal Swedish Ballet. It's not a bad company, but it's so eccentric and at the same time so styleless that one plunge and you're whirled away in a vortex of unreason. I speak, of course, as a foreigner. Living with the company for a year, I could possibly penetrate some of its idiosyncrasies, but after seeing two of its three programs at the City Center I could barely walk a straight line home.

As classical dancers the Swedes are mediocre whizzes—not middlingly competent in all things but great at one end of the scale and terrible at the other. Some were not as great or as terrible at the same ends of the scale as others, but in general the technique seemed insecure in the whole middle register, where most companies are so solid. Backs were weak, knees unstretched; wrists and hands were excitable. Beats were fine, jumps good; turns were poor, partnering was very poor. The Swedes appear to have learned dancing from the extremities in toward the center rather than the other way around. Common sense tells me this can't be true, but it's the impression I have of them in performance all the same. In performing, they found all kinds of odd things to stress or to leave out. They are turned out, but they don't always use their turnout. A few steps are sketched in; then the next few, not necessarily bigger or more important, will be done full force. The current flickers on and off all night long. What the dancers expressed instead of a style was a habit of selection. I could make no sense of the habit, it was so unpatterned, but each Swede as he or she danced seemed perfectly relaxed, beyond strain even at high speeds, and this made them look attractive, at times winningly attractive. Surprisingly, there were no actors among them, and the ballets, most of which were drawn from the international repertory, contained no revelations. One of the home products was a bundle of excerpts from *The Sleeping Beauty*, with a corps de ballet in spinach-green cobwebs and Phyllis Diller hair. If the Swedes ever became reasonable, they'd probably be very good dancers. At the moment, the best dancer they have is Walter Bourke, who happens to be an Australian.

The New York City Ballet's new *Coppélia* has been enhanced by two additions to the choreography. One is a first-act solo for Frantz, set to music from *La Source*, in which Helgi Tomasson hurtles about the stage in a moment of callous exuberance following Swanilda's exit in tears. Her dismay at not finding the rattle in the ear of wheat that tells her Frantz's love is true is lost on Frantz, but the audience expected that. It doesn't expect her to return, all emotion spent backstage, and top Frantz's solo with an even more sensationally joyous one of her own. Last summer, when the production was first staged, at Saratoga, without Frantz's solo, I thought Swanilda's abrupt change of mood unprepared for; I still think it is, but the insertion of the dance for Frantz's distracts me from the thought. To the extent that the dances distract one from the story, which is one of the strongest ever written for a ballet, the piece falls short of what it might be, but it is still better than the Ballet Theatre version, in which the story distracts one from the dances. The other new passage is a coda for the Frantz-Swanilda pas de deux in Act III for which Balanchine has borrowed music from the last act of

Sylvia—music he once used for a memorable Tallchief-Eglevsky pas de deux and to which he has now composed entirely new choreography. Where, when the orchestra crashes into the soaring melody, there used to be soaring lifts, there is now Patricia McBride in a series of huge, slow double pirouettes in attitude front swinging to attitude back—a magnificent demonstration of Swanilda's sovereign power.

Other developments in the production are less happy. It's a shock to discover that what I took for underfulfilled intentions in the design of Act III are really the whole conception. Rouben Ter-Arutunian's backdrop—a vast, empty plain burning with sunset colors—is no better than an undressed cyclorama would be, and the addition of some garish new costumes turns the modest and friendly village pageant that Balanchine has devised into a carnival of bad taste. The gold tunics for the two dozen children who dance in this act have been replaced by stiff pink ballerina-doll tutus. The tunics had no particular tenderness to them, but they did have the kind of accidental innocence that hard functional uniforms often have in real life, and the children, who appear in the ballet as official marshals for the pageant, looked charming in them. In the same stream of "real-life" fantasy, Ter-Arutunian first clothed the principal soloists of the divertissement (Merrill Ashley, Christine Redpath, and Susan Hendl) in "nice" knee-length pastel dresses, identical in design, that suggested three prom queens or local debs. The only questionable effect of these costumes was their resemblance to party dresses of the 1920's, but instead of retaining the lightness and sociability of their mood, Ter-Arutunian—or more likely Balanchine—threw out the whole idea. The girls in their gaudy and graceless new costumes and the children in their scandalously cute pink outfits seem to be taking part in an anonymous ballet happening in a nowhere world. The first set of costumes had asked questions: Where are we? What are we doing? The second set gives the wrong answers—wrong not only for this ballet but for any ballet. The heavy skirts of the soloists conceal their movements— movements that in Ashley's case are electrifying. (She alights from a jump in plié and on point, poses, and darts away.) The choreography for Hendl's quieter solo gives her a new suppleness and graciousness—much the best role she has ever had, but I don't expect anyone to see this now. Redpath is a beauty who can't compete as a dancer with her colleagues, so the ballet's makers give her a bare midriff, hardly a spiritual conception for Prayer. Misadventures of this sort take their toll of the divertissement as a whole. Discord and War used to look like the only really outlandish fancy-dress number; now everything up to that point is heated to the same level and does its deadly little job of regularizing the variable temperature and flow of the dances.

It's been vilely said that Balanchine has a cynic's enjoyment of cheap decoration and that he really cares for nothing but choreography, but in fact the cheap decoration blankets the choreography, and the audience can't catch on to some of his finest conceits. As an example of the fragility of Balanchine's "pastoral" poetry in *Coppélia*, take the hobbled fifth-position jumps in the Jesterettes number that echo the equine references in Ashley's bolts toward and away from the earth. These are evocations we should at least be allowed to see as clearly as we saw them last summer at Saratoga (where programs of ballet used to be preceded by trained Lipizzaner horses performing on the lawn). It might have been imagined at that time that Ter-Arutunian would fill in his blank backcloth with a suggestion of wheat-bearing fields instead of the mindless Cinerama sunset he has given us, and it might have been hoped that he'd resist all further tendencies to artificiality and cuteness.* Ter-Arutunian is almost as much his own enemy as Balanchine is. For the children's polonaise that now opens the second act of *Harlequinade* he has designed some lovely variations on his own commedia-dell'arte costumes. But the Day-Glo costumes for the revelers Balanchine has insisted on adding to this ballet scarcely seem to come from the same hand. The State Theatre must do strange things to people. Perhaps, from time to time, Balanchine likes to think of the place as the family entertainment center of New York. In his lavish, family-style ballets, such as *The Nutcracker* and *Harlequinade* and *Coppélia*, he certainly seems to be jollying up the general audience, saying to it, in effect, "See, it's like Radio City, only better." But his own taste in design is exactly like Radio City's, and in some matters it's worse. The uncomfortable dim lighting of *Coppélia* and *Harlequinade* would never be permitted at a commercial palace, and when we need a few fireworks, as in the Discord and War sequence, the lighting board at the State Theatre is strangely inactive.

It's customary in Balanchine ballets to be torn one way by the choreography and another by the décor and costumes and light-

* *Postscript 1977:* According to a later program note, the new costumes in *Coppélia* were the work of Karinska.

ing, and it's also customary to suffer this rupturing in silence rather than utter feckless complaints. The one man who should care most about such things—Balanchine himself—not only doesn't care but collaborates in the mangling of his work. What he gives us with one hand in *Coppélia* Act III—a beautifully proportioned suite of allegorical dances that belong to the mythical provincial world of *Coppélia*—he takes away, indirectly, with every new stroke of Ter-Arutunian's brush. Why this is so is one of the great conundrums of our theatrical life. —*December 9, 1974*

Over the Rainbow

Eliot Feld's new ballet, *The Real McCoy*, suggests a work in progress about show dancing of the thirties. For the most part, Feld chooses to evoke rather than imitate; there's no tap-dancing in the piece, and where the thirties spectacle was typically extravagant, Feld's is sparse—perhaps too sparse. The nature of *The Real McCoy* is fantasy—a finer thing than parody—but if the ballet lacks the smugness and the vulgar appeal that outright parody might have, it also lacks the sweep. It's weak the way so many of Feld's other ballets are weak—in the projection of a consistent poetic idea. Because the elements of Feld's thirties fantasy don't combine to form a clear statement and other elements seem to be missing, the foreshortened perspective of fantasy doesn't really appear, and the ballet just looks unfinished.

But even in this state it is worth seeing for the way it misses and then scores. Feld assembles the basic ingredients of a thirties-type show (the solo, the romantic duet, the production number), and he tries to re-create their essence by means of a few necessary figments (song-and-dance man, dream girl, male chorus). But Feld hasn't in every instance found the magic formula, which wasn't a formula so much as it was an imaginative process, that made these numbers vintage spellbinders. What's fascinating about *The Real McCoy* is that when Feld finally involves himself in that imaginative process he produces original, gleaming choreography— pure Feldian fantasy, or genuine parody so remote from piracy as to amount to the same thing.

The piece starts badly, like a tinny fake-thirties knickknack. Feld, in contemporary sports shirt and slacks, dons a topper, glances up at the rainbows on the backcloth, catches a cane thrown from the wings, and begins noodling ineffectually about the stage to a piano blues by Gershwin. The noodling continues, on wheels, when a rolling couch appears with a girl on it and Feld jumps onto it with her. The two glide and swivel around and across and all over the stage, with the piano playing the "Walking the Dog" number from *Shall We Dance*. The absurd, dreamy locomotion, smoothly timed to the music, is beguiling once it gets to you, but I think Feld intended it to be more. I think he intended a crystallization of the animate props and décor of thirties movie musicals, and I'm not sure he succeeds. For one thing, the couch remains a couch, whereas a thirties choreographer would have played "let's pretend" with it, turning it into a bandwagon, a sailboat, Washington crossing the Delaware. Feld can turn the couch into a canoe, but he certainly doesn't let his imagination run riot. Much of the strength in the thirties sense of design lay in the play of allusions and resonances; it was a marvelous bond between entertainers and their audiences, and we think of it as "thirties" only because it is dead. Doesn't a modern audience seek this kind of bond, too? Watching ballet especially, we cling to bits of references and build on them unconsciously. We look to the choreographer to control the way we're building his piece in our minds. When he doesn't give us enough to go on, we go on what we've got. For me, Feld's would-be Busby Berkeley couch became irretrievably cross-circuited with the driving rod of the engine that slowly bears Keaton and his girl away in *The General*. In the lulling, vacuous charm of what Feld put on the stage, I couldn't help what I was thinking, and when I knew I was thinking it I loved it. Feld has something Keatonian in his face and in his quick-wittedness as a dancer. I had never noticed the resemblance before, and I probably wouldn't have noticed it now if Feld hadn't cast himself as Fred Astaire. Aiming at Astaire in my mind, he hit Keaton. Although there *was* something of Keaton's character in the early Astaire—in his resourcefulness and total harmony with the universe—Eliot Feld is better at being tight and still and obsessive, like Keaton, than relaxed and mild and free, like Astaire. I don't know what he thought he was doing in that opening solo—it wasn't hoofing; it wasn't anything—but a moment after the couch disappeared he and the girl (Michaela Hughes) were presenting a very creditable Astaire-Rogers pastiche, and Feld seemed at last to have jumped over the rainbow into the thirties.

Whereupon the strangest thing happened: the thirties themselves disappeared and we were in Feld's own imaginary world of romance-as-illusion. There is a chorus of five men with walking sticks, turning, bending, pausing to tap the floor or probe the upper paths of air. They make a swing of their sticks, and Feld lightly seats the girl on it. Lightly he lifts her down, and the sticks continue to circle slowly, like a Ferris wheel. The gradual flowering of the image, set with great delicacy and precision to the Gershwin Prelude No. 2, is a great achievement for Feld, and the unforced sentiment is, coming from him, remarkable. Though he's been brilliant in the past and sometimes sweetly lyrical, too, he's never before given us a dance that spreads like slow honey, all in its own measure of attainment. The dance is evocative in a way that relates to the spirit of the thirties, but the meaning of it isn't confined to the thirties. Feld has titled his ballet after a Cole Porter song (although his music is drawn from the non-Tin Pan Alley Gershwin). The song, "At Long Last Love," runs, "Is it a cocktail, this feeling of joy, / Or is what I feel the real McCoy?" In other words, just how potent is cheap music? Do we fool ourselves by believing in the reality of its emotions and in the grace and beauty of the theatre they inspired? Is any of it good for more than nostalgia?

Feld hasn't given us his answers, because he hasn't handled the whole ballet with the degree of careful attention he's given to its parts. When the ballet is at its liveliest and most fertile, he actually seems to be drawing new substance from his subject. At other times, he's brash, familiar, and unconvincing. Maybe he started out to make nothing much and then ran into more; maybe he found his nuggets first and then couldn't find their setting. However it was composed, the piece has no internal consistency. After the Ferris wheel, the male corps do an obligatory chorus-boy routine. Feld doesn't define their relation to the girl or to himself, and he doesn't show us why Rouben Ter-Arutunian has dressed them like poolroom sharks. Nor does he account for the absence of other girls by making Michaela Hughes into the one girl who stands for them all. This final part of the ballet is set to the "Jazzbo Brown" music that was deleted from *Porgy and Bess*, and, from the sound of it, it should have been the most exciting scene in the ballet. Feld gives us nothing to conjure with. The men vanish, somehow, along with the girl, and Feld time-travels back to the present, yearning before his rainbows as the curtain falls.

The Real McCoy is not all there, but it's an important ballet for Feld to have attempted. A lot of his recent work has been insular, dried-up stuff, and although he's built a repertory on the models of other choreographers, he hasn't often found the inner mechanism that made his model ballets work. In the atmosphere of the best American popular art he seems to have uncovered an instinct for formal allusion, and for the first time he makes a metaphor real on the stage. Many young choreographers haven't developed similar instincts, and I suspect it's because they're afraid of seeming decorative or dated. It may be that in its simplest forms of expression, allusion is a dead convention. But holding up a bunch of sticks and having an audience breathe back "Coney Island!" isn't such an easy thing to do, and Feld has done it, after years of waste motion. Encouragingly, he hasn't pushed it as a big moment; he's let it announce itself as the happy event it is. If he can do this, perhaps he can go on to richer and more complex forms of metaphorical expression. Perhaps he'll even make a coherent ballet out of The Real McCoy.

Another problem with the piece is that Ter-Arutunian's backcloth has no distance and no glow. It ought to be relit or maybe rethought. In the tiny, cramped auditorium at the Public Theatre where the Feld Ballet plays, the audience sits banked above the stage like internes watching an operation. How can we go over the rainbow when we're already on top of it?   —December 30, 1974

Old Acquaintance and New

The orchestra for Rudolf Nureyev's performances at the Uris is amplified in the bad Broadway fashion, but otherwise the evening, which is called Nureyev and Friends, is in quiet good taste: a little too quiet and—except for that gnawed hambone The Moor's Pavane, which I had hoped never to see again—a little too good. Nureyev is no longer the bounding Tatar, nor at the age of thirty-six could he be, although audiences still gasp hopefully at his every jump. Such hopes might be satisfied if Nureyev were doing, say, the pas de deux from the third act of *The Sleeping Beauty* instead of the one from *Flower Festival in Genzano*. Bournonville has never been comfortably within his powers, but he is still magnificent circling the stage in Florimund's coupés jetés. And I wish that for the nine other dancers he has gathered about him he had selected an ensemble capable of performing some such rousing classical excerpt as Balanchine's old *Pas de Dix* (from *Raymonda*). Nureyev seems to have chosen his program to display his versatility, and his choices are overexquisite. A Broadway audience would, I think, have preferred a hotter show, and so would I.

The hit of the evening is Paul Taylor's *Aureole*, and this is due as much to the Taylor dancers, who share the performance, as to Nureyev, who is much looser and more elastic than he was with the Taylor company last fall. He's better, too, in *The Moor's Pavane*— less inclined than he used to be to convert Limón's lunges and straddles into carefully placed ballet positions. The hollowly booming "epic" style, of course, is quite opposite to the paper-kite lyricism of *Aureole*, and, if you like, both these pieces on one program show Nureyev's flexibility as a "modern" dancer, just as, presumably, *Flower Festival* is coupled with *Apollo* to show his range as a classical dancer. Actually, *Apollo* is more modern—it is even more "modern-dance"—than *The Moor's Pavane*, which might reasonably turn up any day now as a Bolshoi "Highlight."

Nureyev's version of *Apollo* is the one he gave last spring with the Royal Ballet, and it's a misrepresentation. Not that he takes liberties with the choreography; he is in a few passages inaccurate, but this is a minor fault compared to the one overriding sin of slowing down the tempi to the point of extinguishing all life from the ballet. *Apollo* has succumbed to misplaced reverence in the past, but never has it taken so long to die. Nureyev is not actually bad as Apollo, and he might be fine if he quickened his pace, relaxed his oversculpted phrases, and cut loose with some of the swinginess of *Aureole*. But probably he'd consider that sort of treatment sacrilegious. *Apollo* to him is obviously a great and exalted ritual whose mysteries must be unfolded at maximum leisure. Meanwhile, the Broadway crowd is going numb and hating every minute. Who could, given the spectacle that Nureyev puts on, hope to persuade a patron of the Uris that Balanchine's youthful masterpiece is not overrated tediola? If Met audiences yawned through Nureyev's rituals last spring, why should a Broadway audience cheer? And where the

Met audience was provided with an explanatory note on the ballet's subject by Eric Walter White, the Uris audience, which must include many people who have never seen *Apollo* before and many others who have never seen a ballet, is given a few facts on the ballet's history. It's always wrong to present *Apollo*, even to a ballet-wise audience, without identifying the characters and explaining something of the story. Most people are familiar with Apollo and Terpsichore, but Polyhymnia and Calliope?

It was good to see Merle Park dancing so well in *Flower Festival* and miming so intelligently as the Emilia figure in *The Moor's Pavane*. I thought her grandly misguided as Terpsichore. And except for *Aureole* the rest of the casting was subserious.

Nothing galvanizes the general public like the advent of a new male star in ballet. Baryshnikov evenings at the American Ballet Theatre are sellouts and surpass in the feverish excitement they arouse even Nureyev's first American season with the Royal Ballet, in 1963. In those days, the hard ticket was Nureyev-Fonteyn. Nureyev by himself didn't sell out the Met until the Hurok office released its publicity barrage in 1965, and it must be remembered, too, that Nureyev's star had already ascended partly via network television. If Ed Sullivan and the *Bell Telephone Hour* were still in business, Mikhail Baryshnikov would be known to millions more Americans than know him today. As it is, he's on the verge of becoming a national household name, and only New York, Washington, Houston, Denver, and Atlanta have seen him. In the current City Center season, the clamor is as much for Baryshnikov solo in *Les Patineurs* as it is for Baryshnikov-Makarova or Baryshnikov-Kirkland in the ballets he performs with either or both ballerinas—*Coppélia* and *La Fille Mal Gardée* and *La Sylphide* and *Giselle*.

So far, if I'd had to give my scalp for one ticket, I'd have given it for *Les Patineurs*. In this transcendent Baryshnikov performance (which, alas for the scalpers, he gave exactly twice), one didn't have to wait around for him to dance. Each appearance was an instantaneous string of firecrackers, a flaring up of incalculable human energy in its most elegant form. The Ashton ballet, thirty-eight years old, is still a model of construction. The central role is so well designed that a dancer can get by on neat execution alone. Baryshnikov embellished it like a bel-canto tenor, and, as often happens, he made the choreography look as if he had invented or at the least inspired it. A now famous Baryshnikovism, the split tour-jeté, looked right for the first time in the context of this ballet about ice skaters, and Baryshnikov produced the step as none of his imitators so far have done—coming out of a double air turn. Curiously, in the performance I saw (the second of the two), the role had none of the brash extrovert character that is associated with it. It had instead a sense of spiritual dissociation, as if the Green Skater's isolation were to be attributed to his genius. He—the "character" as Baryshnikov assumed it—suggested a boy who builds dynamos in his attic; he had that kind of tragic happiness.

Up to now, *Patineurs* is the only role in which Baryshnikov's dazzling dance power and the diffidence of his personality seem to fit together, but it isn't the role Ashton created. (Not that it matters.) As it happens, Ballet Theatre already has a superlative show-off Green Skater in Fernando Bujones, and Bujones is dazzling in an altogether different way—sharp and arrowy, while Baryshnikov is soft and sinuous. With Bujones leading what is now the strongest male corps in American ballet, and with Natalia Makarova and Cynthia Gregory and Martine van Hamel leading a female corps that includes such exceptionally talented soloists as Kim Highton and Marianna Tcherkassky, the company didn't need Baryshnikov to put over its winter season. But it has got him, and it has Gelsey Kirkland, too, who left the dwindling Sugar Plums at the New York City Ballet to be the icing on Ballet Theatre's top-heavy cake. How Ballet Theatre was to handle its load of talent was a problem *before* Baryshnikov and Kirkland joined; the company's ability to attract stars isn't matched by an ability to attract choreographers, and the disproportionately small shareable repertory means that dancers are either waiting to get into a part or waiting to get out of one. A Makarova-Baryshnikov *Coppélia* this season wrung the material for all it could give, shook out a few extra gags (Makarova popping an elastic band under her chin), and wrung some more. Makarova's showmanship doesn't fail her even when her dancing does. Baryshnikov's dancing *is* his showmanship. His acting tends to be a cover for his personality, not a revelation of it. In comic roles, he's less guarded than he is in roles like James and Albrecht, in which he contorts his face and his playing is heavy and confused. He hasn't Ivan Nagy's gift, in *La Sylphide*, of putting the audience in his place. Nagy, the company's best actor in classical roles, is also Makarova's best partner. Makarova's solos were finer in the *Giselle* with Baryshnikov, but in the duets she didn't have the unearthly halation she had when Nagy lifted her.

And Baryshnikov is better with Kirkland. They did one *La Sylphide*, he in his kilt and Frankenstein makeup, she looking like a French chambermaid, yet it was wonderful—the evident climax of this first phase of their partnership. In the first act, Baryshnikov seemed to be trying out different interpretations of the role in a kind of Stanislavskian attempt to make sense of it. James is a character of stormy temperament, but his dances are light and airy. Ironies of that sort, which abound in Romantic ballet, make contemporary Russians impatient. They gave us a Stanislavski *Giselle*, and they probably can't understand how we can live with that and the light insincerities of *La Sylphide* at the same time. In the second act, Baryshnikov actually forced a new element into James's solos. That element was passion. James's buoyancy and speed were overtaken by the fury of frustrated desire. This was dark "Russian" Bournonville, but it was very different from the undirected violence that marks Nureyev in the same part. No other dancer alive could have done it.

Kirkland's Sylph is the first great performance this production has seen since Toni Lander's. She has a lot of natural assets for the role—her size, her years, her baby face—and she has the boneless arms, the plastic waist, and the light, springy jump, which got lighter and higher as the ballet went on. But Kirkland wasn't only physically right, she was theatrically perfect. Unfortunately for the company's star-rotation system, not everybody was born for *La Sylphide*. Cynthia Gregory, for example, can outdance any other woman in the company, and her Bournonville style is admirably conscientious. In the second-act crescendo variation she was unbeatable. But the Sylph eluded her. The tilted head positions, the capricious transitions in mood, made her look dotty, and the character lost tension. Makarova gave us the lightest and most billowy jumps of all, and she's one of the finest actresses on the ballet stage. But although this season she was playing with a new simplicity and directness, she still looked like much too sophisticated a woman to be taking such a part. She's about as at home in it as Gertrude Lawrence playing Peter Pan. Kirkland has the total unity that one wants to see in a stage character. She's a true sprite—a particular kind of imaginary creature with an imaginary nervous system. No one else showed such musical mime, such distinct, untrivial pathos in the death scene, such an unclouded consistency of movement in every aspect of the role. A weakness at the moment is the vague port de bras in jumps, but this performance—as I had to remind myself forcibly throughout it—was, after all, a début.

The City Center—which, incidentally, has too small and dark a stage for *La Sylphide*—is full of star-gazers, and this annoys some of the dance addicts. But the general public that buys into a dance event only when some new comet is passing across the heavens knows what it is doing. It is looking to have explained to it something about an art form which it has never understood. True, it can't be counted upon to "support ballet," but people to whom most dancing is meaningless can't be in on the struggle; they can only be in on the glory. The better dancing is, the more nearly universal is its appeal. —*January 20, 1975*

Back to the Forties

If the number of fine ballets that American Ballet Theatre had to show for its thirty-five years of existence equaled the number of fine dancers it currently has under contract, its anniversary gala, on January 11, would have been a night to remember. But numerically and stylistically the equation is unbalanced. The handful of illustrious ballets that made the company's name can't support dancers like Baryshnikov and Kirkland and Makarova and Nagy and Gregory and Bujones, and even if it could, it's patently impossible to build a gala retrospective around *Fancy Free* and *Pillar of Fire* and *Romeo and Juliet* and *Three Virgins and a Devil*. All but the last are legitimate masterpieces, and all of them were created between 1941 and 1944. The creativity of that first decade had no sequel in the fifties, the sixties, the seventies. When you are seeing Ballet Theatre choreography at its best, you are almost always seeing a picture of the forties. The dancers of the seventies don't fit into that picture. The ballets are still interesting and they're a challenge to perform, but their aesthetic is dead. Often the sentiment is dead, too. Audiences can't get excited about them in the old way because the life of the period that produced them has receded and they're insulated from the way we think and move today. When they are presented as they were at

the gala—deliberately disconnected fragments of the past—it's hard
not to see their position in a contemporary repertory as an extended
irrelevance. They're really "gala material" in a quite specific sense—
not part of the ongoing gala that Ballet Theatre's apologists pretend
its history has been, right up to the present.

The programmers for the gala didn't try to force a continuity between the company's bygone achievements and its current resources.
Mostly, they exhibited Ballet Theatre as a performing collective that
had once been a company. They gave us sections of Tudor's *Pillar
of Fire* and *Romeo and Juliet* mimed by the original casts. They
put on some of the earlier dancers, such as Igor Youskevitch and
André Eglevsky and Agnes de Mille and Yurek Lazowski, alongside
the present ones. They put on Miss de Mille in a speaking part as
well. But apart from these indiscretions it was much like a usual
night at Ballet Theatre. Bits from the current repertory (*Les Sylphides, Concerto, Etudes, The River*) were mixed with bits that
might become current at any moment, such as Makarova and Nagy
in *Spring Waters*. (The company's foreign stars customarily bring
their old repertories with them; otherwise, they wouldn't have very
much to dance.) Some of the programmers' intentions canceled
each other out, among them the decision to impose four stellar but
aging cavaliers on Cynthia Gregory in the Rose Adagio, a number
she'll probably never get to do in repertory. This one time out, she
was understandably rattled, but in the excerpt from *Miss Julie* she
danced with the relaxed intensity she always has in modern character parts. Erik Bruhn returned in this, flying downstage in one of his
uniquely taut leaps, and won the great ovation of the evening. Baryshnikov in *Le Corsaire* was another miss; the choreography is
simply too tame for him. But Kirkland's first shot at the ballerina
role turned out to be a direct hit. So it went: a familiar Ballet
Theatre progression of ups and downs. There were the nonstar turns
(D'Antuono and Kivitt in the *Don Quixote* pas de deux) and the
nonballets (*Etudes* and *The River*—two excerpts each). We got
Eleanor D'Antuono three times and Martine van Hamel not at all.
The look of Makarova standing and bending on her points in *Concerto*—the look of the leg, with its wonderful upward flow of weight,
and the sense of a further weightlessness in the foot—was for me the
dance highlight of the evening's first half; in the second it was Kirkland's undreamed-of pirouettes in *Le Corsaire*.

Between the halves, we got Agnes de Mille, pointing out that

among performing companies in America only the Metropolitan
Opera has lasted longer than Ballet Theatre but that, unlike Ballet
Theatre, the Met had to go outside its walls to obtain its repertory.
"This," she said, hurling an invisible torch to the ground, "is a
creative institution." Agnes de Mille, arch-propagandist of the dance,
regularly shills for Ballet Theatre, but even for her this is a new
peak of chauvinistic bluster. Since 1950, Ballet Theatre has not commissioned one ballet of lasting merit, and by that I mean a piece
that doesn't yield up all its secrets after two or three viewings. It
has gone outside its walls for every useful ballet from Herbert Ross's
Caprichos on (and for a lot of useless ballets, too). In 1965, Robbins
did his version of *Les Noces* for the company, and Eliot Feld did
Harbinger, his first ballet, two years later. Some would make exceptions of these pieces; I wouldn't. But the point is that neither Robbins nor Feld, both Ballet Theatre alumni, has found it possible to
stay with the company long enough to give it his best. Since the
beginning, Ballet Theatre has also made a point of producing the
standard classics, but it really didn't get into the classics business
until the mid-sixties. Its repertory is too small for the demands its
huge roster of stars makes upon it, and the productions are insufficiently stylish. An original full-evening work has never been attempted. The company has relied more and more on big-name stars
whom the public would see in anything, and it hit bottom with this
policy when it revived its dodo version of *La Fille Mal Gardée* for
Makarova.

Fille is too big a price to pay to see stars, and the stars have to pay
as big a price to put it across—to make the characters real, the action
coherent, the bumbling, tacky humor seem like innocent zest. The
piece has absolutely no dance architecture. The stars slave to build
a bit of momentum in their variations only to have it leak away the
next second into the crevasses of the plot. If they did less, they'd
look like paper dolls. Even the *Coppélia* has to be treated by the
dancers like a theme for ever more expansive dancing and acting
improvisations. The more expansive Baryshnikov and Kirkland become, the more recessive and moldy their surroundings seem. They
dance at full height, so to speak; the rest of the company at half
height. But it's a pleasure to see them trying to live up to the values
this production merely hints at. Ultimately, only Makarova, running
wild this season, gets away with performing at the production's expense. She has the wicked wit for it and the improvisatory flair, but

Kirkland, who has learned so much from Makarova, wisely doesn't follow her lead in this. A pity that Kirkland's second act, grown enormously more assured, had to be truncated at her last performance because of an accident at the rear of the stage. But we got to see Kirkland's instant cool reaction to the accident (the collapse of a dancer who was one of the puppets); she "played" it as part of her conversation with Coppélius and swept on.

It may be because of the unreasonable load of responsibility he has to carry, as much as his unaccustomed intensive performing schedule, that Baryshnikov is beginning to look a little tired. The things he has to do in *Le Jeune Homme et la Mort*, revived for him this season, are a pathetic waste of his resources. The piece, one of those in which, at rise, a young man lies smoking in a cheap room while electric signs blink, is B-movie aesthetics puffed to the pretentious limit of a Cocteau fable. Cocteau conceived it in 1946 for Jean Babilée, the angel-thug of Les Ballets des Champs-Elysées, and Babilée subsequently performed it for Ballet Theatre. The role is full of sustained acrobatic balances, some of them in slow motion, and baroque flights over the furniture. But the style of the piece is wearyingly brutal, and the choreography, by Roland Petit, is in raw, convulsed chunks that keep knotting at the same level of tension. Cocteau, in a famous radical departure, had Petit set the steps to jazz, switching to a Bach passacaglia at the dress rehearsal. The disparity isn't very poetic; because the choreography isn't really dancing, the music need be no more than background accompaniment, and the fact that it's Bach strikes me as one of the more mechanically fabulous gestures of the Cocteau of this period. Baryshnikov, more angel than thug, is physically so vital and radiant, so unstrainingly precise, that he unconsciously undermines the expressive intentions of the ballet. Bonnie Mathis, in Nathalie Philippart's role as Death, has to stand like a rock wall over this shining cataract of energy, and she hasn't the dominating presence for the job.

From *Le Jeune Homme*, as from so many other pieces in Ballet Theatre's repertory, I get the continuous impression of an incongruous enterprise. It's like listening to cracked 78-rpm records being played on the finest stereo equipment. But the forties are hot just now, and so is Ballet Theatre. How often we have had recalled to us the company's opening night, in 1940! (Who remembers New York City Ballet's opening, in 1948?) With so few other landmark evenings at their disposal, the company's publicists have had years to press this upon us. Miss de Mille went over it all again on gala night, trying hard to make the sequence of fortuities that constitute the company's history sound like a success story. For twenty-five years, Ballet Theatre's management has been inattentive to the growth of its dancers as artists so long as the public would buy them as stars. It has dedicated itself to devising ways for the company to survive, only survive. Survival is what Ballet Theatre is best at. It markets ballet, but it specializes in the survival business, and this year business is very good indeed.   —*January 27, 1975*

Farrell and Farrellism

Suzanne Farrell, one of the great dancers of the age, has rejoined the New York City Ballet. She returned without publicity or ceremony of any sort, entering the stage on Peter Martins's arm in the adagio movement of the Balanchine-Bizet *Symphony in C.* The theatre was full but not packed. (Ballet Theatre was playing a one-time-only performance of *Theme and Variations* with Kirkland and Baryshnikov, at the City Center.) The lower rings were thronged with standees who did not have to push their way in. Sanity was in the air. As the long bourrée to the oboe solo began, the audience withheld its applause, as if wanting to be sure that this was indeed Suzanne Farrell. Then a thunderclap lasting perhaps fifteen seconds rolled around the theatre, ending as decisively as it had begun, and there fell the deeper and prolonged silence of total absorption. For the next eight minutes, nobody except the dancers moved a muscle. At the end of the adagio, Farrell took four calls, and at the end of the ballet an unprecedented solo bow to cheers and bravas. There was no distraction, no intemperateness, in either the performance or its reception. The Bizet was never one of Farrell's best roles, but it is probably the most privileged role in the Balanchine repertory. Returning in it, she returns to the heart of the company, and she could become great in it yet.

In that first moment of delighted recognition and then in the intense quiet that followed, the audience, I think, saw what I saw— that although this tall, incomparably regal creature could be nobody but Farrell, it was not the same Farrell. She has lost a great deal of weight all over, and with it a certain plump quality in the texture of her movement. The plush is gone, and it was one of her glories. The impact of the long, full legs was different, too. If anything, they're more beautiful than ever, but no longer so impressively solid in extension, so exaggerated in their sweep, or so effortlessly controlled in their slow push outward from the lower back. The largesse of the thighs is still there, but in legato their pulse seemed to emerge and diminish sooner than it used to, and diminish still further below the knee in the newly slim, tapering calf. Yet the slenderness in the lower leg gives the ankle and the long arch of the foot a delicacy they didn't have before. And it shaves to a virtual pinpoint the already minute base from which the swelling grandeur of her form takes its impetus. Farrell is still broad across the hips (though not so broad as before); in pirouettes she is a spiraling cone. But it isn't that Farrell is so terribly big; it's that she *dances* big in relation to her base of support. The lightness of her instep, the speed of her dégagé are still thrilling. You'd think a dancer moving that fast couldn't possibly consume so much space—that she'd have to be more squarely planted. Farrell defies the logic of mechanics, and in that defiance is the essence of the new heroism she brought to Balanchine's stage a little over a decade ago.

Farrell's speed and amplitude were demonstrated more compellingly in *Concerto Barocco*, two nights after the Bizet. They are old virtues, and I am happy to see them back. Farrell doesn't look muscular or drained, as I feared she might, after five years in an alien and diseased repertory. In the upper body, she is almost totally different, and vastly improved. I miss the lift in the breastbone, and I think her sight line has dropped, but the shoulders, neck, and head have a wonderful new clarity and composure. The refinement of the arms and the simple dignity of the hands are miracles I didn't expect. And here is perhaps the best news of all: a Farrell who dances with a new grace of deportment and sensitivity of phrasing. Of all the changes that have come over her, this is the most significant, the most moving. Farrell sensitive? Back in the old days, in the seasons just before her departure from the New York City Ballet, she was the exact opposite—a superdiva who distorted every one of the roles she danced except those with distortions already written in. The absurd sky-high penchées, the flailing spine and thrust hips, the hiked elbows and flapping hands were as much a part of the Farrell of that period as the prodigies of speed and scale and balance that she accomplished. She wasn't joyously vulgar, like an old-style Bolshoi ballerina; she was carelessly vulgar, with no idea of the difference between one ballet and another. But the concept of differences in ballets was in general collapse, and one couldn't blame Farrell for what the company failed to teach her. Strangely, she returns at a time when those distinctions are beginning to be felt again—when the company can be seen at its best one night in *Tchaikovsky Concerto No. 2* and again another night in the utterly different *Stravinsky Violin Concerto*. But there's a collision in the making between Farrell's new, unaffected, clean style and the style of the dancers who've been replacing her all these years.

Farrell's great promise, in which Balanchine was immersed for so long in the sixties, marks the company to this day. It is saturated with her image. What Balanchine saw in her he has projected onto other dancers, but when she left, nearly six years ago, she was still evolving and obviously under fearful pressure. For many of the dancers who got chances after she left, the Farrell image in all its negative aspects has become rigidified as a norm—even intensified as a norm. Karin von Aroldingen and Sara Leland and Kay Mazzo are much worse than Farrell ever was; they're caricatures of the caricature she had become. Beside their wild, strained excesses, the Farrell of today looks almost conventional. Of course, compared to the ballets Balanchine made for her, *Symphony in C* and *Concerto Barocco* are conventional, and these are the only pieces we've seen her in so far. The rest of the Farrell story, which may well contain contradictions of what I've been saying about her, will unfold this season in *Jewels* and *Don Quixote*. But even without having the mature Farrell around to point up the difference, one can see that the Farrell image has been grievously misconceived. Swinging pelvises, baling-hook arms, and clawing hands have become the new, cruel orthodoxy, and there's a whole cluster of young girls in the corps—thin, long-limbed girls who look hysterically overbred: the ultimate degeneration of what might be called the Farrell strain. Penelope Dudleston is one of these girls. All hinges and splays, she dances the Siren in *The Prodigal Son* with a peculiar, dehumanized force. That is to say, she has no force at all—just a limp, terrifying presence. Dudleston is the first Siren to suggest that she stems from the men's chorus of reveling creeps; she might even be taken for one of them in disguise. (And there, opposite this apparition, was Edward Villella, looking sweeter, more innocent—and more baffled—than ever.) Heather Watts, whose hyperextended joints I rather enjoy, does Allegra Kent's old role in the Webern ballet

Episodes, while Dudleston does Diana Adams's. The great breeding cycle of which Farrell's early NYCB phase was a part has long since run its course and is now exhausting itself in mutations. Bodies like Dudleston's and Watts's are redundant in ballets like *Episodes;* they're the bodies that mad, hyperbolic choreography is about, and they get no antipathetical play—no drama—out of the deliberate awkwardnesses and non sequiturs and extreme dislocations that Balanchine invented for the more resistant bodies of Adams and Kent.

Who Cares? is, like *Episodes,* a landmark ballet, and it, too, is showing signs of erosion. When it finally gets going (with the ten demisoloists doing their relay of Gershwin hits), *Who Cares?* is a ballet I adore, but the moment it marks in the history of the company is a poignant one that I can't get out of my mind. It was Balanchine's first ballet after the break with Farrell, and in it you could feel the whole company breathing easier. Patricia McBride, who is still marvelous in it, was unexpectedly marvelous in it then; it was one of the ballets that consolidated her stardom. One of the reasons it's no longer fresh is that Von Aroldingen has trashed the beautiful part Balanchine gave her—the part that for the first time made her look like an American ballerina and that might well have gone to Farrell if she'd stayed. It was as easy in 1970 to imagine Farrell in *Who Cares?* as it was in 1957 to imagine Tanaquil LeClercq in *Agon,* and that, perhaps, is part of Von Aroldingen's problem. She's a hard-working, thoughtful, not overly endowed dancer who doesn't deserve the unseemly prominence into which Balanchine has forced her, and she hasn't borne up well as the prime custodian of Farrell's image. In her roles, one feels, Balanchine has been creating for Farrell by proxy and not really succeeding. Although on occasion (the *Violin Concerto*) he's used her and Mazzo very well, it's pretty obvious that what has been thrown up in Farrell's wake isn't a new wealth of opportunities for other dancers but a whole flock of surrogate ballerinas. Gelsey Kirkland was the one dancer to have arisen and progressed during this difficult period; when she resigned from the company last summer, only McBride was left to carry on as major star and full-time ballerina. As one of the witty dancers remarked, "Suzanne coming back is the best thing that's happened to us since she left." There are young dancers, as yet below ballerina level, who have escaped the influence of Farrell and Farrellism. Merrill Ashley and Colleen Neary (who is one of the thin, long-

limbed girls, but with a soft, human core) are two of the most rewarding. It isn't amusing to speculate, even in private, on what may
happen to these talented girls now that Farrell has returned, or to
the less talented ones, or, indeed, to Farrell herself. The crisis is a
serious one, and these are family matters. Farrell once precipitated
a revolution in the company. She made audiences sweat, and, indirectly, blamelessly, she's been making us sweat ever since. Remembering those revolutionary days, one can only look with helpless
fascination to the days ahead. This is 1975, a new year in the life of
the most adventurous, erratic, and valuable ballet company in the
world.

Jacques d'Amboise has done a new ballet, *Sinfonietta*, a "heavy"
work to stand beside *Saltarelli*, a "light" work he did last year. I
can't see much difference in the two pieces, and I can't see that
D'Amboise is much of a choreographer. One of his problems is
that he's unable to make roles for anyone but himself; what you get
in a D'Amboise ballet is a flock of surrogate D'Amboises. Another
problem is that he's watched Balanchine's trees too closely to see the
forest. The secrets of classical style which magnify a dancer's presence or a dancer's gesture in proportion to the ensemble, so that
soloist and ensemble become part of the same landscape, aren't really
secrets; they're a legible, extendable code that Balanchine has ex-
plored again and again. In *Sinfonietta*, D'Amboise has methodically
worked out the structure of the score (by Hindemith) on the stage.
But the ballet has no content of its own. Perhaps a fairer comparison to D'Amboise's efforts is *Concerto*, the Kenneth MacMillan
piece that has just gone back into the repertory of American Ballet
Theatre. *Concerto* is as musically overdetermined as *Sinfonietta*,
and its "content" consists of ballet-class combinations, which, no
matter how sterile, an audience always likes to see. But in parts of
the outer movements of the piece MacMillan has given the steps a
kind of comic military erectness, and that's at least a *comment* on
the music, which is Shostakovich's Second Piano Concerto. I'm
happier, usually, to see D'Amboise as a performer, and this season
the way he pulled through *Who Cares?* made me appreciate again
the inestimable rapport he has with audiences. His role, the greatest
he has ever had, came too late in his career. He can't sustain it on
the level of his first performances. Yet, like Marnee Morris in the
same piece, he can sometimes soft-shoe his way through the ballet

without losing any of its values. And his timing as a partner is a wonder.

It's a relief to go to *Coppélia* and get away from all the company confusion. *Coppélia* is self-enclosed, like a bubble. The storytelling is perfunctory in the first act, gripping in the second. McBride and Shaun O'Brien, as Coppélius, carry their duel of monsters to new heights at every performance, Robert Irving conducts Delibes's masterpiece as if he'd written it, and I must also mention Terri Lee Port's uncanny miming of the doll Coppélia. McBride, in the scene of her "awakening," makes it especially clear that the last vital organ Coppélius transfers to her body from Frantz's isn't a heart—it's lungs. This Swanilda has no heart. However, the adagio and solo of the last act, based on the Danilova version, aren't well suited to McBride. The prone position in the shoulder lift is wrong for the line of her legs and back, and in the solo she doesn't really register until she gets to the chaîné turns. Then she registers most powerfully in the Balanchine coda. McBride isn't the kind of dancer who can twinkle and spread charm. She's too elemental. Peter Martins is the current Frantz, jovial and grand. He makes the reduced scale of the sets look twice reduced, which enhances the fantastic perspective of the story. His solos, arranged by himself, weren't the best specimens of his style, either. Why does Michael Arshansky, as the village mayor, not reappear in this act? And why does Coppélius now reappear, carrying a *dummy* Coppélia in his arms? It looks ghoulish. Originally, he wheeled Miss Port on, snatched up the villagers' reparations, and wheeled her off, pouring his unquenched dream of world conquest into her lifeless ear. —*February 3, 1975*

Free and More Than Equal

If George Balanchine were a novelist or a playwright or a movie director instead of a choreographer, his studies of women would be among the most discussed and most influential artistic achievements of our time. But because Balanchine works without words, and customarily without a libretto, and because the position of women in ballet has long been a dominant one, we take his extraordinary creations for granted, much as if they were natural happenings. It is part of Balanchine's genius to make the extraordinary seem natural; how many contemporary male artists, in ballet or out of it, can compete with him in depicting contemporary women? Balanchine's world is pervaded by a modern consciousness; his women do not always live for love, and their destinies are seldom defined by the men they lean on. Sexual complicity in conflict with individual freedom is a central theme of the Balanchine pas de deux, and more often than not it is dramatized from the woman's point of view. The man's rôle is usually that of fascinated observer and would-be manipulator—the artist who seeks to possess his subject and finds that he may only explore it. For Balanchine it is the man who sees and follows and it is the woman who acts and guides. The roles may not be reversed. When the man sometimes does not "see" (one thinks of Orpheus, or the lone male figure in the Elegy of *Serenade*, or Don Quixote, who hallucinates), he continues blindly on his mission, passive in the grip of fate. But when the woman is passive and sightless it is because she is without a destiny of her own. She can belong to a man. This is what the Sleepwalker suggests to the Poet in *La Sonnambula*; it is what Kay Mazzo suggests to Peter Martins in *Duo Concertant* and *Stravinsky Violin Concerto*. In both these ballets, Mazzo is blinded by Martins in a gesture both benevolent and authoritarian. They are the only pas de deux of Balanchine's I know in which the man has a fully controlling role. Even the Sleepwalker does not surrender to the Poet she tantalizes. And even Allegra Kent, who in the roles Balanchine made for her was so supple she practically invited a man to turn her into a docile toy, was uncapturable. Think of *Episodes*, in which every trap her partner sets seems to contain a hidden spring by which she can release herself— or ensnare *him*; or her role in *Ivesiana* ("The Unanswered Question"), in which she is borne like an infanta on the shoulders of four men, lifted, turned in this direction and that, dropped headlong to within inches of the ground, delivered for one burning instant into the arms of a fifth man, who is crawling wretchedly after her, and taken away into the dark whence she came. Like the Sleepwalker, she does not seem to belong to herself, yet she doesn't belong to her manipulators, either—they're a part of her mystery. (In the same ballet, another woman enters blind, groping her way forward; what seems to happen between her and the man she meets is rape.)

| The image of the unattainable woman is one that comes from nineteenth-century Romantic ballet, but in Balanchine the ballerina is unattainable simply because she is a woman, not because she's a supernatural or enchanted being. He can make comedy or tragedy, and sometimes a blend of both, out of the conflict between a woman's free will and her need for a man; he can carry you step by step into dramas in which sexual relationships are not defined by sex or erotic tension alone, and in this he is unique among choreographers. He is unique, too, in going beyond the limits of what women have conventionally expressed on the stage. In *Diamonds*, the ballet that follows *Emeralds* and *Rubies* in the three-part program called *Jewels*, Suzanne Farrell dances a long, supported adagio the point of which is to let us see how little support she actually needs. There is no suggestion here of a partnership between equals, of matched wits in a power play such as there is in *Rubies*, with Patricia McBride and Edward Villella. In *Diamonds* there is no contest, and in a sense the conception is reactionary—the woman is back on her pedestal and the man is worshipful. But that is not the meaning of the dance as we see it today. There's much more substance to *Diamonds* than there was in the days when Farrell first danced it; then it seemed the iciest and emptiest of abstractions with, in the woman's part, an edge of brazen contempt. Farrell, a changed and immeasurably enriched dancer, in stepping back into the ballet has discovered it. She is every bit as powerful as she was before, but now she takes responsibility for the discharge of power; she doesn't just fire away. And whereas she used to look to me like an omnicompetent blank, she's now dynamic, colorful, tender. Her impetuosity and her serenity are forces in constant play, and one may see the action of the piece as a drama of temperament. It is a drama very different from the one I remember. Farrell's independent drive no longer seems unacceptably burdensome to her, and her mastery implies no rebuke.

And what mastery it is—of continual off-center balances maintained with light support or no support at all, of divergently shaped steps unthinkably combined in the same phrase, of invisible transitions between steps and delicate shifts of weight in poses that reveal new and sweeter harmonies of proportion no matter how wide or how subtle the contrast. Your eye gorges on her variety, your heart stops at the brink of every precipice. She, however, sails calmly out into space and returns as if the danger did not exist. Farrell's style in

Diamonds (and the third act of *Don Quixote*) is based on risk; she is almost always off balance and always secure. Her confidence in moments of great risk gives her the leeway to suggest what no ballerina has suggested before her—that she can sustain herself, that she can go it alone. Unlike Cynthia Gregory, and many ballerinas less distinguished than Gregory, who perfect held balances, Farrell perfects the *act* of balance/imbalance as a constant feature of dancing. It is not equilibrium as stasis, it is equilibrium as continuity that she excels in. Although, as in her *Diamonds* performance, she can take a piqué arabesque and stand unaided, she's capable of much more; her conquests are really up there where the richer hazards are. In the Scherzo, going at high speed, she several times takes piqué arabesque, swings into second position and back into arabesque, uncoiling a half-turn that, because of the sudden force of the swing, seems like a complete one. In the finale, her partner (Jacques d'Amboise) is only there to stop her. She slips like a fish through his hands. She doesn't stop, doesn't wait, doesn't depend, and she can't fall. She's like someone who has learned to breathe thin air.

Of course, the autonomy of the ballerina is an illusion, but Farrell's is the extremest form of this illusion we have yet seen, and it makes *Diamonds* a riveting spectacle about the freest woman alive. The title is a misnomer. *Diamonds* finds its entire justification in a single dancer; apart from its presentation of the multifaceted Farrell, the ballet is paste. None of the ballets Balanchine created for Farrell were top-flight, and there is very little besides Farrell to justify the maintenance in repertory of his full-evening work *Don Quixote*. Farrell has little to do until the third act, where she fully recaptures her old brilliance and adds to it a new gift for dramatization. Up to that point she has outgrown the role, and the ballet is stale and boring. It was an interesting failure ten years ago, when it was new, but Balanchine's attempts to straighten out the strands that connect the Don's fantasies to the reality of persons and events around him have led to a succession of ever more futile revisions in the first act, and with the addition two years ago of a classical-Spanish divertissement he abandoned all efforts at mise-en-scène. The story of Don Quixote doesn't really get going until well into the second act, most of which is taken up with another divertissement. The ballet has always suffered from a lack of conviction; maybe it was on account of Nicolas Nabokov's music, maybe it was because giving overt dramatic expression to his theme of the elusive Ideal Woman betrayed Balanchine into unflattering revelations of self-pity. Although Jacques d'Amboise, taking over the role this season, gives the Don modesty and dignity, Balanchine seems to feel very sorry for him indeed.

Farrell's Dulcinea and her role in *Diamonds* suggest that, as a Balanchine conception, she's free and more than equal to any man. In *Bugaku*, she appeared in a contrasting role, one originally done by Kent. Here the woman is seen ribaldly as an object, and though there are moments of satire in the geisha-girl pantomime (as well as some nasty pseudo-Oriental mannerisms), *Bugaku* is the nearest thing in the New York City Ballet repertory to a Béjart ballet. Balanchine seems to have derived his inspiration for the pas de deux from Japanese pornographic prints. Farrell brought out some of the acid below the surface, but not enough. Kent can bring it all out —complicity carried to the point of mockery—so the piece becomes nearly a feminist statement; she can make the movements look insinuating and delicious at the same time. There is a close link between Kent and Farrell that Farrell's absence had obscured, but Farrell in Kent's roles rather emphasizes their dissimilarities.

—*February 24, 1975*

Look What's Going On

What kind of dance capital of the world is it which confines the presentation of a new Merce Cunningham work to his downtown loft studio and lets a Twyla Tharp première happen in St. Paul? Neither choreographer can afford the expense of a New York season in a proper theatrical setting; for exposure, both have come to rely more on out-of-town residencies than on the city in which they create their works and train their dancers. Last spring and again for three weekends last month, New Yorkers saw Cunningham's company in a series of studio performances at Westbeth. The studio is idyllic, but it accommodates only a small audience, and although the studio performance, as Cunningham shapes it, with whole works or

excerpts from different works blended in a seamless display of dancing, is an intensely satisfying and revealing experience, no one pre-
tends that it solves the exposure problem. On the same weekend
that Twyla Tharp's première took place in St. Paul, an unofficial
sneak preview of *Rebus*, the new Cunningham piece, was held at
Westbeth for an overflow crowd of perhaps one hundred. The
Cunningham company is now on tour; Detroit will see the world
première of *Rebus*, together with the décor and score that were
commissioned for it. New York may not see it in this form at all.

In a Cunningham work, choreography, décor, and score are independent entities. This is a well-known fact, and it's what has enabled Cunningham to give stripped-down studio performances that,
for the lucky few who manage to get into them, are more exciting
than many another company's in full panoply. But the fact that the
choreography is conceived independently doesn't mean that it exists
in a vacuum. To what extent dancing and sound and décor impinge
on one another is a question that each viewer must settle for himself,
and about many Cunningham pieces—*Crises, Variations V, Sum-
merspace, Winterbranch, Place, Scramble, RainForest, Canfield* (the
list is amazingly long)—there is no doubt that they were meant
to share more or less equally in the creation of a theatrical subject.
And seeing sections of works like these run into one another without
their production elements and without intermissions raises another
question: Are the various choreographies interchangeable? If they
are, why the bundling together under a formal title of one set of
choreographic studies rather than another? Is this arrangement,
maintained outside New York, a mere convenience for impresarios
and audiences, or does it indicate the presence of identifiable distinguishing features in each work? Is the studio performance an
alternative way of seeing Cunningham's work—of seeing how those
features may be erased or changed in different contexts? Is it actually
closer than a staged performance would be to the fundamental
"truth" of his choreography—its flooding of all formal boundaries,
its mutability, its capacity to seem to be anything the viewer takes
it for on any given night? How different is different, and can we
know the variations without the theme?

Questions like these can't be answered on a prolonged diet of
studio performances. The more I see of Cunningham's work the
more I am interested by qualities of differentiation in it and the less
I care to have these qualities, and their possibly groupable meanings,

blurred by informal, eclectic presentation. Much—and much of it nonsense—has been made of Cunningham's chance operations in the making of dances. To me, his work is no more haphazard than the work of any other fine choreographer. Basically, Cunningham works from the materials he has—the capabilities of his dancers combined with formal or technical concerns that seem to him in need of development. The results of this labor may be illuminated or organized by chance discoveries, but what Merce Cunningham does is not determined by chance. A studio performance gives us the undifferentiated results of different labors—sometimes in the same moment ("I'll wear the *Canfield* jacket, the *Signals* tie, and the *Loops* pocket handkerchief")—and this, although undeniably fascinating as sheer spectacle, makes it difficult to see what integrity, evolution, *process* there is to any of it. At Westbeth, where the company has to fight *not* to draw crowds, the audience isn't even told what works or excerpts it is seeing. Nor will it help to wing out to Detroit and see the piece—if it is a piece—that is called *Rebus*. What we need is an extended New York season in a decent theatre, with works performed separately as theatrical pieces and together as "studio" events. Only in this way can we begin to assemble the dimensions of Cunningham's current achievement. It may be that he's working in a less patterned way than he appeared to be a few years ago, and that works of recent seasons—*TV Rerun* and *Landrover* and *Changing Steps*—and possibly even *Rebus* look as good as they do in the studio because they aren't really individual works at all. It would be useful for New York to know some of these things. Maybe Detroit or Chicago or Minneapolis will tell us.

In St. Paul, where Twyla Tharp and her company were concluding a February residency at the Civic Center Theatre, I saw *Sue's Leg,* the latest of her jazz ballets, and *The Double Cross,* a shorter work, created during the residency in open sessions to which the public was invited. Both as to length (four weeks, which allowed for a luxurious amount of rehearsal time) and as to community involvement (the company offered daily classes as well as open rehearsals, all free), the residency was extraordinary. The major première, *Sue's Leg,* is named for Suzanne Weil, the coordinator of performing arts at the Walker Art Center, in Minneapolis, which sponsored the residency. *Leg* is used in the sense of leg of a journey, suggesting that there are more residencies or more jazz ballets to come. Twyla Tharp, like many other choreographers, loves wordplay, and *The Double Cross* has a spoken text dealing in puns and antonyms which relates to the form of the choreography—a tiny suite of maximal-contrast dances—in ways as difficult to reject as to understand. The high point, literally, of the piece is Rose Marie Wright, nearly six feet tall, dancing to a calliope rendition of "The Parade of the Wooden Soldiers." This bright, staccato, giant-size Coppélia is followed by Kenneth Rinker and Tom Rawe on the floor, doing slow, fluid someraults and pushups to "Träumerei." Contrast is an elementary compositional device, and except for the comedy she gets out of it (which is also elementary), Tharp's special use of it in this case isn't apparent; we don't perceive the dances as antonymous without some prodding from the text. And, while the dances and the music may veer from one wild extreme to another, the cheeky banality of taste in both departments is pretty consistent. The piece is about reconciling contrarieties. Its conclusion is the lovely contrapuntal Bach duet for Rinker and Wright that was first seen last year at the Delacorte Theatre, in Central Park. The duet is all one engrossing serpentine curve unwound from some inner mechanism of concentric spools and shuttles. This fiendishly complex Tharpian invention is a marvel; it's baroque art and it's classical art achieved without reference to the behavior of classical ballet. Tharp knows that you don't have to look like ballet to look classical—that classicism has nothing to do with decorum. (When classical ballet is drained of meaning, nothing is left but decorum and tricks. This is why all those mindless classroom ballets are so popular.) In the duet, Rinker periodically spits on the floor and rubs his shoe in it, as dancers do when the resin has run out. The audience laughs happily each time, glad to have its expectations of the sublime undermined, glad to see so practical a gesture become part of the tightening weave of the dance. Maybe the gesture is the ultimate reconciliation—of art with life.

Twyla Tharp's jazz ballets are so refreshing because they, too, undermine our expectations. *Sue's Leg* is made to the music of Fats Waller, and, like its predecessors—*Eight Jelly Rolls* (to Jelly Roll Morton) and *The Bix Pieces* (Beiderbecke-Whiteman) and *The Raggedy Dances* (Scott Jopin et al.)—it doesn't give you the feeling either of watching concert dancers doing jazz or of jazz dancers in concert. It's a whole new type of show. Except for some choice period references, like Tom Rawe's "tap" solo, the choreography eludes every stylistic category you can think of. Yet it is anthology choreography, incorporating the best of everything. Occasionally, a source will be glimpsed pure, in isolation—a shimmy, a carefully pointed preparation in fourth position, bits of "character" mime; more often, a dozen different circuits combine to light up a single phrase. But deciding what the piece is made of is not as much fun as watching it move. Rigor is the basis of Tharpian movement, yet the dancing doesn't look "worked"—it looks light and easy, like what virtuoso dancers would do for recreation. This deceptive ease has caused some people to think that the dancers improvise or work off their natural skills in public. If this were true, no Tharp dance would be repeatable, and "natural skills" (supposing the very idea is not oxymoronic) aren't something a dancer can rely on to sustain a piece. Tharp dancers work harder than any other dancers I know at preserving the kind of grace in dancing that looks accidental, spontaneous, and private. In St. Paul, *Sue's Leg* was performed twice— once at the beginning of the program, in costume, and once at the end, in practice clothes. Half the pleasure of the repetition was in seeing which were the real accidents and which were the planned ones.

Santo Loquasto has based his costumes on the practice clothes the dancers wear in the repeat performance—a crazed assortment of fatigue pants, pullovers, sweaters, and ankle warmers. But Loquasto has rendered this patchwork in a smooth palette of beige and mocha satin and oatmeal knits. This is a heroic idea and it really works. In Jennifer Tipton's warm lighting, the dancers gleam as if cast in bronze. The performance was marginally better the second time, a shade more relaxed. The dancers—Tharp and Wright and Rinker and Rawe—are an exquisitely balanced quartet; they have enough dynamic variety for a company of forty. There's a schematic dualism in *Sue's Leg* that is stressed by the repeat performance. Waller's version of "I Can't Give You Anything But Love" is set twice— once as a quartet, once as a solo by Tharp. In "Ain't Misbehavin'" Tharp's solo is very different in style, and the difference, to me, is roughly that in the first one she's a "black" performer and in the second one she's "white." "Fat and Greasy," a rhythm number full of riffs, is danced by Wright, Rinker, and Rawe, who follow it with the romantic, legato "Tea for Two." Then there are two views of the thirties. One is Rawe making like Bill Robinson in "I'm Livin' in a Great Big Way." (This is not a Fats number, but it is Fats-related:

Robinson's tap track from the movie *Hooray for Love*, in which Waller also appeared.) The other, "In the Gloamin'," is for the quartet, and it's an album of pictures: line dancing, marathon dancing, the Lindy, the Big Apple, college boys piling on top of each other. The dance twists the thirties through the prism of the seventies.

Sue's Leg is the most tightly focused and most consistently funny of Tharp's jazz ballets to date. From Wright's opening solo, which is set like an ice-skating turn to the big bounce of Fats at the Wurlitzer, you know the piece is going to be a spree. As it would have to be to such music. In jazz dancing, as in jazz music, authenticity is all that matters. Either a performer has the life of jazz in him or he hasn't—there are no two ways about it. Twyla Tharp has rescued jazz dancing; she's got it away from the ersatz, Broadway-Vegas school. And she's rescued it from compartmentalization. Her choreography to Fats Waller isn't unlike her choreography to Bach, and in her suite of Joplin rags she includes a striking duet to Mozart. Today, specialist jazz dancing by persons under sixty is hardly ever done. It's a hobbyist's delusion to imagine that great popular art forms can be reborn in isolation from the conditions that sponsored their growth in the first place. But in working to jazz musicians of other eras, in treating them with the same respect she gives to the constructions of Bach or Mozart and with the same omnivorous idiomatic sweep, Tharp is doing more than salvaging a lost art—she's reconditioning it and restructuring it as a *modern* art. In her solo to Waller's 1940 recording of "Ain't Misbehavin' " there's a moment when he cries out, "Sweet essence of pig bar milk, look what's goin' on here!" I wish New York could have heard him. *Sue's Leg* has since been performed at Wesleyan University, in Connecticut. There are no plans to bring it to New York.

A few days after *Sue's Leg*, the Joffrey Ballet opened at the City Center with a new version of *Deuce Coupe*. The original production had a mixed cast of Tharp and Joffrey dancers and was one of the great hits of recent years. The revision, by Tharp, is for Joffrey dancers alone, and it amounts to a completely new, more mature, less sensational work. Tharp hasn't tried to give audiences back what they think they remember; instead, she's made the piece a kind of nostalgic celebration of the *Deuce Coupe* of 1973. The dancers seem to be about five years older; they're like college kids remembering the joys of high school. Remnants of the old ballet flit through *Deuce Coupe II*, but most of the choreography and many of the recorded tracks of the Beach Boys songs are new. Erika Goodman, as the ballet girl in white, is still there, but her part has been broken up and parceled out to other dancers and her significance considerably reduced. She, too, is a remnant, and although I didn't fully understand her function in the first version, I've no idea what it is now.

Deuce Coupe II has a dark, spectral quality, like the parts of *The Bix Pieces* which also were concerned with reminiscence. It's more a sequel than a revision. The bridge to the sequel appears to be in the costumes. Scott Barrie has designed a new set—white midriff blouse and pedal pushers for the girls, white sailor pants for the boys. The piece begins with one of the girls in the new white costume doing a little solo that seems to say "I remember *Deuce Coupe*." When other dancers appear, they're in their original costumes—orange dresses for the girls, red pants and Hawaiian shirts for the boys. Soon people start reappearing in white, and by the end of the piece everyone has changed to white except Goodman, who never wore anything else. It may be that this costume scheme diverted me more than it should have on opening night, but the ballet as a whole seemed to move too fast and to be more arbitrarily pieced together than the old one was. Although the childlike mood is gone (along with the graffiti; a Pop painting by James Rosenquist has taken their place), the new sophistication is beguiling, too. Lovers of the old *Deuce Coupe* are in for a period of readjustment. Don't give up the ship.   —*March 10, 1975*

Going in Circles

To Steve Reich's very interesting musical composition called "Drumming" Laura Dean has now set choreography for eight dancers, with results that are often pleasant and sometimes powerful. The dance, accompanied by Reich's musicians, had its première in the Lepercq Space at the Brooklyn Academy; the sound was wonderful. The dancing is not as interesting as the music, but for the first twenty minutes or so (the piece lasts ninety minutes) it exerts a pressure of naïve excitement that would be ideal if it could be sustained. The flaw in the dancing is that it tries to be a mirror image of the sound, and though the music and the dance are alike in the simplicity of their processes, they are widely divergent in their resources. Reich's score consists of a single rhythmic pattern enunciated in turn by bongo drums, marimbas, and glockenspiels; to each of these bands are added male and female vocalises, whistling, a piccolo; in the fourth and final section all voices are heard together. Since the instruments frequently play out of phase with each other and introduce further variations in pitch and timbre, the effect is sumptuous—a multilayered sonic veil of which the dance is only able to pick up two or three threads. And Dean's choreography is hampered by the fact that her dancers are not, all of them, as keen as they might be; they're enthusiastic performers, well rehearsed but not well trained in any sense comparable to the musicians, and in a piece of this size they can't stay the course. The most they contribute to *Drumming* as a dance event is a lightweight, peppy charm.

Laura Dean, as she says in her program note, has been experimenting for years with "spinning, steady pulse, repetitive movement, and geometric patterning." To take spinning first: it's the most favored of her devices and the least effective. Dance sociologists may be able to make something of the present moment, which finds so many American concert dancers behaving like whirling dervishes; for me, the whole business is a bore. As soon as a dancer or a group of dancers starts to spin, my attention immediately drops by half, then slides to total indifference. It's like waiting for someone to get off the phone and back to conversation. The first Western dancer I ever saw do this kind of spin was Ann Halprin, in a solo called, I believe, *The Prophetess*. This was in 1955, and in those days even Halprin was conscious of borrowing from an exotic tradition. (Years before Halprin, Ted Shawn, in his *Mevlevi Dervish*, was said to be the greatest spinner of them all.) Nowadays, concert dancers spin for the sake of spinning, as ballet dancers turn pirouettes. But, unlike a classical pirouette, a dervish spin has no reality as bodily sculpture; its entire emphasis is on the dancer's interior state, and the pleasure of it belongs to the dancer alone. When, to the marimba section of *Drumming*, the Dean dancers go into their bobbin-like spins, their faraway trance corresponds to the remote whirr of the music, and their different bodily rhythms correspond to its multiplicity. But maintaining the spell becomes a problem for the spectator. There's no kinetic transference, and one has to struggle to keep the field of focus clear. Later on in the piece, there was more spinning—clockwise and counterclockwise, or in crouches, or with changing arms. No matter how Dean varied the visual pattern, the *dance* effect was unintelligible.

What's surprising about these lapses into mystique is that they occur in the work of a choreographer whose other devices—"steady pulse, repetitive movement, and geometric patterning"—suggest a mathematically precise, even a severe turn of mind. But although she's one of the few really promising choreographers around, Laura Dean doesn't seem to have crystallized an attitude toward her work. She's rigid where she should be rigorous, slack where she should swing. From *Drumming* and from earlier works of hers that I've seen, I get the impression that she'd like to cut loose but can't—that she's trying for the kind of objectivity that will swallow her up. To lose oneself in one's work—is there a greater joy, especially for the performing artist? But Dean's choreographic range is so limited (by choice, it would seem) that as a performer she always looks as if she's holding something back. The few irreducibly basic steps to which she restricts herself—stamps, hops, shuffles, low kicks that barely part the legs—have the weight of intense scrutiny; only primary colors are used, and they're meant to burn us with their purity. In the early part of *Drumming*, the dancing also had a brightness of temper that kept it from looking like a ritual, but planned primitivism seems to be what Dean's work is all about. It's a paradox not easy to survive gracefully, and Dean's tension shows in her neck and mouth. She's not one of the best dancers in the company. At least two of the others throw themselves about with more quasimystical rapture. Dean dances like an agnostic in her own church.

Dean's ambivalence is, just now, the most interesting thing about her. I hope it means that she'll develop her material (along with her dancers). The dance to *Drumming* is far from intricate, but portions of it are already a big advance from *Jumping Dance, Stamping Dance,* and *Circle Dance,* which looked like games invented by the white settlers to keep the Indians amused. The question of why a dancer of intelligence and skill would ever want to hold herself down to such an elementary level can be answered by a glance at the formless attitudinizing, the tackily derivative contrivances that constitute so much modern choreography. But it's not the whole answer. Choreographers of Dean's generation are heirs to the radical experimentation of the sixties, which took Merce Cunningham's rejection of literary and psychological content in dance and inflated it into a revolt against all established forms of dance. The alternative to dance was nondance—or, rather, ordinary movement construed as dance. The idea was so shocking that it captured—and paralyzed—a whole generation. As Steve Reich has described the situation (in his book *Writings About Music*), "For a long time during the 1960's one would go to the dance concert where no one danced followed by the party where everyone danced." Nondance concerts persist in the seventies, only now they are likely to consist of stylizations of ordinary movement rather than the real, raw thing, and to take place on a considerably reduced scale. Just as sixties nondance paralleled Pop Art, seventies nondance parallels Conceptual or Minimal Art. The ordered elements in it often have the look of baby's first steps, which are repeated over and over in wonderment, as if choreographers hoped to discover for themselves the secret of why on earth man dances. Certain dancers have elected not to dance at all. Yvonne Rainer, the best-known of the sixties revolutionaries, has turned to filmmaking; the most recent concerts of Simone Forti and Kenneth King consisted of Forti and King reading. (Forti, widely acknowledged as a primary influence on the sixties radicals but seldom seen in performance, has amassed the biggest legend in absentia since Sybil Shearer.) The Grand Union, a group to which Rainer formerly belonged, counts among its current members Steve Paxton, David Gordon, Trisha Brown, Barbara Dilley, Nancy Lewis, and Douglas Dunn, all of them choreographers in semiretirement. An evening with Grand Union, like the one a few weeks ago at the La Mama Annex, is a free-for-all of improvised dialogue, shticks, and stunts, much of it funny on purpose, all of it inconsequential, none of it more than incidentally concerned with dancing. The format is so amorphous that no two performances are the same, and so discontinuous that no two descriptions of the same performance are, either. Grand Union is a slightly less conventional form of actors' improvisational theatre; its communal permissiveness makes it perfect campus-cabaret entertainment.

Implicit in all this seems to be the idea that unless dancing can be taken back to an embryonic state (before there ever was a Martha Graham, a José Limón, or a Merce Cunningham to impose environmental influences) it cannot be done. The only trouble with this is that the embryo never grows. Two years ago, Lucinda Childs gave a baby-step concert at the Whitney Museum; last month, she gave another, at a downtown loft, in which two of the Whitney pieces were repeated. The new pieces were not much more elaborate. As before, four girls marched forward and backward in circles to a basic count of six. As before, Childs appeared alone to measure the space, walking a slow back-and-forth path, row upon row, until the floor area was covered. The walk was embellished at regular intervals with a turn of the body, a turn of the head, an extended arm. In the circle dance, once you'd observed the tiny variations in recovery of impetus with which each of the four girls switched from forward to backward march, you'd observed all. What made Childs's walk dance interesting (minimally speaking) was nothing organic to the dance; it was, rather, that Childs is a striking-looking woman with a beautiful head. Even in minimal, equalizing, white-on-white dances, those dreaded élitist principles, that horrible star quality can't be ironed out. Like Dean, who in relaxed moments can look ravishing, Childs doesn't like to smile or look her audience in the eye. I was reminded of Rainer's mid-sixties manifesto of renunciation: "NO to spectacle no to virtuosity no to transformations and magic and make-believe no to the glamour and transcendency of the star image. . . ." Childs and Rainer are exact contemporaries who helped make a revolution. Ten years later, it's no to dance.

The embryo never grows because the dancers do not build on one another's accomplishments—they work on as if nobody had ever done anything. And the audience has no memory. In the seventies, the "new" and "radical" choreographers who are repeating the experiments of the sixties play to a predominantly young audience— an audience that, having heard of the firebrands of the sixties, now sits crosslegged in lofts and discovers the scene unchanged. (Laura Dean's audience for *Drumming* contained many people who were evidently drawn by the music; it was a refreshingly adult crowd.) And the young audience gets no help from the dance critics, who are either unaware or forgetful of developments in other forms of theatre. Kei Takei, a young Japanese dancer, recently put on a five-hour disaster epic called *Light* at the Brooklyn Academy. It was full of nameless terrors and indefinable threats, and it was acclaimed as original and visionary. But it might have been produced, scream for scream and grovel for grovel, by the Living Theatre. Doesn't anyone remember the Living Theatre?

Modern dance, American dance, contemporary dance, new dance, free dance, or avant-garde—however you call it, it's currently a scene of chaos and devastation. Laura Dean's use of recognizable dance movement is the first breakthrough it has witnessed since the emergence of Twyla Tharp. Dean has her problems; she's overly possessed by the rudimentary, and when she describes her experiences with spinning she sounds like Isadora discovering her solar plexus. Nevertheless, she's dancing, and she's composing dances of rhythm and pattern. She leaves the others standing still.

—*April 21, 1975*

Hard Work

Attempts to get a ballet about Spartacus, one of Karl Marx's heroes, onto the boards date back to 1950, when Aram Khatchaturian began work on *Spartak*, a four-act ballet. In 1956, it was produced at the Kirov with choreography by Leonid Yakobson. Another version, by Igor Moiseyev, was done by the Bolshoi two years later. It failed, and the Bolshoi brought a revision of Yakobson's production to New York in 1962. Plisetskaya appeared as Phrygia, Spartacus's wife (in the Moiseyev version she had danced Aegina, the villainess); Dmitri Begak and Maris Liepa alternated as Spartacus. The ballet met with a poor reception, and several performances were canceled. In 1968, four years after becoming the Bolshoi's artistic director, Yuri Grigorovich presented a new, three-act *Spartacus*, and it was with this production that he opened the current Bolshoi season at the Met.

A peculiar choice. For the first time since 1966, the company appears in New York at something like full strength, but *Spartacus* is not designed to display its range of expression. What it's designed for is force. It has a massive, pounding corps de ballet— soldiers, slaves, courtesans, etc.—acting as background to four principal roles roughly equal in size. The roles contain no opportunities for the dancers to expand or vary their effects; they're straight tests of endurance. On opening night, Vladimir Vasiliev (Spartacus), Natalia Bessmertnova (Phrygia), Maris Liepa (Crassus, the Roman commander), and Nina Timofeyeva (Aegina) managed to sustain their one-note characterizations, and even to build up the kind of pressure openings need. All of them are top-ranking stars, and all but Bessmertnova are members of the original cast. With long experience and that theatrical instinct which Bolshoi dancers alone seem to possess, they took their support from each other and from the corps, which matched them in energy. No other resource was available. Grigorovich's invention expires with the fall of the first-act curtain; from then on he can only repeat. The audience, turned off by Grigorovich's bludgeoning, was slow to respond. And between the stars and the chorus there is no one—no subsidiaries to start a scene or swell one, to enrich the drama or comment on it. When Crassus plots, he has no fellow conspirators except for Aegina; and Spartacus has no lieutenants—men follow and confer with him in squads, in mass unison gestures. Unless one counts Shamil Yagudin's bit as a masked gladiator in a fight with Spartacus, there are no featured roles, and this deprives us of a sense of the company's middle-level capacities. In the front line of the corps, however, were men like Vyacheslav Gordeyev and Alexander Bogatyrev, who in other roles this season will be dancing leads. Whether starred or in the corps, everyone worked as if to burst the heart. It wasn't the fault of the dancers if one got the impression, as the evening lengthened, that the Russians are pretty damn sick and tired of *Spartacus*.

The story and its setting are dimly felt and indifferently projected. All the anonymous faces and bodies make *Spartacus* a cold and empty drama. Grigorovich has been concerned with pace—pace above all. He drives the action along, never allowing it to halt at a climax; indeed, he often deflects a climax, whipping the tail of one scene into the jaws of another, so that the audience can't relax, or even applaud. All the look-alike scenes ram home a different narrative point, yet who would know it? The plot has no dramatic tension; we're not made to follow a thread that binds the characters' fates—there's no such thing. Several times, I got my cues wrong. Phrygia doesn't become Crassus's concubine, as I thought I was being led to suppose, and Aegina, his mistress, isn't activated by jealousy—or any other motive that was clear to me—when she throws an orgy for the more simpleminded of Spartacus's troops and then betrays them. (Why they never suspect her is another obscure point.)

Choreographically, the ballet is relentless. In his corps dances, and notably in his bashing male ensembles (of which there are about five in each act), Grigorovich accounts in strict patterns for every square yard of music, and everything is screwed tight to the downbeat. Nowhere does one see a free, loose, or broken gesture against the music. In the second act, there's a slow bolero for the corps that looks as if it might relieve the monotony, but before long Grigorovich builds it into another of his blockbuster routines. Khatchaturian's classical-jukebox score abets the choreographer in stamping out complexities before they go too far; I wish someone had stamped out the opening bars of the lovers' theme, which sound exactly like the first measures of "Stormy Weather." Simon Virsaladze's costumes are undistinguished, and his scenery makes Imperial Rome look like a moldy granite tomb.

Still, there were extraordinary pleasures to be had in the quality of the performances. Gripped as he was by the choreography's repetitious, stock patterns, Vasiliev never ceased to pour forth his thunderous rhythm; he was a new man at every entrance, and his split-kick jetés in the last act were his most powerful leaps of the evening. Liepa, although he seems to have declined athletically, was also unequivocally committed. The weak-violent mold of the character set by Grigorovich was always before you, but along with his accustomed partner, the amazing Timofeyeva, he achieved something much more interesting: the two of them suggested a couple of panting suburban pols who have somehow missed out on their success and know it. Timofeyeva, with her long dangle earrings and rich, vehement thighs, amazed me, because I had seen her in 1959 during the Bolshoi's first American tour, when she was already a prima ballerina and Vasiliev was a boy. But here she was, shooting up in jumps and doing it as effortlessly as one might open an umbrella. As for Bessmertnova—is she to become the queen of the season? One of the most ideally formed long-lined dancers in the world, she defines the term "lyrical ballerina." Yet, like so many Russians who fit that category, she defies our notions of type with her charged, floating, superhigh jump. Of all the dancers in the cast, she seemed the least confined by Grigorovich's formulas (which blocked out all of Vasiliev's charm), the least hard-pressed to hold the audience. Not that anyone else exhibited signs of strain. To the contrary: these dancers go the limit and beyond with an ease that shames and delights at the same time. Even in trash like *Spartacus*, Bolshoi dancers can impress you with their love of theatre, their rage to perform. They seem to carry reserves of energy like extra oxygen tanks, and because they believe in dancing as a sensible, unharried undertaking they don't mind letting you see them refuel—like Timofeyeva, trudging to the back of the stage between solos or stopping to adjust her *schmata* in full view of the audience. It's a privilege to have such dancers among us once again.

In *The Mooche*, Alvin Ailey has handed four of his dancers—Estelle Spurlock, Sarita Allen, Sara Yarborough, and Judith Jamison—the job of evoking the styles and eras of Florence Mills, Marie Bryant, Mahalia Jackson, and Bessie Smith. Miss Yarborough has the most thankless task: Mahalia Jackson was not noted for her dancing, and the Grahamish postures Ailey has choreographed are not exactly a correlative to her singing. This number, like the ballet as a whole, is much too restless and glitzy. Rouben Ter-Arutunian has designed a "Deco" set full of splintered mirrors and silver balls and neon and smoke; the dancers prowl through it in overkill period costumes by Randy Barcelo and do their turns framed by a shadowy male chorus.

Even though it's nine-tenths production, *The Mooche* might have succeeded as a slightly stoned vision of the black woman as entertainer if Ailey had dispensed with the name tags and let us make our own connections to figures of the past. Judith Jamison is more like Bessie Smith than she was like Billie Holiday in last season's revival of *Portrait of Billie*, but Jamison in *The Mooche* is irresistibly Jamison, with side links to Josephine Baker. For some of his "portraits," Ailey has made the oddest selections from the recorded Ellington miscellany that forms the score. "Maha" is Ellington's homage to Mahalia Jackson, but used theatrically it seems inappropriate. For "Bessie Smith" we hear "Creole Love Call," to my mind an example of what LeRoi Jones called "the 'jungle' bits of his twenties show-band period, which were utilized in those uptown 'black and tan' clubs that catered largely to sensual white liberals." Definitely not the Empress of the Blues.

Although Ailey doesn't intend his evocations to be literal, he becomes helplessly literal when he dedicates two numbers to women who actually danced. He can reproduce only those styles that have some relation to the way Ailey dancers move. "Black Beauty" was written for Florence Mills, the star of the 1921 revue *Shuffle Along*, which puts Miss Spurlock, whose specialty isn't tap-dancing, at a disadvantage. Marie Bryant was a featured dancer with the Ellington band in the forties, appearing in vaudeville and in two of his shows, *Jump for Joy* and *Beggar's Holiday*. I cannot say how close Ailey's Miss Bryant is to that Miss Bryant; Sarita Allen, in her white beaded sarong and ankle-strap shoes, does a bump-and-grind number that isolates a period and a performance tradition, if not the best of both. —*May 5, 1975*

American Space

The New York City Ballet has brought its *Ivesiana* back to the stage of the State Theatre, a year late for the Ives centennial but in plenty of time for the Bicentennial. The piece is one of those on an American subject in which Balanchine becomes completely an American choreographer—not the Stravinsky Balanchine, or the Balanchine of *Western Symphony* or *Stars and Stripes*, who expresses America from a European point of view, but a Balanchine who sees us at the same distance from which we see ourselves. *Ivesiana* is about that American distance, that equalizing yet comfortless space which separates Americans from Americans under the neutral American sky. It is about the lack of perimeters, and journeys pressing onward despite that lack. It is about situations, not destinations, and in it the stage is a box with no sides. Dancers come and go and disappear and seem to fall off the edges into eternity. Each section of the dance gives us a concise picture of what might be happening in the real world, but the pictures, evocative as they are, are not fashioned after anthropological home truths. They are images of pure drama, disconcerting and melancholy, unlike any we have seen before, and *Ivesiana* is like no other ballet in the repertory.

Balanchine made it in 1954 as a homage to Charles Ives in the year of his death. The choreography reflects the music not in patterned dance sequences but in a kind of epic pantomime suspended in time. All but one of the ballet's four sections have this floating quality. The exception is "In the Inn," which comes the closest to an actual dance. "Central Park in the Dark" and "The Unanswered Question" move very slowly, at about the same speed. The finale, "In the Night," moves only a little faster. And all but "In the Inn" are placed far away in space, looming from odd corners or levels of the blackened stage, deep within their cave of orchestral sonorities. Yet dramatically the piece as a whole persistently throws you off course. When it's over, its shape is still unsettled; it goes on spreading its queer dissonances in your mind. This is wonderful, of course, but *Ivesiana*, which has never been a popular piece, ought to grip its audiences more than it does. In the form it has kept since its revival in the sixties (four sections out of an original six) it is too short—and too short on contrast—to do the damage it was meant to do. "In the Inn," a casual encounter between a boy and a girl who compete to the piled-up, off-center rhythms of many raggedy dances, is so different in mood from the other numbers that it practically throws you out of the ballet. Next comes the end, in which numbers of people walk in different directions all over the stage on their knees—nothing but that for a few minutes until the curtain falls. The particular insanity that the ballet mirrors is consistent. The crazy jazz couple who break off their involved game with a handshake and a farewell merge with the night stream of aimless yet obsessed wanderers who populate the ballet, but that point takes a while to sink in. At first sight, "In the Inn" seems to be a break in style.

The only other direct encounter in the ballet, a violently sexual one, ocurs in "Central Park in the Dark." In a forest of bending and swaying forms, a girl cannot find her way. She touches a man's chest and crumples; he catches her up bodily in a lift and releases her in a groping descent; then they lose each other. There is a panic, a tumble, a suggestion of rape, and she is again lost and sightless as the forest shrinks back to the spongy cluster it was at the beginning. In another circle of Hell, another cluster emerges out of the dark—the totemic cortege of "The Unanswered Question." In this amazing, slow-motion adagio, a girl enters standing upright on the shoulders of four men, who then manipulate her body in a series of passes through space, high overhead or around their waists like a belt or low over the floor on which the questioner stretches himself, hoping for a moment's contact. It never comes —or, rather, she does come once into his arms, feet first, clenched up tight as a ball. With this, his erotic torment is complete. Soon, before the ritual can restate itself many more times, it is disappearing, moving off into the dark.

In Elise Flagg's performance I missed the security that would have enabled her to execute one of the more peacefully startling of the scene's incidents—the slow passé into attitude back, accompanied by formal port de bras, which is performed by the priestess atop her human pyramid. Deni Lamont as the questioner and Sara Leland and Francisco Moncion as the "Central Park" pair repeated the good performances they used to give years ago. Suzanne Farrell appeared in "In the Inn," her hair parted gothically and braided in pigtails, and gave a light-hearted, mischievous performance quite different from years ago. Victor Castelli paralleled her in stealth and wit as well as in some frisky high jumps. The costumes, which have never been credited and have always been effective, are practice clothes in a selection of pungent, subdued colors. Only Moncion's shirt, which looked like something a Technicolor pirate might wear, was wrong. The lighting has never recaptured the atmosphere that Jean Rosenthal once gave it, but it has been better than it is now—especially in "In the Inn," where a harsh, dirty-white light is used instead of the gold of New England on a hot summer afternoon.

Having seen the Bolshoi's present production of *Swan Lake* five years ago in Rome, and having since then seen several *Swan Lakes* that destroy themselves by trying to make Siegfried into the most important figure in the ballet, I am less appalled than I might have been by what the Bolshoi is now showing New York for the first time—a *Swan Lake* in which Siegfried's role is expanded by having him dance almost constantly, to music that was written for mime or ensemble or scenic effects, and by having him dance some of these passages as a double solo with Von Rothbart, suggesting that it is Siegfried, and not Odette, who has fallen under the spell of the sorcerer. Exam question: Whistle Siegfried's Theme from *Swan Lake*; demonstrate its chief movement motif. The Bolshoi production is further disfigured by the wholesale deletion of the old mime scenes, along with their plot connections, so that the hero no longer goes to the lake to hunt swans; he's dragged there, instead, by some mysterious power to see a ballet, all of it stage-managed by the Evil Magician. Siegfried becomes a bigger goof than he is in the standard version.

The best parts of the old Bolshoi *Swan Lake* were Acts I and III. This new production, with its "abstract" monochrome setting and undifferentiated nonstop dancing, sacrifices the electric social stir of Act I, which dancers seated or standing on the sidelines used to create anew, seemingly, at every performance. It was no small achievement, and it projected for miles, even in places like Madison Square Garden. In Act III, the Bolshoi was unrivaled at the national dances; possibly it no longer is. But the suite of point dances for the fiancées which it substitutes has no force either as characterization or as diversion. (Most of it is done to the national-dance music —a miscarriage of Tchaikovsky's intentions.)

Bolshoi swans resemble cranes. The whole lot of them lift and drive their legs, work their arms through the shoulder, and bend back the air they move through as if it were jelly. It's the massive treatment, and in the white acts every step is placed and stressed for maximum impact. Dull but honest work. In *Giselle*, the Bolshoi tries to de-emphasize its hardness of contour, but the production is at its best when its punches aren't pulled, as in the Wilis's sequence of death-dealing dances which begins with Hilarion's second entrance. Elsewhere, the hallmark of the production is vitality filtered through the gauze of Romanticism. The whole company applies itself to the goal of maximum expression within a shortened dynamic range. Instead of hard lights and darks, we get a soft-focus composition in a palette of grays. The gradations in a performance by Natalia Bessmertnova are nearly infinite, but because they all occur within a limited compass it is as easy to feel throttled by the effect as to admire the restricted virtuosity it takes to get it. Russian nostalgia observes the Romantic ballet of the 1830's and 1840's at a ceremonial distance and makes a special icon of *Giselle*, finding it, as Carl Van Vechten wrote of the music, "full of the sad, gray splendor of the time of Louis Philippe." But by Pavlova's time, which was when Van Vechten wrote, the choreographic design of the 1841 *Giselle* had been much modified, and Adam's light scaffolding was being used to support the more fully buttressed architecture of Petipa's revisions of the eighties and nineties. *Giselle* as we know it today is as much a product of Russian late-nineteenth-century classicism as it is of the Parisian classicism that flowered a half-century before. It is, if anything, more fin-de-siècle purple than it is *mal-de-siècle* gray. The Russians, though, seem to cherish what is exotic in *Giselle's* tradition more than what is native; they adore that French perfume. Their own essence is dilute.

I have seen more flavorfully "Russian" performances of *Giselle* by American and British companies. When Ulanova was dancing it, the

Bolshoi's production had an immense influence in the West. Now it seems keyed to Bessmertnova's performance—solid in substance but muted in impact, and also much more "pure-dance" in principle. The mime saga of the first act and the dramatic line of the dances in the second act weren't very interesting until Nina Timofeyeva got hold of them. Timofeyeva remembers. She's an "older" dancer, all too evidently, but she's a livelier one, too—not narcotized; she danced full-scale, and made the story points in both acts earnestly clear. When she rushed to Myrtha with an offering of lilies, one recognized the same brave child who had confronted Bathilde in Act I. And Maris Liepa, her Albrecht, reinforced her at every moment. These weren't inspired performances; they were strong, simple, well-routined ones—but what a routine, and what a world of ardent professionalism it implies.

Behind Timofeyeva, for some reason, was the highly talented Ludmila Semenyaka dancing as one of the Wili lieutenants. Semenyaka had earlier danced Giselle with much more confidence and projection than when we first saw her, two years ago, and she's now bone-thin, which heightens the effect of her long, plastically elegant frame and pulled-out limbs, so oddly raylike in their light transparency and force. Semenyaka, alone of the Bolshoi ballerinas, always stretches and points her feet; her high, small head opposes her shoulder on a neck that arches like a violin's; she has severity and blazing pride. But she was overshadowed by Vladimir Vasiliev, who seemed to have heart and style enough for twelve Giselles. This is the man on whom the new Bolshoi male-dominated ballets seem to have been modeled. He's a boomer, all right, but, as the *Giselle* showed, he can be subtle, too, and he lavished on it every nuance, every inflection in his vocabulary. Mikhail Lavrovsky, the Siegfried in *Swan Lake* and the Albrecht to Bessmertnova's Giselle, is, like her, an exponent of pure dance and a good example of the Bolshoi school, but I find him colorless. Colorless in a pretty, sugar-tipped way was Lavrovsky's Odette, Tatiana Golikova. Some of the most exciting dancing of the season has come from Vyacheslav Gordeyev, that paragon of classical refinement. But to speak of Gordeyev is to enter a region of fertile grace which he alone inhabits. I hope to have the pleasure soon.   —*May 19, 1975*

The Bolshoi Smiles, Sort Of

The Bolshoi has reserved till last the best of its new productions. *The Sleeping Beauty* is an attempt to recapture the pomp of the golden nineties, and in a broad way it succeeds. The efforts at period accuracy are often convincing, the characters and their setting are firmly established, the drama misses none of its main points, the action flows easily and in proper scale to the music. At moments, it casts a real theatre spell. One such moment occurs in the Garland Waltz when, on the first notes of the music, the stage is opened to its furthest depth and immediately filled by a great mass of young people rushing down a staircase. Lines of children, tinily conscientious, thread on tiptoe through the ranks. This is the first climax of the evening and the first real sensation of the whole Bolshoi season. As the music slows and softens, spreading its plush rococo fancy, small Italian cupids implicitly take wing, fanning the bland and happy scene. Another perfect memento of the nineties is the corps in the Vision scene, high-stepping across the stage with latticed arms or doubling itself in rows of reverberant images that rebound on one another like facing mirrors. In the adagio, the corps is used both as Aurora's court and as a metaphor for the thick-woven forest in which she sleeps—a conceit that expands poetically on the similar set of dances that has also come down to us as Petipa's invention in the third act of *Don Quixote*. Part of the opulence the Bolshoi achieves in these effects comes from the sheer numbers of people it puts on the stage—pages and footmen and maids of honor and violinists in livery. The children are recruits from American dancing schools; the dryads are the Bolshoi's own vigorous, even-toned corps de ballet, selected from the world's largest pool of dancers and still one of the dance theatre's greater treasures. But what happens to Bolshoi dancers when they leave the corps or the various schools that feed the company, and start to rise? What accounts for the absence of new life in a company that two years ago, to judge from the appearances here of the Bolshoi Dance Academy, seemed on the verge of self-renewal? In *The Sleeping Beauty* the Bolshoi has a hit it can't dance.

The luxury of the grand manner is beyond the company as it is now constituted. The energy it once possessed in character and demi-caractère dancing has paled. Classical technique of the caliber demanded by the great variations of the Prologue and Act III is in short supply at principal-soloist level; below that, it's nonexistent. The young corps is steadier, more truly on pitch, than the women who dance as fairies or ladies-in-waiting; as the Lilac Fairy's retinue or as Aurora's in the Vision scene, these anonymous long-limbed girls throw off hints of animation and style which aren't fulfilled in the dancing of their seniors. But as soon as one sees how good they are—quicker and more alive than in any of the season's other productions—one sees how far they have to go. They haven't been coached in the style of the piece; no one has. It's a question whether *The Sleeping Beauty* can be danced within the limitations of Bolshoi technique, which stresses big jumps at the expense of brilliance in turns and pointwork. But in the third-act entry for the court and its guests nobody even knew how to dance the polonaise. (Remember the *Ivan Susanin* polonaise this company used to do?)

Yuri Grigorovich has staged the ballet in the sense of having graphed and rehearsed its externals; he has left much of it undirected for content, and this is as true of the mime scenes, the processions, and the tableaux as it is of the dancing. His details tend to be production details—touches like having the four cavaliers of the first act pluck their roses from the flower baskets of the corps girls, or having Carabosse enter hunkered down in a phaeton drawn by rats and exit (in the next act) through a trap in the floor. But since the cavaliers aren't characterized, the casting of Boris Akimov, Alexander Bogatyrev, Maris Liepa, and Mikhail Lavrovsky is a mystery and a waste. Carabosse is played *en travestie*—another production plus; but Vladimir Levashev gives every indication of having worked out his role himself. His mime declamations are rendered in a thrashing monotone, without the modulations good direction might have elicited. Later, *bad* direction makes him completely illegible in a pointless downstage scene in which he's lifted and carried from place to place by his attendants while the orchestra describes the Prince's approach to the castle. Although the two confront one another as Tchaikovsky and Petipa arranged, the Lilac Fairy never gets to make her counterprophecy to Carabosse. The hunt dances are given without mood or comment—and without the symbolic game of blindman's buff—although the peasants in their farandole are caricatured. Why should peasants here be any more foolish than they are in *Giselle?*

Like all productions, this one has its own little anomalies and peculiarities. Grigorovich's interpolations include a solo for the Prince on arrival; in fact, he vaults on like Superman to his entrance music, which, unlike Aurora's entrance music, does not change into dance music. Male stars are always suing for equal time in the classics—it's their nature. And it's the nature of audiences to love what critics deplore. Vladimir Vasiliev was so loved on his entrance that even though he contributed nothing to the ballet at that moment but his own presence and a string of his most overwhelming steps, it was a *great* moment. And it was reprised—steps and all— to the music of the Prince's declaration following the Vision scene. For no obvious reason, since the steps are mostly unchanged, Aurora's variation in this scene is danced to the music of the Gold Fairy, taken from Act III. The rest of the suite of which the Gold Fairy was a part is arranged for a Silver trio with one Diamond soloist. The variations are the familiar ones, badly danced. The Panorama is staged after the manner of the original production: the Prince and the Lilac Fairy get into a boat that remains motionless as a scrim painted with leaves and branches moves sideways across the stage. Karsavina has described the original Panorama, at the Maryinsky, as a thing of marvels; along with the unrolling landscape, such sights as a spellbound group of hunters and hounds were carried past on a moving track in the stage floor. The current Bolshoi version doesn't even impart the illusion of movement. It might have done so if we weren't able to see the bottom of the boat sitting on the stage and if the designer had placed another moving scrim behind the boat. But Simon Virsaladze's scenic ideas are tepid to the point of cynicism. Virsaladze's work is also inconsistent —like everything else about the Bolshoi. His smudgy washes strewn with glitter, which are probably meant to look rakish and modern, don't go with his quite conventional storybook costumes.

At the first performance, the Aurora was Nina Sorokina, a small woman with a large heavy head, splayed extensions, smeared footwork, and a manner both uncertain and strident. The Bluebird was the egregious Yuri Vladimirov, exhibiting his scowl, his slump, his twisted line, and his bad stage manners. It's hard to understand how one company, let alone one ballet, can house such performers and also such exquisite classical stylists as Ludmila Semenyaka and Vyacheslav Gordeyev. Semenyaka, the Bluebird Princess on the first night, danced Aurora on the next, opposite Gordeyev's Désiré. Semenyaka's effortless, snowflake dancing emanates from what seem plural centers of strength so evenly distributed as to be almost invisible. At times, one sees a flash or a wink at a nodal point. In the Rose Adagio, where the melody repeats over a dotted rhythm, the ripple of her legs as she circled in place was a constant vibration all the way up and down, guided from the thigh. Such an impalpable style is not only un-Bolshoi, it's anti-Bolshoi; Semenyaka is in fact Kirov-trained.

Gordeyev reminds me of Martha Graham's phrase "divine normal." He has strength, virile beauty, perfection of style, and also the gift of appearing utterly genuine on the stage—not frozen into a picture. Classical dancing is a language he speaks naturally and with astonishing poetic flair. He can assemble elements of classical syntax in new and surprising formations, as when his passé leg in a multiple pirouette sweeps through rond de jambe en l'air into the opening battement of a series of grands jetés en tournant. And those jumps are thrillingly strong, not only in the forward battement but in the feathery freedom of the back leg. Another typical Gordeyev multiple-pirouette sequence (he commonly does five or six) evolves through développé into rond de jambe to end in a huge, still arabesque penchée. Bolshoi technique has always seemed to me much more handsome for men than for women—more developed, too. But not until Gordeyev has it seemed a sensitive style. Gordeyev is the only great classical dancer I know who uses his exceptional feats to disclose himself to his audience. When he shows us unsuspected relationships between steps, it's as if he were revealing a private discovery, a new treasure from the world of his imagination. For his role in *The Sleeping Beauty*, the révérence in low fondu he finds to punctuate his third-act solo is perfectly in keeping with his character and with the style of the ballet. And while in the air he does new things with his arms—transverse sweeps that I can't recall except for their excitement and pertinence. Some dancers say, "I'm the show." Gordeyev says quietly, "I show."

It was sad to see so many empty seats during the Dance Theatre of Harlem's three-week season at the Uris, especially when the two weeks of preview performances had filled the theatre with enthusiastic audiences. Some of those jubilant previews had been matinées for schoolchildren, but two of them were evening performances for which cut-rate tickets were available, and though tickets sold for as little as two dollars during the regular season, not enough people seemed to have heard about it. Adding to this failure of publicity was the unlucky timing of the season. With a considerable portion of its repertory drawn from the New York City Ballet, the company was playing opposite the New York City Ballet as well as the Bolshoi, and also opposite another black dance company—Alvin Ailey's. The uptown audiences that had attended in force during the previews didn't keep coming, and the intellectual-balletomane circuit, which could have provided some warmth, didn't annex the company. The DTH is in a difficult transitional period—well out of its missionary phase as a ghetto experiment and yet not quite into the big time. The meager publicity it does get monotonously emphasizes what the company is long past proving—that black dancers have a talent for classical ballet and black audiences an appetite for it. But in the Uris season the company didn't succeed in capturing the larger claim it is entitled to as an exciting young company with something to show the general public that buys ballet tickets.

Probably the company won't win this audience until it has the right vehicles to give it a distinctive image. I should hate to see that image overlap more than it already has with that of the New York City Ballet. Although in most of its NYCB-derived works the company gives fresh and powerful performances—its *Agon* is now a total triumph and its version of Robbins's *Afternoon of a Faun*, with Lydia Abarca and Ronald Perry, is the best I've seen anywhere in years—there are dangers in continuing to mount works that are more or less definitively performed at the State Theatre. I enjoyed the new production of *Allegro Brillante* as much as I always enjoy good performances of this marvelous, headlong piece; the small ensemble, cast way up with the top soloists, sparkled. But Abarca isn't the allegro technician the ballerina role needs, and the restaged opening, which has the curtain rising early on an onstage pianist and the dancers running on in pairs, isn't as effective as a curtain rising on a ballet already in motion. It might be more fun and more of a box-office draw if the company were to present works that the New York City Ballet no longer does—Balanchine's *Bourrée Fantasque* or *Pas de Dix*, Robbins's *Fanfare*, Lew Christensen's *Filling Station*.

After Corinth, a new ballet by company member Walter Raines, strikes me as the wrong sort of addition to the repertory, too. A *Medea* piece dealing murkily with black magic and vengeance, it was done Graham-style. I wish they'd done it Haiti-style.

—*May 26, 1975*

It's a Wise Child

By subtitling his version of *Ma Mère l'Oye* "Fairy Tales for Dancers," and by staging the ballet as a series of improvisations dressed in leftover décors and props from other ballets in the repertory, Jerome Robbins accomplishes several things at once: a joke about the New York City Ballet, a commentary on the concept of a ballet company in the act of paying "Hommage à Ravel," a peculiarly shrewd and touching rendition of the power of theatrical fantasy. Ravel framed his *Mother Goose* ballet with the story of the Sleeping Beauty, who dreams a suite of fairy-tale dances—Beauty and the Beast, Hop o' My Thumb, and the Empress of the Pagodas. In the end, the Prince appears, walking down the avenue of brambles that part to let him pass, and the wedding celebration, attended by all the other fairy-tale characters, takes place to the tingling climaxes of the "Jardin Féerique." Ravel took his idea of the Sleeping Beauty's sleep from Perrault—who tells us that "(though history mentions nothing of it) the good fairy, during so long a sleep, had given her very agreeable dreams"—and the idea of her wedding (though history mentions nothing of it, either) probably came from the Tchaikovsky-Petipa ballet. Robbins follows Ravel's scenario closely, but by adding one element to it he colors the whole ballet to such an extent that it appears, from first to last, to be his own creation. He surrounds Ravel's frame with another frame, making the ballet a charade put on by dancers, whom he sees as the scamps of the theatre. This new frame by itself is nothing much; yet the ballet could not have been presented in just this form by any other company or by any other choreographer.

Because Robbins has so personalized the idea of dancers as precocious, amusing kids, in dozens of ballets and musicals starting as far back as *Interplay* and *Look, Ma, I'm Dancing* and *Pied Piper*, he succeeds in turning *Ma Mère l'Oye* into a typical Robbins kid-style ballet. When the Sleeping Beauty enters skipping rope, or when the Good Fairy whistles on her fingers, these impudences specified by Ravel seem like Robbins's inventions. When he throws in chunks of classical mime out of *The Sleeping Beauty*, the satire fits right in. So does the general satire of the New York City Ballet and its uncommendable habit of mounting new ballets in the fittings of old ones. Here is that Horace Armistead garden drop yet again, here are pieces of A *Midsummer Night's Dream* (some of them hung backward), here is the *Nutcracker* bed, the French doors from *Liebeslieder Walzer*, the lanterns and grass stalks from *Watermill*. The whole company and its repertory are jumbled together in a salute to Ravel, but people who don't recognize the bric-a-brac won't miss out on the fun or the self-mockery. The elemental, poverty-pleading tackiness of the piece may be vintage New York City Ballet; it's also a more serious conception of Ravel's ballet, coming from Robbins, than a reverent incense-and-gossamer production would have been.

In the poetic style of *Ma Mère l'Oye*, Robbins returns to those qualities which first defined him as a unique theatre artist. He's once again the New York play-school referee, the maestro of the slum kindergarten, the Peter Pan of arts and crafts. When Robbins speaks with a specifically local accent, when his boyhood origins and his eternal boy-genius Bronx High School of Science sensibility are allowed to resonate with their natural color and size, his art seems universal. When he deliberately attempts big, grown-up, universal themes (as in *West Side Story* and *The Goldberg Variations* and *Watermill* and *Dybbuk Variations*), he becomes parochial, local in a reductive sense: Mr. New School Seminar or Mr. Broome Street Avant-Garde. *Ma Mère l'Oye* is bound to be underestimated because it looks so easy and hasn't a lot of dancing, but it's a New York artifact of wide significance. It catches up the beloved Robbins myth about dancers as children and relocates it in our current world of young dancers' workshops, professional children's schools, and incubators of the performing arts. The point of overlap is the ancillary myth, so real to the stagestruck kids of Robbins's generation, of puttin' on a show.

You can see this clearly in the datedness of the ballet's opening scene—its one bad moment. The corps kids are lying around the stage, propped up on trunks or bits of scenery, listening to Mother Goose reading from her book. Comden and Green are not far off.

(At the première, Mother Goose was Mme. Pourmel, the company's wardrobe mistress, in her blue smock; that shows how thorough Robbins's backstage-musical conception is.) Dancers and audiences everywhere, especially at the New York City Ballet, have outgrown this sentimental aspect of Robbins's juvenile fantasy. Besides, it violates practical reality. Why should a ballet company be sitting around? If they'd been warming up—doing their barres or stretching their muscles—instead of just listening raptly, the scene might not have looked so forced and coy. However, the fantasy rolls: theatre trunks are thrown open, hats with plumes come out, the scenery moves, the traffic rumbles; the tables, if there were any, would be turned. These dancers aren't wistful dreamers; they're sober technicians, as systematic as circus acrobats. They do not try to cajole you with an illusion of spontaneity; everything is mechanical, deadpan, precise, and twice as funny because of it. Twice as real, too, in the normal, everyday dimensions of a child's imaginings which Robbins intended the action to have. In the old movie musicals, child performers have no youth; the hysterical energy of vaudeville has ravaged them prematurely. The young dancers Robbins is using now are old and wise, too, but, unlike the monstrous theatrical children of the past, their youth hasn't been sacrificed to their learning. It's a conception that fits neatly into Ravel's world —the child as mandarin.

Robbins's other ballet in this second of the Ravel programs was a small-group setting of the "Introduction and Allegro for Harp," and it was a highly inconclusive affair, vaporizing even as you watched. Patricia McBride functioned beautifully, as she does in other Robbins works, and seemed on the verge of creating a new character. But none materialized, because Robbins's grasp of abstract drama is incomplete; he doesn't—here, at least—seem to understand how dancing becomes characterization without becoming the stepchild of acting. Balanchine's *Shéhérazade*, a vaguely 1910-ish Oriental character ballet in abstract form, started by making sense to me, then grew evasive. One didn't need real scimitars and platters of grapes to enjoy it, but for music so heavy with suggestions of story and atmosphere one did need something more than the angular patterns Balanchine kept giving us for two principals, two pairs of demisoloists, and corps. In *Alborada del Gracioso*, Jacques d'Amboise conceived a Spanish supper-club adagio for himself, Suzanne Farrell, and an ensemble. It was as messily designed as Robbins's *Introduction and Allegro* and as inconsequential as the Balanchine, but more forthright than either, and it had a few raw thrills. Probably from having worked with her so often as a partner, D'Amboise knows a little more about composing for Farrell than Robbins did in the *Concerto in G*, the week before. D'Amboise made her look hot, twisty, and alive. Farrell has a wonderful way now of complying with all the broad effects a choreographer may dream up and swerving just in time to avoid their grosser implications. She keeps a spiritual distance, and it brings her closer to us than ever.

Sitting through ballets that aren't destined to last isn't hard to do when they're as short as these three were. But John Taras's *Daphnis and Chloe* was a forty-minute throwaway of Ravel's greatest ballet score, and it was something else. On the first night, it looked like a disorganized rehearsal for some kind of glitter-rock ritual on the beach at Malibu. Flame-throwers could not have forced me back for another look. Instead, I went to the Bolshoi for Vyacheslav Gordeyev's sole Bluebird of the season, in the last performance of *The Sleeping Beauty*. Even Gordeyev needs more than one crack at the role to be a great Bluebird, and I would prefer to see him in the extended variation that is customary in the West. Still, his performance, with its high, wide, scissoring leaps and brilliantly sustained turning sequences on the ground, was one not to be missed. —*June 9, 1975*

Through the Looking Glass

The New York City Ballet's Ravel series didn't include a ballet to "Miroirs" (although two excerpts from that suite were danced), but mirrors were a theme nonetheless—especially on the final program. The left-right symmetry of the dances in Balanchine's *Le Tombeau de Couperin*, in which the company is divided into Left Quadrille and Right Quadrille; the multiple refractions of the corps in the *Rapsodie Espagnole*; *Gaspard de la Nuit*, with a variety of scenic elements actually composed of mirrors that bounced light into the audience; Jerome Robbins's *Chansons Madécasses*, composed for a white couple whose movements are duplicated by a black couple. I doubt if any of this was intended as a motif by the makers of the festival, but the coincidences do suggest a pattern in the responsiveness of the visual mind to Ravel's music, and it isn't necessary to go back to the mirror of Death in *La Valse* to see how this strain of visual implication may be entirely reasonable even though it isn't clear. Things are often like that in ballet; one accepts a kind of dream logic in what one sees. The "mirrors" in Ravel are more than an ornament but less than a conceit; though they may haunt the imagination, they do not trouble the intellect, and since it's an imaginative world we enter when we go to the ballet, the fact that we are unable to formulate their meanings only strengthens their power to affect us.

I will leave to those who cannot accept this last statement the problem of puzzling out the meaning of Robbins's *Chansons Madécasses*. The whole ballet seems to turn on the text of the second of the "Songs of the Madagasque," which deals with racist abominations, and the dark-skinned and dark-clothed couple is evidently there to indicate something suspect about the white couple. But what? Bad conscience, sexual hypocrisy, racial guilt? Robbins's mirror images don't come from the world of ballet or of Ravel; they come from the world of Edward Albee. Doubling the roles in a pas de deux and casting the doubles as blacks is a playwright's, not a choreographer's, idea, and a corny one at that. Not involving the two couples is astute corn. The audience for the Ravel festival probably included a lot of people who prefer acting to dancing— who like ballets that make you think. I never saw a good ballet that made me think. But in Robbins's ballet there's no way to think even if one wants to. The reason one can't formulate a meaning for what he has put on the stage is that there isn't any.

In the middle scene of *Gaspard de la Nuit* ("The Gibbet"), some black-bandaged figures hang slowly swaying at the ends of ropes. Two of them struggle in a tortuous and obscure way to make love while processions, cowled and draped, cross the stage holding hand mirrors. The other scenes are not as interesting or as succinct. I have no great objection to the flashy décor, by the French designer Bernard Daydé; the materials and workmanship are first-rate. But Balanchine now seems beyond the steadfast chic of Paris and its appetite for morbid pleasantries. *Gaspard* gives us a taste of Les Ballets 1933. However, Balanchine isn't re-creating what that sort of thing was all about, he's just indicating. Perhaps I could have enjoyed the whole piece more if *Ivesiana* hadn't been revived earlier this season. Next to its flat, equivocal terror, *Gaspard* looks frail, melodramatic, and out of touch.

Mirror oppositions are central to *Le Tombeau de Couperin*, Balanchine's setting of Ravel's eighteenth-century-style court dances. Symmetrical repeats and reversals are an elaborate form of courtesy; intricacy in the figures tests everyone equally. The four dances are performed by a double octet: two sets of four couples each. Not until the third dance does the invisible mirror partition between the sets break down. Followed for its ritual changes, the ballet is fascinating, but the narrow rhythms continuing straight through to the end of each piece keep punctuating those changes in a way that makes them seem sadly inevitable. The mirror maze is a lovely bauble but a claustrophobe's nightmare.

The *Rapsodie Espagnole* is a musical trap of a different construction: a theatrical fantasy of the concert hall. Although it is pictorial music of the most imaginative kind, its images are like mental movies—impractically paced for choreography. Until Balanchine staged it, I wouldn't have believed it could be made into a ballet. Even Balanchine doesn't quite bring it off; the explosive rhythms of the Feria are a little too short-breathed to let him expand the finale to a full-scale sizzling climax, the shifting tone-poem contrasts tend to look fitful and edgy on the stage, and there's an awkward moment at the end of the Habañera, which is set as a pas de deux, when the dancers, subsiding from their tango, have no cover for their exit. But Balanchine is at his most insistent and resourceful; he works at the piece as if it were the first one he'd ever made, and just because the material is so recalcitrant his superb craftsmanship is the more exposed—you can see him preparing his effects, hovering in discreet withdrawals or holding actions, then pouncing in a massed attack. The fun of the ballet is in the suspense of its strategy, in watching Balanchine maneuver. The marvel of it is that so much of it works as a *stage* fantasy; even the edginess becomes at times wonderfully suspenseful. And with music this tricky to handle—and this familiar—the decision to make the ballet not high serious art but wittily ersatz art seems entirely appropriate. The *Rapsodie* is pop Balanchine—Hollywood Spanish; spectral and glamorous, it looks like the most expensive entertainment available at some oasis of a resort hotel.

Balanchine loads the stage with those long-stemmed nymphs of his and arrays them in open, steady poses, balances, and splits to the floor. The girls of the corps de ballet are the heart of the piece, and never have they danced more scrupulously. The opening sequence, with them all spread out in diagonals and one by one converting écarté positions into closed and then open croisés, is like a redoing of the opening of the *Symphony in Three Movements* (also a corps piece); this time, everybody gets it right. Karin von Aroldingen dances scrupulously, too, but apart from some languid hand and arm gestures that recall *La Valse* her role is little more than a projection of the corps. Peter Schaufuss has a more brilliant role and shows off some Baryshnikov-style steps, but neither he nor Nolan T'Sani, as the tango partner, seems to know what kind of presence is called for. Harlequin makeup or a carnival mask might help Schaufuss become the spirit of fiesta, and probably T'Sani should wear a domino—it's that kind of part. The costumes, by Michael Avedon, are boleros and short ruffled dresses in turquoise and black, while the men wear black body tights with touches of turquoise and green. Ronald Bates has achieved his best lighting of the festival—a look of the high desert at dusk.

In Balanchine's *Tzigane*, there was and there can only be Suzanne Farrell. With no one else could this florid gypsy-violin rhapsody find so comfortable a home in the theatre. The first half, scored for solo violin, becomes a five-minute dance solo that touches a new height in contemporary virtuoso performance. Farrell's dancing is a seamless flow, and to isolate certain effects is to give a false picture of what she does, but there were moments in this performance that stopped my breath: a high, motionless piqué balance lightly stepped into from nowhere, a headlong plunge into arabesque penchée effortlessly held as she turned over to face the sky, chaîné turns changing speed, some marvelous in-place pirouettes (triples!) slowing to an insolent balance-finish, which she executed with her hands cupping her head. But so subtle is Farrell's dance instinct that half the time she seems only to be standing there, turning from side to side, slipping quickly onto or off point, and now and then, in a playful deformation of a czardas step, turning in her toes. The daredevil feats pass without a murmur from the audience. Then, after all this dream dancing, she goes on and finishes the piece with a masterful Peter Martins and a wholly extraneous ensemble.

There were three other ballets on this heavy program. Balanchine's choreography for Patricia McBride to *Pavane pour une*

Infante Défunte was, curiously, a miss. Robbins's *Un Barque sur l'Océan* made five boys look sweetly pretty. Jacques d'Amboise's *Sarabande and Danse* was recital stuff, with Colleen Neary performing willingly but wildly. The Ravel festival, which everyone expected so little from, has turned out rather well. Of sixteen premières, there were five that deserve to enter the repertory: *Rapsodie Espagnole*, *Tzigane*, *Le Tombeau de Couperin*, and *Sonatine*—all by Balanchine —and *Ma Mère l'Oye*, by Robbins. Perhaps also Robbins's *Concerto in G*, and certainly, if the right conditions for performing it can be found, *L'Enfant et les Sortilèges*. *Gaspard de la Nuit* will probably be around for another season or two. At a maximum, that gives us eight out of sixteen tries, which is a better average than the eight out of twenty-one ballets that remain from the Stravinsky Festival of three years ago.   —*June 16, 1975*

Personal Appearance

As Lucifer in the ballet of that title made for him by Martha Graham, Rudolf Nureyev wore his hair blown out like an angel by William Blake. His costume consisted of a gold, jewel-studded jockstrap, and an Ace bandage wrapped around one foot, which was injured. His choreography was a recapitulation of all the tortured-hero roles Graham ever created—notably for her former premier danseur Bertram Ross. In spite of the way he looked, Nureyev was not ridiculous. The element of camp in his personality frees him for incongruous undertakings such as this; he gives to the bizarre a touch of authority. And the generosity of his nature (he donated his services for the evening, which was a benefit for the Graham company) gives him a whole-souled dignity. Heroes have always been of secondary interest to Graham; hers is a theatre of feminine tempests. Nonetheless, it seemed fitting—inevitable, even—that Nureyev should work at this moment with Graham and in this way. A knight-errant of the dance theatre, one feels, must come sometime to lay his shield before Our Lady of Silences, Calm and Distressed, and in the smoke of battle we glimpsed the ensign of mutual trust, the sure hope that one pro would do right by another. Like Ross, Nureyev has always been a good man with a cape. There were nearly as many flying textiles in *Lucifer* as there were in *Mendicants of Evening*, a season or two ago. Lucifer's cape, designed by Halston, looked like a bedspread made for a king. The jockstrap, by Halston with the assistance of Samuel Beizer & Associates and Elsa Peretti of Tiffany's, was the same sort of royal affair. It took Martha Graham to finally give us Rudi in the nudi, as his fans used to claim they wanted him, but not many of the shriekers were present at the Uris on this night when the tickets were scaled from $50 to $10,000 and when, to add luster to the beaten bronze of his presence, Nureyev's partner in the piece was Dame Margot Fonteyn.

To look for art in such an event seems an impertinence. Nureyev took a mighty swipe at Graham technique. It wasn't good Graham dancing but it was good Nureyev. He has never created a great modern role and probably he never will. Lucifer is less a role than it is an extended appearance in the landscape of Graham theatre, but there are few places he could have turned his personal magnetism to such warm and glamorous effect. Fonteyn (who also waived her fee) was not quite as mobilized as Nureyev. Together they gave the second-act pas de deux from *Swan Lake*, which it would have been wiser to leave out; at fifty-six, Fonteyn is not giving us the *Swan Lakes* she gave us at fifty. Then, in snake headdress and body tights, she was Night, Lucifer's antagonist. (Lucifer is seen as the bringer of light, after his fall; Night represents all the temptations he is prey to in his fallen state.) Dramatically, the role is butter to her; the dancing looked late-Denishawn Oriental and in that style quite delicious. (A program note explained that the choreography had been worked out on a Graham dancer and "restaged" for the ballerina.) Through it all, one could almost hear a sweetly confident little voice saying "I've been angular" in the same way Barbara Stanwyck, in *The Lady Eve*, says "I've been British." Night did a long solo with a rope, which could have been symbolic. The action of the piece was never clear, although the rhythm was—clearer and more lively than it has been for some time in Graham works. The setting was simple—a giant shell scooped out of a rock promontory, by the Philippine architect Leandro Locsin—and a Graham chorus (Captains of Fear, Daughters of the Dawn) was employed, mostly to bring on and take away the capes.

Actually, of course, Graham technique isn't angular, and its sculptural precision has affected American dancers and audiences profoundly for nearly fifty years. On the same program, the forty-five-year-old solo *Lamentation* was revived. The dancer (Peggy Lyman), sheathed from crown to ankle in a tube of stretch jersey, sits blocklike on a low bench, rocks incessantly, strains from side to side, plunges fists deep between her knees. The form of the dance says it all—solid geometry as live emotion. The same organic principle is seen in the space-slashing design of *Diversion of Angels*, which was also presented. *Seraphic Dialogue*, the Joan of Arc piece, is an old friend whose shoulder can be wept on countless times; I love it as theatre, but I can't admire it as drama. One doesn't weep over *Lamentation*, despite the story Graham tells about the bereaved woman whom the sight of it released into tears. Pure drama is too interesting for that—there is too much to learn. Graham told that story and many others on this occasion, speaking with her customary sibylline charm and looking splendid in a series of Halston caftans. Her good stories always contain a subtle admonition to the audience: Pay attention! Be strict! She is in her own person an embodiment of theatre—at times of drama, too. Perhaps the best she can give us now, besides more historic revivals, is herself, just talking.

When it moved from the City Center to Lincoln Center, a little over a decade ago, the New York City Ballet was seduced by the large stage and overlarge proscenium of the State Theatre into putting on spectacles with décor disproportionate to the human scale of the dancing. *Brahms-Schoenberg Quartet*, with its drapes and tassels, *A Midsummer Night's Dream*, with its oversized forest scenery and second-act pavilion, were doomed attempts to mask the high vault of dead space over the dancers' heads. *Divertimento No. 15*, that celestial Mozart ballet, acquired its ivy-twined ramparts and trellises. Another masterpiece, *Ballet Imperial*, was revived in a setting of painted architecture surmounted by painted curtains in cold, deep blue drawn back in swags; beneath those bulging forms the dancers looked like beetles creeping around on a plate. Eventually, the scenery for *Ballet Imperial* (along with its more attractive costumes) was scrapped in favor of a bare stage—a surrender rather than a solution. Although the State Theatre is still an uncomfortable space for dancing, the company at least no longer draws our attention to the fact by trying so often to disguise it; but it has never really solved the problem of how to make a stage look clean without looking bare. And it is stuck with some of those compensatory mid-sixties décors.

The worst of these is probably the *Brahms-Schoenberg Quartet*, which lingers from the company's swag-happy period, together with a forlorn set of rained-out-bridal-party costumes. The choreography was Balanchine's first full-company all-dance work for the new stage. Using Arnold Schoenberg's orchestration of Brahms's Piano Quartet in G Minor, he composed four self-contained ballets, with no returns by the dancers of each movement. The movements that are musically the best (the second and fourth) come off best as dancing; the rest of the piece seems to me as weakly ingratiating as its music and fussily concerned with filling out space to the last full Brahmsian measure. Despite the padding of the large choral sections, the ballet has sustained itself as an audience favorite on the performances of its stars—Patricia McBride in the Intermezzo (second movement), Edward Villella in the "martial" break in the Andante (third movement), Suzanne Farrell and Jacques d'Amboise in the closing Rondo alla Zingarese. Balanchine has given these dancers material so much their own that it's like a personal signature. The Intermezzo unfurls in a continuous line indistinguishable from the line of McBride's body; the dance just seems to grow out of the curve of her deeply indented lower back and to shape itself voluntarily in a series of unarrested scroll-like plunges. Over and over she plummets and returns upon herself—up through her partner's hands, behind his shoulder, or caught on his chest—and each time the recovery seems to fix both of them momentarily in a new condition, a new intimacy. In this way, the pas de deux never loses dramatic tension, never becomes remorselessly physical, but the illusion of drama is created entirely by McBride's steadiness through the variable sweep of the patterns Balanchine has set for her. In the years when she was dancing it with Conrad Ludlow, the Intermezzo was the greatest McBride performance that one could see. Now, without Ludlow to partner her, McBride is having to take a few risks, and Balanchine has made a few adjustments in the partnering. Bart Cook copes gallantly and knowledgeably, and the season's first two Intermezzos were the best. Later, things got more difficult. But this is still among the greatest dance performances I know.

Without Villella, the Andante doesn't explode the way it used to, like a gunshot from a bouquet of roses. Robert Weiss has the timing the part calls for (this wins him applause) but not the range; Peter

Schaufuss has more range but not, as yet, the timing. Farrell's return to the Gypsy Rondo restores a phase of the evolutionary process that led to her dazzling *Tzigane* in the Ravel festival. The Rondo is a lighthearted whirl—the antics of "Hungarian" floor-show dancing adapted to the temperament and technique of a brilliant young American ballerina. It is lyrical light verse, as opposed to the swelling dramatic periods of *Tzigane*. And Farrell understands so well the semiserious imposture involved in each of her gypsy impersonations —understands it not only theatrically (in the Rondo, the pretense of hauteur in response to D'Amboise's monkeyshines) but conceptually, as a vivid pretext for formal progress. The "gypsiness" of it all is a mode of presentation merely—a way of framing successive stages in the crystallization of a style. Within the ornate European frame there's a hale American girl doing the most advanced classical dancing of our day.

This season, Farrell also resumed such choice roles as *Movements for Piano and Orchestra*, the *Agon* pas de deux, and—to lesser effect, because it is a lesser role—Titania in *A Midsummer Night's Dream*. *Meditation*, the dramatic vignette that she alone performs with D'Amboise, came back with a new undercurrent of sympathy in the performance. As we watch Farrell consciously shaping her roles instead of, as in former days, yielding—sometimes misguidedly— to their basic impulse, we are seeing something of incalculable value on the ballet stage. But the revived powers of Violette Verdy strike me as something special, too, and the advent of Merrill Ashley has been one of the most gratifying events of the season.

Ashley has come along very quickly and by the hardest route— the route of the Tchaikovsky gut-crunchers: *Ballet Imperial* (or *Concerto No. 2*, as it's now called) and the "Theme and Variations" of *Suite No. 3*. The débuts came about a half-year apart; by the time of the "Theme" début, just before the Ravel festival, she had improved to the point of near-invincibility. She has a bold, mettlesome style, newly softened and clarified, and she has unclenched and expanded throughout the upper body. She now has the scale to match her size (she's one of the tall ones), and the delicacy to make you appreciate it. Terrifically strong and fast, Ashley eats up difficult parts. *Valse-Fantaisie*, which she also did this season, is no challenge—it's as easy for her as rolling over in bed. She makes the *Stars and Stripes* pas de deux look easy, too, and in the Rondo alla Zingarese she's technically better than Farrell. The way she emphasizes the lunge attack in the manège of bent-knee piqué turns in attitude and holds the high wide line of the attitude is characteristic of the force she can bring to a role. It's an unharrying, exhilarating force. In *Divertimento No. 15*, she's comfortably relaxed —but in the wrong part. I'd like to see her speed and clarity put to work on the leading role.   —*July 7, 1975*

Separate Worlds

American Ballet Theatre is launching its combinations of Russian and native stars in planned stages, like Apollo meeting Soyuz: Rudolf Nureyev and Cynthia Gregory in Nureyev's production of *Raymonda*, Natalia Makarova and Erik Bruhn (an ABT veteran star returned from retirement) in a new pas de deux, Makarova and Fernando Bujones in *La Bayadère*, and, in the last weeks of the season, Mikhail Baryshnikov and Gelsey Kirkland in the *Giselle* that New York has been waiting for, and in practically everything else except *Swan Lake*. The season is huge box-office, with madness in the air—not only full houses but demonstrative ones that keep the madness going long after the curtain has dropped. Bunches of flowers are pelted across the footlights; shredded programs (a specialty of the Gregory fans) rain from the top balcony. Not every star-coupling has produced chemistry, and except in the case of Kirkland-Baryshnikov, who have already established themselves as a team, none could have been hoped for; it was simply the friction of star rubbing against star. Audiences may think they're getting more for their money when such mismatchings as Nureyev-Gregory or Makarova-Bruhn occur and the size of the ovation is automatically doubled, but the excitement dies with the last bouquet, and sometimes it doesn't begin until the flowers start flying.

In *Epilogue*, the pas de deux created for Makarova and Bruhn by the American-born choreographer John Neumeier, nothing happened until the curtain came down and the fans went into their act, but this wasn't the epilogue that Neumeier had in mind. Leaves falling one by one, rust-colored costumes, Makarova in a turban, Bruhn with his back to her—a neon sign spelling out "The Autumn of Their Relationship" couldn't have made the situation more obvious. We "read" the situation at a glance, feeling foolish because it's so easy but feeling apprehensive, too. Neumeier has set us up before with his literary concepts that go nowhere as dances, yet his choreography is so hermetic and painfully labored that it seems to spring from a revulsion against the very idea of literariness. It wants to get somewhere as dancing, but, for Neumeier, translating a dramatic situation into a dance seems to be chiefly a matter of avoiding paraphrasable content. He keeps emptying the dance of what the characters might be "saying" to each other and substituting the arduous anonymous relations of two dancers trying to work something out in a practice studio. The steps are meaningless; they look as if they could have been composed in any order, and to any music but the music we hear, which happens to be the Adagietto from Mahler's Fifth. At this level, Makarova and Bruhn are more interesting taking class. There's nothing wrong with a choreographer's being literary if he has guts, and although I prefer drama when its revealed from inside the dancing, choreography that works with the drama outside (as in the best of Tudor) is just as difficult to bring off and just as rewarding when it succeeds. Neumeier starts by being Tudor, then crosses suddenly to would-be Balanchine. He plants a signpost, then rips up the path it points to. He's become a successful, in-demand choreographer because some of his concepts are almost-magisterial: the use of Stravinsky's score combined with bits of Tchaikovsky to frame a story about ballet in *Le Baiser de la Fée,* the use of Nureyev in *Don Juan,* or Makarova and Bruhn dancing to the score of the movie *Death in Venice.* But Neumeier's concepts are always stuck on the page, like an undirected script. In his *Baiser* one could all but see the script indications for the blanks in the action which the dances were supposed to fill: "Groom dances with Bride." "Bride dances alone." In *Epilogue,* it's "Middle-aged dancers dance."

Bruhn has always been an insular kind of star. Inwardly rigid, absorbed in his own perfection, he has never mated well with any ballerina, and his best roles were those that placed barriers between him and women—James in *La Sylphide,* Jean in *Miss Julie,* the Poet in *La Sonnambula*—or that accounted for the neurotic tension he projected, and still projects, onstage. Neither of his two new roles this season—in *Epilogue* or in *Raymonda,* as Abdul-Rakhman, the Saracen sheikh—accounts for Bruhn in this way. He remains Erik Bruhn, possibly the only major male star in ballet who can't walk toward a woman and appear to love her. In *Epilogue*, his role seems to be based on *Miss Julie*, which would be all right if Makarova's were, too, but she's all suppleness and entreaties, and when she stretches her lovely silken legs around him she seems to give him cramps. The two are temperamentally disparate dancers who have appeared together before mostly in ballets like *Giselle* and *Les Sylphides*. In a "strange," modern work built around their disparities they might have struck sparks at last, but there's no interest in seeing them unrelate to each other in a piece that doesn't have unrelatedness as its subject. It's the dancers, not the characters, who remain in their separate worlds.

Epilogue is the kind of piece that makes an unintentional joke of expressive form. It reveals by accident what the ballet should have been about. *Raymonda* betrays itself in much the same way, but on a far larger scale. Its accidental subject is the destruction of the ballerina; it should have been titled "Putting Raymonda in Her Place." Nureyev, who appeared as guest artist during ABT's first week, is wrong for Cynthia Gregory not only because he isn't tall enough but because he hasn't any use for her as the heroine of his ballet. This is the version of *Raymonda* he originally produced three years ago for the Zurich Ballet, with Marcia Haydée as Raymonda and with scenery and costumes by Nicholas Georgiadis. Nureyev in recent years has avoided putting himself up against dancers of Gregory's strength and stature; it's been Haydée or Karen Kain or Merle Park or the aging Fonteyn, and he has adopted an unseemly high-handed approach to his classical revivals. *Raymonda* is the most egotistical show he has ever put on, and, as a work of custodianship, the most licentious.

Even without Nureyev's participation, *Raymonda* would have been a dubious addition to the Ballet Theatre repertory. It is a long and prolix work, with a foolish story and a score lacking in theatrical momentum. Petipa conceived it, in 1898, as a series of dance suites bridged by a thin scaffolding of pantomime. The suites —classical in the first act, character in the second, a combination of both in the third—are best seen in excerpt form: a fact acknowledged by every major ballet company in the Western world, including ABT, which until a few years ago gave the old Balanchine version of Act III under the title *Grand Pas Glazunov*. About the only case that one can make for a full-length *Raymonda* (did ABT try making it to Nureyev?) is that it has a great ballerina role. Arranged for Pierina Legnani, the Odette-Odile of the St. Petersburg *Swan Lake*, the role is large and glorious, with a superb entrance that recalls Aurora's in *The Sleeping Beauty.* Running down a flight of stairs, the dancer bends to the floor and rises into high attitude, scooping up six roses in turn. Petipa's detailed notes to the composer warned, "You must pay special attention to this entrance. It is for the first dancer." Poor Cynthia Gregory! In her *Raymonda*, the first dancer is Nureyev, and he enters to her music, leaving her to scoop up her roses almost as an afterthought. Raymonda has no entrance —she's onstage when the curtain rises, fooling around the back of the set in the warm-up-the-house scene. Nureyev leaves her her five variations (he himself has four—three more than Petipa and Glazunov planned for), but he never surrounds her with light and space. The role is that worst combination in theatre: it is difficult and it is drab. The production doesn't build up a special picture of a romantic heroine, or even a star ballerina. Petipa's heroine was passive and dreamy, but Nureyev makes her a masochistic nitwit. He has reworked the plot elements so that an uncomfortable amount of the action takes place in her mind, and the triangle of Raymonda, the heroic knight, and the Saracen sheikh becomes tense with ambiguous confrontations in the manner of modern-dance drama. Neither man is characterized so as to make a choice possible, and the girl is badly pulled about between the two to no expressive purpose. I mean literally pulled about: Nureyev never leaves her alone except in her solos. In their big first-act pas de deux, he partners so incessantly that she hasn't room to expand, and he keeps her bouncing like a marionette. Where is the adagio in this adagio? Bruhn partners in the same callous manner—"Oh, here's an ankle," and he grabs it and cranks her into a turn. None of this is meant to be dramatically expressive, but it says a great deal. As in *Epilogue*, the dancing takes on implications that lie outside the ballet; it tells us more about Nureyev's unconscious than about Raymonda's.

Boxed in by Nureyev and slowed by the conducting of Akira Endo on the first night, Gregory gave an exhibition of virtuosity drained of vivacity. At the next performance, David Gilbert's tempi were more reasonable and the steps were brightly produced, but with a sense of personal dissociation, and with no surge through the body. Nureyev's dancing was like his production—eccentric, excessive, overworked. At this point in his career, Nureyev probably feels he must show as much of himself as he can to his audiences, and his audiences obviously feel the same way. But Nureyev's interests, which mesh with the interests of companies in difficulty at the box office, clash with Ballet Theatre's. It doesn't need Nureyev vehicles; it needs vehicles for its own stars, and it badly needs authoritative coaching in the styles proper to classical revivals. What remains of the Petipa tradition in the first two acts of this *Raymonda*—a string of variations, the choreography for the female corps in the Valse Fantastique, one or two of the character numbers—isn't enough to offset the chaos and gloom of Nureyev's staging. The famous Hungarian divertissement in Act III is by far the best part of the show, but, like the show as a whole, it's inferior to other versions Nureyev has produced. (It includes a particularly incoherent solo that Nureyev has fashioned for himself to the processional music, and the Apotheosis begins with a slow-motion wrestling match between him and the ballerina which, in a sense, apotheosizes their odd relationship.) Ballet Theatre keeps on buying pigs in transparent pokes. Did no one fly to Zurich to see what this production was all about? Since the company was not to get out of it what it most coveted—a long, rich role for Gregory—one wonders why it didn't save its money and revive *Grand Pas Glazunov* instead.

Ballet Theatre is weak in middle-rank female soloists—another reason it should have thought twice before putting on *Raymonda*. Only Martine van Hamel, a principal dancer cast in a supporting role, floated above the storm; her several classical variations were fully pronounced and glowing in tone, and her intrepid Spanish number was the salvation of the exotic "character" suite. In *La Bayadère*, the three women's solos were disastrously handled; we did not get Van Hamel (nor are we to get this season her magnificent performance in the leading role). But there was continued improvement in the work of the corps, and Bujones danced with javelin-like precision, though with perhaps a little too much deliberation in the heroic Russian style. Makarova's Nikiya, the best I have seen from her, was troubling in its remoteness and lack of bite until I remembered that Nikiya is a ghost in a world of ghosts and Makarova the kind of dancer who would insist on that. Her way of taking charge of the meaning of an entire ballet, and not just her own role in it, is one of the traits that make her an artist as well as a star. I happen to disagree with her Nikiya, but not with her Chekhovian Caroline in *Jardin aux Lilas*, where her sorrow encompasses all trapped creatures. And she continually renews herself. This year's *Swan Lake* did more than last year's by doing less. The dual portrait was ravishing in its subtlety and mystery—with an Odile neither wittily wicked nor corrupt but guileless in the purity of her evil—and an audience that had come to stamp and yell was cooled to stillness and attention. Makarova did the impossible at Ballet Theatre: she calmed the beast. —*July 28, 1975*

Sweet Love Remembered

Antony Tudor is so often spoken of as the modern master of dance pantomime that other values in his work tend to be overlooked. When he gives us, as he has this season, a modest yet substantial lyrical work with no story interest, it is taken for a departure, and in some respects it is a departure. Yet *The Leaves Are Fading* is much more a return to the enduring strengths of the classic Tudor ballets. What it requires of its dancers—subtle musicality, sustained line, clarity of nuance within a phrase—are also required by *Jardin aux Lilas* and *Pillar of Fire* and *Romeo and Juliet*. The difference is that in the new work these qualities are rendered for their own interest as pure dance qualities; they're not intended to support dramatic meanings. Judging by the ballet's reception at the second performance—the ovation at the première was largely obligatory—Tudor has handed the American Ballet Theatre audience something of a jolt. The ballet is a suite of classical dances based on the theme of the pas de deux. The boy-girl relationships are flatly stated in the beginning, and they never change; the dance reveals more or less depth in some of these relationships than one might expect at first, but it develops no interest from that, and the fact that some of the girls are without partners isn't dramatically stressed. Nor is there much to be gained from the conventions of the genre the piece falls into—the "sweet love remembered" genre. Though this is a link to the classic "Proustian" Tudor, it is the weakest link of all, and in recent years, in the hands of other choreographers, it has become a cliché. Tudor has set the ballet in a forest grove and opened it with a woman's solitary walk across the stage. The woman (Kim Highton) wears a filmy pale-green gown and sniffs a rose. When she exits, dancers in dappled shades of rose and orange wander on from the same direction. After about a half-hour of dancing, the same music is played again and the opening is, in effect, repeated in reverse, with the dancers and then the solitary woman vanishing the way they came. Still young, she has autumn-tinged memories, but this little fortune-cookie sentiment doesn't affect the way we see the piece. Like the sentiment of the piece as a whole, it's only a handle on the action—a handle without much grip to it. Tudor isn't so much concerned with nostalgia for idyllic young lovers as he is with formal tests he contrives for himself and his dancers. Some of those tests are met and some aren't.

The strongest link the piece has to Tudor's great work is its musical construction. The score consists of some unfamiliar Dvořák written for string orchestra; it never gets very emphatic or very loud, and it exerts almost no independent force. The dances closely parallel the music, but they are not carried by it. They are musically transparent and free of the music at the same time. If the floor opened and swallowed the orchestra, the dance could keep going on its own breath. Yet it is the ambience created by the interrelation of dance and music that is meant to be absorbing—and it isn't absorbing for so long a stretch of time. It's not the absence of a story that causes the trouble, although with no dramatic pressure to anchor one's attention the piece slips back into the complacency of its genre. It's just that both in composition and in performance the piece is uneven. Its sensibility is wonderfully fresh and striking from the start, with an opening group dance that doesn't quite pattern. This is a Tudoresque statement, and so is another dance that soon follows, for two girls circling two couples. But the piece doesn't rise to a *major* statement until the entrance of Gelsey Kirkland, about halfway through. Kirkland and her partner, Jonas Kage, have the second of four pas de deux; they also have a solo apiece, and later another pas de deux—an adagio. It's because of these passages that the ballet will be seen and remembered—it has been more than a quarter of a century since Tudor composed like this—but the other dances, which are distinguished without being nearly so exciting, run far too long. Tudor surely knows this, and, as he hasn't cut the piece, he must be hoping it will lift in performance. Much of the material is too difficult for dancers unused to such delicacy and intricacy. Some of it—especially a waltz for four men—looks awkward rather than intricate. I hear that at the next performance the audience response was warmer. The ballet should stay in repertory for as long as it takes the dancers to master it or Tudor to decide that it's hopeless. It isn't a masterpiece, but in the variety of its classical dance shapes and dance sequences and in its curious musical refinement it challenges the company to a new and modern standard of expression. ABT dancers have nothing else like it.

When the story interest in a dramatic Tudor ballet dries up, you can usually watch the choreography for the oddity and elegance of its musical line—it can be looked at abstractly, so to speak. *Pillar of Fire* years ago went dead on me as a drama of cogency and power, but its beauty of design remained provocative until very recently. (Until this season, in fact, when it seemed to have fallen apart completely.) A large share of the credit for that must go to Sallie Wilson, an unusually musical dancer who succeeded Nora Kaye in the central role. Sallie Wilson could keep the ballet alive by a kind of musical faith. Natalia Makarova, when she took the part, dragged me back unwillingly to the drama—unwillingly because, although she revived the life of that drama, she could not persuade me that it was a part of *her* life. Makarova's Hagar was cosmically tormented; she could never have found a solacing love with the dull gentleman caller. Most dancers in Tudor ballets seem to work into their roles backward—from dramatic motivation to dance impetus to musical cue. The musical cues in a Tudor work are often diffuse, lapped over with complex harmonies of composers like Schoenberg, Delius, Mahler. One can't predict where the dance impetus will spring from, but that is what makes the dance interesting. It's what makes *Romeo and Juliet*, which we never see anymore, more interesting than *Undertow*, which we see all the time. In *Romeo and Juliet*, the shifting accents in the Delius score were troublesome to the dancers, which may be the reason it is out of repertory. In *Undertow*, set to a commissioned score by William Schuman, the orchestra keeps up a steady, page-turning parade of motifs for the drama to attach itself to, and all the drama can do is develop some meager psychological insights, largely by way of pantomime. The pantomime is not without images of brilliance, but thirty years after the ballet was created one can still sense in it strain and fatigue, as if Tudor were struggling to redirect the energies that had produced the miasmic *Romeo and Juliet*. *Undertow* and *Dim Lustre* are comparatively simple pieces, and they look as if they were made for critics to write about. If *Dim Lustre* was "Proustian" (Tudor had been called Proustian as early as *Jardin aux Lilas*, which remains his masterpiece), *Undertow*, with its cross-section of a city slum and its characters with names from Greek mythology, was "Joycean"; but the critics got more wrapped up in its subject matter, which deals with the history of a sex murderer, than in literary precedents.

Tudor's eclipse since the forties has not been much written about. He remained active but worked in out-of-the-way places. In 1963, he was welcomed back to glory with a piece created for the Royal Swedish Ballet—*Echoing of Trumpets*. A few years later, he did *Shadowplay* for the Royal Ballet, and, it, too, was clamorously well received. The weakening of dance impetus in respect to story had occurred in Tudor's work long before. The sixties pieces showed also a collapse in respect to music. With that went the keynote of Tudor's style. *Echoing of Trumpets* and *Shadowplay* look like anybody's ballets. The anonymity of these works shocked me the first time I saw them, and when Ballet Theatre revived *Shadowplay* the week after the première of *The Leaves Are Fading*, it shocked me again as the work of Tudor. There has always lurked within Tudor a furtiveness that could be mistaken for sensitivity; *Shadowplay* exploits that aspect to clownish lengths. It's like something done by one of his imitators. An enigma supposedly lies at the center of the ballet's events, but the events are manufactured with such coarse efficiency that long before you know you're not going to guess the secret you don't care what it is. This rusting hunk of junk jewelry was acquired for Mikhail Baryshnikov, with Fernando Bujones scheduled for two performances. Although the Boy with Matted Hair suggests Bujones more than Baryshnikov, it's really a beauty role with little dancing, and it doesn't suit either of them. Gelsey Kirkland, as the Celestial, is as poorly used as she is gratefully used in *The Leaves Are Fading*. The new work is a world removed from *Shadowplay*. Kirkland is more than a leading dancer in it—she's a resource. After twenty-five years, Tudor is composing again for Ballet Theatre, and to see him doing it with confidence and absorption and in such a straightforward manner is as much a pleasure as it is a surprise.

New York City Ballet and American Ballet Theatre have developed specialty acts by which to dramatize their prevailing strengths and their need of money. New York City Ballet flashes its world-championship certificates in choreography by putting on Ravel festivals; Ballet Theatre flaunts its unparalleled roster of stars in gala performances. Last week's ABT gala was like an all-star version of a Moscow or Varna international competition, and for those who couldn't get in, two recently available films of the Moscow (1969) and Varna (1966) competitions may provide partial consolation. There is really not much more substance to Baryshnikov's celebrated solo *Vestris* than there is in the fragment we get of it in the Moscow film, *The World's Young Ballet*, and its so much a mime solo that it might better have been called *Garrick*. What's thrilling about it is Baryshnikov's ability to switch in the flash of a second from absolute frenzy to absolute calm, or from states of hilarity to states of gloom, or from buoyant youth to doddering old age. It's a kind of mime equivalent to the invisible preparations in his dancing. Martine van Hamel's dancing in Kenneth MacMillan's *Solitaire* won her a gold medal at Varna and portions of her performance can be seen on CBS's *Camera Three* on August 24. The solo is about a girl who imagines her friendships. At the gala it was done against a black backcloth that opened into portières. Using no other visual aid, Van Hamel populated the stage. Both in imaginative projection and in the fullness of the dancing (there are two superb sweeps through rond de jambe into a high penchée arabesque on a flat foot) it is a remarkable performance.

Kirkland in *Le Corsaire* is not on any film I know of; but she's as much an exemplar of this role in the seventies as Alla Sizova was in the sixties. In her solo, Kirkland several times swings from high développé in second into a double pirouette en dedans into arabesque into another double en dedans. It's all from one preparation and it's only the beginning. Her partner on this night was guest artist Rudolf Nureyev, at his grandest and most gracious. Nureyev was the world's greatest *Corsaire* hero in the sixties, and he is the greatest today. He may lurch a bit going into a turning jump, but the role draws from him the animal intensity that his own sappy choreography in *Raymonda* and *The Sleeping Beauty* obscures. At the end of the ballet, he slams himself to the floor at the ballerina's feet and yearns upward from the small of his back. No one else does it so well.

A gala program like this takes in a quota of formless stunts along with the fine dancing, and someone should have put an embargo on fouettés. Still, it was needlessly self-critical of the management to open with the first scene of Tudor's *Gala Performance*, a savage satire on the backstage manners of three hypothetical divas of the 1890's, and it was especially hard on Noëlla Pontois, who was making her American début, to be introduced as one of these silly monsters minutes before having to perform the *Don Quixote* pas de deux with Baryshnikov. If I were a ballerina, I would avoid this grimly exhibitionistic number like the plague. Little Miss Pontois is a seasoned professional but not a ballerina of class, and she can't pump iron as if it were crystal. On the next evening, she had a fine role in *La Bayadère*, but her weak insteps deprived her of spring and balance.

Other novelties of interest on the gala program included *A Promise*, a romantic pas de deux choreographed for Kirkland by a New York City Ballet colleague, Robert Weiss. The material is pretty enough and hard enough, nothing more; but Kirkland, partnered by Ivan Nagy, made it look like gala material. New to me was a Bournonville trio from *La Ventana*; staged by Erik Bruhn, it gave Cynthia Gregory a chance to show how well she can dance Bournonville and Nureyev a chance to show how well he can't. The evening closed on a grand sentimental note with the return of Alicia Alonso to her former company after fifteen years. Now in her high fifties, Alonso has legs and feet that would be a credit to a ballerina thirty years younger. Tenderly assisted by her partner, Jorge Esquivel, she went through the white adagio from *Swan Lake*, and then through an amazing series of choreographed bows while the crowd paid her a queen's homage.   —*August 11, 1975*

An American Giselle

Last summer, Mikhail Baryshnikov made his American début partnering Natalia Makarova in *Giselle* with the American Ballet Theatre. Makarova "sponsored" Baryshnikov in that performance, and a year later almost to the day Baryshnikov did the same for Gelsey Kirkland in her New York début as Giselle. In different ways, both débutants enjoyed a triumph that seemed guaranteed in advance. There was nothing to do but wait for the performance to bring it about. Baryshnikov would have had his triumph in any role that let him soar, but in Kirkland's case it was the perfect apposition of star and role that was a fait accompli. In the nearly forty years that we have had *Giselle* in the American repertory, we haven't lacked great interpreters, but we have lacked a great American-born Giselle. Kirkland may be the first totally credible American Giselle since the ballet was first danced here, in the nineteenth century. The role has been taken by brilliant American ballerinas, but none seems to have fit inside its Russo-European tradition as Kirkland does. And this isn't just because, partnered by Baryshnikov and modeling her conception on Makarova's, Kirkland has made herself look almost as if she, too, came from the Kirov; it's because she's a natural Giselle, whose chrysalis is the immediate influence upon her of these two great Russian stars. I wouldn't be surprised if, as she grows accustomed to the part, she were to shake off some of the more pious Kirovisms, such as the very slow tempo of the second-act adagio. A deliberate act of emulation, the performance is already impressive for its lack of excrescence. Kirkland has borrowed only as much as conforms with her instinct, and that instinct is profound. I predict that when she reaches her full wingspread in the part, she will have made the connection between the Russo-European Romanticism of the ballet and the romantic mythology of American melodrama even clearer than it is now.

Kirkland is a natural Giselle the way other Americans are natural Myrthas—by reason of Freudian biological destiny. But it's not only that the role underscores her airiness and fragility; it also enhances the archetypal echoes in her personality. As Giselle, Kirkland is more Lillian Gish-like than ever; she even seems to be playing a Gish role. She also has, again by nature, a plainness and stringency of manner in the way she presents a role, a fastidious taste that withdraws before "romantic" excess. All this has, I think, a peculiar appeal to Americans, especially to young Americans new to ballet. For old-timers, Kirkland just now brings no burst of originality to the part, but that is as it should be. She doesn't jar the marvelous singular clarity of the picture she presents; she awakens an extinct cameo image and lets us play with its reverberations. There is no suspense over "interpretation." She forgives her Albrecht as she dies, and that's that. Though it by no means sets the capstone on what she has achieved as an artist, Kirkland's appearance in *Giselle* is a promise fulfilled. Every ballerina, they say, dreams of dancing Giselle, but very few of them can, as Kirkland has, take the role as if by birthright.

In the first performance, there were a few technical uncertainties, most of them having to do with the spacing of entrances and exits

within the set. Erratic conducting marred the first-act solo. There
was a moment at the start of the solo when eye contact between
Kirkland and Baryshnikov lapsed, but it's an indication of how well
they were performing together that the lapse should have been felt.
I expect that by the second performance these errors had been corrected. So, too, the descent from the two overhead lifts, which on
the first night was chancy both times. Baryshnikov is a much more
relaxed Albrecht than he was a year ago or even last winter. His
acting is free and unguarded, yet rhythmically taut, and there's a
new and keener flow of volubility between him and Kirkland, which
also showed in their *La Sylphide* this season. The dancing pours
out of the mime as if in a fever of pent-up eloquence. The diagonal
of brisés toward Myrtha with open, pleading hands has never been
stronger in its emotional impact, and the lily-strewn ending, with
its symbolic transference of Giselle's spirit into the bouquet that
scatters, never more lucid.

The third member of this superb cast was Martine van Hamel.
Tall and luscious, Van Hamel dances Myrtha as the great ballerina
role it is. The grandeur of her carriage makes even a simple rhythmic
port de bras, such as the one she does standing in a cluster of Wilis,
an exciting dance experience, and when she advances on a majestic
tide of sautés en arabesque those treetop arms of hers both clear her
path and cross it in momentary blockages. She gives Myrtha a
divided nature—she's no one-dimensional dry-ice villainess.

Van Hamel is the company's most dramatic classical dancer. She
shows us the drama of classicism as a drama of poetic suggestion, not
a drama of peril. At Ballet Theatre, you frequently see dancers,
gifted and ungifted, trying to reduce classical phraseology to one
bright element—the piqué balance or the extra twirl—that the
audience can read as a blanket meaning. They have acrobatic daring, but they don't have the large understanding that Van Hamel
has of the compound imagery of a classical phrase—its ability to
express several meanings at once. At times, at ecstatic peak moments,
Van Hamel gets swept away on the crosscurrent of her text; she
goes emotionally high on the movement and, apparently, regrets it
later. Recently, she told a *Soho Weekly News* interviewer that she
felt her Black Swan was "too young and too happy." But the multi-
dimensional logic of classicism allows for Van Hamel's happiness,
and we're as happy as she is that she can express that logic so well.
Van Hamel uses her weight and size fearlessly to magnify the fluid

changes of balance and proportion of which she is such a mistress. She is the perfect Petipa dancer—squarely based, obliquely reinforced, yet temperate, rounded, and soft. In the title nonrole of *Raymonda*, she made sense of every moment that fell to her; and every moment that didn't—and there were quite a few—found her cheerfully content. Van Hamel's movement is big and honest "commenting" movement. Very beautifully, she showed you the exact point of all the *Raymonda* variations and also the exactness of the monotony with which they are arranged. She couldn't save the ballet, but it was one of her largest and sunniest performances, and at the end there was an ovation. As the season closed, the audience seemed at last to be catching on to Van Hamel's magic. Several fans even threw flowers—a sure sign.   —*August 18, 1975*

The End of the Line

The Broadway shows *A Chorus Line* and *Chicago* are dance musicals, in the sense that both were devised and directed by choreographers—*A Chorus Line* by Michael Bennett and *Chicago* by Bob Fosse. I don't think anyone is going to the shows just for the dances, because these aren't distinguished and, curiously enough, they don't aim to be. Choreographer-directed shows, in which the choreography works as an element in the staging, have been with us for a long time, and so has the choreographer as a triple threat—not only arranging the dances and directing the show but also in whole or in part "conceiving" it (as the credit line usually says). But not until now has the viewpoint of the choreographer-director-conceiver taken over the function ordinarily assumed by the writer of a show's book. *Chicago*, which is based, not very soundly, on Maurine Watkins's 1926 play of that title, has a book by Fosse and the lyricist Fred Ebb, but anyone who has seen such former Fosse productions as the film *Cabaret* and the show and film *Sweet Charity* will immediately recognize in *Chicago* the imprint of Fosse the *auteur*. And the circumstances that led to the creation of *A Chorus Line* are already famous. In a *Times* interview shortly after the show opened, downtown at the Public, Mel Gussow printed the following:

Mr. Bennett, who began his career dancing in the chorus (at seventeen in Subways Are for Sleeping), *met with twenty-four dancers. "We danced for hours," he recalled, ". . . and then we went into a room and talked about it. I wanted to know why they had started dancing. In a sense, I wanted to know why I had started—and hadn't I lost something along the way?"*

From this original, long rap session gradually grew A Chorus Line. *Before a word of the show was written, he chose his cast. . . . "It is their lives," Mr. Bennett said, referring to the performers, "although they are not necessarily telling their own stories. A couple of stories about my youth are there." From this material and their own imaginations, James Kirkwood and Nicholas Dante began fashioning a book.*

The book that Kirkwood and Dante fashioned may be said to have the banality of truth, but it also has the banality of show business. The show takes the form of an audition: seventeen dancers line up, give their résumés, and answer questions put to them from the dark by the choreographer-director (Robert LuPone) about why they started dancing. This inquisition is never rebelled against; one might almost think it part of any Broadway open call. And in fact it has been a part of Bennett's continuing auditions for replacements in the show and for second casts. A *Times* follow-up story reports, " 'How did your family feel about your being in theatre?' Michael Bennett, who conceived the show and was running the audition, asked." In the real as well as the staged audition, the dancers respond to Why did you start? and How did they feel? with the stock answers: I used to dance in front of the mirror. I put shows on in the garage. I got interested in my sister's dancing classes. My mother pushed me into it. My parents were unhappy. I had to get out of Buffalo. I saw *The Red Shoes.* But this small change of dancers' biographies grows into the common currency of commercial theatre when the contestants start hitting the "truth" part of the game. In quite a few Broadway and Off-Broadway shows of recent years, the action consists of people coming together in tight situations and confessing. In Harold Prince's *Follies,* a musical that was choreographed and codirected by Michael Bennett, the characters spent a great deal of time raking up the past and accusing themselves and each other of misspent lives. *A Chorus Line* is nothing like this orgy of disembowelment, but it takes its cue from it, both in the setting (a dark, empty theatre) and in the assumption that recitals of past humiliations are synonymous with character revelation. The dancer-characters of A Chorus Line are in their twenties or just past thirty, and what they reveal of their lives are their childhood encounters with sex or the pain they felt at being "different" or their resentment of parents and teachers who did them dirt—all fairly innocuous stuff by Broadway standards but mediocre stuff by any sterner standard. When the show is over, we have our choice of two conclusions—either that we haven't discovered who these people are or that they're actually as shallow as the show makes them out to be. Those who go to A Chorus Line hoping to learn something about chorus dancers, their life and work, will gain approximately as clear an insight as could be had from the All About Eve musical adaptation Applause, in which the same sort of energetic, desperate, hard-bitten youngsters were on view playing supposedly fresh and charming chorus boys and girls. A Chorus Line is a little like Applause crossed with The Boys in the Band; as in the latter show, there's an array of representative types—the cast is a statistical sampling of ethnic and geographical origins, class divisions, and levels of professional experience—but all this variety has no expression in the performances. Nearly everybody is overearnest and strained or cute-tough; the only character who doesn't fit the Broadway-juvenile mold is the cool, wisecracking Miss Been Around, and she's a fixture of long standing in the backstage musicals we used to know.

The powerful illusion of this show and the source of its appeal are that dancers are onstage playing out their own lives. Bennett keeps the pressure-cooker intensity of the audition building even unto the final judgment, when the dancers who are asked to step forward turn out to be the ones who have been rejected. (Good old false suspense; it worked in The Red Shoes, too.) One illusion the show can't sustain is the worthiness of a dancing career on Broadway; especially at the chorus level, conditions haven't been so bad since the days when show dancing consisted of hack routines that the able-bodied could pick up overnight. Vocational miseries creep into the show in the plight of Cassie (Donna McKechnie), a failed star trying to come back by starting again in the chorus, and in the plight of Paul, who loses his place in the lineup when he injures his knee, and in the plight of all of them when they hold a solemn symposium on the subject "What do we do when we can't dance any more?" (with lines like "Dreams don't pay the rent"). There's a polemical tinge to the aggrieved feelings that pile up, and Edward Kleban's lyrics—which, together with Bennett's staging, are the best element in the show—make sardonic use of these feelings in several comedy numbers. One girl sings about a Method-acting course that nearly destroyed her, but nobody sings about the aesthetic content of the dancing that they are asked to do. It doesn't take more than a few visits to musical shows to see what the real tragedy of the dancer is. He's inherited a vacuum. His training, compared to what it was even ten years ago, is weak, his tunes are uninspired, his choreography is stale, and his performing style is corrupt. *A Chorus Line* is one of the shows that reveal this sad state of affairs, and one of the saddest things in it is the dancers' vision of Broadway as a refuge for talent, a haven where you can still shine even though you won't become a ballerina or a star. The emotional tone of the show isn't rousing—it's sweaty and sad—and when the cast recovers its spirits with a hymn to the theatre which is meant to wipe away all anxieties and regrets ("What I Did for Love"), and when those spirits are pumped still higher in the grand finale ("One"), I don't believe in it.

This finale and a solo for Cassie are the only two real efforts at choreographing dances which Bennett makes, and his craft is nothing a dancer can live on. "One" is a conflation of Rockettes-style line dancing and the kind of supercool mannerisms that are primarily associated with Fosse (in fact, it looks very much like a Ben Vereen number from *Pippin*). The solo, in which Cassie tries to prove what she's got if only she can have a chance to use it, is one of the sorest letdowns of the show. The choreography is frantic and unfocused, and McKechnie, who has the most evenly developed technique in the company, *can't* show what she's got. The firm, lifted upper torso, clear waist, and columnar neck that look so lovely when she's standing still are never brought into play by the dance, and she stiffens her back against the jagged phrasing. The other dancers are technically weak in every kind of movement that they can't use peak force to control, such as a high kick or a turn; they have neither an easy rhythm nor a convincingly nervous one. The Fosseisms, which glue the feet to the floor and keep the center of the body pinched against the pelvis, conceal their awkwardness, but they're also seen competing in the various combinations that form the obstacle course of the audition (ballet, Latin jazz, tap).

These combinations are given just the way they would be in a real audition. In the ballet combination, which is taken across the floor four dancers at a time, each lurching quartet performs a gag extraneous to the dancing, though it would be more honest to let the dancing be the gag. For a show built around dancers, A *Chorus Line* is loath to release any of its meanings through dance. Perhaps Bennett doesn't feel much of a commitment to dance as a source of expression. There's a terrible dialogue scene, painful in its factitiousness, in which Cassie and the choreographer-director, who are former lovers, have one of those career-versus-romance quarrels, and he tells her she never understood what his career meant to him— how if he succeeded he wouldn't be "stuck just making up dances." The dances in A *Chorus Line* show us exactly how dreary a fate that would be.

Bennett's talent is evident in the tight pace of the show and the smooth integration of the various confessional arias. Some of these are spoken or sung without interruption; in others the staging splinters and intercuts the material in such a way as to transcend its bathos. And Bennett's staging of "One" transcends his own trite choreography. His device is repetition. So many repeats take place before Robin Wagner's mirrored backdrop (which reverses to disclose a gold-and-silver sunrise) that the formula steps are dramatized into an eternal ritual, an apotheosis of routine. The chorus line seems to stretch into infinity doing its same dumb dance—the only dance that Broadway knows.

Although the limitations of Bob Fosse's dance style became obvious long ago, it is still the pervasive style of Broadway. Its method of closing down and hugging the figure so that the only way it can move is by isolating and preciously featuring anatomical parts makes it a good vehicle for narcissistic display and slithering innuendo. *Chicago* cheapens the style even further, but the style is only part of the décor in a generally cheap and vicious show. The tale of a dizzy chorus girl who shoots her lover and then showboats to fame on the publicity surrounding the trial might have made an excellent musical; the song-and-dance styles of the era come practically ready-made. But Chicago in the twenties was probably too easy a subject for Fosse to get wound up in. He has expanded the yellow press and the shyster lawyers of Cook County's worst decade into malign forces with perennial roots in American life. You won't catch anyone doing the Charleston in Fosse's *Chicago*; this is a universal allegory, and Roxie Hart is Arturo Ui.

Even with this preposterous overload to carry, the story might still have worked if there had been some wit and tension in the writing, but there isn't one line that scalds, one clever characterization or turn of plot. Instead, there are wormwood jokes in the staging, like the one about the innocent imprisoned girl who goes up a circus ladder while the band plays merrily and then swings from the gallows in silhouette. *Chicago* goes beyond *Cabaret* in the putrescent horrors of the life it puts before us; I think it goes beyond any other show I have ever seen. Fosse tells us that we not only permit evil to flourish in our midst but actively enjoy it and love making stars out of scheming whores like Roxie Hart. In both its shock imagery and its scabrous text, the show is a frontal assault on the audience. The lawyer (well played by Jerry Orbach) sings a song called "Razzle Dazzle," the burden of which is that with a little glitter before its eyes the public can always be fooled and any no-talent can get by if he knows the tricks. When Roxie and her girlfriend from murderesses' row reach the big time in their vaudeville act at the end of the show, they toss roses to the audience, because "you made us what we are." The cynicism is appalling, but the audience takes the bait and applauds as if it were really being complimented. Fosse knows all the tricks; does he want us to think he's a no-talent whose success has been too easy?

With Fosse, as with many choreographer-directors, the image seems to come first, then the meaning that will support it. Many of his images in *Chicago* are unsteadily supported, because he is trying to force a correspondence between Chicago and pre-Nazi Berlin which has no basis in reality. Roxie's husband, a sad fat man, is given a solo in a clown rig that makes him resemble Emil Jannings in *The Blue Angel*. *Chicago* is full of odd, elusive conceits like this, which keep it from being boring and may cause people to think of it as a well-staged show, but it's really an overstaged show—the height of theatrical decadence; everything that we're meant to react to is in the staging. It's strange to think of Fosse as the last German Expressionist—strange that his own decadence as an artist should take such a visually corny and alien form. With Liza Minnelli in the role of Roxie for the next few weeks, the link to *Cabaret* is strengthened, but Liza Minnelli is so easy to take that Fosse's conception of the role is vitiated by her presence. Minnelli is a warm, happy performer whose eagerness to please the audience contradicts Fosse's intention of affronting it. She just can't offend. When she throws the roses, at least part of the applause is a response to her personally. I haven't seen Gwen Verdon do the part, but she doesn't seem to have had much dancing in it; all the strenuous stuff is handled by the hard-working, cheerless Chita Rivera.

Dancers and choreographers were once credited with raising the standards of the musical, but that was in an era when those standards were already high. Music on Broadway has declined along with dance; the two are interdependent. When an art form is in trouble, its practitioners may grow self-serious in an effort to assert the stature of their work. Many show people are looking deep into themselves for something to say and finding that the only subject they know is show business. A *Chorus Line* and *Chicago* are about show business, and each reflects an attempt to make the subject rise to some level of significance above mere entertainment. Musicals are proclaiming their stature; now they're being taken with solemnity by people who never could take them at all.   —*August 25, 1975*

Momentous

A masterpiece by definition transcends its time, but even masterpieces are created in response to some need of the moment. Perhaps it would be more true to say that a masterpiece doesn't so much transcend its time as perpetuate it; it keeps its moment alive. In *The Four Temperaments*, revived at the New York City Ballet after some years out of repertory, the moment is luminously there. In *Danses Concertantes*, the moment eludes me. Although Eugene Berman's frontcloth says 1944, the program says "New choreography by George Balanchine," and what Balanchine in part created and in part reconstructed for his revival in 1972 doesn't add up to a major work either of the forties or of the seventies. To read about the original *Danses Concertantes*, which starred Alexandra Danilova and Frederic Franklin with the Ballet Russe de Monte Carlo, is to anticipate a joyous tease of a ballet—modest, light, and playful. The new *Danses Concertantes* is clearly modest, but it's also remote and sourish, and the Berman décor, much praised in its day, is something of a shock. (At the last performance of the ballet's run this season, the unaccountably gloomy backdrop had been removed.) Of the pas de deux for the two stars, I can only assume that it has been entirely rechoreographed, and indifferent casting from 1972 onward hasn't helped me see what Edwin Denby in 1944 described as a "happy flirtation." The much improved Robert Weiss and the highly promising Daniel Duell both danced the man's role this season, but neither as yet has the impact of a star or the quality that Denby said Franklin projected in the part—"the fatuousness of a happy male." Even if they'd had those things, that's still only one half of a flirtation.

Yet if there is a time capsule embedded in this remade *Danses Concertantes*, I would guess it to be the third pas de trois (which Berman dressed in lavender). With one man supporting two stork-legged women in doubled arabesques penchées, it has the robust chic and the rippling erotic tension we associate with high-style Balanchine, and it has also a kind of systematic visual punning, an intertwining of echoes and cross-references, that distinguishes his greatest work of the forties. What a monumental decade it was! Balanchine by then was established in America, but not solidly established; from *Concerto Barocco* and *Ballet Imperial* on through *The Four Temperaments* to *Theme and Variations* and *Symphony in C* he is on the attack. His objective: to make plain to American audiences the dynamics of classical style. In each of these ballets, the dancing grows from simple to complex structures, and every stage of growth is consequentially related to every other. It is partly because of their structural logic that his ballets make such great sense—or such vivid nonsense—to us years after they were completed, but it's also because such logic isn't the featured attraction; it's only the means by which a particular kind of entertainment is elucidated. What *is* featured is human variety.

This is true even of *The Four Temperaments*, one of the earliest works in which the elements of logic are arrayed in a form so brilliantly consequential that they nearly become the whole show. The relation between the continuity of the piece and its subject, which is the four varieties of human temperament (melancholic, sanguine, phlegmatic, choleric), is truly a magical one, consisting of a dance logic Balanchine has made look uniquely ritualistic. It isn't ritualistic in an exotic sense, it is ritual achieved by the most radical exposure of classical style Balanchine had provided to date. *The Four Tem-*

peraments, created in 1946, marks one of Balanchine's several "beginnings," and, like *Apollo,* his first collaboration with Stravinsky, and *Serenade,* his first ballet for American dancers, it is a messianic work, which conveys to this day the sense of a brilliant and bold new understanding. Hindemith's score, subtitled "Theme with Four Variations (According to the Four Temperaments) for String Orchestra and Piano," was written to Balanchine's commission in 1940, but it was not until the formation of Ballet Society, following the Second World War, that Balanchine composed his choreography. After years of working on Broadway, in Hollywood, and for ballet organizations not his own, he was again in charge of a company, and in his first ballet for Ballet Society (the direct predecessor of the New York City Ballet) he made a fresh start, reestablishing the bases and the direction of American dance. Nowadays, *The Four Temperaments* (carelessly billed without the *The,* as if there could be more than four) doesn't appear novel in the way it did to observers of that time; its "distortions" and "angularities" have been absorbed into one important stream of Balanchine ballet and have been imitated the world over. But its style, in both root and blossom, is so consistent and so consistently keen to the eye, and the scale on which it flowers is so active in its leaps from tiny to enormous and back again, that one follows the progress of the ballet in wonder; it never fails to surprise and to refresh. And so it is new every time.

Going back to basics in 1946, Balanchine concentrated his attention equally on the smallest details and the largest resources of classical dance and on making transitions from one to the other clearer, perhaps, than they'd ever been before. When, in the opening statement of the ballet—the first part of the Theme—we see a girl, supported on her points, turning from side to side and transferring her weight from one foot to the other as she turns, we see her do it with a finicky grace: she lifts and lowers the free foot, curls it around the standing leg, and carefully flexes it before arching to full point. We see, in short, a foot becoming a point—nature being touched to artificial life. The detail looms for an instant, then quickly takes its place in the grand scheme of the ballet. The Theme is full of elementary particles, jostling, caroming, crisscrossing space in strokes that define the boundaries of the territory Balanchine will invade. In the Theme's second statement (there are three such statements, each a pas de deux), the side-to-side turns have become full revolutions, rapid finger-turns marked off by the girl's point as it taps the floor. In the third statement, the finger-turns are taken in deep plié with one foot held off the ground in passé position. The weight on that one supporting point looks crushing, but, as we have seen, there is something about a woman's point that makes it not a foot —that makes it a sign. The image created by the third girl as she is spun is blithe, even comical; could Balanchine have been thinking of the bass fiddle the forties jazz player spins after a chorus of hot licks?

The developing sense of the passages I've cited is analogous to the process that takes place in the molding of a classical dancer's body. The "story" of *The Four Temperaments* is precisely that story—the subjection of persons to a process and their re-emergence as human archetypes—but these citations may make it seem as if that process happened all in closeup, and if that were true we would be in a crazy man's world. The world of *The Four Temperaments* is wide and swarming with possibilities, yet if we could pass the choreography through a computer to see how many core gestures there actually are, there would probably not be more than six— maybe eight. Balanchine has built a large and dense composition on a handful of cellular motifs, and it's this economy that allows us to perceive the ballet and survive it, too. There are gestures that seem to cluster in family relationships and that recur subtly trans- formed. How many elaborations are there on grand battement en balançoire? How many derivations from, adaptations of, combinations with? Some of these we see clearly, others hang just at the edge of vision. There are gestures that do not change at all—they're like stabilizing props that keep back the tide. One of these is the "Egyptian profile" with squared elbows; another is the women's splits across the men's thighs (but this, too, is an evolution—from the first pas de deux: the girl dropped in a split to the floor and slid into the wings). Balan- chine's control of the action's subliminal force allows us the most mar- vellous play in our minds; we're torn in an agony of delight between what we see and what we think we see. Metaphoric implications flash by, achieve their bright dazzle of suggestion, and subside into simple bodily acts. The way the women stab the floor with their points or hook their legs around men's waists or grip their partners' wrists in lifts—images of insatiable hunger, or functional necessities? Balan- chine gives us a sharp pair of spectacles to see with, but he occasionally fogs one of the lenses. If he didn't, we'd perish from the glare.

And that lens we see with—isn't it a moving lens, a camera eye? Darting in for details, withdrawing to lofty heights, it views the dance from as many perspectives as the body can indicate in its manifold placements within space. Space itself is liquefied, and planes on which we observe the dance rise, tilt, descend. Sometimes we are launched and roving in this liquid space; sometimes we are pressed, riveted, to the floor. Out of these volatile perspectives drama is made. In the first variation (Melancholic), we have an expansive field of vision, but the solo dancer does not seem to know how much room he has. His space is penetrated by menacing diagonals for the entries of the corps. The corps is a few small girls, a small menace. But they are enough to block and frustrate his every attempt to leap free. He leaps and crumples to earth. We recognize this man: his personal weather is always ceiling zero. (It's a nineteenth- rather than a seventeenth-century conception of melancholy—Young Werther rather than Robert Burton.) In the Sanguinic variation, for a virtuoso ballerina and her partner, the vista is wide, the ozone pure and stinging. The ballerina is an allegro technician; she is also a character. She enters and pauses. Her partner is expectant. But she pauses and turns her gaze back toward the wings. For a moment she seems to wear a demure black velvet neck ribbon, and then she is bounding like a hare in the chase, an extrovert after all. The Sanguinic variation takes us to the top of the world, and twice we ride around its crest, its polar summit (a circuit of lifts at half-height). In these two thrilling flights, the camera eye pivots on the pinpoint of a spiral, once to end the trajectory, once to start it. We see, as in some optical effect of old cinema, a scene spread from the center of its compass, then respread in reverse.

The topography of the ballet shrinks in the Phlegmatic variation to the smallest it has been since the Theme. Phlegmatic is indolent, tropical, given to detached contemplation, to pretentious vices. The male soloist languishes, and loves it. Slowly he picks up invisible burdens, lifts them, and clothes himself in their splendor. Slowly, self-crowned, he picks up his right foot and studies it. His little dance with the corps includes cabalistic gestures toward "his" floor, and he hovers close to the ground, repeating his mumbo-jumbo (a syncopated time step) as if he expected the ground to answer him. The confined, floor-conscious world of Phlegmatic and Melancholic returns redeemed in the next section, when Choleric, that angry goddess, executes her climactic ronds de jambe par terre. Here we have the traditional dénouement of an eighteenth-century ballet (or such a nineteenth-century one as *Sylvia*), in which Mount Olympus hands down a judgment on the mess mortals have made. Choleric enters in a burst of fanfares and flourishes, kicking the air. Her fury must be appeased, assimilated by the ballet's blood-stream. The entire cast collaborates in the process. Key motifs are recapitulated in tempi that charge them with new vitality. We are racing toward the finality of a decision, and then it comes. Those ronds de jambe are a space- and air-clearing gesture. Three circles traced on the ground: it is the most wonderful of the ballet's magic signs; the vastness of it incorporates all bodies into one body, all worlds into one planet. After a silence in which nobody moves, the great fugue of the finale begins its inexorable massed attack. All the parts the ballet is made of are now seen at once in a spectacle of grand-scale assimilation. Apotheosis. We see a succession of sky-sweeping lifts; we see a runway lined by a chorus of grands battements turned to the four points of the compass. The lifts travel down the runway and out as the curtain falls.

As a conception for a ballet, the four temperaments, or humors of the blood, have been realized with a profundity that doesn't depend on the intellectual powers of either the audience or the dancers. Balanchine has interpreted the subject in the form of a dance fantasy, but never so literally or so schematically that we need fear, if we miss one element, having missed all. We can trust the ballet in performance because it is built of the things that dancers as a race know about. No small part of its moral beauty comes directly from the dancers, from their fastidious concentration, their ghetto pride. Yet in *The Four Temperaments*, as in every ballet, casting does make a difference. This season, the perfect cast was Bart Cook in Melancholic, Merrill Ashley in Sanguinic, Jean-Pierre Bonnefous in Phlegmatic, and Colleen Neary in Choleric— all of them new to their roles, and all hitting new highs in their careers. For dancers and audience alike, the ballet represents the cleansing and healing that Robert Frost speaks of in "Directive" when he says, "Here are your waters and your watering place./Drink and be whole again beyond confusion."   —*December 8, 1975*

She That Plays the Queen

Hérodiade, a Martha Graham ballet of 1944, is a dialogue between two women, one of them conceived on the scale of the passionate heroines of French classical drama, and the other a secondary figure just as classical—an attendant who is both maid and confidante. The first woman is poised on the brink of her destiny (the nature of which we do not discover); the second acts as a focus of the ancestral forces that would drag the heroine back from that brink. The action follows a strict classical sequence: long movement "speeches" in turn by each woman, with little or no physical contact between them. The two never dance together, and the drama never assumes the character or the clarity of an intimate struggle. We are meant to have instead a continuous throbbing sense of the enormous fate, ever more rousing and more ominous, that is engulfing the heroine, and a sense, too, of her stoic courage in embracing it. And although the scene is set for two dancers, it is really a picture of one consciousness that we get. Toward the end, the maid dresses her lady, or, rather, undresses her: an outer garment is removed, revealing the martyr's robe, with its pierced heart and pendant drops of blood; a black cloak is prepared for the final investiture. *Hérodiade* is less a drama than it is a dramatic poem—austere in its devices, noble in its aspirations, and in its human perspectives implicitly tragic. It deals with one of Graham's great themes, the attainment of selfhood. But its special distinction is that it is transparently and perhaps preeminently a Graham vehicle. Without her, it lacks substance—it lacks a text. What Graham contributed in the way of a text was her own presence. The steps themselves are a vague notation of the way she must have looked and moved. They don't even constitute the material of a role; they are—or were for Graham—a series of opportunities for creating the material in performance.

Hérodiade is not a young woman's ballet, and Pearl Lang, who danced it in the Graham company's revival at the Mark Hellinger, is only a few years past the age Graham had reached when she first did the role. Graham training has a tendency to breed young hags;

Pearl Lang is an elder ingénue. Always one of the blandest of dancers, she remains in her maturity Graham's antithesis. Her dancing is not feeble; it has the vigor of docility. But she seems made for peaceful elegies, not these large, ideal images of self-immolation. In her performance, the Woman was defined statically as a victim; the twisting paths of what the current program calls "a dance of choice" were illuminated only in flashes. When she posed downstage right in profile to the audience, she didn't make it apparent that Noguchi's home-base prop, a standing mirror (actually, a construction resembling Picasso's *Girl Before a Mirror*), *is* a mirror and that it holds some significance for the Woman. Still, this production, the first revival by the company since Graham's own performances, was better than the one by the Batsheva company of Israel seen here a few years ago, in which nothing at all was illuminated. The Attendant was given a strong performance by Susan McGuire, and Robert Irving's conducting of Paul Hindemith's score had tension. Miss Lang was at her most convincing in passages of persuasion or consolation directed toward the other character, when she could draw support from the exchange. (It was almost as if she wished there were something at issue the two of them could thrash out.) And she reacted—and allowed us to react—to Graham's catalytic use of costume, especially to the implications of reversing a skirt to sheathe the body in a new color. These were clear moments of "choice." The balance of force between the two women was very clear. But about half the ballet was uncreated. The exceptional austerity of its design turned arid and featureless. The dialogue of self and soul—that monodrama of the isolated superior mind, which was surely Graham's objective in composing the work—was not on the Hellinger stage.

Hindemith wrote and titled his score after Mallarmé's poem "Hérodiade," which has speaking parts for Herodias, her Nurse, and John the Baptist, who appears in a brief monologue at the end. Graham's original title for the ballet was *Mirror Before Me* ("Tiens devant moi ce miroir," Hérodiade commands la Nourrice); it was changed at Hindemith's request. Her choreography bears as little relation to Mallarmé as Nijinsky's for *L'Après-Midi d'un Faune.* She takes the poem's characters and its iconographic setting and transforms them into elements of her personal mythology. The tragic queen in her bedchamber, the lady-in-waiting, the mirror, the rite of preparation for "une chose inconnue"—all the things

that in Mallarmé converge in a meditation on the venereal abyss
—become in Graham a fused set of attitudes, an apparatus for the
projection of heroic theatre as a vocation. Vocation implies ordeal,
self-election, sacrifice. Even John the Baptist is a part of this unified
conception; his blood flows in the heroine's martyrdom. *Hérodiade*
the ballet is about aspiring to grandeur in the theatre and becoming
worthy of it. Graham in 1944 was recognized as America's greatest
tragedienne, and in this work we see her casting herself in the
classical mold of greatness—some Rachel or Bernhardt entering
upon Racine. The queen's apartment, the actress's dressing room
are the same arena of choice. But it is the dancer's genius to
demonstrate choice, to show being and becoming. What dancer
but Graham could have done it? Who else would have used
performance as rehearsal?

Graham in a different way had done the same thing the year before
in *Deaths and Entrances*. In that work, the heroine liberated her
consciousness; she shook the bars of her Victorian prison, swallowed
her purgative drafts, fought madness, and became more and more
herself. Graham wrote her own nineteenth-century script, imagining
herself as if produced by Belasco. In *Hérodiade*, she is as if produced by Lugné-Poë. These are vanities to which she was entitled
by reason of her gifts, but she was aware of their dangers—that
they could seem tainted, however deliciously, by the glamour and
hysteria of stardom. In *Dark Meadow*, also revived this season, she
achieved her largest and most direct statement of sacrifice and
renewal, and without recourse to the histrionic traditions of the
past. *Dark Meadow* (1946) is an extravaganza of preconscious
emotion, all rumbling subterranean fantasy. There is no way to
grasp its meaning unless one allows its intense subjectivity to meet
one's own unrestrained conscience. Although *Dark Meadow* is an
enigma, Graham, like so many great women artists, withholds
nothing; she shows you everything, whether she understands it or
not. *Dark Meadow* is at first sight an easy test of one's formal
knowledge. It's a fertility rite taking place in some southern territory
such as primeval Mexico, and it describes the acculturation of an
alien individual (the Graham figure) through sex. Some parts of it
—the phallic symbolism in particular—look blatantly prefabricated.
But the most interesting aspect of the piece is the aspect Graham
herself doesn't understand. Her insistent openness and blind intuitive connections are deeply engaging; we can follow her in the dark.

Graham's submergence in the piece has the dual effect of reducing her own authority and elevating the pressure of the work as a whole on our imaginations. That is what makes it revivable, whereas *Hérodiade* is extinct. Though the Graham solos in *Dark Meadow* aren't as compelling in Yuriko Kimura's performance as they might have been in Graham's, they aren't intimidating blanks. One senses behind Kimura's fine performance the honesty—her own and Graham's—of a commitment to the unachievable. In *Dark Meadow*, Graham pushed subjective experience to a new extreme, and I think she pushed it into a dead end. But in its extremity the piece stands as a testament to what sincerity really means in the work of a serious artist.

At its finest, *Dark Meadow* hits you so directly you don't even feel Graham mediating the blow. I didn't feel Graham in *Adorations* or *Point of Crossing*, two new works introduced this season, but that is because they are impersonal rather than suprapersonal—quota-filling productions from the Martha-Graham-Martha studio. *Adorations* is a dress version of the lecture-demonstrations she has programed with such success in recent years. I find the material more dramatic in its undressed state. *Point of Crossing* resembles one of those wooden epics of the mid-sixties which in turn resembled chunks of old Denishawn exotica arriving by slow freight. Late Graham returning to her roots.

There have been two other revivals. *Acrobats of God* was an acceptable trifle in 1960; Graham satirized herself in the throes of creation, surrounded by such dancers as Paul Taylor, Robert Powell, Ethel Winter, and Mary Hinkson. Even with that cast, the brittle, fussy "antic" humor went just so far. Today, the piece looks directionless, and a raffish Linda Hodes in Graham's old, nondancing role is self-incriminating. *Frontier*, the famous solo of 1935, deserves a more detailed performance than it can get from Peggy Lyman. This is the dance that began with Graham braced on a fence before the diverging lines of the horizon. One eyewitness, Roy Hargrave, wrote this account of the first production: "With a curious quick shuffling movement of her feet, she makes her apparently motionless body move rapidly over the stage, cutting sizable geometric squares from its surface; and what seems to be a miracle has happened, for the squares are no longer cut from the floor but from measureless Western areas and the theatre is filled with a sense of speed and travel and wind." The soloist no longer cuts squares (I'd like to see a dancer of Kimura's caliber attempt it), but she is an authentic dance pioneer; her fence is also her ballet barre. This lovely suggestion brings up a troublesome point. As far as their contribution to dance history is concerned, there is an ever-present hazard of distortion in reviving these old triumphs of Graham's. The dancers of today are too lightweight and glib, and we get very little idea of how the technique worked itself into expression through its use of the body's weight as an obstacle. But the revivals are necessary to the historical record. If nothing else, they are chapters in one of the most overwhelming theatrical biographies of our time.   —*January 5, 1976*

More or Less Terrific

The big question about Twyla Tharp's *Push Comes to Shove*, for the American Ballet Theatre, is whether it is a very complex, very radically evolved piece of choreography enjoying itself as a send-up of conventional ballet or whether all its ingenuities of construction only go to service a few jokes about the style of *Giselle, Swan Lake*, and the institution of ballet in general. After two performances, I believe it is a real work of art and an entrancing good time in the theatre. But the play between the primary and secondary interests of the piece—the real invention versus the spoof material —is maintained in so careful a balance that, as in one of those optical illusions that can be looked at with equal conviction from two perspectives, I have difficulty deciding which end is up. *Push Comes to Shove* (the title is no help) is to Ballet Theatre as *Deuce Coupe* is to the Joffrey Ballet—it's a comment on the company as well as a gift to its dancers. But in *Deuce Coupe*, in both the premiere version and the one that Tharp prepared for the Joffrey repertory, there is a subject that carries the piece home to audiences who know nothing of what it comments on. That subject is popular songs and dances, and what audiences are not expected to know or care about is how it pertains to the Joffrey's self-styled pop image. In the Ballet Theatre piece, the subject is more elusive. The ballet satire is double-edged. It works for a general audience but not, I daresay, in its freshest form. And in its freshest form—the embedded jokes of construction—it ceases to be satire and becomes pure wit.

Tharp's wit is literally devastating. She finds so many ways for the dancers to keep moving it's as if she had no time to keep order. This illusion—and it is a brilliant illusion—widens into the spectacle of a ballet company in the process of a breakdown, and Tharp several times reinforces the point with moments swiped from the classics: the Wilis's arabesques voyagées, Giselle leading Albrecht into the villagers' dance, the danse des coupes from *Swan Lake*. The anthologizing of such moments is good fun; we know why they're there, and we know why in the middle of the last section of the piece we suddenly get the ritualistic curtain calls that are part of any evening at the ballet. But I don't think we experience the comedy of these things as a product of the highly original eruptive force that produced the ballet; they're really no different from the standard gags about ballet that people of far less talent than Twyla Tharp have been pulling for ages. When Martine van Hamel goes into her hard-to-partner act with Clark Tippet, it's funny all right, but the funniness is too far up front—too far from the nervous center of the piece. Tharp at her best—and she is here at her best about eighty-five percent of the time—produces an audacious logic out of dancing which is its own form of comedy. In *Push Comes to Shove*, some of the gag material goes beyond the discipline and self-sufficiency of her style, and despite the abundant flow of creative juice throughout the piece, the final impression it makes is a bit slender. When Twyla Tharp gives us more than she has to, she actually gives us less than we want.

Still, she gives us a lot, and she spreads it around. Tharp has a logician's mind and a vaudevillian's heart. The tension between the two is her hallmark, and if it occasionally leaves traces of ambiguity in her work (as I think it does here), it gives her a tremendous advantage over every other young choreographer working today: she can be as abstruse as she wants and yet reach the big audience. *Push Comes to Shove* takes a very odd form, but it would be odder coming from anyone but Twyla Tharp. She has composed as if the form had been suggested to her by the title of the company that hired her. What's American about American Ballet Theatre? What's ballet to it, or it to ballet? What's left over that has to be theatrical? Isn't American Ballet enough? So the piece starts with an American rag—Joseph Lamb's "Bohemia," of 1919—and a shuffling turn in front of a forecurtain by three entertainers whom we recognize as the ballet dancers Mikhail Baryshnikov, Martine van Hamel, and Marianna Tcherkassky. There are Tharpian shrugs, slouches, and pelvis bumps for Baryshnikov ("Tharpian" because no one else uses this defunct style of black American dancers in blues performance), and there's also a derby hat that the girls keep stealing from him. When you've seen Van Hamel deliver a high développé kick from under the hat, you've seen the beginning of the synthesis that is Tharp's answer to the proposition "American Ballet Theatre." The synthesis involves an amalgamation of high and popular art which no other choreographer except Balanchine has achieved in this country. Tharp's creative bent in recent years has been toward rephrasing the whole process of amalgamation in her own terms. That may be why she follows the rag with Haydn's 82nd Symphony. They have nothing in common except formal lucidity and refinement. But Tharp likes rags and she likes Haydn; she has used both before. And in the 82nd, subtitled "The Bear," Haydn was becoming the master, as Charles Rosen notes, of a "deliberately popular style," incorporating the folk songs and dance rhythms which up until then had been marginal to his inspiration. What Haydn achieved, Rosen says (in his book *The Classical Style*), was "true civilized wit, the sudden fusion of heterogeneous ideas with an air paradoxically both ingenuous and amiably shrewd," and it's what Tharp achieves in passages of this new piece, with her omnivorous dance wit. Some of the heterogeneous ideas come right off the wall. In Baryshnikov's solo to the opening movement of the symphony, in between all the sensational power-packed spins and jumps and off-center balances, he stands with folded arms and contracts his middle, or else walks around in circles running his fingers through his hair. The dancing gives us more of Baryshnikov, the twentieth-century "American" Baryshnikov, than anything else he has done so far, and the "rests" give us more of him, too—more than we normally see in the walking and posing that come between the step sequences in a classical ballet. His personality does not go behind a cloud, as it often does when he isn't dancing; it continues to radiate.

Tharp takes offstage behavior and rehearsal behavior and choreographs them into the dance. She does it again in the Allegretto, when the corps of girls change place in mid-dance merely by walking across the stage (having previously proved how nicely they can *dance* into place). The contrast may be delicate, as it is here, or violent, as in Baryshnikov's stop-and-go solo; it is funny both times. And it makes the sane point that ballet can be as much as a personal style or as little as a habit of performance cultivated by real people. The lifelike, humane manners of the piece are one way Tharp shows her class as an artist. And she shows sound audience sense by providing something, besides dancing, for people to look at. We can follow that derby hat (which shortly becomes two hats) all around the stage. We can enjoy the farcical speed of the jokes, the unpredictable timing of entrances and exits, the differentiated roles of the stars, the happy zest with which the entire company performs. Although no one else could dance Baryshnikov's part, the piece is not a personal vehicle. His is the igniting spark that starts the ballet on its steep ascent, but then the others—Van Hamel particularly—carry it up and away.

Once aloft, it never looks back—or, rather, it never stops to look back. What I have called the subject—the comedy of big-time ballet conventions—keeps advancing while the structural motifs organize themselves more and more tightly around the music's core. It feels like being caught in a whirlwind. Those of us who care about dance values have to look sharp. The big symphonic ballet in the Allegretto is a space-filling geometrical composition in the style of a drunken Petipa. Yet it's also a triumph of the daintiest musical craftsmanship. Like all of Tharp's group choreography, it is best seen from upstairs (where, at the Uris, the orchestral sound is stronger, too). In the finale, the stage is an arena of profuse activity—a ballet circus. There is a great deal to see as the piece rushes by—too much to take in at once. In between movements there are choreographed episodes danced in silence or to a nattering metronome which stretch the time the ballet happens in (not just its running time but also its temporal landscape); even so, it seems to be all gone in five minutes. Fortunately for us all, it is a great big hit, and it will be around for a while. On the first night, there were ovations for everyone—for the dancers, for Santo Loquasto, who designed a charming and curious array of costumes, and for Jennifer Tipton, whose lighting ranged from pastel brights to her warmest darks. The corps de ballet, which has its most exacting task since *La Bayadère,* was cheered. But the loudest roars were for Twyla Tharp. She has given Ballet Theatre a flash act, and left us yelling for more.

—January 26, 1976

Changes

The curtain rises on a dark stage, its horizon lit by a full moon. In the shaft of moonlight, a man is lying on the ground. Figures enter, three or four at a time; they approach the man and attempt to revive him with incantatory gestures. Eventually, they lift the body and carry it to another part of the stage, where they surround it in a circle dance. The men, including the "dead" one, wear strange little backpacks made of fur; the women's leotards are fur-trimmed. After a bit, the group begins a sequence of body rolls on the floor. When the circle reappears, a girl is lying in the man's place. The moon has moved a little distance to the left.

This is a very rudimentary description of the beginning of Paul Taylor's latest work, *Runes*, but not an unjust one. The steps and gestures I have left out do not change the totally routine impression the piece makes in its opening minutes. For a major creation, *Runes* has a most unprepossessing start, and it may catch others off guard, as it did me. Even after the first silky stroke—the substitution of the woman's body for the man's—I didn't see how Taylor could rehabilitate the exhausted modern-dance/primitive-rite genre he was dealing in, and though I didn't notice how he had managed the substitution, I could guess. A moment later, when the girl who is substituted (Monica Morris) has a duet with one of the men (Elie Chaib) and the process of substitution happens again in plain sight, I still didn't see that Taylor had established a theme—merely that he had rehabilitated the acrobatic duet. The two dancers are interlocked on the ground, and when the man starts a somersault the woman finishes it. Their bodies have become one body—hers; she sits with *his* legs akimbo. It is a bravura effect, but Taylor is prepared to go beyond bravura. In the very next section, he again uses acrobatics, but in a way completely different from before. In another of his invisible transitions, Linda Kent appears perched on Nicholas Gunn's shoulders; she climbs around to his front and keeps climbing until, with a heave like a weight lifter's, he deposits her fully outstretched body on top of his head and balances it there for about twenty seconds. It is the large, awful, and preposterously factual demonstration of what in the first duet was just an illusion. Morris's body only *seemed* to have Chaib's legs attached, but Gunn doesn't just look like a man with a woman on his head, he *is* a man with a woman on his head. The wrong way to do things on the stage is sometimes the right way.

In *Runes* we see the same thing happen over and over in different ways, and we see differences producing the effect of sameness. Mutations large and small, bodies vanishing to be replaced by other bodies, the finesse of an illusion exchanged for the nightmarish ponderousness of a fact—this is Taylor's material. The primitive rite enacts the passage of spirits from body to body. There are phenomenal incidents in the action (I've mentioned a few) to which one can pin a story line. But we don't grasp the nature of an incident without seeing it first as a dance. One might define the poetic process of *Runes* as the transubstantiation of dance energy. We read Gunn's duet with Kent not as a bald stunt but as a naked metaphor, like the contortions of the Prodigal Son and the Siren in Balanchine's famous ballet. For an old-fashioned genre piece, *Runes* contains nothing predictable—not even Taylor's variations on his theme. Carolyn Adams's solo is one such variation. She materializes out of Gunn, and her dance, summarizing the "magic" ingredients basic to Taylor's dance design, looks like a private recapitulation of a public ceremony. Occurring exactly midway in the piece, it is about integrity and duality, constancy in the face of change. Taylor's soft, peculiarly bowed croisés and effacés are offered not as counterpositions but as obverse statements of the same position. Dancing by herself, using no charm other than a meticulous scale of dynamics, Carolyn Adams brings the ballet to its focus in the form of pure dance. She is not the agent of transformation— she is transformation itself. And she is changeless. The dance goes on until with a suddenness she breaks it off and paces slowly into the wings.

Runes is an ensemble work, the group of dancers an orchestral body. They do not have the dramatic color of actors; they have the neutral color of instruments. Yet Taylor always chooses the right instrument at the right time. He uses Ruth Andrien's androgynous quality as a tonal value in a section in which men appear with women branching from their bodies. Like images out of Ovid, these double-sexed deities cross and recross the stage, now and then dislodging the soloist, who is Andrien, from her dance. But through a series of substitutions the dance itself goes on. If there is a single chord that is sounded in all the exhilarating variety of *Runes,* it is the idea that the dance goes on. Out of few resources, out of many, out of any; in the centered calm of one body, in the divisibility of another, in the combinations and permutations of an ensemble, it goes on. The enormous pathos that arises in the final moments of the work, when all the elements of the piece are combined and restated and still the momentum leaps ahead—this pathos comes from the unstoppable energy of what Taylor has set in motion. The curtain falls on a company still in labor, their dance unable to end, discharging its force in all directions. And the moon, which has steadily risen during the piece, is at its apogee.

For this striking heroic poem, which had its local première at the Mark Hellinger, Taylor was assisted by George Tacit's costumes, Jennifer Tipton's lighting, and an unusually fine piano score by the young American composer Gerald Busby, who played it at every performance. The score is spare and rhythmic—a little like one of Hunter Johnson's or Louis Horst's for Martha Graham but more independently interesting than Johnson's or Horst's dance music cares to be. Taylor's choreography is musically more complex than it has been for some time. (I may be doing an injustice to *Esplanade,* the Bach extravaganza that was last year's outstanding novelty, but its musicality, though uninhibited, is not complex.) And do I imagine it or is the company's dancing actually better than when Taylor himself was leading it? The dancers have the same objectivity as performers that Taylor has as a choreographer. They use a kind of projection that doesn't aim directly at the audience but aims at a point closer to where the dance actually is. It makes the dance into something real that is happening between the spectator and the dancer—something we both can contemplate—and it draws an audience in. What a pity it is that some way still hasn't been found for the Taylor company to play more than one program on Broadway for more than one week at a time. At the Mark Hellinger, the program also included *From Sea to Shining Sea* and *Esplanade.* The first, which was made in 1965, is a series of deft screwball pantomimes about Americans as a people who can't get their act together. It is savage but not gross, and the audience is not humiliated; Taylor realizes he doesn't have all the answers. *Esplanade,* which expands simple walks, runs, and falls into a baroque playground, has some grand bits of madness in the final movement. Along with the rest of the audience, I loved it as much as before.

A pity, too, that Merce Cunningham chooses to play repertory out of town. Not long ago, he took a week at the Roundabout, which seems an appropriate theatre for the staging of whole works and whatever production elements go with them, but the week was devoted to the Event—Cunningham's name for the format that combines various choreographies in one performance. I have nothing against Events, but one would like a nodding acquaintance with repertory, and so at the McCarter Theatre in Princeton I at last got the chance to see *Sounddance* and *Rebus* produced separate and entire in their official East Coast premières. (Another première, *Torse*, had to be missed.) Mark Lancaster's settings for these pieces explained some things about them. In *Sounddance*, his backcloth is a low-hanging drape with a vent from which the dancers emerge one by one to be swept into the rapids of the choreography; then they disappear into the vent. Cunningham's cryptic poses upstage right in *Rebus* and his several changes of costume are "explained" by the décor Lancaster provides for that piece—a clothes rack placed next to Cunningham. David Behrman's score for *Rebus* is vocal; David Tudor's for *Sounddance* sounds like an excavation going on next door. In *Sounddance*, the sections of nonstop allegro motion, the quieter sections of linked poses, the fast editing interested me as much as they did in the Events. It is a piece that looks as if it had been choreographed in one day. Perhaps because of its score, which implies musical support where none actually exists, *Rebus* left far less of an impression. (Since Cunningham does not use music, let us have not-music.) Its large, loosely spread groups and long, extra-slow adagio sequences make it a companion piece to the taut, restless *Sounddance*.

In both works, the company performs evenly. Cunningham's own performing is remarkable. But as his dancing has become more and more confined to solos, his interest in composing for other soloists seems to have diminished. No one in the group is featured, although Chris Komar and Robert Kovich consistently distinguish themselves. The group effort has increasingly taken the form of extended unison work, and very difficult work it is. Perhaps that is why Cunningham thought it time to revive a 1959 piece called *Rune* (as it happened, in the same week as the Taylor première); it is one of his most demanding works, and a lot of it is in unison. The performance in Princeton was weak. *Rune* was made for a small galaxy of intensely individual performers, among them Carolyn Brown, Viola Farber, Remy Charlip, and Judith Dunn, and its method, involving a dramatic use of space with invisible lines of force zizzing back and forth among the dancers, is one that Cunningham has discarded. Only Komar, in Cunningham's old role, had enough power, dancing with that fanatical precision which makes us instinctively trust his every move. If the company were a gang of safecrackers, he would be the one to carry the nitro.   —*February 2, 1976*

Two by Balanchine

Balanchine's two premières of the season, *The Steadfast Tin Soldier* and *Chaconne*, came in that order and without an intermission on the same program. They are two well-contrasted pieces, even contradictory. If you like me, says one, you can't possibly like the other. But the New York City Ballet audience, which seems to have grown more acutely responsive in the past year, wasn't drawn into that game. Despite some blurriness of intention toward the end of the first ballet and a prevailing blurriness in the second, it welcomed both warmly. *The Steadfast Tin Soldier* comes from the same confectionery as *The Nutcracker* and *Harlequinade* and *Coppélia*. Based on an Andersen tale, it tells of a dancing doll and a toy soldier who carry on a hearthside flirtation. The flames of passion leap higher, a gust of air blows the doll into the fire, and there is nothing left of her but her red enamel heart. Bravely, the soldier mans his post. Although it's only an excuse for a pas de deux, the story might be stronger than it is. I think Balanchine means to tell it earnestly but blithely, without sentiment. However, it isn't clear that the doll runs into the fireplace because she's blown there; nor is it clear that she's incinerated. The music (the galop from Bizet's *Jeux d'Enfants*) contains no motive for the doll's death, but, properly staged, it could sound the exact note of heartless whimsy the piece is aiming at.

Doll dances have a perennial fascination. The overt simulation is a release from the conventions of theatre; it plays upon our need to judge empirically, rather than through a tolerance of fiction, what is "real." And every doll-dancer invents her own pseudo-personhood. Patricia McBride has invented one pseudo-person called Coppélia. She now invents another, without a name, warmer and sillier than Coppélia. The mechanics of the part are not undertaken as a great feat (unlike those mannequins in store windows which really set out to fool you), and they soon vanish into conventional fiction: we must take flesh and bone for wood and sawdust, when a moment ago we were mesmerized by the proposition that wood and sawdust were plausibly there. *The Steadfast Tin Soldier* is a dance and not a puppet show. The dance is continuously absorbing, stringent even in its moments of coyness, and McBride brings an ageless vitality to the doll's character. She has the sparkle of an experienced soubrette. Playing opposite the relatively inexperienced and still tentative Robert Weiss, she resists the temptation she often yields to when her partner is not a match for her—the temptation to compensate for him by exaggerating her own authority. It is a beautifully tempered performance.

The Steadfast Tin Soldier had its world première last summer in Saratoga. It is not a new ballet but a revival of part of *Jeux d'Enfants*, set by Balanchine and other choreographers to Bizet's complete score in 1955. David Mitchell has designed flattering new costumes and a new set, showing a sketchy Victorian parlor with toys piled on the hearth and a row of life-size cardboard sentinels in forced perspective. The choreography for the ballerina looks as witty to me now as it did in the fifties except for one small detail: then she applauded herself *after* the audience applause had begun. The Soldier has entirely new choreography, and it is this role, made for Peter Schaufuss, that should really justify the revival. Schaufuss, a talented Danish dancer, joined the company not long ago and had been going through the period of adjustment that always confronts a dancer new to Balanchine's style. The Soldier was his first custom-built leading role, and presumably it tells us something of how Balanchine sees Schaufuss and proposes to use him. I regret not having seen the Saratoga performance; Schaufuss has been out with an injury since the start of the season. Weiss projects no character; he remains a stick figure.

Chaconne is not a new piece, either. It is a suite set to the ballet music from Gluck's *Orfeo ed Euridice*, and it derives from a production of the full opera mounted by Balanchine at the Hamburg State Opera in 1963. Gluck customarily ended his operas with dance finales

in the form of a chaconne; they are seldom staged today. Balanchine's score was the Paris version of 1774, which Gluck had expanded by adding dance numbers from his other works. In 1973,
Balanchine restaged the production, with cuts in the chaconne, at
the Paris Opéra. Rouben Ter-Arutunian's Louis XIV-inspired costumes for Hamburg were replaced by Bernard Daydé's in the
style of Gustave Moreau. Costumes—especially eighteenth-century
dance costumes—are strongly implied in the line and sense of the
choreography, but the New York City Ballet *Chaconne* uses plain
white tunics for the women, white tights and shirts for the men.
(This is the company's impartial "Greek" look.) Suzanne Farrell,
in an overpowering role, wears an off-white chiffon shift.*

We begin with Farrell, her hair unbound, and Peter Martins
alone on a dark-blue stage. Their dance—a romantic "swimming"
duet to the flute solo from the Dance of the Blessed Spirits in
Gluck's second act—is less a prologue to the ballet than a puzzling
preliminary. What follows is completely different in style—a rococo
divertissement with entries for the corps de ballet and demisoloists.
(The scene in the opera is a court ballet in the Temple of Love.)
There is a gracious and supple, long-limbed pas de trois—Jay Jolley,
Renee Estópinal, Wilhelmina Frankfurt—in which the boy holds
an invisible lute or mandolin. (In Hamburg, the instrument was
actually carried.) Two more courtiers, Susan Hendl and Jean-Pierre
Frohlich, have a vivacious and somewhat taxing pas de deux. A pas
de cinq to music that sounds like the chirping of birds would be
more interesting metaphorically if we could tell that the five short
girls are cupids—cupids with wings. But then Farrell and Martins
return, and the court ballet fades away, to be continued by other
means. Farrell (now with hair classically knotted) is high-rococo
expression in every limb and joint. Architecturally and ornamentally,
her dancing is the music's mirror, an immaculate reflection of its
sweep and buoyancy, with no loss of detail. Farrell's response to
music is not to its moment-by-moment impulse but to its broad
beat, its overarching rhythm and completeness of scale. When people speak of her as the perfect Balanchine dancer, this is probably
what they mean. The blurriness I complained of is not in what she
does. The trouble is simply that such poise, such angelic transparency, is a law unto itself. What happens in the middle of *Chaconne*

* *Postscript 1977:* Karinska later designed an effective set of white-and-blue
costumes, and Balanchine added a prelude with nine girls pacing the stage in toast
chiffon.

is that a whole new ballet crystallizes, a new style in rococo dancing appears which in 1963 was unknown. Balanchine turns the clock ahead so suddenly that if it weren't for Farrell's and Martins's steadiness we'd lose our bearings. Their first pas de deux gave no hint of what was to come. Now, in a minuet, they present a solemn façade or gateway to the variations for them both that follow in a gavotte. These are like sinuous corridors leading one on and on. It is excess, but it is controlled excess—never more than one's senses can encompass, yet never less. Farrell's steps are full of surprising new twists; her aplomb is sublime. And Martins achieves a rhythmic plangency that is independently thrilling. (When people speak of him as the perfect partner for Farrell, this is not all they mean, but it's part of it.) Together, from the gavotte onward into the concluding chaconne these two dancers are a force that all but obliterates what remains of the divertissement. Balanchine's ensemble choreography here is musically focused, but visually it is unrhymed. His yokes and garlands and summary groupings don't quite manage to gather and contain the new material for Farrell and Martins within the shell that remains from Hamburg-Paris. Evidently, Balanchine has restored the musical repeats he cut in Paris, but instead of giving them back to the corps (or, as seems more likely, to the demisoloists), he assigned them, with new choreography, to Farrell and Martins. The two-sidedness of the ballet is a problem.

On première nights, the audience always applauds persistently, waiting for Balanchine to take his bow. After the double première, on January 22, he came before the curtain wearing one of his sprucest blazer-and-silk-scarf combinations, and it was hard to believe that it was also his seventy-second birthday. Not merely because he didn't look his age but because, measured against his accomplishments, his age seemed not nearly great enough. How many in the audience could remember what ballet was like without him? Generations of dancers, of audiences have received his imprint. The epochs unreel in their diversity, showing where he's been and with whom: Diaghilev and Cochran's Revue; Sam Goldwyn and Tchelitchew; Stravinsky and *Cabin in the Sky*; *Where's Charley?* and *The Nutcracker* and again Stravinsky. *Chaconne* reminds us of his many encounters with Orpheus: not only the two European productions of Gluck's opera but Offenbach's operetta and Stravinsky's ballet. Last December, he staged the dances—minus the chaconne—for yet another *Orfeo*, at the Chicago Lyric Opera. And there was his production in 1936 at the Metropolitan, from which only George

Platt Lynes's photographs remain: a ballet-pantomime with offstage voices, Hell pictured as a concentration camp, allusions to judo and nudity, and an attendant scandal in the press.

In those days, Balanchine had just started to build an American ballet company. He must have been as unpredictable then as he is now. Where he stands today, what aspect of his art he will emphasize next are questions to which the two "new" pieces he has just given us don't supply answers. Probably they weren't meant to. But the split in *Chaconne* reflects a vast impatience to be moving ahead. There's a motor racing inside this vehicle which is determined to shake it to pieces, and as a goad to performers what could be more exciting? A week after the première, I saw another performance. There was such euphoria onstage and in the pit that the final chaconne, loose ends and all, came together and held as if by miracle, and stars, demis, corps, orchestra, and audience were wafted together into Tiepolo skies. —*February 9, 1976*

And Round About We Go

The Dance Umbrella seasons at the Roundabout Stage One are the best reminder we've had recently of what a lot of bad and mediocre choreography is being turned out by the very people with whom the future of American dance is supposed to rest. The last time a number of these little dance companies were drawn together under one roof was in 1972, when the City Center sponsored an American Dance Marathon at the ANTA Theatre. Because dance leaves no trace of itself behind, people's memories have, apparently, to be recharged periodically, and there are always new audiences with no memory at all of what the last such event was like. The Roundabout Stage One, formerly the RKO movie house in Chelsea, is a better space for small companies than the ANTA, having a broad, deep stage, fine sightlines, and a seating capacity modest enough to ensure a sellout at nearly every performance. But at Dance Umbrella and at Dance Marathon there was the same clubby atmosphere: the audience seemed to be composed of other dancers, students, and believers. You go to these affairs not to enjoy dance but to study your own relation to it. It's like an audition in reverse. At Dance Umbrella, I had the impression that the overwhelmingly young audience was looking the companies over before deciding which one to try out for.

Naturally, there are some rewards. The Dance Marathon produced Twyla Tharp's *The Raggedy Dances*, and Dance Umbrella brought Merce Cunningham partway uptown for a week. But of the other attractions I saw at the Roundabout—the companies of Viola Farber and Cliff Keuter last fall, and those of Jennifer Muller, Kathryn Posin, and Dan Wagoner this spring—I retain a bright-edged memory only of some things by Kathryn Posin and her group. Posin is a hard-hitting, flashy choreographer. Two years ago, when I last saw her work, she was sprawling amateurishly—not in her phrasing, which was exceptionally tight, but in her sense of the line a whole piece should take. Now she seems to have found a consistent impacted energy and the beginnings of a company style. Posin is refreshingly terse (a piece ends almost before you want it to), and she risks the unfashionable. Her opening number was a shimmery group-motion study in green and blue called *Waves*. Solidly made, perfectly serious, it may have been the piece in which the new consistency was first achieved. *Light Years*, a première, was more like the het-up Posin I remembered, but with none of the indecision. Set to a jazz-rock score, it starts with a boy working an invisible pinball machine, but then it goes on to reflect an inner-city glare and squalor through entirely abstract dancing. There are no clichés, sociological or theatrical.

Viola Farber's company is built along the lines of old-fashioned "lady star" companies. It has two or more dancers of every physical type—two tall horse-faced boys, two short feisty ones, three small brunette girls—but only one Viola. Farber, formerly a Cunningham dancer, is one of the finest soloists of her generation, and despite their Noah's Ark symmetry her dancers are clean executants, engaging and forceful. But their individual qualities are blanketed by what they're given to do. The biggest losses are Farber herself and her partner, the excellent Jeff Slayton. Farber composing for herself becomes rambling, inchoate. In a solo for Slayton, *House Guest*, she succeeds in summarizing his assets but not in making them expressive. Her ensemble choreography, though not as violent as it used to be, is vague, choppy, confused. It's obvious that Farber is aiming for the beautiful discontinuities of Cunningham. But, like Nancy Meehan, a disciple of Erick Hawkins, she reduces juxtaposition to stalemate; it's the master misconceived. Farber's dances aren't about discontinuity, they're about disintegration.

Farber's is the familiar case of the extraordinary dancer who simply has no head for choreography. But among younger choreographers she is atypical. Dan Wagoner, Cliff Keuter, and Jennifer Muller were not good dancers to begin with. Dan Wagoner's difficulties start with his physical limitations. He has an immobile thick torso, a heaviness in plié and relevé which leaves him no means of occupying space except by running or skittering through it. But he's a furry, crinkly-eyed Teddy bear, and he has built a style on presence alone. Although his choreography suggests that he, too, is a mini-Cunningham (a bit better organized than Farber), its outstanding characteristic is audience manipulation. Because he's so butch and huggable, he can get the audience involved in the dilemmas of composition—in the "What'll we do next?" suspense of it all. But though Wagoner is manipulative, his work leaves a cleaner taste in the mouth than the dim, saccharine romanticism of Cliff Keuter or the Dada hooliganism of Jennifer Muller. Wagoner seems to yearn after the missing frontier in American art. When you're a fourth-generation choreographer (Wagoner danced with Cunningham and Paul Taylor, who danced with Graham, who danced with St. Denis), there aren't many claims left to stake out. In a couple of his dances, Wagoner wears fringed buckskins, but I seem to see him in Sunday denims—a suburban tinkerer fumbling with spare parts. Nothing fits together; nothing can be made to fit. Wagoner takes the audience into his confidence, so that we don't question his lack of coordination. One of his most jumbled-together pieces is called *Changing Your Mind*. A new piece, *A Dance for Grace and Elwood* (you remember Grace and Elwood), evokes a rusty nineteenth-century American atmosphere, and that seems to be enough. The dances are a mockery of serious intentions, but then Wagoner knows—and we know—how futile seriousness is.

What is remarkable about these younger choreographers is precisely their tacit acknowledgment—through coyness, obstreperousness, or insularity—of how devitalized and directionless their kind of dancing has become. And yet there they are, season after season, bringing on premières. Many of these premières are supported by funds from the New York State Council on the Arts or the National Endowment for the Arts, and there are those who argue that it would be healthier for dance as an art if such aid were discontinued.

A Draconic solution. Better a "benign neglect" in which the government is benign and the dance public is neglectful, just as it is now. There's no point in bludgeoning the second-raters, because they don't stick up far enough. They play to a minority; their budgets are as small as their audiences, and they're immune from the most common form of corruption. No choreographer who tries to develop a repertory and maintain a company of his own can be doing it for the money. But the counterproposition—that he's doing it for art—isn't necessarily true. Non-artists may suffer as deeply as artists from a sense of compulsion and self-election, and they are sometimes more persistent in pushing themselves ahead and capturing attention. The great argument against arts subsidies used to be that they would only float the unworthy, because real artists never sank. But there is no direct correlation between worthiness and unsinkability; if there were, only those who were truly deserving would have survived to be caught up and carried to safety by the initial wave of government grants, residencies, and tours—which occurred not so very long ago. That did not happen, because the capacity to make sacrifices, to survive despite baleful economic conditions, was not then and never can be a test of merit. And the point about government arts subsidy is that there can be no test of merit—not in a democracy. We have only to look at the Soviet Union to see what happens when merit tests are applied; there the system that began by supporting the best ended by claiming that the best were those who were supported. So there is no choice for government subsidy but to be indiscriminate. Talent cannot be judged by government agencies; only productivity can be judged. And the artist's compulsion to produce new work, to fill out new application forms is the same as the non-artist's. Compulsion—it's the great equalizer.

It would be a bleak twilight indeed that did not have one deadpan comedian. I enjoy Senta Driver's concerts (the last was held a few weeks ago at the American Theatre Laboratory) because she seems, in a grim sort of way, to relish the directionless state of her art. Senta Driver is plumpish, sly, unsmiling. She barely has a company —one smaller girl, one taller—which she calls Harry, and why the hell not, and she barely makes dances; the three of them run about in rings or roll on the floor. Occasionally, Harry produces a straight, necessarily minimal piece of choreography, but its heart (or mine, anyway) is really in its inscrutable satires, such as *Kschessinska Variations*, a seated toe dance, or *Memorandum*, in which all Driver does is stalk in a circle, calling out the names of legendary dancers, from Taglioni onward, in impeccable accents. I was sorry not to see again, on this program, *The Star Game*, which turns the frailest of dance routines into a sporting event, complete with excitable commentary ("Well, look at that! I've never known Bachmann to establish that diagonal this early in the dance"). Driver manages to cast suspicion on the very act of dancing. The weight of the past, the pressure of competition, the certainty that one is no genius —in view of all that, she seems to be asking, how can an intelligent person like me *move*? Her work, if one can call it that, is trifling in the extreme, but she doesn't beg excuses for it. (And her programs carry no government-support credits.) A touch of Harry is a touch of wit in a leaden scene. —*March 29, 1976*

What You See Is What You Get

Of his popular "Pavane pour une Infante Défunte" Ravel wrote, "It is not a pavane for a dead child, but rather an evocation of the pavanes which could have been danced by such a little princess as painted by Velázquez at the Spanish court." Ravel's princess is dead in the sense that she is lost—a remote, archaic creature. Kurt Jooss's *Pavane on the Death of an Infanta* brings her back with a modern sensibility and then kills her off—a literal death caused by the clash between her joyous, free spirit and the callous pomposities of court life. The ballet, which was created in 1929 and is revived this season by the Joffrey, is one of those period pieces for which the phrase "of historical interest" was invented. Like its companion revival, *A Ball in Old Vienna*, it has the look of high-class revue numbers that were once thought exquisite and now seem quaint. *A Ball in Old Vienna* (1933) has five gentlemen in waistcoats of different shades of slate blue partnering five ladies in white crinolines and pantaloons. There is a smooth couple, an awkward one, a minty dancing master. Two maiden aunts kibitz. It is very ballet-Biedermeier and very *bouffe*. The music is by the waltz master Josef Lanner, and the choreography is jolly but not more distinguished than that of *Graduation Ball*, with which David Lichine followed

Jooss, evidently much in his debt, seven years later. As the dancing master, Gary Chryst demonstrates agitato toes and wrists with the caricaturist's wit that in the Joffrey is his alone. I can say little more about the piece except that, like last year's Jooss revival, *The Big City*, it surprised me by being so short. Somehow, Joossian schematics prepare me for a long haul.

Jooss's attempt to give dance the expressive qualities of mime (as a substitute for mime "speech") had a certain influence in its day; in the *Pavane* one sees the roots of Tudor's *Jardin aux Lilas*. But, unlike Tudor's, Jooss's method of classifying movement and assigning meanings to it has no delicacy of allusion, either psychologically or pictorially. Jooss can paint a propaganda mural like *The Green Table*, but his strokes are too broad for "exquisite" miniatures like the *Pavane*. His courtiers move in closed ranks, locking their legs in adamant fifth position. The hapless infanta, who keeps trying to melt this frosty frontage with tripping bourrées, light bounds, and ever more crippled révérences, is finally crushed, as the program says, "beneath the burden of its elaborate etiquette." Onstage, it happens almost that clunkily. There's even a moment when the ladies and gentlemen of the court change places and the heroine gets caught in the crossing lines. You needn't have seen what Jerome Robbins does with the same idea in *The Concert* to know that any choreographer who uses it has got to be kidding. You'd think, too, that anyone choreographing for a dancer who must wear enormous panniered hips and corkscrew curls that jut six inches from either side of her head would have limited her jumps to changements and low pas de chats. Jooss's chipper choreography makes the infanta look like a gamboling sofa.

With what she has been handed in this role, it is a miracle that Francesca Corkle did not put over the comedy of the season. But the miracle has no mystery to it. Audiences now are so passive and suggestible that they won't laugh unless they are cued to; they respond to what the dancers want, not to what they do. These audiences are great respecters of that classroom piety the artist's intentions. And when the tone of entertainment is as uneven as it is right now, it's no wonder that audiences react as they do—by not reacting until the go-ahead signal is flashed. They restrained themselves at the Dance Theatre of Harlem's *Manifestations* when the Snake whipped out a real apple for Adam and Eve to bite into: restrained themselves because by that point in the ballet they'd guessed—

correctly, alas—that the choreographer, Arthur Mitchell, and the composer, Primous Fountain III, were serious. (The real apple in Paul Taylor's Adam and Eve ballet *So Long Eden* is an obvious joke and gets obvious laughs.) In the DTH's *Carmen and José* (choreography by Ruth Page), Bizet's music and characters are transferred to a Caribbean setting and given the hot treatment, with lots of gyrating to a calypso beat. Because the piece is such a muddle of intentions, nobody thinks it ludicrous when Escamillo appears with his entourage—matadors all and classical danseurs, too. (The appearance of Micaela in horn-rims, carrying a load of schoolbooks, would be ludicrous in any setting.) Sometimes audiences never do get that go-ahead signal until the curtain comes down and they are called upon to applaud. Often I sit among palpably disengaged audiences, imagining that they'll beat me to the exit, but I always leave them behind, cheering. This happened with the William Dollar ballet that the DTH put on in its season at the Uris as *Mendelssohn's Concerto* (implying he wrote only one). Certainly it is better danced than it deserves to be, but, in spite of that, nothing emerges. One sits there thinking, All these dancers fitting all these steps so neatly to all this music: it must be adding up to something. What it adds up to is applause.

The audience applauds *The Combat* lustily while I streak for the lobby, but that is a clear difference of opinion. Audiences love *The Combat* as much today when it's done by the Harlem dancers as they did years ago when Melissa Hayden danced it as *The Duel* with the New York City Ballet. (She also performed it with American Ballet Theatre, as did Lupe Serrano, and with concert groups.) *The Combat* is Dollar's best-known ballet. It has a male and a female role of about equal strength plus a small male ensemble, but it's the girl's ballet, because she is in disguise—as one of the boys. It also has another attention-getter: all the dancers are as if on horseback. This makes the piece delectable in an idiotic way; you can follow the prancings and pawings and the showy jumps (split jetés, or ballottés and soubresauts, which suggest dressage) with a keener technical pleasure, perhaps, than you might take in some other ballet, but then you realize they really mean no more than they'd mean in some other ballet, and you feel like a fool. You've been watching horses instead of dancers. The problem for performers of *The Combat* lies in joining the technique to the story interest in such a way as to turn a staid academic exercise into a flashing demi-caractère piece. Lydia Abarca and Paul Russell didn't meet the problem; they performed the steps and played the story (of Tancred, the Christian crusader, discovering that the Saracen warrior he has killed is Clorinda, the girl he loves) without sensing how the one might spontaneously illuminate the other. It helps to be magnificent at the technique. But, lacking technique, one can make suggestions about it. After all, the Bluebird pas de deux is more exciting when you are really made to think of a bird and a princess, both of them enchanted, even though it's a piece that doesn't need to be saved from itself, as *The Combat* does. The DTH performance was decently danced, in a glow of sincere effort. Clorinda, with her plumed helmet and her breastplate and black tights, is the ballet equivalent of the principal-boy roles actresses have loved to play. The sexiness of the role—the Joan of Arc sexiness —that accounts for the ballet's popularity is enhanced by strong, well-turned-over legs and feet, which aren't among Abarca's assets. She has the glamour the part needs, but basically she's a soft, stretchy, lyrical dancer, and as the hard-driving Clorinda she's miscast. If *Carmen and José* had been a good piece or only as good as *The Combat,* she would have had a triumph. As dancing, the role of Carmen is underconstructed; as drama, it is tame; but as a set of anatomical configurations it revealed more about Abarca's softness and pliancy than any other role yet has, and there was not a moment in it that didn't find her looking magically beautiful.

The value of trusting to what you see rather than to what you've been instructed to see was illustrated a few weekends ago at the Brooklyn Academy of Music by the brilliant acrobatic-mime troupe that calls itself Pilobolus Dance Theatre. "Dance" is not what I would say Pilobolus does, and it is not what I would want it to do. Its art, which is based on gymnastics, is already complete. Gymnastics present the body in complicated feats of coordination without reference to what dancers call dynamics—the play of contrasts available between extremes of pressure, speed, and direction (hard-soft, fast-slow, up-down). A gymnast wants to get from one move to another as smoothly as possible, and his rhythm—another distinguishing factor—is adjusted to his efficiency. He can have dance timing, but he is moved more by functional logic than by dance impetus. Of course, theatrical dancing has always renewed itself by going back to this functional logic, and Pilobolus has caused the boundaries between dancing and gymnastics to overlap even more by its use of poetic imagery. The company gives us something to look at besides prowess; it makes pictures, and its best pictures are of a very special trompe-l'oeil variety. Added to the sense of physical dislocation that clever contortionists can convey is a sense of visual paradox and allusion. We get to see two ways at once or to see correspondences between things. The performers turn themselves into animals, organisms, machines. They do not emphasize the turning-into process as much as the result—the accomplished image—but there are a few numbers in which process is all: *Ocellus*, a band of athletes linked and tumbling slowly in wavelike progressions; *Ciona*, an acrobats' circus; and those marvelous solos that deal in gradual or instantaneous conversions. Pilobolus often uses double-barreled illusions (like *The Combat*) but in such a manner as to enlarge our perceptions rather than to titillate them. And it uses no coercive form of choreography—no planting or sustaining devices to show us how to see. The performers themselves rule the pace of events. Sometimes they linger obsessively, sometimes they move ahead too quickly, zooming past an effect that a choreographer might have frozen or repeated. They are pretty precious in the titles they give their numbers, but when it comes to performance they don't ask us to attribute more meaning to what they do than they can provide right there in front of us. What we see is what we get. We can take Pilobolus at face value—that is, if in the welter of duplicitous images we can determine what that face is.

Pilobolus numbers four men and two women, and although some have had more dance training than others, their stage presence is different from dancers'—it's more sexually realistic. The men have a touch of goatishness that is agreeably collegiate; it can lead at times to a kind of cultured ribaldry, but I never found it offensive. In duets (always male-female), there's a lack of conventional sexual sentiment; the performers are more likely to show symbiosis than sentiment—one lives as two, two live as one, under the bamboo tree. Just as any focused dance company is a microcosm of the world, there's a Pilobolus world view, compounded of imagination, physical daring, and humor. That it should have developed outside the etiolated modern-dance tradition is not surprising. That certain of its elements, notably the physical daring, should now be imitated by dancers is not surprising, either. Margo Sappington's new ballet for the Joffrey, *Face Dancers*, attempts some Pilobolus-like lifts and convolutions, but they're as badly worked out as the rest of the choreography. Imitating actual Pilobolus stunts is not the answer. Dancers, as much as the rest of us, have to learn to see.

Dance photographs taken between 1940 and 1975 form the greater part of an exhibition by Fred Fehl in the Amsterdam Gallery of the New York Public Library at Lincoln Center. Fred Fehl's eye is an instructive one. His photographs, all of dancers in performance, show with amazing consistency his expert selection of the moment— the moment that will be as right for the camera as for the dancer. They show also the dancer in correct relation to his space—never a fragmented, impressionistic view. When I look at Fehl's shots of a ballet I have seen, I feel I can say, "Yes, that is the way it looked," but it's the ballets and dancers I haven't seen that are the most interesting—Markova in *Romeo and Juliet* or *Pas de Quatre*, Danilova in *Coppélia* or *Raymonda*. Fehl is able to put before us the same moment in performances years apart—sometimes with the same dancers, sometimes with different ones—and I wish the exhibition had concentrated more on this specialty of his. The mounting is not all it should be, and some captions are incomplete, but in place of a Fred Fehl book, which has yet to be published, it serves very well. —*April 5, 1976*

The Royal Line

The Royal Ballet opened its season at the Metropolitan with an unusually dull first week, all *Swan Lakes* and *Romeos*. Interest centered in the casting of a new guest artist, Natalia Makarova, with Anthony Dowell, and in the return of Lynn Seymour after a couple of seasons' absence. Seymour's first Juliet opposite David Wall's Romeo was not a performance to set beside her memorable ones of a decade ago opposite Christopher Gable. She looked nervous and, from the first moment, adopted an exaggerated sweep and high fioritura that clouded rather than colored the steps. Wall, to whom falls the greater share of dancing, performed with a listless efficiency; his Mercutio was Dowell, who seemed to be holding himself back. Kenneth MacMillan's production, like John Cranko's, is indebted to the Bolshoi version that introduced Ulanova to the West. It has

the advantage of superior designs by Nicholas Georgiadis, newly
refurbished. Thick with texture and detail, Georgiadis's Renaissance
sets reveal his talent at its ripest, before the decay that set in with
The Sleeping Beauty, The Nutcracker, and *Raymonda.* Or is it that
Georgiadis works better for MacMillan than for Nureyev? Georgiadis's *Manon* is comparatively graceful, light, and airy. In *Romeo
and Juliet,* he is ponderous, but he is so in direct proportion to
Prokofiev's ponderous score, and he's alert to its un-Italian accent.
In the chapel scene, he gives us Byzantine saints, and, in the marketplace, hints of a Verona on the Bosporus. The new costumes are all
good ones. It is the Royal's handsomest full-length production.

Leslie Hurry's old *Swan Lake* sets look like platters of frozen food,
and his costumes in Acts I and III don't rhyme with the ones he
designed for the Ashton dances that derive from a subsequent production. Still, this is a solid, workaday *Swan Lake;* its lapses reflect
a universal professional exhaustion with the problems of staging
Tchaikovsky's unwieldy score. (Next year is the centennial of the
Moscow première, but there is no rush to mount a commemorative
production.) Makarova does not do the mime in Acts II and IV—
no Russian ever does—but she seems to come from the same magic
world as Anthony Dowell, and it is a pleasure to see them together.
Dowell gives all his miming a carefully posed but elastic, dancelike
quality; not a shred of naturalism attaches to it. The largo solo of
Act I benefits from the extra stretch he can always produce to sustain
line in switches of direction and balance, and in that "little bit more"
there is never a suggestion of thinning power; the line does not at-
tenuate. Makarova, too, has reserves of stretch and pliancy to draw
on, and she constantly unmolds and remakes her role, sometimes in
mid-performance. This was one of her unsettled "interpretations,"
with lovely paradoxes; her Odile was obdurate yet impalpable, and
Dowell at moments seemed unsure of how to deal with her. But in
a *Romeo* the following week both dancers were as marvelous,
separately and together, as I have ever seen them. Dowell's dancing surged with self-challenge. Double piqué turns in attitude were
a commonplace, and at the end of the baiting-the-nurse scene he
carried a circuit of tight chaîné turns through several changes of
direction to a perfectly composed dime-stop halt. The dancing was
not only musically and academically flawless, it was impassioned.
Dowell is a wonder, but he is twice a wonder when he loses himself
in a role. He seems to be going through a transitional phase, throw-

ing out glints of darkness and deviltry that none of his new roles take advantage of. The world needs to be shown, forcibly, that he is no longer the fetching boy god or passive youth of his sixties repertory.

Makarova built up a second-by-second rapport with Dowell, and she showed the steady absorption in her surroundings that alone can justify the lightning decisions she loves to make. The performance, with all its wiry dartings and surmises, was planted in fertile terrain —it wasn't an extraneous growth. And it was helped—as Dowell's was helped—by a company that looked freshly and painstakingly rehearsed. This enlivened *Romeo* scarcely resembled the tired and blurry one of the previous week; it had the tautness of a first night. The role of Juliet, constructed for Lynn Seymour, is two-thirds mime. The Ulanova mementos in it include a kittenish entrance with a doll (Seymour used to look not kittenish but puppyish) and a cloak-streaming headlong run to Friar Laurence and back with the potion. But these were never the touchstones of the role that other moments, designed by MacMillan for Seymour, were. The runs and dives in the balcony pas de deux are one example; most of the others are clustered in the third act—Juliet's act—which begins with Romeo's leavetaking. The farewell duet is the last big dance number of the evening. After that, it is all mime—the runs to and fro, the wild jump onto the bed as Juliet rejects Paris, and then the long stationary sit, center stage, staring at the audience as the music crashes and eddies. A mime role is porous; it has options a dance role doesn't have. And Juliet has served numbers of Royal interpreters. It serves Makarova not so well as she serves it. In so much that is literally flat-footed, I miss her expressive points. (She inserted one detail—first pulling herself onto point before crawling, drugged, into bed—that I was grateful for.) But no one has exceeded the young Seymour in the bluntness and recklessness of her passion. Her acting was different from standard ballet acting. She never tried to remind you that underneath it all she was still a ballerina. She showed that emotion, even on a ballet stage, can be clumsy. She was the Magnani of dance actresses. In the performance that I saw this season, she got much of her own back in the bedroom scenes, but by the tomb scene her passion had cooled to a mere relish for effects. Was that silent scream part of the original performance? If so, it's to her credit that I don't recall it.

A Month in the Country, Frederick Ashton's new ballet, based on Turgenev's play, was the first première of the season. It is a flashing pendant to the enormous looped lavaliere that was *Enigma Variations*. In that piece, which was produced in 1968, Ashton created a series of intensely individualized dance portraits that were uncanny reflections of Elgar's musical portraits of his family and friends, and he created also a moving portrait of Elgar himself at the time of his "Variations"—of the artist who must endure the pain of being a modest success, lamented by those who love him most. There were many British virtues sealed into the piece—love of home and countryside, reticence, tolerance of eccentricity—and, although New York has not seen it since its first season, it remains a work of nationalist art and the masterpiece of Ashton's later years. His depiction of Elgar's circle against sunset rays foretelling the doom of Empire reminded many at the time of a Chekhov play, but even Chekhov was never so beautifully oblique, so free of conventional dramatics. The one incident in the ballet occurs at the very end, when Elgar receives the telegram that tells him his "Variations" will be performed—and we leave him calmly posing for photographs, on the brink of international renown. That the telegram could only be read in the program notes was typical of the freedom Ashton chose deliberately to exercise in this piece—the freedom to be ironic at the expense of clarity when irony matters more than clarity. It is the highest form of poetic license. What is the Enigma? Is it the artist's reward? Then, to paraphrase one of Ashton's former collaborators, an enigma is an enigma is an enigma.

Although the themes on which Ashton has lavished his taste, skill, and invention in *A Month in the Country* are intellectually and emotionally seductive, the ballet doesn't pour forth meanings, enigmatic or otherwise. One can't keep savoring it in one's mind, as one can even so innocent a piece as *La Fille Mal Gardée*. Turgenev set his play on a country estate near Moscow in 1850. The mistress, Natalia Petrovna, has a charming little son, a steadfast admirer who has never been her lover and never will be, and a loving but oblivious husband. When she thinks that her ward, the seventeen-year-old Vera, and her son's young tutor are in love, she plans at first on marrying the girl off to a middle-aged landowner. But the tutor, Beliaev, doesn't return the girl's love, and Natalia, her jealousy appeased, is now at the mercy of Vera, who has realized that she and Natalia are rivals. The storm breaks. The admirer, Rakitin, whose position in the household has become insupportable, decides to leave. Vera throws herself away on the landowner. And Beliaev, who might have loved Natalia, leaves, too. Natalia's youth is over. The action of the ballet is necessarily more elliptical (and, of course, the subplot, which cast the central disaster into relief, has been dropped), but it's a reduction rather than a distillation of the play. It may be that, turning to an actual drama, Ashton found himself turning away. Possibly he prefers to achieve drama through undramatic means. Certainly the most wonderful section of the ballet is the suite that introduces five of the six main characters he has retained from the play. The solos for Natalia Petrovna (Seymour) and Vera (Denise Nunn) start the action with a bang. Both are placed high in the allegro register—but in Vera's solo, vivacity is stepped up all the way to hysteria. We see that the two women are excited in the same way but that one has more emotional control—more guile—than the other. And so it will prove to be in the course of events. Between these solos and one for the ten-year-old son (Wayne Sleep) with his ball, there comes a pas d'action, built around the husband, Yslaev (Alexander Grant), who has lost his keys. As he turns the house upside down, we begin to learn just what kind of house we're in, what the people are like, how close they are. It's precisely the information we need at that moment. The entrance and variation of Dowell as the tutor—a thoroughly sensible young man from the provinces—brings an abrupt change in mood, and it's just what we need at *that* moment. And so it goes—on through a coda with more solos for the tutor and his three "dependents": Natalia, Vera, and the child Kolia. The vein of *Enigma Variations* is open and gushing again, and the first portion of *A Month in the Country* is resplendently complete.

The rest of the ballet is as finely wrought, and the dances are on Ashton's highest level. However, the mysterious liquid dilation of character and conflict through dance does not occur. The ballet is stuck with the play's situation, and what's interesting is not this situation but Natalia Petrovna's reaction to it—her moral dilemma. The ballet jettisons Turgenev's characterizations and reverts to the conventions of farce he clothed them in. There is no question that Ashton feels Turgenev's irony here, and he uses the farce material just as Turgenev does—for a consistent bittersweet tone of self-mockery. People are always coming in on other people, catching them unawares. But the tragedy that mounts through the superficiality is not expressed. Ashton appears only to be moving the pieces very elegantly around the chessboard. A key figure is Rakitin, but Ashton really can't use him, and can't get rid of him, either. So

Derek Rencher hovers on the sidelines, an unweighted presence. The sole triumph of the ballet, from the dramatic point of view, is Beliaev. In the play, he is not a lover but the object of love. Ashton has interpreted him as an unconscious Don Juan—the Don Juan of whom Kierkegaard wrote, "To see him is to love him." The ballet's Beliaev takes pleasure in giving pleasure. Sexually, he is open, unformed (as he is in the play), yet he is almost criminally responsive to women—all women. Dowell partners three women in turn—Natalia, Vera, and (in a scene that builds very effectively on a passage in the play) the maid Katia (Marguerite Porter). He is different with each of them—he is *her* Beliaev—but Ashton has made us feel that he is really committed only to Natalia, and Turgenev's ambiguity in this regard is swept aside. (Interestingly, in the play Beliaev departs leaving Natalia a note the contents of which are never revealed. Very *Enigma Variations*, that.) And the ballet's final scene dashes pathos on the rocks of sentimentality, as Beliaev returns at the last moment and, unseen by Natalia, kneels to caress each of two blue ribbons that trail from her peignoir. He drops the rose she has earlier given him; she finds it and is left facing a bleak future as the curtain falls.

Seymour dons the peignoir just for this scene, and those two blue ribbons somehow symbolize the failure of the ballet—its decline into fussiness and artificiality. But no element is as crucial to the failure as the conception of Natalia Petrovna and Seymour's performance. As Seymour dances and plays her, Natalia is affected and self-dramatizing *at all times*; she has not one sincere moment. Is it because the incident-crammed plot gives her no time to draw us to her or because Ashton actually does see his heroine one-dimensionally—as he made her sound in a London interview? The essence of his remarks was that "she's a bitch because she's in love." But Turgenev's Natalia knows she's a bitch. She is, with all her cruelty, a woman of honor, and that is what tortures her. Natalia's emotional and moral disarray might have been shaped into a fine role for Seymour, but Ashton appears either to have misdirected her or to have cast her unthinkingly. Seymour's dancing has always been on the flamboyant side, but her acting was unusually honest and straightforward. It was the tension between the style and the mental attitude that made her Juliet, her Giselle, and (as recently as 1972, when she last danced it here) her Anastasia so fascinating. Now it seems that there's no division left. She's becoming a flamboyant actress, but neatened up, as if she couldn't bear to bloody herself as she used to in her wonderful mad scenes. All that would be stained is this new false image of a grand tragedienne. Whether the slightness of the drama would be so disturbing—or so slight—with a more sympathetic Natalia is a ponderable question. Dowell, Nunn, Sleep, Porter, Grant—even Rencher, in his perplexing nonrole—are all very fine. But perhaps the essence of the matter is that Ashton's skill as a dramatist is invested mainly in his dances. Such characteristic passages as the meandering bourrées for Seymour at the end of her pas de deux with Dowell (and the recurrence of this passage in her final solo) or the muted military flavor of the tutor's steps when he dances alone—steps that seem to be tokens of his manliness—give us more "story" than any official scenario could.

The setting and costumes were designed in what appears to have been a dither of intoxication by Julia Trevelyan Oman. A very realistically ornate interior, filled with furniture and pictures, and painted in pale blue, ivory, and beige, is backed by a rural scene that, strangely, neither she nor Ashton has managed to make real, as they did the Worcestershire of *Enigma Variations*. The costumes are effusions in frosty white, pearl gray, and blue, with several too many windowpane plaids. There seem to be blue ribbons everywhere. It is all scrumptiously pretty, and it reinforces the impression that we're watching pretty people with pretty feelings. Since the ballet is really a dance suite disguised as a dance drama, it could go very well without its fancy wrappings.

One more thing about the ballet puzzles me. In his program note, Ashton credits Isaiah Berlin with "suggesting that Chopin was the right composer for Turgenev." Had Ashton forgotten Turgenev's stage direction that, at rise, Vera be heard playing a Chopin mazurka? In any case, Ashton and his arranger, John Lanchbery, have drawn from the early piano-and-orchestra Chopin a perfect score—one that sounds unlike any other Chopin ballet and supports the action at every turn. The Variations on "Là ci darem," from Mozart's *Don Giovanni*, under the opening scenes is a special feat.

—*May 17, 1976*

Put Out More Flags

Union Jack, a new ballet by George Balanchine, is an hour-and-ten-minute salute to the ritualistic folk theatre of Great Britain. Part I consists of Scottish military tattoos and dances performed by seven "regiments," of ten dancers each, in clan regalia; Part II is a fragment of Cockney vaudeville ("Costermonger Pas de Deux"); and Part III brings back the dancers of the first section in Navy whites and blues for an extended hornpipe festival in the form of a musical-comedy revue. Although he's used Scottish folk dances and musical-comedy dances and military marches in other ballets, Balanchine has never done anything like *Union Jack* before. He's "classicized" many of the steps in his customary fashion, but it would be difficult to call *Union Jack* a classical ballet in the same sense as *Scotch Symphony* or *Who Cares?* or *Stars and Stripes*. It has the impact of a forthright character ballet. Working with traditional folk and popular dance forms, Balanchine has this time exalted them through a process of scrutiny rather than of adaptation. We have the feeling of seeing things in deep focus, and of only now and then seeing double: two dance forms, classical and vernacular, in mutual exploitation. In the first section of *Union Jack*—"Scottish and Canadian Guards Regiments"—Balanchine, through devices of isolation and repetition, fastens our attention to certain fixed formal values: the hypnotic drag-step walk, the suddenly struck pose with a foot profiled in piqué position and balanced by one upflung arm, the drag step resumed, or taken up by the entrance of another regiment. The values are not Balanchine's invention, but the emphasis on them is. He extracts the essence of a form and gives it expansion. He prepares us for its expression in dance. Scottish dancing opposes the liveliness of the feet to squared shoulders and "dead" arms, but when Balanchine gives us the flashing, slicing footwork of a Highland fling executed by two competing male regiments, Scottish feet seem livelier than ever before.

Everybody, both men and women, wears kilts in "Scottish and Canadian Guards Regiments" (the clan designations are based on the authentic tartans that are worn), and at the outset—a succession of long, slow entries to a sustained tattoo—everybody does the same steps. But the women, who wear toeshoes, do them very differently from the men, in their character shoes and regulation gaiters. With wider turnout and flexed arches, the women's feet look more selectively placed, more cultivated, than the men's; they're like a feminine melody set against a masculine drone bass. The distinction, absolutely mesmerizing, is something you will see on no parade ground in the world. So is the calculated difference between the swaying walk of the women and the massive tilt of the men. Another difference is that the men, led by Helgi Tomasson and Jacques d'Amboise and Peter Martins, are in their evenly measured tread only somewhat the same, while the women, led by Sara Leland and Kay Mazzo and Karin von Aroldingen and Suzanne Farrell, are precisely the same. (An extracalculated sway in Farrell's movements underlines the fact.)

Such rudimentary elegancies make the close-order drills of the seven regiments spellbinding, and the drills themselves—the marching and countermarching—are as magical as card tricks. Balanchine has anatomized the mythological power of parades. His changing of the guard, which happens differently each time, is like a series of incantations. There is some obligatory taskmasterishness in what he changes it *for*; the individual dances that the regiments do once they're on are not of equal strength. The weakest is the "ballet" of Sara Leland's regiment, the first of the women's dances. After the modulated thunder and flash of the marches and flings, the wispy toesteps look like a retraction of graven testimony. Theoretically, they build on what we've seen, but in reality they niggle and spread false sentiment. The music that Balanchine's arranger, Hershy Kay, has used here is a set of three variations on the ballad "Caledonian Hunt's Delight." Balanchine goes doggedly through all the changes of rhythm, but the variety accumulates no drive of its own, and the stylistic unity of the piece is impaired. (So is the unison of the ensembles, which the girls, on point, can't hold to strictly.) What should have looked like *Scotch Symphony* turns out more like *Irish Fantasy*. The mixed ensemble that follows, a combination of the Martins and Mazzo regiments in an elaborate Scottish reel and running set, is a partial recovery, a return to folkloristic roots. The dance has a droll formality, and, as a sample of ballroom etiquette, it reminds us of the intrinsic variety of the folk material. But the next dance, which is sheer invention, is the most persuasively folklike of all. "Regimental Drum Variations" is the wild-warrior number, and Balanchine has set it for Von Aroldingen's group—entirely for women. A mélange of hammering points and thunderbolt leaps, it takes the house by storm, stops dead, and adds one more tornado twist before a final dead stop. After this, a more sedately girlish number, full of large shapely hops and kicks, can only be anticlimactic, even if the music is by Handel and the dance led by Farrell.

"Scottish and Canadian Guards Regiments" has a formula Balanchine ending for which the State Theatre stage is too small: all clans but one melding, composing themselves into male-female couples, and steadying themselves for a mass grand adagio to the anthemic "Amazing Grace." The excluded clan, or regiment (Mazzo's), joins in time for one last fling; first the seven principals dance it alone, then they're echoed by the chorus ("A Hundred Pipers"). The recessional, set to a reprise of the opening tattoo, looks as stately as the grand défilé of the introduction, but it is accomplished in about half the time, with rank upon rank half-stepping to the footlights, swerving, and moving off row between row. The stage blacks out into silhouette.

Seventy dancers have come and gone, having given us a great spectacle the secret enchantment of which has been its regularity of pattern and fastidiousness of detail. Balanchine's theatre sense has told him that these quintessential elements of folk art have to be developed and featured in some organic relationship to his own genius for pattern and detail, and it's here that one can fault his collaboration with Hershy Kay and with the designer Rouben Ter-Arutunian. Kay and Ter-Arutunian miss the organic connections between Balanchine and his subject matter about fifty percent of the time. Ter-Arutunian seems more intent on expressing the connection between *Union Jack* and *Stars and Stripes*. (The two are, of course, related, and, with a ballet on French themes to be added next year, will form a trilogical program called *Entente Cordiale*.) He has designed stationary borders and two backcloths—one depicting the Tower of London and the other some sailing ships, water, and sky —all in a characterless hard-edged and hard-colored pop style that screams "Made in U.S.A." Kay's arrangements, too, sometimes sound like a pop-concert "fantasia," particularly in the Scottish section. With the lighter-weight music-hall songs, hornpipes, and marches of Parts II and III he does better. And Ter-Arutunian's costumes for these two sections are first-rate. (The kilts for Part I were provided by military tailors in Toronto.) Originally, there was no scenery for the "Costermonger Pas de Deux," but at the third performance Ter-Arutunian's red-and-gold-painted curtain for *Harlequinade* was lowered behind the action, and, while it isn't right for the raffish music-hall atmosphere Balanchine evokes, it does give us some semblance of a locale. (*Harlequinade* is designed after Pollock's "penny plain, tuppence colored" toy theatres. Diaghilev first used the style fifty years ago for a Balanchine ballet based on traditional British pantomimes, called *The Triumph of Neptune.*)

The "Costermonger Pas de Deux" is danced through an implied reek of tobacco and stale beer. Patricia McBride and Jean-Pierre Bonnefous mimic a couple of music-hall entertainers, a husband-and-wife team (it is further implied) who have immortalized themselves playing the Pearly King and Queen on the stage. The pearlies were the legendary street people of Cockney London who covered their clothes with pearl buttons, and Ter-Arutunian's costumes, suitably decorated, are the baggy street clothes, in satin, of the Edwardian era. McBride wears a large feathered hat, Bonnefous a cap. Balanchine, who evidently spent time in the music halls in the days when he was devising revues for Charles Cochran, has given us a character-mime picture of just such an act as he must have seen then. And the Pearly King and Queen appear to us much as the music-hall performers must have appeared to him, a foreigner whose command of English was less than complete and who had to divine, from dance step and gesture, what song and story had to say. There's a bustle-on entrance with plenty of time for greeting friends in the audience. (It looks ad lib.) There's a sentimental adagio in which much is made of three props—a rose, a hanky, and a bottle of gin. Bonnefous's eager, imploring mime is all staccato bursts (an extension of his performance last season in *Harlequinade*); McBride doesn't believe a word of it. There are two soft-shoe solos: one for Bonnefous, with his brolly (which sprays buttons when opened), the other for McBride, with "talking" mime that is like a hail of patter. The coda brings on the children of the act and a real donkey and a cart and anything that may ensue from donkeys on the stage. As yet, the act is too loose. The gag material needs some filling out, and both of McBride's exits should be repaced. But this chummy limelit interlude, unlike anything ever seen before on the New York City Ballet stage, is so quick to establish its own highly particularized world that we're immersed before we know it, and by the time it's over we've become part of it. "Good old Mavis and Alfie," we say. "They've done it again."

Part III, "Royal Navy," is yet another set of customs, curiously reflective of the first two. It combines anecdote and spectacle in a stream of pell-mell motion. The first dance, a hornpipe trio, sets the pattern: chattering, razorlike feet, vivid splashes of pantomime (swimming, hauling rope, tying rope, peering through spyglasses— the lot). While the band bangs along with "We'll Go No More A-Roving" and "The British Grenadiers" and "Colonel Bogey," the dancers keep hurdling the four-bar phrase, landing on different beats, so that the pattern never grows monotonous. From toytown scale, a few simple dance shapes billow to a flood of hilarious images. In "British Grenadiers," sailors swarm in the shape of a Navy bean; then they link hands and make waves. Somewhere in the backwash, Peter Martins appears as a matey bos'n, a pipe between his teeth; Suzanne Farrell leads a flock of Wrens in yachting caps and shorts. Balanchine polishes clichés till they shine like certitudes, and he's economical, too. For the finale, which has the full company wig-wagging "God Save the Queen" in maritime semaphore, he uses the hand-over-hand rope-hauling gesture as a way of equipping the dancers with hand flags without having them leave the stage; the flags are just spirited on from the wings with a few rhythmic heave-hos. The semaphore is set, a letter a bar, to "Rule, Britannia!" The sixteenth bar is a salute. *Union Jack* is that kind of show—grand, foolish, and full of beans.   —*May 31, 1976*

The Theatre of Merle Marsicano

From looking at pictures of Merle Marsicano, I had formed the impression that she was a dramatic dancer. The photographs showed a figure that was thickish but tensely active, strong fingers, short, spiky, windblown hair. The face was the mask of a tragic queen. Merle Marsicano emerged as a concert recitalist in the early fifties, one of those dancer-choreographers in touch with the then burgeoning world of New York avant-garde painting, sculpture, and music. In the following decade, her concerts were less and less frequent; then they stopped altogether, and in the last few years even solo "guest" appearances have been rare. The weekend before last, she returned with a company of three women to give a series at the American Theatre Laboratory. Marsicano is not dramatic—not in the sense conveyed by those early photographs—and, for a performer whose reputation is still high among poets and painters as well as dancers, she seems not at all concerned with presenting or projecting herself as the object of attention. In a 1954 review for *Dance Observer*, the sculptor Richard Lippold wrote of one of her solos, "It sustains a magical quality throughout, and succeeds best in accomplishing what seems to be her intent in all her works: a convincing emotion, compactly stated with such expert abstraction that the presence of the performer is forgotten, and the audience is transported by the experience of pure movement."

The solo, *Figure of Memory*, was the opening dance on the ATL program, and, with the body become bulkier and the face heavier and sadder, it was all the more remarkable in its emotional detachment and clear emphasis on form. Marsicano's art begins in self-effacement; she is the catalyst of meaning, not its vessel. What that meaning is may be hard to understand, and after *Figure of Memory*, which was my first glimpse of Marsicano, it would have been impossible for me to say what had been interesting about the dance except the displacement of emphasis. The dancer had begun standing still, lifting her forearms, then turning her shoulders, then lightly treading. The fluid arm gestures continued, there was some play with the hands and a passage in which the treading turned abruptly into a rapid pounding. It was the only obtrusive moment. The whole dance came and went, without otherwise raising its voice, to the sounds of a sparse piano score by Morton Feldman. The gestures were specifically defined both separately and in sequence, they weren't dull, and the rhythm was pleasant. But for its objectivity—the kind of objectivity one recognizes with a tingle in every artist who has a gift for it—the solo had made no impression; the dancer had receded and, as in a conjuring trick, left you holding the dance. Later, after reading Lippold's words and reflecting on the concert as a whole, I began to think it more than possible that the "meaning" of *Figure of Memory* (and its title) referred to Marsicano's disappearing act. Placed at the head of a program that might have borne the overall title *À la Recherche du Temps Perdu*, it seemed to lay out a path to a private world.

The Marsicano world, in dance terms, is severely circumscribed, but the fact is not as immediately striking today as it must have been before the trend to pared-down movement took over in the sixties. Marsicano, though, has nothing in common with today's primitive minimalists. She is interested not in ritual process or in fundamentals but in the flow and vibration of subtleties, and she uses and re-uses a limited vocabulary of steps to create a kind of pressure in concentration, the way a poet uses a strictly controlled verse form. The pressure builds up slowly, and the momentum is such that without reaching a climax of any sort the piece ends or trails off just as its figurative implications become clear. When you think about them, these implications seem to have been what the dance was about all along, even though they've never crystallized. Marsicano avoids that kind of overt imagery; she prefers to build a dance out of tenuously linked phrases that will be satisfying and beautiful in their own right. But you see what you see. Another solo, to another Feldman score, is as mild and uninsistent as the first but with more keenly differentiated rhythms. Titled *March* (*The Month*), the solo presents opening and unfolding gestures in a formal pattern with no amplification in scale. As the pulsing of energy within a closed bud, or as an image of nascent heroism, or simply as a nonobjective statement—however you wish to see it, the dance supports you on all levels.

Marsicano was apparently always a miniaturist and always passionately devoted to the proposition that form tells. The ATL concert was her first since 1970. It would have been good to have her quiet example before us more often, but then, just as she seems not to have been influenced by any dancers who came before her, she is unlikely to influence others. How she obtains her tiny, graded effects, how she uses the wit of narrow means to create complex, suggestive poetry that doesn't rely on suggestion to make sense— these are secrets of discrimination and require a delicate balance that is rare in any art. In dance it is unique. It isn't surprising, then, that what emerges as "meaning" in her work has a highly personal color. The concert's theme of memory, or meditation on the past, was prefigured in the first solo and established in the second number, *Disquieting Muses*. This was a group dance for Peggy Spina, Diane Broman, and Jolinda Hulse to a tape of Debussy's "Sirènes"—

music composed in the 1890's. The three dancers wore black tights with one thigh encased in a bright-colored silk-jersey sleeve and with a scarf looped around one shoulder. Their hair trailed down their backs, and with one hand from time to time each girl would pull her hair "out to a fan-like spread." (The image is Jill Johnston's, from a notice of a 1962 dance incorporating the same gesture.) The dance was a slow bending and winding of the three along separate paths to different counts, all of them musically valid. The disparity gave the dance its largeness of expression, though its scale remained small. *Disquieting Muses* looked like a dancing symbolist poem or a hothouse view of Parisian aesthetics in the nineties—a slow, wavy frieze of sirens singing songs of decadence. *On the Half Shell*, a solo performed by Peggy Spina in apricot tights with a wisp of organza around her middle, had a sprightlier and homelier air, and no music. Its unheard rhythms were those of a very far-off, turn-of-the-century music hall. Last and best of all was another dance for the group, *They Who Are Not Named*. The costumes were dark satin shifts with contrasting sleeves, ballet shoes, and dominoes or half-masks made of netting. The music was Varèse (selections from "Ionisation," "Intégrales," and "Hyperprism"), and the implied locale was again Paris—the Paris of the apaches, of l'Art Nouveau, of *Les Vampires* (who were not named, being a secret society), and of the dusty yellow dance halls celebrated by Toulouse-Lautrec. As in the other dances, allusions were as irresistible as they were untendentious, but here they were more specifically evoked. A flamenco pose echoed the sound of castanets in the music, and "act" followed "act"—revenge melodrama, tightrope walking, magicians, mind reading, sword swallowing—each as faint and as distinct as a smoke ring. *Disquieting Muses* had recalled Loie Fuller, and *On the Half Shell* an early skirt dance by Ruth St. Denis; *They Who Are Not Named* was the whole bygone Paris theatre. But this collection of theatrical cameos, so astonishingly ample and varied, is preserved in a rhetorical setting that belongs to no one but Merle Marsicano. She never breaks the stride of her style to strike a note of authenticity or of parody; she is never arbitrary. Her evenness of pace and her consistency of design (which extends to her strangely effective patchy costumes) are instruments of terse efficiency. And the rhythmed melting phrases that occur within this inviolate structure have the conviction of a personal memoir.

It is the least exhibitionistic, least athletic, least *strained* dancing that may be imagined. Its most mysterious quality is its incisiveness: all those soft edges, yet how they cut. For the three pieces that I take to be new work, Marsicano has rehearsed her dancers scrupulously; they're individual embodiments of her style. And in the group dances she seems to have taken her magic even further than in her own solos. Watching the group, one sees what power limpid unpretentious gesture has. (My guess is that Marsicano rehearses the exactitudes of movement instead of saying to her dancers, "Now let's be Spanish.") Almost without meaning to, the undeclared subject comes through with such provocative dazzle that the dance itself disappears.   —*June 7, 1976*

Home to Bournonville

The Guards of Amager is one of the dozen or so works by the nineteenth-century master August Bournonville which survive in the repertory of the Royal Danish Ballet. Until the company presented it here at the tail end of its Met season, the ballet had never been seen in New York. Visits by the Royal Danes are rare (the last was in 1965), and although one can see more or less authoritative performances of Bournonville ballets danced by other companies or by student groups, there's nothing like seeing a "new" Bournonville danced by Bournonville's own company—danced and mimed. The Danes bring a quality to miming that endows that sick art with new life. This isn't simple declarative mime in *The Guards of Amager*. This is visual conversation, paragraphs of it, running in counterpoint, overlapped and interrupted to complicated beats. It is done in ensembles all over the stage at once, or in intimate duologues or triologues, and so fast that if you drop your eyes you miss a vital narrative link. Yet it isn't what the characters are "saying" that tells the story—it's the characters themselves. The story that is being told is an operetta-ish affair about the skirt-chasing commander of the guards and his wife, who by way of reprimand seduces him at a masked ball. There are two lovely moments in this story. When the wife finds the sheet of music her husband has been playing, she touches her temple and nods, as if saying to herself, "He's been thinking of me." When she discovers that he's in fact faithless, and later when he faces her, unmasked, at the ball, neither of them takes it big. Louise and Edouard are grown-up gentlefolk, a species we seldom see on the ballet stage.

The Guards is late Bournonville; he made it in 1871, six years before he retired, and eight years before he died. It has the wisdom and buoyancy of old age, a fragrance of nostalgia that still penetrates. The frontcloth bears the subtitle "An Episode of 1808." The prologue consists of five spotlit scenes, each shorter than the one before. First, the guards stationed on Amager are seen in unguardly attitudes surrounding their commander, who plays a spinet. To their left, we see a sewing circle; to their right, townsmen dipping snuff. Next, a huddle of gossips. A line of villagers skips through the darkness, and then a doorway in Copenhagen lights up: two ladies in Empire gowns receive a letter from a postman. Louise will visit the garrison. Almost before we have taken it in, the scene blacks out, the scrim rises, and the ballet proper begins at a daunting pace. It never slackens. The whole first scene is played in what looks like the vestibule of an inn. Though poorly executed in places, this set and the following one, of a provincial ballroom, are good contemporary pastiche of nineteenth-century semirealistic design. Scene I combines an effect of mullioned windows and painted woodwork with overhead borders and side pieces covered in a floral pattern. A large hole in the back wall reveals a winter landscape. It is not a doorway. Through the actual door troop more characters than most companies have in their entire repertories. They're quirkily individualized characters, but they aren't farcical; they have interior as well as exterior life. And the ballet doesn't tell us all there is to know about them. It leaves some of its life behind the scenes.

In the ballroom scene, Bournonville gives us a set of social, folk, and demi-caractère dances, ending in a classical ballet number for two girls and a jester. Louise (Vivi Flindt) appears in disguise: first as one of a quartet of vivandières, then in a coquettish solo with a veil. Henning Kronstam, who plays Edouard, changes his costume to dance a hornpipe with two other sailors, but the lack of a plot motive for the change suggests that this may be a performance tradition. Possibly, too, Louise's masquerade was originally limited to the veil solo. It's unlikely that the ballet we see today is the same in every respect as the one Bournonville composed. In the adagio of the classical trio, the boy holds a girl by the waist, but it is she who promenades him by bourréeing in a circle. The idea is incredibly modern for 1871, yet who if not Bournonville would have had the wit to think of it?* And the boy's solo must surely be one of the most difficult ever created, even by Bournonville. It was danced one night by the practiced Flemming Ryberg and the next night by the young and talented Ib Andersen. Both times, it looked as if it contained no linking steps and no rests.

Unfortunately, there was no opportunity to sort it out. *The Guards of Amager* was a novelty of genuine interest—the only novelty, in fact, of the Danes' entire season. New York got two performances. Washington had four. That speaks ill but, I fear, all too truly of New York. It is in New York that the Danes encounter steep prejudices about what does or does not constitute ballet. In the coarsest New York terms, *The Guards* doesn't qualify as ballet; it has too much mime. The more elegant and responsible New York attitude holds that *The Guards* is simply old-fashioned—very dear and charming in its way and, because it once *was* a ballet, worth preserving. You could probably raise more support for a Bournonville Landmark Preservation Society in New York than you could in Washington, but you still couldn't get four performances. Worth preserving, yes, but not worth inhabiting as a theatrical experience.

On the question of mime: Mime is a legitimate resource of the dance theatre (and not only of the dance theatre). The impatience of audiences when faced with extended mime sequences reflects a suspicion that the meanings being expressed so directly in such easy-to-read sign language are superficial, and that if the characters had something important to say to each other they'd be dancing. The idea that dancing makes a profound statement and mime doesn't may arise in somber ballets with a tragic expression, like *Swan Lake*, but even there, where the fantastic plot is only a pretext for a dance entertainment, it does no harm to refer to the plot now and then in mime. I find that it refreshes concentration. However, in most modern story ballets if the plot is to be taken seriously the choreographer avoids mime. Often these ballets are weak because he does no more than that. He doesn't invest the dances with dramatic content; he relies on the dancers or the audience to translate dance figures into stylized description. Modern audiences are as pleased to puzzle out these

---

* *Postscript* 1977: Evidently, Bournonville had thought of it before. The same promenade appears in the pas de deux from *Kermesse in Bruges* Act I (1851) and *Flower Festival in Genzano* (1858).

bottomless riddles as audiences of former days were to guess the meanings in a well-wrought mime passage. Formally coded mime of the "unless I marry I die" variety is not the only kind of mime there is. There's the Bournonville kind, which the choreographer himself defined as "a harmonious and rhythmic sequence of picturesque attitudes taken from nature and classic models, suitable to character, costume, nation, and epoch. The sequence of postures and movement composes a type of dance, but without the turnout (en dehors) of ballet. Its attitudes are aimed at effects of plasticity and characterization entirely apart from virtuoso academic technique." One might add that *The Guards of Amager* is a comedy deeply rooted in the life and lore of its time, and the lively and differentiated pantomime that fills out the whole of its first scene is as much an expression of the Bournonville ballet d'action as the lively and differentiated dances of the second scene. There is no question of frivolous mime versus earnest dancing. The whole ballet is consistently light and consistently vivid in terms of its characters and setting.

On being old-fashioned: Bournonville is well aware of the degrees of theatrical intensity on the scale between pure mime and pure dance. The ballet exploits the whole diapason, from the opening vignettes to the climactic classical pas de trois. The delay in the outbreak of dancing is a calculated effect. When the hero takes a girl on each arm and flirts with her, it's almost but not quite a waltz. The second scene is almost but not quite a straight divertissement, for it is danced by the characters of the ballet, and the plot reaches its dénouement in the dances. This is really a very modern approach. Perhaps what people mean when they say the ballet is old-fashioned is that, for what it is—the prototype of ballet bouffe—it isn't very exciting. It doesn't swirl with uniforms and petticoats. It doesn't make temperatures soar. Apart from the classical pas de trois, the only dance image that stays with you is the amusing side-to-side chassés in the hornpipe. It's also true that the Met is much too big a place for it. But that many of the cultural references in the mimed action are obscure is not a reasonable objection. There is one very broadly played character, a large nursemaid or granny who trundles mechanically like a mama doll. A Danish audience undoubtedly recognizes her; I took her for some ancient folk figure (though her fame may have originated in the ballet). The action occurs during a Shrovetide festival, as in *Petrouchka*, and the significance of the few customs that aren't familiar is easily guessed.

(One, the blindfolded swatting of a container to release a shower of goodies, is related to the Mexican piñata game.) But the larger point to be made about all this is that the Danish cast, which includes dancers, ballet children, and character mimes, plays with such precision that a time and place of which one knows nothing are brought spiritually to life. Because the ballet has meaning for the Danes, it has meaning for us. (It is this kind of life, incidentally, that is missing from all performances of *Petrouchka* I have ever seen. Until it is done by a Russian company—if it is not too late for a Russian company to do it—I may never know why the ballet, not just the music, is a classic.) Ballet bouffe is a dead genre, buried by the Ballet Russe in gobs of Viennese schmalz. *The Guards of Amager* is indigenous art. Perhaps that's why, after a hundred years, it remains a theatrical image one can believe in.

Its historical background shows how close to life Bournonville worked. A passionate Francophile, he had mourned the fall of Paris to the Prussians the year before. Twenty years earlier, he had written of his hero Napoleon, "It is not only because there flows French blood in my veins that his memory is so dear, but also because I connect his name with many of the feelings I have for my Danish fatherland—the Danes were, after all, his most faithful allies." In *The Guards*, Bournonville is looking back on his parents' genera- tion in the time of the Franco-Danish alliance (in 1808 he was three years old), and the Danish home guards, bravely marching up and down as if hourly expecting the return of the British fleet, are seen with a mixture of childlike affection and skepticism. Edouard pom- pously dedicates his sword. All the officers flirt with the locals' wives. They also have snowball fights. Edouard du Puys, whose full name is used in the cast of characters, was a real person, a friend of Bournonville's father who had been a lieutenant in the Amager volunteers. Famous for his love life, he was once exiled from Den- mark because of an affair with the Princess Charlotte. Du Puys was also a composer and a baritone—the first to sing Don Giovanni when Mozart's opera was given at Copenhagen's Royal Theatre. Vilhelm Holm, who is credited as the composer of the ballet's score, is more properly its arranger. Some of the melodies—notably the one that the ballet's Edouard plays on the spinet—are by Du Puys. The program note might have furnished more of this kind of informa- tion. (The souvenir-program note by Svend Kragh-Jacobsen should have been included.) And it might have avoided the patronizing description of "a little ballet which, though rich in mimed effects, is still eminently entertaining."

Would the company ever use such a line about Flemming Flindt's *Triumph of Death?* Though hardly "rich" in mimed effects, Flindt's ballet falls into the pantomime category simply because no other category would accept it. And Flindt's purpose is not to entertain but to instruct mankind. He harangues us for nearly an hour with shapeless anecdotes in the course of which a man in a black cloak appears and people fall down dead. Flindt's source is said to be a play by Eugène Ionesco, *Jeux de Massacre,* which tells of a city stalked by death. This is not the snickering domestic Ionesco of *The Chairs* or *The Bald Soprano* or *The Lesson* (which became a Flindt ballet in 1963) but the cosmic, eschatological Ionesco of *The Killer* and *Rhinoceros,* who pronounces verdicts of stentorian banality upon whole societies. Ionesco's material may have invited the kind of amorphous treatment it gets from Flindt, but Flindt doesn't seem as intent on adapting another man's work as on staging a series of freak-outs in the manner of the Broadway and Off Broadway acid-rock musicals of the sixties. *Triumph of Death,* which had its première in 1972, eventuates in an absurdly overrated nude scene, which doesn't lift the tedium but only alters its tone. (The mime episodes prepare you for the "orgy" the way watermelon prepares you for Jell-O.)

Flindt has been the company's artistic director since 1966, and, judged by his New York repertory, he has yet to respond to the dancers' needs, either in terms of their strengths or their weaknesses. The women badly need to develop their pointwork, but too much of their choreography leaves pointwork out of account. Flindt's own ballets sometimes seem hostile toward women. In *The Lesson,* a pathological ballet teacher tortures and then murders a girl student. Flindt still takes the teacher's role on occasion, and gives an especially brutal performance. In *The Four Seasons,* an otherwise tepid full-company work, he gets a sadistic laugh out of the audience in the Autumn "hunt" scene, when two girls are carried across the stage slung on poles like dead game. And the use that is made of the entire company—its men and its women, its dancers and its fine mimes—in *Triumph of Death* is degrading.

Another new ballet seen this season was John Neumeier's *Romeo and Juliet,* to the Prokofiev score. It was the most relaxed Neumeier piece we've yet had; it didn't toy with heavy conceits or subject the dancers to hard labor. But it wasn't a ballet, either. Neumeier appeared to be directing an unfinished production of the play during the music. In this way, he accomplished a few effective scenes in *verismo* style: news of Juliet's "death" reaching Romeo in the middle of a clogged road; a tomb scene refreshingly concise and free of histrionics. Jürgen Rose contributed resourceful scenery. But the best of this *Romeo* came from the company—a long list of Cousins and Servants and Handmaids who not only swelled the scene but effortlessly enriched it. The Strolling Players, though, onto whom Neumeier kept shifting the burden of narrative, were an excrescence.

The rest of the Bournonville repertory consisted of *La Sylphide* in a new production, with a very beautiful forest set, and the dance portion of the third act of *Napoli*, in its same old glorious set. Filled with Danes young and old, it still creates one of the happiest stage pictures in all theatre. And there was Niels Kehlet, still dancing the central role and still producing his sensational jump at the indecent age of thirty-seven. Peter Martins returned to his home company in *La Sylphide* and showed how, with his ample, easy rhythm, clear beats, and command of natural gesture, he could have become the dominant James of our day. The production differs in several respects from the American Ballet Theatre version—musically and rhythmically it is superior—but the other differences weren't as interesting as I'd hoped they'd be. Sorella Englund was a waiflike Sylph, with the beginnings of impressive style. There were no other ballerina prospects, and despite two very good young men, Arne Villumsen and Ib Andersen (and Johnny Eliasen in mime), the company seemed to be losing ground in Bournonville. The young women have all learned to jump like Russians; none could produce the grand jeté in attitude that is one of the glories of the Danish school. Technique aside, the appeal of Danish dancing has always been partly philosophical. It's the appeal of a kind of ballet that is not a branch of show business. In the overheated climate of professional ballet in New York, the Danes can't really compete. They tried to, but the season was not hot box-office, and since that might have been predicted, it is a pity the company did not go down fighting, with a complete *Napoli*, with *Konservatoriet* instead of *Etudes*, and with perhaps one or two more of the Bournonvilles that have never left home. Danish dancers have been struggling to get into the twentieth century almost as long as there has

been one, and they've tried every kind of wrenching alternative
to their own classical style and repertory. That style and repertory
should have eroded but didn't. Only now, with Flindt one lap
behind the Zeitgeist, are signs of erosion starting to appear. Yet of all
the dancers who have visited New York in the last decade the Danes
have changed least. Doing what they do best, they are still the
gentlest and most tasteful dance company in the world.

—June 21, 1976

Beauty *in* Distress

Seeing *The Sleeping Beauty* done by American Ballet Theatre,
with Oliver Messel re-creating the settings and costumes he designed for the 1946 Covent Garden production, is a little like
visiting the *Queen Mary* in drydock. It's better than no *Queen Mary*
at all, but it isn't the same as taking an ocean voyage. The new
Sleeping Beauty hasn't gone anywhere yet, although at the end of
its first week of performances at the Met, engines were starting to
turn in the orchestra pit. I have never heard the score played slower
or more rudely than it was on opening night; the conductor, Akira
Endo, made matters worse by following the whimsical lead of the
ballerina, Natalia Makarova. The two other performances I saw
were led by Michel Sasson (with Martine van Hamel as Aurora)
and Endo again (with Gelsey Kirkland). In both, the music had
picked up speed and transparency; it sounded like Tchaikovsky.
The conductor is more important to the success of this ballet than
the ballerina. Spectacles the size of *The Sleeping Beauty* aren't
ballerina vehicles, and they aren't launched in one week. That's
why I'm inclined for the moment to discount Makarova's muddled
performance, along with Van Hamel's far more proficient one and
Kirkland's promising but underachieved début. In spite of the
legendary aura created around the central role by Margot Fonteyn,
one goes to *The Sleeping Beauty* not for one star but for a display of dancing and pantomime by a company schooled in the full
range of classical effects the ballet calls for. Everybody, from

Aurora down to the smallest page, has to show the brilliance of this classical school, and show it, moreover, with the consistent force of a common heritage. Ballet Theatre's weakness is that it isn't able to make this kind of ensemble declaration. At best, it is a polyglot company, with a roster of stars trained to differing aesthetics of classicism. At worst (and best and worst are mixed up together in *The Sleeping Beauty*), it can't muster the technical strength to fill the ballet's many subsidiary roles. As performed at Ballet Theatre, the variations for principals and soloists with which *The Sleeping Beauty* is studded look like a series of guest shots or shots in the dark. The Carabosse (Dennis Nahat or Marcos Paredes) was performed in Trockadero hoodoo style. King and Queen, Catalabutte, courtiers, servitors, suitors were left pretty much to their own devices. Stylistic deficiencies cramp the production at every turn, and these extend from dance manners to court protocol. Just as a sequence of six supported pirouettes into attitude (performed seriatim by six fairies) should agree as to the amount of light and shade in épaulement and as to the level and angle of the leg, backs should not be turned on the royal presence, suitors should doff hats on being introduced to a princess, and a princess, fatally punctured, ought not to be left lying unattended on a bare floor.

The production was delivered unfinished. Oliver Messel, who never got to mount a Panorama at Covent Garden, now does so at the start of Act III, with the Lilac Fairy's boat crossing the stage against a distant shoreline. The moving scrim that would have made the scene work was missing. So were the effects of rising foliage at the front of the stage which, in the old production, used to shut the castle from view at the end of Act I. As I remember that production, the Lilac Fairy did not exit, as she does now, but remained onstage, drifting on her points from side to side, bending, weaving, urging the scenery upward until the curtain fell. Maybe this moment will be restored. And there were other moments—outstanding and treasurable ones in which Messel's settings also played a part —that should be restored, too. One of them was Aurora's entrance; another was the onstage scenic transformation that elided Acts II and III. Even companies to which the ballet is better suited than it is to Ballet Theatre have difficulty holding us throughout the course of a long narrative that ends before the last act. Diaghilev, in producing *The Sleeping Princess* for London in 1921, avoided the anticlimax by joining the Awakening (normally the end of

Act II) to Act III, the Wedding. The designer, Léon Bakst, provided an onstage transition. In Cyril Beaumont's description:

*He bends over and kisses her lips. There is a crash of thunder, the
Princess opens her eyes and slowly sits upright. The Prince takes
her hand and lifts her to the ground. A burst of triumphant
music, and in a moment the palace is ablaze with lights. The
tomb disappears below the floor, and the web and the spiders
crumble to powder. Now, the scene presented is one of unparalleled magnificence. The apartment is bounded by towering groups
of gilded columns. The background is occupied by a flight of
broad curved steps which leads to a massive colonnade. . . . The
Prince and Princess walk toward the dais, where they are greeted
by [Catalabutte], who wears a rich gown of gold brocade. The
lofty roof echoes to triumphant fanfares and an imposing procession files down the left-hand staircase.*

And so on. We are into the Wedding. Messel, who undoubtedly
learned from Bakst, prepared a stage set part of which could remain
in place while the rest, cobwebs and all, lifted away to disclose *his*
scene of unparalleled magnificence. At Ballet Theatre, the two acts
are still merged, the basic architecture is still in place, but, following
the crash of thunder (a gong stroke), there is no burst of triumphant
music. Instead, there's a blackout. The orchestra slices the top off
Tchaikovsky's crescendo and after a moment of silence proceeds
with the overture to Act III as a frontcloth descends. Visually, the
transition is dull; musically, it is barbarous. The allegro agitato that
capped the crescendo has been transferred to the moment earlier
in the ballet when the Prince boards the Lilac Fairy's boat. Since
the allegro agitato is an elaboration of the music it replaces—in
other words, originally an intentional repeat—why not play it again
in its rightful place?

Aurora's entrance, recalled by all who saw it in the old version,
was very simple in its design but electric in its effect. She came
through the colonnade and struck a pose in arabesque under the
arch, but then, instead of entering the stage, ran off. Her "real"
entrance was a bound out of the wings into the pas de chat/pas de chat
sequence. Why has Ballet Theatre acquired the Messel décor if not
to stage the great moments that went with it? And why hasn't it
also acquired some better dances? Mary Skeaping has staged the
choreography on the plan of Nicholas Sergeyev—presumably the

one used for the 1939 revival by the Sadler's Wells Ballet. It includes none of the revisions by Frederick Ashton which were part of the 1946 version, but does include certain revisions and additions made by Nijinska for Diaghilev's 1921 production and its spinoff *Le Mariage d'Aurore* (1922). Miss Skeaping was ballet mistress at Covent Garden from 1948 to 1951, and has mounted many ballets for many companies. The name of Sergeyev, the régisseur of the Maryinsky ballet from 1904 to 1917, has become synonymous in the West with the Petipa classics. But Petipa never set a Garland Waltz as threadbare as the one we have here, and surely it is no blight on his name to characterize Catalabutte and the aristocrats in the Hunt scene a little more distinctly. The ballet needs the hand of a choreographer as well as that of a régisseur. It needs a standardized Rose Adagio instead of the optional versions we are now offered, it needs a coda to the pas de deux of Aurora and the Prince which is danced by them rather than by the Three Ivans, and it could use a seventh fairy in the Prologue. Miss Skeaping's staging avoids the irrelevant interpolations that have become commonplace nowadays, but it does not always distinguish between accretions in the Petipa tradition and mere waste product. The fairies' adagio and some of their variations in the Prologue are a little on the bald side. The Hunt scene is given with a full set of court dances, one of which becomes a charming solo for the Prince, full of small changements. This solo is a post-Petipa Russian tradition, and it happens that we have never seen it before. Could it be that Miss Skeaping is eliminating post-Petipa *British* tradition? Ashton's Garland Waltz, at least, is a necessity.

A classic revival invariably commemorates the era in which the classic is revived. Bakst's designs for *The Sleeping Princess*, probably the grandest ever conceived for this ballet, have about them the look of the twenties. I believe that Messel's designs used to be admired for their emulation of Spanish and French court painters of the seventeenth and eighteenth centuries. Now, though amplified and elaborated for the large stage of the Met, they look ineluctably forties and ineluctably British—Slade School of Art British. The costumes do not "pull together" in the current fashion. They have an eccentric, teasing glamour, each trying to outwit the other, as if they'd been designed to pass in review at a soirée and make the gossip columns by morning. Even under Nananne Porcher's bad lighting, the Messel contribution is the best part of this show. It reminds us how far the British had already come by the mid-forties in their commitment to the grand style in ballet—so far that they could afford to confuse it with very high-camp social entertainment and still remain innocent in the quality of their devotion. For the London dance public, trained in the isolation of the war to respect its young dancers and their native classicism, *The Sleeping Beauty* at Covent Garden marked a generational divide; it was the moment when ballet, which had been Russian, became British. For Americans, that production stood for THE *Sleeping Beauty*—the masterpiece that Tchaikovsky and Petipa created. What it preserved of the old ballet was, owing to the restricted budgets of the postwar years, a partial picture. We came to know this over the years as the picture gradually disintegrated, having periodically to be overhauled, and not always for the better. Ballet Theatre's reproduction is, in other ways and for other reasons, also partial, and so the picture is shrinking just when it should be expanding. It neither repeats the past nor evokes the present. It says nothing of what American classicism in the seventies may make of *The Sleeping Beauty*. But we can hope that the company will one day find its identity in the shelter of a monument. —*July 5, 1976*

Isadora Alive

In *Homage to Isadora*, a solo made a year ago for Lynn Seymour, Frederick Ashton staged from memory a dance image he had often cited in speaking about Isadora Duncan—the image of the dancer releasing a stream of rose petals from either hand as she ran forward. Ashton set this to No. 15 of Brahms's Waltzes, Opus 39. It was the briefest of homages. Now the dance is the last of five numbers, all drawn from Opus 39; under the title *Five Brahms Waltzes in the Manner of Isadora Duncan*, the extended solo was the highlight last week of American Ballet Theatre's gala at the State Theatre. Ashton's dances are not reconstructions but evocations of a personality and a style. Unlike the actual Duncan studies that Annabelle Gamson performs so vividly to the same music, they do not reveal a technique. Neither do they conceal it. But without being any less simple than Gamson's performance Ashton's choreography places far less emphasis on the symmetrical oppositions, the big, plain contrasts by which Duncan dance demonstrated its constancy of motivation from the body's center. Those things, stated in the most instructive way by Annabelle Gamson, tell us how Duncan saw dance. Ashton tells us how she saw herself. For him, "the manner of Isadora Duncan" is inseparable from the person of Duncan, and it may be that at the time he first saw her—1921, when she was past forty—she was giving a less active and clear-edged account of what was purely prescriptive in her work. The Isadora of *Five Brahms Waltzes* asks to be taken on her own terms as a magnetic performing artist, and because she is danced by Lynn Seymour, that is how we do take her.

Seymour's rightness for the part isn't measured only by her magnetism. If there had been a poll in the dance world on the question of whom to cast in the movie of Duncan's life that was made a few years ago, the choice would have been Lynn Seymour— Seymour the actress, the performer of epic daring, but most of all Seymour the dancer. She has always possessed the roundness and fullness of contour, the plastic vigor, and the coherent rhythm to express the sculptural depth that Isadora's dancing must have had. Beautiful in classical effacé positions, Seymour is heroic in Duncan plastique. The back yields, the chest lifts, the arms expand and float, and then from this open aspect the figure suddenly withdraws in a crouch or a stance braced and turned in on itself. The reversal seems miraculous each time, because Seymour is so securely centered. She doesn't have to stop and relocate, and she doesn't tighten up or rigidify or signal ahead; she simply arrives in one piece, loosely disposed, the arms coiled about the head, the hips angled, the turned-in knee relaxed. The whole scroll-like motion is carelessly light and free, yet it's indelible. Ashton's and Seymour's Isadora is a virtuoso.

Duncan at her recitals often had pianists of renown; Seymour's accompanist at the gala was Malcolm Frager. After a short prelude, the curtain rises. A scarf of pink silk hangs from the piano, and, in a pink puff-peplum tunic, Seymour lies on the floor, one knee cocked, one hand toying with invisible pebbles. Like the costume and the tousled red hair, the monumental thigh is Isadora's. The pebbles are on Nausicaa's beach. The image recalls the photographs of Isadora ensconced in her Grecian mood, but then, as Seymour rises and advances in slow balancés with outspreading arms, the photograph suddenly liquefies and becomes three-dimensional. And, from there on, stage space becomes the landscape of the performer's imagination. At first, it's that Homeric beach where nymphs play; then it's the abstract architectural void redeemed and dramatized by its lone tenant. Seymour "acts" the drama of space as if such a drama had never occurred before, as indeed it hadn't. Isadora's recitals marked the advent of the dancer as a personage encompassing all scenery, all events in a series of autonomous gestures. The vault of space expands or contracts and the dancing figure itself becomes voluminous or tiny, sheltered or exposed, as if by impulse. One variation on the theme: the silk scarf held aloft in a headlong run becomes "this canopy the sky"; in the next moment, it sheathes the body, a second skin. Then, when it is cast decisively aside, it is as if intimacy with nature had been checked, and the august impersonal world returns. That the dancer can alter the proportions and the investiture of space without the aid of a corps de ballet, without scenic decoration, is a presumption with metaphysical implications that would repay serious study. There are historical implications, too, in the fact that this idea dawned in a period when, despite Darwin, people still believed in man's hegemony over nature. But what an enthralling theatrical idea it still is! Ashton and Seymour have brought it back alive.

Gala evenings usually program a lot of gadgety pas de deux that sock the audience. Twyla Tharp and Mikhail Baryshnikov dancing to Frank Sinatra songs promised to be an exception, and they were. But Tharp, who devised the choreography for *Once More, Frank*, played things too far down and close in. She and Baryshnikov, in unisex shirts and shorts, might have been doing their supercool duet for themselves alone. The first two numbers ("Something Stupid" and "That's Life") were full of dancerly challenges that often weren't clear to my eye and buddy-buddy jokes that unfortunately were. The third dance, to "One for My Baby," cut the cackle and got down to business. It had a slow-rolling mood of tension, with erratic shifts of emphasis which, though hard to anticipate, were not at all hard to follow—a lot like the densest and most dream-logged portions of *The Bix Pieces*. The material was royally served by Baryshnikov (in the first two numbers he had seemed technically unsure), but there was nothing in it to indicate why he had been used. Tharp seemed to be co-opting him not, as so many other choreographers have done, to punch up a line of goods but to keep her company while she worked out her newest choreographic puzzle. There should be some level between Baryshnikov submerged and Baryshnikov exploited, and there is—in a piece called *Push Comes to Shove*. —*July 26, 1976*

Premises, Premises

The Pennsylvania Ballet has completed another of its seasons at the Brooklyn Academy, this time an extended one, and it marked the occasion by bringing along five new ballets, all by American choreographers and all but one made specially for the company. Like many other products of the Bicentennial Year, two of the homemade works seem to have been created to fill artificial needs. The other two filled needs more or less valid but sought to disguise the fact by dredging up artificial pretexts. Both of these interesting but deceptive ballets were by Benjamin Harkarvy, the Pennsylvania's artistic director. Harkarvy regularly turns out pieces that serve his dancers without adding up to much as ballets. They're useful work-outs for audiences, too—dance études made with the fluent skill and perception of a good teacher. Though their poetic content is not high, they often have a heartfelt academic wisdom that makes them stimulating to watch. Yet with these latest efforts Harkarvy seems to have decided that we need the lure of a fake premise for the action. *Four Men Waiting* is a sample of Harkarvy's energetic lyrical prose which seems like blank verse because of its scheme: it reduces the four men to one, who is still waiting at the end, after women have claimed the others. All this scheme does is channel the choreographer's options; it doesn't present a poetic subject, and the piece turns out to be nothing more than an arrangement for different combinations of dancers to some rippling Saint-Saëns. It's the kind of ballet that thirty or forty years ago would have been done with moonlight and tulle, a strong Russian accent, and a vague perfumy title that didn't lead an audience to expect more drama than it got. And instead of standing around gripping their lapels or crouching in yoga postures the four men would have decorated the stage in melancholy *classique* poses with beseeching port de bras. We'd have known from the start that it was all nonsense.

In Harkarvy's ballet, the women are "classical," the men "modern" and in trousers, not tights. His other piece, a pas de deux, is also ballet kitsch, and though he confines his defensiveness to a program note, what he says there is revealing: that the piece is a tribute to "the film musicals of the past—when any moment, or any situation, seemed an appropriate excuse to burst into dance." What takes place on the stage is a scene in a rehearsal studio: a boy coaxes a girl to dance; she refuses him wearily but then complies. The substance of the piece is not in this most familiar of all contrivances but in the dances, which Harkarvy has fitted, with more than typical care, I thought, to the music of Copland's "Four Piano Blues" and to the talents of Marcia Darhower and Dane LaFontsee. Harkarvy has even made LaFontsee's tightness expressive. Surely we don't need an excuse for that. And the piece doesn't need a title—*For Fred, Gene and M-G-M*—that conjures up not only a false dance image but also the wrong movie-musical era. Movies did create the feeling that dance could burst out of "any moment, or any situation," but that was in the thirties, and it was done by making the stories and characters and settings as fantastic as the lyrical outburst, or by using a backstage plot, in which event the moments and situations came ready-made. In the forties and fifties, which is the era Harkarvy seems to want to invoke, movies were more preoccupied with fitting dances and songs into naturalistic contexts, and it took in most cases a lot of heavy labor. Why a professional choreographer, working with a professional ballet company of stature and playing to an audience that expects to see dance unapologetically presented, should feel the need to inveigle us with pretexts is a question that only Philadelphia, perhaps, can answer.

The three other premières were all Philadelphia stories. Gene Hill Sagan, a Philadelphia choreographer, originally made *Sweet Agony* for an Israeli company; it is a monotonous, hard-driving Talley Beatty-ish affairs, worthless except for the scrupulosity with which the Pennsylvania dancers perform it. *Eakins' View* and *Under the Sun* derive their reasons for being from the fact that Thomas Eakins and Alexander Calder were born in Philadelphia. The idea of basing ballets on the work of these two artists must have seemed attractive as well as pertinent to those who thought it up. But in neither case has the idea been made to assume a theatrical form. In *Eakins' View*, Rodney Griffin takes on not only Eakins but also Charles Ives—his Third Symphony. Following Ives's lead appears to have thrown Griffin off the track of Eakins, and the choreography never gets much beyond its initial presentation of the artist figure (based on the portrait called *The Thinker*) surrounded, as in a reverie, by his life models—boxers, rowers, street folk, various undifferentiated ladies who come and go. This tranquil, twilit world is not Eakins's view but a view of Eakins, a strangely selective one. The reality of Eakins's life was his unrelenting fight against the proprieties of the academy. However, the air is filled with the look and sound of distinguished American art, and most of Whitney Blausen's costumes have unusual style.

Alexander Calder might be the ideal designer of a fantastic-toyland ballet, but *Under the Sun* isn't a Calder ballet. Like *Eakins' View*, it's pastiche, and it's not as good. The designers are Robert Mitchell (scenery) and Willa Kim (costumes), and their adaptations of Calder's work lack the organic wit that a "Calder" stage fantasy should have. The action starts promisingly, with the heroine, who is called Corolla, emerging head downward from the mouth of a gigantic grinning sun, but the other engines and props are perfunctorily used, and the stage never comes to life with Calder's special sense of fun. In fact, the opposite happens: Corolla's adventures take place in an inanimate ice-cold Calderland. Of the two designers, Mitchell appears to have had an easier time translating mobiles and stabiles into décor than Kim had projecting sculptural conceptions onto the human figure. Her costumes tend to wired pompons and polka dots; one dancer has a hula hoop, and that's as far as things go. The difference between the scenery and the costumes is like the difference between Pure and Applied Calder. The dancers in their white body tights touched with streaks and frills of color look like those painted airplanes. Between the museum and the airport, there's no theatre.

One reason the design elements are as poorly integrated and unversatile as they are is that Margo Sappington's scenario is aimless, like her choreography. Corolla, the Sun Child, visits the domain of Etincelle, Queen of the Mobiles. Etincelle makes her appearance in a standing pose inside a blue hemisphere. She alights and is carried about by four handlers. Then she makes another appearance exactly like the first and is carried about some more. Etincelle is pretty obviously the Moon, and though Sappington must have intended some sort of correspondence to Corolla, it never becomes evident in the ballet. About midway, Sappington seems to switch her style from "character" to "abstract," and a temporary correspondence does occur, when mobiles are suspended above the stage while the dancers go through some slow cantilevered balances and hook-on lifts to the shoulder. But at no time does the ballet break free of its resemblance to those indoctrination tours of the art world which are inflicted on schoolchildren. Michael Kamen, whose score might have been written for a television documentary on California freeways, was once involved with Sappington and Kim in a "Rodin" ballet produced by the Harkness company; all I remember of that is an assortment of marbleized tights and bronze-stained rags. Where will the trio strike next—Tinguely, Arp, Nadelman?

Square Dance, the Balanchine ballet that may or may not be about square dancing, is back this season in two versions. The Joffrey Ballet has presented a close copy of the original New York City Ballet production, with the musicians playing in shirtsleeves from a platform at one side of the stage, the male dancers in red neckerchiefs, and an authentic country caller in striped trousers and red flannel shirt. The caller is the same Elisha C. Keeler who originated the role in the first *Square Dance* and performed it in subsequent revivals. Except for a few topical references, his spiel is just what it was in 1957: "Gents go 'round, come right back, Make your feet go wickety-wack." Next week, the New York City Ballet presents its own revival, from which all production elements have been dropped. The string band is in the pit, the costumes are pale-blue and gray practice dress, there is no caller. The choreography, with extra stage room, expands; in spatial terms, it is squarer than ever. The friendly colloquial flavor of the steps is still there, but it's remoter than it was, something scented on the wind. Without words to hammer it into our heads ("wickety-wack" is entrechat quatre), we can perceive why the piece is called *Square Dance* and also why it might just as reasonably be called *Balanchine/Corelli-Vivaldi, 1957.* The ballet contains twin sets of superimpositions: traditional country dancing, American style, superimposed on classical ballet steps and set to seventeenth-century string music that, in its turn, superimposed the elegance of a courtly style on ancient folk dances. Everything locks together naturally—so naturally that Balanchine's first thoughts about the ballet were that the public would miss the point. For years, he insisted on an obvious wickety-wack production. "Otherwise," he is reported to have said, "it will be only another ballet, with Vivaldi music."

But it took Balanchine's eye to discover elegance in American square dancing, and his creativity to ignite the double strands of suggestion in both the dancing and the music. The ballet is one of his brilliant covert jokes. Its premise is that basic square-dance patterns are as old as the Renaissance. He has always loved to raid the vernacular, and square dancing—the only formal ensemble dancing still performed in American society—has been a particularly liberal source. In *Western Symphony*, there's a kind of square dance executed sur les pointes to cowboy tunes. It is breezier and funnier than anything in *Square Dance*, because its irony works only one way: it puts classical ballet up on stilts, as in a cartoon. The irony of *Square Dance* is more bilateral, closer to the deadpan classic-nonclassic ambiguities of *Agon*, which in point of time followed *Square Dance* by only two weeks. In the current, stripped version of the ballet, Balanchine has inserted a new solo for the principal male dancer, Bart Cook, danced to the Sarabande from the same suite that furnishes the other Corelli portions of the score. In its way, the solo is as radically inventive a response to the music of Corelli as the Sarabande in *Agon* is to the music of Stravinsky (who used seventeenth-century court dances as his models). The *Agon* Sarabande (which Cook also dances) is curt, springy, with sections of intricate crossweave built up by a zigzag pelvis over fidgety feet. It's both ceremonious and mocking of ceremony. The choreography to the Corelli Sarabande is in a different rhetoric, more like the officialese of the music, yet drawn far out of range of orthodoxy. Slow, deep, with widely planted feet and serpentine torso, this dance wrings the convolutions of the Sarabande from what seems a single long phrase sustained by momentary adjustments in the leverage of the body. Cook's copper-wire frame supports suspensions and circlings of the leg which press the logic of such steps beyond its normal span or its point of connection with a succeeding step. The connection is mysteriously abridged, so that as we begin to anticipate a step's conclusion it reappears already recomposed and heading in a new direction. The unusual conception is a slow-motion version of what happens in the step-lively sections of the ballet, with their buoyant attack and elliptical continuity. I don't think there's a single preparation or interruption for recovery in the entire piece.

With this 1976 interpolation, and with a filling out of the male soloist's role in the ensemble sections, Balanchine has created a new character in *Square Dance*. Cook's "courtier" is a poet, his solo the poem that such a courtier might address to his lady. In its exploration of the nonpercussive aspect of male dancing, the Sarabande is unique in the Balanchine repertory, and it stems from an evident decision to make the man's role an adagio counterpart to the ballet's allegro heroine. But the New York City Ballet hasn't found the right ballerina to put against the quietly magnificent Cook. Kay Mazzo has been doing the part in braids; many of the details are blurred or deleted, and the show is stolen by Cook and the excellent ensemble of six couples. At the Joffrey, Francesca Corkle is the more forceful, Denise Jackson the more demure interpreter, but the role has been simplified even more than in Miss Mazzo's performance. Patricia Wilde's original performance, recorded on a television film in 1963, is a reminder that in her day Wilde was the *whole* show, and that clarity, precision, and—never to be underestimated—an invincible, cheerful repose were an integral part of her bravura. Wilde's footwork was so delicious that even in a murky kinescope one can relish every feat as it flies past. And the ballet itself flies past in about half the time it now takes in the theatre, with or without the new solo. (This is not an illusion but a fact.)

A Wilde role that has moved more easily into repertory than *Square Dance* has is in *Raymonda Variations*. The Pennsylvania company dances the *Variations* with a uniform deliberation that I find appealing, and this year Martine van Hamel was invited to dance the ballerina role for the first time. Van Hamel, the best Raymonda at American Ballet Theatre, was ready for the greater challenge of the Balanchine version—greater not merely in its development of the Petipa style but in its elaboration of the original Petipa character. Raymonda, created for Pierina Legnani at the age of thirty-five, is a mature woman, and in his great adagio Balanchine carries forward Petipa's conception of a robust and settled femininity. A variety of images are suggestive, among them the many supported turns and poses which seem to stress a certain distance between the man and the woman and also their happy adjustment to it. This is not a youthful passion. In contrast to Raymonda, the other female soloists are girls. (The same relationship obtains between the Swan Queen and the corps—Legnani was then thirty-two—whereas the first Aurora was the twenty-three-year-old

Carlotta Brianza, and youth is reflected in that role to this day.) Van Hamel in her début looked large but slim (far slimmer than in *Concerto Barocco*, where the surgical line of the choreography seemed to want to cut into her midriff) and very festive; it was one of her most beautiful appearances. If she could only have this role to work on and perform often, she could have a triumph in it. The pas-de-chat/pirouette ending of the second variation, nowadays done at the New York City Ballet as a line of brisés, gave her no difficulty; she has the same step sequence in the same tempo in *Theme and Variations* at ABT. The original triple-pirouette/promenade/penchée ending of the adagio was seen in Suzanne Farrell's performance last season at the New York City Ballet for the first time in years. No other New York City ballerina attempts it; neither did Van Hamel or the Pennsylvania's admirably bold Michelle Lucci. Van Hamel's partner was Burton Taylor, also a guest—gallant in support, handsome but violent in his variations.

Another lovely Balanchine ballet—lovely but, I had thought, lost—turned up in a series given by the Eglevsky Ballet at Queens Theatre in the Park, near Shea Stadium. This was the first version of the Glinka *Valse-Fantaisie*, made in 1953. It is cast for three ballerinas and one danseur, who mostly partners but does get to do some leaps ending in a drop to the knee. His arabesque-salutes turning to each of the three girls near the close of the ballet are also quite wonderful. *Valse-Fantaisie* is Balanchine's rehabilitation of the banal genre that *Four Men Waiting* recalls. The current version, for a female and a male soloist and a corps of four girls, retains some features of the old number—the ballerina's manège alternating pas couru with split jeté is one—but on the whole the old *Valse-Fantaisie* is nothing like the new one. It is a warm, romantic "Russian" work, and in certain respects—the involvement of the three women with the single male—it is, like parts of *Serenade*, a valentine to adolescence. Balanchine rechoreographed it, apparently, in order to make the man's part stronger, but the outcome was a piece that is little more than an effective perpetuum mobile with virtuoso passages that bring applause. The performance by the young Eglevsky company was hampered by a shallow, noisy stage with no wing space, but the dancers (Netta Blitman, Salli Silliman, Kim Vickers, and William Starrett) got through it more than decently and should flourish in their parts.   —*November 15, 1976*

Denishawn Without Spirit

The Spirit of Denishawn is an evening-length reconstruction of technical exercises and dances dating from the archaic teens and twenties, and most of it has the same relation to serious dancing that *September Morn* has to serious painting. The honorable place that Denishawn occupies in American dance history has tended to obscure its actual character as dance entertainment. We think of Denishawn as the first institutionalized dance theatre in the United States. Through its branch schools and extensive concert tours and vaudeville bookings, and not least through the illustrious reputation of its founder, Ruth St. Denis, and the evangelical persistence of her partner, Ted Shawn, it had a nationwide impact, which has been amply chronicled. Denishawn opened its first dance school, in Los Angeles, in 1915; it toured the Orient in 1925–26. Martha Graham had already quit the company; Doris Humphrey and Charles Weidman were to leave it shortly afterward. In 1931, St. Denis and Shawn made their last joint appearance with the company, and its dissolution is generally dated from their separation. Although many of the schools remained active, the aesthetic, or "spirit," of Denishawn was by then already dead. But it was a hit in its day, and it is a hit again—the kind people seem to have been hungry for. Staged by Klarna Pinska and performed by the Joyce Trisler Danscompany, *The Spirit of Denishawn* was besieged for four performances at the Riverside Theatre last month; it is now having a two-week run at the Roundabout Stage One.

Klarna Pinska, a lifelong disciple of Ruth St. Denis, came to Denishawn in 1919 to study and then to teach. The program she has assembled appears to be a cross-section of the curriculum and repertory as they were in that year and in 1920 or a little later; it is very much a teacher's program, limited to teachable things. I have always thought of high Denishawn as those historical pageants enacted by the two stars in heavy makeup with lots of extras and scenery, but Miss Pinska gives us instead a straight choreographic revue. We are plunged into a workaday Denishawn technique class, with battements tendus and other classical barre work quickly displaced by decorative attitudes in a number of exotic styles. Dancers flatten their hands to look Egyptian or bend them back at the wrist to look Indian or Javanese. This section ends with the swirling scarves that were a Denishawn trademark. In the two other sections, "Music Visualizations" and "Orientalia," the most effective numbers are those in which the scarf does all the dancing—*Dance in Space, Red and Gold Sari,* and *Soaring*—and in which the music does not resist the dancers' attempts to turn it into a springboard for so many Mickey Mice. (The verb "to mickey-mouse," denoting abusively literal musical treatment, came from Disney's Silly Symphonies, which were often more imaginative, in their extension of Denishawn "visualizations," than Denishawn.) *Soaring* is set to Schumann's "Aufschwung"—which means the same thing, after all—and stars a square of silk supported by five girls, who make it billow like a canopy or shimmer like a waterfall. *Dance in Space* is Miss Pinska's version of Doris Humphrey's solo to the Chaminade *Valse Caprice,* and, like *Soaring,* it suggests that no Denishawn dancer contemplated an invasion of space without a length of cloth in her hand. The concept of a dance as a bodily construction in space and time was not a Denishawn concept, although it appears to have been at the basis of most civilized dancing for two hundred years.

It's tempting to think that what made Denishawn dancing a popular attraction in its time is making it popular now—the placid sweet dreams of "pure" art, the wispy dilettantism. But most people, I think, don't take the dances seriously in that way. (Those who might probably don't know that that's the kind of "serious" they're going to get.) What they do take seriously is Denishawn's legend—its historical place. They want to get at the facts. Dancers seldom investigate their own past, and Klarna Pinska's reconstructions, which give us a chance at long last to inspect the origins of an art form, come at a time when even the general public has realized that an important movement in dance history—what we have called modern dance—has run its course. Contemporary choreographers like Merce Cunningham, Paul Taylor, and Twyla Tharp are so individually accomplished and so far above the competition that we no longer think of them as part of a genealogical line. (Actually, another genealogy emerged in the sixties from Merce Cunningham, but that, too, seems to have run its course.) The death of fertility in the house of dance has inspired new interest in its founders. But we should beware of working up too much compensatory appetite. The past can only be made to yield what the present is equipped to see.

What we see is a suite of dances that make very little sense as dance. We look at these period pieces through eyes at once sharpened by the art of dancing as it has evolved in the twentieth century and dulled by the cultural dispossession that has accompanied our speedy advance through time. For us, dance is the preeminent art in any ballet; it is more important than acting, than music, than décor and costume, and it is the self-sufficient art, too, supplanting the functions of most, and at times all, of these other arts. Naturally, the Denishawn dances look empty by our standards, and some of them (Ted Shawn's swaggering or constricted solos in particular) look unpardonably foolish by any standard. But even the best of these pieces were meant to be seen not as dances in the modern sense but as theatre in the late-nineteenth-century sense. Dancing was just one element in the concerted achievement of a theatrical image. Although they were a chief force in establishing dancing as an independent art form (independent, that is, of sponsoring art forms such as opera or musical comedy), the Denishawners didn't have our appreciation of what dancing alone could do, and if we could time-travel backward to an actual performance of 1920 these dances that strike us now as affected and vague would look very different. The point is, though, that they do look affected and vague. They're inescapably part of the debris of history, and for as long as the present aesthetic moment lasts they're unsalvageable and unseeable.

The greatest loss is that we can no longer perceive the theatrical images that Ruth St. Denis personally set in motion. It has been said too often and too lightly that Denishawn emphasized theatrical over dance effects; not until now did we know what that meant. And it has been said far too often that St. Denis's performances projected a mystique compounded of many Eastern and Western philosophies. How unnecessary it seems now to think of such things when the greater mystique of St. Denis's *theatrical* projection has been erased from view. The St. Denis form of projection consisted in animating an illusion of inhabited space. In her solos, she was never really alone on the stage; her scarf or her sari could become her partner, and we, the onlookers, were partners, too. In the *Nautch* solo there are gestures that imply the noise and derision of a marketplace. The dancer who now performs the solo has obviously been told something of the sort, but she instinctively converts the gestures into those of an Eighth Avenue stripper. Time and again, it's the knowing response rather than the knowledgeable one which we get from the Trisler dancers. I found myself wondering whether a superior company—say, Martha Graham's—could have made more sense of the material, but in the end I realized that the gap in sensibility between our generation of dancers and our grandfathers' was too great to be patched over. All the St. Denis solos call on a gift for dramatization. Many seem provisionally constructed for a dancer with a glamorous, teasingly aloof presence. They were made to be transcended in performance. Dancers who can't act, can't wear a costume with effrontery, can't impose a convincing plastique upon a weak composition are the dancers we are breeding today. They expect the choreography to carry the performance for them; when it doesn't, they wrestle with the choreography, and that only carries a little way. The most one can hope for is clues from which to make translations. In *Nautch* there was such a clue; in *Liebestraum* there was nothing. The dancer did a flowing waltz-walk around and around the stage, now and then striking a high-breasted pose on a musical climax. At the end, there were a few indistinct mime gestures directed to a person unseen. The transitions between the waltzing, the poses, and the mime were unclear as well.

It was through objectifying or animating space that the soloist of fifty and sixty years ago communicated her dance to an audience. Now there is nothing left of that communication or of the sensed bond with an audience out of which it grew. In Annabelle Gamson's recent concert at the Roundabout, the principle was demonstrated so vividly that its existence as a tenet of the old dance is no longer, I think, in dispute. Annabelle Gamson is a dancer of middle years who seems to have caught the echoes of an older tradition. Lately, she has offered interpretations of Isadora Duncan's solos which have done much to clarify our thinking on Isadora and her era. She has now added to her repertory several more Duncan solos, both early and late, as well as a pair of dances by Mary Wigman. In Duncan's *Valse Brillante* (Chopin), she bounded repeatedly toward the audience, shaping with her arms an enormous ball of air; then she'd dissolve the solidity of the thing and on an arpeggio escape backward in pitterpat runs. It was interesting, too, to see the logic of Isadora's musical response: when the arpeggio lengthened, she didn't change the step but merely ran backward longer and faster. Duncan's vocabulary was as sparse as any Denishawner's, but by shifts of weight and emphasis Gamson filled the repetitions with nuance. In "Prelude" (the one Fokine took for his *Chopiniana*) there was only one gesture—a slow walk in four directions with an arm lifting now to this, now to that corner of the stage. This time, it was a question not of repetition but of a single idea stated with complete conviction. The gesture means "Here is my space." Fokine's dance, composed a few years later, is a rhapsody on the same idea. In general, the clearer Duncan's dances are made to seem, the closer grow her associations with her contemporaries. *Mother* is a Duse-like pantomime with cradling gestures for an imaginary child. One feels Duncan to have been part of a worldwide artistic revolution and to have embodied, as a privilege of the revolution, the freedom to rove among a variety of effects, switching, say, from dance to mime and back without losing clarity of motivation. One senses a similar impulse in the St. Denis solos but also a degree of specialization unlike Isadora's. When St. Denis says, on one of the tapes we hear during the Denishawn program, "I was an idea dancer, not a music dancer," I'm not sure I know what she means, but it seems likely that she was better at animating space dramatically than abstractly.

Gamson's portrait of Wigman is drawn from two companion pieces of 1929. *Pastoral* and *Dance of Summer* are schematic music visualizations in the German manner: the arms account for the "theme," the feet for the accompaniment. Aside from the Duncan works, the most interesting parts of Gamson's recital were some new pieces of her own choreography, called *Five Easy Dances*. Gamson's work has occasionally been fastidious and intellectual, like Wigman's, but the new dances are simple, if not easy, and free— more like Duncan's.   —*December 6, 1976*

Selling It

Probably no form of hucksterism is as embarrassing as cultural hucksterism. Shakespeare in the flesh turning up on television to plug the plays at Stratford; that campaign on behalf of the Metropolitan Opera to "strike a blow for civilization"; the lady who once sang Rinso commercials and wound up at that same Met now advertising herself as "Bubbles"; the American Ballet Theatre ads that say "Fall in love again": whether the tone is coy or grim, the appeal of these messages is always indirect, as if the hucksters dared not have us look what they're selling full in the face. Art is something they back us into with a rearview mirror rigged so that we'll keep catching flattering reflections of ourselves. A lot of the time, what we see is the fat, scared face of publicity.

Philistinism—the basic disbelief in the values of all art—accounts for some of that fright, but uncertainty accounts for more of it. Ten or so years ago, when we first began hearing the phrase "the new audience," the Ballet Theatre ad would have said simply, "Fall in love." How to sell what people are already buying is a problem. The market analysts might define the promoters' task as having to deal with an uprooted philistinism that hasn't yet settled into a visible pattern of taste, but since ballet has been increasing in popularity in this country for the last forty years, not just for the last ten, it seems unwise to attribute to social change what may in fact represent expansion on a stable base. The high performance arts aren't susceptible to social change in the same way that popular entertainment is; though they are connected to the way we live, they don't give themselves up to transient values. The Dance Theatre of Harlem wouldn't have been possible even twenty years ago, but its reason for being isn't centered on the conditions that made it possible. There have been commercial coups in ballet, and there's a theory that ballet as a whole has directly profited from the demise of musicals on Broadway and in the movies. What has arisen in the last ten years is a subgenre of ballet which we might call pop ballet: whole repertories (the Stuttgart Ballet) or parts of repertories (the Joffrey, the Ailey) devoted to slick approximations of the higher article. The success of pop ballet, which is very probably related to the demise of musicals, may have caused a slight swelling of the statistics that belong to ballet proper, but if you shear off that success the statistics are still impressive. They always have been.

Everyone knows that ballet is too expensive to support itself on box-office alone. The devious sales pitch serves no purpose; it fools no one. The thing that has sold ballet to the American public is ballet itself. People who market ballet haven't been keeping pace with the public; their methods don't reflect the public's sophisticated interest in a special kind of event. ABT used its line about falling in love again in a season at the City Center which consisted of just two ballets, *Giselle* and *Coppélia*. The ad might have been written by someone who thought that the term "romantic," as in Romantic ballet, meant amorous. Well, ABT does produce *Coppélia* as if it were *Blossom Time*, but *Giselle* is still *Giselle*—the sole surviving work created at the Paris Opéra during the golden age of Romantic ballet. And *Coppélia*, coming nearly thirty years later, was the masterpiece of the silver age. The two ballets are hereditarily linked through their composers. Adolphe Adam, who wrote *Giselle*, was Léo Delibes's teacher, and had himself written an opera on Delibes's subject, called *The Nuremberg Doll*. Is it too much to imagine an ad campaign built on those links? Or, if that seems too stuffy, I think I'd have preferred "Adorable Adam" and "Delightful, Delicious Delibes" to Falling Flat Again.

The score of *Coppélia* is given by ABT with cuts in the first and third acts. In the third, the Discord and War music is used for a men's ensemble with an entry for Frantz—one way of supplying the solo that Delibes didn't compose for *his* Frantz, who was played by a girl. The ending of Dawn, which Delibes left unresolved, to be immediately followed by Prayer, has been newly provided with a closing cadence, for no reason other than to encourage applause for the soloist. The production as a whole is juvenile burlesque in style, with simplistic daisy-chain choreography that a ranking company should be ashamed of. Even so, it takes repeated viewings, because of its transcendent score. How many times can one listen to *Giselle*? Adam does not falter; he's certainly charming, but he never penetrates, and his schematic structure—the celebrated leit-motivs—envelop the ballet in an atmosphere of unyielding efficiency. I speak of the score as it has come down to us, with not only Burg-müller's interpolation (Peasant pas de deux) but the interpolations and revisions that are thought to have been contributed by Minkus to various Russian revivals. Adam's original score had more variety in the first act, with a formal pas de deux for Giselle and Albrecht. (In the ABT production, we get a trace of this when Giselle leads Albrecht into the villagers' dance.) With just two exceptions, the abridged and modified second act is not greatly different in effect from the original version. The exceptions are Myrtha's waltz varia-tion—Adam's is more extensive, more exciting, and more delicately scored—and the Wilis's fugue, which describes a moment when the Wilis attack in waves in an attempt to drive Albrecht from the cross. Mary Skeaping's production for London Festival Ballet restores this deletion, among others. But the fugue sounds like nothing else in the score, and that is probably the reason it was cut. Minkus's editing tightened Adam's scheme to the point where we can speak of Giselle as a dance drama in the modern sense of united elements serving a single purpose. And subsequent revisions altered the libretto to suit the modern sensibility. Albrecht is no longer reclaimed by Bathilde in the end but remains alone at the grave.

Perrot, one of the ballet's original choreographers, and then Petipa mounted the St. Petersburg revivals; the second act as it appears today seems to date from the period of Swan Lake, which was Romantic-revivalist in inspiration. This act is a masterpiece of dance architecture, but in modern performance it often doesn't keep up the plot suspense its authors meant it to have. The idea of the cross as Albrecht's sanctuary isn't maintained, and his motive on leaving it isn't made clear—that in choosing to remain with Giselle he chooses death. In a love-death climax, Albrecht's dances would exalt rather than exhaust him. We never see this happen, nor do we see an ambivalent Giselle torn between her love for Albrecht and her loyalty to her queen.. These possibilities, which can be sensed from the design of the choreography, are options that thoughtful interpreters can adopt as they see fit. At Ballet Theatre, everybody does the ballet the same way, with only tiny modifications of the ritual. Since Baryshnikov's début, the matter of the lilies has become clearer than it was. But if they are tokens of Giselle's living spirit— her sign to him that she's really about to materialize—then they shouldn't be the flowers that Albrecht is carrying when he appears. In pure dance matters, there is likely to be much experimentation. The Giselles fool with the tempi; the Albrechts change the steps. In a guest appearance, the solemn Peter Schaufuss, bursting into high cabrioles and dazzling renversé spins, won the crowd that had come to cheer Makarova.

The role of Giselle is a piety. Dancers believe that until they've done it they haven't really met the test of the ballerina. At ABT, there's further pressure on its top ballerinas to compete in the classic roles; sometimes they seem to be competing for the sake of their fans. Martine van Hamel has already triumphed in the roles that test the kind of ballerina she is—Theme and Variations,

Odette-Odile, Nikiya in *La Bayadère*, Raymonda, Aurora. She doesn't need Giselle. However, as Giselle she had more of a chance to convince us than she had in the title role of *La Sylphide* a season or two ago; that is, she might have turned the traditionally frail and pathetic Giselle into someone we could believe that only Van Hamel could portray—a big, sturdy country girl who goes mad when she's betrayed, and kills herself. But Van Hamel played within the tradition, and she didn't kill herself—she just wisped away. Van Hamel's dramatic gifts are concentrated in her dancing, and it is difficult for her to rise in a role that doesn't have a yeasty dance lead. In *Coppélia*, where that lead is reduced to a trail of crumbs, all she could do was force her animation. In *Giselle* Act II, she was more freely expressive, but here again it was the conventional Giselle who danced rather than the true Van Hamel, and it was impossible not to regret that her presence as Giselle deprived this production of the greatest Myrtha it has ever seen.

—*February 14, 1977*

Old *Master*

As the sole première of its truncated winter season, the New York City Ballet is giving *Bournonville Divertissements*, with a collection of prize performances by Danes and non-Danes alike. There is the astonishing dancing that one gets from Peter Martins, the King of Denmark; there is the authoritative dancing of Adam Lüders, another Danish soloist, who joined the company not long ago; there is the limpid, meticulous dancing of Helgi Tomasson, formed in part by Danish training. But for the American dancers *Bournonville Divertissements* marks a professional début in an un-accustomed style. Peter Schaufuss, the third of the company's true Danes, is not in the cast; it is Robert Weiss who dances in the trio from *La Ventana*, and Daniel Duell who takes the principal role of Gennaro in the Ballabile from *Napoli* Act I. Duell, whose career has been accelerating lately, confirms the strong impression he has already made. But Weiss, in a more demanding role, is a surprise. He has always had the stretch and spring necessary to Bournonville and to his repertory roles, but his flaws, which include a bad hunch, helpless arms, and a two-dimensional torso, are miraculously corrected here. In *La Ventana*, Weiss is careful, relaxed, and stylish; it's the best performance of his career.

There are other surprises. One of them is that the women are as good as the men. This seldom happens, even today, at the Royal Danish Ballet. Bournonville choreography consists of some of the most difficult combinations conceived by the mind of man, and most of them are for the body of man, too. August Bournonville (1805–79) danced until he was forty-three. His fertility and ingenuity as a choreographer, which dominated Danish ballet to the end of his days, sprang directly from his strengths as a dancer and from his methods of disguising personal deficiencies. He was also a teacher, and undoubtedly a great one—scientifically wise and artistically unimpeachable. His studio in Copenhagen was a dancers' lab, hothouse, and proving ground, and it was the necessary link between Paris, where Vestris had once nurtured male dancing, and St. Petersburg, where it was, with Nijinsky, to rise again. A second after the curtain is up on *Napoli*, the first of the *Bournonville Divertissements*, we see Jean-Pierre Frohlich soaring into a sequence of double ronds de jambe sautés and beats, and the male ensemble behind him leaping as exactingly and as lustily, and we know that the men of the company are on to Bournonville's secrets. The proof that the women are on to them, too, isn't in Merrill Ashley's waltz variation in *La Ventana*, tough as it is and brilliantly as she dances it. Ashley is, after all, the strongest female technician in the company. But Nichol Hlinka in *Napoli* and Kyra Nichols in *La Ventana* are revelations in featured roles, which, as corps girls, they seldom get. Little Hlinka, the Teresina to Duell's Gennaro, reveals herself softly but roundly. She does many of the daunting steps he does, including a turning jeté into high, still arabesque, which, in the enterprising Bournonville manner, shuts and reopens itself in reverse (assemblé, sissonne). What a lovely illusion this is, constant in Bournonville, of the dancer finding his feet only to throw them away only to find them again. Miss Nichols's variation is very much a point variation, however, in which the repeated relevés emphasize constancy in the feet themselves. The date is 1854, and use of the full point in unblocked shoes was not extensive. One can feel Bournonville pushing for a feminine touch. Modern ballerina technique was, of course, a post-Bournonville development. It arose from sustained pointwork, which made possible the supported adagio, with its aura of sexuality in partnering. This is something we never see on Bournonville's stage. In point technique, the difference was like going from plucked strings to bowed strings. The beginnings of a major discovery are apt to have a peculiar beauty and dignity. Kyra Nichols, emerging from her historical cocoon, could be a major discovery, too.

I don't know whether to call Colleen Neary's performance a surprise or not. This greatly talented but erratic dancer tends to rush her audience with effects that she can't always control. Yet the tendency is also a part of her charm. The excerpt from *A Folk Tale* is the dashing "gypsy" pas de sept; it releases all of Neary's exuberance while containing her technically. She has length, breadth, and ballon—bounce—to spare. She and Adam Lüders do one of Bournonville's signature variations on the grand jeté dessus en tournant, in which the body pivots on the landing foot to face the raised one. The way Neary does it, with a strength equal to his, but with a yawning port de bras that seems to bring a flush to her cheeks, makes you want to burst out laughing. She gives the wittiest performance in the ballet.

The most curious performances are given by Patricia McBride and Suzanne Farrell. These two, Balanchine's star ballerinas, bring out the connections that exist between Balanchine and Bournonville, but, because they're fully formed and matured dancers who, in a sense, make their own rules, they don't bring out much that isn't superficial. It's the other dancers, still growing and learning, who show the profound connection between the two masters—a connection that makes us speak of Bournonville, despite his period, as a "modern" choreographer. In Bournonville as in Balanchine, correct training prepares the dancer for nonstop continuity, complex combinations, neatness and fullness of execution. Visually, the experience of Bournonville is high-density, like Balanchine (and, one might add, with *Torse* and *Rebus* in mind, like Merce Cunningham). The steps are joined together with infinitesimal links and preparations and are launched from the front of the foot. The raised heel, the quick and powerful instep create speed, vivacity, mercurial contrast. Bournonville was to dancing in the nineteenth century what Bellini and Donizetti were to singing: there is no separation between substance and decoration. But isn't that almost a definition of Patricia McBride? McBride's troubles in Bournonville are purely technical. Her turnout is not great, and this dims her croisé positions and deprives the extended leg of the arrowy sharpness it should have. She lacks ballon, an essential element in Bournonville. In her pas de deux with Tomasson (from the first act of *Kermesse in Bruges*), Tomasson keeps us wondering whether he has ballon or not, and he fakes the elevation he doesn't have by using his arms to lift himself skyward in the big jumps. McBride has no such opportunity; she's cursed with the neat-petite, percussively bounding style, and though one sighs in relief when she finally gets some air into a big pas-de-chat series, her range seems pinched off at one end. There are Balanchine ballets that evoke Bournonville in which McBride has been wondrously successful—*Donizetti Variations* and *Tarantella*—and in the second performance she even wore her *Donizetti Variations* costume, a kind of talisman, perhaps. It didn't help much. McBride is too unorthodox a ballerina—unorthodox even in Balanchine—to exemplify any school.

Suzanne Farrell, who dances with Martins in the famous pas de deux from *Flower Festival in Genzano*, is a study in contradictions that are resolved almost before you have time to be bothered by them. In the second performance, she was less noticeably nervous (she'd stopped bouncing her wrists, an infallible sign), but she still overscaled the steps and phrased them—well, peculiarly. And there is nothing for her to do with the period coquette manners of the piece but guy them. Still, every effect that is wrong for the piece is right for her, and strangely interesting. It's Farrellized Bournonville—an independent show within a show.

Stanley Williams, who staged *Bournonville Divertissements,* is a master of the style, a former solo dancer of the Royal Danish Ballet who has taught at the School of American Ballet since 1964. The staging is a climax not only to his career at the school but also to the Balanchine-Bournonville alliance. Williams's coaching emphasizes principles that are common to the two choreographers, but he sees to it that we do not even momentarily confuse two very different styles. It's unusual for this company of turners to be jumping so often and turning so seldom. (Bournonville himself was weak in pirouettes.) It's odd to see those "flat" Bournonville turns—more like reversals of direction than turns. The NYCB audience is finding that it takes more than one viewing to absorb this exotic spectacle. Once we get used to the range of the choreography, the ratio of large to small effects becomes clear, and steps that had seemed obscure take on variety and distinction. Bournonville steps are beguiling. They're like traps to catch the eye. Watch how they keep their openness through an entire variation, how they sail along on the upbeat, how instead of resting or closing the feet are free to find new paths, veering this way and that, amazing and confounding us, until with a sudden finality they spring shut. The dancer who has been bounding like a flea stands there innocently still in fifth.

The production has been handsomely mounted—with costumes, by Ben Benson, after the original Danish models, and with gathered velvet drapes framing a cyclorama lit, by Ronald Bates, in changing colors. *Bournonville Divertissements* is an enthralling show of dancers deeply engaged with assemblé, emboîté, rond de jambe, ballonné, batterie—in short, with dancers' material. The period style and the prescience of these dances will fascinate us for a long time to come. —*February 21, 1977*

Higher and Higher

The New York City Ballet closed its New York season on a recent Sunday night and reopened the following Tuesday in Washington, where it played through the end of last week. When this annual New York–Washington season was initiated, a few years ago, I remember hearing with some surprise about the sold-out houses and enthusiastic audiences with which Washington greeted ballets that had gone stale in New York. This year, the houses were still sold out, and the company needed its three weeks at the Kennedy Center, having lost six weeks in New York to the orchestra's strike. But what made the Washington extension really gratifying was the new level of performance the company has reached in the past year. The level was still rising when the State Theatre engagement ended. The ballets on that last weekend included some of the same ones that Washington had applauded three years ago—only they were no longer stale. A fresh wind seems to have seized the dancers and scattered all traces of the slump of the early seventies.

Individual careers soared during that low period—Patricia McBride's, Peter Martins's, Gelsey Kirkland's, Merrill Ashley's, to name only the most spectacular—but everyone knows that the real strength of the New York City Ballet is not in its featured dancers;

it's in the fertilizing genius of Balanchine. The depression—and those intermittent "hot" spells that made the depression seem even bleaker—could plausibly have been keyed to Balanchine's creativity. After *Who Cares?* (1970), Balanchine seemed generally disinclined to do very much for the company unless he could work himself up to the challenge of a tour de force. There were blahs on either side of the Stravinsky Festival of 1972 (for which he staged nine ballets), and then a restless, inconclusive period until the Ravel festival injected another giant dose of choreography. Inside and outside both festivals, he produced the work of junior choreographers and gave Jerome Robbins carte blanche; he also supervised the staging, by Alexandra Danilova, of two works from the past, *Chopiniana* and *Coppélia*. On *Chopiniana* he imposed an experiment in distillation which failed. The *Coppélia* combined the best of its tradition with some new dances by Balanchine. Apart from an almost wholly original third act, he seemed to be following a policy of selective intervention. (Although the production is a great success, I wish he would intervene a little more.) Some of the dancers took handily to the opportunities that these new ballets provided for them; a few throve on general repertory; others did neither. The company as a whole moved full speed ahead only when Balanchine or Robbins did, and the long-held theory that it looks its best in their latest inventions certainly seemed realistic at a time when *Stravinsky Violin Concerto* was being more authoritatively performed than *Agon*. The theory still makes a lot of sense, since the latest inventions are those with which the dancers feel personally identified. But the classics of the repertory suffered. It was a time when one could see a better *Evening's Waltzes* than *Liebeslieder Walzer*, a better *Suite No. 3* (its first three movements belong to this period) than *Serenade*, a better *Dances at a Gathering* or *Goldberg Variations* or *Duo Concertant* than *Symphony in C* or *Divertimento No. 15* or *Apollo*. I think I first felt the fresh wind that seems so strong now when *The Four Temperaments* was revived in 1975, with a cast that had never done it before—a revival that is still holding its ground despite a major piece of miscasting in Washington (Peter Naumann in Phlegmatic). In 1973, there had been a revival almost as startling: *Ballet Imperial*. But this was more properly a revision than a revival. Balanchine had scrapped the Imperial Russian décor, rechoreographed a passage in the Andante, and redirected the ensemble into an easier and fuller flow of movement. He also gave

the ballet new and awful costumes and a new and unepigram-
matic title, *Tchaikovsky Concerto No. 2*. But a company that used
to fight its way through the piece now found that it could relax and
command it. The ballet came up more beautiful, more nervously
powerful than ever, and looking as much a New York City Ballet
classic as *Concerto Barocco*, which was created in the same year, 1941
(for American Ballet Caravan).

Concerto Barocco is singularly blessed; nearly everyone who has
ever danced it in this company has done it justice—at least, as far
back as I can remember, which is back to its black-bathing-suit era
at the City Center. By its consistently high standard of performance
the company conveys its understanding of this ballet as the corner-
stone of the repertory. Yet there have been performances—recent
ones—that went beyond stewardship into revelation, and these were
the performances of Gelsey Kirkland just before she left the company
and of Suzanne Farrell just after she returned. If these two quite
different dancers could bring so much to a ballet that could be
great without them, was it really impossible for the company to
revitalize a repertory full of established masterpieces, nearly all of
which had been created before most of the dancers were born?

Balanchine dancers talking about Balanchine's repertory will
usually praise it in terms that have nothing to do with their own
contribution to it—or even with the possibility of their contribut-
ing to it. The general belief is that Balanchine's great ballets are
dancer-proof—that they'll carry their message to the audience right
through whoever happens to be dancing. One of the dancers
has said, "You could put a fairly bland dancer in the second
movement of *Symphony in C* and it would still be effective." You
could and it would, but although an experienced Balanchine audience knows how to adjust its connoisseurship to levels of performance, no audience in the world likes having to keep adjusting
downward. In time, the viewer comes to accept his connoisseurship
as an idiotic form of Platonism, and he may stop going to the
theatre, or go elsewhere for the thrill of a star performance. With
other companies, one has a right to demand star performance,
simply because it's the only thing that makes going there worthwhile. New York City Ballet dancers believe in Balanchine devoutly,
but they have sometimes appeared to be leaning too hard on the
Great Provider and forgetting that the audience is really looking at
them. (Many times, I have wished the balcony would let down a

banner that reads "WE SEE YOU.") The good side of this, of course, is that the dancers aren't tempted to woo the audience egotistically or play into its hands. Farrell exemplifies this ethical severity; she's not indifferent to the audience, but she lets us know she'd dance just as marvelously if we were not there to applaud her. We have come to demand from her everything she has to give because she demands it from herself. It's absurd to think that in respect to stars audience expectations may be greater at other companies than at the New York City Ballet, but unfortunately, because of publicity, they are. And a starstruck audience will confirm its expectations by applauding mightily even when stars haven't given a star performance. The policy at NYCB is not really antistar; it's not to build expectations. Casts aren't publicized in advance, and the roster doesn't isolate the principals from the corps except in out-of-town engagements. It's an anti-New York policy—the New York of the tyrannical, smothering, fall-guy audience. In New York, the job the New York City Ballet is uniquely equipped to perform is to tell us what real stardom is all about. These past few seasons, for the first time in more years than I like to remember, the whole company has begun to come alive to its responsibility.

Balanchine made *Chaconne* and *Union Jack* during this period, revived (or revised) *Square Dance*, and fiddled with a number of repertory pieces. The new additions are remarkable and fascinating in their different ways, but I'm not sure that they have very much to do with the strength the company is now displaying. For once, the dancers don't seem to be feeding off Balanchine's latest enterprises; they're showing their form in places where one might have stopped looking—in standards like *Symphony in C* and *Serenade*. Earlier in the year, there were a few performances of *Agon* that restored to it the tension and wit of shining memory. It was a triumph for the whole company. The latest triumph may be the most offbeat one the company has ever had. *Bournonville Divertissements* is a selection of highlights from the classical repertory of the mid-nineteenth century. The style is strange, the technique difficult. Dancers who were used to custom-fit roles could be expected to flounder. With his misbegotten *Chopiniana*, Balanchine tried to force the connection between Fokine's masterpiece and his own method; possibly it's a connection that can only be sensed, not demonstrated. With Bournonville, he lets the dances, as staged by Stanley Williams, speak for themselves, and we can really see that they're part of his heritage. The dancers all seem to realize this; when last seen, they were still polishing their brilliant performances. In the first performances, which I reviewed a few weeks ago, Patricia McBride looked out of her element. By closing night in New York, she'd found some magic key to the buoyancy she needs for the part, and was transforming herself into a feather-light Bournonville soubrette. Farrell had made comparable adjustments in her performance. Though these developments were unpredictable, and even unnecessary (we don't expect the grandest of Balanchine's ballerinas to be wonderful in an alien tradition), they show us how stardom can be earned.

In Washington, I saw Merrill Ashley's début in *Square Dance*, and it is the performance the ballet has been waiting for—full of sharp, bright photoflash pictures. The old version of the role was more complex than the version Ashley has been given to do; she could be the one to restore the exploding passage of beats in the finale or, in the pas de deux, the opening into arabesque that ends each sequence of double turns under the boy's arms. In an earlier début, Ashley showed her long keen line in the *Symphony in C* adagio—that "surefire" role. It was an enchantingly correct performance, but her forthright power had little chance to show itself in the Violette Verdy role in *Emeralds*; with little piquancy and no rubato, she was *only* correct. One of the major depressants a few years ago was the dearth of ballerinas in a company that has usually enjoyed a surfeit. Besides Ashley (who is still officially a non-principal), there's a flock of juniors who can give performances of ballerina quality. The male wing at the same level has acquired vigor and variety; I see no new Villellas, but the male ensemble of *Bournonville Divertissements* wouldn't have been possible in Villella's day. In *Symphony in C*, *Brahms-Schoenberg Quartet*, and *Jewels*, the corps work was smooth and zestful; in *Serenade* it outshone the principals. The girls are not as spikily eccentric as they used to be, or as ragged in ensembles—except, of course, when Balanchine betrays them with configurations that emphasize those frailties (as in *Symphony in Three Movements*).

Balanchine's tinkerings have effected some changes in the Elegy of *Serenade*, none of which strike me as happy ones. The two girls whom the male soloist lowers to a reclining position, with their feet braced against his, now take a lunge pose before subsiding to the floor. It's a minor detail, and I can only explain my objection to it by saying that the interrupted descent to the floor is emotionally insignificant. I feel the same way about the moment when one of those girls turns a series of stabbing pirouettes and then collapses sideways in her partner's arms. Years ago, she would collapse while turning and would continue to turn spastically while he held her a foot above the ground. The three female principals in the Elegy now go through it with their hair hanging loose, which may be the way it was done once upon a time but looks out of place today. The sisterhood of the corps in *Serenade,* which has expanded through the years as Balanchine expanded the choreography, is in its anonymity one of the most moving images we have in all ballet, and the three new heads of hair in the last movement violate the image. And, as the two lines of girls cross behind the soloist in the Waltz, what has happened to the Jessie Matthews backbends they used to do?

In *Emeralds,* a new epilogue for the major characters in the ballet consists of a strainingly supported adagio in which all seven of them seem to be trying to hold together the remnants of a fragile dreamworld. After the women have vanished, the three men—poets or troubadours from an age of chivalry—sink to one knee and lift an arm in tribute. At the final matinée in New York, the conductor (Hugo Fiorato) adopted a tempo that brought the ballet to a fine slow boil, and then held to a more moderate beat than is customary for *Rubies* and *Diamonds.* This spacious and clear way of performing *Jewels* makes it glow rather than glitter; everyone danced with untaxed transparency. And at the previous matinée Robert Irving performed one of his miracles of versatility by following the rattling batch of nineteenth-century dance scores for the Bournonville— a kind of multigaited music in which dancing is implicit—with Schoenberg's orchestration of Brahms, a complex, *schmalzig* concert-hall score that becomes dance music only because we have a Balanchine ballet to go with it. Neither *Jewels* nor *Brahms-Schoenberg Quartet* is a Balanchine masterpiece, but that hardly matters when they're given de-luxe treatment both onstage and in the pit. We have the ballets that *are* Balanchine masterpieces, and the company has reserves of dance power it has not yet completely displayed. We may be entering a golden age of performance.

—*March 21, 1977*

PART
TWO

By the Month
1969-1971

The Three-Cornered Hat

Of all Robert Joffrey's revivals, none caused more advance excitement than *The Three-Cornered Hat*. The ballet had not been seen in New York since 1945, when Massine was performing it with Toumanova for Ballet Theatre. Massine's reputation died a heavy death in the fifties, but in recent years a new generation has grown curious about him. It is not the symphonic Massine of the thirties that interests us (we cherish our notions, perhaps misguided, of what *Choreartium* and *Rouge et Noir* were like) so much as it is the Diaghilev Massine—the Massine of *Pulcinella*, *Parade*, and *Le Tricorne*. These were Picasso collaborations, heralded in their day as models of revolutionary stage design, but no one has ever answered the question of exactly how, choreographically speaking, the stage picture *worked*.

So, at last, *The Three-Cornered Hat*, restaged by Massine himself with help from Tatiana Massine and Yurek Lazowski, and technical supervision (or, as the program puts it, "American supervision") by William Pitkin. The production is a disappointment. Was this Spain—these hairdresser pastels, this somehow too sweet, dirty, and *yellow* arrangement of blocks and arches crawling with black lines? My imagination had expected sharp sunlight, a few architectural strokes in a vaulting space. As well as looking discolored, the set looks cramped on the small City Center stage. But before we see the set, we have a long moment during Falla's rousing fanfares to look at the frontcloth, that beautiful and queerly formal eighteenth-century scene of spectators turned momentarily away from the bullring. The picture is framed like a window in an expanse of neutral beige cloth. It seems to want to take us back in time.

We didn't really expect the revival to take us all the way back to 1919; 1945 would have been good enough. At that time, Massine's theatrical tradition was diminishing, but it was also being renewed by other choreographers. In the films of his ballets that Massine has presented to the Dance Collection of the New York Public Library, you can see dancers of the late thirties and early forties moving with sweep and sensual precision. The pantomime is conspicuously large and clear, carrying a full-throated force like singing. When the classical distinction between pantomime (or speech) and dance (or song) is blurred in this way, the ballet can either leap along on a volatile current or it can hobble ineffectively like a mechanical toy. It was Tudor's genius, in the period 1936–46, to perceive this danger in the Massine style and to circumvent it by creating a choreography that lowered the lyrical pitch of Massine spectacle. In the forties, Tudor was hailed as a revolutionary realist, but he was actually an introverted Massine. The Tudor ballet remained, like the Massine, transposed opera. In Massine, mime tends toward the condition of dance; in Tudor, dance tends toward the condition of mime. Tudor didn't abandon the Massine style. Ingeniously, he inverted it.

For a time, the two styles, Massine's and Tudor's, had no trouble coexisting. But both are equally remote from the dancers of 1969. Young dancers do not know how to make dancing look like mime or mime like dancing. New York City Ballet has trouble with Tudor's *Dim Lustre*, and the Joffrey dancers have an extra problem with the buoyant mood, the unshadowed psychology of a comic fable like *The Three-Cornered Hat*. It's such a square proposition and they're all too tense—with fear, I think, of being laughed at.

And yet, the ballet is worth reviving. Perhaps revivals only succeed in telling us more about our own time than we thought we knew. That in itself is a value. Then, too, it would be wrong to say that our curiosity about the piece goes entirely unsatisfied. It's true that the finale—the jota where all those famous costumes come to life—is more Picasso's show than it is Massine's. But Massine the artist does emerge. After the Wife rebuffs the Corregidor, she and her husband do a fandango which shows how solid their marriage is beneath its surface banter. In this dance, and in the equally wonderful and poetic solos for the Miller and the Wife (in one of which she flutters her hands in a reference to the caged bird we see at the beginning of the ballet), Massine's art is at its peak. The characterizations are enthralling in their size, in their physical and spiritual energy. We can imagine the conviction in performance they once carried.

Twyla Tharp used the immense acreage of the Great Lawn in Central Park in *Medley*, a work that literally extended the horizon of avant-garde dance (unless you count as dance—I don't—those experiments that have people moving in different parts of the city or in different cities). At one point during the work, with dusk falling fast and some forty dancers spread out down the field and working to separate slow counts, one suddenly saw a human speck in the distance, dancing rapidly by herself. The rest of the dance remained calm and gradually dissolved as one dancer and then another left the field, but not before it was already quite dark. The dancing speck was only one incident in the piece, but it looms up impudently in memory like a joke in scale. Almost everyone I know who saw *Medley* remembers it, too, as they remember the moment in the middle when the original performing nucleus of seven is suddenly joined by the big group rising in a wave from the spectators' section. Almost no one remembers how the dance began, which was imperceptibly, at about six P.M., like a change in daylight or in the weather. To anyone to whom this sounds unbearably desultory and boring I would stress something that occurred to me as I was leaving and walking in the lamplight toward Fifth Avenue: It was a very *happy* event. And happiness is a virtue one doesn't encounter often in the avant-garde. —*November 1969*

The Case of Alwin Nikolais

Gian Carlo Menotti's latest one-act opera was inspired, he tells us, by the theatre of Alwin Nikolais, "which has fascinated me since its very beginning with its unique combination of eeriness and humor." *Help, Help, the Globolinks!*, billing itself as "an Opera for Children and Those Who Love Children," was staged over the Christmas holidays at the City Center for Music and Drama, and it is, as you might imagine, a work of suffocating archness, concerning some Martian-like invaders who, accompanied by electronic beeps and burbles, descend on an American school and are put to rout only when the teachers and children play conventional musical instruments at them. What is really dismaying about it, however, is its demonstration of the incapacity of a developed "art" theatre like that of Alwin Nikolais to function in a commercial context, not because its resources of expression are too many and thus inhibited by that context, but because they are too few and thus exposed by it.

To create the Globolinks, Menotti got Nikolais himself, and though the electronic music that is used to identify them is apparently by Menotti, it sounds exactly like the scores Nikolais creates for his own works, or perhaps I should say score, since the synthetic blurgelating which is Nikolais's idea of electronic music hardly ever varies in its effects from one Nikolais work to another. The same, transposed to traditional vocal and orchestral composition, might be said of Menotti, and, indeed, Nikolais might be thought of as the avant-garde Menotti in more than the musical sense. Both men are showmen who seem to suffer from an exacerbated pride in their own seriousness as artists. Menotti's operatic ventures are generally accompanied by polemical outbursts against the musical establishment. (In the present case, the polemics are in the libretto.) Nikolais's tack, on the other hand, has been to overextend his talents in ever longer, more repetitious and pretentious extravaganzas that seem designed to shore up a reputation as an all-purpose avant-garde genius. What Menotti sees as "eeriness and humor" are there, of course, but less and less frequently in combination; they've become separable and increasingly unstable elements in the media compound that the Nikolais "sensorium" uses nowadays to impress us with its abstract beauty. It's odd that what Menotti tries to make ridiculous and villainous in his little parable about the crisis in modern music should show up on the stage as nothing more harmful than Nikolais's familiar bag of tricks incorporated all but whole —odd, not because the Globolinks are about as detestable as the Blue Meanies in *The Yellow Submarine*, but because they're really nothing at all; the eeriness and the humor are latent in what Nikolais has devised, but neither he nor Menotti has bothered to make these elements dramatically suggestive or exciting in terms of the story that is being told. The show is just an abstract parade. What we get for a Globolink horde is only a typical Nikolais corps de ballet, the men this time looking like concertinas in top hats, the girls like unsprung paratroopers; and what we get for choreography in the action scenes is a simple business of diddling around in these costumes.

No effect is ever so magical on the stage that it can't destroy itself by giving away its secrets too soon or, worse, by failing to have any. Children's entertainment owes its audience a standard of invention as high as, if not higher than, entertainment for adults simply because children are prepared to believe in and therefore question what they see. A lot of what passes for children's entertainment in New York—generally it's presented around Christmastime and generally it centers in dance of some sort—doesn't survive imaginatively beyond the barest presentation of its materials, and I suspect the children know it even if their parents don't. *Help, Help, the Globolinks!* was preceded by *Amahl and the Night Visitors,* Menotti's now classic Christmas variation on the story of the Three Magi. It has parts for dancers, but its biggest part is for a crippled boy soprano— it's that kind of classic. Coming out of the theatre afterward, a little girl asked her mother, "Which one did you like better, Mommy?" "Well," said this buck-passing mommy, "I guess the first one was a little sad. *You* liked the second one better, didn't you?" "Well," said the child, "well . . . yes, I guess so." This child knew she'd been let down by *Globolinks,* and I think I know just when it happened. Like most of Nikolais's pieces, it had opened splendidly, with the overture interrupted, Welles-style, by an almost-for-real loudspeaker bulletin announcing the arrival of the Globolinks. Following this were five minutes of sheer enchantment; Ming Cho Lee's radar towers revolved in the pulsating void of Hans Sondheimer's lighting, and Nikolais's dancers alighted in shadow projections. Then the dancers emerged (as always thereafter from stage right—the girls' 'chutes must have been hooked up there somewhere), and, after the first giggle or two, the rest was that questioning silence which tells us that no answer will suffice. Nor was any answer offered; this host of Globolinks had nothing further to show us, no demonstration beyond the minimality of being. After that, we were in Menottiland, with its static, puppetlike recitatives in which people call attention to feelings they can't otherwise express: "Where am I? What's happening? I feel so funny. How strange!"

I'd gone to this entertainment of Menotti and Nikolais because I expected something from it, more on Nikolais's part than on Menotti's. Nikolais, I thought, would survive commercial pressure very well. Liberated at last from his experimental art-for-art's-sake lab, he might turn out something in support of Menotti's gassy little fable that would be the making of him as a popular artist. Nikolais's real business is, unless I mistake him profoundly, neither choreography, nor décor, nor lighting, nor sound-engineering, but the amalgamation of all of these arts (which other men have mastered better than, or at least as well as, he) in a plastic, totally manipulatable palette of effects that could service popular theatre, if a popular theatre worthy of him, and worthy of the name, could exist.

Nikolais evenings are not in themselves theatre but brilliant suggestions of what a new theatre might consist of; they're trips into
dimensions of sight and sound that are like a perennial World's Fair
of possibilities; they're spectacles en route to an experience which
Nikolais, as playmaker or theatre poet, cannot achieve because he
thinks like a technician, not a poet. If you believe in Nikolais's
genius, you have to believe in its promise—in the possibility of his
yet becoming a poet of the theatre rather than a technician who's
hypnotized by his own inventions and obliged to repeat himself
endlessly because the novelty wears off almost as quickly as the
novelty of color TV. Nikolais by himself has no staying power—
it's great the first time but never so great again—and it may be that
his wizardry is increasingly self-absorbed and remote because no
broad avenue of expression has been offered it. Promise is not the
same as opportunity.

There is always a crisis of definition at the point where art and
commerce intersect. The last man of comparable stature and gifts to
survive this crisis was Busby Berkeley, but now that movie musicals
are dead (and Berkeley is an "artist"), his successor, whoever he
may be, has no place to go. Nikolais has always done well on television, and before the debacle of *Globolinks* I would have thought
he'd go down extremely well at a place like Radio City Music Hall.
But the Music Hall is committed to enervated, dim spectacles fifty
years behind the taste of the vast audiences who patronize it. Even
if it weren't, Nikolais has overdrawn his account with the avant-
garde. All those rarefied evenings at the Henry Street Playhouse—
what have they come to? A few weeks before the Menotti event,
the City Center presented Nikolais's own company in a week of
performances, and it was revealing and dispiriting to see. There were
undeniable marvels: stages made magically high, wide, and deep by
tricks of lighting, darkened to pinpoints or irradiated with a suddenness that took the breath; dancers made to appear or vanish in a
flash, or to loom four times their natural size, or to inhabit ghostly,
inhuman forms; dead materials made animate; static elements
(scenery, props) made liquid and evanescent. One also saw fantasy
without depth, visions without majesty, poetic energy without poetic
purpose. The new work, *Echo*, used the Moog Synthesizer (as if that
made any difference) and dealt at interminable length in optical
paradoxes of number and scale, with dancers constantly filing off and
on, between and around and through their own images, and audi-

ences constantly wondering whether they were here or there, or two or twenty (and finding out, alas, long before the dance was finished). The engagement was well attended and obediently sat through and duly acclaimed, but the only real excitement was caused by two excerpts from a very early work, *Masks, Props and Mobiles* (1953). In one, three dancers sheathed in red stretch fabric made like teeterboards, and in the other, the company, manipulating long cords, rocked the stage in a brilliant series of cat's cradles. These dances, both very famous, were wildly, and I mean wildly, applauded. Their logic and charm were perhaps the last clang of Bauhaus functionalism in American theatre art, but they started Nikolais on his way, and his way now seems to have become irretrievably lost.

One can only dream. Nikolais needs someone to produce him, yes, but producers of latitude and zest and sound commercial instinct are as unemployable as the avant-garde. A Diaghilev, a Ziegfeld, a Disney, even a Billy Rose or Mike Todd might have found vehicles that would have changed Nikolais's life and our own. Maybe another director would have got more out of the Menotti-Nikolais collaboration than Menotti himself did. (Menotti always seems to be directing in a church basement.) But that would have been sheer luck, out of·phase with the times. What we have today in the American theatre is a bleak middle ground where dandified art meets "elevated" commercial intentions—it's not even vulgar with conviction—and you can't grow upward from either. In his latter-day films like *Neptune's Daughter* and *Jumbo*, Busby Berkeley was still able to make complicated, grand gestures without the pop songs that had always been his springboards, but Nikolais hasn't been able to get enough life and force out of avant-garde freedom to hit Broadway. As an initiation into his kind of theatre art, the ballet of the Globolinks isn't even fun the *first* time.

Other happenings: At Lincoln Center, Balanchine's *Nutcracker* passed its fifteenth year as an annual holiday event and, despite my reservations about Rouben Ter-Arutunian's production, about the break-leg speed at which the score is conducted, and about peculiarities in the performance (e.g., hearing the orchestra chime nine times, Drosselmeier invariably hobbles over to the grandfather clock and resets it—at ten minutes to seven), I love it like oxygen. It's New York's version of a Christmas pantomime and succeeds magnificently where all the other kid entertainments fail—that is, in arousing emotional expectations of a high order and then satisfying them. Very little has happened to it since last year: Laura Flagg is still the most spontaneous of little heroines, Jonathan Hochberg as Fritz (in the alternate cast) still steals scenes, and in the grand pas de deux there is now that great moment, new last year, when the Sugar Plum, in arabesque, is drawn slowly forward by her Cavalier on a traveling disc on the floor of the stage. There was a new Sugar Plum this season in Gelsey Kirkland, and the début was typical of New York City Ballet débutantes: strong head, cold heart. The ice does melt; I can recall Allegra Kent and Patricia McBride, who are now so warm and enveloping, looking much the same in their débuts.

Paul Taylor, in a much too brief season at City Center, presented a new work called *Churchyard*, with music based on medieval pieces by Cosmos Savage and with a cast of characters apparently consisting of the recently dead or the living dead. These characters work out their destinies in a somber, remorselessly moral work whose epitaph might well be *Memento mori*, but Taylor's sense of damnation seems to me deeply nineteenth-century American rather than medieval, and the discothèque flavor of some of the movement makes a contemporary allusion unmistakable. It ends in a dance of death and a welter of images from Dürer, Cotton Mather, and Killer Joe Piro. . . .

In two weeks at the Brooklyn Academy of Music, American Ballet Theatre presented four premières it would have done better to lose on the road. About the worst of these (though in some ways my favorite) was Michael Smuin's *The Eternal Idol—A Tribute to Rodin*, which set body-beautiful poses for Cynthia Gregory and Ivan Nagy to sacrilegiously inappropriate music by Chopin when, with any justice, it could have had tom-toms. Both dancers, shyly draped, took three terrific curtain calls in alternate tableaux on a rock. I don't know how they order these things in Las Vegas, but Ballet Theatre plainly hasn't got the touch. No gilt body paint, no blue spotlight. No justice. The fans' favorite new thing was the *Corsaire* pas de deux. When Lupe Serrano came on (rejoining the company after several years), I thought they would get up and sing "Hello, Dolly!" When, in the coda, she did double fouettés alternating with pirouettes in second, I'm sure they did. Ted Kivitt's part in this now immensely popular pas de deux doesn't become him (it doesn't any American dancer except John Prinz), but his leaps and turns had the fans rolling. Another noisy night at Ballet

Theatre brought Tudor's *Gala Performance* back into the repertory
in an overgenial and overgenteel revival supervised by Sallie Wilson.
The same qualities marked her own portrayal of the Russian Ballerina; she gets the butterfly, but misses the iron. Wilson's great performance is in *Pillar of Fire* and it is now one of the great
performances in contemporary ballet. Wilson's power in this role
is a conundrum of the dancer's art. She's musical and fluent and
strong, but she moves with a beauty that conceals beauty (so to
speak), and all that remains—and survives in your memory—is an
image of blunt animal pain. I also liked Cynthia Gregory in *Theme
and Variations*, but the audience doesn't care as much for this
great showpiece as it does for *Etudes*, which is a little like preferring
a boxful of Gorham's silverware on blue plush to a Fabergé service
on ermine.   —*December 1969*

Dreams That Money Can Buy

The first time I saw the Harkness Ballet, in 1967, I thought it
looked European. It doesn't look European anymore, but it does
look stateless. It's a company from nowhere, unless there's a place
on the map called Excrescenceville. Nobody needs the Harkness
Ballet, especially when all it does is remind us how dull affluence
really is if money is all you've got. There might be some point in a
spirited expression of excess—in showing surfeit as exuberance—
but the Harkness hasn't the style for that. Its wealth shows in the
corps, which is exceptionally well rehearsed. Such are the harried
conditions of professional dancing in New York that this modest
achievement passes for brilliance and becomes a selling point. But
the goods the Harkness puts on display aren't unwanted in the
luxury sense, they're simply uncalled for—drab, obsolete Brand X
merchandise that fills a seemingly unappeasable need for a democratic alternative to art. The notion that art is aristocratic and
élitist offends the democratic spirit of American philanthropy.
Theoretically, you should be able to get art for the people *from*
the people. Just throw money at it. Vain hope. Whereas money—
with taste—could buy art, what the Harkness money buys is
simulated art and the incompetence of good intentions.

And good intentions are worse than bad ones, sometimes, as fake art is worse than non-art. The artlessness of such a ballet as *Monument for a Dead Boy*, by the Dutch choreographer Rudi van Dantzig, at least gives the Harkness one trash masterpiece. Amid all the more insipid monuments to dead art that make up the repertory, it's a triumph of whole-souled vulgarity. But Van Dantzig's naïve, painfully sincere ballet, with its dated symbolism and grotesquerie, is untypical of American low taste. Though it was done originally for the Dutch National Ballet, it has no specific locus or intonation. It's nondenominational, like the Harkness itself. Even in its biggest hit, the company can't claim to be probing our roots. (That it's also an international hit, a favorite of Rudolf Nureyev's, suggests that the roots *Monument* does probe are pretty widespread.)

Jerome Robbins's *N.Y. Export: Opus Jazz*, which the Harkness acquired this season, is more like *us*, even though it's a rearview-mirror image of the fifties and a distorted one at that. The distortions—Robert Prince's pit-band jazz score, the too-pretty Ben Shahn scenery, the Dead End Kids–style group humor, the violence of teenage gangs rendered with a kind of sentimental envy—bothered me less than when the piece was new. Either I've been pacified by time or it's been softened in revival. The most jarring episode in the ballet, when five boys trap a girl on a roof and then pitch her off it, was done by the Harkness as a completely harmless diversion. The girl's vicious provocation, the boys' frenzied response—the whole sexual element was missing, along with the rotten taste it left in your mouth. Have we become so hardened to violence that sex murder can be rendered as mere acrobatics, or is the truth just the opposite: that we prefer a "dry," abstract statement because it acts as a shield against the brutality of the experience? In any case, the tossing of the girl's body into the wings looked like the sensational cliché it has now become instead of the shock effect I remember from Ballets U.S.A., and the piece seems much more dulcet and restrained as a whole. It was even possible to feel something like warmth for 1958, when the young were sullen but not mutinous. When Robbins's playground athletes started snapping their fingers slowly (the girls so strangely androgynous, like the flagrant Anybodys of *West Side Story*), my mind filled with early Elvis Presley, terms like "shook up," "crazy, man," "cool" (not yet a noun), and like, like that. Besides, the organization of these dances is brilliant, no matter how specious their base in reality. "Improvisations," the third section, should really end the ballet. Its rhythmic drive and comic invention are so exciting, even Robbins can't top it.

The Harkness gave its best performance of the season in this slightly dubious classic of the fifties (even stressing its age in a program note). *La Favorita* had nearly everybody in the company dressed up and doing a classical divertissement to a Donizetti miscellany. The curiously discontinuous, rambling classical phrases were assembled by Benjamin Harkarvy well below his usual standard. As a rule, Harkarvy's academic choreography is trimly patterned, but it would take a company of magicians to make sense of *La Favorita*. Harkarvy's *Le Diable à Quatre—Pas de Deux* was a hit when his former company, the Netherlands Dance Theatre, danced it here last year. This commemorative piece, to the Adam music, has a distinct period style, but the Harkness dancers don't seem to have any idea what that is. I can only think back to my brief glimpse of the Netherlands' Gérard Lemaître and Marian Sardstädt and wonder what they did, especially what Sardstädt did, to make it so interesting. The other new work, *L'Absence*, was handsome and dead. The only action came from Robert Mitchell's décor, which consisted of a number of steel chairs and an enormous box with mirrors that moved. The box sat there and winked while Milko Sparemblek's choreography played a gloomy game of musical chairs ("A woman sits alone, caught in the grief of loss," etc.). It's at least as sad that the Harkness's experiment with kinetic art should be by a Central European choreographer as that its best American ballet should be a Jerome Robbins rerun eleven years too late. Can there be any justification for the company's existence apart from the fact that it employs good dancers (Lone Isaksen, Lawrence Rhodes, Helgi Tomasson)? For all its riches, it operates on the cheap, buying back numbers and foreign-language reprints instead of first editions. It's the coffee-table, discount-house idea of culture. The Harkness offers its dancers everything except a chance to participate in reality.

The repertory was creatively lit by Nick Cernovitch, and Gilbert Hemsley performed that invaluable service this season for the Alvin Ailey company, which followed the Harkness into the Brooklyn Academy. Hemsley's lighting, Christina Giannini's costumes, and an uncredited tavern set containing a jukebox, a neon sign, a convex mirror, and some beat-up wicker furniture were the best things about *Masekela Langage*. The stage had so much presence it was a pity the dances Ailey put on it didn't clarify our sense of place. To Hugh Masekela's South African jazz (on tape, as were all the scores used during the engagement), the company did angry, anguished, flippant, or drunken dances and bits of business in Ailey's familiar body-sync, act-it-out style, but I couldn't tell whether it was all supposed to be happening in Johannesburg, Watts, or Savannah, Georgia. It's a problem I have often with the Ailey company, and the pains he takes to set the scene just add to my difficulty. The company is integrated in an official sense, but the dramatic fact of the matter is that you frequently have to "read" white dancers as black, and a piece that ends, as so many of his company's pieces do, with a black man running on from the wings all scared and bloody begs the question: If the white folk on the stage are part of the society he's running to, then who's chasing him?

Ailey's use of ethnic materials is widely overrated. The range of movement is not much beyond what the modern-dance tradition had achieved by the mid-forties, and though his performers all have remarkable individual flair, you couldn't call what they do "Negro" dancing in any sense comparable to Negro performance in blues, jazz, or rock music. What some people call "soul" in the best of the Ailey dancers (who tend to be black) is more likely their spectacular animation in performance and their sexiness, which is related to their way of emphasizing the literal implications of a dance gesture. It looks witty and rude. The style is at its best in the dances that Ailey arranges which look like numbers from a Broadway show; it doesn't show in the solemn conservatory-dance pieces to Vivaldi, Barber, and Ives, and, this season, it had no chance at all in Pauline Koner's *Poème*, a pastel pas de deux out of the dilapidated twenties with about four miles of honest-to-God pink chiffon. Of the other novelties by white choreographers, I missed Richard Wagner's *Threnodies*, but Michael Smuin's *Panambi* exploited the sleek surface of the company's style to perfection in what began as a superb exotic nightclub act for Judith Jamison, magnificent in a Josephine Baker turban, and four seminude men. But then respectability broke up the act and we had a boring, "sensitive" ballet. Smuin, himself a former nightclub entertainer, is being encouraged in directions opposite to his talent, which is considerable.

Differences between the New York City Ballet and Local 802 of the musicians' union have been repaired, at least for the time being. Relief, succeeded by regret that the company couldn't have started its season in better condition. But the sentiment is idle, like wishing the air were cleaner. Balanchine's repertory, performed by Balanchine's company, is a national treasure and should be treated as such, first of all by Balanchine, but most of all by the public. The audiences at Lincoln Center are the dullest in the world. They know that Balanchine is a fully accredited institution, so they attend his classes. They must be taking notes because they don't applaud. Brilliant and bad performances are equally rewarded: moderate handclap all around, then out to the bar. The company is past caring, and there are nights—for instance, the opening—when it shows.

The season had to open cold, with fewer rehearsals and more injuries and absences than usual, but the labor dispute didn't materially affect the dancers' performance; it only darkened their mood. *Symphony in C*, a ballet that was at its performance peak in the fifties and early sixties, has drifted under a cloud. Balanchine has opened up the cuts in the music and restaged whole sections of the choreography. It's bigger, longer, *more* than ever. But just as the new cadenza in the glorious Andante of *Divertimento No. 15* gives us more glory when we've already had enough, the expanded *Symphony in C* doesn't have the effect it was intended to have. The big stage at the State Theatre is also a peculiarly withdrawn stage. *Symphony in C* at the City Center used to meet its audience dead-on. Now it looks remote, crowded, rushed. Then, too, the new generation of dancers doesn't seem to have found a way of making the ballet its own; they're correct, even brilliant, but not relaxed and happy. The simple happiness of *Symphony in C*, its almost careless exuberance, is no longer with us. Maybe it should be dropped, as great works should be when their legends are too hard for performers to live up to. Perhaps, like *Ballet Imperial* and *La Valse*, it could find a new form in revival. Other Balanchine ballets that I suspect would benefit from cold storage: *Agon, Apollo, Western Symphony, Stars and Stripes, Prodigal Son, Liebeslieder Walzer*. They're all ballets that I love, but they're either weak from undercasting or stiff from overperformance. The tradition of rediscovery and renewal is not honored at the New York City Ballet. Ballets are kept on long past their first freshness, largely because the subscription system demands it. So they change before your eyes and usually for the worse. As a result, the company has become a fixture to its haughty, impatient audience.

Robbins's *Dances at a Gathering*, the great hit of last season, is still history in the making. This long, ambitious ballet used to hit its peak of excitement when it was only half over, and the struggle to recover from that climax made the ballet seem even longer than it is. But Allegra Kent's absence forced recastings and revisions, and the experience this season is altogether a new one. Limiting Violette Verdy to just one solo was eccentric and ingenious but perhaps too whimsical of Robbins. Now he has her come back immediately following the show-stopper (the waltz pas de six) and do the flirtation-walk number with the boys formerly done by Kent; then she vanishes as before. Not only does the number fit the Verdy "character," it's exactly what's needed to refresh the interest and set the ballet moving again, so that the major accent now falls where it should—in the scherzo, on the pas de deux of McBride and Anthony Blum. The dramatic concentration of these two dancers is miraculous; because of them, Robbins is able to effect the transition from a gay mood to a tragic one that makes people compare the ballet to *Liebeslieder Walzer*. The extension into tragedy gives *Dances*, to my mind, a rather bogus "stature," as if Robbins felt he could no longer impress audiences by being his sunny, funny old self; and I can't help suspecting the ballet of a misty-eyed view of human relations. But there's no question now that this former whiz kid has the authority to go for the big things in life, or that *Dances* is as amazing a demonstration of his ingenuity in the sixties as *Fancy Free* was in the forties and *Afternoon of a Faun* in the fifties.

Because Robbins suffered an injury while rehearsing his new ballet, the first première of the season was, unexpectedly, *Reveries* by John Clifford, using movements from the first orchestral suite of Tchaikovsky. This now completes the run on Tchaikovsky suites which began with Balanchine's own *Mozartiana* in 1933, continued with his *Theme and Variations* (from the third suite) in 1947, and was resumed last year when he gave *Tchaikovsky Suite No. 2* to Jacques d'Amboise to choreograph. Clifford's ballet is a good deal better than D'Amboise's. Unlike D'Amboise, Clifford knows how to arrange a dramatic stage picture in relation to the music, and how to change it on a musical cue. The ballet is full of dreamy stage pictures, a very strong Tchaikovsky soup indeed. Clifford is like an art-struck boy listening to the Philharmonic with his head inside the loudspeaker and visualizing! vizualizing! And the music isn't easy for anyone working under Balanchine; the first movement sounds like *Serenade*, the fourth like *The Nutcracker*. But Clifford doesn't anthologize helplessly, and only the ending comes off with less than complete command of the style. There's a swooning pas de deux for Conrad Ludlow and Johnna Kirkland, and a delicious entrance for Johnna's sister, Gelsey. The Kirkland girls are the new rages; Johnna is intelligent and grave, like Merle Park, and little Gelsey is bold, with the clear eyes of a huntress. The company has bred two generations of dancers in ten years with no sign of diminishing strength, and despite its clammy audiences and overextended repertory, there is reason to hope it will rise again.   —*January 1970*

Balanchine and Gershwin

The title of Balanchine's Gershwin ballet, *Who Cares?*, has a double significance. It means, Who Cares what we call it ("as long as I care for you and you care for me"), and it suggests that the piece is an elegant throwaway. That's how it looks, too—like nothing much. The curtain goes up while the orchestra is playing "Strike Up the Band," and we see a double exposure of Manhattan's skyline projected in a pinkish haze on the backcloth. An excellent idea, but it stops there. The rest of the stage looks bleak. The girls wear their very well-cut Karinska tutus, this time in turquoise and lemon yellow. The skirts have pleats and look 1920's and mod at the same time. So do the boys' black bellbottom slacks. Like the title and the skyline, everything has a double impact, with one effect or style superimposed on another—Now on Then, ballet dancing on show tunes. The two planes of meaning are so shuffled that we're never completely in one world or the other; we're in both at once. Or, rather, we're in four worlds, since *Who Cares?* scrambles two elements, classical dancing and show dancing, and two eras, the twenties and the seventies, with equal paronomastic facility. And since the twenties was itself a period of classical revival, the play of references can grow almost infinitely complex. When Balanchine has five boys do double air turns (one boy at a time) in "Bidin' My Time," we're pleased with ourselves for thinking of the boys' variation in *Raymonda* Act III (the metrical swing of the music is pretty much the same) and even more pleased when we remember the masculine ensemble that made the song famous in *Girl Crazy*.

That's simple enough. But when toward the end of the ballet the four stars fly across the stage to "Clap Yo' Hands" in what is unmistakably a series of quotations from *Apollo*, we catch an unframable glimpse of the multiple precedents *Who Cares?* is made of. It's then that we see, for just the flash of the moment that he gives us to see it, how comradely the links are between the Gershwin of *Lady, Be Good!*, *Tip-Toes*, *Oh, Kay!*, and *Funny Face*, and the syncopated Stravinsky of *Apollon Musagète*. We notice that the dancers in the ballet wear necktie belts in homage not only to Astaire but to the Chanel who in 1928 knotted men's striped cravats around the waists of Apollo's muses. But the allusion to 1928 isn't end-stopped; it reverberates with *Apollo*'s own recapitulations of the nineties and Marius Petipa—high noon at the Maryinsky... and so we are borne back ceaselessly into the past. To the question "What is classicism?" Balanchine responds with a blithe shrug and a popular song. Classicism is the Hall of Fame viewed as a hall of mirrors. The Fun House.

The only thing I can't account for is the bleakness. (Well, I can: Poverty décor is the only décor at the New York City Ballet; its vulgar opulence in other productions is a form of poverty, too.) I hope they fix it soon, along with the opening ensemble dances, which look like a cheerless audition. These dances are standard pop Balanchine, which is to say a lot of jaunty, bright high kicks and pointwork—a little square, a little heavy with repeats, and too impressively ironical in the manner of *Western Symphony* and *Stars and Stripes*, two of the Fun House's major exhibits. It's a slow start and a wrong one. The ballet suddenly picks up, finds its own life, when the boys and girls start dancing out in pairs to " 'S Wonderful," "That Certain Feeling," "Do Do Do," and "Lady Be Good"; the dance invention tumbles forth, so does the applause, and we realize that what we're going to see is not a clever foreigner's half-infatuated, half-skeptical view of a popular American art form; we're going to see the art form itself, re-energized. But this spectacle we see isn't like a musical comedy, it's more like a lieder recital with a few social mannerisms mostly in the pleasant, sappy, ingénue style of Old Broadway. Just when you think that maybe the dancers do represent a musical-comedy chorus full of stock types (with Linda Merrill as the company's inevitable wild redhead), they vanish and another ballet or musical or recital begins.

The second half of *Who Cares?* has an *Apollo*-type cast—one boy (Jacques d'Amboise) and three girls (Patricia McBride, Marnee Morris, and Karin von Aroldingen). Each girl dances once with the boy and once by herself, and then the boy dances alone. They are all four together in the Apollonian coda. The music is the same parade of Gershwin hits that has been going on since the beginning, only now, with the lights blue and the stars out, we listen more intently. If this is a musical-comedy world, it's the most beautiful one that was ever imagined. In "Fascinating Rhythm," Patricia McBride holds a high extension in second and then in two or three lightning shifts of weight refocuses the whole silhouette while keeping on top of the original pose. It's so charming to see in relation to that unexpected stutter in the music which unexpectedly recurs, that it hits the audience like a joke, but that's fascinating rhythm, and that's *Who Cares?* Classical syntax, jazz punctuation. I couldn't begin to say what D'Amboise's solo to "Liza" is composed of, though— it suggests soft-shoe, virtuoso tap, and classical lift and amplitude all at once—and D'Amboise, whose style in classical ballet has characteristically a casual, crooning softness played against sudden monkeylike accelerandos and sharp bursts of detail, dances it in total splendor.

Everywhere, the tight choreography sustains an almost unbelievable musical interest. As if it weren't enough for Balanchine to give us dances of extreme tension and wit and elegance, he also gives us back the songs unadorned by their usual stagey associations. "Stairway to Paradise" isn't a big production number, it's one girl (Von Aroldingen) covering ground in powerful coltlike jumps and turns. And in the duets, the emotion is more serious (the sense of receding hopes, for example, in "The Man I Love") for not being acted out. It isn't emotion that dominates the stage so much as a musical faith that the choreography keeps, and this is what convinces us that the songs are good for more than getting drunk at the St. Regis by— that they have theatrical momentousness and contemporary savor. Gershwin in 1970, in the age of Burt Bacharach, has no trouble sounding classical, and that is how Balanchine hears him.

I am also persuaded that Balanchine hears Gershwin the way Gershwin composed—pianistically—and this brings up the subject of orchestration and Hershy Kay. Kay had been set the task of orchestrating sixteen of the seventeen songs that Balanchine uses in *Who Cares?* (One number, "Clap Yo' Hands," is a recording made by Gershwin himself at the piano.) But because of commitments to the Broadway show *Coco*, Kay has so far orchestrated only the opening ("Strike Up the Band") and closing ("I Got Rhythm") songs. The remaining fourteen songs were played, for the three performances of *Who Cares?* that were given this season, with his customary sensitivity and attack by Gordon Boelzner, from arrangements based on Gershwin's published piano versions. These piano arrangements were unvaryingly simple: verse followed by chorus followed (sometimes twice) by chorus repeat. They are beautiful reflections of Gershwin's highly developed keyboard technique. Gershwin's pianism in his time was comparable to Gottschalk's in *his*, and I hope Kay's further orchestrations of Gershwin are as good as the ones he did for the Gottschalk ballet *Cakewalk*, by far his best orchestration for ballet. To my disappointed ear, his "Strike Up the Band" and "I Got Rhythm" were in the vulgarized idiom of his *Stars and Stripes*—hotcha added to heat; and while the musical format of *Who Cares?* precludes his "symphonizing" Gershwin in the style of *Western Symphony*, orchestral thickening could destroy the bone-dry delicacy, the tonal transparency of this music, and should be avoided like temptation. The more so as Balanchine has taken such evident delight in choreographing the counter-melodies, cross-rhythms and abrupt syncopations out of which Gershwin built his compositions—it isn't all razz-ma-tazz—and not since the heyday of Fred Astaire have such felicities been observed. (In the title number, a loose-rhythmed pas de deux for D'Amboise and Von Aroldingen, there's an echo, for those who tune their echo chambers that way, of Astaire and Ginger Rogers.)

Fred and Ginger, Fred and Adele, George and Ira, George and Igor . . . it's easy to be seduced by the nostalgia of it all, but the remarkable thing about *Who Cares?* is how infrequently it appeals to that nostalgia. It certainly makes no appeal on the basis of period glamour or period camp. The multiple images, the visual punning, the sense of a classical perspective—all of that sweeps by with a strength of evocation more powerful than any individual moment of recognition. It's mysterious, the mythological intensity built up by a ballet that doesn't seem to have a thought in its airy head. No single cultural myth seems to be at the core of it. Manhattan in the Golden Twenties, penthouse parties where composers of brilliance entertained at the baby grand until dawn, are lovely to think about but aren't the subject of *Who Cares?* any more than a rainbow on a wet afternoon is. To put it as simply as I can, this wonderful ballet enriches our fantasy life immeasurably, as works of art are meant to do. It's tonic, medicinal, too. Its fresh, unclouded feeling seems to strike with special directness at the city's depressed spirits. Just before the première, Balanchine received New York City's biggest award for cultural achievement, the Handel Medallion, on the stage of the State Theatre. He made a number of jokes in the disreputable manner of his hero on such occasions, Bob Hope, had what they call in show business a "good roll," and then rang up the curtain on a Gershwin march. The Higher Seriousness didn't have a chance, but who cares?—the ballet was a beaut.   —*April 1970*

A *New* <u>Firebird</u>

The New York City Ballet production of *Firebird*, with designs by Chagall, was never one of Balanchine's masterpieces, and the costly new plumage provided for it this spring emphasizes the trifling view of the piece that he seems always to have held against a wondering world. The people who would have preferred him to produce a masterpiece in 1949—his own or, better, Fokine's—are enraged all over again by what he has unveiled: rescaled and repainted scenery, a new set of costumes executed by Karinska after the original sketches, entirely new choreography including a Danse Infernale by Jerome Robbins. Not one cut has been opened in the score. Beneath the new trappings it is the same old unserious, childish, gaudy little ballet. Its weak points have been strengthened and its strong points, I fear, weakened. The choreography for the Firebird is not as good, and the tender little dance of the maidens with the Prince has been elaborately rearranged. On the other hand, Robbins's Monster Scene is really funny, and the finale has been enlarged and visually orchestrated so that the stage looks like a great big Russian Easter egg. I rather like this sort of sweet, but it seems to give most people the hives. The taste of the production as a whole is probably as awful as people say it is, but it's so crazy and extravagant that it becomes amiable in the way that good taste usually can't be and entirely appropriate to the clownish spirit that remains the most remarkable thing about Balanchine's conception.

The new production salutes the sixtieth anniversary of Fokine's ballet, but Balanchine's version never had more than a passing resemblance to the original. What it did have, choreographically speaking, was a very sensuous, suggestive pas de deux for the Firebird and Prince Ivan which could have been numbered among Balanchine's greatest essays in the pas-de-deux form. In the old days when the company was dancing at the New York City Center, a brilliant ballerina (Tallchief or Hayden), made the ballet worth seeing. At the City Center, too, Jean Rosenthal's lighting helped disguise the increasingly threadbare look of the scenery. But what could be made to look good at the City Center looked less than credible on the much larger stage of the State Theatre at Lincoln Center. By the end of the sixties it was a pretty sick little bird indeed. Over the years, the Monster Scene had undergone several revisions, none of them quite right (monsters are not Balanchine's specialty), while the most powerful effects in the pas de deux gradually disappeared. New sets of costumes kept turning up, none of which served to lift the ban imposed by Chagall, in 1952, on the use of his name in connection with Balanchine's production. (Chagall had designed *Firebird* not for Balanchine, but for a Ballet Theatre production by Adolph Bolm in 1945; Balanchine inherited the décor four years later, along with the shortened version of the score prepared by Stravinsky.) Whatever may have been Chagall's objections to Balanchine's use of his material, Stravinsky seems to have been perfectly satisfied. He conducted the ballet at the City Center in 1950, and I have long supposed that Balanchine's chief reason for retaining *Firebird* is that the recension of 1945 enables Stravinsky to collect royalties on its performance, a right he does not enjoy when the ballet is mounted, as it has been the world over, to longer versions of his 1910 score. As for Chagall, the present production proudly bears his imprimatur, but it doesn't bear his handiwork and that makes quite a difference. I never saw his original costumes, which he hand-painted, but even in tatters his frontcloth was iridescent and his magic tree glowed like stained glass. The scene painters have duplicated the flaming ruby-red backcloth for the Wedding, but elsewhere the painting is dull.

Balanchine's new choreography is dull, too. The new pas de deux, with its use of Gelsey Kirkland as a canary-size Firebird, emerges as one of his more inscrutable ventures. The idea here seems to have been to reverse the proportions of the old production, which, when the ballerina could still dominate it, made the Firebird look big and grand and everything else look tiny and meager. The turnabout doesn't work, although Jacques d'Amboise, as the Prince, and his equally statuesque Princess (Gloria Govrin or Karin von Aroldingen) have the enormous overreal presence that children have in their own stories and drawings. The old pas de deux bore out one of the central motifs of Chagall's décor in its suggestion that the Firebird somehow figures in the Prince's sexual coming of age. The drop-cloth shows Bird and Bride as twin aspects of the same being, and I used to think the ballet showed that, too, for when the boy frees the Firebird—releases the female in her—a real woman soon emerges in the very next scene (the Princess) and he at once claims her for his bride. Balanchine underlines the relationship in the new version by having the Firebird present the Prince with a wedding ring for his bride rather than with a magic feather to wave at monsters, but then Balanchine doesn't do anything else about it. In the old pas de deux, it was possible to think about masculine tenderness gradually quieting and lightening the bestial angers of the forest, and about the Firebird, a demon perhaps once a woman, turning and becoming a benevolent blaze that brings peace to the realm. The new pas de deux is simply uninteresting, and Gelsey Kirkland, in her first big part, just looks miscast. Her costume, with its feathered pannier and smart little hat, is a failure, too.*

Hershy Kay's orchestration for the Balanchine-Gershwin ballet of last season, *Who Cares?*, has passages of sensitivity, but it lays down too thick a carpet for the dances, which last winter seemed to rebound from Gordon Boelzner's keyboard like rubber knives. In their slightly muffled state, the dances still succeed, though, and audiences respond in a frenzy. Nothing whatever has been done about the décor, and the lighting has two moods (lights up, lights down) while the dancing has about two hundred—not only day and night but all times of day and night in all kinds of weather in all seasons of the year. (At the end, I think I see a rainbow, but it's only the afterglow of Karinska's costumes.)

Jean-Pierre Bonnefous, of the Paris Opéra Ballet, has signed with the company and has flagged through three ballets in his first week:

* *Postscript* 1977: The role was changed again in 1972 to make the Firebird a tall creature but also a relatively inactive one. She now wears a full-length gown with wings and a train, and carries a red bouquet. The conception, based on the Bird-Bride of the frontcloth, remains a painter's, not a choreographer's.

Swan Lake, *Tchaikovsky Pas de Deux* (both opposite Patricia Mc-Bride), and *Raymonda Variations* with Violette Verdy. So far, he has dropped his ballerina only once. In fairness to Bonnefous, these partnering assignments are among the most hellish in the repertory. As a soloist, he has fared better: his *Raymonda* variation—the one with the flying beats and turns—was excellent. Helgi Tomasson has also joined the company, and Peter Martins has signed as a permanent member. —*July 1970*

The Moiseyev in America

The Moiseyev Dance Company has come and gone once again, and though the season was a sellout as usual, with a return engagement scheduled for October, there are signs that for New Yorkers a lot of the magic has gone out of the Moiseyev. The company presented substantially the same program with which it first electrified Americans in 1958, but this time around the press took a slightly less rhapsodic view of things. The sight of men leaping eight feet into the sky or lashing out with priziadkas in piston-like sprints across the Met stage is no longer a novelty. There were even some critics who went so far as to suggest that the knee-boggling feats of Igor Moiseyev's trained acrobats have little or nothing to do with actual folk dance. If someone had really pressed that point in 1958, the whole package would have come unstrung.

We have come through a lot with the Moiseyev. When the company first toured America, the clean, simple, healthy look of everything they did prompted a lot of adverse comment on the comparative decadence of American dance and American culture in general. Quick to seize the propaganda point, the Moiseyev in their next visit brought us a parody of teen-age rock-and-roll dancing that epitomized the American intellectual's nightmare vision of his own country. That was in 1961. Today, rock music and dancing are the intellectuals' delight; pop, pot, and pornography are everywhere embraced as tokens of identification with élite values. The abominations of 1961 ("their faces going slack, their behinds protruding obscenely, their lips wrapped loosely around dangling cigarettes, their gaudily costumed bodies plastered together and swaying narcotically to the idiotic rhythms of rock-and-roll"—to quote one critic's description of the Moiseyev dancers in their "American" number) are, *mutatis mutandis,* the fads of 1970. How American taste came to shift so radically over the past decade is a complicated subject, an itch in the body politic waiting for the scratch of satire. As far as the Moiseyev is concerned, its rosy peasant lads and lasses no longer provide an image by which to judge American society and its failings. The company didn't bring its rock parody this time, and in any case the sterner breed of anti-American American critic wasn't looking anymore.

The lesser breed that files the routine press notices was mostly content to point out that, if the Moiseyev's repertory wasn't actually authentic folk material, it was certainly representative of the Russian folk spirit, which nothing, apparently, can suppress. How marvelous to be able to jump so high after fifty-three years of totalitarianism.

The Moiseyev is still selling "folk spirit," but why are we buying it? Do we want to think Russians are happy simply because Moiseyev dancers leap high and smile? (That's like citing the antics of well-adjusted performing seals to discredit the stories about the plundered herds of the polar icecaps.) Or is there something in the spectacle that we envy even while disbelieving the political message? The energy that the critics attribute to a still vigorous folk heritage is undeniable, but its roots may be more tangled than the critics suspect. Igor Moiseyev's art is a mixed thing, an art compounded of the folk festival, the circus, and the music hall, but also an art officially sponsored by the state. It is popular entertainment constrained by official party-line wisdom. We can see that quite clearly in the excerpts from *Pictures of the Past,* where vignettes of prerevolutionary Russia are presented with all the accuracy and tenderness of a *Krocodil* lampoon. (One of these, a charmless skit called "Sunday," has the effrontery to invoke the name of Chekhov in a program note.) But the mixture is so volatile that the effects of art, when they do occur, are out of proportion to the ingredients of the formula. We might expect an out-and-out propaganda number like *Partisans* to be dreadful. It isn't. It's glamorous, the only really exciting number—apart from such leaping and bounding items as the *Gopak*—in the show. We might expect that the relatively straight pieces, the sentimental, sweet-as-pie "festival" dances, with roguish boys ogling blushing girls, to be delightful, but they aren't

—they're synthetic and vulgar. And where we might expect some uncensored sex interest, as in a piece called *Gypsies* (*Bessarabian Dance*), there isn't any at all—not even in the anthropological spirit of the thing. The whole show is remarkable for its sexlessness. You get the impression that everyone in Russia has been gelded.

In the quality of its human expression, the Moiseyev is remote from any living people who ever really lived. It's a clever, rather mechanically assembled dance show of the species that used to be called "nice, clean, family entertainment," and I suspect that nostalgia has a large share in the affection that American audiences feel for the company. It's the fantasy land of old movie musicals, the derring-do of dead vaudeville acts, of which the Moiseyev reminds us. And it gives us a picture, too, of the kind of scrubbed, safe entertainment that can be had when parental authority has some weight in the world. That kind of authority is gone now in America, where parents are ruled by their children and by their children's advocates. The Moiseyev, Soviet Russia's proudest "folk-dance" ensemble, has been with us all through this giddy pendulum swing of our recent history. Once the pet of intellectuals, it has been abandoned to Middle America, who loved it on sight—not for what it told us of Russia, but for what it recalled to us of our own traditions, slipping so rapidly away.

There were three new numbers in the Moiseyev's program this season, all in the completely inoffensive ecumenical spirit of cultural exchange to which the changing times have accustomed us. One was *Sicilian Tarantella*, which was about as poetically evocative as something one might see in a street festival celebrating the opening of a new supermarket in Los Angeles. Another was *Gaucho*, a moderately beguiling number in which three boys in black-and-silver cowboy regalia took turns drumming their heels in a spotlight. The third boy also did a series of body-slaps (like the third sailor in *Fancy Free*) ending in an air turn, after which he slammed a bolo knife into the floor of the stage. Best of all was *Dance of the Buffoons*, a completely off-beat non-"folk" dance to Rimsky-Korsakov, which began with a clown poking his head through the backcloth, as in *Carnaval*, then another head appearing above his, then a third above *his*, and so forth—straight up like a row of buttons. This then exploded into a bizarre masquerade in which there were corny things, like the villian being repeatedly jabbed with a pitchfork, but also beautiful things—men leaping or falling in contorted poses that were clear and easy to the eye, without the crabbed look that deprives comedy pantomime of its bite.

While the Moiseyev was on, the Radio City Music Hall revived its perennial *Ravel's Bolero*, choreographed by Florence Rogge back in the 1940's. Here was old-style presentation-house spectacle on a par with the Moiseyev—an army of dancers in gilt spangles slowly coiling around and across the vast stage. It was led by two guest artists formerly of Antonio's company, Carmen Rojas and Paco Ruiz, who with their own small company contributed an excellent but brief cuadro flamenco as a sort of curtain-raiser.

—September 1970

Graham Without Graham

Martha Graham, the greatest American dancer of this century, is seventy-six. She has been performing professionally for over fifty years. On October 1 she announced her retirement from the stage. *The New York Times* ran the story on page one. On October 2, the night her company opened a week's engagement at the Brooklyn Academy, she came out onto the stage and said, in effect, that the news of her retirement was a lot of talk. "When I retire," she ended dry-icily, "I'll probably go to a Greek island and you'll know nothing about it." It was a perfect exit line and brought a palpitating first-night audience to its feet.

The fact of the matter isn't worth pondering. Graham is one of those whom Cocteau calls *monstres sacrés*; in common ordinary American terms, she's show people. Living up to the moment—to a kind of wild sense of occasion that audiences may inspire but never anticipate—is a task she fills with magnificent, seemingly impromptu precision. These days, one mostly sees her in the role of a national treasure, accepting awards and addressing the public in those non sequiturs—she can go from moral philosophy to mini-skirts without, so to speak, taking a preparation—that set spines tingling. Last May, nursing a foot injury, she clutched the podium while a host of literati—it was the National Institute of Arts and Letters—subsided from standing applause to hear what she would *say*. She has always been charming in print and before a microphone. On October 2 it was her turn to receive the city's Handel Medallion. With her regal scuttle, lit on this night by flashes of black-and-gold brocade, her airy hand gestures, and her small, beautifully set teeth making a tasty tiny morsel of every word, she did everything the audience could have asked.

She is, of course, not only a dancer; she is also, perhaps principally, an actress, and she is a supreme mistress of the stage. Irreplaceable as a performer, she remains a great choreographer. In the brilliant pieces revived without her this season—*Deaths and Entrances* and *El Penitente* and *Letter to the World*—you see what Stark Young meant in 1948 when he said, "Miss Graham has a sense of stage projection, based on intensity and absorption and strict elimination of the unessential, that is rarely found anywhere in the theatre." And you see again how sharp is her sense of timing and how that timing remains dramatic whether the kind of pressure the piece is building is dramatic or abstract. *Deaths and Entrances* is a narrative spectacle without story progression of any usual kind; *Letter to the World* is more episodic and anecdotal; but the pacing of each piece—the first so driven, the second so methodical—invents for each a kind of dramatic contour that makes you pay closer attention to the events as they unfold. In *El Penitente* she invents— apparently—nothing. The work concerns three actors who present a Mystery Play and takes the realistically simple shape of a presentation such as one might actually see in a village festival. How it happens that *El Penitente* is poetic drama rather than prose ritual I can account for only by saying that it is also Graham theatre.

The October season was the first season the Martha Graham company has attempted without Martha Graham. Naturally, in the revivals it was the secondary soloists who had the greatest success. We are always tempted to look *through* whoever dances the Graham character to see, if we can, how Graham would have danced it. A clear exception to this is Mary Hinkson, who gives the performance of her career in Graham's old role as the heroine of *Deaths and Entrances*. In *Letter to the World*, the company hedged its bets, bringing in Jean Erdman and Jane Dudley to reassume their famous characterizations of the One Who Speaks and the Ancestress, and featuring Pearl Lang as the One Who Dances—the role that clinched Graham's reputation as the foremost actress-dancer of her time. Since the 1940's, all three women have built careers as soloists, choreographers, and teachers. This occasion seemed to stress that their enduring fame would be as Graham alumnae. Pearl Lang, a beautiful woman, no virtuoso, has not Graham's sense of stage projection. She couldn't be Martha and she couldn't hold us on her own. Late in the piece, when the character (based on Emily Dickinson) undergoes the torture of bereavement, she was convincing, her reticence and general blandness at last acquiring a kind of poetic humility.

Jean Erdman's role is the weakest in this distinguished but uneven piece. She speaks the lines from Emily Dickinson's poems that cue the action—speaks them while taking part in the action. The device isn't exactly defeating, but it remains a device, sliding frequently into the quaintness of caricature. And since, at its peak, the work achieves spiritual portraiture of a high order, I regret all the more that Miss Erdman's readings of the lines invariably accent the frailest and most impetuous side of Emily Dickinson's sensibility while the choreography does so only now and then. *Letter* is a very strange piece of work, intermittently mannered and trite yet rising in its realest moments to a passionate and eccentric beauty that reminds us of great primitive art. (Stark Young again: ". . . as Cézanne said of his painting, she is a primitive in her own kind of dancing.")

Richard Gain is very good as March, the shy, buoyant image of juvenescence that was Merce Cunningham's best role in the Graham repertory, but the great performance is Jane Dudley's in a stupendous role. The Ancestress is the stock figure of Death (as March is the stock figure of Pan) conceived as a nurse—a heavy, mannish-looking nurse with tremendous swinging arms and a peculiarly divided nature. At one point, she sits blocklike on a bench and takes the heroine in her arms and rocks her like a child. That Miss Dudley, now fifty-eight, has an arthritic limp only adds to the massiveness and dignity of her characterization.

The old Dudley role in *Deaths and Entrances*—the role that I persist in thinking of as that of the oldest sister—is brilliantly taken by Matt Turney, but then, everybody is good in this revival and the piece emerges, twelve years after Graham herself last played it in New York, as an exhilarating, highly polished nineteenth-century-style melodrama. The twentieth-century-style discontinuous narrative is no longer as baffling as it once seemed, and though it's still pretty opaque in some places, it's clear as bells in cold weather in others. No other Graham work sets so pregnant a mood, and no other work in the modern theatre this side of Eugene O'Neill gives us so fearful a glimpse of domestic insanity. The three warring sisters may or may not be the Brontës; if you think that they are (a program note makes the suggestion), you may miss the sharp contemporary bite of the piece. The heroine looks to me like a woman who can't accept a fully sexed male as her partner (the Tragic Beloved); she goes for the Poetic Beloved instead—someone who parallels her own inner nature without relieving her of its burdens—and she winds up with neither man. Throughout all this the household is alive; we sense, rather than observe, whispered conversations, footfalls in the dark corridor; upstairs a shutter bangs in the rain, a lamp burns all night. And it's all conveyed by dancers in Victorian costume crossing and recrossing the barest of stage sets and now and then lifting a prop. The whorl-of-memory structure, containing the tragic perception that we are dominated by the past, lets us see how situations develop without changing the conditions under which we may deal with them. It's not only a lesson about life but a very complex theatrical idea.

Every Soul Is a Circus, the fourth of these much-looked-forward-to revivals, was not a success in the performance of it that I saw. It is an elegant, very lightweight piece about female vanity, and it needs an expert comedienne at its center. Patricia Birch, the company régisseur and a not overly magnetic person on the stage, disported herself at length in the Graham part; determined to be funny, she killed every laugh. —*November 1970*

Hung Up

"How good *is* Eliot Feld?" people ask me, as if they distrusted all the acclaim that has gone to ballet's latest boy wonder and were looking for a way out of going to Brooklyn to see his company. Their caution is understandable; they've learned that the epiphanies experienced by critics every nine weeks are part of the general hokum of the times, and that, much as we'd like to believe we're living through an unprecedented Golden Age of dance, gifted young choreographers aren't dropping out of the sky on schedule. One would like to protect Feld from this cynical backlash, but, simply because he is so talented, and because like all honest talents he can be very disobliging in the working out of his artistic destiny, one can't just say, "He's great, it's all true—go, go at once." One has to say, "You can trust Feld," and hope that one is being understood.

Just now he seems peculiarly hung up—peculiarly, that is, to anyone who hasn't followed his work from the start. He obviously has it in him to create what we routinely call, with a bland contempt for routine, "major works." Yet, although he has produced seven new ballets since his company made its début a year ago, only one of them, *Intermezzo*, is the kind of piece you should take your relatives to when they're in town for a visit. Last spring's *Early Songs*, set to a lieder cycle by the young Richard Strauss, is also very fine, in some ways more sensitive and more richly molded than *Intermezzo*, but it's also unfocused and theatrically dull. And *The Consort*, which is the best of the new pieces seen this fall, is similarly diffuse, developing no tension in performance until the end. All three of these ballets are dance suites, a form that Feld, with his innate musicality and ever-deepening sense of classical style, seems to find most congenial at the moment. But it's a little as if he were standing too close to his subject. Except for *Intermezzo*, which has a grand sweep that carries us from one number to the next, the style is all concentrated in details; it's interesting minute by minute, but we never draw back for a full view, never achieve the perspective which can make those details meaningful.

The linear construction of Feld's recent work, its lack of centrality and of cumulative impact, could be intentional, of course. But it could also be a by-product of craftsmanship. As a craftsman —and he's one of the few emerging choreographers who deserve to be called that—Feld is now at the stage where he makes better parts than wholes. Formerly, as in *Harbinger*, *At Midnight*, and *Meadowlark*, he was good at sustaining a single gesture or color throughout a piece or throughout a section of a piece; but his details were somewhat too large and splotchy. Now these weaknesses seem overcorrected. *Cortège Parisien*, another of the new pieces, looks like a determined corrective to *Cortège Burlesque*, which has been dropped. The new *Cortège*, like the old one, is a giddy send-up of the grand manner, set to Chabrier, but whereas in the former ballet there was a lot of offside capering and very little dancing, in the new one the dancers (three couples) are dancing, and probably counting, every second. It's a little too rigorous for him, and Feld takes every jolt and lurch in the music (the Fête Polonaise) so literally, and his dancers look so intent and busy, that the parody misfires—again.

The steady, devouring, inchwormlike concentration that even his failures reveal tells us that Feld is growing, as an artist. He doesn't work from facility; he chooses the hardest kind of material to make ballets out of (art songs, for example)—material that risks self-exposure—and he works only the hardest side of that. In a dramatic ballet about early sexual experience, called *A Poem Forgotten*, he seemed to run himself deliberately into a wall. Motifs that appeared destined for large-scale dramatization were barely presented when the curtain came down. But they were so vividly presented that the audience got the point and cheered—loudest for dancer Daniel Levins as a kind of wandering foetus in a red cap. But I don't think that story ballets are as much of a challenge to Feld as they are a trap. *A Poem Forgotten*, representing the short end of his talent, was —like last year's *Pagan Spring*—Choreographer Feld working on orders from Artistic Director Feld to balance the repertory.

Gerald Arpino's new work for City Center Joffrey Ballet is a smash hit, as one might have predicted from the easy-to-hand materials it is made out of: rock music, rock dancing, and political protest. Unlike Feld's audience, a growing one which enjoys rising keenly to a challenge, Arpino's audience just seems to lie back and let itself be tickled by a series of familiar strokes. *Trinity* is one big masterstroke, doing for the Joffrey company in 1970 what *Astarte* did for it in 1967. It substitutes peace candles for *Astarte*'s now outmoded psychedelic décor, and instead of one static pas de deux it has a whole stageful of dancers twitching away to a rock beat. The music (by Alan Raph and Lee Holdridge) is the latest brand of art rock, using baroque polyphony, plainsong, and a children's chorus in addition to the usual sonic booms. The whole point is that the Joffrey is the hippest, youngest, most "relevant" company around and don't you forget it.

You can miss the point if you look for any real dance invention in the ballet. When the dancers aren't snapping their pelvises and rolling their heads—gestures borrowed without being transposed (as they were in Paul Taylor's *Churchyard*) from the discothèque —they are leaping scores of invisible hurdles or doing superhigh lifts and running carries across the stage. Even in quiet moments their bodies look galvanized. The vocabulary of movement is so small yet so propulsive that watching the ballet is like getting a love letter from an illiterate, all in capitals. *Trinity* isn't the worst ballet that Arpino has done, and it's almost beguiling in a mindless sort of way. The audience starts grooving with the action the minute the curtain goes up. But before too long, the feeling in the house is more like that of a political rally than a ballet performance. Arpino's supporters keep saying that he's found a new audience and turned it on to ballet, but I can't believe things like *Trinity* turn anybody on to ballet. They just turn you on to being turned on.

After the Joffrey season, coming back to Brooklyn for Merce Cunningham was like rising into the upper ether. To the most brilliant pieces in the current repertory—*Scramble, RainForest,* and *Canfield*—Cunningham has now added *Signals,* which is unlike anything else. The sense of space in it—it seems to be placed far downstage—reminds me of the spaces out West. The piece as a whole has the intensity of country silences; it is a very *quiet* piece, and the score is half silence and half back-porch music (crickets, a car engine, a music box, a Bluegrass guitar). And when we watch the small group of soloists moving, for the most part very quietly and slowly, in their big space and in the atmosphere that the lighting wraps them in—a blue smoky atmosphere like highways and prairies at dusk—the associations and recognitions that play through our minds can be extraordinary. They are, I think, what *Signals* is about.

Signals changes on a week-to-week schedule. That is, the elements it is made of are variable, but the strong poetic spell they combine to cast is always there. Different performances give us different moments to enjoy. The story is always the story of *Signals.* Richard Nelson's beautiful lighting (actually he has devised a set made of flickering or glowing lights) is a large part of this story.

When the New York City Ballet opened its winter season, everyone rushed to see the scenery for *Who Cares?*, commissioned from the veteran designer Jo Mielziner. We expected skyscrapers and that's what we got. Skyscrapers leaning this way and that like a barroom mural in a third-rate hotel. The lighting has also gone from feeble to garish, and the girls' dresses have been tarted up, and the whole ballet looks like the Hotbox Revue, and in spite of it all, the audience loves it more than ever, and so do I.   —*January* 1971

Makarova with Ballet Theatre

American Ballet Theatre didn't need Natalia Makarova to show us how far it has let *Les Sylphides* deteriorate, but it did import this marvellous Russian star, and her dancing in this supposedly definitive version of the Fokine classic pointed up to a painful extent the deficiencies of style and execution displayed by the other dancers in the same performance. I'm not referring to Ivan Nagy, who supported Makarova effectively and danced with sensitivity and dignity; the men of Ballet Theatre are generally quite good in this part, having Erik Bruhn as a more or less constant stylistic model. But the women have had no one since the long-ago great days of Markova who could show them how the ballet should be danced, and the result is that, in the same performance, we get a Makarova whose every movement reveals the perfect security in both outline and continuity for which her training had prepared her, dancing alongside a Diana Weber and a Mimi Paul whose movements reflect only utter bafflement or a pretty notion of how sylphides comport themselves. Makarova's zephyrous lightness, in the leaps that were scaled down for the small stage of the City Center, or in the magnificent weightlessly ascending lifts with Nagy, would have been impressive in any ballet, but here one was struck even more by the vividness of her head and arms in poses that seemed to belong to this and to no other ballet, and by the continuous active impact of these poses as a means of focusing the attention of the audience not upon Makarova as a person but upon the meaning of the ballet. That meaning is what Mimi Paul toyed with in her Prelude but couldn't project because her arms kept losing tension in a step-by-step definition of the dance instead of sustaining that tension like a charged current throughout the dance as a whole. It was Makarova's ability to do this at both fast and slow tempos that gave her dancing its sculptural grandeur, its sense of a smooth unbroken relationship to the architecture of Fokine's choreography. And when I say that she made the other dancers look one-dimensional and childish, I mean merely that she presented herself completely, not that she had ideas about the ballet that the others didn't have or couldn't have looked up in a book. Paul, for example, was far more a "fantastic" creature than Makarova; with her lily-stalk neck and tendril arms and Beardsley slump, she satisfied a large part of the audience, which mooned right along with her in *fin-de-siècle* rapture. Members of this part of the audience, as they later told me, found Makarova "cold" and "remote." This is what one used to hear about the other Kirov ballerinas, notably the great Kolpakova, and about the Kirov's own production of *Les Sylphides*, which commits the fatal offense of being performed in broad daylight. But I suppose the Kirov thinks that this ballet, like any other, is first of all a construction in time and space and was meant to be *seen*, not mooned over; and the differences between Makarova and her Ballet Theatre colleagues are physical differences that one can *see*, not matters of literary interpretation. Not that Makarova didn't "interpret"—she did. The arms were always making important wreaths around a necessarily light head, and I found, too, that her connection with other persons onstage was always stronger than theirs was with her. But this was so because her connection to the whole graphic world of Fokine's ballet was stronger. The perfection with which she could place herself, at any moment, in absolute harmony with the total stage picture—could draw one's eye to the idealism of that picture and not to some insular variant of it—was what made Fokine's fantasy work for me.

And she made Tudor's fantasy in *Jardin aux Lilas* work, too, though in a very different way: by bringing to the part of Caroline such an outpouring of tragic emotion that the ballet surged with life as it rarely does. Makarova's intensity was almost too much at times—the emotion reaching floodtide couldn't always recede in time to preserve the stoic façade of the social code Tudor's choreography captures so brilliantly; and though John Prinz met her more than halfway (in a performance much improved but much too violent), one couldn't really believe in them as a natural pair of lovers. But Makarova's sincere grief, which seemed to extend beyond self-pity to all trapped and suffering creatures, made the ballet a rich and thrilling experience and confirmed the impression I had of her in *Les Sylphides*—that of a ballerina concerned with the whole ballet and not merely her own part in it, and of an artist who can express this moral concern in beautiful movement.

It was interesting to see again the Ballet Theatre production of Balanchine's *Theme and Variations*—to see not only how badly it suffers from the company's lack of first-rank classical dancers (one would like to see Makarova have a crack at it, with Bruhn), but how different in style it is from the new version that Balanchine has mounted for the New York City Ballet. I think there may be some different steps, in the man's variations particularly (though it's hard to say on the basis of one viewing), and there are obvious differences in the entrance of the corps at the end of the pas de deux. But the main difference is one of tone and emphasis. Ballet Theatre's is a spectacular, glamorous affair; the New York City Ballet's is decorous and contained, a grand ballet de cour in miniature, its compactness and delicacy heightened by the casting of Edward Villella and Gelsey Kirkland in the leads. And it takes place after an extended prologue composed to the first three movements of Tchaikovsky's orchestral Suite No. 3 to which the fourth movement, the Tema con variazioni, is both contrast and climax. Balanchine calls the whole thing *Suite No. 3*.

The prologue is set on a darkened stage behind a scrim on which a vast spiral is painted. As the music begins, we seem to move into the cone of the spiral, which vanishes as a faint light comes up on the architectural outlines of a palace setting. When the first movement (the Elégie) is over, the floor of the stage dissolves in blue and reappears for the Valse Mélancolique together with columns and arches more distinctly seen. It is still about midnight. After this, again there is a blue-out, and with the Scherzo we are in a great hall. The moonlight streams in. At the final notes of the Scherzo, the scrim is raised, the lights come up brightly, and behind the back wall of this ballet, which also flies upward, we find another ballet—*Theme and Variations*, with the dancers all drawn up in ranks, ready to begin—and another set, a ballroom painted honey and gold and cream and plum.

Theme and Variations has always had, for me, strong overtones of *The Sleeping Beauty*, and here, in his twenty-minute approach to the ballroom of the magic palace (or perhaps to the stage of the Maryinsky), Balanchine has produced a kind of foreshortened or telescoped *Sleeping Beauty*, from the Vision Scene through to the Wedding divertissement. The conception is so striking and, what is more unusual for a company whose record in matters of production is generally poor, so strikingly well realized (by Ronald Bates, who did the lighting, and Nicola Benois—the son of Alexandre— who did the scenery) that the dances of the first three scenes all but evaporate in the memory like the gradually clearing mists they seem to represent. But I think on further acquaintance they will come to be very interesting, especially the first one, which is performed barefoot and has to do with a lonely, wandering lady (Karin von Aroldingen, looking her most elegant) who gently tortures Anthony Blum with her comings and goings. Benois's costumes for these scenes are romantic loungewear for the girls and bellbottoms for the boys, and, like the formal classical costumes for the finale, they are not very distinguished. —*February 1971*

Out of the Storeroom

Warm-weather ballet has been with us a few years now, but it took John Cranko to devise the perfect fruit punch for a hot summer night at Lincoln Center. *Poème de l'Extase* contains so much exotic frou-frou—so many fluttering capes and drapes and boys in their skimpies—that it almost revives one's faith in ballet as a pleasure garden for sensitive youth and quaintly vicious old men. The trouble is that there's no one left on earth who will buy this sort of starched-collar decadence—certainly not at the original price. Even if we can still succumb to the Scriabin score, there are those Gustav Klimt designs hanging all over the stage like yard goods in a Third Avenue showroom. These days an artist like Klimt is automatically devalued by the passion for period camp, and I'm afraid it's this sort of passion that has gone into the making of the ballet. Cranko and his designer, Jürgen Rose, are dealing in cut-rate material; what they offer us is not Old World vice and sensuality but the fake sensibility of the boutique.

For that, I guess there are enough takers. With the hints on how to decorate your living room this fall, you also get Margot Fonteyn in a role that trades on her legend without adding to its luster. She's supposed to be a great lady contemplating the prospect of a last affair while reliving four former ones, but all that happens on the stage is a series of acrobatic adagios in which she is lifted and swung in turn by Egon Madsen (as a Nureyev-Armand figure) and four exceedingly implausible males (as the ghosts of the former lovers) who are harder to tell apart than the four princes in the Rose

Adagio. Perhaps the whole thing is a send-up of the Rose Adagio; when the curtain falls and Fonteyn presents roses to each of her partners, it's hard to resist the feeling that things have been going in reverse since the start of the ballet. Or that Cranko's imagination is now a helpless victim of what used to be a gift for parody.

Poème de l'Extase was the main event of the Stuttgart Ballet's two-week return engagement. The event of the American Ballet Theatre season and one of the great events of the ballet year was the revival of Tudor's *Romeo and Juliet* with the Eugene Berman scenery and the Frederick Delius music, and with Carla Fracci and Natalia Makarova heading alternate casts. The ballet is not Shakespeare's tragedy but a shimmering vision of the Renaissance, weighted by one of the most splendid architectural sets of modern times. Tudor's choreography curls around it like an insinuating growth. Last seen in New York in 1956 and unknown to many of us until now, the ballet seems to retain an uneasy tension between the elegance of its period (the forties of the war years) and the so-to-speak "eternal" poetic values that inspired it and that made people call it a masterpiece. But the tension between what it wants to be and what it had to be is not unbalanced as in *Poème de l'Extase*. Tudor doesn't exploit his period; he reveals it, and at this distance in time his ballet is almost as interesting for what it can tell us of the forties as for what it evokes of quattrocento art and culture. Its deliberate aestheticism, its almost too exquisite touches are as absorbing as a brilliant nightmare, and the several deliberately ghastly costumes that Berman has provided are affectations of exactly the right kind. The lovers in this ballet are aesthetic objects rather than characters. Ivan Nagy understood his part less well than Carla Fracci, who could become a great Juliet. I did not get to see Makarova, whose Romeo was John Prinz. Dennis Nahat was an epicene Mercutio and Bruce Marks a strangely reticent Tybalt. The rest of the large cast performed with devotion.

Looking back over the ballet year, I'd say that most of the best works have been revivals—the Graham pieces of last fall, the "Theme and Variations" portion of Balanchine's *Suite No. 3*, and his *Donizetti Variations* revived this spring, the Australian Ballet's production of Ashton's *Les Rendezvous*, Tudor's *Romeo and Juliet*. *PAMTGG*, the latest Balanchine novelty, might have been better put off indefinitely, but it cost too much to abandon. *PAMTGG* is an aimless spectacle about space travel, with troops of dancers crossing the stage in Irene Sharaff's science-fiction costumes, against Jo Mielziner's backdrops of runways and planets and skies. The music is sweet, brassy Hollywood stuff, commissioned from the Hollywood composer Roger Kellaway, who used the commercial jingle "Pan Am makes the going great" as a motif (hence title); it's probably the cheapest score Balanchine has ever used, and he gets nowhere with it. Buried somewhere in this disaster is a small joke about the breezy grandeur of someday taking off for Mars or Venus; but the dancing, in an incoherent discothèque style, isn't very amusing. In an interview printed in the *Times* the day of the première, Lincoln Kirstein offered the opinion that "the big direction that really established him [Balanchine] came with Rodgers and Hart, and Goldwyn. The quality of that experience and Stravinsky's music have determined the quality of what we've done." There may be truth in this, but it's also true that when Balanchine works directly with the materials of popular culture, as he does in *Slaughter on Tenth Avenue* and *PAMTGG*, he produces junk, and only when he works with them indirectly, as in *Who Cares?* and *Western Symphony* and in countless ballets with "classical" scores, does he produce art. —*September 1971*

PART
THREE

Quarterly

1966-1972

The Other Royal Ballet

New Yorkers have a fantasy about the Royal Danish Ballet, which is that the company comes straight from Arcadia and is good for the nerves. When the Danes are in town, we all take the cure; and it's tonic, ozone, and country butter to the tired balletomane. The Danes don't rape the senses; they tend to withdraw before massive effects of any sort, as if modesty did not permit. This strange modesty, or diffidence, is a Danish trait. And their style, like no other in the world, *is* powerfully refreshing when you get it full strength. When you do not get it—when, in short, the ballet is not *Coppélia*, *Konservatoriet*, or *Napoli*—nothing else they do seems very important.

Half the repertory that was brought to New York showed the company trying to rise to a kind of importance it doesn't have to command. I had the feeling the Royal Danes were challenging the Royal British for European hegemony; perhaps Hurok had decreed such an impression should be given. The opening, Ashton's *Romeo and Juliet*, to Prokofiev's music, guttered like a spent candle in comparison with the well-fueled British production seen last spring. Ashton's choreography is superior, but it is not superior to other Ashton choreography; Danish diffidence was made to appear positively recessive. What was brilliant was the line of invention for the Danish men and Henning Kronstam's extension used as a kind of dramatic signature and annunciatory phrase (with varied emphases for "But soft!" and "Then I defy you, stars!"). This is one ballet that is not *Juliet and Romeo*; on the other hand, the pas de deux for the lovers had my least favorite Ashtonian devices—the bouncy half-lifts en manège (with running hops or toe-flutters) and the "Fonteyn cameo"—points twiddling in place as the ballerina languishes against the portières or in the crook of one arm.

The Ashton was the one contemporary work of eminence the Danes did in their four-week season. But the applause went to Roland Petit's *Carmen* and Birgit Cullberg's *Miss Julie* and *Moon Reindeer*. *Carmen*, in fact, had sold-out houses shouting far into the intermissions, and not for Niels Kehlet, Solveig Østergaard, and Jørn Madsen (the season's heroes), who got what fun was to be had out of three kibitzing roles, but for the two Bruhnettes in the lead, who were as bad as the ballet. The company was able to get greater ovations by descending to Petit's expressive level than they got by raising Cullberg's to meet their own—which illustrates about as well as anything I can think of how standards come inevitably to be debased in a company run by dancers.

Stark Young's confession—that "in my experience of the American theatre, I should say, after much thought in the matter, that the greatest single moment I ever saw was . . . in a silly Clemence Dane play that went to pot long before the last curtain"—gives me strength to observe that there is some good in *Miss Julie* after all. If only because the most surprising and consistently absorbing performances in their modern repertory are given in this ballet, the Danes are wise to retain it. The piece itself is a shameless revamping of the Strindberg play musical-comedy style (pity it wasn't also retitled—*Julie!* would do, or maybe *Me and Julie*), but there are bad ballets that can be salvaged or even remade through personal force, and Cullberg's *Miss Julie* is one of these, as was her *Medea*. Erik Bruhn's Jean is now his greatest performance, better even than his James in *La Sylphide*; Frank Schaufuss's arrogant loutishness is as good in its way as Bruhn's neurotic self-disgust; and Vivi Gelker, coolly vicious, gave what I'd thought was the best Julie after Toni Lander's until Lander herself gave the worst, in Ballet Theatre's January–February season.

Lander, a beautiful dancer a beautiful lot of the time, is the Danes' prima *in absentia*. Neither Kirsten Simone, an excellent technician in a variety of styles, nor Margrethe Schanne, an excellent stylist in a single technique (I regret, now that she is retiring, never having seen her as Balanchine's Sonnambula), quite holds the repertory together at the top. Lander has the right talents, the right experience, and is the right age, to do so—and to provide Erik Bruhn with the partner he has long needed.

Bruhn, who answers Nureyev in the tournament of Royals, did in the absence of a prima ballerina what a prima ballerina customarily does. He provided a heightened demonstration of his company's best skills and stylistic manner, at the same time advancing them to the limits of his own capacities. One saw the company in Bruhn and, what was less to be expected, one saw Bruhn in the company. As a concession to his prominence, the management added two nonscheduled numbers to his three repertory roles. These were the *Nutcracker* and *Don Quixote* pas de deux. (Why not the

Genzano pas de deux?) The choreography, especially in the former, was messy, the ballerinas were determined but undazzling, and the conductor was less than determined. Presumably, it was all needed to show what the other roles didn't—that Bruhn now does a quick dégagé after his air turns where formerly he would stop dead in perfect fifth position; or that his grandes pirouettes in the air (in *Don Q*) are no longer of the size, sweep, and finish to leave the Russians breathless (as they were in 1960). But I was less distressed at these first fraying threads of technique than at Bruhn's new stage mannerisms, which I don't recall his exhibiting in his last New York appearances with the New York City Ballet in 1963. Here he was, lifting and extending monumental palms in an apparent parody of danseur-noble deportment. The stage mask, too, seemed frozen and enigmatic beyond any expressive need. And though he danced his other roles with his old murderous accuracy and no affectations (Don José aside), I got much the same impression of a wish to appear grand and important in a way even the dullest member of the audience would not miss. At times I thought what I knew could not be true—that Bruhn was very much afraid of seeming part of a family spectacle New York could dismiss.

Not that this detached him from the company, on the contrary. Everyone else wanted to impress New York even more mightily than he. They began by leaving most of what they could do best at home. The marvel is that they were able to keep enough sweetness and spirit for what they did bring, and so ultimately to redeem the mistakes in the other half of the repertory—mistakes that included Robbins's *Fanfare*, performed as cute trivia instead of dead-pan ceremony—which would have made it funnier—and Flemming Flindt's *The Private Lesson*, an attempt at making Ionesco quirkiness work in a ballet; as well as junk like *Moon·Reindeer* and *Carmen*.

In view of all this, I'm sorry I didn't enjoy *The Whims of Cupid* or very much of *La Sylphide*, which, despite some of the loveliest dancing of the whole season, seemed in this production no more imposing than *Iolanthe* in kilts. But if it hadn't been for *La Sylphide* we would have seen very little of Bournonville—no *La Ventana*, no *Flower Festival in Genzano*; only *Konservatoriet* and *Napoli*, of which we were given but the third act. On this evidence, we can only begin to form an idea of Bournonville the artist. During the season, I heard him described as the Moiseyev rather than the

Petipa of Denmark. Compared to *Giselle* (erroneously dated 1841; it is Petipa's revised version that we know), *La Sylphide* (1836) looks underchoreographed at first, but soon we see in the emptiness a materialization like the equivalent of a painter's negative space. The important thing is to be sure you are looking at the right picture and not taking it for a bad imitation of the wrong one. The right picture is the right spectacle.

Bournonville a glorified folk dancer? I find that for a folk dancer he had an unusually high opinion of classical dancing. Often the two styles are used in dynamic contrast. The sylphides are classicists right out of *Konservatoriet*. They do a very strict class in Bournonville technique. But what the Scottish clansmen do, and what the Neapolitans do, is closer to folk dancing. The folk quality isn't so much in the steps, however, as in a concept of mass action you don't see in the classical-conservatory dances. Everybody dancing at once all over the stage in complicated figures and cross-patterns is a folk motif. In *La Sylphide* there's a poignant tension between the domestic intermingling of a big social dance and the decorous unilateral motion of beings from another world, a still world like one seen at the bottom of a lake. When the hero forsakes the one for the other, he forsakes society with absolute decision.

Konservatoriet is simply morning center practice, brilliantly arranged for stars. As the class is being given sometime in the 1820's by August Vestris, the ballet is also a historical miniature, but it has not the least trace of self-consciousness. The same is true of the *Coppélia*, a folk ballet few companies could undertake without converting into insincere ballet bouffe. The company's spirit in these ballets is beyond the trivially charming. The dancers don't rely on charm anyway, but on conveying their happiness in doing something they are used to hearing spoken of highly if it is done well. That spirit isn't like a harassed professional virtuosity with which one takes one's chances. It is more like an aristocratic sense of security—a meritocracy, yes, but more. I was reminded of Tivoli, with its thoughtfully graded and diversified amusements where Danes of all ages and conditions can have fun or improvise their own fun without feeling the slightest social pressure to give way to someone else's. In America we are at present all teen-agers. But in the younger soloists of the Danish ballet you can see the endearing gravity a real teen-ager has when he's not being made hysterical through overattention. They all dance beautifully with a free and open airiness, and nowhere more beautifully than in *Napoli*.

As they dance the brilliant steps, the abundant virtuosic sequences, stepping out one at a time or in combinations, they watch each other with responsibility. When they bow, it is to the rest of the company onstage. When they stand on the sidelines awaiting a cue, they continue to watch, to applaud, to beat time. And on the bridge at the back of the set children look down, watching, too. They see themselves later in life getting to dance this or that variation and don't imagine they are part of one of the oldest traditions in world theatre. *Napoli* demonstrates the way a dance tradition stays alive and pertinent for generations. At the same time, it is a great signature work, and is to the Danes what *Serenade* is to the New York City Ballet, *Symphonic Variations* to the Royal British, and *La Bayadère* to the Kirov. (*Konservatoriet* is less such, as *Symphony in C* is less than *Serenade*—less intimately revealing.)

This large companionable spectacle has the warmth but not the tension of a cuadro flamenco. It is presexual, and that is why, despite its name, it suggests nothing Latin. We would be wrong to condescend to Danish ballet as the world's most brilliant toy theatre. It is far too human. But I find that the Danish sensibility at its best often seems that of an undeceived child, and there is nothing sweet or charming about that, as there isn't about the tales of Hans Christian Andersen. The Sylphide's amorality; the isolation of the hero, James; Swanilda's perversity—these are serious and coherent theatrical conceptions.

The *Coppélia* isn't the usual painless diversion. It has cruelty, passion, moments of icy terror. It manages to make these startling shifts by staying so modest and simple in performance you don't expect hard-hitting realism. Looking back on the two performances I saw, I realize they were almost entirely surrounded by Solveig Østergaard, the company's most outstandingly gifted demi-caractère ballerina, but Østergaard's unflaunted great performance was the measure of a great production in which a comic parable of sex and power is told with typical Danish dryness and lack of urgency. It's so dry, in fact, that some people thought it wasn't a ballet at all but a pantomime with folk dances. The third act is utterly plain; it hasn't even a grand pas de deux. Delibes's great waltz, with its long, curved phrases unrolling like scrolls, seems to go undanced. One could make a good musical case against all that this production is. One could; but I wouldn't choose to. Rather, I choose the Danes, because in the great age of camp their peculiar inability to imagine E. T. A. Hoffmann's characters indulging in tutus and Paris frills and the danse-d'école choreography Delibes's score calls for has a powerful imaginative thrust of its own and an almost spiritual power to satisfy. (Ten years ago I might have thought it a puritan aversion; today a direct statement in almost any medium is in danger of being called utilitarian.)

The Danes have made a great *Coppélia* by putting into it so much of themselves. The Swanilda is a bully—one of the hyperactive, half-grown little-mother bitches that a fair-favored society indulges. Her boyfriend isn't so much a straying lover as a disobedient subject. When, like all ballet heroes, he falls to dreaming of an ideal love, she gets busy and works overtime like a plant executrix who senses the corporation philosophy is being undermined. When all aggressions fail, she resorts to subterfuge. She destroys the competition—Coppélius, a crazy idealist (a Hoffmannesque tautology) trying to get a patent on mechanized brains—by impersonating (literally investing with a person) the male-made robot her friend Frantz has fallen for. She shows how much better—i.e., worth mauling—a person who can be like a thing is than a thing which can be like a person. The male world of things, the perfectible world, falls before the female world of persons. Maternal theory wins. Swanilda saves the race.

Even in bad productions of *Coppélia* you can have fun trying to discern its meanings. The ballet has sex war, business ethics, romantic heresy, political prophecy. Edwin Denby detected in the Ballet Russe version a Shavian parallel; the perfect American production would have to have been designed by James Thurber. What I love in the Danish production is its clear view of a real world of dramatic conflicts and of their utter naturalness. Swanilda is the only girl on point, but she isn't a ballet heroine or even a ballerina, as in the Russian-derived versions. The production doesn't glorify her —she's a part of its world. But we know that the bland, unchanged exterior of sunshine and dancing peasants to which we return in Act III is secured solely by her courage in having penetrated the shuttered malevolence of Coppélius's laboratory. We know also that there in the dark alone, where Frantz, asleep, cannot see her, she becomes fully as evil a monster as Coppélius, tormenting him only as one can torment those most like oneself. But his wrathful dreams of domination are no match for her controlled and confident tyrannical lust. The people of the town console him with reparations and end the ballet by cynically rejoicing in the victory of feminine realism.

Østergaard is magnificent—not heartless as Swanildas generally are, but with a child's ardent heart for destruction. Swanilda's rightness, her invincibility, is in Østergaard's bold, floating, high-chested jump, the most beautiful jump any woman in ballet has, next to Kolpakova. But when she did her doll dance, all mad yellow curls and quivering, contorted wooden limbs, I thought of Chaplin's dance with the balloon in *The Great Dictator*, in which he becomes *its* partner. With Niels Bjørn Larsen, perhaps the perfect conventional curmudgeonly Coppélius, I didn't think Øster-gaard was able to suggest as much of this strangeness as she did with Frank Schaufuss, and the black comedy of Act II was more comic than black. With Schaufuss, playing far out of convention and looking shatteringly like Søren Kierkegaard crossed with Uriah Heep, the stage came alive with intimations of psychopathology. An agonized young hunchback, power-drunk, stumbling about his bachelor digs in search of the whip hand his genius meant him to have, Schaufuss gave the season's most impressive mime perfor-mance. As Frantz, marvellous Niels Kehlet—pumpkin face, button eyes, frayed hair, an eellike sinuousness to his leaps—was the perfect folk-tale hero; one would like to see him as Tyl or as a Danish Petrouchka.   —*Spring 1966*

Ballets Without Choreography

If you are a balletomane in New York, you can be happy much of the year. But if you are seriously interested in choreography, you're a different breed of dog, and you haven't had much to chew on recently. The past season has brought substantial pleasure in parts of Balanchine's *Jewels*, in Ashton's *Monotones*, Cunningham's *Place* and *How to Pass, Kick, Fall, and Run*, and Taylor's *Orbs*, perhaps the most charming work in the modern-dance repertory. There have been some outstanding revivals, notably one of Nijinska's *Les Noces* by the Royal Ballet, and, way off Broadway, one or two interesting new works. And there is always basic repertory to return to—even Graham offers a few of her older and better pieces—but now we are getting down to subsistence rations. Choreography is not all that dance is, of course, but if it is not to be the primary organizing impulse behind what we see, then we have surrendered a medium to its constituent attractions. Balletomanes surrender the dance to stars, and while stars are wonderful, they are twice as wonderful dancing good dances. To speak of dance as choreography is to take a narrow look at the broad action of the medium in space and time, but perhaps it's necessary to look narrowly, even suspiciously, at choreography as the big ballet companies produce it. A lot of it is vile, and most of it is vile on principle.

If more bad ballets are being produced each season than there used to be, possibly it's not because there are too many bad choreographers but because too many choreographers are making the same kind of bad ballet. Having devoted themselves to a single ideal of expressive form, they are falling into a misconception of the ideal. The ideal is absolute expression, dancing for its own sake —what might be called dance totalism; and it has become a major international trend. Dance totalism is everywhere taken to be the sign of an art in its purest state. I have no argument against it. *La Bayadère*,* *Les Sylphides*, *Primitive Mysteries*, *Serenade*, *Concerto Barocco*, *Agon*, *Moves*—these are all examples of dance totalism in successive epochs, and one could add to the list those new works I mentioned at the start of this article. My quarrel with the form is with its fetishistic reductions, with the fallacies and confusions that surround its present-day practice, with audiences and critics so seized by visions of "autonomous" movement that they cannot tell purity of expression from poverty of means.

The pressure these puritans exert is tremendous. Companies from New York to Moscow are thought to be moving ahead if they produce more ballets composed entirely of dance movement without reference to story or characters or scenery. This has been the norm of acceptance for so long that it is difficult to recall just when a mechanical totalism began to replace story lines, star turns, mood pieces, and three-act fables in fancy dress. I would guess it happened sometime in the fifties, when Balanchine ceased being merely a great choreographer and became a climate of inspiration, to para-

---

* In the single act that is all we know of it, an extended "vision" scene with divertissement similar to that in *The Sleeping Beauty*. The nineteenth-century audience was no stranger to dance totalism, simply switching gears in the course of a long evening. Dance totalism was the continuation of spectacle by other means. It still is, not by convention but by inference. The modern preference for full-out "abstract" expression was conditioned gradually; milestones such as Nijinsky's *Faune*, Balanchine's *Apollo*, and Tudor's *Jardin aux Lilas* looked totalistic in their day but were condensed evocations of the representational gestures which were no longer taking place.

phrase Auden on Freud. In a 1955 essay called "The Position of Balanchine," Lincoln Kirstein summed up that position: "His stories are his dances; his characters are his dancers." This is still true, however marked Balanchine's interest since then in areas Kirstein ruled out ("storytelling, character-building, *tableaux vivants* or the historical-picturesque"). The younger generation of choreographers came in those days to observe what Balanchine could afford to do without. They saw that what he worked with—the irreducible physical material of absolute dance—produced beauty. Before Balanchine, Martha Graham had composed dances entirely of personal non-associative gesture. There must have been in Graham at that time a creative impulse acting to liberate movement as Gertrude Stein had sought to liberate words. It was a purely local instinct responding to a felt need—the American reformative conscience in action. (The concern with what was native and primordial is apparent in many of Graham's titles from this period: *Primitive Mysteries, American Provincials, Frontier, Horizons*, etc.) And in Balanchine, Diaghilev's erstwhile "American" choreographer, the need to free native performers from the impedimenta of an exotic (i.e., European) ballet tradition gave rise to a concentrated choreographic expression that left the dancer nothing to do but dance.

Through foreign tours in the fifties, Balanchine's precedent and Graham's repertory (no longer so primitive or so mysterious) became available to the world at large at about the same time. Merce Cunningham came on later to administer the final shock to fixed ideas of form and content. And there were others. But for the past decade George and Martha, parents of the American movement in choreography, have been the prevailing global influences, with what paradoxical and deleterious results we now see on all sides. All-dance ballets were good because they trained audiences to see meaning in movement. But today it is possible to speak of overtrained audiences who presuppose meaning where there is *only* movement. And what dull, derivative, formula-fed movement it is. If I refrain from labeling dance totalism the new orthodoxy, it is only because the formulas have kept its products looking disparate and old-fashioned; never was there so ill-managed a renaissance. Means have been imitated, but meaning has been confounded. Choreography with a capital C has been the vitiation of choreography.

The totalist formulas are applied across the board. Story ballets like Gerald Arpino's *Nightwings* or John Taras's *Jeux*, and full-length productions like Kenneth MacMillan's *Romeo and Juliet*, have long passages of undifferentiated temporizing action which, for lack of a better definition, we have to call dance; it isn't mime or stylized gesture; it's empty rhetoric seemingly designed to keep the medium intact. But the mind wanders. What price purity? Meanwhile, in *Don Quixote* the archtotalist Balanchine has filled an evening-long entertainment with an array of effects employing the full resources of the dance theatre, each gripping the attention in a new way. In *Elegy*, a recent short ballet of Arpino's, a subject which seems utterly concrete (the life story of a Confederate officer told at the moment of his death) vanishes before your eyes into Choreography, and nothing happens—neither story nor dancing, neither life nor death.

Good choreography fuses eye, ear, and mind. This fusion is itself the complete experience one looks for, and it takes place in delight —the perfect intellectual delight, as Proust says somewhere, of seeing a pattern. This is why dancing is so hard to discuss with sobriety. Nothing one can think of to say about it afterward is adequate, since the appeal is not to the analytical but to the assimila- tive faculty. Watching Balanchine's modern classical ballets—ballets like *Agon*, *Ballet Imperial*, *Liebeslieder*, or *Jewels*—which are as lucid as narratives can be without being stories, I often find myself thinking, like Alice, "It seems to fill my head with ideas, only I don't know what they are." Watching the ballets of Arpino or MacMillan or Taras, I get ideas, too, but I don't care what they are. It is impossible to take an intelligent interest in *Nightwings* or *Incubus* or *The Song of the Earth* or *Jeux* because no interest is being generated at an intelligent level, which is to say at the level of choreography. What these ballets offer isn't choreography—i.e., movement filling an expressive need; instead, they appeal to an intellectual interest, to a prior knowledge; they offer situations which are supposed to be interesting in themselves. The movements the dancers do merely state the situation without developing it, and you realize as the piece wears on that there is no reason why they should be moving at all. And the more sterile the means of expres- sion, the more compulsive the effort becomes to create excitement through kinetic emphasis. These ballets are full of overenergized kinetics, of the *will* to choreography. Like sex in the head, the movements are overreasoned at the expense of reason itself.

Take the Taras production of Debussy's *Jeux*, the best work that he has done for the New York City Ballet. (It should get Best Music and Best Décor awards for its season, too.) It is all over in the first five minutes. Once the initial situation has been stated, the ballet goes static. The story interest dries out, but the music goes on and so does the dancing. Lots of music and, as always in Taras, lots of steps—too many to act around, yet too few to create any change in dance interest. The dancers try to carry the emotional changes in the Bolshoi manner, by intensifying their feelings toward the music ("I *feel* this, it must be real"). What is happening? Is nothing happening or is this happening nothing? Finally, long after you are ready for it, the curtain comes down. Taras strikes me as undanceable and unplayable both. His ballets are all terribly sincere harangues on this dilemma. He appears to think that the emotions, the dramatic color of human relations, flow as a logical consequence from dance steps. But if that is how things happen, there is nothing logical about it. In dancing, there is no logic of solutions.

Of course, it is easier to accept the idea that dance expression is irrational and divine than it is to accomplish expressive dances. Tudor has recently told a story about *Jardin aux Lilas* which illustrates the dilemma very well. There is a moment in the ballet when three girls come forward and raise their arms to heaven. One day in rehearsal, Tudor took it into his head to tell the dancers that this gesture meant "wishing upon the morning star." The girls thereafter came forward very literally and wished upon the morning star. A poetic image had reverted to echoless pantomime.

In its struggle to avoid literalism, the younger generation of ballet choreographers has plunged into the opposite doctrinal snare of totalism. Anything less than total dance metaphor seems proscribed. But metaphors are only presumptive figures which cannot be understood unless we know their provenance. In Kenneth Mac-Millan's *Song of the Earth* for the Royal Ballet, we are subjected to an hour of stripped "dance metaphors" paralleling Mahler's poetic texts. The problem is immediately apparent: If you don't know or can't hear the songs, you can't "enjoy" the dancing *unless* the dancing is clear and expressive in its own right (as it is, for example, in *Liebeslieder Walzer* or *Les Noces*). It could be argued that Mac-Millan has a right to presuppose our acquaintance with Mahler's song cycle; it is one of the best-loved classics in the modern repertory. But having presupposed it, is he then free to superimpose an

independent free-fantasy of dance figures whose textual connections
depend not on our perception of the music, but on our ability to
"read" Macmillan's own system of piled-up inner and outer references—just as if the music were something he alone could hear?
Such efforts as this, which start with large communal baths in the
accepted classics, are as liable to result in cultural dispossession
as in cultural synthesis. As if the aural flow were not complex
enough—the Chinese texts full of distinct pictures of people and
things, the German music with its romantic pathos—MacMillan
adds a third element which is utterly disjunct: bright eager steps
and attitudes from the various gymnasia of the American modern
dance. The atmosphere is a little Chinese (the frontal silhouettes
en plié, the flattened palms), a little German (*Caligari*-like faces,
dead grayed-down décor, balm-of-roses lighting), but why also
American? Because it is in America that the tradition of dance
totalism has developed, out of all proportion to the creative need
which impelled it. Just watch the movement, we are told, and the
meaning will take care of itself. Yes, but whose movement? We
all remember Paul Taylor's dramatic stasis of 1957. He presented
a dance in which he did not move one muscle. He was in self-
imposed exile from the world of preconceived dance forms which
he had inherited. The danger was not in making literal movements;
the danger was in making the figurative movements which belonged
to others and not to Paul Taylor. Today we see Rudolf Nureyev,
in *Paradise Lost*, making the same idiosyncratic "free-form" movements Paul Taylor makes now. Progress? I should have preferred
Nureyev standing still for half an hour.

The Americanization of English ballet strikes me as unfortunate
at a time when Ashton's work is refining more and more touchingly
its beautiful transparency of national style. *Monotones* is English
dancing at its most luminous; and devotees of Balanchine's *Midsummer Night's Dream* could compare its thousand-and-one Neo-
Classic Varieties to Ashton's very Old Vic version, with its nonsensical lovers and skimming faery band. Ashton was outflanked in
the Royal Ballet season by a Tudor whose *Shadowplay* showed,
among other things, how American he had become, and by the
transatlantic testaments of MacMillan and John Cranko, the latter
setting *two* Brandenburg concertos with a determined forward look.
Cranko has finesse without conviction; MacMillan, conviction without finesse—you can see, a friend remarked after *Song of the Earth*,

where Monday's composing leaves off and Tuesday's begins, which fault seemed even more conspicuous later in the season when Ballet Theatre put on *Concerto*, to the Shostakovich Second. (I will say here that every ballet I have ever seen to a Shostakovich score has been bad. MacMillan has done two of them.)

I would imagine that *Jewels*—three acts' worth of solid dancing —is Balanchine's answer to his own imitators: See if you can do *this*, my lads. However, the rapturous audience response to its first season seemed to me a little overdone. Balanchine isn't that easy to love at first sight. The challenge of his novelty is the same for his oldest fans as for those who have never experienced him. *Emeralds* strikes me as novel in the context of the repertory he has fashioned over the years. *Rubies*, to Stravinsky's 1929 Capriccio for Piano and Orchestra, is like Old Home Week in a funhouse, refracting elegant perversities of mood and behavior from previous compositions— *Agon, Jeu de Cartes* (perhaps also *Danses Concertantes?*). I accept it, with the audience, as unconditionally marvellous. But *Diamonds* seemed all imminently burgeoning climax. The climax itself never showed up. If much was expected, much was promised (Tchaikovsky, Farrell, D'Amboise, and a cast of thirty-two). As usual, Balanchine refused to deliver the expected. Yet if Homage to Petipa wasn't in order, shouldn't one have had a right *not* to expect Homage to Gorsky?

Traditionally, Balanchine ballets do not achieve their full impact until their second or third season, and there has never been one I haven't profited from by seeing repeatedly. Though the pleasure they give is obvious, there is nothing simple about his best ballets. I wonder, therefore, at the facile connections that are constantly being made between Balanchine and these nonballets that are being constructed in the aura of his example. Choreographers, both American and European, of nonballets have inherited an audience that knows dancing isn't suspectible to verbal formulations— knows, in short, that dancing is movement. Only, these same people who respect movement couldn't be less concerned with whether the movement is expressive or not. Having stopped looking for literal sense in what they see, they've stopped looking for any other kind of sense and stopped trying to distinguish real invention from pointless ingenuity. It's widely assumed that the Joffery company at City Center has taken over a large part of Balanchine's old City Center audience; certainly Joffrey encourages the link by borrowing heavily from the repertory of the New York City Ballet. But if this is really a Balanchine-oriented crowd, how is it they are able to tolerate the phenomenon of Gerald Arpino? The last time I saw Arpino's *Viva Vivaldi!*, here is what took place in the pas de deux from the third movement (boy and girl face to face):

1. *She: Steps into arabesque on point, arms extending backward (the "swan" position). He: Takes her under the armpits.*

2. *A slow pull away from one another.*

3. *She: Falls forward, still fully extended.*

4. *He: Lowers her to the floor as she holds the pose.* (Picture this, please. It's the Swan Queen flat on her nose.)

5. *He: Kneels. Bends. And places his left ear to her buttocks.*

I wonder if they are still doing it.

The case for Gerald Arpino and his awful ballets is usually presented together with the information that new choreographers are as rare as new planets. Is Arpino a new planet? I find that his work is full of opinions, more or less violent, about choreography. It has no imaginative reality of its own. And yet the ballets themselves are real enough, they hold the stage, they constitute a repertory of sorts, and there is an audience that finds them worthwhile. I don't deny that Mr. Arpino's ballets exhibit impressive powers; what I do deny is that they have anything to do with works of the imagination as the imagination translates nature. Mr. Arpino's bent is to translate other ballets. I think he is pretty good at this. Assuming you have never seen Robbins's *Afternoon of a Faun*, *Sea Shadow* is a pretty good ballet. Assuming you have never seen *Square Dance*, *Viva Vivaldi!* is good, too. Assuming you have never seen *The Cage* or just anything by Roland Petit, where the sleaziness of the subject matter receives more nearly its ideal treatment in expressive technique, *Nightwings* will strike you as a fine piece of work. Assuming you have never seen anything by Martha Graham, *Olympics* will seem full of ritual purgation and grandeur. Actually, *Olympics* is as hollow and unconsoling as the puny Greek-style effeminacy of so much popular religious art. While Greek effeminacy, in the context of contemporary manners, might just as well be the point, the compulsively restricted dynamics of the choreography (it is all hard-UP, hard-DOWN, smash-RIGHT, convulse-LEFT) are so defensive that it probably isn't, and only those who wish to see, instead of heroic immolation, all those . . . boys doing . . . things with one another will be consoled.

Quite a few boys are left lying seductively about the stage in
Viva Vivaldi!, too, and this brings up a point. Here the idea seems
to be not translation from other choreography, but simple sex
translation: girls into boys. Boys pose instead of girls; instead of
ballerinas, ballerinos compete in dazzling solo work.* (Remember,
all this is happening in front of Balanchine's old audience.) Well,
what is wrong with that? we say. Balanchine said one day, "Put
sixteen girls on a stage and it's everybody—the world. But put sixteen
boys and it's always nobody." It's true of *Olympics*. The unilateral
sex leaves you clutching in an existential void. And even in *Viva
Vivaldi!*, where some of the boys have girls, those who don't look
strangely lost and unaccounted for—males without real attachment
to their function who do a job because they're being paid to do it.
Poor little ghost-boys of the ballet!

Do I exaggerate? Well, I think you cannot exaggerate the necessity of maintaining seemliness in the classical tradition once it is invoked. Much of what seems to have been derived from convention
and expediency in the classical tradition is in fact a profound honor-
ing of a certain philosophy of life, a way of looking at the world.
So the difference isn't technical; it's philosophical—a question of
attitude. And you can have the attitude without the technique. Why
should Merce Cunningham, for example, while venturing as far as
anyone has from the matrix of conventional ballet technique, still
express (as clearly, sometimes, by negation and indirection as by
affirmation) a sense of connectedness, of philosophical engagement with classicism—while Gerald Arpino, who works from the
conventional classical syllabus, creates ballets which are philosophi-
cally deranged? Is it because Cunningham is a master and Arpino
a novice at best? If so, what is there that the novice must learn?

Seemliness is a poor word by which I fear I have unintentionally
conveyed a prudishness insisting on nicety. I mean this: Seemliness is what you feel is right. It is a tragedy of the modern sensibility that no one dares suppose he knows what is right or, knowing,
dares think someone else may spontaneously agree. Thus I work
and overwork childlike distinctions, distinctions we are not even
aware of in authenticated works of art which give us joy but which,
it seems, cannot be presupposed in our experience of what we are
seeing for the first time. The first effort of art is an ordering of our
sensations; perception begins when we have confidence in that order,

---

* *Postscript* 1977: The soloist competition in *Viva Vivaldi!* is now performed by a
boy and a girl.

and that is what we mean when we say an artist draws us into his world. In the classical dance as its masters have ordered it, in that world which is classical dance, men may play a part, but they may not play women. Clive Barnes has suggested that women belong in the ballet *Olympics*. But Arpino's *Olympics* is a ballet, not a sports event, and women athletes are no more concerned with classical style than men athletes are; they'd look just as phony as Arpino's men do now. This is what I find uniquely unpleasant in Arpino's work —its arrogant assumptions in regard to classical style. The misplaced, jarring look of a lot of his emphases have the same vulgar effect as Plisetskaya's bird imitations in *Swan Lake*. Whatever else it can be taken for, the result is not classical. (If it's swans you want, go to the zoo.) Like Plisetskaya, Arpino wants to make the style do *more*. Supposedly, the sex emphasis in *Viva Vivaldi!* is justified by its Spanish flavoring—a Vivaldi concerto arranged for classic guitar. Supposedly, the choreographer's use of boys conveys machismo, manliness, as in flamenco. It conveys nothing of the sort, and for much the same reason that *Olympics* conveys not athletic virility but its opposite. The only subject of classical dancing is classical style. It is the thing that is not insisted upon and that anyone clear of eye can see. But Arpino is not willing to let it alone. He must have opinions about it. He must employ extraneous usages, which fall from the classical dancer's body like rags.

I don't suppose that, beyond protesting its absence or its mishandling, there is much that one can do toward defining classical style, it is so nonrational a thing. The best discussions of it are in Edwin Denby's work—see particularly "Some Thoughts About Classicism and George Balanchine"—but even Denby avoids hitting the point head on. He will tell you all the places he has seen it; he will speak of its "power," its "secret radiance," he will even say that "classical ballet is . . . based on an ideal conception of expression professionally called 'style.'" But that word "professionally" seems to withdraw it from the public gaze. Perhaps Denby knows that you can't hit the point without crushing it. Better not to try. The beauty of Denby is his beauty of inference. He assumes people know in advance what he is talking about. But I wonder if they do. Isn't it possible that the privacy and privilege of Denby's attitude are bought at the price presently being extorted from us by the solecisms of Arpino and other young choreographers—who, for all we know, read Denby with pleasure?

I have been speaking rather blindly (you must accept certain blind categories in ballet as in life) of the kinds of distortion which are the unmaking of style. I hope it is clear that correct style has nothing to do with mental or moral health—see *Rubies*. In *Rubies*, conscious manipulation of sexual distinctions in style produces something we can recognize as decadent art; the difference is that the decadence is produced on a scale of human consequence. It is alive to its own meaning; it is a joke about style, whereas *Viva Vivaldi!* is a disfigurement of style, a mistake.

Well, then, if we can't watch the choreography, let's just watch the dancers. Yes, but are not dancers, while they are dancing, creatures of choreography? We have all seen dancers whom we know well nullified by steps that are bad and wrong, dance designs that are dim. In another of those aristocratic throwaways of his, Denby says of the New York City Ballet dancers that "the more correct their style the more their individual personality becomes distinct and attractive on stage." Here is something that is very close to the point, so let us snatch it up.

For three seasons now I have been watching the Joffrey dancers and I don't know who they are. Of course they are beautiful, personable, and dedicated, but to the degree that they are, they are also innocent. And so I seek refuge in the illusion that they are free just because they ought to be—personalities free, unspoiled, detached from the surrounding crumminess. So long as I keep up that illusion while watching the stage, I can keep up an interest. Many ballet enthusiasts survive in just this way—they have to. They take the third- or quarter-spectacle and extrapolate the rest. But isn't it better when the dancer's personality is expressed to you rather than being conveyed fortuitously like stray luggage? Isn't it better when he cannot stop himself from being what he is? And isn't that, subject to the authority of an educated technique, what classical style is all about? I myself cannot identify Lisa Bradley beyond the quality of her looks, competence, and devotion in different ballets; nor can I identify in any sense that interests me any other dancer wriggling in Arpino's fancy traps. Of *Sea Shadow*, a vague pas de deux in which Lisa Bradley appears as a sort of mod-style undine, it was said that perhaps the point of the ballet was that it had no point. Perhaps. But, surely, intending not to make a point is different from not being able to make one; and it is in this atmosphere of lifeless ambiguity that *Sea Shadow* and Miss Bradley pass before us while the critics exercise all their best pastel adjectives ("exquisite," "sensitive," "searching," "lyrical").

I have often wondered why the greatest classical ballets don't look great but just look natural. And just as you, when you are sitting in the theatre, are just yourself sitting, neither standing nor kneeling, so the dancing is just what it is, something to which we dreamily assent and then go and smoke cigarettes. We don't assent mindlessly, of course, but neither do we, unless we are asses, dissent to the point of questioning those grand ultimates in which classical dancing deals: Man is, Woman is. Life contains. We don't dissent because we realize that classical style leaves us free to fill in the blanks and it's nobody's fault if we can't do it. This is very different from having to extrapolate a whole order of significance so that we can squeeze some meaning out of what we see; this is very different from being a balletomane. This is the freedom that a whole generation of choreographers can't extend to us because they don't know how. Choreography keeps getting in their way. One wishes more of them would try standing still.

Other Choreographers

ROBERT JOFFREY is more musical than his principal choreographer, Arpino, and has taste. The best theatrical moment in the whole Joffrey repertory comes in *Gamelan* when the full company takes the stage. But *Pas de Déesses* is bland and uncomfortably patronizing toward its historical models, and *Astarte,* the new mixed-media presentation, is a *Life* Magazine recap of the avant-garde (and so is the avant-garde).

ANNA SOKOLOW. One of her ballets about spastic teen-agers is much the same as another. One of her other ballets about lost souls is also much the same as another of her others. Sokolow belongs to the elder generation of social-content choreographers. Her dances are about society's victims. This would be refreshing but for the method of composition, which peels off one parsimonious phrase at a time and passes it obsessively around the stage—j'accuse, tu accuses, il accuse, nous accusons. . . .

ERIK BRUHN, JACQUES D'AMBOISE, EDWARD VILLELLA are about as good at choreography as star dancers usually are, and D'Amboise, since *Prologue,* is somewhat worse. An outsize production with literary pretensions ("Othello" courts "Desdemona" in a heavy Renaissance set) inflated what might have passed as a minor showcase for dancers into minimal significance. Coincidentally, both *Prologue* and Bruhn's *Romeo and Juliet Pas de Deux* (for American Ballet Theatre) used Shakespearean themes. Bruhn's balcony scene had a Romeo (Bruhn) deriving almost as much excitement from his cloak as from Juliet (Carla Fracci). Villella's first full-length ballet, *Narkissos*, created a more convincing dramatic web and did so without recourse to D'Amboise's conglomerate idiom and Bruhn's egotistic projections (to which a Narkissos might have been tempted).

JOHN BUTLER, GLEN TETLEY. Their subject matter is always more interesting than its realization in dance. The quality of movement is body-beautiful, yet almost mystically unrevealing. This isn't choreography, it's aesthetic wrestling.

ELIOT FELD. "The most important new talent in American ballet since Jerome Robbins" (Clive Barnes). It may be because I saw it only once that I missed the apocalypse in *Harbinger*. What I saw seemed a very hip aggrandizement of the contemporary generational revolt in terms that looked very much as Robbins himself might have contrived them. But I prefer to remain out on this one until it is done, together with Feld's second ballet, in Ballet Theatre's fall season.   —*Summer 1967*

Dancers and Dance Critics

Shuffling my list of topics for the last quarter, I find it disheartening to begin with A for *Aleko*, of which admittedly not much was expected and still less can be said. Revived by American Ballet Theatre, it proved to be an unsortable series of choreographic "scenes" in which writhing lovers, stamping gypsies, and bounding barnyard animals cavorted to an indistinct Tchaikovsky score before thunderously beautiful cloths by Marc Chagall. It ended in one of those phantasmagoric swirling ensembles, typical of the 1940's, in which everyone reappears trailing clouds of kitsch surrealism. The whole thing has been sufficiently dispraised as a bad choice by which to restore Massine's reputation, and it is hard to see why the choice was made, given Massine's past productions for Ballet Theatre. We would all have preferred to see *The Three-Cornered Hat*. Massine's production for Ballet Theatre in 1942 had Massine himself in the lead, with Argentinita and later Toumanova in the role of the Miller's Wife. It is not for me to say whom Ballet Theatre should cast after these titans. I'll only note that the last date I can find for a production of the ballet is 1956, when Massine staged it for the Royal Swedish Ballet (the company of which Erik Bruhn is now Artistic Director) and the Miller was danced by one Willy Sandberg. We are long overdue for another look at the greater Massine; as for *Aleko*, I'd like to think that it was the No. 2 choice everybody fell back on, because that's just the way it looks.

Speaking of Bruhn, the Ballet Theatre season exhibited his absorption, in both *Giselle* and *La Sylphide*, in a kind of private ritual. While this may represent all that these roles presently mean to Bruhn, it doesn't, in my view, express all that they might mean to an audience. The mime portions of the performances were all self-enclosed rhetoric, exemplified in his stance, which he would arrive at by a halting step-together, back-together. These silkily undulant lurches he would often accompany with a propounding gesture of the hand. If you watched Bruhn for clues to the story or the character, you saw his figure standing apart, looking at times curt as a drawn dagger, at other times politely frozen. It was more than mannerism, yet less than the broad play of a pattern by which a performer can sometimes fix his own context. Story lines, for all that they are only pretexts for dancing, are not so easily gotten around. It is interesting to read (in *Dance News*) that Bruhn's own production of *La Sylphide* for the Royal Swedes makes it clear that in the first act the Sylph is invisible to all save James. This isn't true of the Ballet Theatre *La Sylphide*, but that is how Bruhn plays it. A similar kind of disharmony occurs in *Giselle*. David Blair's new production not only omits the passage which tells the audience that Albrecht is a duke posing as a commoner, it goes out of its way to suggest that the villagers have long accepted him as one of them.* Yet Bruhn's handsome rigidity, as Citizen Albrecht, would seem excessive even in a court setting.

The contrary view is that the logic of ballet scenarios is never so tight as to foreclose the terrific options of star temperament, and with this I agree in part. It depends on the ballet. And the star. An article by Elena Bivona contends that Bruhn's performances this season constituted a unique process of self-exploration which

---

* *Postscript* 1977: These innovations of Blair's are no longer part of the production.

transcends or nullifies any discrepancies between performer and production. What I see in Bruhn's *Giselle* Act I as rigidity and remoteness, she sees as constraint rooted in monomania. Now, Albrecht may be a monomaniac, and James may be similarly insane, if Bruhn makes them so, but it isn't, I think, necessary to agree that he has done it. What's necessary is to agree that Bruhn is doing something strange in those ballets, which ought not to go unnoticed.

Close analysis of a star's onstage behavior, especially a star of Bruhn's caliber, will often seem to draw fantastic conclusions for an audience accustomed to critics whose treatment of dancers is generally eyeless. Critics who see straight when it comes to choreography or décor are often apt to have blind spots about dancers, the ones they like as well as the ones they don't. To know whether Critic X likes Dancer Y is less important than to know whom Critic X thinks he's talking about; this would seem elementary, yet how many critics can you name who take it as any part of their responsibility to identify the dancer in question and describe what he does? There is a sense in which classical technique, with its equalizing standards, protects the lazy critic, permits him to slot performers in simple good-better-best categories. There is another, neglected, sense in which classical technique can only heighten those personal qualities that make dancers interesting and interestingly different from one another. Of Bruhn's eminence the critics have left us in no doubt; of his oddities, which are pronounced (for me, they are encompassing), they have nothing to say. The question we ask is not How good is he? but What is he doing?

The critics are lazy, and they are also timid. Complimentary notices about almost any dancer of rank abound, but the compliments are apt to be vacant, the adjectives interchangeable: so-and-so's "icy beauty" or "thoroughbred line"—that sort of thing. What about "thoroughbred beauty" and "icy line"? And just which icy thoroughbred is being evoked here? Blot out the name and you can take your pick. The worst thing about such compliments is that they're neutral; you can't really tell how the critic is responding —whether excitedly, evasively, sentimentally, or good copy-ly. The out-and-out adverse judgment is so seldom made that you'd think all dancers now performing are about equally fine on about the same level. I get the feeling that many critics think reviewing dancers just isn't good form because it may get personal, but surely criticism is a personal act, intimately personal, just as dancing is.

A critic who feels ethically burdened by the need to say something about dancers does one of two things: either he indulges in catchy epithets, handing out artificial flowers all around and feeling like a generous, open fellow who lets the audience make up its own mind, or he makes a headlong attempt to depersonalize his opinions about dancers by electing them to immortality, or consigning them to oblivion, with the same grand show of disinterestedness. The "disinterested" critic is the sort who will frequently say, in effect: It isn't my opinion, it's the public's. My favorite example of this was the unfortunate occasion a few years ago when Walter Terry reported on how the audience favorites at the New York City Ballet were running, and ended with: "There is only one Tallchief!" (There are of course two.) The worst kind of critical ninnyism is the everlasting urge to say something nice out of a wish to encourage the performer. Critics who cannot be cruel even to be kind don't realize that their kindness is a form of cruelty, if not to the dancers, then to the readers who only hope to recognize something of the evening's performance in what is written. And I do not see how it helps a dancer to read that he danced "with commendable spirit" in a role he does not understand. It is possible to encourage performers without resorting to meaningless accolades. And speaking of meaningless accolades, I would much prefer a grouch to the enthusiast who sometime, somewhere, every single season commits to print some variation of the line, "Fonteyn *is* Juliet!" "Ulanova *is* Giselle!" I do not know what this means. If intended as a compliment, surely it cannot be much of an accomplishment to become Juliet if you are Juliet. Fonteyn is Fonteyn. Ulanova is Ulanova. (Probably what the critic means is that he was moved.)

The critic who makes the most serious attempt to discuss dancers is B. H. Haggin, and he does so with the full weight of his authority as a music critic of some forty years' standing. Haggin's musical knowledge led him to an early appreciation of Balanchine above every other choreographer, and he has expressed preferences for some of Balanchine's dancers (at the expense of others) which lead one to suppose that they are based on the same principles as his judgments of Balanchine and the musical artists he admires. But I find that Haggin's taste in dancers is often as uninstructive and indulgent as anyone else's who happens to have strong opinions about the performers he sees, and that it gains nothing from Haggin's special gifts as a critic of music (but does gain a great deal from his vocabulary).

Instead of the insights one would expect from a distinguished music critic, Haggin applies a vocabulary of praise words ("bodily configuration in motion and pose whose beauty and perfection were achieved with . . . elegance—in the sense not only of grace but economy," etc.—to quote a review of Fonteyn in *Swan Lake*) which is virtually the same for every performer he finds worthy of praise, and which works for you if you see what Haggin has seen but doesn't if you don't. The difference in Haggin's treatment of musicians and dancers is that his judgments of the former are backed up by extensive analysis of the artist's powers as they illuminate or obscure or distort the musical values of the score that is being performed, so that what Haggin calls "the operation" is brought before you even if you haven't experienced it. But I know of no comparable attempt at elucidation in his dance criticism, or, rather, I do know of one, in which Haggin resorted to extended quotation of other dancers' remarks about Violette Verdy, to back up what he referred to as "her unique and exciting combination of exactness, enchanting elegance and style, dazzling brilliance, and dramatic power"— a series of qualities hardly unique in that they can be claimed for any dancer one happens to find powerful and exciting, and hardly reinforced, as qualities belonging to Verdy alone, by the remarks of the professional dancers Haggin chooses to quote. For the curious thing about these remarks is that, while they do to some extent bring Verdy's "operation" before us, they seize upon aspects of her style which one might as easily find irritatingly mannered as beautiful and impressive—the bit, for example, at the end of the variation in the *Tchaikovsky Pas de Deux* where she "stops, but doesn't really stop," a detail that has always struck me as preciously adorable with that calculation I sometimes hear in the singing of Elisabeth Schwarzkopf, an artist I admire, as I admire Verdy. And although Verdy is generally known to be especially admired by musicians, Haggin himself doesn't give an elucidation of her musical qualities, but again defers to the same dancer (apparently Edward Villella, who made many of these same points when he presented Verdy with her *Dance* Magazine award), who cites the (to me, unfortunate) example of her dancing in the first movement of *Episodes*, where "she lunged and turned" and "I saw a motivation for the lunge and turn—both in visual terms and in relation to the music." To which it might be suggested that what Verdy provides by way of "motivation"—she "acts" the movements with her face

and body, as if to imply an emotional context—is simply unnecessary and in conflict with the intention of Balanchine's choreography in this and other sections of *Episodes*, which is to make dance
statements as utterly disassociated from emotional and dramatic
contexts as Webern's music. And if Verdy's way of "making you
see" this music is in harmony with Balanchine's intention, it is
notably out of harmony with the company as a whole as it dances
the ballet. And the rest of the remarks Haggin reproduces only
reflect an encomiast's tribute to Verdy, about her backstage preparation, etc.—interesting if you are interested in Verdy.

What is objectionable in all this is that a bias which would
be perfectly acceptable if rendered as such is presented instead as
certified truth. And getting a professional dancer to "authenticate"
one's own feelings only shifts the burden of responsibility for them
into areas where, presumably, non-experts cannot follow. The whole
business has that ring of pseudo-objectivity whereby critics are
forever disclaiming the very personal response to art which led
them to be critics in the first place. If there exists a universal, objective standard by which to judge the experiences that dancers
create in the theatre, then let us hear about it, but I do not suppose
that Haggin thinks that there is. So very redoubtable a critic should
not undermine the pleasure we take in his expression of *his* pleasure
by making a naked imperative of our agreement with him; for
though he customarily adds that "you are free" to disagree, his
implication is that there is no basis for disagreement.

With the situation as it is, then—with most critics either not
paying attention to dancers or giving misleading accounts of their
work—it is not puzzling that there should have been no indication,
in what has been written about the New York City Ballet, of the
steady degeneration of its prima ballerina, Suzanne Farrell, into the
absurdly vulgar, routinely unexpressive performer we have been
seeing for the past few seasons. In her earlier seasons as a featured
soloist, starting about 1962, Miss Farrell was an altogether different
dancer—sensitive, light, fluid, and simple without, as yet, much
projective force. This force began to appear in *Meditation*, with its
new, for Balanchine, use of emotionally expressive gestures and poses
that seemed more in the vein of Bolshoi *moderne* than the NYCB
repertory at that time. The Farrell of that period was not only a
beautiful dancer in the variety of styles that Balanchine had established in the ballerina roles of the repertory, she was obviously the

dancer whom Balanchine had chosen to lead him into fresh areas of composition and to set a further style of her own. She was one of the few dancers I have ever seen who could make any movement, no matter how unorthodox, look classical, at any speed. Expression seemed to pour from her. She was incapable of ugliness or insecurity. Today, in the dances of the third act of *Don Quixote*, she can still persuade me that she is among the greatest dancers on earth—in the great sighing lifts in which she holds the shape of her pose in its continuing arc, in her entrance a moment later with the torso twisted to the back as she breaks into fleet, low jumps, both feet lifted and held above the ground like an illusion in stop-time photography. These moments, for me, sum up Farrell's greatness, a greatness which the critics still write about, and the public pays to see, as if it were present in everything she does.

The break came in the Rondo alla Zingarese movement of the *Brahms-Schoenberg Quartet*, which Balanchine set for Farrell and D'Amboise as a rowdy escapade with the kind of amorous, tongue-in-cheek byplay that might have been staged for a floorshow in a Hungarian restaurant. In addition to flashing through the movements, which were a sophisticated version of the backbends and heel-and-toe work common to that style, Farrell apparently decided, or was encouraged, to play for powerful climaxes and sexiness on a big scale. This wasn't inappropriate, but soon it began to seem as if this role had become the expressive norm for her entire repertory. One now saw, in almost every part, the same worked-up shape to every phrase, everything delivered with utmost impact, no subtlety, no coherence. One saw a formerly fluid line distorted for maximum dynamic thrust in every direction, continual flaunting and flailing through the spine and neck, limp wrists, dismissive hands. Worse than this, there were movements that were repeated from ballet to ballet, whether they belonged there or not: simple arabesques were converted into extreme arabesques penchées (in, for example, the second movement of *Concerto Barocco*, where the distortion was blatant), and I was astounded to see her kick her hand (in a grand battement) even as Terpsichore in *Apollo*.

All this is not only vulgar, it is immodest. It exhales self-importance. Paradoxically, it contracts the expressive range of her personality. Currently, her best roles, the ones in which she seems to function most happily, are the flashiest ones, like *Slaughter on Tenth Avenue*, the most enjoyable parts of which are her two dances on the little stage. The moment when she removes her garter and shies it past her derrière is worthy of Ann-Margret.

I have called Farrell the company's prima ballerina, and she is that by virtue of the number of roles which she performs exclusively—thirteen. The only other ballerinas who own roles are Hayden and McBride (tied at four apiece) and Verdy (one). Farrell is obviously to be closely watched, and she is. But not, evidently, by the critics. —*Fall 1968*

The Avant-Garde on Broadway

Apropos of Andy Warhol, Hugh Kenner remarked a few years ago that it was enough to hear about what the avant-garde was up to, to grasp the point. An eight-hour film of a man sleeping doesn't have to be seen; it simply has to have been made. A great part of the audience to whom avant-gardism appeals still doesn't seem to believe what's going on—to believe, for example, that boring material can be presented just because it is boring. It's as if the artist were saying, "Look, if I'm boring you, admit it's not the first time you've been bored." After all, it's not much different from the mental tuning-out that we do when we come to those sections in great works of art that bore us, and who hasn't his private list of dull patches, or whole dull masterworks, that he'd rather skip or sleep through?

If artists now acknowledge boredom as a condition, indeed a convention, of modern life—as avant-garde dance artists do at least once an evening when they start presenting effects that are apparently going to go on forever—they also expect us to know how to handle it. Of course, you may elect to stick around for amusement's sake, but if you do, you have to know you're being worked on. Tweakiness is the original sin of avant-gardism; we might as well acknowledge that, too. Right in the middle of Merce Cunningham's *Walkaround Time*, the house lights come up, the sound track switches to light cocktail-hour Muzak, and the dancers come back to stroll or lie around on the stage, napping, conversing, massaging their muscles. When is a performance not a performance? But it would have taken cattle prods to move the audience at the Billy Rose.

Walkaround Time doesn't, as they say, "work." I took it as one of Cunningham's lesser projects in demystifying Art. It has something to do with a Jasper Johns assemblage (which is assembled only in the last minute by the dancers, after they've used it as environmental décor) based on the Marcel Duchamp construction called *The Large Glass*—which Duchamp himself quit work on because it bored him. There's a curious solo for the choreographer in which, not quite hidden from the audience, he removes and re-dons all his outer clothing while running in place. After a while, the lived-in look of the piece becomes not so much a comment on the commonplace as an expression of it—and that includes the Victor Borge-like joke in the middle.

At its best, Cunningham's style in this vein (I think of *Field Dances, Variations V,* and *How to Pass*...) is not only humble, serene, and charming, but also beautiful and edifying. His dancers are dancers, and they always dance. You are (I am, at least) edified by the technique which makes dancers beautiful people. Strip them of their technique and you have something which goes further than Cunningham's delicate or shocking operations on the sanctity theory of art; you have an attitude which comes close to saying, "Art is bunk." Some impatient snort of this kind seems to me barely concealed in the work of Yvonne Rainer. Her people often do not look less than beautiful, they look less than ordinary. However well trained they have to be to execute movements of which the inner mechanism, at least, requires a pretty sophisticated technical approach, they don't *look* any more interesting than an ant farm. And in the same way I would watch ants, or six-year-olds in some inordinately supervised sandbox, I watch Rainer's group for its psychology. If only once in a while one of them would break up, as sometimes happens in the "straight" theatre, the humanity of the whole enterprise would become clearer. But no, all the pans stay dead.

The consistent compulsive logic of a Rainer group concert can be as perversely fascinating as the look of her beat-up performers, some of whom are former Cunningham dancers. In John Cage's statement (often reproduced in program notes), that Cunningham "can be said to affirm life, to introduce an audience not to a specialized world of art, but to the open, unpredictably changing, world of everyday living," you find the credo for what Rainer in *Rose Fractions* has reduced to a kind of communal all-ye-in-free, the formal elegance of choreography displaced by various kinds of team spirit and sweated labor. Previously, in the dance portions of *The Mind Is a Muscle* (circa 1966), I had thought her most gifted in the kind of open-space abstract choreography that Twyla Tharp has developed. Now I see that her compulsion is more strictly ideological; she and her colleagues have become the sans-culottes of the Cunningham revolution, clomping through the back wall of the theatre into—everyday living? More likely that same spotlit underground that Warhol first put on the culture map. Yet to know about Rainer is not the same as to know her; she has to be seen. In the first place, no description can impart the duration, calculated shock, or graded monotony of her effects. Second, there are times when Rainer herself, who has a strong, fresh, cryptic presence (most of the time she seems to be wearing a self-protective mask of melancholy), appears to be taking a satirical delight in what she does. (Not that she doesn't mean well by it, too: certain of her concerns, as Jack Anderson has noted, have the force of a scourge on the prurient-minded.) Those bits of autobiographical material, for instance, as bewildering if you can recognize them as if you don't: are they a comment on her own brand of democratized, depersonalized "anti-art"? on the counterproposition that "if everybody is somebody then nobody is anybody"? She's her own heckler and, to be perfectly fair, deserves to be, because she's invented her own necessity.

No matter how casual or accidental avant-garde expression seems to the viewer, it no longer bears many of the earmarks of haphazard consequence or "chance." We are past the era—largely male-dominated—of happenings and into a phase of planned activity whose most prominent organizers are women like Rainer, Twyla Tharp, and Deborah Hay. Rainer's compulsive logic is a trait common to all three, as it is a trait of most women artists. Women make good avant-garde artists. (I threw out my copy of *The Second Sex* long ago or I'd make you a list, showing how the Brontës, Steins, and Woolfs outnumber the Austens, Cathers, and George Eliots in any competition between innovative and traditional. And in American dance, the roll call, from Loie Fuller to Isadora and onward, is virtually all-woman and all-pioneer.) It was not, certainly, to prove the corollary point—that no good avant-gardistes are men—that the Ford Foundation put Don Redlich on at the Billy Rose Theatre in the same week with Rainer (and Hay, who shared the Rainer program) and Tharp and Meredith Monk; but, in any event,

Redlich did not qualify. Juxtaposed to the joyously wayward Miss Monk especially, he betrayed a fatal neatness of intention versus an equally fatal faintness of execution. His films were just films and his dances, just dances—surely mixed media is more mixed than that?

Solipsism, the most common charge against female artists, is in Meredith Monk a kind of nascent glory. Not a choreographer, only in the academic sense a dancer, Miss Monk has managed to make of herself and her personal fantasies the focus of a new aesthetic in the theatre. With the help of a handful of background figures, most of whom were to be glimpsed during intermissions at the Billy Rose as "lobby exhibits" inside corrugated drums—by the end of the performance they'd all been hatched—she has mastered a unique form of homemade entertainment which is perfectly daffy and perfectly serious by turns. Chez Monk one may see such re-cherché avant-garde visions as a woman in eighteenth-century dress inching across the back of a brightly lit stage while a plastic tank slowly fills with water. In a moment the woman will return with a man, both of them wearing army fatigues bloated with padding. They will each sit in the tank. Another girl will cross the stage on the run. Meanwhile, one will hear a *Candid Camera*–like conversation about something hilarious which is not entirely clear. One may get the impression that the main action is actually taking place offstage or that *this* is offstage, and one may be wrong. The performance will open with a record of Ethel Merman singing "There's No Business Like Show Business."

Such genial sadism is offset by such genuinely perplexing works as *16 Millimeter Earrings*, one of the most beautiful mixed-media presentations that I have seen. This is a solo with films and props, a large-scale theatrical self-portrait for which the audience is delightfully prepared earlier in the evening by a middle-aged woman who crosses the stage and announces, "I'm Meredith's mother." The heroine of *16 Millimeter Earrings* is presented in multiple manifestations of adolescence, like Picasso's *Girl Before a Mirror*. She is (and these are the meanings I see as I watch the piece—for others they may be different) precociously self-enchanted, dreaming on sex, self-expression, heartbreak, mutilation, and suicide. The meanings come from recurrent or parallel images in an inter-play of films, objects, sound, and the performer's actions as she moves about the stage—which (as in Graham) suggests both a psychic interior and a real place, perhaps the girl's bedroom. The climax comes when, having put on a long, tattered flame-red wig (from a white tabletop there erupts a comet of red streamers, blown upward by a fan), she lowers a white drum onto her shoulders and animated film images of her own face appear on its surface, the hair tormented, one eye hugely distorted through an optical lens. At the end, flames rise again in a color film projected on the backcloth. In the film, a doll seen in silhouette is slowly cremated. As it falls, the heroine on the stage rises nude to take its place in the inferno. Over the sound system, her voice, singing "Greensleeves," breaks on the words "Alas my love—alas my love you do—" and *16 Millimeter Earrings* is over.

The difference between this piece and one like Robert Joffrey's *Astarte*, which uses the mixed-media bag in a work of startling conventionality, is the difference between having ideas for which mixed media are the only appropriate form and having an idea that mixed media are exciting per se. A better work than Joffrey's, Don Redlich's *Reacher*, still gets so lost in its own sensuous excitement that the form stays vivid only in theory. One clue to the weakness of weak media-mixes is that you think you've seen those effects before—and you have, in your own mind, in the very notion that such effects are possible. What you haven't seen are works like *16 Millimeter Earrings*, which has the *wit* of its means and an emotion like that of Jacobean drama.

Twyla Tharp is the first of the new generation of avant-garde choreographers to develop a choreographic style ordered entirely by considerations of time and space. Her group pieces employ an allover pattern, with the dancers moving to simultaneous but disparate counts in a determined space, preferably not proscenium-bound but open on all sides, like handball or tennis courts and gyms. There is no décor, drama, or music, and often no sound but the amplified beat of a metronome. Lacking any semblance of glamour or of journalistic immediacy (such as may be projected by the Rainer-Hay use of nonprofessionals), Twyla Tharp's work holds the mind to ·an amazing degree in obvious contradiction to its ostensible aim, which—to put it naïvely—is to torture the attention span of even unconventional audiences. It takes a formula for boredom and turns it inside out.

Watching a piece like *Group Activities*, one has the feeling of having emerged on the other side of some barrier to perception. The ineffable-abstract vanishes into the palpable-concrete. Bodies of girls (it's an all-girl troupe) move near and far on shifting planes of action, in disjunct but uniform phrases. One notices a marvellous anatomical variety. There are all sorts of differences in bodily impetus—patient, impish, sharp, steady—and in rhythmical accent. The flow of movement is neutral but by no means featureless. But that's all there is to style. I wish there could be more. The Tharp company is spectacular, but its virtuosity is mostly mental. It works like a feat of visual ventriloquism. It isn't, however, very attractive.

At the Billy Rose, Tharp presented three pieces, only one of them intended for the conventional theatre stage. The program looked best when viewed from the balcony, but the no-walls, no-focus look of the choreography was largely lost, along with the subtler qualities of impact that make each work distinct within an unvarying systematic approach. A few weeks later, at the Brooklyn Academy, she seated her audience on bleachers along both wings of its large stage and gave two more pieces, *Group Activities* (a première) and *Generation*. The former, like most of her works, is performed on a floor squared off and divided by lines of tape. *Generation,* on the other hand, makes free use of space and appears to be five solos occurring simultaneously rather than a work for five dancers. (Miss Tharp never appears as the leader of her group, only as one of its members, thus collapsing the dramatic principle of hierarchy.) In *Group Activities,* you grasp immediately its difficulty and then its beauty of precision. It's so complicated that a time-keeper has to sit by, clocking the "score," now and then calling out the main count. The individual counts (in relation to the main one) and individual paths of movement of the ten dancers are uncanny in their symmetrical and asymmetrical play. The ten dancers are divided into two groups of five. Mirror-image opposites are offset by irregularities that keep the eye jumping. Oppositions occur in time as well as space. The animation is so intense, the stop-and-go action of the piece so unpredictable, that one hangs on in quasi-dramatic suspense. The unforeseen logic of these calculations has a peculiar relation to the imagery of abstract ballet. I mean, no matter what they are on paper or in the dancers' heads, they look—the near-collisions, the sudden crowding or circling in a gang (in a jumping phrase), the as-sudden dispersals—brilliantly irrational to the eye. I know only two other choreographers who give the same effect, and they're Mr. B. and Merce.   —*Spring 1969*

Stuttgart's Ballet, New York's Myth

THE WÜRTTEMBERG STATE THEATRE BALLET, otherwise known as the Stuttgart Ballet. (1) Organized as a court ballet and administered 1760–67 by the French ballet master Jean-Georges Noverre, whose revolutionary *Lettres sur la danse et les ballets* was promulgated during this period throughout Europe with lasting effects on the development of the classical dance. (2) In the nineteenth century, a brief flowering (1824–28) under the Taglionis—Filippo, Marie, and Paul. No significant activity until (3) the twentieth century, when Stuttgart was the scene of Bauhaus experiments in stagecraft by Carl and Oskar Schlemmer (*The Triadic Ballet,* 1912–1922). (4) From mid-fifties to 1961, Ballet of the State Theatres directed by Nicholas Beriosoff. (5) 1961 to present, directed by John Cranko. First presented to the American public June 10, 1969, Metropolitan Opera House, New York.

JOHN CRANKO. British dancer and choreographer, b. 1927. Created *Pineapple Poll, Harlequin in April* for Sadler's Wells Theatre Ballet. For Sadler's Wells (now Royal) Ballet: *The Lady and the Fool* and *The Prince of the Pagodas,* first evening-length all-English ballet. Conceived and directed two revues, *Cranks* (1955) and *New Cranks* (1960). Resigned from the Royal Ballet, 1961. "While I was pleased to see Walter Terry ("Steps from Stuttgart," *World of Dance,* May 31) alerting American audiences to the importance of the phenomenal Stuttgart Ballet—a job long overdue ... he might 'have mentioned that classical ballet was in fact virtually born in Stuttgart when Jean-Georges Noverre worked there in the latter part of the 18th century ... making Stuttgart the center of the ballet world then as it is rapidly again becoming now under John Cranko."— Ernest Bernhardt-Kabisch, Bloomington, Indiana, in a letter to the editor published in the *Saturday Review,* June 12, 1969.

WALTER TERRY. Dance critic for the *Saturday Review.*

PHENOMENON. An exceptional or abnormal person, thing, or occurrence; prodigy.—Webster's Dictionary

MARCIA HAYDÉE, RICHARD CRAGUN. Stars of the Stuttgart Ballet. "These two artists, together, make a brand of theatre magic different from but as potent as, say, that of Fonteyn and Nureyev."—Walter Terry, SR, May 31, 1969

FONTEYN, NUREYEV. Two artists who, together, make a brand of theatre magic different from but as potent as, say, that of Haydée and Cragun.

CLIVE BARNES. Dance and drama critic of The New York Times. "About five years ago I first called the Stuttgart Ballet 'Germany's ballet miracle' and it was a term so apt at the time that it has become tagged to the company."—C.B., NYT, June 8, 1969

NEW YORK. A city where "Germany's ballet miracle" is advertised by S. Hurok as "the ballet miracle."

MIRACLE. An event or effect in the physical world deviating from the known laws of nature, or transcending our knowledge of these laws; an extraordinary, anomalous, or abnormal event brought about by superhuman agency.—Webster's Dictionary

S. HUROK. Presented first American season of the Royal Ballet, 1949, first American season of the Bolshoi Ballet, 1959, first American season of the Stuttgart Ballet, 1969. Onward and upward.

1

Everybody who lives in New York believes he's here for some purpose, whether he does anything about it or not. Otherwise, there's no reason to put up with the city. It's common to hear talk of the "death of" New York; not so common to hear about the deterioration of New York's myth. Do we still believe all that stuff about New York being the center of things—where quality comes to be judged, reputations made or broken, etc.? We do for publicity purposes, anyway. But really we know that it's just something else about the city that has been given away. That's why it's so painful when visiting ballet companies drop that regulation curtsy on our doormat: "We know that New York will be our most difficult test," writes Professor Dr. Walter Erich Shäfer, General Administrator of the Württemberg State Theatre in Stuttgart. "America's knowledge of great ballet companies is unprecedented." (For "America" read "New York"; there speaks a true mythomane.) This statement, appearing in the souvenir program of the Stuttgart Ballet's American début season, was considerably more than we deserved. The Stuttgart's New York success was assured long before New York laid eyes on it, but no New Yorker would have wanted to believe that. New Yorkers—Hurok subscribers, dance fans, people from the Bronx and Queens who like a nice June evening at Lincoln Center—apparently need to believe that they made the Stuttgart Ballet the way they made the Royal Ballet twenty years ago at the old Met.

It's so nice to hear about the old days. Open your souvenir program quick, the other one, the one you bought at the Royal Ballet only weeks before the Stuttgart season, and live it all again. There it is: Twentieth Anniversary New York season. October 9, 1949— *The Sleeping Beauty*. Take another ride on the Manhattan merry-go-round. "We were terrified of you!" says Ninette. "Lady, you're in," says the Mayor. Screaming motorcycle escort all the way to Gracie Mansion.

Yes, New York knows its apples and, baby, you're a pip. But if we grant that the then Sadler's Wells company was only an obscure local legend—its obscurity much exaggerated in retrospect—let's also admit that New York was longing to canonize it. And let's admit further that the Stuttgart Ballet in 1969 scarcely held out the same sort of promise. It was genuinely, totally obscure. You had to be a fairly devoted reader of *Dance and Dancers* to know anything about it at all. Here, after twenty years at the game, was a chance for New York to show what it knew about apples. Here would come the Stuttgart, whatever that was, opening with some sort of long ballet about Eugene Onegin which did not even use the music from the opera. (*The Sleeping Beauty*, even in 1949, was *The Sleeping Beauty*.) It would come at the tail end of a long and congested dance season. It would follow the beloved Royal into the Met. And as for the dancers, were they German or what? New York sniffed the air. Box-office was slow. There were rumors of well-papered houses.

Well, you don't want to hear this if all I'm going to tell you is that Sol Hurok pulled it off, which he did. But not even Sol Hurok could have wrought the kind of success the Stuttgart had, because impresarios alone do not make ballet companies; critics and audiences do. And Stuttgart had the critics. The mythical "New York" had nothing to do with it. The Stuttgart was a hit because the critics of New York had said so and had begun saying so before it had so much as set foot on the Met stage. From Walter Terry had come a typically fulsome preview of the company in a *Saturday Review* cover story. From Clive Barnes, far more ominously, several columns of his Sunday space all but giving it away then and there: "On Tuesday [the] Stuttgart Ballet...opens....It could be a night to be recorded in ballet history." By whom? Well, by Mr. Barnes, of course, since nobody else does that kind of recording around here. As for the opening-night audience, do you think it's going to take the subway home when it could stick around and make history? There never was a more dispensable opening. It only remained for the curtain to fall (on a ballet so dull, incidentally, that one wanted to cry out like Hector Hushabye, "Fall! Fall and crush!") and for New York to wake up and read that it had taken the company in its hot embrace. At least, that's what "history" will say, but I will say that it was raped in its sleep. Except in the ads and the reviews, the Stuttgart isn't a "great" company, isn't a "miracle," isn't "of major international status"; it's just a modest little company and now it's got a great big head.

Too modest, gentlemen, too nondescript. Too many gaseous, depleted, bottom-of-the-bill ballets by bottom-dog choreographer Cranko. (But he's been in the business so *very* long, and it was *so* brave of him to go to Stuttgart....) The Stuttgart, a young company, is at that stage where the oppressive search for novelty has worn it down to a premature weariness. It looks rapidly decomposing from old age. I don't mean the dancers, who are bouncy enough, but the effect of their exertions, which is always disproportionately weak. Cranko's choreographic style is characteristically linear; mass is beyond him. You get a choreography of constant calligraphic squiggles. You get mass by multiplication and counterpoint by restless shifts of line and direction. The result is bulk without solidity and animation without energy. A night of this is a nightmare of inconsequentiality. The dancers can't seem to control the space they move through, they never seem to be getting anywhere. Individually and collectively, their actions don't gather any cohesive force. You could watch Cragun and Haydée and Madsen all night and never see what they had obviously come onstage to do—never see, that is, the images for which their gifts seemed to have prepared them. Egon Madsen I thought terribly trivialized by most of his assignments, and Richard Cragun, with all his flash, lacked dimension in an almost palpably physical sense. Haydée was always charming. A skillful actress, she carried *Romeo* alone. But what kind of choreographer is it who sees his ballerina as either Margot Fonteyn (*Onegin, Romeo*) or Imogene Coca (*Shrew, Présence*) and makes aging tadpoles out of his leading male dancers?

And the ideas! *Jeu de Cartes,* highly praised for its brilliant wit and style, takes Stravinsky's own suggestion of a score "designed for German tastes and German audiences" as a cue for painfully enervated sausage-thumbed farce. The wit, mostly on a level with "stories mein grossfader told," has, I suppose, its moments of happy moronism—the takeoff on Balanchine's *La Valse* is one such—but how much happier if this would-be farceur could put his own stage in order before spoofing the ballets of his betters. *Présence* jams the eye, ear, and mind with an assortment of contemporary culture totems: multimedia settings; silence alternating with Webernisms and musique concrète; three protagonists who are supposed to be Don Quixote, King Ubu, and Molly Bloom; but beyond some grand otiosities about life, death, and dreams, it develops no content at all. *Eugene Onegin,* a three-acter to miscellaneous Tchaikovsky compositions arranged and orchestrated by Kurt-Heinz Stolze, is a pallid bore, its hero reduced to a featureless cad, its heroine to a stereotype of das suss mädel, and its meaning to a synopsis of the opera's libretto, which is then "danced through" in the manner of Ruth Page and her Opera Ballet. In the course of this evening-length "spectacular" (Barnes's word for all of Cranko's long ballets), less happened that bore a relationship to Pushkin or Tchaikovsky or, for that matter, to Russia than happens in an approximately ten-minute pas de deux by Balanchine called *Meditation,* and I do not invoke the invidious comparison, Barnes does. "Of all the world's choreographers," he wrote, "only George Balanchine has the actual range of Cranko, which permits him virtually to create a repertory single-handedly. Perhaps he [Cranko] takes things too far, but then perhaps so does Balanchine." Perhaps so does Barnes.

Romeo and Juliet. Anyone who has seen the MacMillan production for the Royal Ballet has a good idea of how Cranko's looks, which is to say not good. The former was recently correctly characterized by Barnes as "feeble and derivative"—i.e., derivative of Cranko, which certainly doesn't leave Cranko's the best of all *Romeos,* as Barnes again would have it; it leaves "feeble" as the adjective appropriate to both. MacMillan's even has the edge in certain respects: in the Georgiadis sets with a wide central staircase that gives his production the multilevel sweep in Acts I and II Cranko can't obtain because Jürgen Rose's scaffolding cuts straight

across the back of the stage; and in some superior strokes of characterization that make Mercutio, Friar Laurence, Rosaline, and the
Duke of Verona more memorable or imposing than in the Cranko
version. Apart from those things, there are the same faults in both
versions: tedium in the marketplace (three whores flaunt themselves interminably in the MacMillan; in the Cranko, there is an
eternity of that awful "Shakespearean" mirthless mirth and merry-
making, and I don't think it's the Prokofiev score that forces a
choice between these evils), torpor in the love duets. The best effect
in the Cranko production comes quietly in the third act when the
stage is cleared after Juliet's presumed death and we gaze for a long
moment into a mackerel sky lit by the moon. Along the bridge
comes the funeral procession. Midway it stops and Juliet's body is
lowered on ropes through the planks onto her bier. The procession
passes on. But in a minute Paris walks calmly into the "tomb" from
the wings. Why, then, the bridge and the ropes? The effect we've
just witnessed turns out to have been only that, an effect. As in the
Royal production, the stars of the show can make up for a lot. But
I couldn't see, in the Cragun-Haydée match, beyond the distance in
style that separated them: a beach-boy Romeo and a quick little
tragic sparrow of a Juliet seemed to come at each other not from
warring houses but from opposite worlds.

The Taming of the Shrew. In the New York press, it wasn't
enough for Cranko to present full-length ballets, he had to present
"spectaculars," and it wasn't enough for Haydée and Cragun to be
stars, they had to be "superstars." If expectations hadn't been
kited so high, maybe the really bad stuff in the repertory, like this
production, wouldn't have caused so much embarrassment. *Shrew*
looked like a backwoods summer-stock production got up by the ex-
dance captain of a Gower Champion show. The suggestion, widely
put forward by Crankophiles, that the inspiration here owes something to *Kiss Me Kate* is a slur on the good name of Cole Porter
and the professionals who created that entrancing musical. In fact,
if professionalism is any criterion, I snatch back the slur on Gower
Champion. *Shrew* could have used him, mostly to cut and edit.
There were about twelve too many giddy ensembles—shrieking visual hubbub passing for effervescence. Two pas de deux, one "woo-
ing" and one "taming," might have got by, had they not been
embedded in the prolix, straining-for-stature full-length format. The
comedy was as relentlessly unfunny as in *Jeu de Cartes*. I laughed
twice: at (1) Marcia Haydée splaying her knees in one of the duets,

and at (2) the other joke. Something about a horse. Cranko's resources of comic style are remarkably scanty. He's a cabaret artist, basically, with a snarky wit. When he tries for rougher, more conventional stuff like burlesque, he's shrill, ballet-masterish, and incompetent. In *Jeu*, he puts a ballet skirt on poor Egon Madsen, but it might as well be a lampshade for all Cranko gets out of it. No shticks. (Madsen's shtick in *Shrew* is appalling.)

There was worse. Was there better? *Opus One* could be accurately but uncharitably described as a clever pastiche of *Ivesiana* and *Episodes* (its music is Webern's Passacaglia Op. 1), but, pastiche or no, its superiority to the rest of the Cranko repertory was clear. I wondered why Cranko should have succeeded with material of this kind and not with the long ballets he was being touted for, but then nothing about the company was turning out as advertised. *Présence* even misrepresents itself, with its pretentious literary allusions and turgid pretext. Once the culture dust had got out of my eyes, it turned out to be a more or less simple series of blackout sketches in the manner of *Cranks*, Cranko's revue of 1955; some of them weren't bad at all. Interestingly, this piece, which had moments of real fun, was least liked by the nouveau-chic audience (it's hard to characterize such raw enthusiasm any other way) that patronized the Stuttgart all season. Just before the curtain went up, the man to my right asked me who Ubu Roi was. He and his wife didn't laugh or applaud once. They hated the ballet. They loved best the formless but endlessly tricksy plotless ballet that Cranko choreographed to a Mozart concerto for flute and harp. Ten or so years ago, I would guess, a work like this would have been received with bored inattention. But today audiences are more than patient with abstract ballets. They want either No Meaning ("It doesn't *mean* anything, it's just to look at") or literal meanings which are graspable on sight, as in famous stories like *Romeo*, *Shrew*, and *Giselle*. It doesn't seem to occur to them to look for meaning *in the movement* and to reject meaninglessness in abstract as well as story ballets. (They didn't get the *La Valse* reference in *Jeu de Cartes* either, but it didn't keep them from enjoying the ballet as a string of pointless lowbrow escapades—unlike *Présence* with its Ubu-Who?s.)

2

There is a sense in which reviewing should function like a Food and Drug Administration, even if that function is largely futile. The only trouble with that statement—which the reviewers themselves believe—is that their function is futile because they can't be trusted. At least once a season, you'll find them issuing warnings against things like *Pelléas and Mélisande* (Fonteyn-Nureyev's worst vehicle yet) or clumsy productions of *Swan Lake* and thinking they're living up to the stern ideals of their calling because people flout them and go. The rest of the time they spend bumbling around the test kitchen, getting their labels all mixed up. For what do you do with a F&DA that is well-nigh omnivorous? That can't tell the difference between nectar and treacle, and brown gravy with no lumps in it and glue? That will one week say, "If you don't like *La Bayadère*, you don't like ballet" (a formulation harsh but true) and another week call Cranko's *Mozart Concerto* a "near-masterpiece"? (It isn't even a near-ballet.) Is it possible that choreography at a certain aggressive but untalented level beclouds the reviewing mind with images of grandeur that aren't there? Are all white ballets equal to each other? How can a mind that perceives the perfect formal clarity of *La Bayadère* miss the formal desperation of *Mozart Concerto*? Or is clarity of form something one doesn't ask of a near-masterpiece?

Mozart Concerto is a classical ballet in the style that has come down to us from Petipa through Balanchine. There are two, to name only two, great lesions in Cranko's sense of classical style that should be obvious to anyone who has seen what that really is. The main one has to do with unsound structure in relation to the music. Cranko will begin a figure—say, the ballerina supported seriatim by a line of men. On she will go, lifted by each man in turn—until the musical pattern closes before Cranko has had a chance to complete his figure. The rest of the men who haven't done any partnering stand there in position while he hurries the ballerina off or to a new part of the stage to start something else. In this way, the dance keeps setting up pins and not knocking them down. Seeing this sort of thing over and over, the observer might ask himself if the effect, whether intended or not, means anything—whether it has any power of poetic suggestion. But his common sense or, more than that, his imaginative anticipation will tell him that he isn't watching a drama about lack of fulfillment, only choreography that cannot get where it wants to go. And by the time that Richard Cragun comes on in the last movement and does a solo that looks like something out of the Hungarian divertissement from *Raymonda,* to utterly un-Hungarian music, he may very well conclude that Cranko simply doesn't give a damn where he's going.

Abstract academic choreography is no ground for amateurs, but it is very tempting territory for semipros who know a thing or two. Not the least of its charms is that it provides a focus of expectation for decorum-starved audiences (vide the popularity of classroom-set ballets like *Etudes, Ballet School,* and *Konservatoriet*). It *behaves* in a way that is pleasant to look at, and with no pressure of programmatic content. The general audience may still be so innocent-eyed that it takes just these things for the source of its pleasure, but people well acquainted with the genre want something more—they want something happening, and that's exactly what Cranko's *Mozart Concerto* (like Arpino's *Cello Concerto* and MacMillan's just plain *Concerto*) doesn't supply. It's a beguiling sham. There is always something to watch, but there is never anything to see.

But then, it's silly to expect John Cranko to provide high art. He's the bargain-basement Balanchine, and what he deals in looks old, is old, but comes out new and shiny. It's pop ballet.

Pop ballet is not only high art in dilution, it's inauthentic kitsch, too. It represents the appropriation of high-art procedures and materials to fashion a classier kind of show biz than Balanchine had in mind when he made *Stars and Stripes* out of chorus lines and patriotic revues. The Stuttgart's repackaging of *The Nutcracker* (judging from the divertissements that it showed here) is pop ballet on its lowest level of vulgarization. More seductive are Cranko's "new" ballets like *Onegin* or *Romeo* or *Mozart Concerto.* They aren't, or aren't often, vulgar, as Arpino's and Brian Macdonald's ballets are; there is more schooling in their technique than there is in MacMillan's and more vitality than in Joffrey's or Taras's. They are disarmingly cool, if you eliminate from that classical attribute any suggestion of classical discipline or chastity. The temperature is right. They look as if an event, like classical dancing, is going to take place, and in that look is everything. Cranko doesn't create serious choreography, he imitates it, and there's always some gimmick around the next bend to give the whole thing "go." Some of the gimmicks are so arduous they have the look of artistic enterprise: a duet for Tatiana and Olga which binds them together like Siamese twins; a trio, done to utterly discrete musical numbers (in *Nutcracker*), in which the male dancer's body is crisscrossed like an intersection at which the two ballerinas are determined to collide; innumerable pas de deux imperiling a girl's breasts in sensational lifts and plunges. The audience, sensing disaster, thinks "Choreography!" and gives it a hand. These malformations are typical of pop choreography in its current state, aping the advanced manner of genuine masters. Like all those Picassoesque "portraits" of a generation ago, which represented front view and profile with unfailingly displaced eyes, they convert a mode of analysis into a conventional trick. In modern art, it's only a short step from the atelier to the department store. Ballet has now taken that step.

3

No other city in the world offers dance in the abundance and diversity that New York does, but activity by itself means nothing important. The dance season, once a spotty affair, has steadily expanded in the sixties until now it runs from September through June, with a good deal of unconscionable overlap in rival attractions. The patient looks healthy. The deadly infusions of silicone don't show up in glamorous soft-focus. Box-office statistics, smart publicity, and adjustable reviewing standards have set the whole ballet scene ashimmer with lesser lights, disguising the inconvenient truth that ballet is only good when it is great. Go below a certain level—the level, say, reached by most of the new and rediscovered talents of the sixties—and it does not exist at all. The ballet-lover knows very well that what he loves in his heart cannot be given to him except by a very few who—alas for democracy—are by no means evenly distributed among the world's peoples. Existentially determined modern dance offers a wider safety margin—and weaker resistance to egotism and chaos. No, it is not a certain good that so much goes on for so many. One could write as I have written about Cranko— irritably, intolerantly—about sixty percent of what is exhibited in New York, in whatever form, as professional dance entertainment. (Half of that is so bad even the critics condemn it.) But if not New York, where?

Let's stay with New York as long as what's good is still too good to be missed, and not trifle with it by implication, as when Mr. Barnes writes that the Stuttgart is the world's "seventh-ranking ballet company"—which, I guess, places it just below American Ballet Theatre and just above (I guess again) the Joffrey—and then reviews it as if it could stand comparison not with Ballet Theatre or the Joffrey, but with the New York City Ballet and the Royal, which —to make comparisons even more odious—had just finished playing six weeks side by side. One might have expected Barnes's sense of hierarchy to restrain him when seeing things at the No. 7 level, but it didn't.* What happened was that No. 7 became instant legend, and the last time we had instant legend in the ballet world (I'm quoting the experts now) was when the Royal came to New York in 1949 and the New York City went to London in 1950. However, instant legend is also a New York phenomenon, a latter-day Broadway specialty, in fact, and its main characteristic is sheer mystique: it operates independently of the worth of a person or a thing. That's why the sudden apotheosis of the Stuttgart is suspect. In ballet, we want to have things judged on their merits, and the Stuttgart, considered as ballet, is in no way meritorious. Like its own production *Présence*, it's perfect culture-vulture bait, a trap for audiences socially or culturally on the make. Underneath the camouflage is a Broadway show, triumphing by virtue of the Broadway mystique, and that's what the fuss is about. Up to now, The Ballet, with its arcana of tradition and prestige, its downright irrelevance to the acquisitive needs that shape the Broadway mind, had been in about as much danger of becoming a hard ticket as tournament chess. Broadway had come to ballet in the past—to Jerome Robbin's Ballets U.S.A., to the Bolshoi, to a number of Balanchine hits (*Nutcracker, Agon, Seven Deadly Sins, Jewels*), to Fonteyn-Nureyev; it had come for a long, curious stare at Martha Graham—but it had never owned anything outright. In this light, the Stuttgart phenomenon is certainly fascinating, but reviewing it isn't criticism, it's market analysis. What critics should recognize in it is the definitive arrival of pop ballet and a pop-ballet audience.

And another jolt downward in the decline of New York as tastemaker to the world. The Stuttgart season was a disaster for anti-Broadway New York. The company brought us the least distinguished repertory of ballets since the San Francisco Ballet was driven out of town in 1965, and it got away clean. And on the strength of its New York notices, *Variety* is now reporting, it can go home in triumph and maybe collect a national charter from the Federal Republic of Germany. Well, West Germany no doubt deserves a ballet. Maybe (not having been there, I won't insist on it) it even deserves this ballet. But I live in New York, and there was a time

* It never does, come to think of it. Barnes gave us a heavyweight in Gerald Arpino only a few seasons ago; now he gives us John Cranko. If the Stuttgart does outrank the Joffrey on the charts, the reason probably is pop-audience snobbery. As a precursor of pop ballet, the Joffrey repertory must be given its tinselly due, but it was somehow too collegiate—not substantial or conservative enough, and not *foreign*.

when one of the things life in New York was supposed to protect you against was being made a fool of in certain matters, like the ballet. New York wasn't foolproof, of course. We'd gone quite silly, at times, over a lot of Russians. But the pressure in those cases was unique, and, whatever one may say about the Bolshoi and the Kirov and the Moiseyev, they undermine one's taste with brio. But the Stuttgart? Not failed art or out-of-fashion art, but simply stale, unnourishing pop. An astute impresario sponsored it, a radically schizoid critical establishment promoted it, an eager, pleased-with-itself, arriviste audience bought it. The other audience that buys ballet may yet have to sweat out the after-effects of its crazy success, for New York ballet life is now divided in separate paths. One leads to the gold (and over it mists are closing fast); the other is the path of cultural blackmail, the hard sell, the hard ticket, the complacent, with-it swinginess of Ballet, Our Thing. The question is, Can two such audiences coexist in peace—that is to say, in full knowledge of one another—or does the future point only one way, and if so, which? Which world awaits us? Is it Granada or Asbury Park?

—*Fall 1969*

Eliot Feld and Company

When the luckless little Manhattan Festival Ballet disbanded last year, a lot of people who had got into the habit of attending its performances on Monday nights at the tiny playhouse on St. Mark's Place wondered why they were sorry to see it go. The performances were hardly ever good; the repertory, with few exceptions, was dismal; and the theatre was barely big enough for puppet shows, let alone ballet. It was a distinctly abnormal atmosphere for dancing, which generally takes place in circumstances of high theatrical tension, but the trouble with the MFB was that it was not abnormal enough. It didn't take its cues from its circumstances, which were much like those of a modern-dance troupe that is prepared to fail honorably, far from the bright lights and the press notices. When the company finally gave up, it was possible to feel regret that it hadn't tried harder—hadn't really taken advantage of the good will the audience held out to it (some patrons even going so far as to be put in mind of Rambert's Mercury Theater). It could have tried anything down there in its Old Village-style experimental hideaway, and it didn't try much of anything at all, and pretty soon it folded and its wistful audience drifted away to the Brooklyn Academy of Music, where a genuine Off-Broadway ballet company is now in residence.

At least, I hope Eliot Feld's American Ballet Company is Off-Broadway ballet, and not just another reduction of things better supplied uptown. In its October début season at the Academy, a season remarkable on many counts, it certainly looked like a company that could be trusted to work out its own destiny. What strikes me as most hopeful about it, and already unique, is that it's a classical-ballet company built along the lines of a modern-dance one. Each of its twenty dancers looks hand-picked. Each seems to have found his place in the company from the start. And though many of the dancers are very young (the babies had no stage experience before joining Feld), they have a modern-dance troupe's unanimity and tenacity of spirit. Audiences for both classical ballet and modern dance are ready to appreciate them; and, in fact, it's a measure of how closely connected these two audiences have come to be in the sixties that Feld, himself a product of the modern dance, could have formed a resident ballet company on almost nothing but his own talents as choreographer and first dancer without too much notice being taken of the precedent.

The providential remoteness (emotional as well as geographic) of the Brooklyn Academy from the big-time Broadway audience will enforce the company's independence, too. The season was underattended, but to have had it attended by a fashionable frenzy would have been worse luck. The Brooklyn Academy isn't exactly a refuge from Broadway; it's easy to get to and conspicuously pleasant to visit—the best theatre for dance in the city. But it is at least temporarily a refuge from a certain damning kind of success. *Meadowlark*, a quite respectable ballet and Feld's third effort at choreography, was indifferently received by British critics last year only because his advance notices had led them to expect a masterpiece. Until he produced *Intermezzo* for his own company, Feld's gifts as a choreographer really hadn't announced themselves, and even with *Intermezzo*, the most brilliant piece of work by an under-thirty choreographer since Paul Taylor's *Three Epitaphs*, it's not possible to predict how they will develop. We push new choreographers at their peril; the sixties, that oversold decade, have seen more deaths than entrances. To go by the publicists who love to write about the "dance boom" of the sixties, you'd think all comers were first-raters. Maybe, from all the talk about "nonverbal theatre," you'd even think some sort of new, indigenous mass art were being born. The loss isn't only in reputations that don't hold up. There's an economic backlash, too, that has nothing to do with box-office. The New York City Ballet, with the heaviest advance sale in its history, and with a militant musicians' union to feed, may be going out of business as I write this.

No artist likes to feel he's being floated in a cultural Hellzapoppin, and though Feld's arrival in Brooklyn may have been largely for-tuitous (I can't hear him saying, "I want to be ballet master of my home borough"), at least he's been spared his second Kiss of Death. His company had a very decent success under considerable backstage pressure. On the eve of the opening, a foot injury put Feld out of the season except for one partnering role. Edward Verso of the Joffrey, Bruce Marks of Ballet Theatre, and Richard Rutherford of the Royal Winnipeg Ballet all pinch-hit. But, again by reverse luck, Feld survived. The accident threw his contributions as choreographer and artistic director into high relief, and these are, after all, what will make the company.

Of his own ballets, only two were out-and-out misses. *Pagan Spring* had musical difficulties with Bartók's schizoid Dance Suite. It seemed to want to say something neo-expressionistic about cave men in squats and cave girls on points, but the music rushed it. Though it had an uncharacteristically heavy, unbudgeable look (a little like *Harbinger* in glue), it failed less interestingly, to my mind, than did *Cortège Burlesque*, whose miscalculated satire seemed to contain the seeds of self-betrayal. Like most of Feld's repertory (and I don't disparage it for this), *Cortège Burlesque* is "one of those" ballets, a grand pas de deux that makes fun of grands pas de deux. He's working very studiously at an anthology of repertory attitudes and seems to have got a fix on most genres of ballet-making. But the attitudinizing in *Cortège Burlesque* (the title is from Chabrier's piece, lumpily blended with "Souvenirs de Munich") is harmful and silly because the dance structure of a classical pas de deux hasn't been absorbed to a comic purpose. It's just been hastily dabbed to-gether with a lot of superpompous, cute mannerisms and then laughed at. Feld has John Sowinski take bullfighter-style bows after a near-nonexistent variation. He has Christine Sarry fluffing out her tutu. Their behavior doesn't remind us of anything we've ever seen unless our acquaintance with classical ballet is very, very slight. Feld may have gotten the idea from the *Pas de Quatre*, where the mannerisms of the ballerinas are very special. Or he may have gotten it from Tudor's *Gala Performance*, or from certain Balanchine pas de deux where the dancing is funny whether or not the performers care to enlarge upon it. The point is there has to be a dance before there can be a joke, and Feld's travesty pas de deux makes us wonder if he knows how to do one straight. If he can't, then he's taken unfair advantage of himself (and of his dancers, too), and if he can, then why not do it—or rather, do one that really wins applause if applause is supposed to be so funny?

But of course it's not that simple. I suspect Feld may be uneasy in his mind about his control over classical technique, and sending up the whole thing, or seeming to, is one road out of a dilemma. In *Meadowlark*, his biggest trouble comes from his inexperience with steps and phrases out of the classical school. The choreography holds together, but largely because of force. It lacks the small connections (especially in footwork) that give brightness and variety to the classical phrase; it lacks the developed detail that makes classical technique the most sophisticated form of dance. And though *Meadowlark is* a classical ballet with a pastoral setting and a Haydn score which it takes very seriously, it has a bit of a where-are-we-what-are-we-doing look, much as if the cast of *Oklahoma!* had got hold of *L'Elisir d'Amore*, rammed it around awhile, decided to kid it, and then ended by showing how very honored they were to be doing bel canto. It's not surprising to find a young American choreographer with Feld's varied background (Broadway musicals, modern dance, Ballet Theatre) skittering all over the stage in a classical work, being impudent, working at musical-comedy depth, trying to be inside and outside the piece at the same time. What's surprising is that the brashness, the slippery intentions, aren't allowed by Feld to sell the piece, as in *Cortège Burlesque*; they're absorbed into, communicated by, vivid dance structures that make a distinct statement in relation to the music, and though these structures don't maintain a convincing continuity, they're sound enough to make the ballet pleasant and peaceful to watch. I find nothing to object to in *Meadowlark*. It's coarse, both in texture and in taste, but it isn't offensive, and there are none of those disfiguring solecisms we see being offered as hopeful ingenuities by the wonderboys who are supposed to be inheriting contemporary ballet. Feld's style may be adulterated, but it isn't faked; it doesn't try to be more than it is, so there's no feeling, when the ballet is over, of deceit or of things introduced and left unused.

This feeling—that there's nothing left unused—is one I get consistently from Feld. It makes me think that nothing in the world matters to him so much as form—the logic of classical form in particular, which is the hardest kind to master. He has taught himself how to choreograph in basic units of movement and how to expand on that base. He dares, as Balanchine said of his own work on *Apollo*, "not to use everything." I can't think there could be a better lesson for a choreographer to learn. And you can see the sense of form in spatial design, advancing from the elementary witticisms of *Harbinger* to the careful sectoring of the stage in *At Midnight* to the bumptious rondo of *Meadowlark*, in which the ballet rides to a close, taking every repeat in the music and varying the dance pattern each time with new virtuoso twists.

Intermezzo is as great an advance from *Meadowlark* as *Meadowlark* is from the first two ballets. It's an extended, tightly packed classical composition, mostly in the form of pas de deux, and it tries nothing it doesn't achieve. It's interesting, the way Feld has chosen to teach himself his craft: he seems to have set out to do his own versions of ballets he's admired, an exceedingly dangerous game. But while *Intermezzo* invokes *Liebeslieder Walzer* to an unnerving degree (even to the Karinska-style coloring and cut of the girls' costumes), it nowhere, once it is under way, reminds you of it—unless, again, your acquaintance with ballet is very, very slight. *Liebeslieder* is a drama of erotic affliction, and *Intermezzo* is light social dancing, adolescent and bold, with a tender finish. What I think it represents is Feld's challenge to himself, to see if by capturing a masterpiece's technical secrets he could learn what he had to know about making dances. If it's inevitable that young artists imitate, and I think it is—there aren't that many pages in the sample book, after all, and there's a Beethoven who sounds like Mozart—then it does seem that Feld's is the right way to do it: not by quoting steps or copying the surface, but by going to the architectural foundation and trying to build a similar structure of one's own in the dark. What we're waiting for now is for Feld to put the insights he's gained from *Intermezzo* to work on a new ballet that will be just as good and like nothing ever before seen on land or sea.

The non-Feld half of the repertory says much for his abilities as artistic director. It contains revivals of Donald McKayle's *Games* and Herbert Ross's *Caprichos* and *The Maids*—all examples of excellent small-scale works. There was also a much-disputed revival of Fokine's *Carnaval*, supervised by Richard Thomas and Barbara Fallis. *Caprichos*, with its famous dirty girls and dead woman, and *The Maids*, with boys cast as girls according to Genet's wishes, were done with appropriate brutal directness. The Ross ballets have perfectly sound audience appeal, though I find *The Maids* compromises Genet's ambiguity by not dressing the boys as girls. Sowinski, the company's lighthearted danseur noble, was terrifying in it. In *Carnaval*, which Feld had the temerity or the touching good faith—depending on your reaction to the result—to revive without ever having seen, the dancers looked sweeter and more precocious than they did in anything else. Never having seen it either, I can only report from the picture books what was missing: the striped settees (this production substituted terracotta-colored ones), the border on the curtain that separates the inner from the outer stage, exact replicas of Bakst's costumes. The orchestration was the one by Konstantinov explicitly repudiated by Fokine. Those things are in the books, but the spirit of the piece, the continuity and flavor of the choreography aren't in any book I know of, and what Feld's dancers did looked wonderful to me. Sowinski was the jubilant Harlequin, Sarry had her best role as Papillon, and a beautiful dark-eyed teen-ager named Olga Janke impersonated Karsavina to the life. The American Ballet Company in *Carnaval* may have been dead Bakst and Schumann, but it was living Fokine. —*Winter 1969*

The Royal Ballet in New York

The Sleeping Beauty

The Royal Ballet's production of *The Sleeping Beauty*, new last year, just doesn't work. I think they've forgotten it's a fairy tale and accepted too meekly the proposition that spectacle on the stage isn't as interesting to modern audiences as stories about lovers in which the boy gets to dance as much as the girl. It's suspicious how many of the Royal's evening-length ballets tell the same story about enchanted or doomed lovers, with the dance scenes appropriately divided into His and Hers. The rest of the production tends to drop into low relief while one or another popular dance team hogs the foreground. *The Sleeping Beauty* has a narrative sweep and a spectacular tradition utterly different from *Swan Lake* or *Nutcracker* or *Romeo and Juliet*, yet the principle behind these various productions seems to be that they should all look as much alike as possible and keep the stars out front all night long. The male star of *The Sleeping Beauty* gets to do the same meditative largo solo he does in the first act of *Swan Lake*, and in all these ballets there now seems to be one pas de deux too many. The superfluous pas de deux in *The Sleeping Beauty* not only sounds like *Nutcracker* (Ashton used music originally discarded by Petipa, part of which Tchaikovsky later recast as Christmas-tree music) but looks like it, too, with the dancers moving in the broad parallel steps that Nureyev uses for the last-act duet in his version of *Nutcracker* (in which, incidentally, Nureyev has given himself and his ballerina two roles apiece).

Because it also looks like an Ashton pas de deux, it's interesting to watch, but it interrupts the ballet at the worst possible moment, when the audience's attention should be not on the lovers (we already know they're in love, we saw it in the Vision Scene) but on the awakening of the castle—the lifting of that century-old cobweb and the bestirring of the court into fresh activity. These are the things that I ask to see in *The Sleeping Beauty* because they are there in Tchaikovsky's music. It is all there—his magical intimacy and his expertly judged distances, too—in the moment when the Prince bends down with his kiss of life. We see the private moment, and then we "see more" as the music begins that withdrawing motion in which, with a mighty relief, all nature stirs and wakes. Actually, we should see this, or something close to it, on the stage, but unless you're very quick you'll miss the poor little clump of waxworks royalty on their throne being whisked out of sight in mid-yawn. The action is much too simple for what the music is doing—which may be the reason the audience giggles and then hastily recomposes itself when it realizes it's going to get another! a new! pas de deux.

If we're lucky, we see it performed by Antoinette Sibley and Anthony Dowell, on whom it was set, but we may wonder why on earth it was set on them in this ballet. It would look better out of context. The music that Petipa discarded is entr'acte music (which it becomes in Balanchine's version of *The Nutcracker*). Originally, it was to bridge the moments between the Panorama and the Awakening. We have followed the Prince's long journey to the sleeping forest, and now we await the lifting of the spell. To compose a pas de deux to this music is not to misuse it—like so much of Tchaikovsky, it is very serviceable dance music—but the kind of dance music it is is not the kind of dance music that characterizes the ballet; and the kind of choreography that goes with such music is not Petipa's kind of choreography. Ashton's pas de deux, even when danced by Sibley and Dowell, makes no sense as part of the production. It's a rupture in style.

This little-known between-the-acts musical fragment is such a beautiful example of Tchaikovsky's ability to express a certain kind of event in the theatre that I cannot resist quoting those lines from *East Coker* of which it has always reminded me:

> *As, in a theatre,*
> *The lights are extinguished, for the scene to be changed*
> *With a hollow rumble of wings, with a movement of darkness on*
> *darkness,*
> *And we know that the hills and the trees, the distant panorama*
> *And the bold imposing façade are all being rolled away—*

I believe it was customary in the imperial theatres to employ virtuoso violinists or cellists to whom would fall the task of accompanying the dancers in the high moments of the evening—in, for example, the second-act pas de deux of *Swan Lake* or the Vision Scene of *The Sleeping Beauty*. We can imagine with what relish the long violin solo of the entr'acte would have been played in the darkened theatre by Leopold Auer, soloist to the Czar. Tchaikovsky's ballet is not so far from us in time that its conventions can be violated even if they cannot be reactivated. The same with Petipa: you can stick with him or abandon him completely, but you cannot cancel him at convenient moments. It's surprising to see a choreographer like Ashton, so sensitive to period style in his Garland Waltz and in the new "Fairy of Joy" variation, collaborating in such a blunder.

This isn't the only blunder in the new production. In general, the ballet strikes me as badly edited, indifferently staged, and decoratively coy. But the entr'acte pas de deux is a key weakness and one from which the production never recovers, unambitious though it may be. There were plenty of holes in the old version, but it held the stage. This one barely holds the attention. It doesn't, as seems to be its pathetically wistful intention, reconstitute Tchai-kovsky in a lazier, more domestically fragrant English vision of an Arthurian romance; it only punishes and confines him in a theatrical perspective more suited to the wilted dimensions of a Delius or a Sir Arnold Bax. The production is at best a handsome caprice; at worst, it is an insult to the militant sincerity of Tchaikovsky's imagination and of his temperament, which was Russian, pessimis-tic, and aristocratic to the core. I don't find any of these qualities at variance with the "French" delicacy, the ecstasy and childlike direct-ness of emotion which are mirrored in this music. I do find them at variance with the peculiarly faithless spirit of the production and can only conclude that the people responsible for it either (a) haven't listened to the story Tchaikovsky is telling, (b) don't know how to produce it, or (c) imagine they can tell a better one.

a) *Haven't listened.* Tchaikovsky's music throughout the ballet is, like Dickens's writing, protocinematic in its pacing of events and in its clear and continual opening-up of imaginary perspectives through which the action assumes color, size, and detail in our minds. It makes you *see.* The extraordinary visual suggestiveness of Tchaikovsky is present in other scores of his, too—in *Swan Lake* notably, but also in music not intended for the stage: the *Manfred* Symphony, the orchestral suites, the overture-fantasy *Romeo and Juliet* are especially tantalizing. The difference between *Swan Lake* and *The Sleeping Beauty* is that in the latter ballet Tchaikovsky's natural powers of visual suggestion are focused in the second-by-second shaping of a dynamic theatrical fantasy that could really be expressed on the stage. *Swan Lake* suggests more about the dance theatre than that theatre can express, which may be why it's the favorite ballet of people who have never seen a ballet. The one ballet of Tchaikovsky's written without Petipa's collaboration, it did not find its form until it was revised under Petipa's supervision, and in Ivanov's conception of the swan it acquired a transfixing image. Yet even today its poetry seems more hypothetical than real. *Swan Lake* is a dramatic poem written for a medium that does not exist.

The Sleeping Beauty, on the other hand, was written for a theatre capable of the kind of ambient spectacle that was overtaken by the movies. Strangely, the score is faster and more fluid than *Swan Lake.* If the fantasy in *Swan Lake* is still largely mental and abstract, in *The Sleeping Beauty* it is of an absolute pictorial distinctness, the stage pictures now melting and flowing, now packed with detail, now void and still with one figure moving toward us as if in closeup. One of the wonders of the score is the extent to which it suggests the plasticity of theatre—suggests separate resources of dance, pantomime, and architecture, and suggests also what the secret potency of their proportions is. Of the fairies, Carabosse only mimes. The others only dance. The Lilac Fairy alone both mimes and dances. The speed we move at in this imaginary world would be impossible without the particularized sensation we get from everything in it. The abrupt shifts in scale the ballet makes between intimacy and grandeur, the many shifts in mood and subtle leaps in rhythm, are movielike in their flexibility, yet they are every one of them of and for the stage, exactingly composed to the requirements of the particular theatrical technique it takes to render them. One could not make a decent movie of *The Sleeping Beauty*. I may describe its effects of speed and emphasis and contrast as movielike; one might as well say they are dreamlike. It is only description, a metaphor for their emotional reality.

Metaphorically, then, I suggest that Petipa wrote a script and Tchaikovsky directed it. The score is the ballet. We still have some of Petipa's dances and they are glorious. We have, besides, in the Royal Ballet production some exceptionally careful restorations. What we do not have is the details of Petipa's actual production—his mise en scène*—but even if we had nothing, we have the music for which he provided an excruciatingly detailed minutage. This is expert dramaturgy. This is precision engineering in the ballet. It is what Tchaikovsky produced on orders from Petipa ("Give me four bars of yes and four bars of no, three-four time")—not only filling out the expressive content of a scene but flooding it with meaning —that is our main text. In a sense, the ballet comes to us pre-staged. When in doubt, we need only listen for a cue.

* *Postscript* 1977: Since this article was written, we have seen a Bolshoi revival which confirmed an earlier Kirov production in having children participate in the Garland Waltz and Aurora's ladies-in-waiting, either by themselves or paired with her suitors, participate in a section of the Rose Adagio. These details we now assume to be authentic. The Bolshoi also adhered to Petipa in having Carabosse enter in a low, three-wheeled phaeton ("wheelbarrow" in Petipa's original instructions to the composer) instead of on foot, as in the Kirov and the Royal Ballet production under discussion. In general, details of staging and production have turned out to be easier to authenticate than details of choreography. This article of mine takes most of the dances of the earlier Royal production on faith as pure Petipa and assumes that the music's scene-painting is the only guide to all the rest of the action. Certainly, it is the only guide that matters, but it's also true that *Sleeping Beauty* research turns up ten wheelbarrows to every pirouette or rond de jambe.

When we listen, we realize that we are in the grip of a master dramatist who with equal skill places us now within his characters' minds and hearts, now on a great height viewing the design of an allegory as it unfolds. Thus, in Act I, the music cries out with Aurora when she is stricken, a few moments later drawing down the deep, sweet darkness of her sleep and the sleep of an entire kingdom. In the next act, the music by its pronounced eighteenth-century intonation places us in another world a hundred years later and gives us a sharp, almost satirical depiction of the kind of court life out of which the Prince steps. The present production suggests not the slightest sense of the passage of time, and its hints of decadence are limited to having the Prince borne on in a sedan chair. The characterization of the Countess (formerly so interestingly vicious, especially in Julia Farron's performance) is limited to having her borne out, rather early, in the same chair. Scenically, it is exotic to the point of having no point, suggesting some odd country where people wear furs and disport themselves in the middle of a slag heap. The period is the same as in the Prologue and Act I—and in the pre-Raphaelite wing of the Tate Gallery.

After the Vision Scene, Tchaikovsky gives us a wonderful moment when the Prince's heart leaps in his eagerness to be off on the journey that will take him to the woman whose existence has just been revealed to him. This music—so crucial to the Prince's character (in the score Tchaikovsky writes, "Désiré implores the Lilac Fairy to take him to Aurora") and so suggestive, in its agitato reprise of the Rose Adagio theme, of the pairing of his destiny with Aurora's—used to be given by the Royal Ballet and given again when Tchaikovsky has it recur after the kiss. In the later years of the former production, it was given only the second time. Now it is not given at all. Similarly with that moment in Act I when the Lilac Fairy reclaims Aurora's life from Carabosse. The transition—the modulation toward the light and peace that the Lilac Fairy stands for—is cut.

The passages that I have cited take only a few seconds, yet their omission deprives us of vital links in the action. These minor cuts, like others that occur throughout the ballet, are harder to understand than the major ones that dispense with whole characters like Gallison the tutor or Red Riding Hood. Such penny-wise deletions have the effect not of tightening up the action but of forcing it in fits and starts. The directors undoubtedly think that twentieth-century audiences are quicker of eye and instinct than nineteenth-century ones. If that is true, it is true only in relation to twentieth-century entertainments. When we are going at nineteenth-century pace, we need nineteenth-century detail. We don't accept abridged editions of Dickens. We don't cut out and frame bravura patches of Delacroix's brushwork because the action painters of the fifties sharpened our fancy for such things. But we do cut the scenario of *The Sleeping Beauty* without regard for a dramatic structure which carries us up to and away from a succession of climaxes carefully distributed over the course of a long evening. Interfering with that structure shortens the clock time of the ballet but not that other time in which the ballet happens in the imagination of the audience. When structural cuts are made, we experience a disintegration of our nervous sympathy that makes the ballet more difficult to endure than if it had been allowed to happen in its own time. We open the first act hard on the Garland Waltz, omitting the scene with the knitting women that prepared us for the fatal spindle. We start Act III with the Polonaise. But such is our folly that the ballet actually seems to grow longer. The new *Sleeping Beauty* is not only dramatically perfunctory, it's a bore.

b) *Don't know how.* I suspect the knitting-women scene was cut not because it saved time but because the directors of this production didn't know how to put it right. A truncated version of the scene Tchaikovsky wrote, it always looked frantic and crabbed and unintentionally somewhat hilarious. Here were these three crones down near the footlights with their elbows pumping to beat the band. Couldn't the designer, Henry Bardon, or whoever it was who put those ladies with their beautiful medieval tapestry screens into the Prologue, have found a way to get them back into the first act, and couldn't Peter Wright (who is credited with overall production of this version) have styled their movements *against* the music, maybe even suggesting a kind of mildly insane abbess-like detachment from the affairs of the court? Nor is there any reason why the lethal object should be a spindle; it could be a plain, ordinary ivory or bone needle (in which case it could be picked up and flourished by Carabosse in the Prologue and banned on the spot). There are many possibilities. Any would have been better than introducing and hastily dispatching a harmless old lady whom we've never seen before and who doesn't even turn out to be Carabosse in disguise.

In producing *The Sleeping Beauty*, the hardest part is knowing where to put the intermissions. In that respect, it's harder to produce than *Swan Lake,* in which usually only the last act is anti-climactic. The great series of stumbling-blocks is in the second, Vision-Panorama-Awakening-Wedding, half of the ballet. Compared with what lies ahead, the Prologue and Act I go like a song.

The dilemma lies in deciding whether to sever Act II from Act III after the Vision Scene or after the Awakening. If after the Vision Scene, the Panorama may or may not be given by the orchestra as a prelude to the next act. It may or may not be played to a dropcloth (as it was in the Bakst version for Diaghilev*), but the chances of staging it are next to impossible because the stage is already burdened with machinery for the transformation that must take place between the Awakening and the Wedding. If the break occurs after the Awakening, as in the original production and the present Royal one, the big transformation scene can come with the end of the Vision Scene, leading into the Panorama and then out of it to the Awakening. But here the ballet runs the risk of an anticlimax much worse than *Swan Lake*'s. Even if the audience can be coaxed back into the mood of the lakeside story after the glittering ballroom scene of *Swan Lake,* in *The Sleeping Beauty* there's no story to get back to. Another difficulty is that for *Swan Lake* Act IV Tchaikovsky wrote not enough music, while for *The Sleeping Beauty* Act III he wrote almost too much. In *Swan Lake,* the story, unless pieced out by additions to the score, winds up almost in the fashion of an epilogue. In *The Sleeping Beauty,* the dance divertissement of the Wedding Scene is such a sharp departure from the kind of spectacle we've been watching all evening that it's almost like another ballet—almost like *The Nutcracker,* in fact. But *The Nutcracker* has only two acts. It's hard to get a fresh grip on our attention so late in the evening—and then ask us to watch anything close to a full suite of the dances that Tchaikovsky wrote for Aurora's wedding. My memory tells me that that is exactly what the Kirov did ask us to do, but then the Kirov didn't bloat the pre-

---

* From contemporary accounts of the Bakst production it is clear that no break took place between the Awakening and the Wedding, although one most certainly did occur either before or after the Panorama. Cyril Beaumont suggests that the break came after, and that Bakst actually contrived to stage the Panorama, a very vivid one in Beaumont's description, right after the Vision Scene. But, as in many descriptions of *The Sleeping Beauty,* it is not clear whether the vivid pictures we get are of things that actually happened on the stage or of things suggested to the mind of the writer by the music. Sacheverell Sitwell, another constant observer of that 1921 production, states explicitly that the Panorama *followed* the intermission, and that it consisted merely of the music played to one of Bakst's dropcloths, in the manner of an entr'acte.

vious act with an irrelevant pas de deux. (It put its irrelevant pas de deux in place of the Vision Scene.) And the charm and novelty of the Kirov's Wedding was worth staying for. The Royal's present production calls us back from intermission for a Wedding the only apparent purpose of which is to hurry up and finish the ballet.

Most people object to this new Wedding not only because it's so curt and claustrophobic (it takes place in a kind of *Ivanhoe*-like mead hall or pavilion with a diminishing perspective like a wind tunnel) but because the festivities are unbalanced between classical and character dances. There is only one character dance—Puss in Boots and the White Cat. I agree with the objection, but then I object to the cats, too. Out of so much that is so seldom seen, I would have preferred Red Riding Hood, or Cinderella, whose music is so lovely. But the strongest objection that can be made to this act is that it has obviously been worked on with an exasperation known only to people who have seen it and dealt with it too long from the inside and are now looking worriedly at their watches. Yes, the hour is late. Florestan and his sisters were charming (whoever invented them?), but they've been replaced by somebody and her brothers, who dance to even less of the music that Tchaikovsky wrote for this episode. The Bluebirds (so called) come on much too soon and do a fussily worked-over version of their formerly beautiful dance, and then there are those damn cats. Here's the grand pas de deux (what, again?), and before you have a chance to notice the absence of the Three Ivans and be grateful for it, the ballet is over. Not enough charm, wrong kind of novelty.

What shows appallingly in this act—exasperation and exhaustion —shows also, I think, in the big decision to stage the Panorama in Act II. This decision forces everything that follows onto a downhill path—the phony pas-de-deux ending of the act, the anticlimax of Act III. It needn't have.

For the twenty years that the Royal had to dance it (1946–66), the production that Oliver Messel designed served every purpose but this—it had nothing to show for the Prince's journey by water, with its long cantilena gradually subsiding into the murmurs of the enchanted forest. This journey (the Panorama) the company now stages for the first time with one of those dry-ice mists that covers the stage (in preparation for which the whole of the act takes place annoyingly behind a scrim). The stage becomes an underground river; the Prince steps into a small motorboat driven by an anonymous helmsman and chugs off to the Tunnel of Love. A ripple of green light on the scrim shows us the movement of water while concealing a change of scenery.

This is exciting in a whimsical sort of way, but the idea uses itself up too quickly. Karsavina tells of a Panorama of 1895 in which a succession of sights came into view. One of them was of hunters and hounds frozen in their tracks by the spell in the middle of a great park. The mixed-media proponents of the sixties have lived in vain if dry ice is all we have to challenge the painted forests and living tableaux of the nineties. Why not an actual movie on the scrim (a better excuse for a scrim) instead of a stage effect that is exhausted long before the music? If the Royal had used a movie or a series of projections for the Panorama, the stage would have been left clear for the only transformation scene that really matters —the one between the Awakening and the Wedding. And the way would have been open to try something really novel and worth trying in an era when even movies are getting longer: the presentation of Acts II and III, Vision through Wedding, without a break. At the very least, a movie would have allowed the Prince really to go somewhere. Where he goes is back to the set of the previous act. The script has him fight off some monsters at the foot of it (giving the unnecessary impression that Aurora is being held captive when it's enough that she's comatose), climb a wall, and at length bestow the kiss that revives her for their big new pas de deux. The awakening of the court is barely indicated, and the curtain drops on the diminuendo ending of the pas de deux.

The comic-book excitement of this scene doesn't compare, to my mind, with what used to happen in the old Messel version. There, to a succession of light-changes and scene-shifts that brought him closer and closer to his objective, with details of the castle and its surroundings getting ever clearer and larger to the eye, the Prince simply crossed and recrossed the stage, and in a few moments he was standing in the bedchamber. It was the very ease and freedom of his entry that thrilled—as if all this had lain for a hundred years asleep, awaiting only his appearance to be brought back to life. The Messel version also had a diminuendo end to the second act, but it came earlier, when the Prince embarks on his journey with the Lilac Fairy. The Royal then used to give the Panorama music (sometimes) as an overture to Act III, which commenced with the approach to the castle and continued through the Awakening to the Wedding, a brilliant transformation scene in which we were allowed not only to watch as the entire court participated (as Sacheverell Sitwell wrote of this production, "... the veil lifts, the cobwebs and the mists are dissipated and we behold the palace of the Sleeping Beauty in all its pristine splendour") but also to settle ourselves for the great dance divertissement that was to come. It was all one superb theatrical gesture, from the moment the curtains parted on the sleeping forest to the moment when, on a brightly lit "pristine" stage, Florestan and his sisters stood in place for their pas de trois. The ballet then rose to its natural peak in the bridal pas de deux.

By contriving to have the ballet rise to a false peak in the Act II pas de deux, Wright-Bardon-Ashton satisfy the jaded audiences who long ago began turning this most complicated of ballet spectacles into a star vehicle. Any great classic has three separate lives: what it was for the men who made it, what it meant to the history of its art (i.e., its "legend"), and what it became in the process of revival. Sometimes a revival is so successful or so important historically that it starts another series of incarnations—a subclassic, as it were. The model for the Messel production of 1946 was obviously Diaghilev's London revival of 1921, but it is doubtful whether the directors of the company at that time sensed the significance of what they had in *The Sleeping Beauty*. They thought they were prolonging the afterglow of the Maryinsky twilight (Diaghilev had already done that) when in fact they were seeing the dawn of a great new classic for English dancers. At her New York début in 1949, Ninette de Valois wanted to open not with *Beauty* but with the contemporary ballets by herself and Robert Helpmann which to her represented English dancing. But she did open with *Beauty*, and the result of that opening was that the ballet became more important to the life of the company than any other. Still the company didn't see what they had. They kept it up loyally, believing both the people who said it was a "museum piece" and those who said it was an English classic, really. It was all a great strain. The present production capitalizes on the ballet's "Englishness" but in the dreariest way possible. It's like a revolution carried out from within by petty bureaucrats bored with their jobs. And considering how long the English have been in the *Beauty* business (thirty-one years if you go back to the Nadia Benois production of 1939; longer if you start with Diaghilev's passing of the torch in 1921), it's no wonder that they should have become more than a little bored with it by now. Besides, the Messel production was falling apart, and not for the first time. So the Royal called in Peter Wright, an all-around Mr. Fixit of ballet, and said, Give us something new, make it English if you can, and while you're at it . . .

c) *Tell a better story.* Don't destroy the ballet, Mr. Wright, just make it "now." They would have done better to call in Zeffirelli or Visconti. Mr. Wright's reputation is inscrutable. The story his production tells is one of simple lack of confidence—in the ballet, in the company. In a sense, it's the inside story of the company and something of a scandal.

It's understandable if the company had really come to identify the Messel production with the ballet that Tchaikovsky and Petipa created and to assume, furthermore, that it was theirs for the changing. This was the ballet in which Margot Fonteyn reached international stardom, pulling the company up after her. Fonteyn was *Beauty. Beauty* was the Royal. And the Royal didn't believe in *Beauty* as much as it believed in Margot. Now, with Fonteyn on the threshold of retirement—panic. Smash the image. If international audiences were silly to rave over just one ballerina out of a stageful of spectacle (such as it was), the Royal makes matters worse by reducing the spectacle still further and splitting the action between female and male stars. It's a His-and-Hers ballet. The ballerina still possesses Act I with its Rose Adagio and variations. In Act II, Florimund gets a new solo (we've had Her, now let's have Him) and, after the Vision Scene, gets to ride around the stage in that little boat and fight monsters. And to make sure our interest isn't taken by extraneous persons, the Lilac Fairy, a five-star general in the former production, is broken to the rank of master sergeant. The role of Carabosse loses almost all its force for no longer being played *en travestie* and on wheels (wooden wheels, as I recall, on which the black coach bore down like a thundercloud upon a suddenly foolish, suddenly dear little court). The idea of Carabosse as a heavily aged, insulted old queen was simple dramatic counterpoint; you didn't need a star to put it over, although star mimes would often be cast in the part—Frederick Ashton, Ray Powell, Stanley Holden, Alexander Grant. In the old days, Robert Helpmann would often double the role with Florimund.

And you don't need a star for the Lilac Fairy if the production treats her as one. It's wonderful how in the Prologue Mr. Wright contrives to keep losing her by changing all the diagonals. Once the apex of any triangle, the capstone of any arch, the Lilac Fairy is now more like the fairy nobody invited than Carabosse is. The seventh fairy whom this production adds to Petipa's train of six takes a lot of the play away from her. Mr. Wright does the rest. And her movements following the Awakening bear all the earmarks of "We've got her on, now how do we get her off?" Of course, in Maryinsky days the Lilac Fairy was a star, Petipa having assigned the part to his own daughter and Tchaikovsky having clearly made her prominence and importance one of the major motifs of his score. Musically and dramatically, the ballet is a duel between the Lilac Fairy and Carabosse. In this production, they are barely tolerated.

Still, and for all its mangled notions of hierarchy, the Prologue is the best part of this show. It's the one act that still looks like *The Sleeping Beauty*, that still has space and light in it. I think it also looks like a beehive. But the oddities of décor and costume are just fanciful enough to be interesting in a positive way; they don't spoil things as much as they will later. And the grand design of Mr. Wright's new-style *Beauty* ("It's just a story of young love, folks") hasn't yet emerged.

With all the protection they get, the current young Auroras and Florimunds of the Royal Ballet don't make a more exciting show of their parts than they did in the old production. Except for the dull entrance she now has to make, the ballerina's part is basically no different from what it was before. You'd think that, with Tchaikovsky setting the scene, no ballerina's entrance could be really dull, least of all this one, and yet . . . In place of the exciting entrance Aurora used to make—a fake one followed in an instant by a real one—we now see her come over a bridge and down some stairs. The old entrance was like nothing else in ballet. The new one is, too—it's like everything but ballet (operetta, Broadway, old film musicals). If Mr. Wright thinks he's making it easier for a ballerina to live up to our expectations by toning down her entrance, he isn't; he's making it harder. But maybe he doesn't think he was toning it down, maybe he thinks he was toning it up? With Mr. Wrights like this, the Royal Ballet doesn't need any Mr. Wrongs.

Anthony Dowell, obviously the star for whom the new Florimund was choreographed, is the finest classical stylist before the public. In the Vision Scene, he really seems to be seeing an apparition come and go. (Nureyev, charming everywhere else, looks as if he's playing hide-and-seek.) The new bits focus on Dowell's specialties as a dancer. When he and Miss Sibley do the new pas de deux, we see two stars who have already been typed—Sibley as the fearless plunging instrument of Dowell's archery—and who will be doing *The Dream* forever because that is what people are paying to see.

The Sleeping Beauty isn't, of course, about one star or two but about a parade of stars. It's the grandest classic a company can own. I used to think the English dancers in the old version most wonderful at the very end, doing the mazurka (the leads don't join in now—infra dig) and getting quite carried away with it until Tchaikovsky interrupted them with his heavy Czarist anthem. Then they would all line up and pose as much like Russian royalty as they could. But it wasn't the Romanov court and it wasn't Louis XIV's; it was the Court of St. James's. Or it was all three at once. I don't see these things any more. The production wants me to see something else—Camelot, I guess; all this Franco-Russian energy forcing a wilted briar rose.

Since I've rhapsodized certain of its effects, I want to make it clear that I don't think the Messel production was all that much better. (Franklin Pangborn voice: "Thank heaven! If I see one more colonnade or one more plashing fountain on the stage of this theatre, I think I'll scream.") But its horizon was right. The fake opulence of 1946 should have led on to something more nearly real in the 1970's; it was a halfway house, not the dream castle itself. Significantly, the new production was staged on the eve of the twentieth anniversary not of its London but of its New York première. New York was the making of the company, they say; but it was the start of the unmaking of the ballet. I remember a remark of Richard Buckle's at the time, something to the effect that "the fate of a company is poised on the slender point of one ballerina." Is that what *The Sleeping Beauty* had become? Not really, but everyone thought so. Since we can't do *Miracle in the Gorbals*, dear Margot, it's all up to you. Was it? Not really, but everyone thought so, Margot most of all, perhaps. I wasn't there, but I believe she was perfectly splendid; and we and the company and the ballet are in debt to her to this day, and debt, as Pound said, is slavery. Fonteyn's magnificent effort made fine publicity, but its effect was finally narcotic. The ballet went to sleep, snoring over its press notices by the library fire.

It was in New York that everything began to go wrong, at first subtly, then drastically. In its second most important reincarnation in our time, a masterpiece was being surrendered—ruinously—to a whole new legend. *The Sleeping Beauty*, that dear old crock, had saved the company when it didn't want to be saved, it wanted to shine in vital modern works. The male dancers of the company, gaining strength after the war years, grew tired of having to worship the star image that the part of Aurora had become. And the company's notorious policy of scaled casting—putting stars in support of the stars who were really Stars and dropping everybody down a peg when the lowercase stars danced in place of *the* Stars—kept things permanently on ice. This pecking order has ruined the life of more than one ballet, and it stops careers dead. Ann Jenner has advanced to dancing a Bluebird to Fonteyn's Aurora rather than just to Sibley's or Park's, but we should have seen Jenner as Aurora years ago. By the time we do, there'll be another potentially great young dancer being held back at Bluebird level. And if you don't think it matters to a dancer which "great" part she gets to do in *Beauty*, ask one. Ask the Lilac Fairy. The company in 1970 has become more anxiously star-conscious than ever; it has even rescaled its greatest classic to the proportions of secondary stardom—the whole thing has been dropped into lowercase. Naturally, it isn't terribly exciting in performance.

All ballet companies are crazy, but each is crazy in its own way. It's almost justice that the new production has gone to Rossetti and Burne-Jones for its visual style. All these years asleep and *Beauty* wakes up bonkers.

Repertory

The Ashton who over the years has put so much of his talent into little pockets of the nineteenth-century classics, into emendations of this and interpolations of that, is the same Ashton who created *Birthday Offering* in 1956, a ballet that has the charm of a nineteenth-century divertissement. The failure of this ballet to win an audience this season is surprising, for, though a minor work, it has been a durable one in repertory, changing casts many times over the years. Five years after its première, for example, only Fonteyn remained of the original seven ballerinas and there was much switching about of ballerinas from one variation to another. Although these variations have a custom-built look, they must long since have lost their associations with particular dancing bodies. It does not appear to have been Ashton's habit to alter his choreography to suit different dancers. (John Percival's company chronology printed a few years ago in *About the House* lists new solos only for the male star, when Blair did the role in 1964 and Nureyev in 1967.) The original piece seems to have stood up rather well at Covent Garden, establishing a consistent if thin record of performances. Only New York does not like it.

The impact of *Birthday Offering*, or, rather, its lack of impact, tells a lot about Royal Ballet style and about the style of New York audiences, too. New York does not understand the diffidence that is one rather delicious aspect of Ashton's wit. This diffidence runs to self-mockery, to the little stylistic inversions and precious nonsense that Ashton seems to love to insert in places where a New York audience does not expect such things—in a classical variation, for example. When we see seven ballerinas sweep out onto the stage with seven cavaliers, we don't imagine that they're going to St. Ives and that, like the seven wives with all the baggage, they're just going to tease us. We're more used to variations with a straightforward look, as in Petipa or the Balanchine of *Raymonda Variations* —clear-spoken, level-eyed variations that make the dancers look beautiful. But Ashton seems to enjoy fuss. His variations in *Birthday Offering* chatter on outrageously: sudden stops and changes of direction, flowery ports de bras, many little appurtenances to style that another choreographer might edit out. Every ballerina has seven cats. Cats, kits, fits. But instead of relaxing and enjoying it— enjoying how well each little bit of nonsense is stitched onto another—the audience gets impatient and hostile. These affected women look utterly brainless! Trying to impress us! The only girl who gets solid applause is Monica Mason with her big swinging jumps that look so sincere.

There are other reasons why the piece doesn't work. It doesn't set its own stage. It's a created antique, something that belongs to the mauve era of the Alhambra, not something that happens in between a couple of "nowhere" candelabra and in dresses that suggest nothing but another of those awful ballets by André Levasseur. And the bland, impassive opening waltz is like a dim corridor that no one would suspect led to a marvelous attic full of crazy furniture. After the furniture (the variations), when the audience is good and mad, there comes a dance for the seven men it can take or leave, and then a very strange, washed-out pas de deux. No way to save the piece now. The orchestra plays the waltz again and everybody goes home.

The low theatrical vitality is related to the quality of Ashton's wit. His wit is not dangerous. If it were, there might be more sex and drama in his ballets than there generally is—a real tempest in the Tirrenio scenes in *Ondine* (instead of the amusing and charming waterfall ballet that we get), and real social comedy in *A Wedding Bouquet* and *Façade* instead of the inoffensive high-level vaudeville comedy that tells us nothing really serious is at stake. *A Wedding Bouquet* either presumes too much on our knowledge of what turn-of-the-century French provincial weddings were like or presumes too much on Gertrude Stein's knowledge of, or intention to convey, the same thing. Cryptic Gertrude Stein lines that make a joke of communication and clarity are spoken over the action (by Robert Helpmann) in an arch, knowing voice as if they were crystalline epigrams that really made sense in relation to what we see. Whereas what we see is a series of bustling, giddy, and broadly comic dances and characterizations that are not at all related to the deadpan, taciturn style of Gertrude Stein and that might have been composed without her collaboration and for any other ballet. When the narrator says, "She has made no plans for the summer," or, "Not in any other language could this be written differently," the audience laughs because it catches a momentary "straight" correspondence in the words and the action. To explain "Josephine may not attend a wedding," Ashton has invented an elaborate drunk scene for this character. As played by Deanne Bergsma, it's the ballet's funniest section.

But these are all easy laughs. The nonpertinent lines in the Stein script ("They incline to oblige only when they stare") are pressed upon us in the same way, only there's nothing to laugh at. These dances make conventional jokes in a conventional way, like those in *Façade*, but they're weaker because the jokes are all at the expense of propriety; and propriety—absolute, straight-faced, not-letting-us-know-that-*they*-know-their-slip-is-showing propriety—is something we never see for a minute on the stage. Ashton was right not to use Edith Sitwell's words in *Façade*—it left him free to compose little dance satires, however harmless their sting—but his English-style larks, like Lord Berners's "impudent" score, are no match for Gertrude Stein's wit, which *is* dangerous and which in this piece, I think, reveals at its core a Bohemian schoolmistressy hatred and tragic perception of middle-class heterosexual functions. It is dangerous and funny. I'm unable to believe in a line like "Bitterness! Bitterness! Bitter, bitter, bitter! Ness!" could come from the pen of Gertrude Stein, although I could believe such scansion came from the pen of Lord Berners. Berners set Stein's script the way he understood the subject—as a comedy of roguish manners. Anything more would have been beyond his capacities. But I think you don't enlist Miss Gertrude Stein in the service of conventional farce.

A *Wedding Bouquet* and *Façade* are both very pretty trifles, and *Façade* can be hilarious, too. The one performance the Royal Ballet gave of it this season, a special performance for the Ashton gala on closing night, was the funniest I've seen. It's interesting that English dancers can still be funny when American dancers seem to have completely lost their sense of humor. I think it has to do with composure, or resignation perhaps—a less driven attitude toward one's work. Ballet Theatre has some good comedians in Dennis Nahat and Michael Smuin; the New York City Ballet has none, the Joffrey none. In the Joffrey's *Façade,* the only consistently funny number is "Popular Song" because it's the most relaxed— the more dutifully limp the boys look, the better it gets. But in other ballets where one might have expected the Royal dancers' unaggressiveness to work beautifully in effects of pathos (in *Daphnis* or *Giselle* or *Romeo*), they gave very boring performances.

Nureyev alone moved into a new grandeur. In *La Bayadère,* his physical force makes everyone around him seem even more wraithlike. I don't want to belabor his new vehicle too much except to say that, since that is obviously all it is, it might have been more grateful. In *The Ropes of Time,* by the Dutch choreographer Rudi van Dantzig, Nureyev does a great deal of rolling and writhing and open-mouthed posing, and seems to take an inordinate pleasure from it. There is always a small but highly vocal portion of the public that is ready to encourage "experiments" like this by the big established companies and that greets with enthusiasm the most wanton distortions of a great classical dancer's technique and style, especially if they're accompanied by an electronic score and presented in the name of progressive choreography. I suspect Nureyev's wasteful exertions in this are his answer to the New York critic who a few years ago implored him to "come to grips with the age in which we live." Owing to felicitous programming, he was almost always able to appear in *La Bayadère* before coming to grips.

In *La Bayadère*, he partnered Margot Fonteyn, and partnered her also in *The Sleeping Beauty, Swan Lake, Giselle, Romeo and Juliet, Marguerite and Armand*, and *Raymonda* Act III. When the season was over, it was hard to believe that there could be any Hurok subscribers left to complain about not getting to see enough of Fonteyn and Nureyev, who appeared in nineteen performances as against fourteen for the next most popular team, Antoinette Sibley and Anthony Dowell. (This is out of the forty-eight performances that were given during the six-week New York season. In London, during a recent three-month period, thirty-three performances were given and F&N appeared in nine.) More likely, the subscribers, after first satiating themselves, were passing the experience on to their children. Nureyev gave them their money's worth and more, but what these same children were seeing in Fonteyn I can't imagine. In the performances of hers that I saw, she certainly didn't look like the greatest ballerina in the Western world and sometimes didn't look like herself either. At fifty-one, she can no longer move us with the consistency of which she was capable even five years ago when she last did *Daphnis and Chloe* here. Without her, that ballet seems to have lost its "voice," especially in the scene where Chloe, her wrists bound, confronts her captors with the unspeakableness of their crime against her. From Fonteyn I had the impression that the crime was as much or more against nature, and that she couldn't understand how it could be happening; whereas with Sibley I just saw a girl who demanded her rights.

Ashton's choreography is still beautiful, but it remains beautiful only as an aesthetic hypothesis, so to speak. The characters behave in a manner that does not express them as persons, but does express what they are in the world they live in. It's a Platonic world like that of *Symphonic Variations*, and the trouble with *Daphnis and Chloe* is that it has no more need of a plot than *Symphonic* has and, specifically, no need of the melodrama associated with Ravel's score. Done another way, without its Picassoesque Mediterranean décor and costumes (which look old-fashioned and touristy anyway), its dramatic inertia might become interesting. As it is, the unachieved localized melodramatic effects make the delicate dance design look weak and callow. It is hard to deal with a scenario that involves jealousy, rape, and pillage by pirates and still keep the audience hanging on to a doctrine of essences. Ashton has trouble with it, and so do the dancers. Five years ago, Fonteyn and her partner, Christopher Gable, managed to convey that they were live divinities and inviolable because they were in love and loved by nature. It's a very old idea, but the current casts don't seem to know how to be very, very beautiful and responsible for the story at the same time. Dowell, who might have been born for Daphnis, looked as if he wished he were doing Romeo.

Except for the corps, which was wonderful all season, and Fonteyn and Nureyev, who are just Fonteyn and Nureyev, the Royal left the impression of a company of dancers unhappy in their jobs. The stars are getting farther and farther out of tune. Merle Park looks miscast in everything. Her stage personality has developed a strange contradiction, like thick cream poured over acid. You get interested in that, and look for places in her ballets where it might be expressed directly, but then her manner of appearing to be above anything an audience might ask of her defeats you. She's not sinister, after all; she's a Great Lady. So many of the Royal girls are pursued by Doppelgängers it might be interesting to make use of. Sibley, for instance: it doesn't seem to have occurred to her that the hints of sluttishness that Ashton drew from her Titania might be useful to her Juliet. She's a pious, wronged Juliet; a pious, wronged Chloe.

Like the girls, the men are conscious shapers of their images, but they're less distinct. Michael Coleman is still faceless. He has a sickly tension in classical parts (and some bad technical faults) that leaves him as soon as he enters a character part. Dowell and Donald MacLeary are both beauties, but one has style and tautness; the other doesn't. Both seem to be competing in some sort of mooncalf derby. When either does *Symphonic Variations* surrounded by his stuffy ladies (Park or Sibley with Jenner and Penney), it is all this one milky, even tone—the ooze of the transcendental holy cow the ballet has become.

The dullness of the Royal Ballet in its off seasons is a patronizing dullness only British dancers can inflict. Not that I think there's any connection, but I would like to make a political protest:

On the closing night of the engagement, we had to endure from Sir David Webster one of those traditional Royal Ballet curtain speeches which rehearse the early circumstances of the company's début in New York more than twenty years ago. These English-Speaking Union speeches are accepted in good grace by the audience as the obligatory fatuities they are; nothing could be more harmless than hands-across-the-sea and all that. But ah, these English. Give them half a chance and they'll always slip it to you. Ninette de Valois, a past mistress of the needle, used regularly to congratulate the stupid Americans on their ability to appreciate fine classical dancing (meaning her). I remember the speech of hers that ended the Royal season that followed the first New York season of the Bolshoi Ballet. How relieved she was, she said, to find that New Yorkers could still love the Royal after we'd seen the Bolshoi. And Sir David this year chose to remind us yet again (we've heard it dozens of times) how, long ago, he'd been offered a "most unsuitable theatre" for the first appearance of the Royal in America, and how he'd held out for the Met, and how the rest was history, etc. Even if you didn't know that the theatre in question was the New York City Center, which, unsuitable or not, became the home for fifteen years of the New York City Ballet, the remark was ungracious. One may mention the unheated guest room to one's host—but one doesn't go on mentioning it for twenty-one years, especially if one has never slept in it. But do these people think we have no ballet life of our own, nothing to warm us on the cold winter nights when the Royal (or the Bolshoi) is out of town?

This is a crucial year for the Royal Ballet. Ashton is leaving; the entire company is being reorganized under new directors who are going to have to decide what course the company takes in the next decade. Signs of disrepair and demoralization were evident in the season just past. There is a lot for the Royal to do. Let them stick to their knitting women.   —*Summer 1970*

Folies Béjart

"Beige art! Beige art!" the standees were yelling the night the Ballet of the Twentieth Century closed its season at the Brooklyn Academy. Well, it might as well have been beige or any other pastel; anyone expecting bold colors, a raw palette, or some form of sensational vulgar display was bound to be disappointed. Béjart's art is vulgar, all right, but not enjoyably so; it has the vulgarity of the provincial guru in self-enchanted exile from the world where ideas are formed and tested. Advance publicity had led us to expect a contemporary fauve, a wild man of the arts who broke all the rules. The only rule Béjart doesn't break is the wiliest in show business: Never try to outstrip your audience. Béjart keeps pace with audience expectations, but a lot of the time he lags behind. Most nights the audience put on a better show than he did. The heralded revolutionary production of *Firebird* was living-room fantasy, performed to a booming stereo in two sets of kiddie costumes— dungarees and Captain Marvel. The fantasy falls apart at the end, just when it should rise and strangle us. Such isolation may be childlike, but it isn't privileged; an "unsophisticated" number like the Bolshoi's *Walpurgis Night* comes about through insularity, too, but there's more excitement and vitality in that ballet than there is in the whole repertory of a company that reminds us where it's at by putting "Twentieth Century" in its name.

The mystical encounters, social commentary, and sexual fantasy that Béjart deals in are the same ones we've sat through in ballets, movies, Broadway shows, and nightclub acts for a hundred years. With Béjart, these experiences seem at first peculiarly significant because he doesn't seem aware of their decomposition into kitsch. We wonder if he is going to accomplish the final mutation that turns kitsch back into art. But solemnized kitsch is what we get. Béjart's ballets are like serious parodies of things that are no longer taken seriously. In the piece called *Bhakti*, Béjart does to Jack Cole what Jack Cole did to Hindu dance. *Bhakti* turns the Copacabana back into the Holy of Holies. A straight Jack Cole number would have been more fun, but unlike Jack Cole's dancers or the Bolshoi's in *Walpurgis Night*, Béjart's dancers don't seem to want to have fun. They are out to instruct mankind.

Instructing mankind at a trash level of taste can be a very amusing business. I was surprised, as the season went on, at how little there was to be amused by. The pretentiousness didn't outrage, the sex didn't titillate, the sham didn't have theatrical dignity. Béjart's old-fashioned ideas derive from a kind of wishful modernism—a wish to distort, a wish to explore, a wish to shock, to offend, to be "relevant"; he has any number of faintly disreputable intentions. And all of them are pale and thin in execution not because of any delicacy of presentation but because Béjart never takes any chances. He sticks to the text of his lecture. The showmanship displayed in *Les Vainqueurs*, the most sprawling and "decorative" of the works presented, is about what you'd expect from the small-bore professor who writes in the program, "What is the meaning of this 'ceremony'? The dance is a rite. A ballet which descends to the roots of its origins is always a ceremony." Except that the origins to which *Les Vainqueurs* descends are the Folies-Bergères and Béjart doesn't even get to the roots of that.

This work mixes up the Tristan legend with Buddhist myths. Béjart's taking-off point is Wagner's interest in Buddhism at the time that he composed *Tristan und Isolde*. The subject would make a fascinating doctoral thesis, but it's limp as old lettuce on the stage. The ballet's best moment—one of the few good theatrical moments in the repertory—is the scene in which a figure, an idol or a priestess, stands motionless in a cloth cape extending in enormous swags to the sides of the stage while a number of men dressed like spook acrobats snake-dance slowly around in front of her. For a moment, it seems as if P. T. Barnum and Aleister Crowley are shaking hands across time. Four of the men shinny up ropes for no reason, it seems, other than that four ropes are hanging there and ropes are what you shinny up. They shinny right back down. Meanwhile, the lady in the cape is getting off her perch, which she does by stepping on the necks of her attendants, but this bit of action is so clumsily handled it doesn't even seem staged. It has no sensuous interest at all. Then the cape collapses like a parachute, is taken away—the whole scene is taken away and nothing has happened in it. When we read further in the program that we may, if we wish, see in this inane tableau "nothing but a magic universe of shapes and colors," we can only wonder what else Béjart thinks he's providing when he can't even get us up to this level of mindless satisfaction.

Some of the things he thinks he's providing: "a wondrous fairy tale, a romantic and exotic love story, the psychoanalytic version of the Tristan myth, or the initiation voyage toward illumination." I saw some crablike swimming motions on the floor of the stage. I saw Isolde balanced like a ship's prow in drydock on the knees of Tristan. I saw some bad paintings of sailing ships with their viscera blown apart in surrealistic style. All this was apparently "voyage toward illumination." Most of all, I remember seeing what Béjart does to express "cosmic love." The company rolls on the stage in bluejeans, making waves ("The Ocean") and getting fondled, each in his or her turn, by the two leads, also in bluejeans. After a long time, all the kisses and hugs are distributed, the last and most pointed buss being reserved for the one black member of the company, and then everybody assumes the lotus pose in their bluejeans and it's the end of the ballet.

Béjart is famous for his appeal to youth, and one can see why. Youth appeals to Béjart; the theatrical gestures of political youth give him something to put on the stage. His company, Brussels-based, is made up of young dancers from all parts of Europe and from England and the Americas, too. They have and use different techniques. Only the men have anything approaching a uniform style. The spectacle of this company on the stage resembles a World Youth Festival in Belgrade or Helsinki, everyone doing his thing for peace, love, and the Revolution; the fervor is like that of Moral Re-Armament. This is different from the enthusiasm that young dancers project when they are dancing with strength and style—it's more baleful, like the Bolshoi at its worst. And the polyglot techniques reinforce the impression that anyone with a passport can play. The Academy program carried an ad for Mudra, the school in Brussels that Béjart runs. (Mudras are the symbolic hand gestures of the Hindu dance; Béjart never uses mudras in his quasi-Hindu choreography, possibly because they mean something and Béjart's Orientalism is completely phony, a more narcissistic form of kooch dancing.) To qualify for Mudra, the ad tells us, the applicant must be between fifteen and twenty-one years old, with a background in classical or modern dance. But those without background can still apply, if they're under eighteen, "have a flexible body and good coordination," and want a professional performing career. There is no tuition. Many of the young people who attended the New York season also came to audition for Béjart. The Academy offered specially reduced ticket rates for "students"; they even had their own box office. One boy to whom I gave a ticket at a sold-out performance said that, since the beginning of the season, it had become the dream of his life to get into Mudra. When I pointed out that he could get better training right here in New York, he said that what Béjart offered couldn't be had in New York, and he was right. Béjart's accommodationism certainly seems odd to local viewers. No American choreographer, for example, would use a black dancer the way Béjart uses Dyane Gray-Cullert, an American trained in the Graham technique. It's much the way Hollywood used Sidney Poitier. She's always front and center when he wants to make a political statement. And when she appears with the company in *Choreographic Offering,* she's the only girl who isn't on point. Maybe being black excuses one from pointwork?

In its latest hit, *Trinity,* the Joffrey Ballet brings peace candles onto the stage. It's what the Béjart dancers do at the end of *Messe pour le Temps Présent* and what the Living Theatre used to do in exactly which one of its mystic orgies I now can't remember, and what for one performance several seasons ago, mercifully never repeated, Balanchine had his dancers do in memory of Martin Luther King. Serving to an audience in the theatre the theatrical gestures that people make in life out of a need to express themselves psychologically or politically carries the Theatre of Piety one bathetic step forward to the Theatre of Ritualized Piety. Audiences pay to see their pieties confirmed in the same form they themselves have invented to express them. Theatre adds nothing to the ritual act; it merely provides one more place where it can happen. And since theatre is not quotation but transformation, it can't speak in the sentimental—because unexamined—colloquialisms of "people" theatre (peace vigils, marches, love-ins, encounter sessions, etc.) without becoming by that much less a place of art and by that much more a place of worship. Indeed, that is how the theatrical ritualists think of their art—as a religion—and how they think of the theatre: as a place to celebrate, by enacting, the formalities of right-mindedness.

But that isn't all. Transplanted "people" theatre represents the Theatre of Ritualized Piety in only one of its forms, the lower one. Higher up in consciousness comes a transplanting—from backstage, from the rehearsal studio—of the theatrical gestures that *theatrical* people make in life. What actors do in order to act and what dancers do in order to dance—improvisations and exercises—are carried out and laid before an audience. This is still quotation, but this time the performers are quoting themselves. Theatre itself becomes a form of belief, a faith to be practiced. It is right-mindedness imbued with the mystery of a professional calling. The flames of worship rise higher.

The Brooklyn Academy sponsored the last New York season of the Living Theatre, it brought Grotowski to America, it extended Peter Brook's production of *A Midsummer Night's Dream* after its successful Broadway run, and it introduced the marathon pantomimes of Robert Wilson. Not all of these things are equal to the same thing, nor are they equal to each other; and I can't believe the directors of the Academy think that Béjart's little weasel gestures amount to anything like the Grand Guignol joke that was performed by the Living Theatre on New York's Cloudland intelligentsia. Yet I can believe that they thought the time was right for the pop version of avant-garde "ritual" theatre to make its appearance. Béjart doesn't have much to do with our own dance traditions, as the reviews were quick to observe. But this is beside the point. Béjart's whole enterprise is elaborately beside the point of what professional theatrical dancing has meant to us in our time. I don't even think he's much interested in choreography; he'd rather expound a message about "the dance as rite." Political rite, mystical rite—it all holds the same giddy enchantment for the kind of born-yesterday audience that was attracted to the Academy this season in unprecedented numbers. This audience is used to playing out theatrical roles in life, even if it's only a matter of dressing up funny, and what they see on Béjart's stage is a theatre they can imagine themselves taking part in. From watching the stage, you get the strong feeling that the dancers are not only performers but initiates. They all seem to be undergoing a life-adventure—the boys in their bluejeans and long, sweat-matted hair, the girls with their crazily painted faces. They pound around in mandala rings, and drink from the springs of knowledge with cupped hands, and lie on the floor with their legs spread, and cuddle close to one another. Above them, the Zeitgeist, a dove of peace, spreads its large and silent wings. And how long it all takes! *Les Vainqueurs* is nearly an hour; the *Messe* takes all evening, no intermission; *Actus Tragicus* (a Bach rite) seems to go on forever. But to be bored is to be not with it. If none of it has any theatrical interest, that's because it isn't a show, it's a religious service and you have to believe.

No one seems to have scored so well off the attitudes of the younger generation since Jerome Robbins stopped making his teen-age ballets in the fifties, but Béjart doesn't present his heroes as alienated and rebellious, he enfolds them in a warm, positive vision of ideal friendship. I suppose the hectically applauding adults in the audience were relieved to find they weren't being assaulted or punished or even cut down with a Sokolow Stare.* It was like a return to 1967 and the first wave of affection for the flower children. But one doesn't know whether Béjart has eschewed the more

---

* Devised by choreographer Anna Sokolow as a theatrical expression of the Age of Confrontation. Once an evening, the performers come to the footlights and stare out accusingly. It has become such a cliché that it can be used only by black choreographers, who give it a bit of animation by putting guns in the performers' hands.

extreme tactics of shock and confrontation or whether he hasn't found out about them yet. The tactics he does use—having the dancers warm up in view of the audience before *Choreographic Offering,* having them speak (in gibberish), having an actor harangue the audience in a stentorian Comédie Française voice during the *Messe*—are so trite as to serve no function. The version of the Sokolow Stare that he uses (at the end of *Choreographic Offering*) is what that Stare was when it was a pup back in the thirties. It belongs to something like *Babes in Arms.*

2

In the way I see dance, everything is included: relaxation, love, purity, health. I've been searching for total theatre for a long time. I think I have found it in dance. I am entering a new period. Dancers give me everything I need in life.
> —BÉJART *in* Dance News, *January 1971*

In recent years there has been a movement toward the blending of dance and traditional, spoken drama. Béjart, who has studied with both Brook and Grotowski and who probably saw "Le Living" when it was in Paris, is not the only one who conceives of dance as a basis for total theatre.

When the mystique of Theatre encounters the art of Dance, it moves onto its most grandiose plane. Dancers, more than actors, are exciting to watch in class or in rehearsal, for obvious reasons. And dancers, especially when they are members of a strict *école,* do seem to be celebrants of some mystical rite of perfection. Not only do their skills seem all-encompassing, their discipline looks monastic. It's easy to romanticize their absorption as religiosity, and to go from this into a fantasy of dance as a rite and even to prefer the ritual repetitions of exercise and rehearsal to the once-through-and-be-damned effort at transformation which is the performance. I remember a lecture-demonstration Martha Graham gave with her company about seven years ago at Philharmonic Hall in Lincoln Center. The Graham class, as everyone knows who has seen it, is extremely exciting; the Bolshoi were bowled over by it. It's exciting because it incorporates the techniques that Graham invented for her choreography; it's halfway to theatre already. But it is not theatre in itself; it *means* nothing without the Graham theatre. On this occasion at Philharmonic Hall, the lecture-demo was followed by *Secular Games,* which didn't look very good on that stage and isn't a very great piece anyway. Most of us in the audience, I think, were more impressed by the first half of the program. If we were, it was because the untheatrical space (there were bleachers on the stage, as I recall) didn't diminish it; it would have looked good anywhere—in a parking lot, on television even. But because the audience could follow the simple progression of exercises with unblocked eyes, and because the exercises seemed to form themselves into theatrical units, the class accumulated an almost terrifying theatrical power. And this is what happened: Graham, who must have sensed the audience's tension (it was during the breathing exercises), suddenly turned to the microphone and said, "If it frightens you that this looks so very ritualistic, remember that the practice of every craft, all crafts, is a ritual. It's not done for metaphysical reasons."

The practice of a craft is a ritual, but when the craft is as imprecisely defined as it is in Béjart's company, the ritual becomes mere affectation. Béjart's theories about the dance as a rite would be more persuasive if he had invented his own form of ritual dancing. Instead, he leaves it up to his dancers, who sink themselves into their meager store of technical equipment—a little Western classical baggage, some scraps of Central European expressionism, a few Asian trinkets—and find their cheap versatility crowned with ceremonious significance. It doesn't seem to matter whether they are potentially good dancers or not. Bortoluzzi and a few other boys are very talented, and Suzanne Farrell's gifts are unparalleled. Any available technique, even highly developed technique, is exploited as mere ceremony next to any other available one. The ceremony presumably comes to a focus in the choreography, only it doesn't. The choreography just burns a lot of incense to the dancers, who are left exposed in their "come as you are" shreds of temperament and technique. To Béjart, master of rituals, letting dancers do whatever they can seems to embody some universalist vision of East meeting West, classical meeting modern, and so on.

The natural corollary of Béjart's exaltation of dance as a rite is his cult of the dancer. An impressive passage in another of his program notes (he is an indefatigable writer of program notes) runs: "Choreography, like love, is done in pairs / In a choreographic work, the dancer is more important that the choreography, for it is the dancer who is the author of the work; the choreographer merely fits it together / To the extent that the choreographer strives to understand the shape, rhythm and will of the body one may create a work that appears original. The dancer's body, which is the interpretator, is always right. When I say body, I mean the whole intuitive and spontaneous being, and not the mind of the dancer. The dancer should be carefully observed, not only for the steps he makes, which he believes favor him, but because, despite what he says or thinks, his whole being is impelled to express itself in that very particular way." (All this by way of explaining why the credit line for *Choreographic Offering* is "Choreography by Ballet of the Twentieth Century" instead of "Choreography by Maurice Béjart" —but why don't the dancers get credit for the other works as well?)

This business about the dancer being the author sounds heavy, yet it is nothing but a pompous description of the way most choreographers, the bad ones as well as the great ones, work. There is no mystery, no special tender deference, involved in observing dancers to see what they can do, how they like to move, and then "fitting it together." But Béjart leaves one room to doubt that he ever edits, ever attempts to draw from his dancers the best that they can do and delete the worst. From the effects he gets, it's tempting to conclude that he does the opposite, but I rather think he is indifferent to any effect. Béjart is like all bad choreographers who don't analyze their dancers' gifts but take the most striking movements they make, however banal, and fling them onto the stage. Unlike the others, he does it because the movement is not only "right" but "rite." He's more than a choreographer; he's a theologian. Béjart technique is mannerism surrounded by mystification. It is Paolo Bortoluzzi forever folding his leg into passé from a high extension in second, but it is also the cult of Paolo Bortoluzzi doing it. It is Jorge Donn in perpetual fondu, curving his naked belly and parking one foot on the other shin, but it is also the cult of that belly and foot and shin. It is Maina Gielgud turning in her knees and her toes, it is Suzanne Farrell shouldering her leg to 180 degrees or dipping into arabesque penchée or doing split kicks or doing anything, so long as it is to 180 degrees, and it is the cult of 'the grotesque in the female dance. If dancers have freedom in this company, it is the freedom to drain themselves with monotonous self-repetition. On that basis, it's easy enough to attract a following; these foolish things remind me of you.

3

A popularized version of extremist technique in the theatre tends more to expose the technique than to vulgarize it, since it is often self-consciously vulgar to begin with. Béjart is Ritualized Piety, and so is Peter Brook. Because Brook has obviously so much more talent than Béjart and appeals to a classier audience, we don't associate the two, but there are ideological similarities. The most striking is the way the work of both men reincarnates aspects of the thirties. Béjart exploits contemporary fashions in theatre, especially political theatre, and Brook appears to be setting them (remember his production of *US?*), yet these fashions are thirties revivals. Brook has brought back much of the experimental theatre of the thirties—the documentaries and pseudo-documentaries and the innovatory productions of Shakespeare. In *Messe pour le Temps Présent*, Béjart provides a travesty of the "social-consciousness" theatre that Brook has also drawn upon. Béjart's attempt to span the thirties and the sixties is so crude you hardly know which agitprop era you're in; the effects tend to backfire confusingly, as in the "Mein Kampf" episode. I should explain that the *Messe*, dated 1968, is subtitled "A Ceremony in Nine Episodes." After giving us an extended ceremonial tribute to the beauty of the Body (the corps de ballet at the barre), Béjart brings on a flock of gymnasts, marches them up and down, and makes Nazis of them all. The facile identification of sports with militarism and Nazism takes your breath away—not only as one of the flimsiest clichés of the era it sprang from, but as a dumbfounding non sequitur coming from the man who venerates physical culture and loves to book his company into sports arenas.

Nazis are always good for a good hate when you can't arouse an audience any other way. When you look into Béjart's work for dance meanings—and you're often tempted to simply because the programmatic meanings are worthless—when you look for the meanings that the body can express as metaphors of the spirit, you find that they aren't there. Here the mystique of Le Corps is converted into its own ideological opposite, and without the slightest suggestion of irony. I can imagine a Mass for Today well worth celebrating which posed in some coherent way the dilemma of a faith in the purely sensual or physical ends of existence. A poet of the dance might have a unique ironic awareness of how such a faith can support its own stream of mechanistic terrors. But irony is the last thing Béjart is equipped to convey. Even if he had wanted to say that cultivation of the body can be directed toward perverse as well as sublime ends, he'd hardly be the one to talk. Often, what he offers us as sublime is—perverse. It's like having a natural gift for Doublethink.

The spectacle of *Choreographic Offering* is that of Béjart being ironic. This big company number, created especially for the New York season, does go so far as to outline a dilemma of sorts, but those with short memories will recognize it as one of the formulas of old Broadway and Hollywood musicals—the "Jiving the Masters" and "Swinging the Muses" kind of thing. Classic Ballet, personified by a young man in his underwear, performs classroom exercises to Bach. His antithesis is a joker who keeps horning in to an accompaniment of washtub thumps and slide whistles. The corps de ballet has a cute time trying to decide whether to follow Cecchetti or Mickey Mouse. (Their synthesis—if you can call it that—seems to be Harriet Hoctor.) But don't laugh; at the crucial moment, a sloe-eyed girl in army fatigues brings a peace offering (a rose): this is no joke, it's in dead earnest. Whither ballet in Our Time?

I had gone to the Béjart season thinking it would have some of the trashy glitter of the good old Ballets de Paree with maybe a little incense-burning on the side. I had not expected metaphysics and unisex and dirty fingernails, nor, seeing that that was what I was going to get, did I think it would turn out to be so ridiculous and so *mild*. Béjart has been called a romantic. "Sentimentalist" is better. The only interesting thing about him is that he has set up shop so successfully as a choreographer when it's mystagogy that he's selling. The dance, as they say, has many faces, and these days it has many false faces. Maurice Béjart is the false prophet of the ballet.

—*Spring 1971*

Twyla Tharp's Red Hot Peppers

Twyla Tharp's subject is not your life or hers, and in that sense she is a classical artist. She doesn't present herself as a force for change or as a vehicle for new ideas, and her aggressiveness is not the least bit hostile in its attitude toward the audience. She is radically different and radically new, but, whatever else you may think of it, after about a minute her kind of dancing doesn't even look strange. You find you can take more and more of it.

The Tharp dancers give us so much more to see than most companies ever think of giving, and they let us see them giving it. At peaks of furious activity, they may get breathless and a little giggly, but they stay calm—they have to, because they're being so carefully objective. It's this objectivity that fascinates and carries us from one moment to the next. We get interested in the task they have set themselves; we try to follow the intricate logic of it. But we can also enjoy the dancing another way as a burst of nonsensical excitement. We can leave the dancers to their purpose and wrap ourselves in the illusion that it's all happening spontaneously. I wouldn't suggest that one or the other way of watching is better. I find that I watch both ways, and that as the dancing flickers between its two aspects I become convinced that I'm watching the most exciting performing in the theatre.

Tharp dancers work to an elaborate system of counts and meet danger with the predetermined nonchalance of trapeze artists; nothing is left to chance. Usually, when they perform without music, their intensity of planning and purpose is more exposed; one can see they wish to use no other charm. Yet we are seduced by a paradox: it's obvious that they're executing programmed movements, but what makes the routine difficult and exciting to watch is that the movements themselves look utterly wild—forced from some extreme necessity in the calculations you hadn't thought it possible to foresee, much less calculate. This is the reason that the dance doesn't become a grind to watch; it is always attacking, and it can (or so it seems) keep up the force of its attack indefinitely. Three girls can hit the stage like a thundering herd; they go in all directions and stop on a dime, in a nerveless silence. Then they can do it all again in reverse, or in limitless variations; they will attack one at a time or all together in or out of unison. The end comes without warning. The dance's only subject is itself; there are no pictures in it, at least none that you have seen before. And because there are no concessions either to what an audience might want from an all-girl cast or to what it might settle for, the dance goes way beyond the limitations of conventional sex differences in dance expression and into the neutral "white" territories of abstraction.

There are no pictures in it, or else one huge and rather frightening picture forms in your mind. Such is the effect of virtuosity emptied of conversation: we are overwhelmed, we can't question it or answer it back. The dance I have been speaking of is called *The Fugue*; it might as well stand for the quintessential Tharp dance. It's so "white" I have nothing to say about it; I thought it was what it was, clearly a series of fugues and possibly a classic of Tharpian form. (Or I could try to break it down a bit more. Let's say I dreamed the Nicholas Brothers were three girls and were doing a routine choreographed by Merce Cunningham whose mentor is Bach this time and not Cage—that's *The Fugue*.) But a man who also saw it had a picture. He said it was like a war dance of Women's Lib. And I have nothing to say to *that*, except that if, in looking at dancing, you are assailed by a notion, then you must surrender to it.

Basic Tharp body movement—the spiraling twists and off-balance lunges and kicks, the shuffles and stomps that look exclusively hers —is nonevocative. That is, it takes itself more seriously than its several obvious origins: tap-dancing, rock dancing, track and field sports, ballet. We see the stylistic residue of these things, not the things themselves. *The Fugue*, for example, "comes from" tap-dancing; the stage is even miked to bring up the sound of the dancers' boots on the floor. But it has about the same relation to a flash act that, say, a Louise Nevelson wall has to somebody's attic or barn. Tap-dancing has never been a congenial style for women; it seems to defeminize them. Twyla Tharp's performance transcends this limitation as it transcends tap. The difference between the Eleanor Powell-Ruby Keeler school and the Twyla Tharp dancers is the difference between performers and gladiators.

Strange things happen when this basic, unchanging, highly individual, compressed *mélange de styles* is set to music. *Eight Jelly Rolls* is danced to the music of Jelly Roll Morton's Red Hot Peppers—great jazz music of the late 1920's. The dancing doesn't revert to "jazz" choreography; it keeps its neutral texture. And yet it's as exact an expression of this music—as funky, as blue, as coarse, and as elegant—as the finest jazz dancing imaginable. There are incidents in the choreography—splat falls, competitions between the dancers, waves to the audience, Sara Rudner pulling an invisible tape measure down Rose Marie Wright's back, Twyla Tharp becoming a wailing drunk in the appallingly funny "Smoke House Blues" (surely one of the great individual set-pieces in modern dance)—but the dance as a whole is still an abstract dance, a musical landscape. It's so exhilarating a musical experience that one is tempted to call *Eight Jelly Rolls* a breakthrough for this company. And yet it probably isn't that so much as it is a logical development from *The Fugue*.

Tharp dancers are obsessed with time, but until *Eight Jelly Rolls* it had seemed to me that they were more interested in static divisions of time than in patterned ones; that is, in rhythm. I really didn't know what I was missing until *Eight Jelly Rolls*, and now it seems to me that a new rhythmic subtlety has entered the company's style and that it must have been already present in *The Fugue*, where the dancers are self-accompanied by exquisite Paul Draper-like detonations of heel and toe. In *Eight Jelly Rolls*, it's as if you were seeing a brilliant *a cappella* choir transform itself, with orchestral backing, into another set of musical instruments. The dancers are up to anything the music proposes. In the slow blues passages, they are cool rising above cool or the stranded hulk of melancholy washed by a tidal despair. In the fast dances, they go all-out, a pack of zanies shot from guns. Their habitual way of moving lets them cut loose as if the music were inside them—tickling, teasing, jabbing to be let out.

The piece has a slow, easy start. Rose Marie Wright, the group's long tall Sally, does a lazy, slew-footed shuffle, the arms lifting and falling in an imitation of shadow-boxing with now and then a leg opening wide in a ballet extension. Right in the middle of this, at an entrance for two gravel-throated trombones, two other dancers make an upstage cross in a state of high spastic agitation, like a marionette act being pulled slowly across the scenery. They disappear. A moment or two later, back they come again, a precise repeat in the opposite direction. Wright meanwhile has gone straight on with her own act. She finishes decently and stands in position with Sara Rudner for "Shreveport Stomp." It starts with a bang and they fly off on separate paths. Rudner falls dead once, twice. Rudner and Wright now become the comedy sensation of the year. Here is the measuring tape. Here are the off-beat claps and stomps ("Betcha can't!" "Betcha can!"). When the dance ends, they drop it like a used-up toy and walk away; there is no freeze-pose for applause.

Sara Rudner's blues solo is next. It's the most beautiful thing in the whole piece. Rudner is a fine round lyrical dancer, slipping bonelessly into her turns and out again. Her dance is a ribbon of such spiraling movement; the hip-wiggles and shoulder-shakes are ironic, subtle rather than juicy. It's the other side of her style, the side that goes with her grave bearing and rosebud face. This curvilinear soft-shoe ends and we are into insanity, a *very* fast rag in which three dancers again create, as in *The Fugue*, the sensation of a crowded dance floor. And then, from far offstage right and not exactly on cue, come straggling two more members of the cast. They're too early and have to go back. All right, *now*. And all of them are on, but the dance is over.

Five dancers become a funeral. The music is downhearted, a leaden thump, too defeated for words. It's Twyla's turn and she's loaded: sick, filthy drunk. She's flat on her nose and can't get up. She's up and off balance, legs spraddling, knees sinking, keeling and careening the length of the stage. The cortège passes, an icy current. She is staring up now; surely the sky is falling. The music makes a two-beat cadence and stops. Another and stops. How can she get off? No way. A silence. She makes one more desperate fling. The last two-beat cadence nearly catches her, but she's off.

Three sextets follow. In the next-to-last, there is a statuesque parade across the back of the stage as one dancer, then another, breaks out against the group. They are all glamorous. The last number, "If Someone Would Love Me," is six solos, a discothèque scene. We descend to total anonymity, no smiles now. One by one, the dancers leave the stage. A spotlight is killed on each exit, and at the end the stage is in darkness. The sky does fall, and the sweet night rolls on.

Since the great age of virtuoso tap-dancing ended in the 1940's, most of the jazz dancing we have seen has been some form of souped-up, thrust-pelvis ballet, and this has been true, for the most part, whether the choreographers were black or white. *Eight Jelly Rolls* is a complete break with that ersatz tradition. It puts the humanity back into jazz dancing, and the humor, but this considerable triumph is only a part of what Twyla Tharp has accomplished. I think it's a great jazz piece, dynamite; but the most impressive thing about it is that Twyla Tharp brought it off without breaking stride in her own development as a choreographer. Although it is more conventionally arranged than most of her pieces have been (here I mean floor plan, exits and entrances, the handling of the ensemble in relation to the soloists, etc.—all of which strike me as brilliant by any standard), it is a typical Tharp construction. In a way, it "proves" the strength of this singularly unemotional, objective art of hers, an art that can absorb jazz without getting carried away by it, that can release and even galvanize the senses without ever slipping into self-indulgence or going out of control.

"Avant-garde," with its connotations of élitism, is, I think, a miserably inadequate term of description for Twyla Tharp's special atmosphere of novelty. I should prefer to call this atmosphere baroque, bearing in mind that the original meaning of "baroque" was "bizarre." Her love of paradox, of radical possibility and permutation, is a challenge to any lively audience. It makes the bond of communication one of a mutual respect for form. Years ago, James Agee criticized the makers of a famous avant-garde film for "underestimating the audience and the difficult, considerable art of entertaining." Twyla Tharp's position on the leading edge of modern dance represents a flight from its banalities. It also represents, I think, an impatience with minority cliquishness and discontent. She's farther out than most people, but in many ways she's closer to home.

—*Winter 1971*

The Relevance of Robbins

What now seems to happen is this appalling thing of artists asking themselves "Is this relevant for 1971?" Well, it may be important what I wrote at the age of sixty-four, but it's absolutely unimportant what I write in 1971. This slavery to the moment is far more tyrannous than any other constructions I can think of. The artist ceases to ask the personal question of "What is right for me to do?" and asks instead, "What is right for 1971?"

—W. H. AUDEN, *interviewed in* The New York Times, *October 18, 1971*

I have never before noticed anything Japanese about the sensibility or the imagination of Jerome Robbins, yet I wasn't surprised when *Watermill* appeared on the stage of the State Theatre decked out in the trappings of Nōh drama. In terms of its style, *Watermill* is the most pretentious Robbins production yet and the most banal in terms of its subject matter, and if it really is the personal testament that its admirers take it for—personal in the sense of autobiographical—then it is even worse than I think it is. It's not that I'm unable to relate the events depicted on the stage to Robbins's life—I haven't got any information on Robbins's life—it's that I'm unable to relate them to anyone's life. The ballet is almost frighteningly anonymous; its basis in human experience is so solemnly universalized that it rings false at every moment.

The Nōh treatment is one of the "universal" touches, and it also lends a certain authority to the total effect of austere contemplation and ritual and suspended time that Robbins wants to create. Actually, time isn't so much suspended as it is manipulated in strained ambiguities that have nothing to do with Nōh. The paradoxical time checks that Robbins provides aren't real bafflers; they're just mutual cheats. The ballet, which is almost wholly performed in slow motion, lasts about an hour. In the course of the action, a year passes or maybe just a month. Or maybe just a day. A moon rises and sets; it also waxes and wanes. Two of the episodes are flashbacks to spring and summer—i.e., the childhood and youth of the hero; when we return to the present, it is autumn, and the piece ends with intimations of winter, or old age. All this playing around with calendar and clock time is deceptive. Robbins, in placing the cycle of a man's life against the cycle of nature, has worked hard to intrigue us, but he hasn't ensnared us. I think he may have intended a meditation on sterility, but it is the ballet that comes up sterile. The slow-motion pace, the long periods of stillness work on the audience's nerves rather than on its imagination; you do more waiting than watching, and as you piece the fragments of the narrative together, you may wonder at the inordinateness of it all. Do these programmatic events really add up to an experience in the life of a man—any man? If someone sent you a Rod McKuen lyric through the mail, one syllable at a time, it might indeed seem like haiku, and for days on end.

It's interesting that such a "controversial" piece as *Watermill* is not discussed in terms of its content but only in terms of its style. Perhaps that's because the style is not just a mask that prevents us from getting at what the piece is about, but a mask of a mask. Most people are aware that Robbins has used two types of stylization and overlapped them so that the piece is both Japanese-medieval and American-contemporary at the same time. The tendency, therefore, is to assume that some latent meaning exists in *Watermill*—something having to do with time—that is common to the two worlds Robbins has joined. This is foolish and dangerous nonsense. Kyoto and New York may meet, but not here. The profound poetic correspondence that is said to have been discovered by Robbins is nothing more than a superficial resemblance exploited by him.

He gets plenty of play out of the resemblance and a nice array of double exposures. Water Mill, for example, is a beach town on

Long Island and, as they say, "may or may not" be the scene of the ballet. There are long moments when the set, with its austere clumps of marsh grass (wheat? barley? corn?), its waxing and waning moon, and with people poling across the back of the stage as if on rafts, seems straight out of the film *Ugetsu*. The amorphous score composed by Teiji Ito, a Tokyo-born New Yorker, and played by his group from a corner of the stage, sounds like arty film music. There are even sound effects—barking dogs, an airplane engine. Robbins doesn't follow Nōh forms very closely; he uses them because they are convenient to his purpose and because they are emotionally attractive to him, as they are to many Westerners. Americans in particular feel reverent toward the theatres and civilizations of the East—they even like to feel emptily reverent. (One had only to attend the last New York season of the Kabuki—sold out—to know just how far this can go. Thousands of people in the upper reaches of the City Center, who couldn't see, hear, or understand a thing, mystically applauding with the downstairs house a timeless wonder.) There could not have been many in the audience at the State Theatre with the heart or the learning to upbraid Robbins for his aesthetic blunders in *Watermill*, in which Nōh devices are mixed into the general atmosphere like so many tatami mats at a rug sale; and, besides, we know by his program note that he means no harm: "The ballet . . . is influenced by the music and theatre of the East. However, its world, people and events are not construed as Oriental." "Not construed" is odd wording. I think it is Robbins saying, "I know what I'm doing here, I know I'm not Japanese." All right. And yet why do it Japanese? Why, if we are only about as far east as East Hampton, set up this ambiguity in the first place?

When Western artists throw off the forms of Western dance and drama and turn eastward, as Yeats did in some of his plays and Martha Graham in some of her dances, it is because they feel disinherited by them, but anything less than this sense of a compulsive aesthetic choice and we are faced with mere theatrical coquetry. The Oriental setting may reflect Robbins's own confusion about the expressive method he is using in *Watermill* or it may be a strategic decision. Beneath the Orientalia is an attempt to create something in the way of the contemporary New York–American avant-garde ritual theatre. The nearest things to *Watermill* are the static evening-long pantomimes staged at the Brooklyn Academy by Robert

Wilson. The second of these, *Deafman Glance*, was given in Paris last year, wringing from Louis Aragon the appropriately pleonastic tribute "I never saw anything more beautiful in the world since I was born." There's nothing Japanese about Wilson either, so far as I can see. To me, his work is distinctly European, a throwback to the Surrealism of fifty years ago. In a Wilson play, the stage will generally be crowded with scenes of activity, the action in each scene inching along at the pace of a glacier. Men in dress suits appear along with men in frogs' heads. A handkerchief-headed Negro plays the "Moonlight" Sonata. To men like Aragon, it seems a dream come true, the fulfillment of a prophecy, Surrealism re-born as a living allegory of the seventies. (How can he, who helped stuff the pantheon with live heroes, recognize them in Wilson's ceremonial waxworks?) He rhapsodizes with the innocence of his seventy-five years the relevance of this gaudy diorama to *our* time, not his, and in this way he—unconsciously, to be sure—makes clearer than anyone yet has the psychic connection that exists be-tween obsessively slow, repetitive motion and the perennial amnesia of the avant-garde. His description of time passing in *Deafman Glance* is accurate:

> *Imagine that there is also a problem of time, with the human being as clock: these boys there, and those girls, who pass at the deepest limits of the stage and of the unknown . . . is it a beach, a track . . . as a simple runner goes from left to right and right to left, and perpetual return, and who serves as the clock of human time; or else these fish-men crawling on their bellies in the fore-front of the stage, elbows for fins, from one side to the other of the theatre, and then beginning again; or even the time object— a chair which takes longer than four hours to descend from the height of the balconies to the floor, at the end of a rope. No, Distinguished Professors, it is not surrealism, that is to say, for you something to be classified, a subject for a thesis, for a class at the Sorbonne, no, no, no. But it is the dream of what we were; it is the future which we were foretelling.**

It isn't often that one of the Grand Old Men of Surrealism will say such things about a made-in-America product. However, the man who said "Everything changes except the avant-garde" makes

---

* "Open Letter to André Breton, on *Deafman Glance*, Art, Science and Freedom," by Aragon, *Les Lettres françaises*, June 2, 1971.

more sense to me at the moment. Avant-gardists who always want to go back and do it again, just as if no one remembered anything, are taking longer and longer to go about their business. Those who last the night out at one of Wilson's events usually speak of *one* rewarding moment of "pure theatre"—a handkerchief-head chorus in *The Life and Times of Sigmund Freud*, an ape chorus in *Deafman Glance*. A long run for a short slide. *Watermill* is not long at all by avant-garde standards, and not even very boring, again by those standards. By any other—which is to say, more useful—standards, it is pretty bad but not as bad as *Les Noces* or *The Goldberg Variations*, two ballets I cannot bring myself to see again. Is being non-entertained preferable to being over-entertained? It's certainly less painful. Actually, underneath all the fancy wrappings, *Watermill,* is a conventional and quite painless experience—it's *palatably* boring. Knowing that Robbins has interested himself for some years in the work of Wilson, knowing that he appeared on one occasion in the title role of *Sigmund Freud*, I expected more things to happen on the model of those Brooklyn evenings than in fact did happen.

Still, quite a lot of things happened. Robbins borrows from Wilson the slow motion and the gloomy-sweet mortuary look of the stage picture; he even borrows certain elements—the boys and girls on the is-it-a-beach, the "simple runner [who] goes from left to right and from right to left." He has, in fact, produced a foreshortened and somewhat bowdlerized version of a typical Wilsonian spectacle and impulsively drawn a discreet Japanese veil over it. In place of Wilson's heterogeneous assembly of frog-men and fish-men and Southern mammies, there are tillers and sowers and reapers in coolie hats. There is Eastern order, Eastern mystique, Eastern *time*. There is, at any rate, the illusion of all those things, and I think the illusion is what counts. The Eastern overlay is no more crucial to an understanding of *Watermill* than it is to Balanchine's *Bugaku* or Ashton's *Madame Chrysanthème* or the other bits of ballet japonaiserie that one could mention. *Watermill*, however, is different from those ballets in one important respect: it is an antidance, anti-motion ballet whose technical origins in New York Dada Robbins seems to have felt the need to disguise. His impulse—I call it an impulse, although it may have been calculation pure and simple—was to substitute a prestigious order of tackiness for a defunct one. That hanging chair (a hanging *chair!*) has become an Oriental moon. Was this only because he wanted to work uptown and for the big

Lincoln Center audience, or does he really feel he has this height-ened-consciousness, static-motion business of ritual theatre "placed" better than Wilson has with his old-time Surrealist lumberyard? Whatever Robbins is "into" in *Watermill*, he is not into it very far. The suggestion that some basic relationship exists between Robbins's musings and the time sense of Asian music and dance surely helps him more than it does us. His notion of this time sense seems to go no further than the idea that any commonplace action will take on a heavy significance if it is performed slowly enough. Yet in a strange way the strong Japanese identification marks make *Watermill* more acceptable to a certain kind of New York audience than it would have been without them. The question of where we are in the piece if *not* in medieval Japan is as naïve as the symbolism that runs through it. We are where Robbins thinks he should be just now. We are not at the old address; we are far out, culturally relocated, flying new flags, keeping up with the Zeitgeist. Must we ask where *Watermill* is? It's in Cross-Cultureland; and insofar as it perpetuates and plays up to the cultural confusion and semiconscious snobbery that is reflected in the values, tastes, and what I suppose we have to call the life-style of so many fashionable New Yorkers, it is a per-fectly disgusting piece of work.

Like Patricia Zipprodt's costumes, which cannily suggest both Asian bazaar and hippie boutique, Robbins means to have it both ways. *Watermill* is a demonstration of how to stay on your macro-biotic diet and have your schmalz, too. In this "innovative," "experimental" piece, Robbins indicates calendar time in the manner of calendar art—by having peasants pass across the back of the stage sowing when it's spring, reaping when it's fall, and generally tilling till ready. My mother used to have calendars like that hang-ing in the pantry, with scenes from Millet, and the phases of the moon printed on every date. As a skeleton key to *Watermill*, a pantry calendar won't work, although it does come close to suggest-ing the kind of cornball symbolism the piece is made of. The pro-tagonist is a man who pauses in the middle of life's journey to review his past. This includes seeing himself as a child doing fancy leaps to tinkling music while the chorus flies kites. Then, in an A. E. Hous-man-like interlude, he sees a vision of fair youths running in some athletic meet. With phallic batons (or knives—they could also be hunters) they poke the earth. One of the runners, presumably the hero as a young man, returns to re-enact Sexual Encounter with

Woman (anal penetration), and this is followed by an episode involving another hero-surrogate and homosexual rape or perhaps castration. After these flashbacks to spring and summer, we have the mature hero facing his hour of crisis. There is a harvest scene during which a passing peasant ceremoniously hands him two long stalks of grass, which he accepts in an X across his shoulders. From the cruciform position, he gradually manipulates the stalks in a slow dance of affirmation and acceptance. Snow starts to fall. Four figures from his past return—the child, the woman, and two of the runners —and withdraw. In the final scene, old age enters in the form of a bent hag with a cane, whom the hero acknowledges with a bow. He resumes his journey. As the curtain falls, big paper bundles are released into the air, like Magritte's floating rock. Experience is a burden no longer.

If there were anything to this tedious hokum, there might be some point in raising questions about the less obvious goings-on. For example, who is the second runner (Robert Maiorano) and why is it he who returns toward the end rather than the victim of the rape/castration (Victor Castelli)? Who are the creatures with the plumes (Deni Lamont, Colleen Neary) dancing through the snow? But these occasional obscurities arise only in contrast to the numbing predictability of everything else. The Christian-Freudian symbols, the Martha Graham-style props and frame-of-memory format are so facile and familiar that one's curiosity isn't even aroused. One just sits there dutifully ticking off déjà-vus. Must we have that clinical-demonstration pas de deux yet again? And that other staple of shock theatre, the homosexual rape? The only novelty is that, except for one or two sequences, it all happens in slow motion.

In stylized theatre at its greatest (like Nōh or Western classical ballet), a dramatic statement and its presentation are inseparable. When we look for the dramatic core of *Watermill*, we find that it is not contained in its method of presentation. The protracted nuances, the slow pace, the visual monotony do not constitute a new form, but, rather, the intense scrutiny of an old one—decomposing fifth-rate Graham theatre. The material can't bear the pressure Robbins puts on it. The third layer of *Watermill* (under its Eastern layer and its simulated avant-garde layer) is one more surface; under that —nothing. In a way, the Christian-Freudian-Grahamesque themes-symbols-techniques are Robbins's subject, substituting, by virtue of his fascination with them, for a true subject. The story of the man who becomes reconciled to his life as part of the natural process is not the true subject but a sentimental correlative of this sort of theatre, and that's why it's so phony and mechanical and "universal" and dull. It just happens automatically, like fag-end Graham—gestures invoked for the sake of the meanings they once had. Robbins even uses gestures for meanings they never had, as when he has Villella, after ten minutes of standing and mooning about the stage, do a slow-motion strip down to a white satin bikini. What is this bit of Broadway glitz doing in a serious, advanced, "innovative" work of art? And what can be made of the moment when Robbins brings on the Woman?

There are theatrical archetypes and then there are theatrical stereotypes, conceptions so crushingly unoriginal that the mind drops its assemblage and sits down in disbelief. In Robbins's *Afternoon of a Faun*, when the boy reaches out to stroke the girl's hair, or later, when he kisses her on the cheek, we let the incidents pass as "classic"; and though the emphasis that Robbins places on the kiss has always seemed to me disproportionate (after what the involvement of their bodies has told them about each other, what could a mere kiss mean to this boy and girl?), it doesn't really disturb our picture of a dreamy, narcissistic world. In *Watermill*, the Woman (Penny Dudleston) lets down her long and yellow hair, and then the Woman *combs* her long and yellow hair, stroke upon stroke, slowly, deliberately, caressively . . . as Villella gapes from his end of the beach. The image is beyond the classic—it's "mythic" in the hokiest sense. It doesn't even get us over to the territory of a Renoir or Degas *baigneuse*, because Miss Dudleston's face and figure and hair suggest nothing so much as those languorous models who toss their locks in TV shampoo commercials. Is Robbins being witty? But no, he means it: this is Woman, this is Nausicaä, this is Narcissa, and he rams in the point by having someone dressed as a peacock cross upstage during the Hair Scene.

And why not a peacock? We have all these other bulbous conceits—the old hag standing for old age, lanterns that shed the light of truth, Calvary, the fructifying earth, the eternal peasants—why not one more? Robbins, who once danced in the corps of Ballet Theatre and who made a breakthrough modern ballet in *Fancy Free*, was quoted then as saying, "I got tired of being an ear of wheat." Well, now he's back to being an ear of wheat.

It has occurred to me that the three big sheaves of grass that decorate the stage might be hemp, and that Villella's long solo with the two stalks might be a celebration of cannabis. This provides a crude kind of justification for the strange drugged consciousness of the ballet, but you have to be desperate to think of what these possibilities can add to its interest. (Maybe then the snow is heroin and Lamont and Neary are pushers?)

Robbins has had the "brilliant" idea of having Edward Villella, the most physically exciting man in the American theatre, move extremely slowly or remain motionless for long periods. It doesn't work—not because Villella hasn't the physical control needed for the part, but because he is unable to relax on the stage and dominate it simply by his presence. Villella brings to the part the same air of overdefended masculine dignity that has been so oppressive in some of his other roles, notably *Bugaku* and *Dances at a Gathering*. He's so concerned with projecting his virility that he seems insincere whenever he isn't dancing. Ostentatious virility on the stage is as offensive in its way as ostentatious effeminacy, and though Villella doesn't go to the pushy extremes of Luis Fuente, his lack of ease has become as much of a problem as it is a mystery. Villella at his best in his greatest roles (*Rubies, Tarantella, Harlequinade,* Oberon in *A Midsummer Night's Dream*) has been supremely wholesome, tough, exuberant, and cocky. At less than his best, he throbs like a sexy steam cabinet. If Fuente is the Anthony Quinn of the ballet, Villella is its Kirk Douglas. Robbins, by calling on the Byronic and brooding qualities that Villella has sometimes displayed—qualities that seem to me to have been largely faked in the interests of giving big "star" performances—hasn't helped him at all, and it would be hard to think of any other credibly male dancer in the world today who could get through that disrobing scene in *Watermill* without embarrassment.

For Robbins as for Villella, *Watermill* is perhaps a tour de force of self-negation; it represents some sort of desire to start again at ground zero and move off in an unfamiliar direction. Neither artist succeeds, and in Robbins's case, disaster is complete. At fifty-three, he has given us a glib, trendy picture-puzzle, as conventionally sentimental in spirit as it is glossily "revolutionary" in style. Robbins has never seemed more of a lightweight. By contrast, *Gypsy,* the best of the Robbins-directed musicals and the best Broadway show I ever saw, is a masterpiece of poetic theatre and radical design. *Watermill* isn't self-negation, it's self-deception. Is this what happens when an artist suppresses his sense of humor in a grim effort to succeed at Serious Art? I'm not suggesting that Robbins should stick to the lightweight stuff, nor am I simple-minded enough to suppose that because he's so good at comedy he ought to be impervious to the fraudulent allure of "masterpiece" art. But I am unable to understand how a lively and sophisticated man of the theatre succumbs to the essentially antitheatrical, anti-audience spirit that Robbins shows in his increasing commitment to monotony and excess. *Watermill* seems to be part of a pattern.

Every work that Robbins has done since returning to the New York City Ballet has been a tour de force of some sort, deliberately taxing the audience's power of concentration. The NYCB audience, used to having its powers taxed by scenically impoverished stages, might be said to be the perfect audience for these experiments. *Dances at a Gathering* has become an international hit, yet even in New York it still seems too long. I would like to see it cut by fifteen minutes—though not the same fifteen minutes—at every performance. *In the Night* is again Chopin. It is not a long ballet, but it is a severely restricted one: all nocturnes, all pas de deux. Robbins has not used the ballet orchestra once, except in his revival this season of *The Concert*, in which the orchestra is heard only intermittently. His décor tends to projections, his costumes to the interchangeable and undistinguished designs of Joe Eula. Eula's costumes actually detract from *The Goldberg Variations*, turning the raison d'être of the piece into a gigantic cliché. The business of the dancers' switching from twentieth- to eighteenth-century drag or vice versa is just a scholastic platitude—"Bach Our Contemporary."

Partly because of the costumes, which illuminate nothing, *Goldberg* is ninety minutes at hard labor. For a work of this size not to have a subject other than what the eighteenth-century music may suggest to the twentieth-century eye and mind of Robbins is—for Robbins—a daring proposition. Robbins working without recourse to story, scenery, and orchestra, and working, moreover, with one of the most exacting and complicated scores in the keyboard repertory, is Robbins working under great and obvious strain. For things like this to come out properly, they must suggest irresistibly the rightness and inevitability and therefore the supreme ease of their conception; they must persuade us that all the resources of theatre are aptly concentrated in one medium of expression—they can't just "do without." Above all, they must give us something to take away from the theatre—some image—that we didn't have when we came in. The trouble with *Goldberg* is that it doesn't exist as a ballet. When Robbins has wrestled every last musical repeat to the mat, we don't come away with a theatrical experience but with an impression of endless ingenious music-visualizations, some of which —like the exquisite dance for Gelsey Kirkland and the many good variations for the boys—stick in the mind but most of which fade away like skywriting.

There's something curiously half-hearted and abortive about *Goldberg*; it seems to draw back from the audience that might have responded to it most—the young audience that flocked to Béjart a year ago. However much Robbins may deny it, *Dances at a Gathering* possesses a story *idea* (if not a story) in its suggestion of communal relations. Although I can't get interested in this aspect of it, a lot of people who like *Dances* like it most for that. It seems to me that the same idea of communal relations appears in *Goldberg* with an extension into a more private and personal world in the second part, when the focus is on the three couples. In *Goldberg*, the canvas is large and crowded; we lose the individual in the mass, and I presume the loss is intentional. The emphasis may fall on anyone; a corps member may shine like a star. In a way, *Goldberg* improves upon Paul Draper's method of democratizing Bach's music by tap-dancing to it—it makes Bach a vast sounding board for a collective morale, and though I find the morale sticky, it gives me something to look at. (I'm speaking of the first part of the ballet; the second part, which is like a week in a suburban domestic-relations court, puts me to sleep.) But the ballet doesn't round out this particular picture—or any other. It loses its way, and the ending is a blitz of surefire ballet routines. I don't believe that *Goldberg* would have been better if Robbins hadn't evaded a subject, but I believe it would have been a *ballet* rather than a Bach recital, and certainly the young people who might have been encouraged to see something of themselves in it would have had a chance to see some good choreography and dancing, too. They didn't get that at Béjart.

Goldberg seems to flirt with the youth culture and then pull back as if unwilling to hand it so massive a victory as the conquest of Bach. (Bach would have survived.) Robbins's own cultural attitudes may be unresolved—I think cultural irresolution shows glaringly in *Watermill*—or he may not care to make himself so accessible as an artist. He has, I think, a yearning to remain elusive, uncategorizable.

He seems to select aspects of himself to suit the occasion: comedy relief, high serious art, Broadway shows. Now that he is working in the ballet exclusively, each project must test a separate area of his virtuosity. *Watermill*, long and static with lots of production, follows *Goldberg*, long and active and raw. And within the context of each work he is subdividing himself, simultaneously pressing forward and pulling back, antagonizing the audience, consoling the audience, canceling himself out, seeking extinction and salvation at the same time. No matter what style the piece is in, the same emptiness yawns from within. And, meanwhile, the constant process of self-revision eats away at the stabilizing elements of personality. After *Watermill*, it is a question just who Jerome Robbins is. I believe that he is fatally attracted to pretentious undertakings—more so now, it seems, than in the days when he used to balance every Broadway hit with a *Facsimile*, an *Age of Anxiety*, or a *New York Export: Opus Jazz*. In those ballets, which earned him points with the highbrows, and especially in *New York Export*, he could still hold the stage with movement, transform it with a touch. The man is like a Houdini of stagecraft, and he seems now to have grown tired of his magic, tired or afraid. In the sense that his technique is a part of him, as much a part of his being as his nervous system, he has grown tired—or afraid—of himself. Perhaps he hoped that by entertaining stasis as a serious theatrical proposition he could construct something utterly unlike himself. A new Robbins, perhaps, would emerge.

This spring *Fiddler on the Roof* becomes the longest-running hit in the history of the American theatre. And *Watermill*—controversial," "difficult," "innovative," "unique"—goes into a second season with the New York City Ballet. The anonymity of a true virtuoso.

—Spring 1972

PART FOUR

On Occasion

The Pleasure of Their Company

With no plot that you can pin a notion to, many of Balanchine's ballets have a festive atmosphere like great parties where everyone behaves charmingly and has a wonderful time. The garden parties of *Divertimento No. 15* and *Raymonda Variations,* the baronial pomp of *Theme and Variations* and *Ballet Imperial,* the gathering of the clans in *Scotch Symphony* (and the "Scottish" reel in the third movement of *Symphony in C*), the hoedown of *Western Symphony,* the Gypsy Rondo of *Brahms-Schoenberg Quartet*—the festivities are practically endless. *Bourrée Fantasque* is the perfect ballet for New Year's Eve. The whirl of high spirits is so irresistible as the piece moves to a climax that, when the curtain comes up for applause, you wonder why the floor isn't littered with the confetti and champagne corks you've been seeing in your mind.

Yet the actual party scenes that Balanchine has staged for his story ballets are likely to be less effervescent, stranger, and more troubling by far in their sensations than these ballets of pure dancing. They are full of disturbing, violent, and even grisly happenings. The mood of *La Sonnambula,* where a poet arrives unannounced at a masked ball, is rich with menace. The poet dies, stabbed in the belly by his jealous host. In *La Valse,* a girl is danced to death and the whole of society pitches crazily after her into the abyss. What looks to the Prodigal Son like the fun of happy voluptuaries turns into a sickening orgy in which he is systematically degraded, beaten, and robbed. Act II of *Don Quixote,* the reception in the Duke's palace, is utterly black, and its grimness is not offset by a dance divertissement which is—most of it—freely sensual but heartless in expression: a dance of pagans reminding us how far, in his confused idealism, the Don has come in his journey out of Catholic Spain. (The resemblance to episodes in both *La Sonnambula* and *The Prodigal Son* is obvious.)

Liebeslieder Walzer is also a party—an all-dance party for four couples at a private house. It is entirely free of incident, and although the mood is ebulliently social in the first half, intimate and dream-like in the second, it contains for those who care to find it a persistent note of melancholy and tragic remorse. I have never been able to experience the rise of the second curtain, on those girls now suddenly frozen on toepoint, without a tightening of the heart. The piano ripples in an upward scale, the pose breaks, and the action begins again at twice the speed of anything up to that point. The toeshoes, the flying lifts give everything extra momentum, and the gesture seems redoubled in size and sharpness. What's odd is that the new sweep and scale of movement don't bring a sense of liberation; they bring a sense of anxiety, maybe because the theatrical tension has been heightened. Something conversational in the tone of the ballet has been replaced by something incantatory and solemn, just as the furniture and candlelight have been replaced by wind and stars. And how wonderfully the change is prepared for, in the last dance of the first scene, as the dancers first break out in listening attitudes, then rush past each other, throwing up their arms in an intoxication of surrender. At that moment, the whole room seems stirred by a fresh breeze like a summons and to be giving itself over to the deepest part of the night. And it may be, too, that what enters the room when the dancers all leave it and the curtain drops is still there when we discover them in Part II, in their pure element of space and time.

But even before this second part of the ballet—the "ballet" part of *Liebeslieder*, when Eros turns to them its other large and at times inscrutable face—we feel that the dancers are involved in something more than a dance—that they're getting more and more deeply into a drama about men and women in love. The Verdy-Magallanes relationship is tragic from the start and has been celebrated by admirers of the ballet for ten years. But the other relationships are no less dramatically charged, although they can be more freely interpreted. More striking than individuals, though, is the drama of the group. The women all make impossible demands on the men—they're powerful, variable, difficult creatures, and the men in turn want them to be, want to submit to their divine inconsistency, to treat them as both goddesses *and* toys. It would be too brutal to speak of the key situation of *Liebeslieder* as an unconscious contest for power in sexual relations, but something like that is close to the surface of its erotic tension, and because the characters are helpless and noble and accepting, it is close to tragedy, too. And if all this is just a fancy of mine, then I don't mind being struck with it, or with other theories that have got into my head, such as that the house where the party is held is Conrad Ludlow's and that Kay Mazzo is not really in love with him.

I have probably exaggerated the sorrows of *Liebeslieder* to the discomfort of those who love it for its beautiful virtuosity and decorous charm (but for whom the final song, with Goethe's text which speaks of art's inability to portray "how misery and happiness alternate in a loving heart," can then have no irony), but it would be hard to exaggerate the bitterness of *La Sonnambula* or the hysteria of *La Valse*. These deliberately melodramatic and richly morbid spectacles are in the vein first proposed to Balanchine by Boris Kochno, Diaghilev's librettist and later Balanchine's collaborator in the Blum–de Basil company and in Les Ballets 1933. Of the two Balanchine-Kochno productions mounted for the final season of the Ballets Russes in 1929, *Prodigal Son* survives. The other ballet was *Le Bal*, with sets and costumes by De Chirico. *Le Bal* seems to have set the pattern for the Balanchine *fête noire*, having as its direct descendants *Cotillon* (1932), *La Sonnambula* (or *Night Shadow*, 1946), and *La Valse* (1951). *Le Bal* was basically a series of divertissements at a masked ball, linked by the thread of a romance between Anton Dolin and Alexandra Danilova, who in the end unmasks twice, revealing first a hideous old hag and then a beautiful young girl. Of *Cotillon*, the most affectionately remembered of Balanchine's unsurviving works, Lincoln Kirstein wrote in 1935: "If Balanchine never read Proust, it is of no importance. He absorbed from Chabrier's brilliant music the acrid perfume of adolescence; divinity felt by young dancers at their first ball, heady with their own youth, shyness and insecurity, masking it all in false boredom, and the frightened indifference of aching wall-flowers at a heartbreak ball." In a famous passage called "The Hand of Fate," a woman guest in black gloves forces a young man to dance with her. The woman is a vampire in disguise. This conceit of Kochno's returns, in *La Valse*, in the figure of Death, along with the black gloves and the finale, in which the company surrounds the heroine in a rushing circle. *Cotillon* was set by its designer, Christian Bérard, in a mansion ballroom ringed by a tier of boxes; the cut of the women's gowns inspired Karinska's costumes in *La Valse*. Although it was revived only once, by the Original Ballet Russe in 1940, it has lingered to haunt the repertory in other ballets besides *La Valse* —notably in the second movement of *Bourrée Fantasque* and in one of the *Trois Valses Romantiques* which actually is *Cotillon* music rechoreographed. (*Trois Valses Romantiques*, one of the most underrated ballets in the current repertory, uses pianos on the stage to set a party atmosphere that doesn't, for reasons Christian Bérard would have understood, quite jell. In any event, it's clear what Balanchine thinks of when he hears Chabrier—he thinks of giving a party.)

La Valse, the *Cotillon* of the fifties, is not a heartbreak ball; it is a Vanity Fair encompassing the death-wish of an egregiously permissive society. As in *La Sonnambula*, the horrible dénouement comes not altogether as a surprise. And it really is horrible, although we're permitted to be amused by a good deal of what comes before, in the first section of the ballet, which is set to Ravel's "Valses Nobles et Sentimentales." The whole social world of the ballet is conveyed in those three girls we see when the curtain rises. They are standing on the threshold of life, tingling with erotic expectancy. They hide their eyes to avoid the fate of which they are such knowing, yet such uncaring mistresses. With their conformist, lah-di-dah sophistication, they're a little comical, yet the music is caressive and tender, and as they drift about the stage, making elegant chit-chat, we see that they're really desirable, too. A few moments later, we see another girl, dressed all in white, exactly like those three but somehow more vulnerable, more challenging. Maybe she doesn't understand what she's doing, maybe she does. She finds a good-looking man with the right touch of fashionable cynicism to amuse her. Together they go to the ball.

At first, we don't know which of the young people we've seen in the prologue to watch for the story of the ballet. The cast includes some fresher, more hopeful boys and girls, but they look a bit simple. It notably includes a young man, a rash young romantic, who drops his date (or is dropped by her) to tangle luxuriously with the three fates, now implacable in their desire. He thinks they're everything a boy could want. He can't choose among them. He does three giddy renversé turns, then another, and bolts out into the night.

The Waltz itself begins like a movie out of focus. It is very dark, and everything is in disarray. Jean Rosenthal's skeletal drapes and candelabra are a Doré-ish ink splotch floating in a sea of bile. We still don't know where to look. Dancers—one, then two and three —cross and recross the stage like swallows. A boy arrives looking for his partner. On a sudden premonition, he turns and a spotlight picks out the deadly trio standing completely still at the back of the stage. (Have they been there all along?) Again they are blind, one arm covering their eyes, the other flung to the heavens. They look like crosses in a graveyard. He approaches and they seize him.

Now a line of boys runs on, and with them, in this movie that is still running, we scan some mysteriously far-off horizon, which begins to pitch and dip as if in a landing on the moon. Then, as the mists clear, a line of girls; they find the boys just in time, for with a mighty crescendo the stage suddenly rights itself, we touch down, and everything coalesces in a smash of *luxe, calme et volupté*. But only for a moment.

I've cited this magical opening of *La Valse* proper, not only because of its sensuous excitement and optical brilliance, but because of what it accomplishes—a plunge across time that links the restlessness of modern society with the rich fantasy and fatalism of another century. *La Valse* sets contemporary manners in counterpoint to the agitated spirit of the Romantic era. Those twin epidemics, infatuation with the Waltz and infatuation with death, are transferred to a modern locale—a party that might be happening in 1951 in Oyster Bay. Karinska's dresses, with their tight bodices and cinched waists, reflect the "cocktail-length formals" of the fifties; they are based on Bérard's star-speckled gauzy skirts just as Bérard's were based on the long muslin tutus of the Sylphides. And then Death walks in the door dressed in an 1820's cutaway. Why not? Ravel is ironic. So is Balanchine. So, said Dostoevsky, is death. Francisco Moncion might be the ghost of Comte de Salvandy (whose epigram, "We are dancing on the edge of a volcano," Ravel adopted for his mock-Straussian score) returned from his age of apocalypse to warn a society that thinks it's got everything, especially the sense to snicker at his approach. The ballet *La Valse* has sometimes aroused snickers—not in the audience; in reviews. And it certainly has a fat element of kitsch. But maximal sophistication always looks like naïveté to the truly naïve, and Balanchine can sweep together original inspiration and kitsch and still come out with a pure product. So Death does his job on the Girl in White (does she expect it? does she *want* it?), and we watch, I think, rather coldly, for a curious crossing of sympathies has taken place. Though we've long since picked her out as the heroine, we've switched away from her viewpoint to that of the young man she came with, now rudely disburdened of his cynicism. Yet if he were to tell us about it afterward, he might say, "I went to this party and met this crazy girl." That's the kind of material *La Valse* is made of —real hellfire under red cellophane.

I've mentioned Boris Kochno, who contributed much to twentieth-century ballet besides his work with the young Balanchine. Another link in the line of descent is the composer Vittorio Rieti, who wrote the music for *Le Bal*. In 1946, Rieti not only arranged the wonderful Bellini score for *La Sonnambula*, he also wrote the book, with perhaps a nod to *Le Bal* and the gothic taste of Kochno. Again, the setting is a masked ball with a suite of entries: a pastoral pas de quatre, two blackamoors, a harlequin. There are some very peculiar ballroom dances—skittery, frantically social, like the people who dance them. Except for its subject and period (the 1830's), the ballet hasn't anything to do with the operas its music comes from. Bellini's Sleepwalker becomes here a typical Balanchine inamorata, reacting with either conscious or unconscious indifference (you're not sure which) to the Poet who wants as much to manipulate as to adore her. The "loathly lady" theme of *Le Bal* and *Cotillon* returns in the form of the Coquette, whose beauty masks a vicious heart.

This is not, like *La Valse*, an easy ballet to get into. It seems chilly and remote. The tone, apart from the melodramatic aura which invests the plot, is edgy and fitful, scraping along an emotional precipice, threatening always to disintegrate into unintentional comedy. As behavior, whether considered naturalistically or parodistically, the ballet looks at every moment completely absurd. But it never loses its balance and it never, even at the end, rewards an audience's curiosity with solid denial of its suspect nature. It just moves to another part of the precipice and hangs there with a frightened smile as the curtain falls. We *really* don't know whether to laugh or cry.

The world of *La Sonnambula* is so thoroughly objectified—caricatured, even—that its tremendous emotional impact is uncanny, way out of proportion to what we "feel" for the characters. We certainly don't feel anything except fascination for this very distinguished Poet who crashes the party, steals the host's girl, and then assumes he has the run of the place; whose first impulse, when he finds he's met a beautiful woman fast asleep, is to try and control everything she does, as a lover would. Yet in the Sleepwalker pas de deux, the ballet's only direct statement, it is the Poet who is pathetic, not the Sleepwalker. We're suddenly admitted to the privacy of his tortured spirit, to his secret burning for beauty he may not possess. When she eludes his every stratagem and he locks himself about her body, straining with a last desperate effort against her forward motion —and in this, too, is defeated—we feel that it's the story of his life.

But for this moment of intense pain, all is caricature, an insistent statement in genre. The emotion of the ballet comes in a series of nervous shocks, as deeply pleasurable as in a horror story. The ending—is there a finer one in all Romantic ballet?—is high traumatic bliss. The pas-de-deux roles are unthinkably reversed. Now it is the Sleepwalker who claims the inert body of the Poet, accepts it in her arms, and carries it away forever.

The ideas in *La Sonnambula* are perfectly clear derivations from the Romantic ballet of the nineteenth century, but they are outrageous, forced even beyond the neurotic extremism of *Giselle* and *La Sylphide*. The Poet's character as a hero who engages a divine force is not morally shaded. When he dies, he is vindicated, but in a manner that anathematizes not only the explicitly antiromantic society on the stage but all humanity as well. The iron-clad arrogance of the gesture makes the real suffering we've witnessed seem like a personal secret accidentally disclosed. It keeps you at a distance, though you may find yourself in tears.

These are Balanchine's greatest parties for adults. But his most famous party is, of course, in Act I of *The Nutcracker*, and though it's danced for and mostly by children, I think it has a few metaphysical *frissons* in it, too: the magic Christmas tree (which glows eerily the first time you see it), like a living talisman in primitive nature magic; the hints of "evil genius" in the character of Drosselmeier; the odd fantasy of the things that happen in the little girl's dream, like the wandering bed. The trend in most productions of *The Nutcracker* is toward demystifying Drosselmeier and playing up the rats (I can't imagine why; do the producers think a child would rather have horror when he can have mystery?), pulling it all together as a love story about an adolescent girl and a transformed prince. But *The Nutcracker* is a child's Christmas or it is nothing. After years of sitting it out, I now think Act I contains the best of the Balanchine version, matched only by the Waltz of the Flowers and the grand pas de deux of Act II. It's the only one of his parties that uses naturalistic pantomime, and it's the only one that shows us any kind of domestic world—even *Liebeslieder* doesn't. And that world—so ordinary, so secure, and so exactly paced, a rapture of routine—has a special poignance in the context of our modern urban desolation. The annual *Nutcracker* has become a liturgical event, one whose deepest significance we celebrate in our hearts and try to keep our children from knowing. —*Winter 1969*

Balanchine's Girls: The Making of a Style

World's thinnest book: *English and American Literary Men Speak About the Dance.* V. S. Pritchett once wrote a piece putting down ballet as "the most foolish and cruel of the arts." Shaw knew enough to detest the rigid specimens of it that he saw. R. P. Blackmur called the New York City Ballet "a ballet of pinheads" after seeing it several times during its tour of Europe in 1956. Not a very good record. The French have a better one—the best. English and American literary critics all seem to have the same complaint about ballet: that it's inhuman. Few have eyes that see beyond their humanistic prejudices. Fewer care to write about what they do see. Blackmur was so upset by what he saw—it was the period when literate Americans were very much annoyed with America for not being beautiful and wise the way Europe was beautiful and wise— that he wrote a long, sensitive, and profoundly irked essay on national style in the dance.* Naturally, he found nothing in the Americans to praise beyond their proficiency, which was exclusively technical. "There were all those beautiful legs," he wrote, "and no one in the company who could walk except Diana Adams and none but her with a proper face. All the rest of the girls made up a ballet of pinheads."

Blackmur's essay, though a masterpiece of impressionistic writing, comes down to not much more than the standard charge against Balanchine that one heard constantly in those days—the charge that he depersonalized his dancers. One doesn't hear it so often now. One doesn't hear very much at all. The New York City Ballet as a gathering point for literati isn't what it used to be. Yet at this moment, Balanchine has possibly the finest company he's ever had— excellent male dancers (a few of whom, like Jacques d'Amboise and Edward Villella, are great stars who never stop growing) and girls who are astonishing. In Patricia McBride, he has the outstand-

* "The Swan in Zurich."

ing American ballerina of our day. The response to all this is
strangely muted. The odd part of it is that the period when all the
complaints were being filed—the late fifties to early sixties—was
also the period when articulate intellectual enthusiasm for the
company was at a peak. Something was happening in ballet that
was safer not to leave to the balletomanes. New York intellectuals
could look at the company and see themselves. If they saw an abstract landscape, they knew how to fit themselves into it. If they
saw tiny monsters, they knew what to make of that, too.

There's a curious echo of Blackmur in the admiring review that
Igor Stravinsky wrote in 1963 of the choreography for his *Movements for Piano and Orchestra*. Stravinsky remarked on "those
extraordinarily beelike little girls (big thighs, nipped-in waists, pinheads) who seem to be bred according to Balanchine's specifica-
tions." The picture also calls to mind another notable description of
Balanchine dancers—Edwin Denby's in his article on *Agon* written
in 1957 ("They hang in the air like a swarm of girl-size bees"). If
Stravinsky's is an accurate picture of the company, it's also, like
Denby's, an accurate reflection of the music. A long-time mentor
of the company, it was Stravinsky who put Balanchine on the track
of the serialists. And it was his own musical personality that provided
the main clue to expression. (One recalls Lincoln Kirstein's charming caricature of Stravinsky as "a platinum grasshopper scooting
ahead of the pack.") The style Balanchine was then evolving, in
the course of his long struggle to get American girls to stop thinking
and start *dancing*, found one of its logical points of culmination
in the condensed, non-sense-making energy of this music. The style
has since changed—one might say that it leans more to the Tchai-
kovskyan than to the Stravinskyan—but there is a certain look the
company had at one time that it can still sometimes recapture when
called upon to fill a certain expressive need. *Agon* is still, today, in
several important respects what these images evoke: the great impersonal bee-swarm of New York. It's like the minute lashing of the
traffic seen from far away but brought unnaturally close as if with
a telescopic lens; it has all the baffling pressure of that kind of
contradiction. When it was new, people went around quoting
Baudelaire's "fourmillante cité"; the resemblance hasn't faded. On
the other hand, I think the later Stravinsky masterpiece, *Movements*, has lost much of its sting.

As for the bee-girls themselves, it's as if they'd turned into the flowers. With marvelous intuition, Blackmur in 1956 singled out Diana Adams as the only girl who had a face. Of course she had a face—so did the others; but she had a wonderful face and wonderful legs like calipers, and she was a real person in the same sense that Fonteyn and the English ballerinas at Covent Garden were real to Blackmur. She made humanists breathe easier. Yet it was Adams who led the company in the final consolidation of the pinhead style. The groundwork had all been laid by Tanaquil LeClercq, also a real person but more skeletal in her body line, more frangible in temper. LeClercq was a delicious comedienne, too, one of the few genuine wits the company has ever possessed. One felt she enjoyed being a dragonfly or a spiderwoman or a gooneybird—she could make the comedy as well as the drama of it real. But in the late fifties and early sixties, Balanchine's chief instrument was Adams. They were momentous years. Starting with the commissioning of *Agon*, in which Adams had the grand pas de deux, he made a series of ballets to the music Stravinsky continued to write or to recommend, and he developed a generation of young dancers who could do anything this advanced music demanded. These girls didn't seem to think; they acted. They didn't walk; they swam and hovered in balances and dove with a perilous insistence; or they moved one muscle and froze the time they moved it in, as if time, by catching up, might force it to move by itself. Balanchine's choreography in this style, after *Agon* and up through *Movements*, was increasingly microscopic, cellular: tight phrases exploding like crystals in a confined space. Many people believe it derived from the hours of therapy Balanchine spent with his wife, LeClercq, whose muscles had been deadened, and her career cut short, by an attack of polio on that European tour of 1956. But the style was also a uniquely local New York view of things; it wasn't recondite. Like *Concerto Barocco* (Bach, 1941) and *The Four Temperaments* (Hindemith, 1946), the new ballets to the new music seemed to seize on qualities of architectural scale and anatomical deployment that made sense to New Yorkers. And they made sense in an era of affluence. These were richly concentrated, high-protein ballets, with more "grip" per measure than anything that had been seen up to that time. At the huge old City Center, "Twelve-Tone Nights" (as the company billed programs made up of its avant-garde specialties) were always sellouts.

When we first see something new, we don't see all of it at once, we see one part of it and fasten on that. It's the part that looks most like us, the part we can recognize from inside or from what we already know. With a Diana Adams crooking her beautiful length of leg in its female arch of complicity, with an Allegra Kent stretching her spine in kittenlike contortions, Balanchine was able to draw miracles of erotic suggestion from the sparse structures of serial music. Or so it seemed. After one of the first performances of *Agon*, a well-known New York writer said joyfully, "If they knew what was going on here, the police would close it down." But being glad to see sexuality so brilliantly arrayed on the stage is a very different kind of response from seeing dancing. Since its early seasons, the *Agon* pas de deux has been given by many different ballerinas. It has assumed a different content each time, and it has never failed. "Content" —i.e., the energy of the personality who dances—is different from "material," which feeds and directs the flow of energy. Choreographers near and far who for the next dozen years sought to copy *Agon* were misled by their own ideas of its content. They improvised mannerism without material. That's why the international "abstract" style in modern ballet—the thin meanderings and grapplings to thin music—is such a bore. (When Balanchine said, in 1957, "A thin style is our style," he put the rest of the ballet world on concentration-camp rations.) It's probably why, although *Agon* and *Episodes* remain popular, the New York City Ballet doesn't put on "Twelve-Tone" evenings anymore. The nervous excitement they used to cause has been blanketed by dull imitation, and the company has gone on to further adventures.

Balanchine never pursues one line of stylistic development, no matter how progressive, at the expense of another, and he sometimes blends several lines in the most extraordinary and unforeseen syntheses. In 1960, the year after the Webern ballet *Episodes*, he made *Liebeslieder Walzer*, one of the great romantic ballets of the century. An hour of dances in waltz time (it is set, without narrative embellishment, on the Brahms songs), it had maximum grip and irresistible sweep. The sublime aura of *Liebeslieder* mitigates any suggestion of harsh experimentation; yet it was, and remains, a tour de force which Balanchine couldn't have accomplished without dancers trained in the most advanced intricacies of his modern repertory. In the second scene of the ballet, Violette Verdy begins a double pirouette in her partner's arms that we think is going to end in a forward arabesque. Instead, she reverses her direction and ends by embracing him, the line of her back and extended leg completed by the quiet pose of her head on his shoulder. This isn't anything we might not see in a conventional ballet to romantic music of which the ballerina might take several luxurious measures before coming to rest. Verdy does it, unbelievably, on one count—in the flash of a single cadence. So did Mimi Paul when she danced Verdy's role in the London season, and so does Sara Leland when she occasionally substitutes for Verdy today. The whiplash timing and the technique necessary to it were *new*, and they were not attributes of one dancer's virtuosity, they were a company trait. The girls didn't have to understand the sentiment of the music in order to express it; they had a technique which did it for them.

In fact, the technique *was* the sentiment. In the performing arts, there is generally some contest between the performer and the thing being performed, and audiences can frequently get their pleasure from evaluating the one against the other. Yet nothing is more exciting to an audience than performing that is so far out of itself and into the subject of the performance that the two can't be separated. When that happens, we have the illusion of absolute art, though we know it is only an illusion. For some people, the idea that poetry can pour from the bodies of hardworking American girls who, from the general look of them, aren't easily distinguishable from fashion models or chic Madison Avenue secretaries, is hard to believe, and occasionally, as we watch one of these girls moving with brilliant clarity, the thought "She doesn't know what she's doing" occurs to us. If she did, though, would she do it better? The question has never been answered. It isn't mindlessness but the state beyond mind that moves us in perfect dancing. It's what moves the dancer, too. And the whole problem in directing a company that plays dozens of ballets in repertory for long periods each year is how to keep that state beyond mind *ahead* of mind. Dancers learn from example and they learn fast. Precedents spread like rumors. *Liebeslieder* is being done today by young dancers, and it probably could even be done by young dancers in another company who haven't been put to the precise series of challenges that enabled Balanchine's dancers to dance it first in 1960. In 1893, Legnani amazed St. Petersburg by turning thirty-two fouettés pirouettes in Cinderella. The feat went straight into *Swan Lake*; later, Russian dancers made it a commonplace. In the same season he made *Agon*, Balanchine also made *Gounod Symphony*, a copious, plushy work full of softened lines and supported figures that would climax in sustained balances. It was too far ahead of his dancers and they failed in it. But by 1962—largely, I think, because of the success of *Liebeslieder*—he was able to choreograph *A Midsummer Night's Dream*, a full-evening work to lots of Mendelssohn, and have it come out a hit. In the dances for Titania and Hermia, and in a magnificent wedding pas de deux, were the first indications of the loose, heroically spontaneous and free style that Balanchine ballerinas would assume in the next decade. All that was lacking was the perfect instrument for it.

Suzanne Farrell, this new-style ballerina, appeared somewhat inauspiciously at the center of the most complicated, most manipulative, and most angular work Balanchine had yet composed—the *Movements for Piano and Orchestra*. When Adams, on whom the ballet was rehearsed, had to retire from dancing (owing to a persistent physical disability), her place was taken at the première by Farrell, then eighteen years old. Farrell was an Adams discovery, and at first (the familiar part of the novelty) all anyone could see was how much she resembled Adams. She was big and strong and handsome, although without much personal force. In her tiny leotard, she looked very like a big bee, but more like a woman-size baby. With that almost perverse precocity that was then characteristic of the younger generation, she could do anything Balanchine asked of her—and do it on a grander scale, at greater speed, and with a silkier recovery and sense of control than anyone else. And then we began to see that, unlike Adams, whose physical quality on the stage was, for all its amplitude, indomitably chaste (a quality she shared with Fonteyn), Farrell had a line that was positively voluptuous. The following season Balanchine produced, to Tchaikovsky music, a ghostly little pas de deux called *Meditation* in which Farrell was the lost love, or muse, or ministering angel, of a grieving Jacques d'Amboise. Its use of lavish emotion and storytelling gesture made it more of a shock than *Movements*. Though few people in the audience realized it at the time, here was the future. Farrell, her stage personality as yet undeveloped, moved at once into a lead position. Our style was thin no more.

In any decently written history of the New York City Ballet, the years 1963–69 would consume several chapters. The Farrell Years saw the company remade in a new, younger, and more romantic image. For Farrell personally they began in glory and ended in confusion and estrangement. Because of her importance to Balanchine —she was probably the most important dancer who ever entered his life—her rise to prima status was spectacular and sudden, perhaps too sudden. *Meditation* led to Dulcinea in *Don Quixote*, the role that made her a star, but Farrell was almost too shy to be a star. When she tried to project across the vast distances of the State Theatre in Lincoln Center, like a soft-spoken person trying to raise her voice over a bad phone connection, she just became shrill. She was the prototypical Balanchine ballerina for her generation—today we can see her even in little Gelsey Kirkland—but, calamitously, she didn't stay with the company long enough to work out her difficulties. When her break with Balanchine came in the middle of the 1969 spring season, her repertory totaled thirty-two roles, as many as Patricia McBride's. She was everywhere and nowhere. Her beauty fascinated more people than were repelled by her flamboyance, and we all have our cherished memories of her at her best—in the last-act dances of *Don Quixote*, in *Liebeslieder* (dancing the Adams role), flashing through the Gypsy Rondo of *Brahms-Schoenberg Quartet*. She transformed the company, freed Balanchine from the excessive braininess of "modernism," and departed, like Dulcinea, who in the ballet is apotheosized, the Queen of Heaven. Her place in the history of the company is sacrosanct.

Patricia McBride, who gained principal-dancer status a few years before Farrell, didn't become a star until just a few years ago. She didn't have Farrell's grandeur or silky, rippling flow of movement; she had a little, sticklike body which she has patiently taught to move deeply and expansively, "in the round." If Farrell was shy, McBride was shyer. Even today, she is the shyest, most tenderly true, bravest, and least corruptible of classical dancers. But it's just by having been all these things, night after night for ten solid years, that she has fought her way to distinction.

McBride has the body of a pubescent girl, the bones of a sparrow, the stamina of a horse. She has a deep sway in the upper back which tilts her upward and outward, so you are struck by the beautiful head and face. In *Dances at a Gathering*, she's the one who seems to be carrying the whole story of the ballet around in her head, but she doesn't give any indication of what's coming; she accepts it along with the rest. She has, I think, two quite piercing moments, one performed solo and one with a partner. The first is like a stroke of anti-typecasting, when Robbins has her bend low in an attitude parallel to the ground and "swim" over it with powerful arms. That downward sink, the whole intent plunge downward, is so unlike

McBride that you remember it. It foreshadows the moment at the end of the ballet when Villella touches the ground. Later on, she is facing Anthony Blum in a supported pose far to the side of the stage. The "storm" in the Chopin scherzo the pianist is playing suddenly returns, breaks into their idyll but doesn't break it up. They hold the pose, and she holds the dramatic focus alone, for a ponderably long moment, while the music pounds them both. McBride always had presence; now she has authority too, the kind an audience silently appeals to. It's the mark of a true ballerina. As for the incredible upside-down lifts, she does them as casually as one might fold a napkin while speaking. Having dispensed with all angles in her body, she appears to be dispensing with her body as well, with recalcitrant flesh. In her other Robbins role, in *In the Night*, she jumps curled into Moncion's arms, and so lightly that he seems to have received nothing but spirit.

How does a dancer get to be so transparent? McBride seems to be acting all through these roles and yet she does nothing of the sort. The pantomime in *In the Night* is completely musical and dancelike in its effect. Her head is all face, a perfect stage face with a brilliant inverted crescent of a smile, though usually it's impassive. New York City ballerinas don't wear the "such sweet agony" expression preferred by almost all European ballerinas, and they don't emote. McBride's face is like a Kabuki actor's, never changing and never the same. In *La Valse*, it wears (or seems to wear) a leer like that of a hungry thrillseeker. (This isn't in the part, necessarily; the Girl in White can be played as the rankest innocent and usually is.) In *Rubies*, it looks complacently pretty as she matches wits with Edward Villella, and in "The Man I Love," a duet she does with D'Amboise in the Gershwin ballet *Who Cares?*, it has a dreamy raptness that, each time she turns and finds him—with perhaps a touch of doubt that she *will* find him—seems to glorify him anew in her mind and in the mind of the audience. With McBride, it's easier to speak of sensibility than of personality. Her "personality" is impossible to pin down. It takes dramatic coloring from a part and projects that color. As Columbine in *Harlequinade*, she has a doll-like role, no color to it at all. The vivacity of it is supposed to be heartless, but what you're conscious of is McBride's affection for the part—"Here's something I used to do when I was a little girl," she seems to be saying—and that saves it; and then she saves it some more in the second-act solo when she shows (metaphorically speaking) how she grew up and accepted her adult responsibilities. And finally, toward the end of this marvellously gentle dance to lullaby-like music, when she's fully grown up, she steps out of the fantasy and out of the part, like a clown in *commedia dell'arte* sweeping off his mask, and opens her arms to the audience and blows a kiss. It's the "Pardon, gentles all" moment after a night of heavy farce.

Because of her simple, matter-of-fact manner and personal reserve, it sounds slightly pretentious to describe Patricia McBride as a dramatic artist. She's not an actress like Melissa Hayden or Violette Verdy or Sara Leland, and her technique doesn't strike you immediately as a dramatic one. Nor is she dramatically "original" like Allegra Kent, whose ineffable personal magic is more effective in roles like Terpsichore in *Apollo*, the sylph in *Scotch Symphony*, the Number One geisha in *Bugaku*, and the title role in *La Sonnambula*, than McBride's practical sharpness. But, like Kent, McBride has a gift for dramatization that looks excitingly spontaneous. She doesn't decide on her effects in advance; they just happen. This quality in his dancers Balanchine seems to adore above all others, and he encourages it by leaving his ballets open to their imaginations. There are no blueprints for "correct" interpretation.

In her earlier years, McBride didn't have the confidence to express her gift freely. Her parts looked a little underfilled. Kent, too, would often look tentative in a role, but her trouble, one felt, came from distraction or lack of interest (a problem that has continued off and on to affect her career). Charming little McBride wanted passionately to be correct—it's a natural thing for a young dancer to want—and held back from simple fright. The way she looked at the time is wonderfully captured in Hermia's strong, woeful solo in *A Midsummer Night's Dream*. (It looks based on Snow White's run through the woods in the film.) Balanchine uses whatever his good dancers can give him. As he used Kent's feyness, Hayden's swagger, Verdy's rhetorical drive, Adams's dignity, Farrell's creaturely impact, he seems to have admired and drawn upon McBride's purity of conscience as a classical dancer. But he also recognized its dangers. Gradually, he coaxed her out of the warm corner she'd settled into (in some relief, one supposes) as partner to the phenomenal Villella, got her to loosen up and punch a little harder. Balanchine likes all kinds of women, but he doesn't like saints. (He doesn't like sexpots either, though he has hired a few from time to time. The greatest —and I don't think it demeans her elegant classical style in the least

to suggest it—was Jillana, who left the company some years ago.)
He's devoted a large part of his creative life to demolishing the image
of the ballerina as nun mentally reciting her vows at every per-
formance of *Giselle*. He seemed to sense, too, that nice little Miss
No-Name was not the true McBride. In *Rubies*, her part is equal to
and fully as taxing as Villella's, and it's also glamorous, witchy:
Mary Astor besting Bogart. McBride's courage in it was fantastic
(Villella still gets all the applause), but I don't think it was until
Dances at a Gathering and *In the Night* and *Who Cares?* that she
let us know what a great star she really was.

In the Night is Jerome Robbins's first ballet to deal with mature
people. (With Balanchine, people generally have no age—they're
divine.) McBride and Francisco Moncion recall the lovers in such
poems of John Crowe Ransom's as "Two in August" and "The
Equilibrists." They fight and then she surrenders, as only McBride
can do it—nobly, without humiliation. *Who Cares?* is a classical
ballet about New York, with songs by Gershwin, dances by Balanchine, and décor and costumes that look designed by Herman
Badillo. Still, it's a brilliant work of art, especially so in the second
part. The three musical-comedy-style heroines are classical ballerinas,
the man is a character dancer. The same arrangement prevails in
the Balanchine-Stravinsky ballet of 1928, *Apollo*, and *Who Cares?*
more than recalls that great work, it quotes from it. The program
doesn't give McBride, who is the Terpsichore of this piece, precedence over the other two girls, but she assumes it because of the
peculiarly thrilling quality of her tension on the stage. She "sings
higher." And the other two, Marnee Morris and Karin von Aroldingen, are marvellous.

Morris is one of the lost-art girls of the stage. She's a perfect lady
who doesn't like to show off, or only the least little bit. When she
dances "My One and Only" with a vanilla-wafer charm and a
technique like impeccably worked lace, it's like having an old theatrical photograph come alive. Von Aroldingen projects something else:
blazing, powerful good health and a kind of plodding animal vigor.
A German girl who joined the company nine years ago, Von
Aroldingen has never really excelled in any of the major roles of
the repertory. *Who Cares?* naturalizes her—she looks like a cheerful,
beer-drinking American college girl—and makes her look like a star,
too. McBride's solo is to "Fascinating Rhythm," and she dances it
possibly better than it has ever been danced. It is one of Balanchine's

trickiest creations, as densely lettered as a Mozart aria, but he meant it to be a wicked charm number as well. In two places where the choreography implies a chorus-girl boomps-a-daisy flourish, McBride couldn't bring herself to deliver. Only lately has she started to come across, pouncing full on the beat, but you feel it has cost her a night or two of spiritual anguish.

McBride at twenty-eight is not yet a great artist; she's merely the most exciting ballerina in America. Natalia Makarova, the great Russian star now with American Ballet Theatre, is unsurpassed in her own limited repertory. She made an affecting début last winter in Tudor's thirty-five-year-old classic *Jardin aux Lilas*, but her future in a company that has been unable to do anything with Mimi Paul and Cynthia Gregory is questionable. Suzanne Farrell when last seen was doing for Maurice Béjart's Ballet of the Twentieth Century a corny imitation of the kinds of roles she did for Balanchine. The spectacle was heartbreaking. Though she made the stupid choreography look beautiful, Béjart cannot return the compliment, and Farrell is still an unfinished dancer who needs to work.

When one considers the odds against success in this kind of career, it is more than ever remarkable that McBride should be where she is. She represents a triumph of sensibility, an obdurate purist whose concessions to vulgar usage only enhance her appeal and her value to the public. Of course, she's been very carefully protected. In one sense, New York City ballerinas *are* like nuns: they're a sisterhood. They survive in the atmosphere of an aesthetic style that happens to exist nowhere else in the world, that absorbs modern tensions and transcends them; and they put up with untold miseries because they know it's the only way to look the way they want to look—ravishing like mortal goddesses, yet reachable. Their exact stature in the world community of ballet is a mystery to society at large. There are no shrieking fans at the stage door—somehow it isn't done. Every five years or so, some big magazine takes a picture of Balanchine surrounded by his rising young dancers, and the world knows that the New York City Ballet is in another stage of its development. Very close behind McBride comes Kay Mazzo, an elegant waif who arouses an audience's sympathetic concern as McBride never could, and the amusingly solemn and inscrutable young Gelsey Kirkland.

The company has bred two generations of dancers in ten years with no sign of diminishing strength. After Balanchine and his organization, the credit for this goes to one group of people. Not to the dancers, who are generally too young to know what they're getting into at the age when they have to get into it, and certainly not to the critics; but to the dancers' mothers. This maligned tribe, and may it increase, has over the years chosen to give its most talented daughters to Balanchine. Ballet mamas are the great realists of the business. If there were anything better in life, in art, in the art of dancing, they'd go for it in a shot. Back in the days when Tallchief was striking across the stage like a cobra and Hayden was developing her coiled puma spring and Wilde was perfecting her gargouillades and LeClercq was gawking it up in a host of *impossible* ballets and Adams was showing everyone else how to walk, these ladies were making their decisions. And when their weary charges came home full of aches and pains, they'd say it, night after night: "Darling, all I want is that you should be a pinhead."   —*April 1971*

Dance in Film

Dance in film is a subject that has taken on a semblance of controversy owing to the insistence of some writers that a conflict between dance and film exists. Many dances designed for the stage are not suited to film presentation, but to assume that dancing is exclusively a theatrical medium is to take a needlessly restricted view of it. People danced long before theatres were built, and people dancing in the movies are demonstrating one kind of human activity the camera can capture as well as any other. Movies can also invent dances that cannot be done anywhere except on film; this method isn't necessarily preferable, because "purer," to photographing dances that have already been choreographed and may just as easily be seen on a stage, in a ballroom, or on the street. Most successful screen dances lie somewhere between total cinematic illusion and passive recording. But it is also true that movie dance has offered the most excitement when it is operating at, or close to, the polar extremes of its range (possibly because here the risks are greater). Partisan debate provides for such extremes by telling us that one or the other medium is being "violated," but it may be a violation that has consistency, purpose, and style. Whether a filmmaker creates a dance out of an array of mechanical effects or whether he photographs a staged routine has no bearing on the validity of the sensation he is trying to produce. A cleanly photographed dance can be pretentious and boring; a complex cinematic extravaganza can be utterly devoid of kinetic charm. We can only look at the results and judge whether we have had a dance experience and a true one.

Though dancing could not achieve full expression on the screen until the coming of sound, the silent film immediately set about developing the two major approaches to dance in the work of a single man, Georges Méliès (1861–1938). Dancers were among Méliès's favorite subjects; he was in love not only with the new medium of film but with theatre, ballet, and the music hall. He photographed dance pantomimes and routines in simple box sets, and he also created optical effects to heighten their appeal for the camera. Sudden transformations, tricks of scale and continuity, things popping out of nowhere, people whose body parts become separated and dance off on their own were the stuff of Méliès's illusions. His films are excellent visual records—though fragmentary ones—of the dance theatre of his day. At the same time, they indicate nearly every possibility that has since been developed in the field of "camera" choreography. Also, with their subtly hand-tinted frames, they are mysteriously beautiful to look at. In one of the most bewitching trick shots, Mme. Méliès (who with her husband often appears as a kind of onscreen conjuror) produces tiny pierrots who dance on point in the palm of her hand. (There is a curious repeat of this effect much later in the history of movies when, with the arrival of sound, movie directors reverted for a brief moment to Méliès's neglected box of tricks. In *The Hollywood Revue of* 1929, Jack Benny as the m.c. pulls Bessie Love out of his pocket.)

At about the same time, Edison, Pathé, and Biograph (among other companies) were busy filming dancers. Theatrical, social, and folk dances were recorded at the turn of the century in the thousands, and a considerable fraction of this footage is extant in paper or film prints. Leading dancers of the day are to be glimpsed in their specialties: Pierina Legnani in *Cinderella* can be seen, if not comprehended, in one of the earliest fragments, and, in one of the most famous ones Pathé recorded Loie Fuller, who enchanted Rodin and Mallarmé, in her *Fire Dance* in 1906. (A cross-eyed woman flailing in huge draperies, she has an impact on the modern viewer as bewildering as the sight of Sarah Bernhardt keeling over in *Camille*.)

Primitive film techniques, which often distorted even the simplest dances, did not keep dancers from recording themselves, less for posterity than for extra money. Stars of the ballet tended to stay away from the camera—they could afford to—but probably it was Diaghilev's intransigence that kept Karsavina and Nijinsky from being filmed. Diaghilev was not opposed to film; he was to use film projections in *Ode* (1928), one of the first mixed-media ballets. But it was a fact that motion-picture film could not capture the clarity of developed ballet technique or preserve the sense of its continuity in space. Diaghilev knew, too—who knew it better than he?—that it was enough to dance in the present without taking risks in the future. Tastes change, styles fade, and what is novel and exciting to one generation may prove incomprehensible and even ludicrous to the next. Both Diaghilev and Nijinsky had ideas about the expressive potential of films. However, Nijinsky, who visited Chaplin on the set of *Easy Street* in 1916, wrote in his diary, "I will leave filming to those who love to do it." No record of him in action has been turned up. Pavlova starred in *La Muette de Portici* in 1916; a straight acting role with passages of dancing, it is her most vivid performance on film. When she was filmed in her stage repertory in 1924, she was past her prime. Still, the test shots taken of her in famous solos (including *The Dying Swan*) on the set of Fairbanks's *Thief of Baghdad*, together with another series of excerpts compiled in 1935 (*The Immortal Swan*), are remarkable and invaluable with all their imperfections. There is a marvellous record of the legendary Spessivtseva in portions of *Giselle* Act I, crudely yet tenaciously filmed from a box during a rehearsal in London in 1932. This fragment has been incorporated into a documentary about Spessivtseva, *The Sleeping Ballerina* (1964), where it is combined with a piano accompaniment and an affecting narration by Marie Rambert. Those who have seen it have had a glimpse of a great dancer still at her peak.

Despite the hazards of filming and the egregious omissions (no extended footage of Isadora Duncan dancing is known to exist), the catalogue of dance films dating from the silent era is an impressive one. It was a period, too, of unusually close harmony between dance and film. Dance trends of the day injected their vigor into an essentially wordless medium. In America, where large ballet academies were just beginning to be established, dancing meant vaudeville, ballroom, or various forms of "aesthetic" theatrical dance.

All had their reflection in commercial film production. Probably the most successful dance film of the period was *The Whirl of Life*, which starred Vernon and Irene Castle. The most popular ballroom dancers of the age—indeed, the team that had done the most to spread the craze for ballroom dancing in the years before World War I—the Castles made only one feature film, but it is almost a complete summation of the era in which they danced. *The Whirl of Life* (1914) was loosely biographical, with a few melodramatic incidents (a kidnapping, a chase on horseback) thrown in to excite their fans. The best part is the exhibition dance sequence filmed in their ballroom at Castles by the Sea on Long Island. Here, as rarely in dance films, we can see what made these dancers great. Their ability to embody and at the same time exalt the spirit of an era was to have no equal until the emergence of Astaire and Rogers as a team in the thirties.

In 1915, the year of the release of *The Birth of a Nation*, Denishawn opened in Los Angeles. To this school, attached to the dance company of Ruth St. Denis and Ted Shawn, came many film actresses, including most of those working for D. W. Griffith. The Denishawn influence is evident in the fluid physical style these actresses used in their film performances. Dancers from the Denishawn school appear in the Babylonian section of *Intolerance*, and Carol Dempster, a Denishawn dancer and later a Griffith star, danced frequently in her films. St. Denis had been filmed as a teen-ager performing a "skirt dance" with bouncing Pickford curls. Shawn started collaborating with Edison in 1913, amassing an extensive library of films which incorporates an important segment of American dance history.

The great dance influences on Griffith's films were not all Denishawn. The greatest was D. W. Griffith himself. Quite apart from actual dancing, of which he appears to have been very fond, Griffith's films contain more dance elements than many of the movie musicals that came later. Films eliminated declamation from classical acting and the declamatory aspects—studied poses—of mime as well. Griffith cultivated this new style by stressing the dance impulse in characterization; he wanted actors who were like live wires. The stress is related to his gift for overall architectural rhythm in the making of a film. *Broken Blossoms* appears seamless to the eye, one tragic gesture. The three principals—Lillian Gish's waif, Barthelmess's Chinese drug addict, and Crisp's slum bully—are each characterized by choreographed attitudes reminiscent of Fokine's

Petrouchka. Barthelmess's angularities derive from nothing naturalistic; their twisted introversion contrasts powerfully with the exaggerated spread stance of Crisp (cf. ballet turnout) and with the helpless slow creeping and curling of Gish's body, which in the closet
scene accelerates in a whirl of terror. Such physicality of characterization has been absent so long from the performing tradition that
one has to search for it today even on the ballet stage.

"Chaplin has always been at his greatest when he approached
ballet," wrote John Grierson. The fine line between acrobatics and
dance is crossed repeatedly in silent film comedy. Chaplin loved
to parody serious dance—the dance in *Sunnyside* is an extended
burlesque of Nijinsky's *Faune*—and Denishawn's nymphs—but his
own dance exploits, such as the globe dance in *The Great Dictator,* the
dance of the rolls in *The Gold Rush,* and the roller-skating sequences
in *The Rink* and *Modern Times,* are almost too beautiful to be
funny. Douglas Fairbanks's athletic feats were designed frankly for
their beauty; Buster Keaton's concealed their aesthetic purpose in
an elaborate rationale of functionalism. Flying from the handlebars
of a speeding motorcycle to land exactly where he has to land to
knock the villain off his feet (in *Sherlock Jr.*), Keaton is like a
fateful bullet fired from a cosmic gun. He does not conquer space
or time, but passes through both in an orderly if unseemly fashion,
and his own motion is graceful because it *works* along with everything else. The whole universe dances.

Laurel and Hardy, greatest of the soft-shoe comedians, continued
well into the sound era along with W. C. Fields, who never danced.
Laurel and Hardy were the opposite of the high-style comedians—
the reverse of brilliance and grace; they flourished through their *lack*
of expertise. They could dance and sing without making a production
number out of it, whereas the Marx Brothers never could. Sound
and the Marx Brothers were made for each other, Harpo's silence
notwithstanding. Interestingly, it is Groucho, the most verbal of the
brothers, who is also the most devoted dancer.

The freedom of expressive movement achieved by the silent screen
suffered an initial setback with the coming of sound. The musical
gave dancing a place it had never enjoyed before in movies, but in
the beginning there was hardly any dancing of note to be seen in
feature films. Dull choreography and substandard execution were
the norm. Good dancers appeared most frequently in two-reelers
and were easier to appreciate away from the interminable dialogue

scenes and rigid production numbers that dominated feature-length films. The musical as a new form of movie underwent a severe trial-and-error process during the Stone Age of sound, and what began in the excitement of novelty ended, all too quickly, by driving audiences away because producers hadn't grasped that the musical *was* a new form of movie. Musicals renewed the careers of such stars as Clara Bow, Nancy Carroll, and Bebe Daniels, but these newfound careers were short-lived. Sound posed key problems of expression to which producers remained indifferent or insensible even after they had conquered the technological difficulties. It meant a whole new way of coming to grips with the attention of the audience. Overhead shots of dance sequences, for example, rapidly became a commonplace, but the position of the camera mattered less than the pace of the action and the variety of moods and situations. The first wave of movie musicals (c. 1929–31) inundated the public with static adaptations of Broadway shows. Apart from some exterior shots, though, these usually didn't pretend to be movies. Some of the better adaptations (e.g., *The Cocoanuts, Rio Rita*), stage-bound though they may have been, were in fact far more shrewdly paced, amusing, and stylish than the "original" movie musicals that were being made at the same time.

Hollywood quickly invented three main types of musical: the stage show at one remove, or "backstage" musical (*The Broadway Melody, On With the Show*); the all-star movie revue (*The Hollywood Revue of 1929, The Show of Shows, Paramount on Parade*); and the modified-operetta movie (*Monte Carlo, Hallelujah*) in which musical numbers were inserted straight into the dramatic action without the usual device of framing them as performances for a theatre audience. These were all versions of theatrical stereotypes and there was nothing intrinsically wrong with any of them. The backstage musical came to be especially despised by purists, but this was because the work of Ernst Lubitsch, René Clair, and King Vidor in the unconfined lyric form made it seem much sillier than it was. It was not the formulas that were faulty, it was the lack of sophistication with which they were applied.

And the cheap ingredients. The technique of the playback had been mastered early, freeing sound stages from the perils of direct recording (the mike in the flower pot, satirized in *Singin' in the Rain,* had been a common resort), but this brought new perils in the cutting room. Film editors were totally unfamiliar with the task of cutting a dance sequence to a prerecorded musical track and would frequently unite dance accents with the wrong beats. Dances that were simple in their relation to music made postsynchronization a good deal easier. However, you didn't need good dancers to perform mickey-mouse choreography, and until the advent of music cutters in the studios you didn't get them. Many more singing stars (Jeanette MacDonald, Maurice Chevalier, Al Jolson, John Boles, Helen Morgan, Dennis King, Grace Moore, Lawrence Tibbett) than dancing stars were launched in movie careers during this period.

Choreographers, however, were considered indispensable. From Broadway came Sammy Lee, Seymour Felix, Larry Ceballos, Busby Berkeley, and Albertina Rasch, all of whom survived when the bottom dropped out of the musical market sometime in 1930. The ubiquitous Mme. Rasch, a Viennese dancing teacher with a strong background in opera ballet, became the queen of the operetta films (*The Cat and the Fiddle, The Merry Widow, The Firefly, Rosalie, The Great Waltz*). Her specialty was toe-dancers doing relevés in strict time and strict formation or fluttering in mothlike droves while the camera peered down from the flies. In England, Gaumont attempted a few dance talkies with ballet star Anton Dolin, but in Hollywood the tradition of ballet was ersatz ballet and was to remain such until the fifties. Busby Berkeley, who became the king of the backstage musicals, was brought to Hollywood to stage the dances for the film version of the Ziegfeld show *Whoopee* (1930), which he did with such finesse that, measured against the prevailing standard, they almost seem too *short*. In that film, he also began the practice of bringing each of his chorus girls into a closeup, a variation on the *Follies* showgirl parade that remained a feature of his style throughout the thirties.

Berkeley's girls were not conspicuously well-trained dancers, and he seldom presented them as such. Ruby Keeler, his dancing lead, tapped with such vehemence that she made up for the bevy that not only didn't dance but often disappeared into kaleidoscopic spectacles choreographed entirely by the camera as it roved through space. By 1933, when *Forty-Second Street* (a remake of *On With the Show*) made musicals box-office again, sound technique had been so perfected that directors could now explore what they formerly only exploited. The title number unleashed Berkeley in the format that was to become his trademark, a kind of visual orchestration of motifs inspired by the lyrics of a song rather than the mechanics of a plot. "Naughty, gaudy, bawdy, sporty Forty-Second Street" was seen in all or most of those aspects, Ruby Keeler pounded away on top of a taxi, and there was a parade of dancing skyscrapers. "The Shadow Waltz" (in *Gold Diggers of 1933*) had a hundred chorines dressed in china-silk lampshades and playing a hundred illuminated violins which then assembled in the shape of one monster violin. In *Footlight Parade* (1933), Berkeley created a series of aquatic images for "By a Waterfall." Photographed from above, his mermaids melted into water lilies or undulating water snakes. From below water level, they suggested the wheel of a paddleboat. And in the title number of *Dames* (1934), he played not only with human geometry but with optical mazes and illogical transitions in scale, reaching the Nirvana of sheer abstraction. The end of the number is a pull-back from a giant scaffold on the several levels of which girls recline. When the screen becomes a grid filled with tiny figures, Dick Powell's head bursts through it in closeup.

Berkeley was still choreographing on a massive scale in 1962 (*Jumbo*) when his thirties period was revived as a precursor of the Pop Art movement in America. Since then, Berkeley has moved from being a semi-fatuous enthusiasm of the avant-garde to being a staple of the thirties-memorabilia addicts and the subject of something like a popular cult. His prestige has never been higher than it is today, and it no longer seems necessary to defend him against the literal-minded ("But it isn't *theatre!* It isn't *dance!*"). Too many television viewings may have taken the edge off the supreme joke of Berkeleyan spectacle, which was that his numbers characteristically are framed by the rise and fall of a curtain, as if the theatre audience in the film could see what we see. A film like *Footlight Parade*, which ends with two of the most colossal numbers played back to back to a cheering audience, loses much of its delicious absurdity when it is fragmented by commercial interruptions and seen alongside TV sit-coms with their canned laughter and variety shows in which we aren't certain which parts the studio audience is seeing live and which parts are on film. As a choreographer, Berkeley can be reduced to his simplest routines (the chorus of marching girls in "All's Fair in Love and War" from *Gold Diggers of 1937*) and still come out in the front rank, but he was probably the greatest choreographer who has ever worked directly with the processed effects possible only in the movies. Walt Disney, whose Silly Symphonies very likely gave Berkeley ideas (and whose reputation inexplicably declines as Berkeley's rises), was not controversial in the sense that Berkeley was as long as he drew his dance material before photographing it. Berkeley, on the other hand, manipulated live people. The only ground on which Berkeley can be attacked is taste, and, strangely, it is Disney's weakness, too. When Berkeley manipulates people, it is much more likely to be in the interests of prurience than of lyrical fantasy. But vulgarity is in some ways essential to the imaginative exuberance that drives these mad productions on. Less primitive taste possibly would not have supported such extremes of invention.

In 1933, the man who was Berkeley's opposite—the man whose screen choreography could consist merely of himself dancing alone in a living room—made his first appearance in a feature film. "Either the camera will dance or I will," said Fred Astaire. "But both of us at the same time—that won't work." When the curtain went up on an Astaire dance (and often there was no curtain—Astaire just danced), it was usually the kind of dance that one could imagine seeing on a real stage, but the experience was so dazzling that the only sane response was gratitude to film for having brought it into existence. Astaire was the first dancer to establish himself on the screen, and the greatest. He raised technical standards in every department—camerawork, cutting, synchronization, scoring. He inspired the best efforts of the best song writers, and his personal style set a criterion for masculine elegance that has persisted through two generations. He did more than anyone else to develop the dance musical. Yet in the forties, when his career was faltering, there were critics who suggested that he wasn't able to get as much out of the film medium as Gene Kelly was. The point about Astaire, though, is that he could always give more to the film medium than he could get out of it. He gave himself as a superb virtuoso whose every gesture was penetratingly clear to the camera. And when he experimented with the capacities of film, it was usually in order to give more of himself by multiplying his image, as in "Bojangles of Harlem" (*Swing Time*, 1936) or "Puttin' On the Ritz" (*Blue Skies*, 1946). In 1938, he used slow motion for the first time; later, he used animation. He danced on the ceiling. None of these things would have been possible on the stage, and none of them improved on the perfection of his dancing. They merely provided new ways for it to show itself.

In any Astaire film, the high spot is his solo. Only in the period

1933–39, when his partner was Ginger Rogers, were the duets on the same level. Later, there were other girls whose technical abilities were more developed than Ginger Rogers's—Eleanor Powell, Rita Hayworth, or Cyd Charisse—but with none of them was Astaire able to achieve the romantic intensity of his dances with Rogers. There have never been wittier flirtatious duets than "I'll Be Hard to Handle" (*Roberta*, 1935) or "Isn't This a Lovely Day?" (*Top Hat*, 1935), or more nobly passionate ones than "Night and Day" (*The Gay Divorcee*, 1934) or "Let's Face the Music and Dance" (*Follow the Fleet*, 1936). Passion—the missing element in just about every "sexy" duet that has been attempted since—is usually confused with emoting or going primitive. With Astaire and Rogers, it's a matter of total professional dedication; they do not give us emotions, they give us dances, and the more beautifully they dance, the more powerful the spell that seems to bind them together.

Astaire and Rogers made nine films for RKO, beginning with *Flying Down to Rio*, in which they introduced "The Carioca," and ending with *The Story of Vernon and Irene Castle*, in which they saluted the great dance team of another era. Astaire and Rogers were never surpassed as dancing idols. The mood they projected in their great romantic duets has become part of the mythology of the 1930's—so much so that, to young audiences especially, the whole decade seems romantic in retrospect. Certainly by 1949, when MGM's *The Barkleys of Broadway* reunited an Astaire who had just come out of retirement (for *Easter Parade*) with a Rogers who had given up musicals, the climate had changed. At MGM, the new vogue in musicals tended toward Broadway parasitism and hard-hearted chic. The studio's big musical that year was *On the Town* with Gene Kelly and Vera-Ellen, adapted by Betty Comden and Adolph Green from their stage hit. Comden's and Green's script for *The Barkleys of Broadway*, like their scripts for *Singin' in the Rain* and *The Band Wagon*, was big on satire, wisecracks, and production *ideas*. Astaire, with his light informality, his classical emphasis on steps rather than ideas in choreography, seemed less suited to these ambitious new musicals than dancer-manager Gene Kelly, who, besides choreographing his films, was already codirecting them (with Stanley Donen). Astaire never wanted to direct whole films or even whole production numbers. Working with an assistant, usually Hermes Pan, he would choreograph and direct the filming of his own dances; the ensembles he would leave to Pan. But where

Astaire achieved dance films with stories, Kelly made story films with dances. In Kelly's best film, *Singin' in the Rain* (1952), the brightest performance is given by a nondancer, Jean Hagen. It could never have happened in an Astaire film.

This distinction between Astaire and Kelly is more important than the fact that Astaire stuck mostly to tap-dancing while Kelly went in for the large-scale effects of Broadway's latest export, ballet. In terms of dance content, *Yolanda and the Thief* (1945), in which Astaire collaborated with ballet choreographer Eugene Loring, is loaded, whereas it's the big ballets that are the least diverting features of *On the Town, Singin' in the Rain,* and *An American in Paris* (1951). Movie critics pressed for their favorite musicals will generally name one of Kelly's or, if it's an Astaire film, *The Band Wagon* (1953)—MGM's magic is hard to resist. It's the nondance values in these films that make them entertaining—the pace and tunes and color and locale, the "literate" scripts and funny performances. Even when the big empty ballets are replaced by a good one—Michael Kidd's "Girl Hunt" in *The Band Wagon* (which isn't all that good, just less pretentious)—the result still isn't a dance film, it's a story film told by dancers and a dance-minded director (Astaire, Jack Buchanan, Nanette Fabray, and Cyd Charisse, directed by Vincente Minnelli). Astaire is an outsider in this film, just as he is in the plot. Times had indeed changed, and Astaire's lack of ease in the new "art" musical is one point the film gains by exploiting. It's fun watching him trying to adjust and seeing how well his style holds through all the nonsense of the "Girl Hunt" ballet, but no dance fan *prefers* a film in which Astaire works this far from his true center.

A dance film is one in which the dance values are more lucid and exciting to the mind than any other kind; it is not necessarily a film in which we see nothing but dance. There has never been a satisfactory all-dance feature film. *Tales of Beatrix Potter* (1971), with choreography by Frederick Ashton, has some delightful dances, but after the first half-hour it has delighted us long enough. The tales never get onto the screen; they're blocked by choreography. This business of eliminating every expressive resource of movies in the conviction that dance will take their place is founded on a mistaken notion of pure expression. Purity of expression is achieved by cutting away excess; poverty results from the cutting away of essentials. In the Potter film, nothing takes the place of Potter's text. The dances are charming but dramatically inconsequential—and would seem so on the stage, too. So we have neither filmed ballet nor a ballet film. In *Invitation to the Dance* (1957), Gene Kelly attempts three ballets which can scarcely be said to fail because he has limited himself to the one form of expression. His material is so routine that the fact that it is mimed and danced rather than spoken or sung makes no difference. Nor is the material enhanced by the "cinematic resources" that Kelly employs: the long animation sequence is a long *bad* animation sequence. It would be a great pity if Kelly's contributions as a choreographer (or "choreo-cinema maker," as the dance profession designates him) should take precedence in our minds over his much more solid contributions as a performer. He came along at a time when the wartime boom in ballet was making everyone conscious of dance as a high art. He was supposed to do great artistic things with dance in the movies and is thought by many to have done them. But Kelly the artist is Kelly the performer, and his best choreography consists of the brilliant solos he invented for himself—the alter-ego dance in *Cover Girl* (1944), the statue dance in *Living in a Big Way* (1947), the newspaper dance in *Summer Stock* (1950), the title number in *Singin' in the Rain*.

For a long time, it was generally agreed that ballet was not expressive in the movies, and in fact (as the Jeremy Fisher sequences in *Tales of Beatrix Potter* show) camera speeds are still registering fanlike impressions of big jumps and rapid steps in the air. In the 1938 *Goldwyn Follies*, Balanchine arranged his American Ballet dancers in a highly effective series of still poses with wind streaming through the shot. Vera Zorina "rode" a statue of a horse. The movement sequences were less interesting. It was the first time, however, that a trained classical corps de ballet had appeared in a Hollywood film. *Goldwyn Follies* was a terrible movie and Balanchine's part of it caused no great stir. Nor did his later film dances for Zorina (*I Was an Adventuress*, 1940, and "That Old Black Magic" in *Star Spangled Rhythm*, 1943), in which he continued to try things that couldn't be done on a stage. It is doubtful that movie audiences unfamiliar with ballet could appreciate Balanchine's effects, and today they appear rather academic. Balanchine's ideas about film choreography at that time were negative in principle—or he was never given screen time to work out dances that were more than negations of stage conventions. In 1948, *The Red Shoes* dramatized many of Balanchine's fancies to sensational effect. In the climactic ballet in that film, optical printing went wild, with seas beating against the footlights, the stage dissolving into a desert or a ballroom, and a slow-motion fall through space. There were not many more times this sort of thing could happen, and even *The Red Shoes* didn't get completely away with the pretense that it was all happening in the ballerina's mind. But it worked because nothing was attempted in dance that could not be seen clearly, or improved upon, by the camera. Robert Helpmann's choreography was thin to the point of misty suggestion. The lovely young classical dancer Moira Shearer was given runs, arrowy arabesques, dartlike passages on toe. She remained in the eye like the point of a flame (an image—life's candle—that actually appears to the audience as the film ends).

What was special about the *Red Shoes* ballet was not so much its free use of movie devices—audiences had seen lurid visual tone poems before—as its assimilation of those devices in a picture of the ballet's stage world. The things that could have happened on the stage were almost as strange as the things that couldn't. The taste of the moviemakers was so consistent—so consistently outrageous —that they made the imaginary happenings seem like plausible (though not, of course, literal) extensions of the behavior of classical ballet. The fetishistic emphasis on toeshoes, red like the color of Moira Shearer's hair, was the most brilliant touch of all. But Powell and Pressburger went even further than this. They enclosed the ballet in a story about a dancer's life and loaded it with a specialized atmosphere that was more suggestive than the fictions it was intended to support—such forties-movie themes as mad genius, the culture-sadism link, the career-marriage conflict. Their dancers looked real, their ballets (gems from the classic repertory, unerringly selected and photographed) looked real, even their fabrications looked real. *The Red Shoes* was a horror story told in the form of a dance musical with dance supplying the main thrills, and it aroused tremendous popular interest in ballet. It had a direct influence on the success of the Sadler's Wells (now Royal) Ballet on its first American tour, and it brought a new and young audience to the support of the crucial first seasons of the New York City Ballet. The whole surge was extraordinary and has never been repeated in just that way. The fans it created realized soon enough that the film was shallow, but they did not feel cheated. The kind of excitement it offered was the excitement of good caricature, of certain presumptions about ballet technique and the ballet *Gestalt* carried to a point of ecstatic involvement. *The Red Shoes* is witty rather than moving, and its wit is distinctly *outré*, as in the point it makes about "spotting" by having the camera do flash pans, seeing what Moira Shearer sees when she does pirouettes. (Hitchcock makes the joke again in *Torn Curtain* when he has Toumanova spot off Paul Newman, sitting in the audience.) Although the kind of power it gets from its subject is not the best that subject has to offer, and although it launched the ballet trend in all the musicals that won honors in the fifties, there really is no other ballet film.

As a *horror* film, it summed up and externalized all the things that had kept ballet off the screen or just barely, cringingly, on it. Before *The Red Shoes*, ignorance and intuition had combined to create a minor movie tradition where ballet was concerned. The movie producers were no more interested in ballet than they had to be. It was just starting to become popular in the thirties, and they used it then because (a) it symbolized culture and (b) it seemed to exercise a malign fascination. Everyone had heard of the mad Nijinsky. John Barrymore had played Diaghilev (and Donald Cook, Nijinsky!) in a film actually called *The Mad Genius* in 1931. Shakespearean adaptations had to have ballets, which were generally scissored to ribbons in the release prints: a Nijinska one in Max Reinhardt's A *Midsummer Night's Dream* (1935) and an Agnes de Mille one in Thalberg's *Romeo and Juliet* (1936). When producers wished to show respect for art, they invariably created a lavish number around some performing freak who would knock the public's eye out. Even Astaire and Rogers in *Shall We Dance* (1937) had to make way for a ballet starring Ziegfeld's ballerina Harriet Hoctor. During this period, in England, Jessie Matthews had forged a lightly idiosyncratic and highly appealing dance style out of ballet steps done in jazz rhythm. There was nothing gloomy or perverse about Jessie Matthews, and her musicals were charming, but she had no American counterpart. In America, you were either Tap or Toe, and Toe was art. Hoctor, who was a contortionist specializing in backbends on point, and Vivian Fay, who was a toe dancer specializing in whiplash turns, made numerous film appearances as stand-ins for Ballet. In 1938, art-house audiences saw European classical dancers in *Ballerina* (*La Mort du Cygne*), a backstage ballet drama in which a trapdoor is opened under Mia Slavenska. Though it contained scarcely any dancing, the Vivien Leigh–Robert Taylor *Waterloo Bridge* (1940) reworked Robert E. Sherwood's play to make the doomed heroine a dancer and her story identical to that of Odette-Odile in *Swan Lake*. (It was remade in the fifties as a vehicle for dancer-actress Leslie Caron.)

The morbid tradition continued into the forties with the Hollywood remake of *Ballerina* (*The Unfinished Dance*, 1947) and *Specter of the Rose*, starring a dancer named Ivan Kirov as a Bronx Nijinsky who did beats with turned-in legs and leaped to his death through the plate glass of a window high over Manhattan. Written, produced, and co-directed by Ben Hecht in 1946, *Specter* is one of the most richly naïve movies ever made, constantly plastering sticky tributes to ballet over the alarming gaps in its author's knowledge. The dialogue is justly famous ("Hug me with your eyes." "I am." "Harder...") and the dancing is justly forgotten. Hecht should be given points for the characters, though, if not for their speeches. There are ineffectual people like this in the ballet world, particularly on its fringes, where Hecht must have run into them and assumed they were doing something important.

Like the rest of these movies, *The Red Shoes* said that ballet dancers were crazy and/or doomed. It capped the tradition of morbidity and raised the status of ballet in the movies at the same time. After that, things got healthier but duller. Goldwyn spent a fortune capitalizing on *The Red Shoes* with *Hans Christian Andersen* (1952), featuring Jeanmaire in uninteresting choreography by Roland Petit. (Originally, it was to have had Shearer dancing Balanchine.) The next film by Powell and Pressburger, *Tales of Hoffmann* (1952), was an overstuffed culture sandwich with one indigestible ruse: it tried substituting dancers for singers, and there was a lot of frantic lip-syncing on the hoof. Chaplin made a ballet film with undistinguished dances (*Limelight*, 1952). Dance sequences by Petit, Loring, Kidd, Helen Tamiris, Valerie Bettis, Jack Cole, James Mitchell, or Herbert Ross turned up in nearly every major musical. The find of the fifties was Bob Fosse (*The Pajama Game*, 1957); like Ross, he turned to directing. The ballet binge produced no stars. Stars of the ballet appeared in special spots, but their appearances were only newsworthy; they were rarely given a chance to do the kind of dancing that made them famous. There was a general attempt to make ballet winsome and cute or cold and jazzy. Leslie Caron, introduced in *An American in Paris*, had a hit in the minor

Lili (1953), but eventually withdrew to straight roles. Because ballet was still thought of as a woman's art, there were no opportunities for male dancers; and a danseuse without a male co-star was hard to cast. It was not only the fear of effeteness that kept male classical dancers off the screen. The technique is too hard to photograph. (Rudolf Nureyev, whose style is measured and emphatic, is more photogenic than the equally brilliant but mercurial Edward Villella.) The wide screen brought two notable attempts to make large-scale masculine movement appealing to audiences. *Seven Brides for Seven Brothers* (1954) had some roughhouse clowning in an innocently gymnastic style, but *West Side Story* (1961) was not so innocent. Perhaps the most overpraised dance film yet made, it tried so hard to generate art from the violence of street warfare that it became bombastic kitsch.

Filmed ballet, a minor category of dance film, is just what it is and no more: a chance to see something of what goes on in the theatre. Unobtrusive camera work and editing can heighten the illusion of a performance (and are rarer than one would think), but they cannot redeem discrepancies between stage and film time. The screen can go dead while dancers labor to build an effect that has power in the theatre. Studio treatments of stage choreography should work, but don't; compromise shows as falsity. The look of a real stage becoming gradually stained with sweat is preferable to the cosmetic smoothness of a performance that is obviously not being filmed in one piece. We can understand more of an event and have more patience with it if we can discount in advance the effects it is *not* going to give us. A *Giselle* or a *Romeo* that is played to a camera still doesn't look like a movie; and what is the point of asking stage performers to modulate their technique for the camera if that technique is what we have paid to see? The films that Paul Czinner has made of the Bolshoi and the Royal Ballet in performance are good examples of the risks and virtues of straight, unpretentious filming, and there have been some enthralling fragments from Russia. (Warning signs should be posted against Jean Negulesco's filming of two Massine pieces, *Gaieté Parisienne* and *Capriccio Espagnol*, for Warner Brothers in 1941. Negulesco competes with Massine in bravura and cancels every choreographic effect. The films are still shown because of the star casts, but *Gaieté* excludes the great Danilova from one of her most famous roles—Warners' thought she wasn't pretty.)

Art films on the dance, from the rhythm-and-motion studies of the twenties down to Maya Deren's experiments in the forties and fifties and the contemporary camera choreography of Norman McLaren, Ed Emshwiller, and Hilary Harris, have traditionally concentrated on abstract, impersonal expression rather than on dancers in performance. The dancers in most of these films have no personalities; they are exactly what one of Hilary Harris's titles suggests they are: themes for variations by the camera. These films are often pleasant and even sensual experiences in their own terms. They would be more exciting, though, if they hadn't lost the point of their tradition—if they'd continued to present a contrast rather than a correlative to general tendencies in commercial moviemaking. Front-of-the-camera performing is now so rare that the starring role in a film biography of one of the world's great dancers, *Isadora*, can be taken by a nondancer with little or no protest from the dance press. With the decline of the movie musical, there seems to have arisen a vague impulse to transplant dance values to other forms of screen entertainment, in extended motion sequences—bike-riding, car-driving, running through woods (in slow motion)—that have no point other than to beguile us with their abstract beauty. The screen is said to be dancing when often it is only temporizing. When musicals of the past are revived, the choices reflect the current taste for impersonal sensation: Berkeley in quantity, the Disney of *Fantasia*. In order to see dancing by dancers, more people are going to the ballet than ever went before. Dance as an experience for the spectator has just about ceased to exist any place else.

The personality of the dancer comes through in the two documentaries that are really performances for the camera by Martha Graham. In *A Dancer's World* (1957), she sits at a dressing table making up for performance, and as she talks to us, with the camera cutting away to her company in a classroom demonstration, we get caught up in her personality and theatrical style as we have no chance to do in the dim and musty films that were made of her stage works about the same time. In a 1943 film study of her famous solo *Lamentation*, which she performed seated, Graham becomes living sculpture examined by the camera from different angles. The camera's explorations don't wipe out Graham. Because of their modesty of scale, these Graham films are among the few dance films of their kind that can be shown successfully on television.*

* Postscript 1977: Since this encyclopedia article was written in 1971, there has been one first-rate dance movie—the version of *Eight Jelly Rolls* made by Twyla

Abstraction need not mean depersonalization. There probably should be a special category for *Olympia*. Although it is not a dance film, it is unsurpassed as a study of physical motion. Although it was made in Nazi Germany, it is not propaganda. It is abstract and yet it does not leave out the personalities of its subjects. Produced and edited by Leni Riefenstahl, a former dancer, and accompanied by a fine musical score composed by Herbert Windt, *Olympia* transcends its obligations as a documentary of the 1936 Olympic Games to become a ritual celebration of beautiful bodies and heroic movement. But it is always moving on two planes: journalism and poetry. It is the most *sensuous* of documentaries. The editing is so lyrical and so exactly timed to the differently charged proportions of regular or slowed motion that we are often displaced before we know it from one plane to the other—from stadium to "theatre." The javelin-thrower dances into his takeoff, the gymnast lifting himself on parallel rings (a slow movement slowed further by the camera) is seen to rise with a massive strength, and each collapse across the finish line of the twenty-six-mile Marathon is an individual aria of pain. The effect has been widely imitated, but no other film of this type has quite succeeded in enhancing the event without blurring or falsifying the record, and certainly none has enhanced it to the extent that *Olympia* does, with its classical nudes, its radiant morning mists, and its high divers falling out of the sun.

The current emphasis on a directors' cinema makes most movie musicals look very bad indeed—and some bad directors look good. Not all directors who have been interested in movement as a film subject have been great. The directors who were concerned with what most audiences wanted to see—great performing in great routines—made musicals that, on the whole, were not up to the routines that were in them. It is the performers whom we remember in these movies; the directors' names may matter less than the choreographers', and some of the greatest moments may occur in movies we wouldn't want to see again—Hermes Pan's dances for *Moon Over Miami* (1941) and *Coney Island* (1943); Robert Alton's "The Lady Dances" in *Strike Me Pink* (1936); LeRoy Prinz's Charleston in *Tea*

Tharp with London Weekend Television, which used a full range of optical effects to orchestrate the dances. But videotape choreography (Merce Cunningham has also made some fascinating examples) is an area of experimentation different from choreography on, or for, film.

for Two (1950); the Nicholas Brothers in *Kid Millions* (1934) and
Orchestra Wives (1942); the astounding Merriel Abbott Dancers in
Man About Town (1939), *Buck Benny Rides Again* (1940), and
Sensations of 1945. There are performers—Bill Robinson, Ray Bolger
—who always seem halfway out of the movies they appear in, as if on
loan from another and better movie that really belonged to them.
For these reasons, film students who are interested in the musical are
less interested in it as a showcase for performers than as a showcase
for direction. But very few musicals that really work all the way
through—e.g., *Good News* (1947, with Charles Walters's direction
and Robert Alton's production numbers)—can be attributed exclusively to good direction—or to good writing or good performing. Musicals combine too many forms of expression to be analyzed in this
way; they're the ultimate fantasy movie.

Not all directors who have been interested in movement were
great, but few have been great who were not. Griffith, Murnau, Lubitsch, Eisenstein, Dovzhenko, Ford, Flaherty, Riefenstahl, Disney,
Clair, Cocteau, Ophuls, Kurosawa, Satyajit Ray—all have different
ways of making films move; each is the way of a virtuoso. Not only
do their films move; their dance scenes—scenes of actual dance or
dancelike movement—are among the greatest ever recorded. With
the death of the musical, the dance-lover's film repertory has almost
stopped growing. Now it will expand only when the best of today's
directors become good choreographers, too.

Index